# Home, Work, and Play

Situating Canadian Social History, 1840–1980

Edited by

**James Opp** and **John C. Walsh**

OXFORD

UNIVERSITY PRESS

# OXFORD
UNIVERSITY PRESS

70 Wynford Drive, Don Mills, Ontario M3C 1J9
www.oup.com/ca

Oxford University Press is a department of the University of Oxford.
It furthers the University's objective of excellence in research, scholarship,
and education by publishing worldwide in

Oxford  New York
Auckland  Cape Town  Dar es Salaam  Hong Kong  Karachi
Kuala Lumpur  Madrid  Melbourne  Mexico City  Nairobi
New Delhi  Shanghai  Taipei  Toronto

With offices in
Argentina  Austria  Brazil  Chile  Czech Republic  France  Greece
Guatemala  Hungary  Italy  Japan  Poland  Portugal  Singapore
South Korea  Switzerland  Thailand  Turkey  Ukraine  Vietnam

Oxford is a trade mark of Oxford University Press
in the UK and in certain other countries

Published in Canada
by Oxford University Press

**Library and Archives Canada Cataloguing in Publication**

Home, work and play : situating Canadian social history,
1840–1980 / edited by James Opp and John C. Walsh

ISBN-13: 978-0-19-542270-2    2.– ISBN-10: 0-19-542270-8

1. Canada—Social conditions—19th century. 2. Canada—Social conditions—20th century.
I. Walsh, John C., 1969– II. Opp, James William, 1970–

HN103.H58 2005          306'.0971          C2005-904153–6

Cover design: Brett Miller
Text design: Janette Thompson, Jansom
Cover image: Stephen Swintek/Getty Images

1 2 3 4 – 09 08 07 06
This book is printed on permanent (acid-free) paper ∞.
Printed in Canada

# Contents

## Part III:  At Play    241

# Acknowledgements

When we were unexpectedly thrust together to teach a course in Canadian social history in the fall of 2003, we had no idea that many of the concepts we set out in class would evolve into this work. Although very few of the articles we used in that course made the final version of this collection, that class sharpened our sense of purpose and clarified how space could be used to structure and communicate the importance of social history. To our students past, present, and future, we thank you for making the classroom a two-way learning experience.

This project came together quickly, thanks to the support and enthusiasm of Laura Macleod and Rachael Cayley at Oxford University Press Canada. Richard Tallman did yeoman's work as copy editor. We also want to thank Joy Parr, Craig Heron, and Karen Dubinsky for their support of this project. Barbara Lorenzkowski was generous and gracious with her comments on a draft of the introduction. Geoff Eley kindly allowed us to read in draft form his own book, *A Crooked Line: From Cultural History to the History of Society* (University of Michigan Press, 2005), and we thank him and our colleague, Mark Salber Phillips, who made this possible. The anonymous referees offered helpful, constructive criticism that sharpened the final version of the book.

We would like to acknowledge the support of Mike Smith, Dean of Arts and Social Sciences at Carleton University, for providing funds to hire two research assistants. Joel Legassie and Karen Gabert took time away from their own studies to unearth many of the images used in the visual resource sections. The sharp eyes of Maja Villarroel, a standout student from our first social history class, brought the Eveready battery ad to our attention. Heather Matheson of Carleton's Maxwell MacOdrum Library provided us with timely access to and free use of non-circulating materials.

*Home, Work, and Play* was developed and produced at a time when the lives of both editors underwent dramatic transformations in all three areas. We are indebted to Karen Reyburn and Pamela Williamson for enduring (yet more) work at home and we are especially grateful to Emily and Nevan for teaching us the true meaning of play.

Figure 1.

# Home, Work, and Play

James Opp and John C. Walsh

In a 1952 advertisement for Eveready batteries (Figure 1), the flashlight is heralded as an essential tool for Canadian consumers, whether at home, at work, or at play. Although the flashlight remains the same in each setting, the context for its use suggests dramatically different social and physical environments. From illuminating the inside of an oven for a housewife to exposing the vehicle engine for an ambulance driver to lighting the way in the forest at night for a group of young adults, the social relations surrounding the device are depicted in very specific ways that shift across space, gender, and age. In this example, the three fields of home, work, and play are deeply gendered; domestic labour is a feminine activity while a masculine mechanical aptitude is required outside the home in order to accomplish paid labour. Leisure activities, such as camping, are defined by young adults, at a stage in life when courtship and sexual relations are in flux, and individuals' own home and work lives have not yet been defined. The ad suggests that the flashlight is useful from 'basement to attic', reinforcing the broad post-war middle-class conception of home ownership. Furthermore, the fact that all the actors in these images are white has the effect of normalizing a particular racial identity as typically Canadian. While the intention of this ad is clearly to sell batteries, it communicates a great deal more in evoking a set of cultural ideals that characterized Canada in the 1950s.

Such idealizations were not, of course, descriptions of reality as much as they were the projections of a comforting social order defined by an advertising agency. Nevertheless, the advertisement serves as a useful starting point for considering how historians situate history in terms of social and physical space, real or imagined. In bringing together a diverse selection of articles in recent Canadian social history, this volume calls attention to how historians, implicitly and explicitly, frame their work in relation to these spatial categories. The inclusion of visual primary sources offers readers an opportunity to go one step further, developing their own analysis of spatial meanings. Home, work, and play are not, as the battery advertisement suggests, self-evident or natural categories. Ultimately, our objective is to unsettle simplistic notions of how such spaces are constituted and made meaningful.

As spatial categories, home, work, and play operate in this collection in two different but complementary ways. First, the articles shed light on how home, work, and play were historically understood and experienced by various peoples in multiple contexts. Annmarie Adams, for example, explains how doctors and architects in the late nineteenth century sought to design the ideal healthy home, a space that would nurture the bodily well-being of families. Steven High explores how factory design in the 1970s sought to change the identity of work, and thus workers, by remaking industrial factories into post-industrial campuses. And Suzanne Morton deftly shows how the gendered spaces of gambling were elements of an alternative social geography of Montreal during the 1940s, where play both reaffirmed gender identities and provided opportunities for men and women to transgress the normal codes of conduct. Despite the different historical settings, all three essays demonstrate that the spatial context in which people lived, worked, and played was an active component of their identities and experiences. This theme can be observed in each of the essays in this volume through different sources and understood from a variety of methodological and theoretical positions. While making no pretense to being comprehensive, the selections reorient how we can and should think about home, work, and play.

Second, as editors we have used 'home, work, and play' as an organizational framework. We expect most readers of this volume will be newcomers to Canadian social history, and our use of these categories operates as a map to help readers navigate what might otherwise seem a dense and incomprehensible field of study. As new faculty charged with designing a Canadian social history course from the ground up, we wanted something more than a strictly chronological structure or an endless list of themes with little in common. At the same time, we understood that chronology is critical to historical understanding and that social history is as diverse as the peoples whose stories it tells. Still, the sheer volume of different topics that one might be expected to cover in an undergraduate class on Canadian social history can be overwhelming. The spatial organization of the course into 'home, work, and play' offered a means for students to see shifts in social relations over time in focused areas.

Although we have organized our selections in three discrete categories, our intent is not to insist on their strict separation. Rather, this structure allows for readers to challenge the very artificiality of such predetermined classifications. Many of the selections point to the permeability of these boundaries. Industries such as tourism and sport fishing might have been 'play' to some participants, but as Karen Dubinsky and Bill Parenteau note, these areas were very much 'work' for Niagara Falls motel operators and Native guides in New Brunswick. While many readers may take it for granted that their home, work, and play lives are interconnected, thinking about these connections historically is unsettling for it compels us to embrace the messiness of the past.

In designing this collection, we deliberately sought out recent work. While new is not necessarily better, we wanted readers to have a clear sense of the diversity of interests, methodologies, and approaches that characterize the field today. We are also aware that in framing our volume in terms of social space, we have shifted the focus away from other major themes such as immigration, industrialization, and urbanization.[1] These large-scale transformations and the dislocations they triggered are not absent from this collection. Instead, they are framed in relation to other concerns, reflecting new directions in social history that have emerged in the last decade.

Another innovative feature of *Home, Work, and Play* is the incorporation of visual primary sources. Historians tend to rely solely on textual sources of information, and images (when noticed at all) often serve as little more than inert illustrations. In recent years, however, visual culture has emerged as an important resource for scholars interested in how social spaces were represented. In paintings, photographs, advertisements, maps, and architectural plans, social space is portrayed, reshaped, and given meaning by producers and consumers of such images. The inclusion of illustrations in this volume is therefore not a means simply to 'visualize' the past—rather, we want to encourage readers to 'read' visual imagery critically in light of the questions raised by the essays. As with the battery advertisement, we need to be aware of how visual images create and reinforce the social constructions of gender, class, and race just as they represent the spaces of home, work, and play.

## Situating Social History

When social history emerged on university campuses in the 1960s, it was often defined against the dominant tradition of political history. Self-consciously revolutionary, social historians declared that they were doing history 'from the bottom up' or writing a more complete 'total history'. Over the past 30–40 years, however, the field has evolved. Perhaps a better way to define social history is as an attempt to relate the social experience of the lived past to the social structures that limit and define such experiences. Karl Marx famously said that individuals make their own histories (what social historians often call 'agency') but that they do so within parameters defined for them by others ('structure'). Most, if not all, Canadian social historians would agree with this basic proposition, although they would differ on the relative importance of agency and structure. Indeed, there is an enduring and underlying tension between the two in the broad landscape of Canadian social historical writing.

Structure and agency were central questions for social historians in the 1960s and 1970s who sought to restore a place for those marginalized by the traditional focus on national politics and the elite classes. For some, the path to recovering this history lay in a social science methodology that mined new and different types of sources, such as wills, baptismal and wedding registers, tax assessment records, city directories, and census returns. Like their colleagues in sociology and economics, historians became adept at statistical analysis and eventually produced a startling array of figures about the historical identities and behaviours of Canadians, from child-rearing to marriage patterns to kinship and community relations. This research was both interdisciplinary and international, as Quebec historians drew upon the work of the French Annales movement while English-speaking historians found inspiration in demographic studies of the Cambridge Group for the History of Population and Social Structure. The use of statistical analysis also owed much to the social scientific history emerging in the United States, which made an explosive entrance into Canada via the work of American-born and American-trained Michael Katz and his well-funded project on Hamilton.[2] These works produced large amounts of data that spoke to large-scale economic structures related to industrialization, urbanization, and family strategies.

For some historians, however, the social scientific approach offered little room for recovering the actual voices of the historically marginalized—the working class, immigrants, and women. A parallel, and occasionally overlapping, impulse within social history sought to go beyond these structures, to explore how people were agents of history in their own right.

In particular, these scholars drew upon the work of a British Marxist, E.P. Thompson, whose classic *The Making of the English Working Class* (1963) is still regarded as the seminal text in the field. In his preface, Thompson famously remarked that his objective was to recover workers 'from the enormous condescension of posterity'.[3] For him, the key to recovering working-class agency lay in taking working-class culture seriously, analyzing class-based organizations, customs, rituals, songs, and poems as expressions of political resistance that 'made' the working class as much as it 'was made' by the economic forces of capitalism and industrialization. Canadian working-class historians followed this lead, focusing on topics such as the organization and rituals of the Knights of Labor, the parades of the Orange Order, and the use of the charivari as markers of working-class culture.

Thompson's influence extended beyond his scholarly conclusions. In his political activism, most famously his campaigning for British disarmament in the 1980s, Thompson demonstrated a social role for the intellectual in contemporary society. Social historians in Canada similarly engaged with Marxist, New Left, and feminist concerns. The creation of the journal *Labour/Le Travailleur* (later *Labour/Le Travail*) in 1976 reflected the interest in creating dialogue between intellectuals and Canada's working class, and the journal actively sought outside contributors and cultivated a broad readership. Social historians' pursuit of agency and voice was viewed as a meaningful contribution to present-day politics. Concerned over the apparent rising tide of subversive activity among historians, the RCMP even sent spies to observe what went on at the annual meetings of the Canadian Historical Association.[4]

In the 1980s and 1990s, the interests and approaches of social historians evolved, but agency and structure remained central. Increased interest in immigration, ethnicity, and women's lives raised questions about whose experience was being reconstructed by historians. Labour and working-class historians had acknowledged the role of ethnicity in shaping working-class experience, but immigration historians focused their efforts on family and community bonds, framing their work as part of a narrative of migration and relocation. Women's historians called attention to the public and private aspects of women's lives, but in turn discovered that women's experiences varied with class and ethnicity. This broad-ranging dialogue called attention to the complexity of peoples' identities, shaped by multiple and overlapping factors, including sex, class, and ethnicity. Textbooks in Canadian history reflected these trends through titles such as *History of the Canadian Peoples* and *The Peoples of Canada*, which implicitly rejected a single national narrative in favour of a more pluralistic perspective.

However, this embrace of multiple voices and identities produced new debates over the moral position of historians and their unspoken assumptions. How accessible are past experiences, and who has the right to speak for those whose voices were denied or lost over time? How do we understand historic actions and events when the only records we have were written by those in power, such as housing inspectors, Indian agents, and criminal courts? The claim to understanding the experience of others was critiqued particularly by historians who worked with First Nations. The representation of Native voices produced heated debates at academic conferences as First Nations demanded a role in representing their own histories. Social historians struggled to bridge a cultural divide between academic interests and collective memory.

The search for agency raised troubling questions for historians in many fields, and, drawing again on similar developments in the social sciences, new tools were developed to differentiate social realities from historically produced social constructions. In the 1980s, gender historians defined 'sex' as the biological entity of women and men, while 'gender' referred to the construction of feminine and masculine identities. Gender history, therefore, is not simply about including men, as many students mistakenly assume, but about analyzing how representations of what it means to be female or male are defined and relate to each other. Gender relations infuse and structure our understanding of social actions and spaces.[5] Whereas women's history sought to give women a voice and narrate their experience, gender history began to examine how masculinity and femininity are negotiated, and ultimately influence or restrict social behaviours.

The use of gender as a category of analysis offers historians a powerful tool to understand the structure of social history at a very different conceptual level. In their study of urban transit in the 1940s, Donald Davis and Barbara Lorenzkowski go beyond the experience of women riding and working on streetcars to explore how work and public space were gendered. From the very design of the streetcars to the battles between 'smokers' and 'shoppers', gendered assumptions lay at the heart of the debate over public transit in the war years. With bodies crowded together in such close proximity, the question of whether passengers' social actions are defined as 'proper' feminine or masculine behaviour takes on heightened significance. Gender historians argue that we cannot grasp the full meaning of individual experience without first understanding the structures of gender that have historically surrounded women and men.

In the 1990s, other socially constructed categories of analysis emerged. In particular, social historians turned their attention to the way perceptions of racial difference have changed over time. Writing about 'race' is not simply a matter of narrating the story of various ethnic groups, but rather of exposing how essentialized notions of the Chinese 'character', or Native peoples, or 'whiteness' were produced. Gender and race are not competing levels of analysis, but overlapping spheres. As Kevin Wamsley and David Whitson point out, boxing promotions in the late nineteenth century hailed the sport as an acceptable form of masculine violence, but did not extend this respectability to black boxers, who were framed as lacking civility and relying on 'brute' force.

Most recently, sexuality has come to the forefront as another site of contested meanings. Mary Louise Adams's discussion of crime comics and pulp novels calls our attention to the post-war anxiety over defining heterosexuality as 'normal', and how these perceptions shaped understandings of homosexuality as a danger to the social order. Against the backdrop of the Cold War, such 'abnormal' behaviour was seen as part of a moral unmaking of the nation through the corruption of children and young adults. Little wonder, then, that the reading of comic books and pulp novels was subject to both social and political forms of governance. Adams's examination of the social and legal context that surrounded the ephemeral, everyday qualities of comic books is a social history encouraged by the focus on the constructed and historically specific categories of sexuality, gender, class, and race.

To explore how meanings of gender, race, and sexuality are produced, scholars have turned to a wide variety of linguistic theories. Broadly speaking, such postmodern approaches to history question the ability of primary source texts to represent 'truths' or 'facts' of the past, and instead suggest that social meanings are ultimately produced through language and 'discourses'. Since the past is unknowable, postmodernists suggest that scholars should turn their attention away from 'reality' and onto questions of 'representation', including visual, spatial, and literary sources. This critique cuts to the heart of the historical enterprise. Can historians truly claim to reveal how others experienced the past when we only know 'reality' through layers upon layers of 'discourse' and language? Indeed, are the historical meanings we draw from these fragments representative of past experience or the product of our own present understandings? Critics warn that an exclusive focus on discourse leaves little room for analyzing experience or for recovering a sense of agency on the part of oppressed groups. They also worry that such a focus pushes us farther away from our historical subjects rather than bringing us closer to them.[6]

While it may never be entirely possible to reconcile such oppositions, many historians are increasingly attuned to the significance of local resistance. For example, in Paige Raibmon's article, Aboriginal domestic space is put on display and carefully constructed as a spectacle of either 'primitiveness' or 'civilization'. And yet Native peoples themselves reconfigured their houses to suit their own needs, subverting the attempt to establish assimilation through domesticity. By viewing space itself as a form of language, Raibmon allows us to envision domesticity as a site where everyday life was both culturally constructed and materially contested. In understanding the surrounding context of representation and performance, agency is not lost, but rather gains new meaning.

These are neither the first nor the last debates within Canadian social history. One of the defining elements of social history has been a willingness to question itself, to ask difficult and sometimes discomforting questions about what social history is and should be. In the 1990s, conservative critics lamented the loss of a national narrative in the face of multiple perspectives and the fragmentation of history into specialized subfields. We would argue that the proliferation of perspectives and new areas of interest testifies to the continuing vitality of Canadian social history. The essays in this collection are derived from fields as diverse as urban history, sport history, Native history, religious history, labour history, cultural history, and rural history. And yet all of them speak to larger issues surrounding themes of class, gender, and race. In addition, they are included in this particular volume because they speak to another overarching theme: space.

## Thinking About Space

The continuing tension between agency and structure, experience and constructed identity, is also reflected in how social historians approach social space. Many focus on how the material conditions of home, work, and play shaped the experience of those who inhabited these spheres. Questions surrounding working conditions, standards of living, and family structures have been prominent in Canadian social history for decades. In this volume, Catharine Wilson traces the value of the work bee for rural economies and analyzes how these work spaces reinforced 'neighbourliness' and particular social interactions that were, in turn, shaped by gender and class.

Recently, historians have also explored how such spaces are conceptualized, socially constructed, and represented. Chris Dummitt examines how barbecues were sold to consumers as a manly form of cooking, rather than probing their actual use in the home. The particular words and phrases used to describe a cooking implement reflected masculine concerns, reinforcing a gendered notion of the 'outdoors' as an acceptable space for men to engage in an activity traditionally considered feminine.

It is worth noting the differences in sources employed by Wilson and Dummitt. Whereas Wilson turns to the diaries and writings of farmers who participated in nineteenth-century work bees, Dummitt focuses on advertisements and the language describing barbecues. This is not to suggest that the two approaches are mutually exclusive; most of our selections combine both perspectives in their analyses. For example, Joy Parr explores how washing machines were portrayed by their manufacturers and, through oral history interviews, compares this representation to the actual adoption and use of new technology in Canadian households. In this case, the social space of the laundry room is both 'real' and 'constructed', existing simultaneously as a sphere of lived experience and as a wider representation of domestic labour and technology.

From these examples it is apparent that social space can be viewed from many perspectives. Spaces are never neutral or empty of meaning, especially those designated as proper sites of home, work, and play.[7] In the very classification of certain activities as 'naturally' belonging to these spheres, a multitude of historical assumptions are brought to bear in defining domesticity, labour, and leisure. Social spaces function materially and symbolically in shaping everyday life. In situating Canadian social history, we want to stress the active nature of these processes. Although not all the articles in this volume directly address the question of social space, they all point to the dynamic negotiation of power, whether imposed from above or resisted and restructured from below.

## Visualizing Space

It is important to note the distance between experience and representation, especially when examining visual sources. The idyllic world portrayed in the Eveready advertisement offers a sense of how the social spaces of home, work, and play were represented to consumers, but without further research this would serve as a poor guide to understanding the everyday experience of Canadians in the post-World War II era. No doubt many working-class women who were employed outside the home relied on flashlights in their work lives, while men certainly used them in the home.

Just as textual sources require a critical eye, so, too, do visual sources. Even photographs, which appear to offer an objective view of the past, are subject to multiple interests and cultural constructions. The photographer selects what to include within the frame and what to leave out. The subjects may willingly pose, or they may resent the intrusion. Technological limitations and cultural aesthetics influence what is captured on film and what is not. Publishers routinely recrop images to suit other needs, often adding captions that may have little to do with the original intention. As James Opp suggests, photographs of Winnipeg's North End do not reflect reality as much as they construct spaces of moral concern. And, as with any public image, what the producer *intends* to portray is not necessarily what the audience takes from it.

Visual sources actively contribute to the construction of meanings that surround and infuse social space. Sometimes they explicitly reinforce existing ideologies, and sometimes they articulate unspoken assumptions and attitudes.[8] By including images for readers to analyze, critique, and evaluate, we hope to encourage discussion of perspective, evidence, and methodology. Ultimately, there is no simple way to determine how such images were received or what their creators intended. However, the insight provided by the articles in this collection may help readers think about the visual representation of social space in new ways.

## Conclusion

The obstacles facing historians in recovering social experience and social structures in many ways mirror the difficulties inherent in drawing out meanings and understandings from images. Social historians face a daunting task in trying to produce historical narratives that capture the multiple voices, meanings, textures, and complexities of past social worlds. The choices we make, as historians, are not dissimilar to the choices a photographer makes in framing his or her subject. In selecting what to focus on, a great deal is left out. The picture, like history, is never entirely complete.

Social history has changed a great deal in the last 40 years.[8] A field once dominated by a focus on labour and the working class has now expanded to include issues of gender, race, and sexuality. Domesticity and home life are no longer marginal areas of concern, but are viewed as fundamental elements of nation-building, colonization, and imperialism. A new interest in popular culture has led to wide-ranging studies in leisure, recreation, the environment, and spaces of play. New sources, including oral history, photographs, and advertisements, have led to new questions surrounding identity and representation. Yet, for all that is new, social historians remain committed to seeking understanding of and respect for the diversity of peoples who made Canada, a project that was as fundamental to scholars in the 1960s as it is today. *Home, Work, and Play* is a testament to the determination of social history to push the boundaries of our knowledge and understanding of the past while remaining unapologetically humane in its concerns.

## Notes

1. For recent social history collections that explicitly approach these topics, see Franca Iacovetta and Robert Ventresca, eds, *A Nation of Immigrants: Women, Workers, and Communities in Canadian History, 1840s–1960s* (Toronto: UTP, 1998) and Ian Radforth and Laurel Sefton MacDowell, eds, *Canadian Working Class History: Selected Readings*, 2nd edn (Toronto: CSPI, 2000).
2. Michael B. Katz, *The People of Hamilton, Canada West: Family and Class in a Mid-Nineteenth-Century City* (Cambridge, Mass.: Harvard University Press, 1975) and Michael B. Katz, Michael J. Doucet, and Mark J. Stern, *The Social Organization of Early Industrial Capitalism* (Cambridge, Mass.: Harvard University Press, 1982).
3. E.P. Thompson, *The Making of the English Working Class* (London: Penguin Books, 1980 [1963]), 12.
4. Steve Hewitt, 'Intelligence at the Learneds: The RCMP, the Learneds, and the Canadian Historical Association', *Journal of the Canadian Historical Association* 8 (1998): 267–86.
5. Joan Wallach Scott, 'Gender: A Useful Category of Historical Analysis', in Scott, ed., *Gender and the Politics of History* (New York: Columbia University Press, 1988).
6. Bryan Palmer, *Descent into Discourse: The Reification of Language and the Writing of Social History* (Philadelphia: Temple University Press, 1990).
7. An important work in theorizing space that has influenced not only historians but also geographers, sociologists, and anthropologists is Henri Lefebvre, *The Production of Space*, trans. Donald Nicholson-Smith (Oxford: Blackwell, 1991).
8. This is particularly strong in the case of maps, as historians of cartography are continuing to explain. See the essays in J.B. Harley, *The New Nature of Maps: Essays in the History of Cartography*, ed. Paul Laxton (Baltimore: Johns Hopkins University Press, 2001).

# PART I

# At Home

Before the 1970s, the question of the home rarely found its way into the pages of Canadian history. Even the earliest works in women's history tended to focus on the pioneering roles of women outside of the home, rather than viewing the home itself as an important historical space. However, in the 1970s and 1980s, social historians interested in women, children, the family, household structures, immigration, and kinship placed the home and household at the centre of their analyses, rather than viewing domestic spaces as marginal to the larger narrative of national (and political) history. For many historians, researching and theorizing the 'private' world of home and family offered a useful way for recovering the voices, work, and actions of women and children, which had been marginalized by historians' traditional understandings of the nation and citizenship.

As scholars delved into new issues such as domestic labour, child care, and women's property rights, the distinction between public and private was itself called into question. The conceptualization of diametrically opposing social worlds, also known as the ideology of 'separate spheres', was itself a historical construction of the Victorian period (*c.* 1830–1900). In the shift from an agrarian society to an industrial economy, the middle classes physically separated home from work, as fathers no longer worked with their families but instead found employment in factories and offices. This separation produced new ideals of domesticity, which reflected middle-class concerns over the nature of industrialization, and established new boundaries of gender. Women were viewed as 'naturally' embodying domestic virtues, such as fidelity, compassion, and moral strength. In contrast, men were seen as the 'breadwinners', most capable of rational thought, and uniquely suited to the public affairs of politics and work. Within this binary context, the home served as a 'haven in a heartless world', a moral centre that counteracted the ruthless competitiveness that marked nineteenth-century economics and politics. This middle-class, Victorian ideology was critical to the work of early feminist historians who focused on the home as the space where women lived and made history, where they were agents rather than passive spectators of historical change.

By the 1990s, however, historians realized that the ordering of society as 'naturally' divided into public and private broke down in multiple ways. Studies of the Victorian era demonstrated that the waged labour of immigrant domestic servants betrayed the notion that 'work' did not take place in the home, while the realities of working-class family economies compelled many women and children to work for wages, both within and outside their homes. Apart from the industrial heartland of southern Ontario and Quebec and the Lower Mainland of British Columbia, the majority of Canadians continued to live in rural settings well into the twentieth century, and it was clear that the ideal of 'separate spheres' had limited relevance for understanding the everyday experiences of rural families, where work and home often remained firmly intertwined. Historians even began to question how urban, middle-class women themselves fit the domestic ideal in light of their 'public' activities, such as participating in religious societies and social reform movements. The conclusions drawn from this research understandably led to a new questioning of the boundaries between the spheres. The simple division of public and private could not be sustained, since most people have historically inhabited some portion of both worlds simultaneously.

But rather than jettison the concept of separate spheres, historians discovered new ways of incorporating it into their analyses of the home. The emergence of gender history, which focuses on the social organization of masculine and feminine identities, has been particularly influential. Instead of viewing 'public' and 'private' as static categories of a strictly defined society, gender historians emphasize the overlaps, ambiguities, and distance between the cultural conceptualization of private life and the material complexities of lived experience. The use of gender as an analytical tool allowed scholars to demonstrate the fluidity of the meanings that surround space, calling attention to the shifting representations of masculine and feminine attached to particular sites even within the home, such as the kitchen, the dining room, the study, and the parlour. Rooms occupied by both sexes could nevertheless be gendered very differently. Further complicating the picture, gendered perceptions of domesticity also intersected class and race. As the following essays demonstrate, the home is not simply a physical place inhabited by people; it is also a space that has historically been embedded with contradictory social meanings.

The gendering of domestic space is a prominent theme of the first article in this section, Annmarie Adams's 'Female Regulation of the Healthy Home', which is the only selection in this book that does not deal with Canada directly. In her study of health reform and middle-class houses in nineteenth-century Britain, Adams addresses a set of concerns surrounding the home that were common in the Anglo-American world. We have included it for its sensitive appraisal of how middle-class domestic space was simultaneously 'private' and 'public', and how masculine questions of 'science' were also a part of the domestic sphere. As with many themes in social history, questions of gender and domesticity are not confined by national borders, but are in fact part of a larger cultural milieu.

Beyond the overlapping spheres of public and private, new questions are being raised about the meaning of the home. How did the material spaces of the home function in relation to everyday life? And why was so much 'political' capital and energy invested in maintaining idealized conceptions of domesticity? These themes run through many of the articles included in this section. The home as a space for raising families was seen as the key to the future of the nation, and domestic ideals were central to middle-class perceptions of Native peoples, immigrant communities, and the working class. As these essays illustrate, inside and outside of the physical space of the home, a broad range of domestic relations were infused with moral tensions, especially marriage, sexuality, and the family. The public surveillance directed at the domesticity of 'others' points to the depth of anxiety that the white middle class felt about the future of Canada and the state of its 'race'. In the post-war period, suburban perceptions of home were closely aligned with the interests of consumer culture. From these articles, we therefore learn that such issues were not marginal, nor were they confined to the private sphere. Instead, the home emerges here both as a site of lived experience and as a space central to the culture and politics of state formation in the nineteenth and twentieth centuries.

# Female Regulation of the Healthy Home

Annmarie Adams

'Woman's sphere', observed Harriette M. Plunkett, 'has had a great many definitions.' To illustrate her idea of women's place in sanitary reform, the author of *Women, Plumbers, and Doctors; or Household Sanitation* included in her book a sectional drawing of a standard middle-class house, labelled 'A properly plumbed house—Woman's Sphere'.[1] Drawn in the manner of Teale and the other house-doctors, it showed the exterior connections of a building to the municipal sewer system, as well as its ventilation and water supply. . . . Woman's sphere 'begins where the service-pipe for water and the house-drain enter the street-mains,' explained the American author, 'and, as far as sanitary plumbing goes, it ends at the top of the highest ventilating-pipe above the roof.'[2]

Plunkett was not alone in designating domestic sanitary responsibilities to women. Ada Ballin, the editor of *Baby* magazine and the author of numerous books for women, also considered the examples set by women in the home to be significant contributions to public health:

It is a glorious thing for us to think that health-science is mainly to be taught and practised by women; that women are now going about among the people as apostles of health, teaching them

how to be well and happy, and that this movement is gaining impetus every day. Oh, yes, my readers may say that is doubtless all very good and noble, but we cannot all frequent the shrines as missionaries of the goddess Hygeia. Certainly not; not every woman is suited, or can have the opportunity to do so; but yet, by attention to herself, her children and her home, she can work in the good cause. Let her make her own home a temple of the goddess, and she will have done her duty.[3]

Sanitarians noted women's supposedly innate interest in health and also their familiarity with the construction and arrangement of the house. 'The men of the house come and go; know little of the ins and outs of anything domestic; are guided by what they are told, and are practically of no assistance whatever', asserted the physician Benjamin Ward Richardson. 'The women are conversant with every nook of the dwelling, from basement to roof, and on their knowledge, wisdom, and skill the physician rests his hopes.'[4]

Plunkett and Richardson were also typical in their focus on the spatial limitations that defined women's place in late nineteenth-century health reform; both sanitarians described women's sphere as being within the physical boundaries

---

Annmarie Adams, 'Female Regulation of the Healthy Home', from *Architecture in the Family Way*. McGill-Queen's University Press, 1996. Reprinted by permission of McGill-Queen's University Press.

of the middle-class house. Throughout the literature of the period, the so-called separate sphere—or woman's sphere, as Plunkett called it—was synonymous with the female-led middle-class home.[5] While men toiled in the city, a public world, middle-class women were thought to live in an essentially private, domestic realm bounded by the exterior walls of the house.[6]

Few historians have challenged this notion of a spatial separation of men and women in English or North American urban life.[7] According to most accounts, the period since the Industrial Revolution has been marked by sharper distinctions between the experiences of men and women, reinforced by the breakdown of the extended family as a unit of production.[8] Since the mid-eighteenth century, the story goes, home and work have increasingly been differentiated by geographical location, architectural style, and gender associations. 'As the workplace became separated from the home,' observed Jane Lewis in a major social history of nineteenth-century English women, 'so a private, domestic sphere was created for women, divorced from the public world of work, office and citizenship.'[9]

As a result, the history of the nineteenth-century home, like the building that is its focus, has been gendered female. Concentrating on the differences between the middle-class house and the city, rather than on their similarities, historians have painted a picture of home that 'assumed a universality of experience and meaning'.[10] A 'cult of domesticity' in the late nineteenth century supposedly made the house antithetical in every way to the city. The city was aggressive while the house was passive; the city was unpredictable while the house was stable; the city was corrupt while the house was virtuous. In terms of architectural style, public architecture relied on universally accepted principles for its meaning. The house was personalized, emotional, exclusive, and sheltered from the public gaze, like the Victorian woman.

'Control' of the separate sphere (the house), in terms of its health, was largely the responsibility of middle-class women. The medical discourse that emerged from the Domestic Sanitation Movement in the 1870s radically changed women's relationship to the home and to the city. The conceptual blurring of the body, the house, and the city exposed women's control of domestic space and their participation in the urban realm. This chapter explores the female regulation of domestic architecture during the period 1870–1900. It also examines the significance of a new field of endeavour for women, domestic science, which focused on the house as a subject of study, debate, and reform. As a feminized component of the medical profession, domestic science provided a significant public arena for feminist critiques of the middle-class house, while at the same time expressing time liberated from the constraints of reproduction and child care. The emergence of this new field at this particular time also illustrates how public debates over the virtues of art and science were simultaneously played out in both the woman and the house. Neither the woman nor the house, then, was as separate as most histories of the period would have us believe.

This idea of the middle-class house as a separate domestic sphere was not invented in the twentieth century. Like Plunkett, many Victorian women described the separateness of their lives from the public world of their fathers and husbands, adopting the metaphor of the sphere to emphasize their isolation. Jane Ellen Panton, the author of more than 30 popular advice books for women in the late nineteenth century, was typical in her description of Victorian women's lot in spatial terms: 'A woman's sphere is domestic, more or less, she cannot alter it by stepping out of it.'[11] Advisers earlier in the century had even noted the exclusion of men from the world of home. It was the right of every wife, said author Sarah Ellis, to have 'a little sphere of domestic arrangements, with which the husband shall not feel that he has any business to interfere, except at her request, and into which a reasonable man would not wish to obtrude his authority, simply because the operations necessary to be carried on in that department of his household are alike foreign to his understanding and his tastes.'[12]

There is no doubt that Victorian women's choices in life were extremely limited, as many excellent studies have shown.[13] Women had no access to property or wages, for example, during most of the nineteenth century. Nor did Victorian women exercise any real political power; they could not even vote in England until 1928.[14] Victorian women were not lawyers, and few were doctors. None were architects.[15] Some were teachers and nurses. Most were mothers and homemakers. In the realm of opportunities, the spheres of women and men were unquestionably distinct.

In most other respects, however, the social worlds of nineteenth-century middle-class women and men overlapped considerably. For example, although women undoubtedly spent more time than men in the home, they exercised enormous power in the so-called public sphere of economics. If a family rented out a room to a lodger, for instance, it was the woman who handled this arrangement, generating a sizable percentage of the family income within supposedly 'separate' space. Middle-class women in the nineteenth century typically controlled the employment of servants; they hired, trained, paid, and fired the men and women who looked on their houses as workplaces as well as residences.[16] They also managed the elaborate round of social events that helped secure their husbands' place in the public world of finance and manufacturing.[17] In addition, most women managed the purchase of food and clothing for their families; they balanced the family books, exercising, in many cases, considerable economic expertise. The rise of the department store in the business districts of cities is testament to women's economic power in the consumption of ready-made goods.[18] The sphere of women encompassed, in a very real way, the public spaces, rural landscapes, commercial enterprises, and private rooms of nineteenth-century England. Gender distinctions

depended on women's behaviour in public places.[19] If anything, the range of spaces accessible to Victorian women was far wider than that open to Victorian men.

Nor was the world of home shielded from the influence of men. The daily lives of middle-class husbands and fathers had an enormous impact on domestic life.[20] Although architectural historians have focused in their consideration of gender on rooms associated with women's experiences—the parlour, the kitchen, the nursery—as many rooms in the house were relegated to men's special use. The dining room, for example, was often occupied exclusively by men when women left the table after eating.[21] Victorian dining-room furniture was often dark and massive in appearance, supposedly satisfying masculine tastes. . . . Decorators Rhoda and Agnes Garrett maintained that the gloomy atmosphere of most dining rooms in London was to 'remind one of the British boast that every Englishman's house is his castle, and that he wishes neither to observe nor to be observed when he retires into the dignified seclusion of this, the especially masculine department of the household.'[22] In larger houses, the library, study, smoking room, and billiards room were designed especially for the man of the house. The separation of these spaces from the family rooms was necessary for the proper transaction of business (and smoking), but their difference was also marked in material terms by the presence of books, maps, scientific equipment, and weapons.[23]

Indeed, the spatial separation of men and women was one of the most prominent features of the typical Victorian house, and the degree of separation was a significant indication of class.[24] While the dining room, study, and smoking room were associated with the husband, the drawing room, boudoir, and morning room were the wife's realm. It was in these rooms that the elaborate ritual of women's morning calls took place, as well as other important occupations for middle-class women, such as reading novels, writing letters, and doing handiwork.

Men's association with the dining room depended on the withdrawal of women to the drawing room after dinner. In plan, the dining and drawing rooms were often set off in direct opposition to express these gendered associations. The 'masculine departments' were commonly located at the front of the house, the more 'public' part of the plan, while women's rooms were in the back or were removed from the street level altogether, apparently protected by this distance from public space. The plan of a typical London house cited by Poore and published in the *Lancet* . . . shows this configuration of rooms. The dining room is adjacent to the main entrance of the house while the morning room is in the rear. The lady's drawing room and boudoir are on the first floor, above the unpredictable and presumably noisy activity of the street.

The prospect of rooms and their means of access in a typical Victorian house were also clearly gendered. Men's rooms, particularly the study or library, often included a separate entrance 'to admit the tenants, tradesmen, and other persons on business, as directly as possible to the room in question, and no other part of the house', while women's rooms often looked out on flower gardens or even on a 'lady's walk'.[25] Men's rooms were thus open and accessible to the outside world, while women's spaces were most often intended to be closed and inaccessible. Most experts recommended the complete separation of men's and women's rooms. Robert Kerr, for instance, considered connection between the dining and drawing rooms 'a clumsy contrivance'.[26] The author of another popular advice book observed that the drawing room and dining room were the reverse of each other in every way.[27] The location of the rooms on different levels, of course, secured separation and guaranteed relatively predictable meetings between men and women in the house.

In terms of decoration, too, men's and women's rooms were directly opposed. 'The relations of the Dining-room and Drawing-room', explained Kerr, 'are in almost every way

those of contrast.'[28] He saw the ideal drawing room as being 'entirely ladylike' in 'cheerfulness, refinement of elegance, and what is called lightness as opposed to massiveness'.[29] Hermann Muthesius, whose classic *English House* of 1904–5 is a perceptive analysis of the contemporary British house plan, said that the drawing room had a 'light, pleasing impression and a general air of *joie-de-vivre*'.[30] The Garretts described the decoration of the drawing room as 'light and airy' compared with the 'heavy and sombre' dining room, for in the former 'the ladies of the family are told that it is now their turn to have their tastes consulted.'[31] According to the Garretts, the drawing room was devoted 'to the lighter occupations of life'.[32]

The entire Victorian house—its location, arrangement, style, and size—also served to situate men (and women) in a culture ordered according to class.[33] Like clothing, language, behaviour, and even smell, the house expressed to the public world the aspirations and economic mobility of all its inhabitants. The healthy house, 'from basement to roof', as Mrs Plunkett described it, was an equally important expression of women's participation in the public urban realm.

The association of middle-class women with health in general was not new in the Victorian period. As many historians have noted, before the rise of the modern profession of medicine, women of all classes had played significant roles as domestic healers in their homes. In the seventeenth century, Lady Anne Clifford described her mother as 'a lover of the study of medicine and the practise of Alchemy'. It was said that 'she prepared excellent medicines that did good to many.'[34] Cooking, brewing, and distilling—traditionally women's work—were closely associated with healing.[35] Sickness and dying were much more private conditions than today, and both were overseen by women within the home.

The expectations of the nineteenth-century sanitarians stemmed from this long-standing belief that domestic health was an innately female concern; women were considered 'natural' healers and nurturers because they bore children. Victorian scientific theories of sexual difference also saw women as passive, intuitive, and tender—qualities that were considered appropriate to caring for the sick.[36] 'Sick-nursing' was seen as a natural extension of domestic labour. As Lewis has noted, it was not until 1891 that the census in England differentiated hospital nurses from household servants.[37] The emergence of modern nursing in the nineteenth century as a profession particularly suited to women is testament to all these beliefs.

By then, too, it had often been stated that women were particularly adept at preventive rather than therapeutic or curative medicine. Their experience in raising a family supposedly endowed them with special abilities in maintaining good health in the household and preventing the spread of disease once it entered a home. Pioneering female physicians later in the century used the seemingly urgent need for preventive medicine to strengthen their campaign for more women doctors. 'We should give to man cheerfully the curative department, and women the preventative', proclaimed Dr Harriot Hunt in 1852.[38] This perception that women's place in the profession of medicine was complementary to men's eased the way for women to enter the predominantly male field.

As in the profession of medicine, so it was in domestic sanitation. Women's role in the reform of domestic architecture focused on preventing the spread of infection within the house—by inspecting and maintaining the sanitary aspects of the house, by caring for the sick according to modern 'scientific' principles, and by keeping the house clean, especially free of dust. . . . [T]he responsibility for repairing or healing the already 'sick' building—like the restoration of sick bodies—was the charge of male physicians.

Women's isolation in the home was used to advance their role in domestic sanitation, as Dr Richardson so clearly stated: 'I press this office for the prevention of disease on womankind, not simply because they can carry it out . . . but because it is an office which man never can carry out; and because the whole work of prevention waits and waits until the woman takes it up and makes it hers. The man is abroad, the disease threatens the home, and the woman is at the threatened spot. Who is to stop it at the door, the man or the woman?'[39] This parallels women's 'progress' in other fields, where their supposed experience as mothers was used to strengthen their position outside the home as practitioners of 'social' or 'civic maternalism'.[40]

But the reformers' enthusiasm and support for female collaboration worked in other ways as well. Teaching women the 'laws' of sanitary science and expecting them to realize these laws in the home meant that any subsequent sickness or death was considered to be the result of women's failure to follow the rules.[41] 'The gospel of sanitation must find its chief preachers and exponents in the women who make the house into the home, or by neglect turn it into a trap for the four deleterious D's, Darkness, Damp, Dirt, and Disease. Slovenly women . . . are factors of disease, and cleanly housewives acting forces against the possibility, or for the suppression, of sickness', reported a reviewer of Dr Richardson's *Household Health*.[42] . . .

The domestic sanitarians expected middle-class women to be amateur inspectors of their houses, maintaining minimal standards of healthy architecture by detecting architectural defects. Typical house inspection covered a wide range of tasks, including checking the connection of the house to the municipal sewer system, the orientation of the building, and the materials used in the walls, as well as inspecting for water purity and measuring dampness and air movement in the interior of the house.[43] A proliferation of books and articles appeared in the 1880s and 1890s instructing women on how to inspect the work of the 'ignorant or indolent plumber', builder, or architect.[44] The authors included tips on drainage, ventilation, lighting, furnishing, and the arrangement of rooms, covering the architecture of the house thoroughly for their female readership. Attention to these sanitary matters, claimed one sanitarian, could decrease the death rate by half.[45]

The inspection of the house was usually conducted in a series of tests, which were spelled out in detail and illustrated in the women's advice literature. The 'peppermint test', to check the drainage system, consisted of running peppermint oil into a drain from the exterior of the building. If a minty smell was detected inside, the house was considered insanitary. The oil could also be mixed with a can of boiling water, as recommended by William Maguire in his popular plumbing manual, then poured down the soil pipe from the roof. Maguire pointed out that this test was 'troublesome' and required 'delicate handling'. The person pouring the peppermint oil into the pipes had to remain on the roof for a considerable time, otherwise one might bring the peppermint smell into the house and ruin the test.[46] Special machines, resembling modern vacuum cleaners, were commercially available to assist householders in the diagnosis of their houses. . . .

. . .

The titles of articles in popular ladies' magazines in the final decades of the nineteenth century suggest that women may have participated in decisions regarding the health of houses long before problems were evident. The authors of 'Where Shall My House Be?', 'The Site of the House', 'Walls', and 'Drainage' provided middle-class women with comprehensive information on building design, including issues of health in the home.[47] The design of domestic architecture was thus a form of preventive medicine regulated entirely by women. 'She may have something to do with the building of the house at some time', observed an expert in 1899.[48]

Again, this gendering of responsibility worked in two ways. If a wife and mother was solely responsible for major design decisions that were thought to affect the health of the family, it followed that any defects or illness that subse-quently emerged was essentially her fault. In addition, it meant that a woman's poor health was regarded as a result of her own actions. By insisting that middle-class women's health had declined rather than improved as the reform of domestic architecture presumably progressed, doctors implied that women's faulty choice or regulation of sanitary systems was more to blame than their own inability to cure.[49]

'House-choosing', as Panton called it, was a standard chapter in late nineteenth-century domestic manuals for women. Selecting a family residence was one of the many tasks that a young couple performed together before (or just after) marriage. According to most authors, women were expected to make most of the decisions regarding the family's place of residence, sometimes but not always with the advice of their husbands.[50] They were always solely responsible for any aspect of the house affecting the family's health. For example, although both husband and wife probably participated in the general inspection of a house before its lease or purchase, the more detailed investigation of plumbing and drainage was the responsibility of the wife. The previous generation of women, reported Plunkett in 1885, had left inspection of the 'semi-telluric' region of the house to their husbands, whereas modern women 'rise above the beaten paths of cookery and needlework to some purpose.' 'A new sphere of usefulness and efficiency opens with the knowledge that in sanitary matters an ounce of prevention is worth a ton of cure', she asserted. 'There is nothing in hygiene that [a woman] can not comprehend.'[51]

As well as becoming amateur inspectors of their houses, Victorian women learned about science and medicine by nursing sick family members, just as their mothers and grandmothers had done. Indeed, the primary location for middle-class medical care at this time was the home. It was even the site for major surgery. Hospitals, especially those in large urban centres, were seen as the causes of death rather than as places to heal, since their mortality rates were extremely high. It was not until the turn of the century that the hospital was considered preferable to the home as a site for middle-class medical treatment, for by then it was understood to be cleaner and more appropriate than the home. As a result of Joseph Lister's explanation in 1867 of the role of living organisms in the putrefaction of wounds, cleanliness and antisepsis were practised so that hospitals gradually became curative places.[52] Around the turn of the century, many operating theatres were redone with new easy-to-clean materials and were rearranged to include specialized sterilizing and recovery rooms, which obviously were not available in typical middle-class houses.[53]

Women's role in the home involved much more than the simple isolation of the patient in a bedroom. As sick-nurse, a woman's responsibility included monitoring the room temperature and humidity, overseeing the patient's meals, and ensuring the patient's isolation from other family members. The difference between the Victorian woman's care for the sick and her great-grandmother's was that the late nineteenth-century sickroom was ordered with 'hints' from a medical expert according to modern 'scientific' principles.[54]

'However skilfully designed the arrangements of a house may appear to be,' commented Mary Ann Barker, author of *The Bedroom and Boudoir*, 'it is impossible to know whether a great law of common sense and practical usefulness has guided such arrangements, until there has been an illness in the house.' Family sickness entailed considerable rearrangement of the spatial relationships between family members, as well as the ways spaces were perceived. 'Many smart and pretty-looking bedrooms are discovered by their sick owner to be very different abodes to what they seemed to him in health', noted Lady Barker.[55]

Women's major responsibility in caring for the sick at home was ensuring the isolation of the family member in the sickroom. The sickroom was an ordinary bedroom that was often set aside and especially furnished in anticipation of illness

in the house. Catherine Gladstone described the benefits of such planning in the book she authored for the International Health Exhibition:

> As we must prepare, in every dwelling-house, for the contingency of illness, how desirable it would be for *all* houses, even of moderate size, to have some one corner suitable for a sick-room! If space admits of such a room being entirely isolated from the rest of the house, so much the better; but much may be done by at all events securing two rooms opening into each other, with windows, doors, and fireplaces where they should be, with hot and cold water supply within easy reach, and a closet properly placed.[56]

Many authors not only recommended the careful planning of special rooms for the sick but also advised that they be constructed differently from ordinary bedrooms, with 'double sashes and double wall', for example, 'to exclude the sound of the elements without'.[57]

Mrs Gladstone did not explain why she recommended having two sickrooms, though she probably subscribed to the widespread belief that a 'change of rooms' improved a patient's health. Children were often moved to a spare bedroom when they were ill, not only to prevent the infection spreading to other children but because it was feared the illness might infect the room itself. Maud Sambourne, daughter of the cartoonist Linley Sambourne, was temporarily accommodated in the spare room of the family home in Kensington. Her mother Marion Sambourne's diaries record the concern she experienced when 12-year-old Maud fell ill in 1887 and the frequency with which doctors visited the family's sickroom. On 10 February 1887, Marion wrote, 'Maudie no better, v. feverish & in pain, Dr O came four times.'[58]

The 'construction' of a special room or suite of rooms for a family member within the home often involved considerable rearrangement of room uses, as previously mentioned. Mrs Panton suggested choosing a room at the top of the house. In the case of a house that was being built to a family's specifications, she advised that the sickroom be separate from the main building—an annex that could be reached by an interior passage and an exterior door. The door between the passage and the sickroom should be of plate glass so that a mother could observe her sick child without risk of infection. As additional protection, Panton suggested that a sheet soaked in carbolic acid should be hung on the door. The doctor would enter the sickroom from the exterior door. The decorations and furnishing should be extremely cheap, Panton advised, because they would be destroyed after every illness.[59]

Most sickrooms were less elaborate than Panton's version. Certainly, most families did not construct special annexes to their houses. They simply 'emptied' ordinary rooms of furnishings, clothing, and any other contents as a way of securing separation of the sick from the healthy members of the family. The back of the house was better than the front, and upper levels were preferable to lower floors, experts said, because of the need for perfect quiet. Too much furniture was believed to 'confuse' sick people. 'As a rule, in a severe illness,' warned Lady Barker, 'sick people detest anything like a confusion or profusion of ornaments or furniture.' Like others, she associated successful nursing with the removal of 'things' from the room:

> I have known the greatest relief expressed by a patient, who seemed too ill to notice any such change, at the substitution of one single, simple classical vase for a whole shelf-full of tawdry French china ornaments, and I date the recovery of another from the moment of the removal out of his sight of an exceedingly smart modern dressing-table, with many bows of ribbon and flounces of lace and muslin. I do not mean to say that the furniture of a sick-room need be ugly—only that it should be simple and not too much of it.[60]

The American author and social reformer Charlotte Perkins Gilman described the sense of confinement, even imprisonment, she had felt in a 'big, airy room' because of its 'smouldering unclean yellow' wallpaper.[61] Her well-known story, 'The Yellow Wallpaper' (1892), recounted her quick mental disintegration while spending time in a former nursery at the top of a rented summer house. The tale has become a classic in women's history and is also significant for the clear links drawn by the author between architecture and women's power, a subject that intrigued Gilman throughout her prolific career.[62] Seldom mentioned, however, is that in 'The Yellow Wallpaper' she blamed her husband John, a physician, for her inability to get better.

An emptier room was also easier to clean, protecting the next occupant from infection. Catherine J. Wood suggested that women should remove all carpets and curtains, retaining only a table and washstand in the sickroom.[63] While every family could not afford to destroy and replace the room's contents, care was certainly taken to clean the sickroom and its contents thoroughly after an illness. Like the regular cleaning of the house, this was entirely the woman's responsibility.

The above advice of Wood and others is evidence of the widespread debate at the time over the role played by household objects in the spread of infection. It also shows that medical experts as late as the turn of the century continued to create an 'atmosphere of constant crisis' in the middle-class home. Articles with titles such as 'Books Spread Contagion', 'Contagion by Telephone', and 'Infection and Postage Stamps', as well as many experts' insistence that diseases were continuing to spread because of women's negligence, must have boosted both the standards of cleanliness (and sales of sickroom furniture) and maternal guilt.[64]

The sanitarians also promoted cleanliness in the home by specifying the use of new materials inside the house. This advice, of course, assumed that there would be considerable renovation to house interiors. The sanitarians' 'prohibition against dust', for example, discouraged the use of upholstered furniture and the elaborate decoration that was popular at mid-century. W.H. Corfield recommended the use of tiles throughout the house; Douglas Galton, an authority on hospital design, suggested that interior walls be made of metal or cement to avoid the accumulation of dust. Most experts' advice was less drastic, suggesting simply that one avoid heavy curtains and difficult-to-clean furniture.[65]

Commercial manufacturers took advantage of woman's role as sick-nurse in the home by promoting health-inducing products that were supposedly less disruptive to the household. The 'Arema' vaporizer, for example, would prevent the spread of all infectious diseases while a woman slept, read, or worked. . . . Not surprisingly, the International Health Exhibition of 1884 brought together hundreds of manufacturers selling devices specially for invalids and sickrooms. Many of these were marketed to women. Messrs Doulton and Company, the major manufacturer of domestic tiles at the time, set up a special pavilion at the IHE.[66]

In terms of material culture, however, health reform had its greatest impact on the design of beds. The most drastic change was the popularity of metal beds, which had formerly been used only in institutions. It was believed that metal, like tiles, harboured less dust and absorbed no humidity; it was thus intrinsically cleaner than wood. The leading manufacturer and distributor of beds in London, Heal and Son, exhibited an ideal small bedroom at the IHE. . . . Although the other three pieces of furniture in the room were wooden, the bed was metal.

Physicians also advised different 'environmental' conditions for the treatment of various illnesses in the home. After about 1870, the authors of articles advising women how to nurse sick family members nearly always focused on the arrangement of the sickroom rather than on the therapeutic treatment of illnesses.[67] Through the arrangement of the 'architecture', women were expected to prevent the spread of infection in the house. A fever, for example, required that

the sickroom have either a small fire or none at all, thorough ventilation, and minimal furniture. A completely different 'architecture' was recommended for the treatment of measles: closed windows and an open door.[68] Victorian women thus practised domesticity, as historian Regina Markell Marantz has noted, 'not as a cult, but as a science'.[69]

. . .

Beginning in the 1870s, women's sanitary responsibilities in the home were professionalized under the name of domestic science or domestic economy. Like medicine and architecture, the new 'field' was configured to follow precise and predictable rules, was subject to examination (not registration), and became the subject of formal programs of education. 'Wifeliness, which for centuries has been attributed to natural charm, is demonstrably a science', proclaimed the pioneers of the new field.[70] As Barbara Ehrenreich and Deirdre English have noted, 'scientific housekeeping' depended heavily on real connections to the male world of science.[71]

'[The home maker] must know a good deal about physics', stated an expert in 1899, 'because that is basal to all the plumbing in her home, basal to the whole subject of ventilation, to the whole material side of the home.'[72] Like Catharine Beecher in the United States, proponents of the new field argued that proper housework was based on scientific principles. 'It is a Profession,' claimed Phyllis Browne, the author of several housekeeping manuals, 'and to qualify for it a girl needs systematic training and methodical practice.'[73] Beecher's ideas were promulgated in England in the 1890s by her sister-in-law, Eunice Beecher. 'There is nothing that can lighten labour', she said, 'like method and regularity in performing it.'[74]

The first annual congress on domestic economy was held in Birmingham in 1877 to discuss the teaching of domestic science as a part of the general education of girls.[75] Several sanitarians, including Edwin Chadwick, read papers to the newly assembled organization. A journalist reporting on the conference noted what he considered a peculiar omission:

> We are not aware if domestic architecture has yet been taken up as a profession by women—but we feel convinced that when this is the case it will prove not only lucrative to themselves, but most valuable to the community. The dreary monotony of our street architecture would be done away with, and our poor and middle-class houses would be built with all the appliances for domestic health and comfort which now are either done without or are subsequently added at great expense and trouble by the inmates themselves. We wish that someone had taken up this subject at the Congress.[76]

This remark was typical of the period. As women gained more and more recognition and confidence in design through their management of the home by 'scientific' principles, they, like the physicians, were seen by an anxious public as alternative 'designers' of domestic environments.

. . .

The invention of the new field of domestic science was part of a broader program to employ women in the late nineteenth century. A 'surplus' of females—resulting from an imbalance in the number of men moving to the colonies, among other reasons—had reached seemingly insoluble proportions by 1891, when the census reported nearly 900,000 more women than men in England and Wales.[77] Ten years earlier there had been recorded 121 spinsters to every bachelor in London.[78] Many of these unmarried women, called 'redundant' at the time, were forced to earn their own living. The new educational opportunities, including programs in domestic science, provided 'professional' opportunities for the redundant spinsters. Domestic science was not threatening: women studying it did not put men out of work. Moreover, its subject matter seemed restricted to women's traditional work within the home: cooking, cleaning, and caring for the sick. Even the new field of

hygiene, as we have seen, was considered a woman's version of science.

A major aspect of the discipline was the systematization of household cleanliness. This meant that women should follow a 'routine' in keeping their houses clean. 'Method and system', observed the housecleaning expert Phyllis Browne, 'are to household work what oil is to machinery—they make things go smoothly and easily.' 'System', she explained, 'consists in having a clear understanding of what has to be done, when and how it is to be done, and arranging who is to do it.'[79] Methods of housecleaning were equally important. Following the general scientific model, this meant the establishment of principles that were to be observed in the cleaning of a house. 'There is a right way and a wrong way even of dusting a room or furniture', Browne asserted, and then explained at length to her female readership how to dust 'correctly'.[80] Again, the threat of sickness and death was upheld as the consequence of 'incorrect' dusting: 'Where dirt reigns, disease, misery and crime stand erect around his throne; liberty, progress, and enlightenment hide their heads in shame. All the great plagues which have destroyed human happiness, broken women's hearts and made children orphans, have held their carnival in the midst of dirt.'[81]

Pointing to dirty houses (and, by implication, careless women) as the cause of illness was obviously not in itself a liberating factor for Victorian women. Through this kind of liability, however, women became 'experts' on the design of houses. Women trained in the 'principles' of hygiene spoke out publicly on the merits of various materials and designs, constructing a critical forum with which to consider the work of architects. In addition, women's accomplishments at home led directly to work in the supposedly public world of men. Having proven their gender-based competence in detecting faulty drains and poor ventilation in their own homes, women were among the first to be appointed sanitary inspectors of buildings as 'health visitors' to the poor.[82] . . .

The overall tone of Victorian domestic advice literature implied that women could detect unsanitary work but could not undo or improve the mistakes supposedly made by builders or architects. Changes to the plans of the houses, at least in England, were beyond their immediate power, which many advisers suggested would be much improved if women were given the chance to design buildings. 'Doubtless the great thing that strikes us when we are house-hunting is that if women architects could get employment houses would be far better planned than they are now', remarked Mrs Panton.[83]

The situation was very different in the United States. There women were encouraged to make extensive renovations to their homes, including substantial changes to the plans of their houses. In the name of domestic cleanliness, the American author Helen Dodd advised the wives of farmers to improve the arrangements of their houses to suit their own needs better. She told women to look critically at their houses and ask themselves whether the buildings really satisfied them rather than being designed to suit the rest of the family. Dodd set out some 'principles of sanitation' for farmhouses which could be realized without employing skilled workmen; 'any strong woman' could do the renovations, she said.[84] Dodd's instructions focused on changes to the interior arrangements of the houses without altering the exterior walls. . . . For example, her renovated kitchen plan increased the direct light of both the kitchen and the dining room, as well as providing a more efficient work space in the kitchen.

E.C. Gardner's manual, *The House That Jill Built, after Jack's Had Proved a Failure*, also encouraged American women to modify their houses.[85] Using the narrative of a young married couple considering various arrangements of houses, Gardner conveyed to women standard architectural information on room composition, sanitary drainage, and decoration. Intended for three groups of people—those contemplating the purchase of a home, those wishing to improve

their homes, and those who had suffered from living in homes based on errors in design—the book's title revealed the author's confidence in the design abilities of women.

No such books were written for English women, though women in Britain may have read the American literature. As noted above, their responsibilities appear to have been limited to the detection of faulty design and did not include the building's physical improvement. This was doubtless because the system of middle-class housing was far more standardized in England than in the United States; it was not necessarily a reflection of stronger feminist impulses among American women. . . .

English novelists described women's familiarity with plumbing as a mark of new-found confidence. In *Pilgrimage*, for example, Dorothy Richardson described a woman's view of a Bloomsbury house in 1890:

> The large dusty house, the many downstairs rooms, the mysterious dark-roomed vault of the basement, all upright in her upright form; hurried smeary cleansings, swift straightening of grey-sheeted beds, the strange unfailing water-system, gurgling cisterns, gushing taps and lavatory flushes, the wonder of gaslight and bedroom candles, the daily meals magically appearing and disappearing; her knowledge of the various mysteriously arriving and vanishing people, all beginning and ending in her triumphant, reassuring smile that went forward outside beyond these things, with everybody.[86]

As we saw at the beginning of this chapter, Mrs Plunkett's assignment of a 'properly plumbed house' to 'woman's sphere' in 1885 was undoubtedly accurate. Women actively participated in building construction and science through their regulation of healthy houses. Their own homes—particularly the drainage—were arenas through which they exhibited their mastery of these concepts, hence the name of the new field: 'domestic science'.

Equally important, however, was Plunkett's qualification of her statement that woman's sphere had many definitions. Although the new scientific and architectural expertise gained by women through sanitary science appeared to be liberating, it set relatively rigid limits on their participation in health reform. Women were blamed for the persistence of disease among the middle class as well as for the unacceptable work of plumbers and architects. In addition to their role as regulators of healthy houses . . . the close association of women and houses between 1870 and 1900 cast Victorian women into passive roles as the objects of scientific research. Like the service pipe, house drain, and ventilating pipe that defined woman's sphere, her body acted as both the protection against disease and the source of infection.

## Notes

1. Mrs H.M. Plunkett, *Women, Plumbers, and Doctors; or, Household Sanitation* (New York: D. Appleton, 1885), title page.
2. Ibid., 94. . . .
3. Ada S. Ballin, 'Health in Our Homes', *Baby: The Mothers' Magazine* 3 (Dec. 1889–Nov. 1890): 3.
4. 'Domestic Economy', *Englishwoman's Review*, 15 Aug. 1877, 350.
5. For an analysis of the literature and language of separate spheres, see Linda K. Kerber, 'Separate Spheres, Female Worlds, Woman's Place: The Rhetoric of Women's History', *Journal of American History* 75 (June 1988): 9–39. See also Linda McDowell, 'City and Home: Urban Housing and the Sexual Division of Space', in Mary Evans and Clare Ungerson, eds, *Sexual Divisions: Patterns and Processes* (London: Tavistock, 1983), 142–63.
6. Men supposedly operated in both spheres. See Leonore Davidoff and Catherine Hall, 'The Architecture of Public and Private Life: English Middle-Class Society in a Provincial Town, 1780–1850', in Derek Fraser and Anthony Sutcliffe, eds, *The Pursuit of Urban History* (London: Edward Arnold, 1983), 326. On the

link between gender and anti-urban trends in British planning, see Leonore Davidoff, Jean L'Esperance, and Howard Newby, 'Landscape with Figures: Home and Community in English Society', in Juliet Mitchell and Ann Oakley, eds, *Rights and Wrongs of Women* (London: Penguin, 1976), 139–75.

7. There are exceptions to this in recent literature. See Mary Poovey, *Uneven Developments: The Ideological Work of Gender in Mid-Victorian England* (Chicago: University of Chicago Press, 1988), 1–23; Elizabeth Blackmar, *Manhattan for Rent, 1785–1850* (Ithaca, NY: Cornell University Press, 1989), 126–38; Leonore Davidoff and Catherine Hall, *Family Fortunes: Men and Women of the English Middle Class, 1780–1850* (London: Hutchison, 1987), 357–96; Mary P. Ryan, *Women in Public: Between Banners and Ballots, 1825–1880* (Baltimore: Johns Hopkins University Press, 1990), 58–94.
8. Many historians rely on the pattern of forces described by Philippe Aries in 'The Family and the City', *Daedalus* 106 (Spring 1977): 227–35, and *Centuries of Childhood: A Social History of Family Life*, trans. Robert Baldick (New York: Vintage, 1962).
9. Jane Lewis, *Women in England 1870–1950: Sexual Divisions and Social Change* (Sussex: Wheatsheaf, 1984), x.
10. Blackmar, *Manhattan for Rent*, 110.
11. Jane Ellen Panton, *The Way They Should Go: Hints to Young Parents* (London: Ward and Downey, 1896), 165.
12. Sarah Ellis, *The Wives of England* (London: Fisher, 1843), 129.
13. There is a huge literature on Victorian women in England. The major studies that subscribe to the 'separate spheres' model include the following: Patricia Branca, *Silent Sisterhood: Middle-Class Women in the Victorian Home* (London: Croom Helm, 1975); Carol Dyhouse, *Girls Growing Up in Late Victorian and Edwardian England* (London: Routledge & Kegan Paul, 1981); Deborah Gorham, *The Victorian Girl and the Feminine Ideal* (Bloomington: Indiana University Press, 1982); Lewis, *Women in England*; Jane Lewis, ed., *Labour*

and Love: Women's Experience of Home and Family, 1850–1940 (Oxford: Basil Blackwell, 1986); Martha Vicinus, Independent Women: Work and Community for Single Women, 1850–1920 (Chicago: University of Chicago Press, 1985); Vicinus, ed., Suffer and Be Still: Women in the Victorian Age (Bloomington: Indiana University Press, 1980); Vicinus, ed., A Widening Sphere: Changing Roles of Victorian Women (Bloomington: Indiana University Press, 1977).

14.  The first women's suffrage committee was formed in 1866; women taxpayers voted in local elections in 1869, following the Municipal Franchise Act. It was not until 1928 that the Equal Franchise Act allowed all women over 21 to cast votes. See Angela Holdsworth, Out of the Doll's House: The Story of Women in the Twentieth Century (London: BBC, 1988), 12–13.

15.  The first woman architect in Britain, Ethel Charles, was accepted by the Royal Institute of British Architects in 1898, just three years before Queen Victoria's death. See Lynne Walker, 'Women and Architecture', in Judy Attfield and Pat Kirkham, eds, A View from the Interior (London: Women's Press, 1989), 99.

16.  Leonore Davidoff, 'Mastered for Life: Servant and Wife in Victorian and Edwardian England', Journal of Social History 7 (Summer 1974): 406–28.

17.  Leonore Davidoff, The Best Circles: Society Etiquette and the Season (London: Cresset, 1973).

18.  On the department store as an institution designed to appeal to women, see Susan Porter Benson, Counter Cultures: Saleswomen, Managers, and Customers in American Department Stores, 1890–1940 (Urbana: University of Illinois Press, 1986).

19.  Ryan, Women in Public, 59.

20.  This question has not been explored fully by historians because of a dearth of sources. Studies that begin to address men's influence at home include J.A. Mangan and James Walvin, eds, Manliness and Morality: Middle-Class Masculinity in Britain and America, 1800–1948 (Manchester: Manchester University Press, 1987).

21.  The major text advising women how to decorate dining rooms was Martha Jane Loftie, The Dining-Room (London: Macmillan, 1878). On the history of the dining room, see Clifford Edward Clark Jr, 'The Vision of the Dining Room: Plan Book Dreams and Middle-Class Realities', in Kathryn Grover, ed., Dining in America, 1850–1900 (Amherst: University of Massachusetts Press, 1987), 142–72; on dining rooms in aristocratic houses, see Jill Franklin, The Gentleman's Country House and Its Plan, 1835–1914 (London: Routledge & Kegan Paul, 1981), 48–51.

22.  Rhoda Garrett and Agnes Garrett, Suggestions for House Decoration (London: Macmillan, 1876), 28.

23.  Most Victorian books on house planning described men's rooms this way. For a typical example, see Robert Kerr, The Gentleman's House; or, How to Plan English Residences (London: Murray, 1864), 101–10, 129–38.

24.  For an analysis of the gender divisions of a house plan published by Robert Kerr, see Matrix, Making Space: Women and the Man-made Environment (London: Pluto, 1984), 64–7.

25.  See Kerr, Gentleman's House, 125; Hermann Muthesius, The English House (New York: Rizzoli, 1979 [1904–5]); J.J. Stevenson, House Architecture, vol. 2 (London: Macmillan, 1880), 57; Dianne Harris, 'Cultivating Power: The Language of Feminism in Women's Garden Literature, 1870–1920', Landscape Journal 13 (Fall 1994): 113–23.

26.  Kerr, Gentleman's House, 124.

27.  W. Audsley and G. Audsley, Cottage, Lodge and Villa Architecture (London: Mackenzie, n.d.), 24.

28.  Kerr, Gentleman's House, 119.

29.  Ibid.

30.  Muthesius, English House, 85.

31.  Garrett and Garrett, Suggestions for House Decoration, 28.

32.  Ibid., 56.

33.  Blackmar, Manhattan for Rent, 128.

34.  Hilary Bourdillon, Women as Healers: A History of Women and Medicine (Cambridge: Cambridge University Press, 1988), 17.

35.  Lesley Hall, Hygeia's Handmaids: Women, Health and Healing (London: Wellcome Institute for the History of Medicine, 1988), 21.

36. On scientific theories of sexual difference in general in the nineteenth century, see Jane Lewis, *Women in England*, 83–92.

37. Ibid., 174. Lewis referred to Celia Davies, 'Making Sense of the Census in Britain and the USA: The Changing Occupational Classification and the Position of Nurses', *Sociological Review* 28 (1980): 581–609.

38. Cited in Regina Morantz-Sanchez, 'The Female Student Has Arrived: The Rise of the Women's Medical Movement', in Ruth J. Abram, ed., *'Send Us a Lady Physician': Women Doctors in America, 1835–1920* (New York: Norton, 1985), 63.

39. Benjamin Ward Richardson, 'Woman as a Sanitary Reformer', in Henry C. Burdett and F. de Chaumont, eds, *Report of the Fourth Congress of the Sanitary Institute of Great Britain* (London: Sanitary Institute, 1880), 190.

40. Lewis, *Women in England*, 91.

41. Barbara Ehrenreich and Deirdre English have noted how the germ theory became a doctrine of individual guilt. See Ehrenreich and English, *For Her Own Good: 150 Years of Experts' Advice to Women* (London: Pluto, 1979), 74–5.

42. 'Reviews', *Sanitary Record*, 15 Jan. 1887, 335.

43. For a typical article, see 'Going Over the New House', *Baby: The Mothers' Magazine* 3 (Dec. 1889): 129.

44. T. Pridgin Teale, *Dangers to Health: A Pictorial Guide to Sanitary Defects* (London: Churchill, 1878), plate 5.

45. Ballin, 'Health in Our Homes', 3.

46. William R. Maguire, *Domestic Sanitary Drainage and Plumbing*, 3rd edn (London: Kegan Paul, Trench, Trubner, 1901), 194–5.

47. These appeared in *Baby* 3 (Dec. 1889–Nov. 1890). A similar series appeared in the *English Woman's Journal*. See 'Modern Housebuilding', *English Woman's Journal* 10 (Feb. 1863): 399–404, and 'House Building', ibid., 12 (Feb. 1864): 27–30, 341–7.

48. Dr Luther Gulick, 'The Home Maker: What She Ought to Know', *Young Woman* 8 (Oct. 1899–Sept. 1900): 64.

49. On physicians blaming women for having poor health, see Branca, *Silent Sisterhood*, 66.

50. This process was expounded by William Dean Howells in his novel *A Hazard of New Fortunes* (1890), in which Mrs March, exposing her 'female instinct for domiciliation', led her husband on a lengthy search for lodgings in New York.

51. Plunkett, *Women, Plumbers, and Doctors*, 10.

52. Lindsay Granshaw has explained how general cleanliness and antisepsis were seen as two distinct methods. See Granshaw, '"Upon This Principle I Have Based a Practice": The Development and Reception of Antisepsis in Britain, 1867–90', in John V. Pickstone, ed., *Medical Innovations in Historical Perspective* (New York: St Martin's Press, 1992).

53. J.T.H. Connor, 'Listerism Unmasked: Antisepsis and Asepsis in Victorian Anglo-Canada', *Journal of the History of Medicine and Allied Sciences* 49 (Apr. 1994): 236–8.

54. See, for example, Benjamin Ward Richardson's suggestions in 'Light in the Sick-room', *Sanitarian* 24 (Apr. 1890): 313–14, and the advice of American physician F.C. Larimore, 'Hygiene of the Sickroom', *Sanitarian* 20 (Mar. 1888): 220–3.

55. Lady Mary Ann Barker, *The Bedroom and the Boudoir* (London: Macmillan, 1878), 94–5. Books on bedrooms typically included entire chapters on how to transform them into sickrooms. See, for example, ibid., 94–109.

56. Mrs Catherine Gladstone, *Healthy Nurseries and Bedrooms, including the Lying-in Room* (London: Clowes. 1884), 124–5.

57. MSA and MRAS, *The Grammar of House Planning* (Edinburgh: Fullarton, 1864), 38.

58. Marion Sambourne's diaries were analyzed in Shirley Nicholson, *A Victorian Household* (London: Barrie and Jenkins, 1988). For this photo and the description of Maud's illness, see ibid., 46. Today the Sambourne house appears much as it did in the late nineteenth century. It is operated as a house museum by the Victorian Society.

59. See Jane Ellen Panton, *Nooks and Corners* (London: Ward and Downey, 1889), ch. 2, 'The Sick Room'.

60. Barker, *Bedroom*, 97–8.

61. Charlotte Perkins Gilman, *The Yellow Wallpaper and Other Writings* (New York: Bantam, 1989), 3–4.

62. Polly Wynn Allen, *Building Domestic Liberty: Charlotte Perkins Gilman's Architectural Feminism* (Amherst: University of Massachusetts Press, 1988).

63. Catherine J. Wood, 'The Sick-room and Its Appliances', *Baby: The Mothers' Magazine* 1 (Dec. 1887–Nov. 1888): 179.

64. . . . These titles are reproduced from Ehrenreich and English, *For Her Own Good*, 157.

65. Judith Ann Neiswander, 'Liberalism, Nationalism and the Evolution of Middle-Class Values: The Literature on Interior Decoration in England, 1875–1914', Ph.D. dissertation (University of London, 1988), 107–9.

66. An illustration and description appeared in Douglas Galton, 'The International Health Exhibition', *Art Journal* n.s., 4 (1884): 294–5.

67. For a characteristic article from the Victorian women's press, see 'Hints on Home Nursing', *Young Woman* 1 (Oct. 1892–Sept. 1893): 415–16.

68. This typical advice for the management of a sick-room is extracted from Pye Henry Chavasse, *Advice to a Mother*, 14th edn (London: Churchill, 1886), 215–20.

69. Regina Markell Morantz, 'Making Women Modern: Middle Class Women and Health Reform in 19th Century America', *Journal of Social History* 10 (1977): 493.

70. Florence Bohun, 'Back to the Home', *Englishwoman's Review*, 15 July 1910, 182.

71. Ehrenrich and English, *For Her Own Good*, 141–81.

72. Gulick, 'The Home Maker', 64.

73. Phyllis Browne, 'The Profession of Housewifery', *Young Woman* 8 (Oct. 1899–Sept. 1900): 223.

74. Mrs Henry Ward Beecher, 'Method and Regularity in the Home', *Woman's Herald*, 16 Mar. 1893, 51.

75. A report on the entire conference was published in 'Domestic Economy', *Englishwoman's Review*, 15 Aug. 1877, 347–55.

76. Ibid., 354–5.

77. Mrs Mallet, 'National Association for Housewifery', *Women's Penny Paper*, 28 Sept. 1889, 7.

78. Allerdale Grainger, 'Census Statistics as Indicative of the Employment of Women in London', *Englishwoman's Yearbook* (1881): 64.

79. Phyllis Browne, 'House-cleaning', in Shirley Forster Murphy, ed., *Our Homes, and How to Make Them Healthy* (London: Cassell, 1883), 870.

80. Ibid., 875.

81. Ibid., 869.

82. See 'Women as Official Inspectors: English Experience', *Sanitarian* 32 (May 1894): 437–43; 'Women Sanitary Inspectors', ibid., 43 (July 1899): 70–1. On American women as inspectors, see 'The Sanitary Inspectress and Her Maid', ibid., 44 (Jan. 1900): 34–9. On the steps performed by both male and female inspectors in England, see 'House Inspection', ibid., 10 (Feb. 1882): 156–61.

83. Jane Ellen Panton, *From Kitchen to Garret: Hints for Young Householders* (London: Ward and Downey, 1888), 4.

84. Helen Dodd, *The Healthful Farmhouse by a Farmer's Wife* (Boston: Whitcomb and Barrows, 1906), 3.

85. E.C. Gardner, *The House That Jill Built, after Jack's Had Proved a Failure* (New York: Fords, Howard, and Hulbert, 1882).

86. Dorothy M. Richardson, 'Interim', in Richardson, *Pilgrimage*, vol. 2 (New York: Knopf, 1967 [1916]), 428. For a detailed analysis of the relationship of fictional spaces to real-world architecture in eighteenth- and nineteenth-century England, see Philippa Tristram, *Living Space in Fact and Fiction* (London: Routledge, Chapman and Hall, 1990).

# 2

# Living on Display:
# Colonial Visions of Aboriginal Domestic Spaces

### Paige Raibmon

Notions of domesticity were central to colonial projects around the globe. They were part of the fray when metropole and colony collided and transformed one another. As Jean and John Comaroff put it, 'Colonialism was as much about making the center as it was about making the periphery. The colony was not a mere extension of the modern world. It was part of what made the world modern in the first place. And the dialectic of domesticity was a vital element in the process.'[1] The colonial desire to order domestic space had its correlate in broader attempts to impose discipline in the public sphere.[2] On the late-nineteenth-century Northwest Coast, this process took shape for Aboriginal people who increasingly lived not only overseas from, but within, the society of the colonizing metropoles. Aboriginal people experienced extreme pressure to bring their lives into conformity with Victorian expectations about private, middle-class, bourgeois domesticity. This pressure came not only from isolated missionaries posted in lonely colonial outposts but also from a broad swath of colonial society. So intense was the interest in Aboriginal domestic arrangements, however, that colonial society brought

Aboriginal domestic space into the public domain as never before, even as it urged Aboriginal communities to adopt the Victorian values of the domestic private sphere. While missionaries and government officials pressured Aboriginal families to replace multi-family longhouses with Victorian-style nuclear family dwellings, anthropologists and tourists invaded Aboriginal homes, alternately in search of a rapidly receding ('savage') past or a slowly dawning ('civilized') future. Missionaries encouraged such voyeuristic investigations in the hope that the object lessons of everyday Aboriginal life would generate a flow of funds from Christian pocketbooks into missionary society coffers. Anthropologists such as Franz Boas fed their own form of economic necessity with these displays, which they hoped would encourage benefactors to provide funding for additional anthropological fieldwork and collecting. In a sense, as they transformed Aboriginal domestic spaces into spectacle, all of the members of these non-Aboriginal groups became sightseers.

Domestic space was transformed into spectacle, and attempts to effect greater separation between private and public spaces simultaneously

Paige Raibmon, 'Living on Display: Colonial Visions of Aboriginal Domestic Spaces', *BC Studies* 140 (2003): 69–89. Reprinted by permission of *BC Studies*.

blurred the two, creating a hybrid public/private domain. Colonialism is riven with such invariably ironic contradictions. But the importance of such contradictions runs deeper than postmodern irony. While with one hand colonial society held out the promise of assimilation, with the other it impressed upon Aboriginal people its lack of good faith. The history of Aboriginal people in North America is replete with 'sweet' promises gone sour; with 'final' promises turned final solutions.[3] How did colonizers reconcile these contradictions, these 'tensions of empire'?[4] A review of their views of Aboriginal domestic space provides an opportunity to address this question.

When curious, often nosy, sometimes aggressive members of colonial society entered Aboriginal homes, they brought the things they needed to make sense of the room around them. The significance of cultural practice may lie in the story we tell ourselves about ourselves, but the insight that the metropole has been defined by the colonies, and the 'self' by the 'other', forces us to acknowledge that culture is also the story we tell ourselves about others.[5] The colonial preoccupation with the domestic spaces of Aboriginal people provides a window onto stories that worked in both of these ways simultaneously. The stories that members of colonial society told themselves about Aboriginal people were also stories they told themselves about themselves. The stories that Canadians and Americans told themselves differed, as did specific policies and conditions on both sides of the border. However, during the late nineteenth century, public interest in 'authentic' Indians and pride in successful Indian policy were important components of both countries' sense of nationalism. Differences in policy did not preclude continuities in attitudes and assumptions. Colonizers' fascination with the domestic spaces of Aboriginal people offers us an important moment of cultural convergence.

The colonial narration of Aboriginal domestic space as spectacle generated a multiplicity of stories about, among other things, Aboriginal savagery, white civilization, colonial legitimacy,

and modernity. Two assumptions of colonial thought recur in these stories. First, from their various, and admittedly diverse, vantage points, members of late nineteenth-century colonial society cast domestic spaces and domestic goods as material markers of civilization. But this alone cannot explain the sway that these markers of domesticity held over the colonial imagination. The second assumption takes us this additional step. The evidence suggests that members of colonial society assumed that the significance of these markers was more than skin deep. They assumed that the markers were straightforward reflections of the inner state of the individual's soul and the family's moral state. They extrapolated from fixed material form to fixed immaterial self. If the space was civilized, then likewise its inhabitants; if the space was uncivilized, then so were its inhabitants.

Aboriginal domestic spaces were put on display in a variety of contexts and along a continuum of consent. Some Aboriginal people willingly participated in the public performance of their private lives, while others submitted somewhat more grudgingly to the public gaze. Sometimes Aboriginal people did not have the opportunity to grant or withhold consent at all, when non-Aboriginal viewers invaded their private homes without bothering to ask permission. All of these interactions were infused with relations of power. Whether they suffered public scrutiny willingly or not, most Aboriginal families could ill afford to forgo the material benefits that accompanied submission to the colonial view. Some form of direct or indirect remuneration usually accompanied the performance of everyday life. This sometimes came as wages, at other times it came from the sale of souvenirs to sightseers hoping to commemorate their excursions into Aboriginal domestic space.

In this article, I explore a selection of domestic spectacles that fall along various points of the aforementioned continuum of consent, and I also address the nature of some of the stories that these spectacles enabled colonizers to tell themselves. I conclude with some brief considerations of the quite different stories that Aboriginal people told themselves about domestic spaces. The transformation and narration of everyday life were central to colonial policy and culture alike. This article takes preliminary steps towards considering why this may have been so.

## Exposition Space

The world's fairs and expositions of the late nineteenth century provide some of the clearest examples of Aboriginal people voluntarily submitting to living on display. Beginning with the Paris Exposition in 1889, colonized peoples became important attractions at world's fairs and expositions. In many respects, exhibit organizers intended these so-called 'live exhibits' to display and legitimate colonial narratives of modernity and progress. Early examples of mass advertising that helped generate public support for foreign and domestic policies, the expositions were themselves grand stories that members of colonial society told themselves about themselves.[6] While live exhibits at European fairs tended to come from distant overseas colonies, North American fairs, beginning with the 1893 Chicago World's Fair, featured displays of internally colonized Aboriginal people. While most of these performers spent at least some time in scripted song and dance performances, the bulk of their time as live exhibits was given over to the performance of everyday life.

The live exhibits at the 1893 Chicago World's Fair invariably revolved around domestic dwellings. Millions of tourists flocked to see Aboriginal people supposedly living 'under ordinary conditions and occupying a distinctive habitation'.[7] These dwellings fed into the fair's organizational theme: progress. They offered a relief against which visitors could measure the architectural achievements not only of the rest of the fair but also of dominant society in general. As one reporter wrote, the Aboriginal dwellings stood 'in amazing contrast to the white palaces

stretching away to the north, that evidence[d] the skill and prosperity of their successors in this western domain.'[8] Against this backdrop of modernity, the Aboriginal dwellings lent themselves to a social evolutionist narrative that legitimated colonial endeavours.

Anthropologists and other exhibitors erected a 'great Aboriginal encampment',[9] consisting of the living spaces of Aboriginal people from across North America. While newspaper reporters might concede that Aboriginal people lived in 'stone, brick and frame houses'[10] when they were at home, they imagined 'authentic' Aboriginal dwellings as something quite different. For the duration of their time at the fair, Inuit families lived in skin tents; Penobscot families in birchbark wigwams; Navajo families in hogans; Menominee families in skin tepees; Winnebago families in 'sugar-loaf' woven reed mat wigwams; Chippewa families in birchbark longhouses; Iroquois families in elm and birchbark huts and longhouses; and Kwakwaka'wakw families in cedar plank longhouses.[11] Anthropologists simultaneously created and fulfilled expectations of authenticity among visitors to the fair by carefully stage-managing the forms of dwelling put on display.[12]

The Kwakwaka'wakw performers from northern Vancouver Island were, in several respects, typical of the live exhibits. Frederic Ward Putnam, Harvard professor and organizer of the anthropology display, explained that the 16 Kwakwaka'wakw participants would 'live under normal conditions in their natural habitations during the six months of the Exposition.'[13] In order to reinforce the aura of ordinary life, Putnam and his assistants worked to ensure that the Kwakwaka'wakw troupe consisted of family units. This principle was applied to most of the live exhibits, although the definition of 'family' in this context was a non-Aboriginal one. Organizers attempted to limit the performers to couples and their children, even when would-be performers expressed a desire to travel in larger groups.[14] The co-ordinator of the Kwakwaka'wakw troupe, George Hunt, arranged for his brother and his brother's wife to join the group, although his own wife did not come to Chicago.[15] Hunt's son and father also came. The group included two other couples and two small children. Another performer came with his brother. Hunt seems to have made an effort to meet the desires of his employer, anthropologist Franz Boas, by recruiting people in such a way as to approximate nuclear families. While the final group was not quite a Victorian nuclear family unit, neither was it an extended family of the kind that would have lived in a cedar longhouse.

Putnam's fixation with producing authentic, 'normal' conditions extended to his insistence that the domiciles be originals rather than faux reproductions. Thus, when the Kwakwaka'wakw from Vancouver Island arrived at the Chicago World's Fair, they reassembled the planks of a cedar longhouse that had been disassembled at a Nuwitti village on the northern coast of Vancouver Island before being shipped by rail to Chicago. The house's authenticity was heightened by the report that, when it was chosen for the exhibit, it had actually been occupied by a Kwakwaka'wakw family.[16] The house may even have been the property of one of the performers, which would have added an extra layer to the exhibit's patina of everyday life. The Kwakwaka'wakw house was situated alongside the fairground's South Pond, which stood in for the waters of the Johnstone, Queen Charlotte, and Hecate Straits. The houses faced a sloping 'beach' upon which canoes were pulled ashore.

The display of everyday life was about domestic goods as well as domestic space. 'Traditional' domestic goods completed the tableaux of Aboriginal domesticity presented by the familial scenes. Visitors could see the Kwakwaka'wakw living among items representative of everyday and ceremonial life, including canoes, house poles, totem poles, masks, and regalia. And if they strolled past the dairy exhibit to the nearby anthropology building, visitors could inspect hundreds of other implements integral to Northwest Coast Aboriginal life. Like other human performers, the Kwakwaka'wakw were living appendages of the vast displays of ethnographic objects, many of them drawn from domestic life.

The Kwakwaka'wakw exhibit in Chicago was an explicit realization of the colonial assumption that the 'normal'—that is, 'traditional' and 'authentic'—state of these so-called savages was most visible in their 'everyday life'. The enormous trouble and expense that exhibit organizers took to ensure that the mock villages consisted of 'real' houses, filled with 'real' goods, was emblematic of their belief that inner meaning was inherent within outward form. They knew that the live exhibits did not 'normally' live beneath the intrusive eyes of millions of visitors. But they nonetheless assumed that the more subjective characteristics of everyday life could be held stable as long as outward conditions and characteristics were replicated as precisely as possible. This assumption was apparent in a number of other settings.

## Migrant Space

The Kwakwaka'wakw who travelled to Chicago did so voluntarily and earned lucrative wages for their efforts. Less consensual examples of the performance of everyday life abound. When the domestic spaces of migrant labourers became spectacles, the degree of Aboriginal consent was much more ambiguous. In the late nineteenth century, thousands of Aboriginal people from British Columbia and Washington converged on Puget Sound for the fall hop harvest. Workers harvested a cash crop that was sold on a volatile world market. Yet while employers may have seen Aboriginal pickers as an emerging proletariat, many non-Aboriginal consumers of spectacle cast the labourers as remnants of a vanishing, authentic Aboriginal past, inexorably dying off to make way for the region's non-Aboriginal future. The migrant labour camps to which the influx of workers gave rise became tourist destinations for non-Aboriginal inhabitants of urban and rural

Puget Sound. Entrepreneurs and sightseers converged to transform the migrants' temporary living quarters into spectacles. Although the migrant hop pickers had not set out with the intention to perform commodified versions of Aboriginal culture, their experiences in the migrant camps around Puget Sound bore striking resemblances to those of the Kwakwa̱ka'wakw in Chicago's 'great aboriginal encampment'.

The workers were sights of interest even before they reached the hop fields. Local newspapers commented on them when they travelled through urban areas on their way to and from the fields.[17] The appearance of the hop pickers in Seattle was said to be as 'regular as the annual migration of water fowl or the rotation of the seasons, and . . . ever a source of attraction and interest'.[18] The most commonly referred to centre of Aboriginal activity in Seattle during the hop season was the waterfront area known as 'Ballast Island'. Aboriginal migrants began fashioning makeshift camps atop this pile of rocks and rubble in the 1870s, and by 1892 *Harper's Weekly* informed readers that Ballast Island was the place to go to see the pickers.[19] Other sites in and around Seattle and Tacoma also became known for the appearance of seasonal Aboriginal camps.[20]

Rural Aboriginal camps in the hop fields themselves provided an even greater spectacle for curious tourists. During the harvest season in late August and early September, each day hundreds of tourists descended on rural towns like Puyallup and the surrounding hop fields, travelling from Seattle or Tacoma in carriages and on the frequent interurban passenger trains.[21] In the late 1880s and early 1890s, day-trippers turned into vacationers as businessmen opened hotels at or near the hop farms.[22]

These urban spectators converged around the domestic lives of the Aboriginal hop pickers. Local papers touted the temporary villages as being 'always worth a visit and study'.[23] John Muir found 'their queer camps' more striking than even the natural setting of 'rustling vine-pillars'.[24] When 400 Cowichan camped in the Puyallup Valley in 1903, visitors and residents alike flocked to watch the 'mode of life and habits of these fish-eating aborigines from Vancouver island'.[25] For tourists, these 'queer camps' were colourful spectacle with a measure of ethnographic education thrown in.

Physical conditions at these urban and rural encampments varied. Tents made of a variety of materials, ranging from cedar bark or rush mats to canvas sheeting, were common in city- and field-side camps alike. Along the urban waterfronts, some migrants erected structures on the ground, while others used their canoes as the foundation over which to hang canvas or mats.[26] At the fields, workers located wood with which to frame the canvas or mats that they had brought with them. Some farmers built houses or temporary huts for seasonal labourers.[27] Cabins, and even 'wooden houses, built after the style of the white man,'[28] could also be found along urban waterfronts. Some Aboriginal people found the living arrangements substandard—even uncivilized. Twana subchief Big John visited the Puyallup hop fields and commented that the people living there had 'small huts, not like our houses, or even barns, but more like chicken coops, while we have houses and are civilized.'[29] For Big John, as for colonial viewers, domestic form and domestic character were interlocking.

For the non-Aboriginal viewer, the fact that these were migrant labourers living in temporarily erected tents did not detract from the attraction of the spectacle. The notion that they were viewing 'real' everyday life rather than reproductions (as they would at a world's fair) likely appealed to many. In the hop fields, they could believe that they were one step closer to the real thing than even Putnam, with all his attention to authentic details, could offer.

The transitory quality of the structures themselves also corresponded with common assumptions about Aboriginal people, who were presumed to be shiftless and wandering by nature. The assumption that Aboriginal people were incapable of permanently possessing property shrouded the self-congratulatory stories immigrants told themselves about the improvements they wrought with their transformation of the Pacific Northwest landscape from primitive (Aboriginal) to modern (non-Aboriginal). As railway investor, amateur ethnographer, lawyer, and (later) judge James Wickersham put it, 'the Indian doesn't care [about retaining reservation land]—clams, a split cedar shanty on the beach, a few mats and kettles, leisure and a bottle of rum once in a while are all he wants—anybody can have the land that wants it. Really why should our govt [sic] go to such enormous expense in trying to make a white man out of an Indian?'[30] Wickersham's bluntness may have been somewhat unusual, but his sentiment was not. North of the border, in British Columbia, newcomers applied a different land policy than that used in Washington, but it, too, systematically deprived Aboriginal people of the land base required to remain self-sustaining.[31] The scene that Wickersham described was much like the ones that non-Aboriginal viewers in Washington and British Columbia, or at the Chicago World's Fair, found when they sought out spectacles of Aboriginal domestic space: picturesque object lessons featuring the notion of the vanishing Indian. The hop pickers reinforced several dearly held assumptions for tourists who ventured forth to view the workers en route or in camp: Aboriginal people used land and resources sporadically and unsystematically; they were inevitably disappearing in the face of civilization and modernity; and investment in an Aboriginal future was an oxymoron.

These assumptions were apparent in popular assessments of how the pickers spent their hard-earned wages. Here again, domestic goods as well as domestic space came under scrutiny. Although Indian agents commented that Aboriginal pickers often returned with 'useful' goods such as furniture, harnesses, sewing machines, and stoves, tourists and reporters focused on items they deemed ridiculous and frivolous.[32] The belief that outer form mirrored

an inner subjective state informed these assumptions as well. It elevated the brief glimpses non-Aboriginal viewers had of Aboriginal lives from anecdotal evidence to generalized and authoritative judgement.

Casual viewers who made afternoon or weekend excursions to the hop fields or waterfront did not see the rough migrant labour camps as a component of a hard-working and highly flexible Aboriginal economy, which is what they were. They read the seasonal itinerancy of the migrant workers as evidence of an underlying lack of connection to any fixed locale. The notion that Aboriginal people had no use for land or resources was a fiction; however, in the hands and minds of a growing non-Aboriginal population, it was a powerful one. As in Chicago, spectacles of Aboriginal domestic space provided a jumping-off point for the stories viewers told themselves about themselves.

## Home Space

As migrant labourers, the hop pickers faced constraints on the level of privacy they could maintain over their domestic spaces. The circumstances of travel would have subjected their spaces and processes of domestic life to a degree of public view, even without tourists' obsession with 'vanishing Indians'. Their presence as travellers was noticeable to local residents. As in Chicago, it had been temporary structures that were on display at the hop fields. Yet, along the late nineteenth-century Northwest Coast, even inhabitants of Aboriginal villages who remained at home had to deal with the intrusions of non-Aboriginal viewers. With the advent of tourist steamship routes along the Inside Passage in the early 1880s, adventurous non-Aboriginal travellers could now journey along the coasts of British Columbia and southeast Alaska. As Sitka, Alaska, became one of the prime ports along the Inside Passage tourist route, the Tlingit residents faced one of the most intrusive forms of assault on Aboriginal domestic

space. For tourists the 'performances' of everyday life in Sitka seemed among the most 'authentic' to be found; the Tlingit, meanwhile, found
themselves cast in the role of involuntary 'performers'. This latter point is of course not unre-
lated to the former. In Sitka the Aboriginal
people stayed put; thus, the display of Tlingit
lives falls among the least consensual examples
of 'living on display'.

Sitka's tourist industry provided visitors
with a dual view of Tlingit domestic life: (1) the
'civilized cottages' inhabited by Presbyterian mission school graduates and (2) the Tlingit village.
The 'Ranche', as the latter was dubbed, was both
the figurative and literal antithesis of the mission
cottages located at the far end of town. Tourists
arrived by steamer, and, as they disembarked,
they had the choice of turning left towards the
Ranche or right towards the mission school and
cottages. This dichotomous division of domestic
space was not unique to Sitka. Farther south,
along the coast in British Columbia, missionary
Thomas Crosby made the same distinction
between what he called 'Christian street' and
'Heathen street'.[33]

Publications for visitors to Sitka invariably
featured the Ranche as a 'must-see' sight. The
local newspaper encouraged visitors to 'get off
the beaten track' and, if possible, to find a local
guide: 'Get some one who knows the village to
conduct you through, as many places of interest
will be otherwise overlooked. Don't confine your
attention to the front row only, go in among the
houses and see those on the back street.' This
reporter urged visitors to penetrate the inner
reaches of Tlingit domestic life, claiming that
'generally the natives do not object to visitors
entering their houses.'[34] At least some visitors
took this advice to heart. As Sir John Franklin's
niece wrote of her visit in 1870, 'We went into
several [houses], not merely to inspect, but in
search of baskets & other queer things.'[35]
Glimpsing the interior was important because
this was sometimes the most distinctive aspect of
the building: 'In exterior appearance [the

houses] do not differ from those of the white
man, but usually there is only a single room
within on the ground floor.'[36] Although some
Tlingit residents undoubtedly chafed at such
intrusions, many took advantage of the situation
that literally came knocking on their door. Pine
doorplates appeared above the lintels of certain
houses, directing visitors towards homes that
gained renown in the tourist literature.[37]

Tourists carried their assumptions about
domestic space as women's space with them to
the Ranche. Although male residents such as
'Sitka Jack' and the hereditary chief, Annahootz,
put up such doorplates, the 'palace of Siwash
Town' had a matriarch on the throne.[38] Mrs, or
'Princess', Tom was the most sought-after resident of the village and was renowned throughout
southeast Alaska. Visitors never failed to scrutinize her domestic situation. In some respects,
her home sounded like the epitome of domesticity: 'a painted cabin with green blinds, and a
green railing across the front porch'.[39] But it was
other elements of her domestic situation that
attracted the most attention from visitors in
search of a savage authenticity: her excessive
wealth in gold, silver, blankets, and furs; and her
multiple husbands, one of whom was reported to
have been her former slave.

While male and female visitors alike focused
their travel writings on Mrs Tom, they told different stories about her. While female visitors
used stories of Mrs Tom to argue obliquely for
women's economic independence and sexual
freedom, male writers decried Mrs Tom's behaviour. Eliza Ruhamah Scidmore's 1885 description
of Mrs Tom was the basis for subsequent writers'
accounts, and its transfiguration over time is
telling. Scidmore wrote that Mrs Tom had
'acquired her fortune by her own ability in legitimate trade.'[40] Later male writers cast aspersions
on her moral and sexual conduct, characterizing
her as 'a disreputable Indian woman' who used
'doubtful methods' to amass her large fortune.[41]
Female writers, on the other hand, viewed Mrs
Tom's accomplishments of domestic economy in

a more positive light. In 1890 a female traveller emphasized that this wealth allowed Mrs Tom to support two husbands and to still live in greater luxury than Chief Annahootz.[42] The 'regal splendor' in which she reputedly lived included silk, satin, and lace dresses, carpeted floors, a mirror, pictures, and a 'Yankee' cooking stove.[43] While female writers, beginning with Scidmore, stressed the neatness of Mrs Tom's home and self, Frederick Schwatka characterized her as a 'burley Amazon of the Northwest'.[44] When these visitors stepped inside Mrs Tom's house, they brought with them the narrative framework of the story they would tell.

Nearly a mile through and then beyond town, at the mission cottages, visitors could investigate the lives of the 'civilized', 'modern' Indians. They lived in two rows of neat, frame cottages built by Aboriginal labour but paid for by donations from American churches. The local, Presbyterian-aligned newspaper articulated the purpose of the cottages: 'With their neat and inviting appearance, they are an object lesson which strongly contrasts with the filth and squalor of the Indian huts in other parts of the town.'[45] Not only were the Ranche houses presumably dirty, they were also said to 'cause trouble'; that is, to encourage uncivilized, tribal behaviour and relationships.[46] Missionaries worried that tourists' romanticization of 'uncivilized' Aboriginal life would hinder their missionary endeavours, but they also saw the money that the tourists spent on curios in the Ranche.[47] The mission came to rely on displays of domestic space in order to convince potential donors that mission work could be successful and that mission graduates had a future other than 'back-sliding' into Ranche life. By putting the object lesson of the cottages on display, missionaries hoped to elicit donations for their work.

The object lesson among object lessons was the Miller cottage (named for the pastor of the Pennsylvania church that donated the funds), in which the mission's star graduate, Rudolph Walton, lived. According to Presbyterian missionary Sheldon Jackson, the Miller cottage was 'a better and more comfortable house' than those of 90 per cent of the Americans in Sitka, 'one of the best dwelling houses in the place'.[48] But the donors were disappointed. When Walton sent them a sketch of the finished cottage, they complained that the structure did not look to have the character of a $500 house.[49]

The donors' concern with appearances makes sense in the context of the assumption that outer form reveals inner state. This non-Aboriginal assumption was as apparent in Sitka as it was at the Chicago World's Fair and in the Puget Sound hop fields. Visitors invariably subjected the domestic arrangements of cottage residents to close scrutiny and paid close attention to the bourgeois furnishings. When the mission doctor wrote an article about the Miller cottage he detailed everything from the furniture to the behaviour of the children. He commented on 'the neat board walk and gravel walks around the side'; the 'parlor and sitting room, about twelve feet square—carpeted, sofa at one side, rocking chairs, table and book case, as we should find in any comfortable home'. Continuing, he noted, 'in a small room adjoining this sitting room we find a cabinet with some pretty china and a few odd trinkets treasured by the family. The dining room and kitchen in the rear though less pretentious are neat, while upstairs the two bedrooms are furnished with bedsteads and the usual furniture.'[50] Such details were evidence that the family within had escaped the 'contaminating influences of the Ranch'.[51] Other cottages received similar evaluations by visitors. 'In many of their homes are phonographs, pianos, and sewing machines', wrote local schoolteacher Dazie M. Brown Stromstadt in her promotional book on Sitka.[52] For Stromstadt, these items were evidence that their Tlingit owners were 'living a "civilized life"'.[53] The cottage settlement was meant to stand as objective material proof of the subjective spiritual transformation that had taken place in the lives of the resident Tlingit. The material circumstances of the cottages were critical measurements of civility and modernity. Missionaries and tourists alike assumed that the geographical and structural opposition between Ranche and cottages extended to the inner lives of the residents.

Needless to say, reality was not as simple as this idealized picture would have it. Close attention to the written descriptions of Ranche and cottage life reveals that some of the similarities are as striking as the differences. Much like the cottage settlement, the Ranche, too, had neat boardwalks and a general tidiness about it.[54] Ranche homes also contained modern domestic goods such as furniture and stoves (often of the 'modern type').[55] The cottages, too, were less severed from Ranche life than many missionaries liked to admit. While living in the cottages, Rudolph Walton and other Tlingit residents sustained familial ties with Ranche residents and participated in important Tlingit ceremonies and community events.[56] They also followed similar cultural practices. The family unit within Miller cottage was not a nuclear one but, rather, included Rudolph Walton's widowed mother and grandmother, who spoke Tlingit to Walton's children.[57] Moreover, it was not just Ranche residents who were likely to offer baskets, carvings, or 'curios' for sale to visitors but also cottage residents.[58] However, in the minds of white observers, the larger context—either Ranche or cottage—of each domestic interior seemed to carry overriding importance.

The notion that outside mimicked inside was less a statement of the status quo than it was a wishful prescription—an interpretation that observers attempted to impose, against the natural grain of the evidence before them. It was the story they *wanted* to tell themselves. Not surprisingly, the contradictions inherent within such an exercise frequently broke through to the surface, rending the oppositional social fabric of Ranche versus Cottage. At such times, observers worked hard to repair the damage and to restore the impression of easy opposition. Visitors might attribute the 'civilized' signs of cleanliness and

order in the Ranche to the influence of white discipline (through the police and military) or white blood (through interracial sex).[59] Either way, they countersunk their narratives in the common plank of domestic space as social text.

The stakes of sustaining domestic space as transparent social text become clearer when we realize that challenges to the Ranche-Cottage dualism came not only from Aboriginal people but also from white frontier residents. While interracial sex and marriage might explain signs of civilization found within Tlingit homes, they might just as easily engender new contradictions when white 'squaw-men' adopted the domestic habits of their Aboriginal wives. In places remote from white settlement such behaviour could be attributed to the poverty that prevented the men from travelling to find white wives.[60] Such rationalizations were less tenable in busy settlements like Sitka. There, the Russian fur trade had given way to American settlement, and the domestic choices of 'squaw-men' became increasingly difficult to reconcile with the standard colonial dualisms of Indian and white, primitive and modern, savage and civilized. Too many white men failed to enact the bourgeois values that middle-class society worked to impress upon Aboriginal people. The narrative power of domestic space could justify the marginalization of men whose race ostensibly should have ensured them a measure of colonial privilege. It could likewise broadcast the price that would-be 'squaw-men' faced if they failed to conform to the bourgeois values of the modern settlement frontier.

Non-Aboriginal viewers used Aboriginal domestic spaces as a trope through which to tell themselves stories about themselves. Even when Aboriginal people did not intentionally or willingly place their homes and goods on display, non-Aboriginal viewers sought them out, often penetrating the inner reaches of Aboriginal home life. The contradictions of such a situation run deep. While the forces of colonial society urged Aboriginal people to adopt bourgeois values of privacy and domesticity, they simultaneously transformed Aboriginal homes and private spaces into public spectacles. Even missionaries, who were among the most aggressive proponents of bourgeois domestic values, encouraged the public to view the Aboriginal domestic space of 'civilized' Christian converts. The homes of families who became mission success stories were as subject to inquiring eyes as were those who resisted missionary overtures. While missionaries promised that Aboriginal converts could earn equality through outward conformity to colonial, Victorian values, they broke this promise from the very start. Aboriginal homes—whether civilized or uncivilized—were *always* subject to different rules than were non-Aboriginal ones. Voyeurs implicitly judged *all* Aboriginal domestic space as savage when they subjected it to a degree of scrutiny that they would never have tolerated in their own homes. The display of domestic space became not just a story white people told themselves but also a story they told *to* the Aboriginal spectacles.

## Aboriginal Stories

Non-Aboriginal viewers were not the only ones who narrated domestic space. They were not the only ones telling stories. While the display of domestic space did not always begin with Aboriginal consent, Aboriginal people invariably took advantage of the situation when they could, catering to tourists' desire for souvenirs and 'curios', thus creating added income opportunities for themselves. 'Traditional' Aboriginal domestic goods circulated as commodities, the returns from which sometimes allowed the vendors to purchase 'modern' domestic goods that tourists would later judge, depending on the context, as either material markers of civilization or laughable markers of pretense.

Aboriginal people did not tell themselves the same stories as non-Aboriginal people told themselves. Aboriginal transformations of domestic spaces, and the adjustments they made to nineteenth-century colonialism, suggest a sto-

ryline out of keeping with any straightforward correlation between outward form and inner nature. Sometimes cottage life was literally a facade concealing traditional practices. For residents of Sitka's cottage community, the outer trappings of civilization fit easily over sustained hereditary obligations and practices. Similarly, the Christian homes in Metlakatla, British Columbia, looked, from the street, like workers' cottages. Past the door, however, they opened up into large communal spaces with sleeping areas to the sides, just like the interiors of old longhouses.[61] Sometimes, when the main floors of houses were conjoined (with only the second storey separate), the communal space extended to more than one 'house'.[62] The model Christian Indians of Metlakatla also refused to relinquish the longhouses they kept at Port Simpson.[63] The outward forms of Christian life at Sitka and Metlakatla distracted missionaries from the continuities of practice and value within cottage walls. Cottage residents could live in accord with Aboriginal values and simultaneously placate missionaries, thus reaping the material and spiritual benefits that accrued to converts.

It seems likely that chiefs mimicked Victorian architecture in order to speak to both colonial and Aboriginal society. When Christian Tsimshian chief Alfred Dudoward built himself a Victorian mansion, he moved in with a large lineage-based group and continued to fulfill his hereditary obligations.[64] His wife, Kate, confused missionary women with her syncretic domestic habits. On one occasion, she concluded a respectable afternoon gathering with a slightly suspect biscuit give-away. When the white women returned the following day, they watched, shocked, while Kate and other Tsimshian women performed in front of them, 'painted and dressed in their skins blankets and other old fixtures', before sending them off with more tea biscuits.[65] Like Dudoward, Musqueam chief Tschymnana built a colonial house; his was in imitation of Colonel Moody's residence. When Bishop George Hills visited the house in 1860, he found the chief's *three* wives at home.[66] These prominent chiefs' houses engaged colonial notions of form and content as well as indicating Aboriginal awareness of colonial scrutiny. They also demonstrate a degree of confidence and flexibility that culture inheres not in the post-and-beam structure itself but in something else: the idea that form can change without foreclosing continuity. Indeed, the forms of these houses may have offered an added measure of prestige within Aboriginal communities.

With the advent of colonialism, high-ranking individuals sought new ways of displaying power and status.[67] Engaging with 'modern' colonial culture is one example of this. Shingles, hinged doors, milled lumber, and windows functioned as status symbols.[68] They marked new forms of expression within an age-old system. This hybrid facility extended to domestic goods as well as to structure. Nineteenth-century photographs reveal Aboriginal interiors to be 'contents displays' of status items of both Aboriginal and non-Aboriginal origin.[69] These new styles and objects joined older symbols of wealth and power that marked the status of Aboriginal homes and their residents. Crest art painted on house fronts or carved on house posts has long asserted the status and hereditary rights of the inhabitants.[70] A house's size, materials, and position relative to other houses rendered the intra-village hierarchy visible—a pattern dating back over 4,000 years on the Fraser River.[71] The spatial distribution within pre-contact longhouses designated the relative status of the family units within,[72] and, similarly, the styles of pit houses can be correlated to wealth and status.[73] Such examples hint at the contours of Aboriginal narratives of domestic space.

## Present Space

Through the twentieth century, agents of colonial policy continued to target Aboriginal homes for transformation. Reserve houses constructed by the Department of Indian Affairs continued in the 'cottage' tradition of attempting to reshape Aboriginal domestic life socially as well as architecturally.[74] At the same time, twentieth-century Stó:lō families who had the means continued to build European-style frame homes that could accommodate the large extended family and community gatherings of Stó:lō social tradition.[75]

The preoccupation with 'traditional' Aboriginal domestic space has likewise survived. The 'Indian house' has remained the ethnographic artifact par excellence, somehow imbued with an unstated yet assumed ability to speak for Aboriginal culture and history writ large. When the Civilian Conservation Corps of the New Deal looked to define a project in Alaska in the 1930s, it chose, at the urging of the local non-Aboriginal population, to undertake a meticulous and authentic restoration of Chief Shakes's house at Wrangell.[76] Some members of Wrangell's Tlingit population initiated a further restoration of four house posts in 1984.[77] When the Canadian Museum of Civilization designed its Grand Hall, which opened in 1989, it decided to construct a composite Northwest Coast 'village' with houses and totem poles from various nations placed side by side, although still in geographical order.[78] The similarity in form with Chicago's 'great Aboriginal encampment' is too striking to ignore. However, unlike the world's fair, the Grand Hall intends to celebrate rather than to condemn Northwest Coast culture. The difficult question comes in deciphering the relationship between this colonial form and its post-colonial message. To pose a familiar question: can new meanings transcend old forms?

## Conclusion

More than just an ironic contradiction of private turned public, an analysis of the spectacle of Aboriginal domestic space reveals some underlying colonialist assumptions. The audiences of Aboriginal people living on display defined themselves as modern through a dialectic of stories: stories they told themselves about themselves; stories they told themselves about others; and stories they told others about themselves. Colonial society presumed that civilization and modernity were as easy to read as an open book. This assumption, although false, shaped myriad interactions. Various groups, Aboriginal and non-Aboriginal alike, have had an interest in the spectacle of Aboriginal domestic life, with money and prestige always at stake. Missionaries' and anthropologists' interests dovetailed in the contrasting displays of uncivilized and civilized domestic spaces. For missionaries, the former demonstrated that reform was needed while the latter demonstrated that it was possible. Anthropologists focused on the former to display the ethnographic strangeness and value of their work and on the latter to establish that such work was urgent because Aboriginal disappearance was imminent. For many other non-Aboriginal members of colonial society, the display of domestic spaces reinforced comfortable stories about themselves and their position in a colonial world. The souvenirs they brought home to their 'curio-corners' played a role of their own in bringing middle-class status to Victorian homes.[79]

Aboriginal people also linked domestic and social space to individual and group identity. Traditional elites might manipulate domestic forms to shore up their personal power and status over other Aboriginal people as well as in relation to colonial society. Ambitious nouveaux riches might play with old and new markers of domestic space in their move to climb the social status ladder. It seems certain, however, that Aboriginal people conceived of the connections between domestic space and identity in a radically different manner than did colonizers. The form and content of domestic spaces did not obviously offer the key to the interior of residents' sense of self and community responsibility. The links that existed were not clearly visible to outsiders. Looks could indeed be deceiving, at least for those with colonial eyes.

Colonial society from the nineteenth century through to the present has focused on houses as representative material forms of culture—as culture in practice. And Aboriginal people have consistently inhabited their houses in ways that prove the simplistic nature of this assumption. Still, scholars today continue to find it remarkable that Aboriginal people can proceed with traditional values and practices in 'untraditional' contexts. Twentieth-century Tlingit potlatches held in 'Western-style buildings' indicate to one writer, for example, that 'the presence of proper joinery and other architectural devices that refer to past form, the "classic building blocks", are not required for traditional practice.'[80] The history of Aboriginal domestic spaces suggests that we should not be taken aback by the realization that the presence of 'knowledgeable people' and witnesses from other clans is more important than are the specifics of a particular architectural form.[81]

The endurance of domestic space as a trope for the narration of Aboriginal culture gives rise to many questions. Why has domestic space proven such a powerful symbol? What is it that imbues domestic spaces with the power to shape judgements about inner selves? How did the fixed material forms of houses and household goods come to signify fixity of character and culture? Perhaps we are more prone to naturalize the values and arrangements of domestic spaces because they are the most familiar environments we have. The intimacy with which bourgeois domestic space has been experienced since the Victorian age may set off the alleged strangeness of other ways of living. And perhaps it is the very changelessness of material form that lends itself to rendering accessible the otherwise amorphous concepts of self and culture.

Members of colonial society have been searching for the location of culture since they first arrived on the Northwest Coast. Just when we think we have it cornered, it escapes out the back door. Maybe what these stories of domestic space tell us is that we should begin looking somewhere other than architectural plans.

## Notes

I wish to acknowledge SSHRC, whose support made this research possible. I would also like to thank Kathy Mezei, who encouraged me to present this as a conference paper and then to write it up as an article; Tina Loo, who offered editorial suggestions; and Jean Barman and Susan Roy, who pointed the way to useful primary sources.

1.  John and Jean Comaroff, *Ethnography and the Historical Imagination* (Boulder, Colo.: Westview Press, 1992), 293.
2.  Dipesh Chakrabarty, 'Postcoloniality and the Artifice of History: Who Speaks for "Indian" Pasts?', *Representations* 37 (1992): 13.
3.  J.R. Miller, *Sweet Promises: A Reader on Indian-White Relations in Canada* (Toronto: University of Toronto Press, 1991); Frederick E. Hoxie, *A Final Promise: The Campaign to Assimilate the Indians, 1880–1920* (Lincoln: University of Nebraska Press, 1984).
4.  Frederick Cooper and Ann Laura Stoler, eds, *Tensions of Empire* (Berkeley: University of California Press, 1997).
5.  Clifford Geertz, *The Interpretation of Cultures* (New York: Basic Books, 1973), 448.
6.  Robert W. Rydell, *All the World's a Fair: Visions of Empire at American International Expositions, 1876–1916* (Chicago: University of Chicago Press, 1984), 6, 8; E.A. Heaman, *The Inglorious Arts of Peace: Exhibitions in Canadian Society during the Nineteenth Century* (Toronto: University of Toronto Press, 1999), 7.
7.  'The Man Columbus Found', *New York Press*, 28 May 1893, Scrapbook, vol. 2, Frederic Ward Putnam Papers (hereafter FWPP), Harvard University Archives (hereafter HUA).
8.  *The Dream City* (St. Louis: N.D. Thompson Publishing Co., 1893), n.p.
9.  'All Kinds of Indians', *Daily Inter Ocean* (Chicago), 20 June 1893.
10. See, for example, *Daily Inter Ocean* (Chicago), 9 July 1893, Scrapbook, vol. 2, FWPP, HUA.
11. Clipping, 8 Feb. 1893; *Daily Inter Ocean* (Chicago) 9 July 1893; *Pioneer Press* (St Paul, Minn.), 15 Mar. 1893, Scrapbook, vol. 2, FWPP, HUA.
12. In a strange wrinkle in the authentic fabric of the fair, the Midway included Sitting Bull's 'log cabin'. The presence of the log cabin was unusual, as all other Aboriginal performers lived in dwellings that fair organizer's deemed 'traditional'. Perhaps Sitting Bull's fame imbued the cabin with the necessary aura of authenticity that, in other cases, only a tepee could have offered. Or perhaps the log cabin conveyed a grudging respect for the Sioux chief. *Official Catalogue of Exhibits on the Midway Plaisance* (Chicago: W.B. Conkey Co., 1893), box 38, FWPP, HUA; Gertrude M. Scott, 'Village Performance: Villages at the Chicago World's Columbian Exposition, 1893', Ph.D. dissertation (New York University, 1991), 329–30.
13. Rossiter Johnson, ed., *A History of the World's Columbian Exposition Held in Chicago in 1893* (New York: D. Appleton and Co, 1897), I: 315.
14. See, for example, Antonio, an Apache, to F.W. Putnam, 25 July 1892, box 31, FWPP, HUA; F.W. Putnam to Antonio, 4 Aug. 1892, box 31, FWPP, HUA.
15. For the most complete account of the identities of the Kwakwaka'wakw performers that I have been able to compile, see Paige Raibmon, 'Theaters of Contact: The Kwakwaka'wakw Meet Colonialism in British Columbia and at the Chicago World's Fair', *Canadian Historical Review* 81, 2 (June 2000): 175.
16. Clipping, July 1893, Scrapbook, vol. 2, FWPP, HUA. Organizers went out of their way to apply this principle to other Aboriginal groups at the fair as well. On the Navajo performers, for example, see F.W. Putnam to Antonio, 4 Aug. 1892, box 31, FWPP, HUA.
17. 'Siwashes Again Seek the Street', *Seattle Post-Intelligencer*, 31 May 1904, 9; 'Great Influx of Indians', *Seattle Post-Intelligencer*, 10 Sept. 1899, 6; 'Indians Returning from Hop Fields,' *Seattle Post-Intelligencer* 1 Oct. 1906, 16.
18. J.A. Costello, *The Siwash: Their Life, Legends and Tales, Puget Sound and Pacific Northwest* (Seattle: The Calvert Company, 1895), 165.

19. W.H. Bull, 'Indian Hop Pickers on Puget Sound', *Harper's Weekly* 36, 1850 (1892): 546.

20. 'Indians Returning from Hop Fields', *Seattle Post-Intelligencer*, 1 Oct. 1906, 16; Photo NA–698, Special Collections, University of Washington (UW); Paul Dorpat, *Seattle: Now and Then* (1984), 45; photo NA–897, Special Collections, UW; photo 15,715, Museum of History and Industry, Seattle, Washington (MOHI); 'Indian Life on Seattle Streets', *Seattle Post-Intelligencer*, 10 Dec. 1905, 7; 'Siwash Village on Tacoma Tide Flats', *Seattle Post-Intelligencer*, 15 Apr. 1907, 20.

21. 'Hop Picking', *Washington Standard*, 24 Sept. 1886, 2; *Puyallup Valley Tribune*, 3 Oct. 1903, 6.

22. 'A Western Hop Center', *West Shore* 16, 9 (1890): 137–8; 'Meadowbrook Hotel Register', Snoqualmie Valley Historical Society, North Bend, Washington.

23. 'Picturesque Hop Pickers', *Puyallup Valley Tribune*, 10 Sept. 1904, 1.

24. John Muir, *Steep Trails* (Boston: Houghton Mifflin, 1918), 257.

25. 'At the Indian Village', *Puyallup Valley Tribune*, 19 Sept. 1903, 1.

26. Photos 2561 and 6123–N, MOHI; photos NA–1508, NA–1501, NA–1500, NA–698, NA–680, Special Collections, UW.

27. 'Hops in Washington', *Pacific Rural Press*, 3 Jan. 1891.

28. 'Indian Life on Seattle Streets', *Seattle Post-Intelligencer*, 10 Dec. 1905, 7; 'Siwash Village on Tacoma Tide Flats', *Seattle Post-Intelligencer*, 15 Apr. 1907, 20.

29. Myron Eells, *The Indians of Puget Sound: The Notebooks of Myron Eells*, ed. George Pierre Castile (Seattle: University of Washington Press, 1985), 270.

30. Quoted in George Pierre Castile, 'The Indian Connection: Judge James Wickersham and the Indian Shakers', *Pacific Northwest Quarterly* 81, 4 (1990): 126.

31. Cole Harris, *Making Native Space: Colonialism, Resistance, and Reserves in British Columbia* (Vancouver: University of British Columbia Press, 2002), 88, 109, 111.

32. Canada, Department of Indian Affairs, Annual Report, 1886 (Sessional Papers 1887, no. 6), 1x; W.H. Lomas to J. Johnson, Commissioner of Customs, 3 Nov. 1886, Cowichan Agency Letterbook, 1882–7, vol. 1353, RG 10; Bull, 'Indian Hop Pickers', 545–6; E. Meliss, 'Siwash', *Overland Monthly* 20, 2nd ser. (Nov. 1892): 501–6.

33. Susan Neylan, 'Longhouses, Schoolrooms, and Workers' Cottages: Nineteenth-Century Protestant Missions to the Tsimshian and the Transformation of Class Through Religion', *Journal of the Canadian Historical Association* 11, n.s. (2000): 76.

34. *The Alaskan*, 5 June 1897, 1. See also 'Sitka and Its Sights', *The Alaskan*, 7 Dec. 1889, 1.

35. Sophia Cracroft, *Lady Franklin Visits Sitka, Alaska 1870: The Journal of Sophia Cracroft, Sir John Franklin's Niece*, ed. R.N. DeArmond (Anchorage: Alaska Historical Society, 1981), 24.

36. George Bird Grinnell, *Alaska 1899: Essays from the Harriman Expedition* (Seattle: University of Washington Press, 1995), 157.

37. E. Ruhamah Scidmore, *Alaska: Its Southern Coast and the Sitkan Archipelago* (Boston: D. Lothrop and Company, 1885), 176.

38. Ibid.

39. Ibid.

40. Ibid., 177.

41. H.W. Seton Karr, *Shores and Alps of Alaska* (London: Sampson, Low, Marston, Searle and Rivington, 1887), 59.

42. 'Journal of a Woman Visitor to Southeast Alaska, ca 1890', fol. 4, box 7, MS4, Alaska State Historical Library (ASHL), 20. See also Anna M. Bugbee, 'The Thlinkets of Alaska', *Overland Monthly* 22, 2nd ser. (August. 1892), 191.

43. Bugbee, 'The Thlinkets of Alaska', 191; 'Journal of a Woman Visitor', 20.

44. Scidmore, *Alaska: Its Southern Coast*, 176; 'Journal of a Woman Visitor', 20; Bugbee, 'The Thlinkets of Alaska', 191; *New York Times*, 3 Oct. 1886. Quoted in Frederica de Laguna, *Under Mount Saint Elias: The History and Culture of the Yakutat Tlingit* (Washington: Smithsonian Institution Press, 1972), 191.

45. *The Alaskan*, 23 Jan. 1891, 4. See also 'A Visit to the Cottages', *The Alaskan*, 30 Oct. 1897, 2.

46. Brady to Rev. J. Gould, 30 Dec. 1905, J.G. Brady, *Letters Sent*, vol. 9, Nov. 1905–May 1906, files of the Alaska Territorial Governors, roll 7, microcopy T–1200, National Archives Microfilm, AR25, ASHL.

47. 'The Orthodox Indian Temperance', *The Alaskan*, 10 July 1897, 1.

48. J. Converse to W.H. Miller, 30 Aug. 1888, Sheldon Jackson Correspondence, reel 97–638, Sheldon Jackson Stratton Library

49. J. Converse to W.H. Miller, 25 July 1888, Sheldon Jackson Correspondence, reel 97–638, Sheldon Jackson Stratton Library.

50. B.K. Wilbur, 'The Model Cottages', *The North Star* 6, 8 (1895): 1.

51. Ibid.

52. Dazie M. Brown Stromstadt, *Sitka, The Beautiful* (Seattle: Homer M. Hill Publishing Co., 1906), 9. See also *The North Star* 5, 8 (Aug. 1892) in *The North Star: The Complete Issues*, 228.

53. Stromstadt, *Sitka, the Beautiful*, 9.

54. 'President's Message', *The Alaskan*, 9 Dec. 1905, 3; Bertand K. Wilbur, 'Just about Me', box IB, no.8, MS4, ASHL 220–1.

55. Wilbur, 'Just about Me', 220–1; J.G. Brady to Geo. C. Heard, Attorney at Law, Juneau, 19 June 1905, fol. 86, box 5, John G. Brady Papers, Beinecke Library, Yale University.

56. For examples, see Rudolph Walton, 'Diaries', 1900–4, 1910, 1919. Private possession of Joyce Walton Shales.

57. *The North Star*, 6, 1 (1895): 1.

58. Wilbur, 'The Model Cottages', 1.

59. Scidmore, *Alaska: Its Southern Coast*, 175; 'Journal of a Woman Visitor', 24; E. Ruhamah Scidmore, *Appleton's Guide-Book to Alaska and the Northwest Coast* (New York: D. Appleton and Co., 1896 [1893]), 120; Francis C. Sessions, *From Yellowstone Park to Alaska* (New York: Welch, Fracker Co., 1890), 92; Wilbur, 'Just about Me', 221.

60. *The Alaskan*, 5 Aug. 1893, 2.

61. Neylan, 'Longhouses, Schoolrooms, and Workers' Cottages', 81.

62. Ibid.

63. Ibid., 82.

64. Ibid.

65. 28 and 29 Jan. 1884, Kate Hendry, Letterbook, 1882–9, EC/H38, British Columbia Archives.

66. Roberta L. Bagshaw, ed., *No Better Land: The 1860 Diaries of Anglican Colonial Bishop George Hills* (Victoria: Sono Nis Press, 1996), 75. Even allowing for the distinct possibility that Hills misinterpreted the exact nature of the relationship between the women and the chief, this domestic space clearly housed an extended rather than a nuclear family.

67. Judith Ostrowitz, *Privileging the Past: Reconstructing History in Northwest Coast Art* (Vancouver: University of British Columbia Press, 1999), 31.

68. Neylan, 'Longhouses, Schoolrooms, and Workers' Cottages', 79–80; Ostrowitz, *Privileging the Past*, 32.

69. Ostrowitz, *Privileging the Past*, 30. See also Tony Bennett, 'The Exhibitionary Complex', in David Boswell and Jessica Evans, eds, *Representing the Nation: A Reader* (London: Routledge, 1999), 333.

70. Neylan, 'Longhouses, Schoolrooms, and Workers' Cottages', 79; Ostrowitz, *Privileging the Past*, 9.

71. Keith Thor Carlson, ed., *A Stó:lō Coast Salish Historical Atlas* (Vancouver: Douglas & McIntyre, 2001), 36, 41.

72. Ibid., 43.

73. Ibid., 46.

74. Ibid., 44.

75. Ibid., 43, 45.

76. Ostrowitz, *Privileging the Past*, 33–9.

77. Ibid., 39–43.

78. Ibid., 51.

79. As one writer put it, 'every well-appointed house might appropriately arrange an Indian corner.' George Wharton James, 'Indian Basketry in House Decoration', *Chautauquan* (1901): 620. See also Lloyd W. MacDowell, *Alaska Indian Basketry* (Seattle: Alaska Steamship Company, 1906).

80. Ostrowitz, *Privileging the Past*, 39.

81. Ibid.

# 3

# Re-imaging the Moral Order of Urban Space: Religion and Photography in Winnipeg, 1900–1914

James Opp

When the Methodist minister J.S. Woodsworth published his first book, *Strangers within our Gates*, in 1909, the 'problem' of the city took up one small chapter. By 1911, however, the city formed the main topic of his second book, *My Neighbor*, reflecting the growing sense of urgency over the new urban space created by the rapid expansion of Canadian cities: 'As we penetrate more deeply into [the city's] life, we discover evils of which we had hardly dreamed. . . . We get behind the scenes; we see the seamy side. We look beneath the glittering surface and shrink back from the hidden depths which the yawning darkness suggests.'[1] Addressing the social conditions of the city required a new way of 'seeing' the 'seamy side' of life 'behind the scenes'. By the twentieth century, proponents of the social gospel such as Woodsworth had decided that the old methods of Christian charity work and a focus on individual salvation needed to be replaced with a collective approach that emphasized building the kingdom of God through new forms of social reform based on more scientific principles. To 'penetrate' the darkness required not only moral courage and converted hearts, but data, statistics, and comprehensive city 'surveys'.

The emergence of the social gospel marked an important transition in the visual metaphors employed by the Methodist Church in Canada. Mission work among the urban poor had traditionally been seen as the light of the gospel displacing the darkness within. But Woodsworth's language in *My Neighbor* operated differently. Now the goal was to expose the darkness, to see through it in order to reveal its very existence. To observe the darkness was the first step towards producing a collective strategy of changing the environment. The act of seeing was in itself a 'light', and so it is not surprising that the language of the social gospel is overlaid with visual metaphors. The Reverend Hugh Dobson wrote that the church's pursuit of 'Social Service' involved two stages: the first, and 'most vitally constructive', was 'to observe and set down and look squarely in the face of the facts of our social life'; the second was to 'establish and fix in reality the vision made visible by the preacher and evangelist, to build cities and plan towns and rural communities patterned after what they saw in the

James Opp, 'Re-Imaging the Moral Order of Urban Space: Religion and Photography in Winnipeg, 1900–1914', *Journal of the Canadian Historical Association* 13 (2002): 73–93. Reprinted by permission of the Canadian Historical Association and the author.

mount, and guided by the knowledge gained by the survey of facts.'[2] In a public recommendation for *My Neighbor*, the Reverend S.D. Chown made the same point, noting that the 'fulness of knowledge displayed indicates intimateness of opportunity for study and observation and gives a satisfying sense of authority to the statements made. It is well that those who are at ease in our Canadian Zion should be made to see so clearly and forcibly how the "other half" lives.'[3] Constructing the New Jerusalem upon a righteous moral order first required an accurate assessment and a visualization of current conditions.

While the principles and theology of social reform have been studied, and the activities of social gospellers like J.S. Woodsworth have been detailed extensively, one area that remains to be explored is how the 'modern' techniques of social reform entailed a new way of visualizing urban space. In carrying out their appointed tasks, social reformers compiled statistics and constructed detailed charts and graphs, but one of the most powerful tools for re-visualizing the city was photography. The social documentary style of photography had evolved from the startling exposés of Jacob Riis's *How the Other Half Lives* (1890), which sensationalized New York slums, to a more 'scientific' form in the hands of social reformers such as Lawrence Veiller, secretary of New York's Charity Organization Society. Veiller incorporated more than 1,000 photographs in his famous Tenement-House Exhibit of 1899, and the power of photography to document social conditions was felt across North America as health departments started to develop their own photographic records.[4] Photography was incorporated into a 1911 study of Toronto's slums by the city's Medical Officer of Health, Dr Charles Hastings, and it was prominent in Montreal's Child Welfare Exhibit of 1912.

For Protestant reformers such as Woodsworth, photographs served an indispensable function in bringing the 'real' conditions of the city to the public mind, creating visual reference points from which the new emphasis on a social gospel could

be launched. In their extensive publishing efforts that incorporated photographs, Protestant churches in Canada played a key role in publicly framing the moral boundaries of the modern city. The Methodist Church in particular, through the efforts of the Young People's Forward Movement for Missions (YPFM), distributed photographs through multiple channels that included its own journals, photographic exhibitions, and lantern slide shows. The YPFM also served as the publisher for both of Woodsworth's books, each of them amply illustrated with photographs drawn from the YPFM's own files. Toronto and Montreal were both featured in the new social documentary style, but the city that attracted a disproportionate amount of attention from the Methodists was Woodsworth's own Winnipeg. As a rapidly growing metropolis, a centre for immigration, and a symbol of the future direction of Canada, Winnipeg embodied the potential dangers of urban growth across the country.

In focusing on the photographic representations of the city of Winnipeg in the published materials of the Methodist Church before the First World War, the purpose is not to assess the real conditions of urban poverty, but rather to analyze the transformation that occurred in visual representations of the city. Although historians have been far from reluctant to incorporate such images into their own books as illustrative material, there has been remarkably little analysis of the photographic medium and the relation between visual representation and social reform. While the choice and placement of photographs were the responsibility of a small group of editors, authors, and publishers, it is important not to underestimate their impact on the public perception of urban space. As Susan Sontag suggests, photographs 'do not simply render reality realistically. It is reality which is scrutinized, and evaluated, for its fidelity to photographs.'[5] The increasing use of photography in the early twentieth century shaped a modern sense of vision, and these images offered particular narratives and realities that were difficult to ignore.[6]

The first decade of the twentieth century marked a definite shift in the visual strategy of representing the city. Photography was not a new technology, but photographic images were invested with a new authority, a power of scientific observation that exuded an 'evidential force'.[7] The appearance of documentary photographs of poverty and unsanitary living conditions in Canadian cities within the context of religious publications marked a conscious attempt to make 'surveying' and 'seeing' society a part of the work of social redemption. And yet, while the value of photography lay in its dispassionate representation, such images were produced and read within a particular moral and spiritual context. To examine Methodist photographic representations of Winnipeg at the turn of the twentieth century is to witness a 're-imaging' of the moral boundaries and order of urban space.

## Picturing Religion

When the aspiring photographer Lewis B. Foote arrived in Winnipeg in 1901, his first foray into marketing his photographic skills was to take pictures of every single church in the city, superimpose the prints with portraits of the ministers, and then sell the pictures to the churches.[8] This photographic narrative, linking the visible landscape of religious institutions with portraits of those called to religious service, was the same framework for photographic illustrations used by the *Christian Guardian*, the official denominational journal of the Methodist Church of Canada, and other religious magazines in this period. Popularized in the 1890s, the half-tone printing process made the reproduction of photographs feasible, and pictures of churches and portraits of the ministers who served them dominated the visual imagery of religious journals, especially denominational organs such as the *Christian Guardian*. There were important exceptions to this pattern, however. Missionary pictures offered both similarities and differences to the standard photographic practices. For the

most part, the focus remained upon heroic missionaries and the mission buildings constructed in foreign lands, but they also strayed into more scenic explorations of exotic landscapes. Occasionally, a direct moral commentary was offered to explain the intended meaning of photographs of subjects that lay, geographically and morally, outside of the church. For example, underneath a 1905 photograph of a 'Vancouver Island Indian Home' in the *Christian Guardian*, the caption noted that its inhabitants had 'grown old in paganism'.[9]

The *Guardian's* use of photography increased noticeably in 1903 when it introduced a new format, transforming itself from a newspaper-style serial into a longer magazine with a smaller layout. With the shift, photographs became noticeably larger and more prominent. However, the role of photography remained the edification of the church and its ministers. In 1906, a photograph of Calgary's Central Methodist Church was featured on the cover of the *Guardian*, with a caption underneath that read: 'Completed February, 1905; seating capacity, nearly 2,000; cost, including furnishings and organ, $75,000. Beginning at the very first, Methodism has been in Calgary only 23 years.'[10] The spiritual health of the church found a direct corollary in the increasing number and size of stone monuments in the nation. Churches, especially large, new buildings in rapidly expanding parts of the country, represented growth, progress, and the post-millennial optimism that shaped Protestant thought at the turn of the century.

In 1907, the *Christian Guardian* devoted a special issue to the city of Winnipeg. The explosive growth of the Canadian Prairies from the waves of immigration in the early years of the new century had quadrupled the size of Winnipeg; between 1901 and 1916 the city's population jumped from 45,000 to 187,000, making it Canada's third-largest city.[11] The *Guardian's* photographic representations offered visual confirmation of the expansion of the city and the fulfillment of its motto: 'Commerce,

Prudence, Industry'. Banks, warehouses, department stores, and the city hall all spoke to the material progress of Winnipeg, while the detailed history of Methodism was interwoven with photographs of the impressive churches that now stood as the monuments and confirmation of spiritual progress. For the moment, the public vision of building the kingdom of God was concentrated upon demonstrating that Methodist work was expanding in Winnipeg just as fast as the city itself.

The growth of the West, and Winnipeg in particular, was an important issue for Methodists. Membership in Anglican and Presbyterian churches was increasing at faster rates in the city and the region because of their direct links to the religious background of a greater proportion of recent British immigrants. Far fewer Methodists were emigrating, and many feared that Methodism would be left behind if the West fulfilled its growth potential.[12] The front-cover status of Calgary's Central Methodist Church and the interweaving of Methodist growth in Winnipeg with the expansion of the city itself assuaged anxieties that the Methodist Church was in danger of losing its pre-eminent position as the dominant Protestant denomination in Canada.

The growth of the city itself, however, posed new social and spiritual problems. In its commemorative issue, the *Guardian* editorialized that Winnipeg could, by most accounts, be called a 'great city'. But at the same time, it cautioned that the 'problem of the great city is one of the most serious that faces an enlightened civilization in this twentieth century.'[13] Indeed, in the same issue, the Reverend S.P. Rose warned that the religion of the city was different than the religion of the country because the city 'demands of the Christian religion that it shall pre-eminently express and apply itself socially.' It was not enough to lift people from despair, 'their feet must be placed upon the rock. A purified environment must be found for the regenerated life.'[14] Visually, however, photographs illustrating the particular social or spiritual problems of

Winnipeg remained off the page. For the moment, the moral uplift of the city was directly connected to the ability of Methodists to raise impressive stone churches that matched the progress of the city itself.

The 1907 pictorial display coincided with an important shift within Winnipeg Methodism that would ultimately mark the beginning of a new photographic strategy. J.S. Woodsworth's arrival as the new superintendent of All Peoples' Mission in Winnipeg's North End heralded the introduction of a social documentary style that offered a very different visual representation of the city. On the verge of resigning from the ministry altogether, Woodsworth saw the superintendent's position as a perfect opportunity to engage in a more 'practical' Christianity, and he dedicated himself to increasing the profile of the North End mission.[15] It was in the course of promoting this work that a new visual representation of the city emerged in Methodist publications. The photographic images produced during Woodsworth's tenure offered bleak assessments of conditions in the North End in the social documentary style; it was no longer a celebration of material progress.

In Winnipeg, L.B. Foote was the most prominent photographer that Woodsworth and other social reformers turned to for photographic evidence to document social conditions of the city. By this time, Foote had established himself as a freelance commercial photographer who supplied images to a variety of newspapers. Although he was familiar with the diversity of Winnipeg's population, Foote himself was no crusader in the mould of Riis or the child labour activist Lewis Hine, preferring to take pictures of visiting royalty than raise awareness of the North End. Nevertheless, it was Foote's work that made its way into the pages of the *Christian Guardian* in August 1908 as social reformers started to reshape the image of the city through documentary photography. In stark contrast to the prosperous, progressive images of Winnipeg laid before its readers only a year earlier, Foote's picture of the back of a double-decker tenement house (Figure 1) marked the first time that a photographic representation of poor urban living conditions had been published in the magazine. The same image had accompanied a *Winnipeg Free Press* story a month earlier on 'Social Settlement Work in Winnipeg', an article which Woodsworth saved for his scrapbook.[16]

The paucity of archival material leaves only speculation as to the actual relationship between Woodsworth and Foote. Even though a number of mission activities were documented photographically by Foote, there is no direct evidence that he was actually commissioned for this work. Woodsworth himself wrote nothing about photography, and was certainly not an innovator in adopting the social documentary style, which had already made significant inroads within the American social reform movement. Many of Foote's images of Winnipeg's North End appear to have been taken primarily for use in newspapers, and only later incorporated within Methodist magazines and books. Nevertheless, Woodsworth clearly embraced this new photo-

graphic strategy, and put the images to use in many different places. The 1908 tenement-house picture was later republished on the second page of All Peoples' Mission annual report and included as an illustration within Woodsworth's *Strangers within our Gates*.[17]

The introduction of a social documentary approach to photographic representations in Methodist publications was neither abrupt nor absolute. Traditional forms continued to dominate, and hybridized versions also emerged. Woodsworth may have wanted to make mission work more scientific in nature, but he still had to raise money and support for All Peoples' through publicity, and photography was an important avenue for demonstrating both the need and the work accomplished by the mission. Even prior to Woodsworth's arrival, photographs of All Peoples' had been printed, largely focusing upon the mission buildings and the types of classes and activities that occurred within. In 1905, an image published in the *Christian Guardian* (Figure 2) displayed a kindergarten class arranged outside of the mission.[18] The traditional progressive vision

**Figure 1.** The back of a tenement house in Winnipeg. Photographer: L.B. Foote, c. 1908. Reprinted from J.S. Woodsworth, *Strangers within our Gates* (Toronto: The Missionary Society of the Methodist Church, 1909).

was confirmed in this representation by placing the class in front of the sign with the English phrase, 'A House of Prayer for All People', clearly visible, while the German text underneath was blocked from view. Assimilation through Canadianization was the goal of such educational efforts, and the bodies of the children are situated as vehicles for assimilation. Pictures of Sunday schools, kindergartens, and 'fresh air' camps were visual images that spoke to the work of the mission itself, and reinforced the message that the hope for the future of Canada, and Methodism, lay in the children of immigrants.[19]

After 1907, however, the work of the mission was increasingly conceptualized as taking place not only within the mission building itself, but also in the homes of the North End, and film was used to capture this form of broader community outreach. For example, a series of images produced around 1910 documented the activities of All Peoples' in conducting Christmas charity drives and delivering baskets to the needy. One photograph (Figure 3) presents the exchange between the Mission and the North End as a personal interaction between a deaconess, helped by a boy, and a needy family who are receiving a Christmas basket. These pictures

were a form of public appeal for the mission, an effort to demonstrate the concrete action being taken by its workers. The class lines are clearly distinguishable between the warmly clothed workers and the poor family, whose faces are marked by dirt. The picture is obviously posed, requiring the mother and children to step outside into the cold in order for the photograph to be taken. Published as part of the mission's 1911–1912 annual report with the simple caption, 'Christmas Cheer',[20] the family and location are not identified.

This type of documentation offered proof that mission workers were engaged in active, 'practical' Christianity, and that the work of the mission was indeed reaching the poor. In their namelessness, the family on the step became the embodiment of poverty in Winnipeg's North End, a passive entity exposed by the camera to prove both the necessity of relief, and the ability of the mission to deliver it. . . .

Such photographs were useful for publicity purposes, but this portrayal of mission workers in action was actually quite rare. . . . The new photographic strategy of 'surveying' existing conditions, such as the tenement house in Figure 1, relied upon an 'objective' visual regime that

**Figure 2.** All Peoples' kindergarten class, Winnipeg. Writing on the image identifies the teachers as Annie Kelly and J.K. Lothrop. Photographer unknown, c. 1904. Winnipeg: Provincial Archives of Manitoba, No. N13261.

required a detachment from the subject. To place mission workers in direct contact with slum dwellers within the frame implied subjectivity and personal connections. The place of the scientific social worker was behind the camera, directing the view, gathering photographic exposures as a form of data, rather than being caught in front of it as a participant or an object of inquiry.

A parallel theological shift accompanied this changed photographic strategy. As the social gospel shifted attention away from individual salvation towards more collectivist approaches to building the kingdom of God, the camera similarly directed attention away from the individual subject and onto the environment that surrounded the body. Unlike the carefully documented pictures of churches and portraits of ministers, which offered a comprehensive, progressive narrative that drew image and text together, the new visual representations of Winnipeg's North End were largely disconnected from direct textual references, and their subjects were rarely identified by name. However, reproducing images of social conditions did not necessarily mark a secularization of the Methodist urban vision as much as it created a new moral ordering of urban space. The presence of photo-graphic images of the North End within religious publications drew an explicit connection between environment and salvation. As Rose wrote in his series of articles on religion and the city, the church should 'intentionally set herself to the correction of specific abuses and evils, which threaten the well-being of modem civilisation, particularly in great centres of population.' Through the teaching and living of the 'truth', a 'purifying atmosphere' could pervade the political, commercial, and social realms. In this way, 'the truth of the Gospel pervades society, corrects its errors, and thus effects marvellous changes in the environment in which men live.'[21]

Before such a task could be accomplished, however, the existing environment needed to be surveyed and documented. Out of the documentary photography of Winnipeg and other cities in the first decades of the twentieth century, a new visual representation of the city entered the public consciousness. However, such images did not simply fill a vacuum; rather, they were read within a particular moral and spiritual context. Despite the perception that the camera was positioned to simply capture an objective reality, the employment of this new visual regime ascribed a moral order to urban space that reflected a wide

**Figure 3.** A posed photograph of mission workers delivering Christmas hampers to a home in Winnipeg's North End. Photographer unknown, c. 1910. Winnipeg: United Church of Canada Archives—Manitoba and Northwestern Ontario Conference, J.M. Shaver fonds, PP53, No. 2484.

range of underlying anxieties and concerns about the city itself.

## The Danger of Urban Space

In their very ability to reproduce detail and context, photographic images made the environment that surrounded the subject an aspect that was impossible to ignore. In many of the examples already given (such as Figure 1), individuals and their bodies practically merge with their surroundings, or become dominated by the conditions around them. Woodsworth argued that if unchecked, the social problems of the urban environment threatened to turn the city into 'a hateful thing, from which we would flee in despair—a monstrous blot on the face of God's fair earth.'[22] Following the lead of the newspapers, church publications participated in a certain degree of sensationalism in publishing images of the 'monstrous blot' of urban slums.

Photography served the purpose of documenting the threatening condition that the city had become, but the underlying danger of this environment was conceptualized not in the mere existence of poverty or slums, but rather as a relationship between urban space and the body. While the city itself was generally seen as an unhealthy place compared to the country, the deeper tension lay in how specific urban spaces could lead to both physical and moral failings. This moral ordering of urban space was explicitly and implicitly related to the bodies that occupied it. Under the new photographic strategy of social documentary, when bodies enter the frame, the bodies are usually those of children. Woodsworth's *My Neighbor* included 44 different photographs, 15 of which were devoid of any human subjects. Of the remaining 29 pictures, 21 included children as part of the subject matter.

Children were prominent in the documentary activities of social reformers for a number of reasons. It was obviously easier to capture images of children than to take photographs of adults, who might have resisted the imposition.

More importantly, however, the bodies of children drew attention to moral codes ascribed to the social space that surrounded them. By the second half of the nineteenth century, Methodists had started to remove the spectre of original sin from children, arguing that their innocence kept them in a state of grace. More controversial views suggested an environment of Christian nurture even removed the necessity of a traditional conversion experience.[23] While the exact theological relationship of children and the church remained in dispute, most agreed that without a healthy Christian home, based on Anglo-Saxon Protestant values, the moral lives of children were at risk. The pliable nature of children in the face of their environment indicated that the space surrounding the child's body held a particular moral significance.

In making children the subject of photographic representations of urban slums, the 'problem' of the city became a problem for the future of the nation. For middle-class social reformers at the turn of the century, children were central to the welfare of Canada,[24] and Methodists, the most self-consciously 'national' Protestant denomination, repeatedly expressed these concerns. The *Guardian* editorialized that slum conditions and neglect would turn children into a 'class of thugs and hooligans and criminals', and the church's greatest task lay in 'safeguarding the moral and physical health and well-being of the children, and especially the children of our rapidly growing cities. The destiny of the church of the city, and of the nation rests upon the way we accomplish that task to a far greater extent than we can at all realize.'[25]

The physical environment of the city, however, posed a number of difficulties to the creation of productive citizens out of children. Rather than offering a pure and wholesome environment, the *Guardian* characterized the atmosphere of crowded downtowns as 'vitiated with smoke and tainted with a thousand inevitable odors that do not make for health'. Children needed to play, but their choices were limited geographically to playing indoors or on the street: 'To shut healthy children indoors to play is little short of murder . . . But, in the cities, to step outdoors is to step into the street . . . And unfortunately the streets are not a school of virtue, but of vice.'[26] To place children photographically in the street was to document the moral boundaries that threatened the nation. Unsupervised children on the street were subjected to the vices of the street. Only the urban reform of cities, creating more playgrounds to provide a safe space for children, could solve the problem. As the *Guardian* put it, 'Let the boys and girls have plenty of vigorous physical exercise, and the probability is they will be far less apt to become lawbreakers, and much more likely to become good citizens.'[27]

But the moral boundaries of urban space were not gendered equally. Parks and playgrounds were necessary reforms to prevent crime and disease, but they were particularly important for boys. As articles in the *Christian Guardian* outlined, the nature of boys made urban space particularly problematic. R.B. Chadwick, Alberta's Superintendent of Dependent and Delinquent Children, explained that 'The boy is a little savage, who prefers the free, natural, simple life of

his aboriginal forebears to the ridiculous customs and conventionalities of civilization . . . His savage instinct demands that he live close to nature.' As Canadian cities became crowded, an 'insufficiency of grounds' prevents the boy from 'finding an outlet for his desire to run and play'. The result was predictable: without a safe space in which to express his natural inclination, the boy would 'become outlawed or a criminal'.[28] The streets of the city were defined as a moral space that produced criminal bodies, an area that threatened the health of boys in particular, and by extension, the manhood and leadership of the nation.

While it was common to find photographic images of both girls and boys in the street, often with captions that commented on the lack of playground space, pictures of girls alone on the street were practically non-existent. The same was not true of boys, however. *My Neighbor* included a photograph (Figure 4) of a line of boys with the caption 'Boys of school age on the street'. The same image was published in a special 'city' issue of the *Missionary Outlook*, the magazine of the Young People's Forward Movement. F.C. Stephenson, secretary of the YPFM, and Woodsworth's publisher, excerpted part of *My Neighbor* for the issue and had some of the pho-

**Figure 4.** This image of boys on the street was used in a variety of Methodist publications. Photographer unknown. Reprinted from J.S. Woodsworth, *My Neighbor* (Toronto: The Missionary Society of the Methodist Church, 1911).

tographs reprinted. Underneath the image of the boys, the caption starkly asked 'NEGLECTED NOW—WHAT OF THEIR FUTURE?' and included a subtitle that implied the voices of the boys themselves, stating, 'We run the streets all day.'[29]

Girls needed parks as well, but the moral space of greatest concern for them lay not in exterior spaces, but within interior spaces. Streets were dangerous, but the greater danger of moral corruption for girls lay in the largely unspoken fear of sex and girls becoming 'fallen' in their morals. At a time when the domestic space of middle-class households emphasized separate bedrooms and offered girls' bodies a private space, the emergence of tenement houses and slums with overcrowded conditions raised fears that the environment was corrupting girls. Families sharing a single room, and sometimes, a single bed, was a sight fearful enough. The greater worry was when families took in boarders, often single men; girls mixed with this uncontrolled element would find their moral state under threat.

Unlike the relatively straightforward campaign for playgrounds, however, raising the issue of sexuality was complicated by social sensibilities. The Reverend James Allen, Secretary of the Home Mission Department of the Methodist Missionary Society, caused an uproar in Winnipeg when he gave a sensational address to an Ottawa audience, claiming that living conditions were so poor in Winnipeg's North End that 'whole sections of the female population were being driven into virtual prostitution.' An outraged Winnipeg newspaper broadcast the headline 'Winnipeg Given Bad Reputation', and the city council was up in arms at the remarks.[30]

Respectable Winnipeg did not want its reputation sullied by such generalizations about prostitution, but the underlying visualization of moral boundaries within the interior of the homes remained. The *Winnipeg Tribune* sensationalized a case in which a fine had been levied against a boarding-house owner with the headline, 'Girls and Men in Same Room'. The item went on to report that 'The house consists of three rooms and a cellar and is large enough to hold seven people, but the accused was found to have 25 people living in his domicile, three of whom occupied the cellar and in one room girls and men slept.'[31] In Toronto, a missionary worker related similar stories on the 'secret sufferings and horrors of Toronto's "Ward"', where girls grew up 'without privacy, without self-respect'.[32]

Photographs taken by L.B. Foote of domestic interiors from the North End were framed within this context of moral concern. One image (Figure 5) juxtaposes the bodies of men, all of working age, with the bodies of children (boys and girls) within the cramped quarters of the home. Although one of the men is holding two children in his arms, perhaps signifying a paternal relationship, the other men remain detached from any clear familial ties. *My Neighbor* reproduced similar images that problematized the issue of gender and beds. . . .

Mariana Valverde argues that for most reformers the 'sexual secret of the slum' was incest, an 'unmentionable vice lurking deep beneath the crust of civilization'.[33] Despite Woodsworth's oblique reference to it through the use of a quotation from Tennyson (included as an epigraph in *My Neighbor*), the general characterization of crowded living conditions in Methodist publications does not substantiate Valverde's claim. Rather, in reports from the North End of Winnipeg of how the 'other half' lived, the greatest expression of anxiety concerned the problem of unattached male boarders. When the Reverend S.P. Rose took readers on an imaginary 'pilgrimage' to some North End homes, he described one domestic household as being occupied by a 'Ruthenian woman' and two children in a room that is 'neat and fairly clean', but in which danger lay, not in the close quarters of the family, but in the presence of five male boarders, which made 'decency and morality . . . inconceivable.' In contrast, another one-room household of two parents and four children, including an 18-year-old daughter, was

**Figure 5.** Interior of a North End home, Winnipeg. Photographer: L.B. Foote, c. 1911. Winnipeg: Provincial Archives of Manitoba, No. N2438. The image was published in the *Winnipeg Tribune*, 28 Sept. 1911.

described as a 'more hopeful' situation largely because there were no boarders.[34]

The moral implications of bodies crowded together extended into images that ostensibly documented environment alone. Foote's photograph of an unkempt bed (Figure 6) was originally published in the *Winnipeg Telegram*, complete with the prominent headline 'Six were Sleeping in This Room'.[35] Without physically placing the bodies onto the frame, the moral implications were read through the context which problematized such conditions on multiple levels. Although the accompanying article on visitations to the poor in preparation for distributing Christmas funds did not refer explicitly to the photograph, it did complain about Winnipeg's familiar problem of overcrowding. Single-room homes that contained both large families and male boarders produced circumstances where the 'sanitary conditions were something to appal one and the moral atmosphere under each surroundings can be imagined.'[36] The same image was reprinted as an illustration for an article on All Peoples' Mission in the *Canadian Epworth Era*.[37] The absence of bodies did not lessen the moral boundaries ascribed to urban space, given the ability of readers to 'imagine' it.

## Conclusion

The meaning of the social gospel is traditionally framed in connection with issues such as secularization, the rise of the welfare state, or class-based theories of social control. However, a deeper epistemological engagement with modernity within the social gospel has been overlooked, especially in the Canadian context. The new focus upon social conditions at the turn of the century required a new way of 'seeing' and 'surveying' the city. The progressive vision of churches and church workers within the photographic representations of Methodist publications had to make room for an objective exposure of how the 'other half' lived. The arrival of the social documentary style produced a dramatic shift in the visualization of Winnipeg within Methodist publications at the turn of the century.

One of the major differences between the two different photographic strategies, however, lay in how the images related to the text. When photographs were used to exemplify the progres-

**Figure 6.** Photograph of a one-room home for six people in Winnipeg. Photographer: L.B. Foote, 1908. Courtesy of United Church of Canada/Victoria University Archives, No. 93.049P/3117N.

sive expansion of the church, they were carefully linked to the accompanying narrative; through captions or references within articles, people and places were carefully identified. In contrast, there was a remarkable discontinuity in the narrative when images that offered a social documentary were published. People are rarely identified by name, and often even the name of the city is absent, let alone more specific indications of place. This absence of narrative reinforced the underlying notion that the subjects were not important as individual people, but rather served as bodies framed by the environment. Such a 'depersonalized' approach was, as John Tagg has noted, indicative of the practices of 'professional social technicians' who believed that social problems could be solved through environmental change.[38] Set within the context of Methodist publications, the namelessness of subjects overshadowed by the details of their surroundings had a particular theological resonance that implicitly downplayed the importance of individual conversion and reinforced a collective moral understanding of the urban environment.

Referring to the photographs within a 1911 study of Toronto slums, Mariana Valverde observed that there were 'many more dirty outhouses than criminal human beings', and suggests that 'this shift in focus from the poor people to their habitat reflects not a shedding of moralism in favour of science but simply the ascription of moral deviance to physical objects.'[39] However, objects in themselves did not reflect a moral order as much as they created a moral space which produced moral bodies. The bodies of children in particular offered social reformers malleable material, but the meanings of these bodies could be understood only as products of their environment. Woodsworth summed up this relationship when he claimed that 'Crime, immorality, disease and misery vary almost directly as the size of the plot, the breadth of the street and the number of parks.'[40] As sin was increasingly seen as the product of an environment, the environment itself required surveillance.

Documenting the shift in visual imagery in Methodist publications is a much simpler task than analyzing its meaning. Peter Burke suggests that visual images are both 'an essential and treacherous source' for historians, in part because 'Images can bear witness to what is not put into words.'[41] While we can only speculate as to the exact intentions of Woodsworth and others who promoted this strategic shift to the social documentary style, the wordlessness of photographs should not obscure or diminish how such images operated within the historical context of their production (and reproduction). This visual ordering was not simply symbolic of social reform ideals, but actively constructed a view of the city through its own technological authority, an objective claim to dispassionate representation of the urban space surrounding the body. In return, the very context in which this re-imaging took place invested the urban landscape with multiple layers of moral boundaries, where the dangers to physical and spiritual health were clearly exposed. Although they were disconnected from the overt narratives of missionary work, social documentary photographs spoke to a broader narrative that positioned the religious response to the city as both a moral and environmental issue.

## Notes

Financial support for this project was provided by a University of Lethbridge Research Fund Grant. The author wishes to thank Janet Friskney for her comments on early drafts of this work.

1.  J.S. Woodsworth, *My Neighbor* (Toronto: Missionary Society of the Methodist Church, 1911), 22.

2.  Toronto, United Church of Canada Archives (UCA), 73.102C, Methodist Church Department of Evangelism and Social Service papers, box 1, file 2, Board of Temperance and Moral Reform, Annual Meeting, 21–2 Oct. 1913.

3.  S.D. Chown, 'Introduction', in Woodsworth, *My Neighbor*, 6; see also *The Missionary Outlook* 31, 8 (Aug. 1911): 177.

4.  As Alan Trachtenberg notes, the 'documentary' label was applied retrospectively to the work of Lewis Hine and Walker Evans as a way to classify an aesthetic that appeared to be neither 'art' nor purely journalistic in its intent. Alan Trachtenberg,

*Reading American Photographs: Images as History, Mathew Brady to Walker Evans* (New York: Hill and Wang, 1989), 190–2. On the transition from Riis to Veiller, see Maren Stange, *Symbols of Ideal Life: Social Documentary in America, 1890–1950* (Cambridge: Cambridge University Press, 1985), 28–46.

5.  Susan Sontag, *On Photography* (New York: Dell, 1977), 87.

6.  On the relationship between photography and a 'modern vision', see Suren Lalvani, *Photography, Vision, and the Production of Modern Bodies* (Albany: State University of New York Press, 1996).

7.  The phrase 'evidential force' is Roland Barthes's, but John Tagg takes the same notion in a different direction by pointing out that the 'very idea of what constitutes evidence has a history.' See John Tagg, *The Burden of Representation: Essays of Photographies and Histories* (Basingstoke: Macmillan, 1988), 2.

8.  Doug Smith and Michael Olito, *The Best Possible Face: L.B. Foote's Winnipeg* (Winnipeg: Turnstone Press, 1985), 2–3.

9.  *Christian Guardian* 76, 40 (4 Oct. 1905): 9.

10. Ibid., 77, 21 (23 May 1906): 1.

11. Paul Voisey, 'The Urbanization of the Canadian Prairies, 1871–1916', *Histoire Sociale/Social History* 8 (1975): 84–5.

12. George Emery, *The Methodist Church on the Prairies, 1896–1914* (Montreal and Kingston: McGill-Queen's University Press, 2001), 104–25.

13. 'Problems and Policies', *Christian Guardian* 78, 14 (3 Apr. 1907): 5.

14. S.P. Rose, 'The Religion of a Great City', *Christian Guardian* 78, 14 (3 Apr. 1907): 6.

15. Nancy Christie and Michael Gauvreau suggest that the threat to resign was not based on theological issues but was rather a 'ploy' to secure the position at All Peoples' Mission. . . . See Nancy Christie and Michael Gauvreau, *A Full-Orbed Christianity* (Montreal and Kingston: McGill-Queen's University Press, 1996), 8–12. In contrast, George Emery reasserts the radical position of Woodsworth, but claims that this was balanced by a mainstream evangelicalism that characterized most of the mission workers. See Emery, *The*

*Methodist Church on the Prairies*, 147–50. Whether mainstream or radical, Woodsworth's ascendance certainly marked a shift at All Peoples' that was reflected in the realm of visual representation.

16. *Christian Guardian* 79. 34 (19 Aug. 1908): 9. The image was published the previous month in the *Free Press*. Ottawa: National Archives of Canada (NAC), J.S. Woodsworth fonds, Woodsworth Scrapbooks, newspaper clipping, 'Social Settlement Work in Winnipeg', *Winnipeg Free Press*, 11 July 1908.

17. NAC, J.S. Woodsworth fonds, box 15.8, microfilm H-2278, *All Peoples' Mission, Winnipeg, Report, 1907–1908*; J.S. Woodsworth, *Strangers within our Gates* (Toronto: Missionary Society of the Methodist Church, 1909), facing p. 262.

18. *Christian Guardian* 76, 40 (4 Oct. 1905): 5.

19. For an even earlier image of All Peoples' Mission, and one that included signage in multiple languages, see *Christian Guardian* 70, 30 (26 July 1899): 467.

20. NAC, J.S. Woodsworth fonds, box 15.8, microfilm H-2278, *Organized Helpfulness: All Peoples' Mission, 1911–1912*, 22.

21. S.P. Rose, 'The Religion of a Great City: Part III', *Christian Guardian* 78, 16 (17 Apr. 1907): 8.

22. Woodsworth, *My Neighbor*, 23.

23. Neil Semple stresses the development of the Christian nurture ideal, while Marguerite Van Die notes that Nathanael Burwash maintained the more traditional evangelical viewpoint well into the twentieth century. Although Burwash reasserted the doctrine as official church policy in 1906, the model of Christian nurture promoted by Horace Bushnell had clearly won out by 1918. See Neil Semple, '"The Nurture and Admonition of the Lord": Nineteenth-Century Canadian Methodism's Response to "Childhood"', *Histoire Sociale/Social History* 14, 27 (May 1981): 157–75; Neil Semple, *The Lord's Dominion* (Montreal and Kingston: McGill-Queen's University Press, 1996), 363–7; Marguerite Van Die, *An Evangelical Mind: Nathanael Burwash and the Methodist Tradition in Canada, 1839–1918* (Montreal and Kingston: McGill-Queen's University Press,

1989), 26–37, 191. As Phyllis Airhart notes, these issues were further complicated by psychological views of religious experience itself. Phyllis Airhart, *Serving the Present Age: Revivalism, Progressivism, and the Methodist Tradition in Canada* (Montreal and Kingston: McGill-Queen's University Press, 1992), 97–103.

24. See Neil Sutherland, *Children in English-Canadian Society: Framing the Twentieth Century Consensus* (Toronto: University of Toronto Press, 1976).

25. 'Giving the Children a Chance', *Christian Guardian* 82, 13 (29 Mar. 1911): 5.

26. 'The City and the Children', *Christian Guardian* 78, 5 (30 Jan.1907): 5.

27. Ibid.

28. R.B. Chadwick, 'The Boys: A Social Problem', *Christian Guardian* 81, 52 (28 Dec. 1910): 9–10.

29. *Missionary Outlook* 31, 11 (Nov. 1911): 251.

30. UCA, 78.099C, Methodist Church of Canada Board of Home Missions, box 7, file 3, unidentified newspaper clippings, 11 Oct. 1909.

31. Ibid., *Winnipeg Tribune* newspaper clipping c. 1909.

32. 'Sad Picture of Toronto's Slums', *Toronto Star*, 19 Oct. 1909, 1.

33. Mariana Valverde, *The Age of Light, Soap, and Water: Moral Reform in English Canada, 1885–1925* (Toronto: McClelland & Stewart, 1991), 139. Valverde also notes the problem of male boarders, but prioritizes the issue of incest.

34. S.P. Rose, 'The Raw Material of Canadian Citizenship: A Closer View', *Christian Guardian* 79, 34 (19 Aug. 1908): 9–10.

35. Woodsworth Scrapbooks, *Winnipeg Telegram*, 16 Dec. 1908.

36. Ibid., 'Some of Children to be Gladdened by Fund', *Winnipeg Telegram*, 16 Dec. 1908.

37. Ibid., *Canadian Epworth Era* (Mar. 1909): 68.

38. Tagg, *Burden of Representation*, 131–2.

39. Valverde, *Age of Light, Soap, and Water*, 133.

40. Woodsworth, *My Neighbor*, 47; also quoted in Valverde, *Age of Light, Soap, and Water*, 130.

41. Peter Burke, *Eyewitnessing: The Uses of Images as Historical Evidence* (Ithaca, NY: Cornell University Press, 2001), 31.

# 4

# Negotiating Sex and Gender
# in the Ukrainian Bloc Settlement:
# East-Central Alberta between the Wars

Frances Swyripa

By the time Maxim Pylypczuk became a *cause célèbre* in the local Anglo-Canadian press for the brutal murder of his 20-year-old wife near Pakan in the heart of the Vegreville bloc in east-central Alberta in 1912, the criminal reputation of Ukrainian immigrants was well established.[1] According to the stereotype which persisted to World War II, Ukrainians beat their wives, drank to excess and ended up in bloody brawls, stole without conscience and engaged in senseless litigation, and figured disproportionately in the country's penitentiaries and insane asylums. This image—popularized and sensationalized in articles, editorials, fiction, and countless discussions of the 'immigrant problem'[2]—reflected in part the reality of Ukrainians' peasant cultural baggage and the dislocation of uprooting. But it also reflected Anglo-Canadians' concerns for the moral fibre of their nation, and was based as much on anti-Ukrainian prejudice as on hard data and research. Anxious to blend in and be accepted, successive generations of Ukrainian Canadians simply preferred to ignore the issue of crime in their community, rather than draw attention to it by subjecting the Anglo-Canadian

stereotype to serious scrutiny. Recently, however, that stereotype has been challenged. Ukrainian-Canadian criminal behaviour has also begun to be examined within the dual context of the old-world peasant culture, patriarchal and materially poor, and the emerging prairie frontier culture that simultaneously nurtured it.[3]

This article uses crime investigation files compiled by the Department of the Attorney General in Alberta between 1915 and 1929[4] to continue the process, exploring how Ukrainian men and women in the Vegreville bloc negotiated issues of sex and gender between the wars. Carnal knowledge, rape, seduction, indecent assault, and wife-beating charges—which formed only a minority of the 1,500 cases to involve Ukrainians in these years—reveal the extent to which attitudes and behaviour imported from Ukrainian villages in Galicia and Bukovyna were retained, redirected, or submerged under the influence of the Canadian legal system.[5] A combination of isolation, ignorance, fear, and physical force would have prevented most victims of domestic violence and sexual assault from bringing their problems before the courts to be solved by Anglo-Canadian

Frances Swyripa, 'Negotiating Sex and Gender in the Ukrainian Bloc Settlement: East-Central Alberta Between the Wars', *Prairie Forum* 20, 2 (1995): 149–74. Reprinted courtesy of the Canadian Plains Research Center.

notions of abstract justice. But in those instances where charges were laid, whether by women themselves or their male relatives, individuals on both sides of the dispute had an ambiguous relationship with the state institutions and laws of their adopted homeland. If they sometimes welcomed outside intervention and saw the courts as an ally, they more frequently tried to adapt and manipulate an often inflexible law to their own ends. Above all, Ukrainians of both sexes tended to turn to mainstream structures for resolution of their problems only after their informal community-based avenues to securing justice had failed.[6]

Criminal activity represents the irregular and abnormal, and never shows people at their best. Moreover, all parties to a dispute that reaches the attention of the authorities naturally structure their stories to promote and protect their own best interests. The first observation cautions the historian against stereotyping Ukrainians in interwar Alberta on the basis of the crime investigation files in the Attorney General's Department. The second warns of potential problems with this material as a historical source. The teenager who thought she had strained herself lifting and did not know she was pregnant until consulting a doctor some five months later is perhaps plausible; her seducer, she said, 'told me he was trying not to have any children.'[7] Less believable is the uncle who claimed ignorance of the condition of the niece in his care until the doctor informed him the day she delivered a full-term baby, and one suspects that he wanted to defend himself from both criticism for inaction and rumours that he had fathered the child.[8] Other problems with the material have nothing to do with the credibility of the actors. Sentences like 'He inserted his penace [sic] into my private parts' and 'You told my learned friend that you called your sister a hoar [sic]' question the literacy skills of the police and court officials creating the written record.[9] Incompetent or biased interpreters intruded more seriously on proceedings. Pressed by the judge to get an alleged rape vic-

tim to recount her experience in detail, one interpreter insisted that 'pregnant' was 'rather a hard word' to translate.[10] A witness's imperfect English, especially without a translator, further complicated the court's efforts to arrive at the truth. It put the plaintiff at a decided disadvantage when she lacked the vocabulary to describe her sexual assault or to understand the precise meaning of terms like 'intercourse'.[11]

Regardless of such limitations, the sworn statements and testimony of the principals in a case, their families, and neighbours registered what people either believed the truth [to be] or wanted to have believed was the truth, and thus how they ordered and perceived their world. Furthermore, while the files under examination constitute official records generated and maintained by the Anglo-Canadian establishment, the actions they documented differed significantly from liquor-related offences that arose from government agents or police officers campaigning against illicit stills.[12] Indecent assault, carnal knowledge, seduction, rape, and wife-beating charges were initiated by Ukrainians against other Ukrainians. As women acted on their own behalf, or as husbands and fathers spoke for wives and daughters, they defined what Ukrainians—and not mainstream society—considered important, morally or legally right and wrong, and in need of 'justice'. In presenting their claims, they furnished inadvertent but valuable insights into the functioning and mindset of the rural Ukrainian bloc settlement as peasant tradition jostled with the values of industrialized North American society.

Emigration and education had not yet alienated Ukrainians from centuries-old rituals and superstitions that governed life and conditioned the peasants' attitudes and behaviour.[13] For example, despite modernity on Ukrainian farmsteads that the telephone and Eaton's catalogue signalled, belief in magic survived. A woman explained that she contaminated her neighbour's well with dead chickens and rotten eggs because he had changed himself into a mouse and stolen a sack of her grain, then turned into a horse and ridden off with it.[14] The complainant in a seduction trial testified that when she rejected the suggestion made by the father of her child that she induce a miscarriage by jumping off the hayloft, he instructed her to tie red string around her wrists and legs and she would escape unharmed.[15] In another incident, a farmer dragged his wife of 30 years off the wagon into the bush, tied her up, and struck her—demanding to know where she had learned 'those mysterious things', and threatening to rape her with a stick if she did not confess 'how your sister learned you to be a witch.' This accusation of witchcraft appeared to arise from a power struggle within the marriage, for the man later complained that for nine months 'since our trouble commenced' his wife had been 'very angry' and 'against my will'.[16] Finally, a recent immigrant denied any responsibility for a schoolgirl's pregnancy. 'How did you get that way?' he demanded, 'Did you take a magnet off me?'[17]

A late-night fracas in an Edmonton rooming house, in which a female resident struck a visitor from Smoky Lake with a poker, reveals the survival of magic in another context—continued belief in the potency of a curse. When the case reached court, the judge was astonished to learn that the man considered his assailant's exclamation, 'Lightening [sic] strike you here', to be swearing and part of his injuries.[18] A squabble over a haystack in a long-standing property dispute near Chipman saw a son actually charged with assaulting his father, not only by hitting him on the nose but also by calling him 'dirty names'. 'Nick', the father explained, 'called me a thief. . . . he said also your mother is a *hour* [whore].'[19] A curse or name-calling was particularly inflammatory if it involved sexual prowess or impropriety. In a second violent altercation over hay, stored on land the complainant's wife rented to the accused, her husband admitted to taunting the man, but only after 'he called me a balled [sic] headed prick.'[20] When several men called a woman 'filthy names' on her return from the toi-

let at a country dance, her brother leaped to her defence. Whether to emphasize his chivalry or to justify losing the ensuing brawl, he explained that 'if I could have got a fence post I would have got the best of it. . . . It was not right that he called my sister a dirty fool' (her testimony specified 'whore' and 'dirty son of a bitch').[21] But an image of retiring womanhood relying on male initiative and gallantry to defend its honour would be a misreading of Ukrainian peasant society. Women not only appreciated the power of a curse but also, quite literally, fought their own battles. This was clearly demonstrated when a Fort Saskatchewan-area farm wife took a club to her neighbour after she ran into her yard yelling, 'You blind woman without ovaries.'[22]

Yet old-world superstitions and practices faced competition from new values, reflecting the impact of immigration and Anglo-Canadian influences. The changing world view of Ukrainian women entailed a reassessment of both their self-image and their rights as human beings. According to folklorist Robert Klymasz, the folksongs composed by Ukrainian immigrant women in Canada—a sensitive barometer of popular opinion—shifted from 'balladic outpourings' to become 'more outspoken in [their] opposition to the woman's traditionally subordinate position in the Ukrainian family and community'.[23] One folksong in particular—rife with anglicisms and preserved in the collective memory of its unknown creator's female contemporaries—revealed how some women internalized and interpreted female emancipation as a Canadian concept. The author describes how her husband beat her, how she eventually had enough, and how she ran away to a woman friend who 'knew the law real well' and immediately called the police. Now, she is enjoying herself while her husband languishes in jail: 'And when he comes out he'll know that he should show respect for a *lady!*'[24] Too few sources in their own words exist to reconstruct the process by which individuals cut off physically and linguistically from mainstream society learned about Anglo-Canadian notions of womanhood and womanliness, or to determine precisely what a Ukrainian immigrant understood by 'lady'. But Alberta's crime investigation files reinforce the message of the anonymous folksong through a handful of women who refused to endure further physical abuse. Equally significantly, these women perceived the Canadian justice system not as an alien interloper in the Ukrainian community or their lives but as an ally to enlist on their behalf. When assaulted by her husband at the breakfast table, a Vilna woman testified, 'I told him for to be careful with the knife or I will put him in the Court for that.' Undeterred by his threat to kill her on his release from jail if she did, she had a charge laid.[25] After her husband beat her with a broom handle and knocked her to the floor while she was nursing the baby, another wife matter-of-factly testified, 'as soon as I could get up I went and phoned the Police.'[26] The actions of these two women reflected the influence of the Canadian environment, but they also drew on established practices in their homeland. Ukrainian women in Galicia, for example, also took steps to escape intolerable situations, initiating the great majority of interwar petitions requesting the Greek Catholic Church to dissolve unhappy marriages.[27]

Ukrainian men, more exposed to the Anglo-Canadian world through work, also exhibited new values. Some—like the defendant in a seduction trial who declared he would not marry the girl because she could not read or write— were clearly status conscious and upwardly mobile.[28] The expectant mother in another seduction case testified that the father of her child promised to marry her if she first went to the nearby Methodist mission 'to learn to cook and talk'.[29] Other men absorbed less savoury prejudices of Anglo-Canadian society. Fisticuffs erupted at the church in Star, for example, after the accused asked the complainant what 'he meant by spreading the story around that he, accused, was a half breed and that his sister was a nigger.'[30] But if Ukrainians quickly identified

and disparaged those beneath them in Canada's emerging ethnic hierarchy, using racial taunts to scare off an enemy, a domestic dispute between a well-known moonshiner and his wife shows they were more circumspect when it came to those above them. The confrontation occurred in front of several witnesses, including a non-Ukrainian neighbour who had reluctantly come to the house at the entreaty of the distraught wife. One of the Ukrainians present testified that the accused 'throwed the bread and meat' at his wife and said he was prevented only by the presence of Bob Coleman from throwing more. Her husband's exact words, the woman recalled, were: 'If it was not for this Englishman here I would show you how I'd fix you.'[31]

Canadian attitudes had a more positive impact as well. While Ukrainian parents were criticized by Anglo-Canadians and the Ukrainian pioneer intelligentsia alike for apathy towards education—particularly of girls destined for matrimony—more than one father objected to the marriage of a pregnant daughter on the grounds that she was too young or still in school.[32] Girls themselves reinforced the notion that schooling was important. The girl who supposedly took a magnet off her seducer had been attacked on the way home from a concert at the local school. Before he knocked her down, she told the court, 'Panko said he wanted to marry me and I said I don't want to get married because I am a scolar [sic] yet.' One of the most telling instances of new values, or at least of female rebellion against traditional roles and parental expectations, involved a young woman who poisoned her father's cattle by putting lye in their feed because she was angry about $20 he accused her of stealing. She had worked for nine years, she explained; her father had taken all her wages and given her nothing for her wedding, so she wanted to see him with nothing too.[33]

The coexistence of old-world and new-world value systems clearly indicates that the Vegreville bloc remained an immigrant society in transition. After some 30 years in Canada, Ukrainians had discarded much but not all of their peasant past. Certain observances, as the puzzled lawyer for a youth charged with seduction learned, were tenaciously kept. His client, even when arrested, wanted to marry the underaged girl but was prevented by her mother, who 'would not permit the marriage during a Russian [sic] holiday season' (she proved perfectly amenable once the pre-Christmas lenten period had ended).[34] The religious calendar joined the agricultural or seasonal calendar in ordering Ukrainians' world. Time was measured and events pinpointed not by the dates and months demanded by Canadian courts and modern urbanized society but by the yardsticks of pre-industrial Christian communities. One girl recalled that the hired hand who seduced her had begun to work for her father 'about Ruthenian New Year', a second that her rapist left her father's employ 'after the spring work'.[35] Others testified that sexual intercourse had occurred 'about a week after the Ruthenian Easter', 'during shooting time, I don't remember what month', 'on the church holiday (Safat)', 'two weeks before St. Peter holiday', 'when people were putting the potatoes in'.[36] Parents first suspected something wrong 'about the time we were digging potatoes', 'about two weeks after the Russian [sic] Xmas', during 'spring work they were ploughing and seeding.'[37] That Ukrainians adhered to the Julian calendar and not the Gregorian (which they identified as 'Polish', underlining how the old country continued to define the outside world) further complicated matters for a legal apparatus intent on establishing time and place.[38]

From the perspective of the female victim of a sex crime, inability to furnish the type of precise information the law required could be disastrous. In the case of the young woman whose uncle disclaimed all knowledge of her pregnancy, the police found insufficient evidence existed to proceed with the seduction charge:

No further proof can be got as to the complainant's age, she does not possess a birth certificate, just her own statement that she is twenty

in September coming. . . . complainant cannot give any definite time or date as to when her marriage with the accused was to take place. . . . she cannot speak one word of English and has no idea what month week or day the intercourse took place, denies having intercourse with any person except the accused.[39]

Sometimes, without the village priest to keep the peasants' records for them, the upheaval of emigration and pioneering meant that events like the birth of a baby had never been registered or were subsequently forgotten. Such negligence had significant repercussions in seduction and carnal knowledge cases, where the alleged victim's age was crucial. One investigating officer did his best. The girl's father, he wrote, testified that

he really did not know how old Yowdoha was, but stated that he has been in Canada since 1899 and that after a little while his girl Annie was born and three years afterwards Yowdoha was born. According to Land Office statistics . . . [X] . . . filed on his farm in 1901 and he had one daughter, and three years afterwards would give him Yowdoha, and this would make the girl just about 15 years in a few more months.[40]

A judge threw out a seduction charge after the 15-year-old girl, the eldest of 10 children, admitted on cross-examination to prior intercourse with the accused, ruling out either chastity or rehabilitation. Defence counsel's attempt to trip up the mother over her daughter's age, however, shows how much the act of moving halfway around the world defined people's lives. The woman remembered neither the date nor time of year of her marriage some 25 years earlier, but she knew exactly how old her daughter was, 'because I came to Canada in 1903 and she was born two years later.'[41]

Nowhere were two not-always compatible value systems more visible than in Ukrainian-Canadian attitudes towards marriage. Twenty of

25 seduction charges formally read 'under promise of marriage', and a good proportion of the carnal knowledge and rape cases also involved a promise of marriage on the part of the accused. If the girls' versions of events are to be believed, it was this guarantee or understanding that convinced them to agree to sexual intercourse. Many subsequently described their hesitancy, shame, fear, incomprehension, or confusion at the act itself. In other respects, their responses serve as a reminder of the need to approach past phenomena within the proper cultural context rather than the prejudices of the historian's own society. These girls saw themselves not as violated children but as young women ready for marriage. One 12-year-old described how the accused had had intercourse with her when she went to his place: 'We had arranged to get married next year, after Xmas we were to be married the accused said. I was satisfied. . . . I like the accused and would like to get married to him. I think that we can make a good home.'[42]

While this girl was exceptionally young, the files under review confirm that early marriage for girls was accepted and normal among Ukrainians in the Vegreville bloc.[43] Statistical findings support this. Through World War I one-third of Greek Catholic brides in the area married at 16 or younger, and fully three-quarters were under 20 (in Alberta as a whole in the same period only one-third of brides were under 20). In the early 1920s a massive shift benefited the 17-to-19 age group in particular, so that at midpoint in the decade some two-thirds of girls were marrying in their late as opposed to mid-teens.[44] But while delayed marriage signified changing attitudes, sex-crime cases show that tradition persisted. Well into the 1920s, as girls agreed to arranged marriages or marriage to men they scarcely knew, economic considerations and parental pressure over love and free choice remained major determinants in conjugal unions. One would-be groom (whom his targeted bride had never seen) arrived at her parents' house at ten o'clock at night with his witness, who would testify that the man 'was going to look at the girl and if he like that girl he was going to marry her.' Presumably he liked her, for he proposed—and, in a Ukrainian version of bundling, proceeded to have intercourse in the upstairs bedroom after she accepted. 'Everybody wanted us to get married', the girl later explained, adding, 'I wouldn't have had connection with him if he hadn't promised to marry me.' When the man failed to appear for the wedding, charges of seduction were laid. The preliminary hearing prompted a change of heart and he agreed to the match, only to discover that the girl had also reconsidered. 'I don't see what is the use of me getting married to him', she declared under cross-examination, 'if he said he would give me a licking every day.'[45]

Her resolute stance shows that Ukrainian girls were not simply bystanders as others decided their future or they acquiesced in family and community expectations. Rather, they developed a range of strategies to negotiate power and to control their own destiny. Some refused to have sexual relations without a wedding ring on their finger; others spurned the offer of marriage that accompanied the sexual assault or was extended after pregnancy resulted. 'I don't want to marry him', one pregnant young woman protested, informing the court that the man had proposed when a charge of carnal knowledge loomed. Either external pressure or the social and economic consequences of single motherhood outweighed her resistance, however, as the pair eventually wed.[46] A second pregnant girl, apparently valuing independence over respectability conferred by a husband, took no action until seven months after her sexual assault because 'I was working in Vegreville and did not want to lose my position.'[47]

. . .

If carnal knowledge, seduction, indecent assault, and rape cases show Ukrainian girls acting in their own interests, the men involved were equally motivated by selfish concerns. Besides the substantial offer of land or the easy promise of marriage, inducements to win consent to intercourse ranged from clothes, ribbons, oranges, and candy, to a trip to the movies.[48] But money, with five cents the base rate, seemed the preferred incentive and pacifier. After an unsuccessful attempt at penetration, one girl testified, her assailant gave her a nickel 'to buy something with'.[49] Confronted by the mother of the 17-year-old he had seduced and impregnated, a neighbouring farmer reputedly retorted: 'We don't owe you anything as I paid you, five cents each time I did it.'[50] A hired hand charged with carnal knowledge of a girl under 14 not only disputed the complainant's chastity, claiming she had admitted to being with 'other boys' who had paid for her favours, but also implied that any obligations on his part had been discharged because 'after business I gave her a dollar.' The investigating officer saw the incident differently. 'The girl states', he wrote in his report, that 'the accused after ravishing this child laid a dollar bill on her leg and told her not to tell her parents or anyone.'[51] The givers of such gifts clearly regarded acceptance as both a contract for services and payment for services rendered. In the men's minds—and more than one defence counsel adopted the same position—it also absolved them of any future moral or legal responsibility.[52] The threat of discovery, however, could raise the value of the transaction from the man's point of view. A girl who struggled free of her captor's drunken fondling in her brother's livery barn was offered $5 to keep quiet. She refused and ran to tell her family.[53]

The number of private bargains amicably struck or not exposed by pregnancy to reach public notice in the courts will never be known. Nor will the attitudes of the intended or actual recipients of the ribbons and nickels before everything exploded and they felt compelled to present themselves in the most positive light possible. Casual sex was perhaps the only way for girls to acquire money and goods independently of the family. But a woman accosted by her neighbour early one morning while she was feeding the pigs suggests that females placed their value somewhat higher than the males who

sought them out. She begged the man to leave her alone because she was tired. 'I told him that even if he paid me $10 I would not do it [consent to intercourse].' . . .[54]

On at least one occasion the male aggressor in a sexual assault enlisted his superior knowledge of Canada, and Ukrainian immigrants' perverted image of a 'fri kontri' (free country) where no restrictions applied,[55] to subdue a reluctant partner. In tackling his neighbour, a recent immigrant out fencing while her husband was in Edmonton, the would-be rapist explained that this was Canada and he could do as he wanted. His assault had serious economic consequences for the needy couple, who rented their farm, as the woman's fear of staying alone subsequently prevented her husband from seeking outside work.[56] Recent immigrants were not alone in having their ignorance of the new homeland exploited, or in feeling uncertain about their rights. In 1926 a woman confined to the farm since her arrival in Canada and marriage 13 years earlier was twice waylaid by a neighbour lad on the public trail that crossed his parents' property. After the first encounter, she testified,

> I was very scared and ashamed. . . . I thought I would forgive him for his act and would not mention it to anybody. I was unable to speak English and in a new country and did not know the language and did not wish to make trouble at home or have the public laugh at me. When I got home from the store I was shaky and nervous at my work. . . . The next day my husband said there was something the matter with me as I was shaky and looked different but I was afraid to mention anything as I thought he would beat me and I would suffer for the rest of my life.[57]

Despite her shame and fear, this woman proved no passive victim. On the second occasion she told her attacker 'to go to Hell' and 'hoped the lightening [sic] would strike him dead.' She also informed her husband (the record does not say if he did, in fact, beat her), as well as the culprit's mother (who said she should have pulled his eyes out). And when neither of them gave her satisfaction, she took matters into her own hands:

> After he ran after me the second time I knew that he would bother me in the future right along and I would not stand for it. When I saw that my husband was not taking this matter very seriously, I started to talk amongst the neighbours and to get advice what was the best thing to do and if it was the law in Canada that a man could attack anybody he likes and I was advised to report the matter to the police, that if a man does anything like that he will be punished and the following day my husband went to make a complaint. . . . I told all the neighbours I met about this trouble, since which all the women who were using this path avoid it or use it when they have somebody with them.[58]

This woman's story raises several important issues. First, it says much about women in her position, unfamiliar with Canadian law and prey to unwanted attentions. Second, for she was not unique in making her case public, it illuminates how Ukrainians in the rural bloc settlement dealt informally with illicit sexual liaisons and their consequences. Lastly, it offers insight into how the various parties in a grievance mobilized and actively involved the community in settling or arbitrating their disputes.

Immigrant women—isolated on the homestead, often illiterate in their own language, for the most part certainly illiterate in English—were at a decided disadvantage when it came to seeking outside help or 'justice'. Victims of domestic violence especially could not look to their husbands to initiate proceedings or to guide them through an unfamiliar and often bewildering legal apparatus. The plight of the woman beaten for being a witch, for example, reached official attention only because her daughter wrote an aunt, asking her to tell the police.[59] One would expect the Canadian-born or -raised generation to be more skilled in dealing with the outside world, but the bloc and farm also isolated adolescents. As late as 1928 a 19-year-old did not know her postal address; queried to ensure she appreciated the gravity of an oath, another girl knew only that the Bible was a book; a third girl, tricked by her seducer to believe that the piece of paper she signed properly married them, defiantly insisted that she knew what weddings were, she had been to them.[60] Notwithstanding such 'enlightening' agencies as the public school, or even their own churches, the female world was often circumscribed.

. . .

If neighbours began the trouble, neighbours also participated in its publicity and resolution. When the woman who balked at being accosted on the footpath complained to the lad's family, the family urged her not to talk about the affair so they would not be publicly mortified for raising 'that kind of boy'. This presumably referred to his age, as the woman's husband later chided him that 'it was not right for a young boy to go after an old woman' (she was 33). The husband had also preferred to suppress the matter and deal with the lad privately, and was upset when his wife went over his head to seek advice from the neighbours. That she broadcast his reluctance to take action, causing him to lose face and be sharply lectured on his duty, he found particularly galling. Neighbours were thus viewed in two lights—one supportive and desirable; the other interfering, censorious, constricting. Often the two roles overlapped. One husband's perceived public humiliation triggered a fight with his wife when he returned home from church and ordered his visiting sister-in-law to leave because 'she had been telling the neighbours that I had not been with my wife for 6 months that I ran away from her.' The wife declared her sister would stay, and announced that she herself, likely in a bid to rally community opinion, had publicized their situation.[61]

That the community was prepared to intervene and take sides in domestic disputes is indicated by a letter to the attorney general request-ing the early release of a husband jailed for beat-ing his wife. The man, his lawyer wrote, was a farmer and property owner with several head of livestock and 35 acres of grain. Incarceration would be ruinous, 'a more serious loss to the country' than the husband's correction, for even if guilty he was 'not a criminal in the ordinary sense'. The lawyer elaborated:

> From what I could gather the quarrel . . . arose over the unchastity or suspected unchastity of [the wife], and her behaviour with two other men of that settlement, which may not be justi-fication for him evoking the plea of the unwrit-ten law, but in these farming communities sometimes things are done in a passion, and with outsider's influences, more particularly in a case of this kind, are brought to bear on the wife to have the husband incarcerated and out of the way for a couple of months.[62]

Ignoring the lawyer's sexism to focus on his primary complaint, meddling 'outsiders', the truth is that these anonymous individuals were really 'insiders', friends and neighbours and fel-low Ukrainians. Moreover, the ethnic commu-nity they represented would determine if and when the real outsider—the Anglo-Canadian law—became involved in its affairs. After a Radway couple were charged with confining their severely handicapped son in a chicken coop, for example, the local teacher (himself Ukrainian) pleaded with the attorney general to deny the rumour he had been the one to notify the authorities.[63] The ethnic community also expected Anglo-Canadian law to do right by it. Although admittedly not an impartial observer, the lawyer, consulted by a father whose daugh-ter's seducer had his conviction quashed on a technicality, twice wrote the attorney general to say he had been sought out by concerned indi-viduals from the district. Persistent rumours about no retrial, they had cautioned, were having 'a rather disquieting effect on the neighbours'.[64]

In a second case, news that a Copernick-area youth had taken advantage of his parents' absence to sexually assault a girl stopping at the house on her way home from school soon circu-lated locally, and on his next visit the Greek Catholic priest was approached for advice. Meeting with several men after church, he advised them 'not to have such matters hushed up', and the girl's mother was told. When insuf-ficient corroboration brought a stay of proceed-ings, the girl's family continued to campaign for justice through both the legal system and com-munity opinion, prompting the youth's lawyer to threaten the mother and grandmother with a damage suit if they persisted in making 'bad statements' about his client, whose reputation in the community had suffered as a result. The grandmother was particularly irresponsible and provocative, boasting that she 'could lay any charge she wanted' against the youth 'because it did not cost her anything.'[65]

Community sanctions and opinion could exert immense pressure. A Chipman-area teenager, seduced by the hired hand, said noth-ing because 'he told me if Father found out he would not let me go anywhere, and people would be laughing at me and Father was liable to kill me.' Finally convinced that the people were indeed talking about her, the girl agreed to run away with the man.[66] Shame and fear of 'a lick-ing' (which often proved well founded) deterred many girls from telling their parents about unwanted intercourse until pregnancy forced the issue. An attacker's threats to 'tell father'—or to 'kill me', 'shoot me', 'cut my head off'—were equally effective silencers. Yet someone told someone, for rumours and gossip flourished as an underground grapevine turned a secret act between two people into public property.

. . .

The implications of community went much deeper than a forum for gossip, rumour, and bragging about sexual exploits, or even the mobilization of public opinion in resolving per-sonal disputes. As people tried to sort out their problems, both 'injured' and 'guilty' parties formally involved friends, relatives, and neighbours in enforcing communal standards. This was particularly true of sexual liaisons and the shame and embarrassment, loss of reputation, or unwanted pregnancy that either attended or ensured discovery. In fact, it would appear that physical relationships outside marriage became rape, seduction, carnal knowledge, or indecent assault—in other words, 'sex crimes' to be decided by the Canadian courts—only when Ukrainians' private system of justice failed. With respect to a pregnant daughter, marriage presumably represented the ultimate form of justice, and in an unknown number of instances a wedding would have been arranged, amicably or otherwise. If need be, a seduction charge could be brandished to help convince a recalcitrant young man that matrimony was preferable to a trial and perhaps jail.[67] But not all girls or their parents saw marriage as the answer. One pragmatic father objected to his daughter marrying the father of her child because the 19-year-old, his former hired hand, had 'no home of his own . . . was a lazy useless fellow and would not be able to support a wife.'[68] When marriage, for whatever reason, was rejected, Ukrainians turned to the community, soliciting its co-operation to correct the wrongs of sexual transgressions.

In such situations, whether giving redress or absolution, justice was understood as concrete and personal, and not dispensed by a fine or prison term imposed by the courts in the name of a nebulous Crown. To Ukrainians in the Vegreville bloc, justice in a 'sex crime' meant a 'settlement' or monetary compensation, negotiated between the male perpetrator and his female victim (or her parents or husband) either directly or with neighbours and friends as intermediaries. Numerous agreements were undoubtedly struck without being recorded. But unless the male refused to consider this option, settlement was seen as the responsibility of the Ukrainian community, with mainstream society to be involved only if the community failed to resolve the problems. Those rape, seduction, carnal knowledge, and indecent assault cases where a settlement was broached, or even purportedly reached, reveal a set of values at odds with Canadian society and the Canadian legal system.

While Canadian law defined a whole series of sexual irregularities as criminal offences to be prosecuted by the Crown on society's behalf, Ukrainians treated them privately like civil offences, with restitution made directly to the victim. Moreover, in taking or threatening legal action, the injured party in a 'sex crime' seemed to assume that the Canadian courts would also treat the matter as a civil suit dispensing material compensation. When their neighbour subsequently charged with rape originally came to settle, a Smoky Lake farmer told his 19-year-old wife that 'she knew what he had done to her and . . . what to do to him. If he had done very bad she could go to court and sue him.'[69] Rape charges were dismissed against a Wahstao man on the grounds that the 17-year-old girl was known to be prostituting herself in the district; according to the investigating officer, the accused had had intercourse with her on several occasions 'and this time she was put in the family way and wanted him to pay her some damages.'[70] There is evidence that the perpetrators of 'sex crimes' also construed any wrongdoing on their part in a civil and not criminal light. 'I didn't kill anybody. I am not going to Gaol', an Edmonton meat-packing plant worker quoted her seducer as saying when she confronted him with her pregnancy and he refused to settle.[71]

Even when couched in terms of innocent and wronged womanhood, the notions of 'damage' and 'damages' bore a price tag, reducing women to male or family property. Aided by an English-speaking accomplice who posed as a detective, the Smoky Lake poolroom operator tricked a local woman into intercourse. 'He said if I did not go with him', she explained, her fugitive husband 'would be caught . . . and then who would give bread to me and my children.' Hearing gossip on his return from the

Drumheller mines, the husband refused to sleep in the conjugal bed until he 'knew what was true', and informed the poolroom operator that 'money could not settle it, as it had spoiled my wife.' Yet he accepted the $500 offered.[72] In another case, the attorney general's office recommended dropping charges against an itinerant beggar accused of raping a farmwife while her husband skinned a cow a hundred yards away. The woman was strong and the man crippled; he had readily admitted to intercourse (and paying $5); and the woman's husband had admitted rejecting $30 to keep quiet because he 'would not settle it up for less than $500 for my shame.'[73] Lastly, the girl who had rebuffed her attacker's offer of marriage because she was still in school was blunt about her priorities, even on cross-examination. On discovering her pregnancy, she stated, she had demanded '$500 to get my honor. He said he wouldn't give me anything because he didn't have nothing and I said if you won't pay $500 you'll pay me $1,000 later.' A letter entered as evidence of blackmail had promised to 'go further' (presumably a criminal charge) if the man refused to settle. Something of the girl's plight, and the practical considerations motivating her actions, can be gleaned from her comment: 'I told him to give me a living or get married because I had no place to stay.'[74]

This girl moderates the image of women as male or family property, ignored and irrelevant as fathers or husbands bargained over 'damage' and 'damages'. At times those most personally affected by the exposed sexual relationship participated actively in the settlement process— consulted directly, allowed by their menfolk to accept or reject the payment offered, taking the initiative. And in representing themselves, they gave their own estimates of their worth. The girl, jilted at the altar after being seduced by the stranger she had just agreed to marry, testified that she was offered $500 to keep quiet. Under cross-examination her brother denied all knowledge of her demanding $3,000 if the accused refused to marry her, or telling him that the family wanted $3,000 in lieu of a marriage.[75] Pressed by a hostile defence, a Bellis farm girl, employed as a waitress in Edmonton, refused to confess to asking for money in return for dropping a seduction charge against the man she found out was married; counsel suggested she had wanted $2,000 to settle the matter.[76]

. . .

But much more than a piece of blackmail or a spur-of-the-moment and furtive response to discovery, a financial settlement represented an accepted mechanism for rectifying the wrongs of illicit sexual liaisons. The deliberate presence and involvement of 'witnesses', who did not simply verify the agreement reached but first participated in its negotiation, attest to the formal and public nature of the settlement process. Although he rejected monetary compensation in favour of marriage for his pregnant daughter, the courtroom testimony of one father suggests how well the procedure and rules of the settlement process were understood in the Ukrainian bloc. It also highlights the central, mediating role of the third party, mistakenly identified by the court as the accused's 'lawyers'. The man had come with his two witnesses, the father stated:

> Q. Was anything said about sexual intercourse with the girl? A. There was no use in talking to stir up the matter. Q. What matter were you settling? A. I simply took it for granted that we knew because he came down and wanted settlement. I took it for granted that we knew what we were talking about. . . . Q. Were you willing to discuss any settlement by money? A. No. . . . Q. Did he suggest it? A. No he never suggested it. Q. Did either of his lawyers [sic]? A. His witnesses said he wanted financial settlement.[77]

Known to both parties and representing one of them, a witness was nevertheless not necessarily chosen for any expected partiality, suggesting that status and respect were more important. One witness said he had to drag out of the accused what exactly he was supposed to settle with the farmer in question. When informed of the sexual advances made to the farmer's 14-year-old daughter, he agreed to mediate—making the offer of $50 that the accused considered appropriate, while the man himself 'stayed in the bush' outside the house.[78] In another case, the local blacksmith—who declined the accused rapist's request to mediate ('I told him I could not be a judge in anything')—also had not known what he was being asked to settle. The alleged victim in this instance, a woman only two years in Canada, was the sole person to appear ignorant of a financial settlement and its mechanism. She had not understood what her assailant and his witness meant by damages or wanted by a settlement, she said, and had told them that there had been no damage apart from her dress. The witness, she continued, offered her and her husband $10, saying it was better 'to pay you poor people than some rich people getting it', and advocated a settlement 'to save court' and to 'save spending money on lawyers'. Yet neither the woman nor her husband were innocents. Under cross-examination they vigorously denied prosecuting for money, and the husband specifically denied telling anyone that the accused 'would pay me for every day I lost work', but the woman had already testified that her husband initially went to the local justice of the peace to sue her attacker.[79]

Although certainly thinking of his 'client' in discouraging legal action, the above witness also showed disdain for a foreign and rapacious Canadian judicial system. Other Ukrainians seemed anxious to involve the Canadian legal establishment (if not the Canadian law) in the settlement process. Still others, voicing doubts about the wisdom or legality of what they were doing, recognized that their idea of justice contravened Canadian practices and attitudes. The man who futilely hoped $5 would buy the silence of the girl he assaulted in the livery barn testified at his rape trial that her father had immediately rushed out to demand $200 to settle; the father, likely realizing this harmed his

case, contradicted him in rebuttal.[80] The husband who refused to settle for less than $500 for 'my shame' ultimately decided to consult a lawyer about accepting the sum he negotiated.[81] The Smoky Lake man and local poolroom operator who had tricked the farmer's wife into intercourse jointly consulted a lawyer after the poolroom operator said he could not afford the $1,000 the husband wanted and suggested four town lots instead But the pair told the Anglo-Canadian attorney, who innocently advised taking out a $500 mortgage, only that the one owed the other money. 'I thought it over,' the husband testified in self-justification, 'and thought that I ought not to settle it myself because there was a law in Canada. I took the mortgage from him because it would be good evidence for me.'[82]

. . .

Most certainly, countless disputes highlighting sex and gender in the Ukrainian bloc settlement of interwar Alberta never reached the Canadian courts to be arbitrated by the law of the new homeland. Those that did, entering the realm of Canadian legal history as official 'criminal cases', comment at length not only on the interaction of Ukrainian immigrant and Canadian concepts of justice but also on the transitional world the bloc's residents inhabited. Men and women confronted with domestic violence or sexual irregularities were prepared to seek help from the Canadian judicial system, but they looked first to their own community to air their grievances and solve their difficulties. While women, both old and young, were often shown in the process to be the naive and impotent objects of male aggression, they often proved to be equally shrewd and forceful defenders of their own interests.

## Notes

1.  The Pylypczuk case received extensive coverage in the *Vegreville Observer*, the *Edmonton Journal*, and the *Edmonton Bulletin* in March 1912.

2.  See, for example, the novel *The Foreigner* (Toronto:

Westminster Company, 1909), by Charles W. Gordon (Ralph Connor); W.G. Smith, *A Study in Canadian Immigration* (Toronto: Ryerson Press, 1920); Charles Young, *The Ukrainian Canadians: A Study in Assimilation* (Toronto: Thomas Nelson and Sons, 1931).

3. See Gregory Robinson, 'Rougher Than Any Other Nationality? Ukrainian Canadians and Crime in Alberta, 1915–29', *Journal of Ukrainian Studies* 16, 1–2 (Summer–Winter 1991): 147–79; also his 'British-Canadian Justice in the Ukrainian Colony: Crime and Law Enforcement in East Central Alberta, 1915–1929', MA thesis (University of Alberta, 1992).

4. Cases involving Ukrainians form only a small part of the crime investigation files, housed in the Provincial Archives of Alberta (Acc. 72.26), and accessed through an alphabetical surname index (Acc. 72.82) that identifies the accused, the locality, and usually the nature of the offence. The great majority of Ukrainian cases focus on the Vegreville bloc; smaller numbers originated in Edmonton, followed by mining communities like Drumheller and the Crowsnest Pass. . . .

5. Christine Worobec, 'Temptress or Virgin? The Precarious Sexual Position of Women in Postemancipation Ukrainian Peasant Society', in Beatrice Farnsworth and Lynne Viola, eds, *Russian Peasant Women* (New York and Oxford: Oxford University Press, 1992), 41–53, uses court documents and folksongs to examine a sexual double standard and women's subordinate position in late nineteenth-century Russian Ukraine. There is no comparable study of western Ukrainian territories, which contributed the bulk of immigrants to Canada.

6. There is a growing body of historical literature, drawing heavily on court records, that examines how gender has affected the treatment of women by the Canadian legal system. Much of it deals specifically with sex crimes. The two major monographs are Constance Backhouse, *Petticoats and Prejudice: Women and Law in Nineteenth-Century Canada* (Toronto: University of Toronto Press and Osgoode Society, 1991); and Karen

Dubinsky, *Improper Advances: Rape and Heterosexual Conflict in Ontario, 1880–1929* (Chicago: University of Chicago Press, 1993). . . .

7. Provincial Archives of Alberta, Alberta Department of the Attorney General, Crime Investigation Files (hereafter PAA), 72.26/2931, carnal knowledge under 18, Vermilion 1919. The case was never tried, the judge concluding that conviction was impossible, and the couple (who were cousins) eventually married.

8. PAA, 72.26/6621, seduction under promise of marriage, Edson 1925; the young woman was a recent Polish immigrant, the accused Ukrainian. . . .

9. PAA, 72.26/4956, rape (amended to carnal knowledge) over 14 under 16, Leduc (Dnipro) 1922; and 72.26/5329, assault occasioning actual bodily harm, Lethbridge 1923.

10. PAA, 72.26/3928, rape, Edmonton 1921.

11. To describe her actual seduction one girl switched from English to an interpreter; PAA, 72.26/3878, seduction over 14 under 16, Carvel 1920. . . .

12. The best discussion of policing Ukrainians for moonshine is Robinson, 'British-Canadian Justice in the Ukrainian Colony', 138–73.

13. Samuel Koenig, 'Ukrainians of Eastern Galicia: A Study of Their Culture and Institutions', Ph.D. dissertation (Yale University, 1935) is a good English-language introduction to nineteenth- and early twentieth-century Ukrainian peasant beliefs and customs. . . .

14. PAA, 72.26/6537, placing poison in wells, Vermilion 1925.

15. PAA, 72.26/6088, seduction under promise of marriage (over 16 under 18), Mundare 1924.

16. PAA, 72.26/2250, assault causing actual bodily harm, Andrew (Wostok) 1919. The man was acquitted, even though the daughter testified that her mother could barely walk when her parents arrived home.

17. PAA, 72.26/7427, seduction over 16 under 18, Leduc 1926. . . .

18. See transcript (file incomplete) in PAA, 72.26/7531, assault occasioning actual bodily harm, Edmonton 1927.

19. PAA, 72.26/3608, assault, Chipman 1921; see also 72.26/3607, unlawfully wounding, Chipman 1921.

20. PAA, 72.26/3895, assault causing grevious bodily harm, Mundare 1921.

21. PAA, 72.26/7589, common assault, Tofield (Holden) 1927.

22. PAA, 72.26/5936, assault causing actual bodily harm, Fort Saskatchewan (Dalmuir) 1924.

23. Robert B. Klymasz, *Folk Narrative among Ukrainian-Canadians in Western Canada* (Ottawa: Canadian Centre for Folk Culture Studies, 1973), 24.

24. Recorded in Shortdale, Manitoba, 1963; ibid. 24–5.

25. PAA, 72.26/3539, assault wife and threaten to kill her, Vilna 1921. Found guilty, the man was ordered to leave town and find work elsewhere, away from his wife.

26. PAA, 72.26/5659, assault and beat wife occasioning actual bodily harm, Tofield (Holden) 1921.

27. See the archives of the Consistory of the Greek Catholic Church in Lviv, Ukraine (Tsentralnyi derzhavnyi istorychnyi archiv Ukrainskoi respublyky, Lvivskyi viddil, fond 201, opys 2a). . . .

28. PAA, 72.26/3422, seduction under promise of marriage (under 21), Vegreville 1920. The case was dismissed because of insufficient corroboration, but only on the promise of marriage.

29. PAA, 72.26/4212, seduction under promise of marriage (under 21), Bellis 1921. . . .

30. PAA, 72.26/4429, wounding, Star 1922. For attempts to slur Ukrainian women by insinuating sexual relationships with 'Chinamen', see 72.26/2909, wounding, Radway 1920, and 72.26/1316, rape, Edmonton 1918.

31. PAA, 72.26/6238, assault wife with intent to do grevious bodily harm, Viking (Bruce) 1924. . . .

32. See, for example, PAA, 72.26/298, seduction over 14 under 16, Radway 1916; 72.26/907, seduction over 14 under 16, Chipman 1917; 72.26/1268, seduction, Vermilion 1917; and 72.26/4018, carnal knowledge over 14 under 16, Smoky Lake 1920. The father of a pregnant daughter crippled since falling and hurting her back as a child did not think the young woman

was 'fit to be married, or to have children'; 72.26/3412, carnal knowledge, Bruderheim (Egremont) 1920.

33. PAA, 72.26/6906, wilfully place poison, to wit, lye in such a position to be easily partaken of by cattle, Spedden 1925.

34. PAA, 72.26/7020, seduction under promise of marriage (over 16 under 18), Leduc (Calmar) 1925.

35. PAA, 72.26/907, seduction over 14 under 16, Chipman 1917; and 72.26/2523, carnal knowledge over 14 under 16, Vegreville 1919.

36. PAA, 72.26/372, carnal knowledge under 14, Fort Saskatchewan [1915–16]; 72.26/1428, carnal knowledge over 14 under 16, Bruderheim 1917; 72.26/3422, seduction under promise of marriage (under 21), Vegreville 1920; 72.26/4956, carnal knowledge over 14 under 16, Leduc (Dnipro) 1922; 72.26/5783, rape, Smoky Lake 1922; and 72.26/6088, seduction under promise of marriage (over 16 under 18), Mundare 1924.

37. PAA, 72.26/2523, carnal knowledge over 14 under 16, Vegreville 1919; 72.26/4956, carnal knowledge over 14 under 16, Leduc (Dnipro) 1922; and 72.26/6536, carnal knowledge, Andrew 1924.

38. PAA, 72.26/907, seduction over 14 under 16, Chipman 1917; 72.26/4212, seduction under promise of marriage (under 21), Bellis 1921; and 72.26/6088, seduction under promise of marriage (over 16 under 18), Mundare 1924. From outside the Vegreville bloc, see 72.26/2129, assault occasioning actual bodily harm, Lethbridge (Staffordville) 1919; and 72.26/4816, indecent assault, Blairmore (Bellevue) 1922.

39. PAA, 72.26/6621, seduction under promise of marriage, Edson 1925; insufficient evidence led to a stay of proceedings.

40. PAA, 72.26/639, carnal knowledge under 14, Wostok 1916. See also 72.26/6475, carnal knowledge under 13, Chipman 1925; and 72.26/7427, seduction over 16 under 18, Leduc 1926.

41. PAA, 72.26/3878, seduction under promise of marriage (over 14 under 16), Carvel 1920; see also 72.26/5976, seduction over 14 under 16, Vegreville 1924.

42. PAA, 72.26/1140, carnal knowledge under 14, Vegreville 1917.

43. Six carnal knowledge cases involved married women. Of the remaining complainants, eleven were under 14, five over 14 under 16, one under 16, two under 18, and two over 20; four had no age given. Eight alleged seduction victims were over 14 under 16, one was under 14, nine were over 16 under 18, six were under 21, and one was 29. The great majority (18/27) of rape charges involved married women; of the remaining complainants, one was under 12, one was 14, two were 15, one was under 16, one was under 18, one was 18, one was 19, and one had no age given. Two indecent assault cases concerned wives. Of the unmarried, two were 14, one was 17, and two had no age given.

44. For a fuller discussion of marriage patterns in the Vegreville bloc, based on the parish registers of the Basilian Fathers in Mundare, see Frances Swyripa, *Wedded to the Cause: Ukrainian-Canadian Women and Ethnic Identity, 1891–1991* (Toronto, 1993), 83–8.

45. PAA, 72.26/6416, seduction under promise of marriage (under 21), Leduc 1925.

46. PAA, 72.26/2931, carnal knowledge under 18, Vermilion 1919; see also, for example, 72.26/1084, carnal knowledge over 14 under 16, Wostok 1916.

47. PAA, 72.26/116, indecent assault, Vegreville (Wahstao) 1915.

48. See, for example, PAA, 72.26/1084, carnal knowledge over 14 under 16, Andrew (Sunland) 1917; PAA, 72.26/2280, attempted rape, Smoky Lake 1919; PAA, 72.26/2532, carnal knowledge under 14, Daysland 1915; PAA, 72.26/3878, seduction over 14 under 16, Carvel 1920; PAA, 72.26/4212, seduction under promise of marriage (under 21), Bellis 1921; and PAA, 72.26/4956, rape, Leduc (Dnipro) 1922.

49. PAA, 72.26/5215, carnal knowledge, Vegreville (Mundare) 1923; the accused was found guilty of indecent assault.

50. PAA, 72.26/3656, seduction under promise of marriage (under 21), Vegreville 1920.

51. PAA, 72.26/5130, carnal knowledge under 14, Tawatinaw (Nestow) 1923.

52. Some men took steps to guard against unpleasant consequences, giving the woman 'pills' at the time of intercourse, for example, or promising 'medicine' if/when she became pregnant. See PAA, 72.26/5783, rape, Smoky Lake 1922; 72.26/6088, seduction under promise of marriage (over 16 under 18), Mundare 1924; 72.26/4491, seduction under promise of marriage (over 16 under 18), Edmonton 1921; and, although the parties' Ukrainian origins are not certain, 72.26/1562, procuring a miscarriage, Meanook 1917.

53. PAA, 72.26/8220, attempted rape, Smoky Lake 1928; the man was found guilty of indecent assault.

54. PAA, 72.26/4862, attempted rape (amended to indecent assault), Bellis 1922. . . .

55. The Ukrainian peasant immigrant's understanding of 'fri kontri', particularly as it was perceived by the Ukrainian immigrant intelligentsia, is discussed in Swyripa, *Wedded to the Cause*, 67–8.

56. PAA, 72.26/8457, attempted rape, Opal 1928.

57. PAA, 72.26/7176, carnal knowledge thereby committing rape, Waugh 1926.

58. Ibid. At the subsequent trial, on the advice of the judge who stated it was the only way to construe the evidence, a jury found the lad not guilty.

59. PAA, 72.26/2250, assault causing actual bodily harm, Andrew (Wostok) 1919.

60. PAA, 72.26/8522, rape, Lamont (Eldorena) 1928; 72.26/6088, seduction under promise of marriage (over 16 under 18), Mundare 1924; and 72.26/7110, seduction under promise of marriage (over 16 under 18), Vegreville 1925.

61. PAA, 72.26/2567, assault causing actual bodily harm, Leduc (Bulford) 1919. Charges were not preferred on the order of the attorney general's office at the written request of the wife, whose letter contained the following: 'Since the date in question my said husband has treated me well, and we have settled all our outstanding differences.'

62. PAA, 72.26/1113, assault (wife beating), Boian 1917.

63. PAA, 72.26/7610, failure to provide the necessities of life, Radway 1927. . . .

64. PAA, 72.26/4696, seduction under promise of marriage (over 16 under 18), Vegreville (Kaleland) 1922.

65. PAA, 72.26/7649, carnal knowledge under 14, Bruce 1927. This was not the only instance where the priest played an active role in bringing sexual impropriety into the open; see also, for example, 72.26/4696, seduction under promise of marriage (over 16 under 18), Vegreville (Kaleland) 1922.

66. PAA, 72.26/907, seduction over 14 under 16, Chipman 1917.

67. See, for example, PAA, 72.26/4696, seduction under promise of marriage (over 16 under 18), Vegreville (Kaleland) 1922.

68. PAA, 72.26/5625, carnal knowledge under 14, Andrew 1923; after hearing the witnesses for the prosecution, the accused changed his plea to guilty. . . .

69. PAA, 72.26/2280, rape, Smoky Lake 1919; the wife refused the $30 offered and demanded $75 instead.

70. PAA, 72.26/4739, rape, Bellis (Wahstao) 1922. According to the crime report, after the girl miscarried her mother told a relative that they had only been playing a joke on the accused about getting her pregnant.

71. PAA, 72.26/6442, seduction under promise of marriage, Edmonton 1924. Although the complainant was identified as German, the accused as Austrian and Roman Catholic, and the court interpreter as Russian, Anglo-Canadian ignorance of Central and Eastern Europe casts at least the two men's identities into doubt. From their surnames, the interpreter was most certainly Ukrainian, the accused perhaps so.

72. PAA, 72.26/3500, carnal knowledge, Smoky Lake 1920.

73. PAA, 72.26/5172, rape, Smoky Lake 1923.

74. PAA, 72.26/7427, seduction over 16 under 18, Leduc 1926.

75. PAA, 72.26/6416, seduction under promise of marriage (under 21), Leduc 1925.

76. PAA, 72.26/3365, seduction under promise of marriage (over 16 under 18), Edmonton 1920.

77. PAA, 72.26/3422, seduction under promise of marriage, Vegreville 1920. . . .

78. PAA, 72.26/5500, attempted rape (amended to attempted indecent assault), Eldorena 1923. News of the assault had apparently not reached the girl's father, for he seemed not to know what the witness had come to settle.

79. PAA, 72.26/8457, attempted rape, Opal 1928.

80. PAA, 72.26/8220, attempted rape, Smoky Lake 1928.

81. PAA, 72.26/5172, rape, Smoky Lake 1923.

82. PAA, 72.26/3500, carnal knowledge, Smoky Lake 1920.

# 5

# Indispensable But Not a Citizen:
# The Housewife in the Great Depression

Denyse Baillargeon

*Translated by Yvonne M. Klein*

## Introduction

In an article published in 1975, the historian Terry Copp, after describing the difficult conditions that the Montreal working class endured during the Great Depression, concluded, 'One of the great mysteries of the depression decade is the reason for the relatively low level of social unrest . . . that these conditions produced.'[1] It is true that, despite especially high rates of unemployment, the 1930s did not see any extraordinary incidence of working-class mobilization. Leaving aside the On to Ottawa Trek that was staged by young single men who were inmates in the Bennett government's labour camps, it must be said that mass demonstrations were extremely few and that protests by the unemployed did not seriously threaten the foundations of the liberal economy or the capitalist social order.[2] Addressing himself to the task of elucidating this mystery, Copp attributes the relatively stable social climate first to the fact that only a minority of wage-earners, which he estimates at 20 per cent, were profoundly affected by the Depression, and second to the decrease in the cost of living, which would have more than made up for reductions in wages. As a result, 'many working-class families were, in fact, better off during the 1930's than they had been in the 1920's.'[3] In essence, Copp suggests that the times were not 'hard' enough to provoke revolt.

Copp may be correct, but the arguments he advances are certainly not sufficient to explain a phenomenon such as this. In the years since Copp wrote this article, a number of feminist historians have made the point that the economic indicators he cites to explain the weak level of social protest actually turn out to be quite imperfect instruments for evaluating working-class standards of living. Hence it would be risky to draw conclusions from these indicators concerning the revolutionary potential of such social conditions. Indeed, if we consider under-employment, small business and shop bankruptcies, and the extraordinary length of time that certain groups of labourers were without work, especially in the

building trades, we might just as easily conclude that the Depression generated a measure
of poverty and of economic, social, and psychological insecurity much greater than that
revealed by official statistics. Wages were not,
however, the sole resource upon which families
depended for their support. From the beginning of industrialization, working-class families
had employed a range of survival tactics that
were based as much on the labour of women in
the home as on that of male breadwinners and
of children.[4] The responsibilities undertaken by
women within the home were indispensable
even during 'prosperous' times such as the
1920s; they turned out to be even more crucial
during the Depression when government relief
measures were far from making up for losses in
wages.[5] For this reason, these women are
unquestionably one of the key elements we
must take into account if we are to understand
properly the weakness of social protest in the
period compared with the economic collapse
that characterizes it.

More recently, several feminist historians
have also observed that the Great Depression
has appeared, both at the time and in retrospect,
as an essentially 'masculine' crisis, as a crisis of
masculinity, in fact, because it undermined the
breadwinner status that constituted the foundation of male power and identity.[6] All the same,
the aid programs, home relief, and public works
established by the nascent Canadian welfare
state operated to support the prerogatives of the
male heads of the household, as married
women, seen as the economic dependants of
their husbands, could not avail themselves of
such relief programs directly.[7] The intervention
of the Canadian government may have been
reluctant and largely inadequate, but it did confirm the privileged access men had to a source of
income, a proof of both their independence and
their status as citizens. In so doing, state policies
simultaneously consolidated patriarchal family
structures and encouraged men to remain faithful to their role as breadwinner.[8] Housewives,

excluded as they were from the job market and
subordinate to the man of the house, were not
regarded as citizens of the developing welfare
state even if, implicitly, the state recognized
women's contribution to family maintenance.[9]
In fact, relief payments were as a rule largely
contingent on good housekeeping, which state
representatives checked up on through home
visits to recipients; likewise, the allocation of
tracts of land to aspiring 'pioneers' in the 'colonization areas' depended upon the ability of
their wives to adapt to a life on the farm.[10] Thus
the state expected women to make a specific
contribution to their families' welfare as a complement to whatever public assistance it might
extend. Governmental measures and the unpaid
labour of women in the home combined to
cushion the worst effects of the Depression not
only on the economic scheme, but also on patriarchal social and family organization. Placed
under severe strain in the public marketplace,
the bases of masculine identity were thus preserved in the domestic sphere, which probably
contributed to calming any rebellious urges on
the part of married workers and fathers.

On the basis of 30 interviews undertaken
among francophone women from Montreal,[11] in
this chapter I will examine the dynamics of gender relationships and the contribution made by
women to the survival of workers' families during the Great Depression. In the 1920s or at the
beginning of the 1930s, these women, from poor
backgrounds, married labourers, white-collar
workers, or small businessmen who, for the most
part, would suffer from periods of joblessness or
underemployment.[12] This 'feminine' take on the
economic crisis will bring to light the dependence of both society and the state upon these
'non-citizens', providing an excellent example of
the interrelation between the public and private
spheres as well as of the ways in which social
policies and private welfare activities are articulated. The latter rely, in particular, on the failure
to acknowledge the citizenship of housewives in
the same way as that of men.

## The Gender of Work

When women married, it was understood that they would quit work in order to take care of the house and the children, while their husbands would work outside the home to earn the money needed for the household. The ideology of separate spheres was so entrenched that this gendered division of labour seemed to spring from immutable natural law, and so the question would never even arise as a topic of discussion between engaged couples. Almost by instinct, these women knew that the male identity depended on the ability of the husband to 'support' his wife and they were perfectly aware of the social prohibitions against paid work for married women. As one respondent said, 'Married women weren't allowed to work in those days. My husband did not marry me for me to support him. . . . Men had their pride. They didn't want their wives working' (I23).[13]

Though the breadwinner/homemaker model was rigid, it could allow certain accommodations. In fact, almost two-thirds of these women worked for a salary or wages even before their husbands fell victim to unemployment or cuts in pay due to the Depression.[14] In reality, at the time of their marriage, only five of the husbands earned more than $25 a week, the level that could be termed a decent salary; more than half were earning less than $20 a week and a few were making less than $10. According to the figures of the federal Department of Labour, it would require $20.18 a week in Quebec merely to cover the costs of food, heating, light, and rent, these outlays representing approximately 65 per cent of the expenses needed by a family of five.[15] From all the evidence, the image of the homemaker wholly dependent on the male wage and exclusively dedicated to housework and child care represented a virtually unattainable ideal for the majority of these poor working-class households. In the absence of a genuine 'family wage', family survival depended by necessity on intensive domestic production and the extremely close management of the household budget, to which were often added the earnings from paid work of the mother of the family.

Unable to make ends meet, especially after the birth of their first children, several of these women sought sources of supplementary income. Five of them worked at jobs outside the home for brief periods; the others worked at home in one or more paid capacities, sometimes several at a time, in addition to carrying out their household responsibilities. They did sewing, knitting, or took in laundry, they took care of boarders, they worked as domestics, managed a small business, sold homemade baking—all ways of transforming their 'feminine' expertise into hard cash. While the amounts they were able to earn from these activities varied considerably—depending on how much they charged and on the customers who used their services (if they were working for themselves, for example), or on the amount of work they did for their employers in a given week—this monetary contribution on the part of women might represent a considerable part of the household income: 'We didn't have enough money. I used to smock baby clothes. Then I had my boarder who gave me six bucks a week. That helped a little, my husband was making ten dollars a week' (I13). Without always representing such a large proportion of the total family income, the money these women earned in their 'spare time', as they put it, often made the difference between living below or just a little above the poverty line. It also allowed them to avoid going into debt: 'It didn't pay a helluva lot, but it was only that it gave me a little something at the end of the week. . . . When [my husband] didn't have enough, then I was the one who paid, I would put it toward the rent or to buying clothes for the kids. . . . It meant that we stayed out of debt' (I17).

If male salaries were largely inadequate before the Depression the financial situation of the majority of families deteriorated even further during the 1930s. Unemployment, underemployment, and pay cuts affected the great majority of heads of households, forcing more than half of them to fall back on relief payments. This circumstance did not, however, lead to a major disruption in attitudes, limited by the patriarchal social norms in force, towards the financial contribution of wives to the family economy. Thus only two women became the principal support of their families while their husbands were unemployed. On the other hand, nine of the men lost their jobs for periods ranging from several months to several years without there being any question of their wives looking for work. Full-time homemakers since the day they married, they pointed to various obstacles to explain this paradox, such as the number of children at home, the impossibility of finding work, even work at home, but also, and perhaps chief of all, the opposition of their husbands. 'I would have liked to go to work,' one of them maintained, 'but [my husband] didn't want me to. Anyway, the children were too little, I couldn't leave them. In those days, you didn't leave your babies with someone else' (120).

For this woman, as for several others, having young children seemed to present a major barrier to her entry into the job market, even if the father, who was unemployed, would have been available to take care of them.[16] Mothering was so profoundly identified with femininity that it seemed unthinkable that it could become a male responsibility. Most of these women also asserted that there was no employment to be had, even if they had not actually looked for work, or that jobs were strictly reserved for men, a discourse that was an article of faith during the Depression.[17] As one woman mentioned, 'There wasn't any more work for girls than there was for men in those days. . . . And I'd never had a job,[18] let me tell you I'd have had a lot of trouble finding work too' (119). Another declared: 'Married women did not have the right to go to work. . . . There was too much unemployment. . . . they would rather hire heads of families' (16).

Underneath these arguments, one detects a strong reluctance, as much from the women as

from their husbands, against bringing about a reversal in roles that would be incompatible with defined and accepted social norms[19]—indeed, in these instances, the sexual division of labour was integrated in so rigid a manner that it precluded any possibility of redefining, even briefly, how responsibilities were shared within the home. The opposition of a husband resolved to preserve his dominant status was probably the determining factor in most cases, but, as Margaret Hobbs suggests, some of these full-time homemakers perhaps were fearful that if they were to stand in for the male breadwinner, they might encourage their husbands to lose interest in their family obligations.[20] In this connection, moreover, the women were anxious to stress that it was the husband's assignment to apply for government aid, a chore they were happy to leave to him: 'It wasn't me who would have gone—I would have starved to death before going to ask for home relief. . . . He knew perfectly well that he was the man of the family—it was up to him to go see them. It wasn't up to me' (119). In this very special circumstance, where it was a question of publicly admitting an inability to take care of his family, having breadwinner status was nothing to envy. The men who had this experience suffered a profound assault on their masculine dignity and came out of it feeling humiliated. Nevertheless, remitting aid to the head of the family left power relationships within the family intact. Those wives who were economically dependent on husbands who refused to shoulder their responsibility to provide for their families, perhaps because they drank or gambled for example, had to stand by while the resources necessary for their survival and that of their children were continually squandered: 'The dole was given in the husband's name, not the wife's. So that meant that he went to collect it and if he spent it, then you had nothing. It happened a lot—he went to get the relief money and when he came home, he didn't have a penny left' (122).[21]

The women who had engaged in one or several paid occupations at home before their hus-

bands lost their jobs continued and even aug-
mented their work as far as was possible.[22] But
none of them imagined replacing the work they
did in the home with an outside job, which, by
their own admission, their husbands would never
have stood for: 'During the Depression, I took in
sewing to bring in some money. I was a big help
to my husband—he did the best he could and so
did I', one of them remarked. But when she was
asked if she had thought about looking for a paying job, she answered, 'My husband would never
have let me, not at all' (I22). Just like the men
whose wives made no financial contribution to
the household before they were unemployed,
those who agreed to their wife's working at home
for pay would never have put up with her finding
a job outside the home. This reversal of roles
would have been a direct threat to their superior
position as man of the house and would have represented too stern a blow to their pride, which
had already been sufficiently shaken by their failure to fulfill this role adequately.

Just as the wives did not attempt to take
over their husbands' place as breadwinner, the
men were not prompted to participate more fully
in the housework because their unemployment
gave them more time on their hands, even if they
already were in the habit of doing certain chores,
like going to the store or washing the floors.
Undeniably, the majority of the women considered the house their domain and they themselves
did not ask for any additional help. To ask for
help was the same as admitting that they were
not able to carry out their part of the husband-
wife contract, and that would bring their own
femininity into question: 'We didn't ask them to
help us—as far as we were concerned, it was our
work. We said, "We don't want to have them in
our pots and pans." We were the ones who
looked after that' (I29). Many others agreed:
'When you're married you each have your own
job' (I7). Additionally, a number of these men
spent most of their time outside the house. Some
of them were employed for short periods on
public works projects or were doing various

kinds of odd jobs,[23] but others stayed away regularly, claiming to look for work. In this way,
they could escape the 'female' universe in which
they had difficulty situating themselves and
which could seem to threaten them—constant
immersion in the world of women could be seen
as yet another attack on their already shaky male
identity, weakened as it was by their being out of
work.[24] The women themselves preferred their
husbands to get out of the house, as they found
their unaccustomed presence rather annoying or
even a bit abnormal, since men did not belong in
the domestic space: 'Oh, sometimes, I'd really get
fed up. I used to think, this is not his place. A
man's place is to go to work, not to hang around
the house' (I19). Even if the wives sometimes
expressed impatience at having their husbands
underfoot, they rarely complained about it to
them. Part of their wifely role was to maintain
their husbands' morale and preserve their self-
respect; they fulfilled this by not seeking to
become the principal breadwinner and by avoid-
ing reminding the men of their failure to provide
properly for the family. Some of these women
insisted that their husbands had also tried to
cheer them up. It is certainly possible that some
of these men had kept their feelings of insecurity
or desperation to themselves in order to preserve
their image as a protector able to cope with any
situation. Still, one of the few men who did participate in part of the interview with his wife
acknowledged that he had often cried in secret.

## Making Ends Meet

According to a tradition that was deeply rooted
in the working class in Quebec as well as elsewhere, it was most often the wife who was
responsible for managing the family budget. As
several feminist historians have observed, giving
over the pay envelope to the wife, far from representing a real delegation of power, allowed the
men to avoid the trial of having to manage on
insufficient wages (a reality that called their status as breadwinner into question) without hav-

ing to go so far as to renounce the definite privileges which that status conveyed.[25] Most of the men in fact kept back a certain amount for their own expenses or expected that there would be something left over for them if they said they needed it. For their part, the women were explicitly aware that they were managing money earned by someone else and clearly felt that it was not theirs by right. Their economic dependence thus induced women to get by on the amount available without complaining about not having enough money, which in turn contributed to maintaining the myth that their husbands continued to be adequate providers.

Despite the additional amounts that women's paid work provided, their families' income was still generally very low because these extras most often added to only the lowest of wages. Making ends meet represented a daunting challenge confronting most of these women. To respond to it, they committed themselves to an extremely strict set of priorities to which they made every effort to conform, no matter what. At the top of the list came the irreducible expenses like electricity and rent, seen as 'debts' that they made a point of honour to pay regularly. The remainder of the money went for food, for wood or coal for the stove, and, in last place, clothing, transportation, and insurance, if there were a few pennies left. Very few among them were able to save anything at all. Households that had succeeded in accumulating any savings had to nibble away at them before resigning themselves to signing on for the dole.

Checking prices, buying only what was strictly necessary, wasting nothing, and not going into debt were watchwords that recurred constantly in their oral testimonies: 'I never wasted anything' (I1); 'You had to really know not to buy anything you didn't need. We didn't waste a thing' (I26). What they got in return for this dedication was the most intense household labour, with a bare minimum of domestic appliances and in housing conditions that were often substandard. On their coal or wood stoves, which

were also the only source of heat, they cooked every meal, from soup to dessert, not to mention pickles, jams, and jellies. Those who had learned how to sew made most of the clothing, at least for the children, often out of old clothes they altered to fit. Most of them sewed the household linen—sheets, tablecloths, dishcloths, bedspreads, and curtains. As well, most of these women had a sewing machine, if only to repair rips and tears. This purchase, more advantageous because it represented a source of savings, often came before a washing machine, and it seems that the majority delayed until the second or third child appeared before buying one of these. Despite the absence of this convenience, very few of the women patronized commercial laundries and none used their services on a regular basis. What this meant was that for some significant time almost all the women did the washing on a washboard in a laundry sink or bathtub, if there was one in the flat.

The amounts that the women could spend on rent, between $12 and $18 a month, restricted them to substandard accommodations, that is, to flats that were poorly lit, badly insulated, with softwood floors that were difficult to keep clean, and sometimes infested with rats and cockroaches.[26] All these lodgings were connected to the municipal water mains and had electricity, but rarely were they supplied with gas; less than half of the women interviewed had always lived in quarters that were equipped with a bathtub and almost none of them could afford to buy or rent a hot-water heater. Their inadequate incomes often meant that these families had to make do with accommodations that were too small, even if it meant sacrificing the living room in order to make an extra bedroom. Some of the children might have to sleep in the kitchen or in the hallway on a folding bed that was put up and taken down daily.

This brief sketch reveals that, for these women, managing the family expenses proved to be an almost obsessive concern, while housework represented a trying, physically exhausting obligation that they had to carry out in difficult circumstances, without always having the household conveniences they needed to do it. Faced with the consequences of unemployment and shortened workweeks, they had very little room to manoeuvre, considering what they were already providing for their families. Indeed, their domestic production encompassed such a range of products and services that, when the Depression hit, it was difficult for them to add new tasks to those that they were already doing. But since they were already consuming no more than necessary, reductions in wages and, even more, the low level of state assistance obliged them to reduce their expenditures in vulnerable areas, which translated into an increase in and intensification of their workload and ever greater deprivation, which they were often the first to experience.

Buying the least possible was already one of the habitual consumer strategies of these housewives. Particularly when it came to food, however, they often found it hard to cut back on quantities. Therefore, the housewives sought new ways to economize by purchasing lower-quality goods and by procuring their groceries in new ways. For instance, some of the women began to buy their meat directly from the abattoir rather than from the local grocery, which permitted them to obtain greater quantities at the same price though they had to travel longer distances to get there. It was also possible to get cut-price meat by buying it late on a Saturday evening, just before the stores closed;[27] a number of grocers who did not have refrigeration preferred to get rid of their stock rather than risk losing their merchandise by storing it until Monday morning. Some of the women would get fruits and vegetables that were on sale or even being given away because they were wilted or beginning to rot, even if it meant taking a little more time to prepare them: 'It was a lot of work to make them all right to eat. Sometimes they were starting to go. But if you picked out what was edible . . .' (I5). Just one of the respondents

tried several times to make bread, but, as she pointed out, it was a long and complicated process, not to mention that her inexperience made it more likely that there would be waste. It was cheaper to go directly to the bakery at the end of the day: 'We would go there at four o'clock in the afternoon when the bread runs came back. We could fill up a whole pillowcase with bread for twenty-five cents. You'd see everybody there—I would see them on the corner, they all had a pillowcase folded up under their arm or some of them had bags . . .' (I20).

Preparing the same amount of food with fewer means and from inferior quality products required a good pinch of ingenuity to create appetizing meals. Sausage, minced meat, spaghetti, and noodles appeared very often on the table, prepared in every imaginable way. Dishes in sauce, made with a base of flour and water, were also an economical solution, since they generally did not contain meat: 'I made potatoes and white sauce, eggs and white sauce, beans and white sauce, and tinned salmon and white sauce. We ate a lot of paste!' (I25).[28] Desserts were skipped altogether or consisted of 'broken biscuits' sold cheaply in bulk or made from recipes that did not ask for expensive ingredients, like the famous 'pouding chômeur' (literally, unemployed pudding, poor man's pudding).

Despite all of these strategies, some of the informants and even their husbands simply had to deprive themselves of food so their children could eat: 'I would make a stew, as we called it. . . . I would make it out of spaghetti and whatever stuff was the cheapest and the most nourishing. But that doesn't mean we were well fed. . . . All it meant is that we had something to eat and even then sometimes we had to leave it all for the children' (I27). One couple often made do with macaroni and butter and sugar spread on bread, while another informant admitted that she had often eaten sugared bread dampened under the faucet. Another explained, 'We often ate mustard sandwiches . . . before the next cheque would come. When we got to the last stretch, we had a little jar of mustard and a few slices of bread and we would say, we're going to have to be happy with that—what do you want, there isn't anything else. . . . My mother-in-law would come and take my little girl. As long as I knew my little girl would have something to eat, it was all right, I knew we'd get by' (119).

During spells of unemployment, buying clothing was the first thing to go. Women, whose wardrobes were already strictly limited, were the most likely to pass up new garments in favour of devoting whatever resources were available to clothing for their growing children or for their husbands who had to go out of the house more often. One of them recalled that during the Depression she had only two dresses to her back: 'I only had two dresses—wash the dress, iron the dress. Two days later—wash the dress, iron the dress. . . . Me, who hates to iron!' (126). Some respondents patronized the outlets run by the Salvation Army or St Vincent de Paul, while others, who had never previously done any sewing, had to resign themselves to learning how: 'That's when I learned to sew because I used to buy ready-made clothes for my kids in the beginning but later on, I couldn't. . . . You had to make new clothes out of old ones. Everybody gave me clothes—I'd take them apart and make them up for the kids. I didn't have a machine—I'd go to my mother's to use hers' (112).

Half of the families also moved, sometimes several times, into ever cheaper housing, which meant smaller, less comfortable, and less well-equipped accommodations.[29] Women were thus forced to give up what little comfort and convenience they had enjoyed. If the whole family suffered from the deterioration in their housing conditions, it was the women, for whom the house represented both their workplace and their living space, who were the most affected. For women, moving to new accommodations represented an increase in their work as well. Not only did they have to find the new flat and pack and unpack the family's belongings, but they also had to clean it from top to bottom and,

if they had the money, repaint or repaper, run up new curtains, and the like.

The Depression likewise deprived a number of these women of their customary amenities, for a number of reasons. One of them, for example, did the laundry for several months in the bathtub because she did not have the money to get her machine fixed: 'I had a wooden agitator with a handle in the side and the wringer was broken, which meant I had to do the wash in the bathtub. And it was only something that cost thirty-nine cents. I did the laundry for I think five or six months in the bathtub like that' (127). Others avoided using their electrical appliances, especially the iron or the washing machine, in order to save on electricity. Those who had their lights cut off because of unpaid bills reported doing some of their chores in the evening, when they could reconnect illegally without worrying about inspectors from the company coming by, but this seriously complicated their housework schedule.[30] Finally, two of the women went back to live in the countryside because their husbands were not able to find jobs and could not reconcile themselves to going on the dole. Without electricity or running water, they had to give up their washing machines and other electric appliances and return to making a good number of items at home, like bread and soap, that they had previously bought. These two women had already experienced this kind of life, which made it easier for them to adapt to their new situation. All the same, it represented net loss in the standard of their working conditions.

In short, even though these women were already doing practically everything they already could to balance their budgets and could only with great difficulty do more, the Depression nevertheless meant an increase in the burden of their household tasks, since they had to accomplish them with less money, less space, and fewer conveniences. Without any extra help from their husbands, they had to shoulder the additional labour occasioned by loss of income all by themselves and they were generally the first to leave the table hungry or to manage without decent clothing. The unequal distribution of resources within the home, already a present reality for these families before the Depression, was only heightened in the absence of a wage.[31]

## Motherhood

More than other Canadians, Québécoises at the beginning of the century were the target of religious and medical pronouncements that exhorted them to have children in order to ensure the future of the 'race'.[32] This pro-birth rhetoric, reinforced by legal prohibitions on birth-control devices and by the notion of 'conjugal duty', which presumed the husband's unlimited and unconditional access to his wife's body, varied by not a single syllable during the Depression. For women starting their families in this period, the intransigence of the Church, which could impose individual control over their behaviour through the agency of the confessional, meant they had but two choices: they could either live in the perpetual anxiety of 'getting caught' or employ 'artificial contraception' and experience a profound sense of guilt.

From their wedding day, these women deeply desired to have a baby, since motherhood represented one of the fundamental elements of their feminine identity. As one of them said, 'Life was having children' (I24). The daily responsibilities of taking care of them and raising them did, however, become a heavy load to carry, especially when money was short. Repeated pregnancies represented a considerable burden for women whose strength was being sapped at the same time that they had to undertake greater toil. If her husband lost his job, she would spend her pregnancy in conditions that were worse for her own health and that of the child she was carrying, as she would not be eating properly or receiving adequate medical supervision. From the strictly monetary point of view, the arrival of another child might turn out to be simply a catastrophe. The doctor's fees alone for a delivery amounted to

at least $10, an astronomical sum in view of the fact that this was the equivalent of a week's wages for the poorest worker. Then there would be another mouth to feed at a time when there wasn't enough money as it was. A birth represented such a drain on the family finances that *Assistance maternelle* of Montreal, a female philanthropy founded in 1912 with the aim of offering material aid and free medical care to poor mothers, was rapidly overwhelmed by the demand: whereas in the 1920s it helped an average of 800 women a year, in the 1930s it aided between 3,000 and 4,000 expectant mothers annually.[33]

After the birth of two or three children, a number of these women wished to space out their pregnancies and, despite the fulminations of the Church, 15 of the couples[34] did indeed take steps to prevent conception. The economic situation certainly played a considerable role in their desire to limit the size of their families, but it should be noted that economic difficulties were not the only motivation underlying this decision and did not always lead to the use of contraception. In fact, if the majority of couples using birth control did rely on home relief for a greater or lesser period of time or suffered from cuts in income, the women also offered other reasons to justify their choice, like the workload involved in a large family and the desire to pay enough attention to each of the children and bring them up properly: 'I told the good Lord to send me children, but that I did not want them to suffer afterwards. Large families always have problems. Someone is always overlooked in a big family, even if it isn't meant. . . . I said, I'd rather have a small family and be able to give them what they need. It was their education that I was thinking about for later' (I16).

On the other hand, other couples, equally affected by serious financial problems, never imagined the possibility of limiting the size of their families. One of the women, who was pregnant 16 times and bore 11 children although her husband rarely worked and drank up a portion of what he did earn, stated, 'I thought that's the way it always was, since I came from a big family' (I22). Another said, 'There wasn't anything, you never heard of anything that would prevent a baby. . . . You'd often think, if I only had something. . . . Some had ways that they talked about, but I only learned about them later' (I3), while a third woman maintained, 'Birth control was out of the question. It was the law of the Church. You had to have babies' (I29).

Ignorance of contraceptive practices and the internalization of religious values could therefore lead to an almost fatalistic acceptance of successive pregnancies, despite precarious economic circumstances. But more often than not, it was those couples whose relationships were the most hierarchical, where the husband's authority was the most heavily felt, and where all discussion between husband and wife was absent who were the least likely to control their fertility. In view of the contraceptive means available—condom, withdrawal, and the rhythm method[35]—the women could not manage without the agreement and co-operation of their husbands. It was the men who had all the freedom to decide how and how often sexual relations would take place and they could easily decide not to worry about any possible consequences. Women who had not sought to limit their families and who were confronted with particularly trying economic conditions spent their pregnancies in anxiety and dread lest they not be able to provide sufficiently for their babies: 'He was working up until 1933. . . . After that there wasn't any more construction. And the little ones kept coming every year. That was really hard. They have to eat, eh? But when the man isn't working . . .' (I12).

On the other hand, given the religious climate of the period, women who did turn to contraception had guilt and reproach to deal with. Even when they were convinced of the logic of their decision, most of the women who limited the size of their families felt they were in the wrong in breaking the rules of the Church and continued to confess their sin, at the risk of being refused absolution, something that happened to

more than one of them: 'Oh, yes, madame, I was refused absolution, yes, indeed, that happened to me. I didn't repent because I was using my head. In my opinion, the priests were there to inform us, but they weren't there to raise our kids. And in those days, it wasn't easy. . . . You know, women always felt guilty because in those days . . . when you went to the retreat . . . we had one evening in the week about it, you were going to go straight to hell. . . . When you came away, you were shook up, let me tell you' (I16). Even if it was the men who actually employed the contraceptive, it was the women who were condemned by the Church. Men seemed to have a much more elastic conscience and, in order to be left in peace, did not hesitate simply to hide the facts from their confessor. One husband recommended that, if his wife wanted absolution, she not tell 'what we do in our own bed' (I6). Another felt fully justified in limiting the size of his family in the light of his income: 'My husband said, I'm the one who earns the money. It doesn't make sense to live like the animals, neither better or worse' (I5). Used to enjoying a large measure of autonomy and to exercising both their free will and their authority, men easily convinced themselves that they were well within their rights, especially as their earning capacity was objectively demonstrable.

For women, more children certainly meant more work, more worries, and greater risks to their own health, but the Church and patriarchal society had taught them that their needs and even their lives counted for little in the scheme of things: 'It was cruel when you went to confession. It was not a small thing to say that you had used birth control. . . . The priests would scold us. . . . We would tell them, "The doctor said that I mustn't have any more children." They didn't care—the baby would live even if the mother died. That's all they had to say to us. It wasn't right' (I5). Whether or not these couples used contraception, their histories reveal that motherhood for these women represented more a source of anxiety than of joy.

## Help from the Family

Even with increased household production and a decision to limit the number of children, most of these families, especially those who lived for a number of years on the dole, could not have coped without the support of their relatives. Mutual aid within families did not of course occur simply in times of economic crisis; rather, it was a common occurrence necessitated by poverty.[36] But what stands out in the histories is the differences in the help provided depending on economic circumstances. In ordinary times, for example, services most commonly rendered would include babysitting during a lying-in or an illness, and the exchanging or giving of clothing, but we can also observe the very frequent practice of sharing certain implements of work, like a sewing or washing machine or the use of the telephone. The tendency of relatives to settle in the same neighbourhood or even in the same street facilitated these exchanges.

An effect of the Depression was the enlargement of the range of services rendered by relatives. Gifts of meals or foodstuffs and fuel increased, as did gifts and loans of money and of shelter for the young couple: 'Oh, they helped me a lot because they brought me lots of vegetables. I had a sister who was married to a farmer and that meant she could bring me lots of vegetables. . . . We would go over to my mother's, sometimes for weeks at a time. . . . If we didn't go, she'd send someone over to us. . . . She'd say, "Come over, I want some company. . . ." Then I'd do a lot of little things while we were there . . . like sewing, knitting. I made a lot of things when I was at my mother's. . . . We were lucky to always have my mother-in-law. . . . If we didn't have enough to eat, we would go and eat at her house, and that was that. . . . My mother-in-law would come for my little girl. . . . Sometimes she'd keep her for three or four days' (119).

All these kinds of help obviously went beyond the framework of customary exchanges, and some of the women who benefited from them felt decidedly dependent on their families: 'It was my mother who had me under her wing. Mama would send over food to eat—we didn't have anything to eat—he was out of work' (127). Another remarked, 'I didn't like it very much. If I had been on my own, that's OK, but there was my husband and my little boy . . .' (19). Even if it came from very close relatives, these women still felt as humiliated to be on the receiving end of this sort of assistance—which exposed not merely their extreme poverty but also their husband's failure to provide for his family's needs—as they did to turn to the state for aid, something which the majority of couples viewed only as a last, and shameful, resort.[37] The ideal of financial autonomy, a measure of respectability, was a value so deeply rooted in the majority of these couples that one of them even hid the fact that they were on the dole from those closest to him.

This case is, however, exceptional. In fact, more often than not, the immediate family played an essential role in supporting those of its members who were afflicted with unemployment. In theory, the state granted aid only to those without work who absolutely lacked any resources and who could not turn to their families for help. In practice, families contributed in many ways to supply those needs that the meagre relief allowances granted to the unemployed could not provide for, especially in regard to clothing, food, and shelter. The amounts dispensed as aid were so inadequate that any hope of surviving on them, not, at least, without going seriously into debt, was an illusion. After having exhausted their own resources and every tactic for cutting down on their spending, these couples then turned to their own families. The Depression thus intensified the importance of the traditional networks of mutual aid that depended on the commitment of women relations. The contribution made by the work of female relatives, most particularly mothers and mothers-in-law, was just as essential as governmental aid to maintaining a minimum standard of living for the families who were helped. In short, it was all of these women, and not merely those wives whose husbands were out of work, who bore the brunt of the effects of the Depression.

## Conclusion

Unlike their masculine counterparts, working-class women were not unemployed during the 1930s as their families counted more than ever on their labour, their dedication, their self-sacrifice, and their ingenuity in order to survive. Of course the contribution they made to supporting the family did not prevent a decline in the standard of living of their households, but the domestic labour of the wives of unemployed men, together with that of the women of the extended family and state welfare payments, meant the difference between poverty and abject destitution and made it possible to cope with material conditions of existence that would otherwise have been viewed as intolerable. In fact, women's private welfare efforts represented an essential complement to meagre public assistance. Women thus acted as an important social stabilizing factor during this troubled period in Canadian history, even though the women themselves were not considered full-fledged citizens. Montreal housewives of the 1930s held only partial political citizenship since they did not have the right to vote in provincial elections. Unlike other Canadian women, they were still deprived of their societal rights by reason of their maternal function, whereas the Bill concerning needy mothers would not be finally adopted until 1937. Both the Church and the Criminal Code prohibited them, at least in theory, from controlling their reproduction. According to the Civil Code, they were subject to the authority of the head of the house and excluded in fact, if not in law, from the job market. They were thus denied full legal competence, self-determination, and economic independence, the bases of male citizenship. Seen as dependent on a male provider, it was only thus that women had access to state

support, because, except for rare exceptions, they could not claim the role of head of the family on which rested the social rights that were conferred on men at the beginning of the Depression. Established as a way of preserving the patriarchal structure of both society and the family order, the economic dependence of women, which was at the core of their non-citizenship, nevertheless camouflaged the interdependence of the family and of society on the work they did, which was unpaid and disregarded. Hidden from the eyes of their contemporaries and from history, their domestic endeavours were crucial all the same to softening the impact of the Depression on the family structure. In the end, it is probably no accident that social protest arose primarily among young single men with no family connections.

## Notes

1. Terry Copp, 'The Montreal Working-class in Prosperity and Depression', *Canadian Issues* 1 (1975): 8.
2. See Andrée Lévesque, *Virage à gauche interdit. Les communistes, les socialistes et leurs ennemis au Québec, 1929–1939* (Montréal: Boréal, 1984) for an appraisal of social conflict in Quebec and especially in Montreal.
3. Copp, 'The Montreal Working-class', 8.
4. Bettina Bradbury, *Working Families: Age, Gender, and Daily Survival in Industrializing Montreal* (Toronto: McClelland & Stewart, 1993).
5. The scale of allowances fixed by the city of Montreal was set at $36.88 a month in summer and $39.48 in winter, the amounts allotted to cover the costs of food, fuel, rent, and clothing for five persons. These sums constituted barely half the minimum considered necessary by the federal Minister of Labour. See Leonard C. Marsh, *Canadians In and Out of Work: A Survey of Economic Classes and Their Relations to the Labor Market* (Toronto: Oxford University Press, 1940), 193.
6. Ruth Roach Pierson, 'Gender and the Unemploy-

ment Debate in Canada, 1930–1940', *Labour/Le Travail* 25 (1990): 77–105; Margaret Hobbs, 'Rethinking Antifeminism in the 1930s: Gender Crisis or Workplace Justice? A Response to Alice Kessler-Harris', *Gender and History* 5, 1 (1993): 4–15; Cynthia R. Comacchio, *The Infinite Bonds of Family: Domesticity in Canada, 1840–1950* (Toronto: University of Toronto Press, 1999), 124.

7.  This was the case except in certain narrowly defined circumstances. On the topic of aid programs adopted during the Depression, see James Struthers, *No Fault of Their Own: Unemployment and the Canadian Welfare State 1914–1941* (Toronto: University of Toronto Press, 1983).

8.  In its report for 1935, the Society for the Protection of Women and Children of Montreal stated: 'During the past five years, "failure to provide" and its companion offence "desertion" by the male parent has progressively and markedly decreased.' The report attributed this decrease (of 33 per cent) to the lack of work and to the distribution of welfare that kept families together. In contrast, in 1946, the same association recorded an increase of 48 per cent in cases of desertion and failure to provide in comparison with the preceding year and concluded: 'We can look for an upswing in these figures, because it has always been our experience, proved by records, that with the return of economic prosperity, desertions, the number of which always tapers off in periods of financial depression, increase markedly.' (ANC, MG281129, Society for the Protection of Women and Children 2 Minutes and 6 Minutes, 1947–1950).

9.  On women as citizens and the specific mode of their integration into the state, see Carole Pateman, 'The Patriarchal Welfare State', in Joan B. Landes, ed., *Feminism: The Public and the Private* (Oxford and New York: Oxford University Press, 1998), 241–76; Sylvia Walby, 'Is Citizenship Gendered?', *Sociology* 28 (1994): 379–95.

10. Denyse Baillargeon, *Making Do: Women, Family, and Home in Montreal during the Great Depression*, trans. Yvonne Klein (Waterloo, Ont.: Wilfrid Laurier University Press, 1999).

11. For summary biographies of these women, see Baillargeon, *Making Do*.

12. Thirteen married between 1919 and 1928, five in 1929, ten between 1930 and 1932, and two in 1933 and 1934. Twenty-six of the spouses were either manual or non-manual workers. One was unemployed at the time of his marriage and had rarely had a job, while the three remaining owned small businesses (a barbershop, a snack bar, two taxi cabs). We must make it very clear that the status of owner did not mean that they enjoyed a standard of living necessarily higher than that of those working for others, since the Depression forced two of them to sell up before bankruptcy. . . .

13. The quotation is taken from interview number 23. Hereafter, references to interviews will be indicated by an upper-case 'I' followed by the interview number.

14. Only three of them looked for a way to make money specifically because their husbands were partly or wholly out of work. . . .

15. Québec, *Annuaire statistique,* 1930 and 1934, 400 and 426; Canada, ministère du Travail, *La Gazette du Travail*, février 1933, 249.

16. The women who did work outside the home had a maximum of two children and someone other than the husband took care of them, even when he had the free time to do it.

17. On this topic, see Hobbs, 'Rethinking Antifeminism in the 1930s'.

18. In fact, this informant had taught for a year before getting married, but she did not seem to consider this a real job.

19. On the impossibility of reversing roles during the Depression, see Mirra Komarovsky, *The Unemployed Man and His Family* (New York: Arno, 1971); Ruth Milkman, 'Women's Work and Economic Crisis: Some Lessons of the Great Depression', *Review of Radical Political Economics* 8 (1976): 85.

20. Hobbs, 'Rethinking Antifeminism in the 1930s', 9.

21. In fact, article 23 of the Montreal Unemployment Commission regulations stipulated that 'If the husband drinks or gambles away his aid cheque, then the registrar should immediately be

informed. He will see to it a new registration is made in the spouse's name or that of another responsible person or Society that can replace the head of the family. . . .' This article does not seem to have been widely circulated, and, in any event, in order to get benefits paid in her own name, this woman would have had to challenge openly her husband's prerogatives and authority, something which seemed impossible to her [Montréal, Commission du chômage, *Renseignements à l'usage des chômeurs nécessiteux et des propriétaires* (Montreal: n.p., n.d.), 6].

22. Which it was not always. During hard times, even professional dressmakers lost some of their private clientele, for example.

23. Before turning to the state for aid, or even while on the dole, six of the men tried hard to support their families by undertaking various sorts of work. . . .

24. Hobbs, 'Rethinking Antifeminism in the 1930s', 8.

25. Meg Luxton, *More Than a Labour of Love: Three Generations of Women's Work in the Home* (Toronto: Women's Press, 1980), 161–99; Veronica Strong-Boag, *The New Day Recalled: Lives of Girls and Women in English Canada, 1919–1939* (Toronto: Copp Clark Pitman, 1988), 133–44; Elizabeth Roberts, *A Woman's Place: An Oral History of Working-Class Women. 1850–1940* (Oxford: Basil Blackwell, 1984), 125–68; Pat Ayers and Jan Lambertz, 'Marriage Relations, Money, and Domestic Violence in Working-Class Liverpool 1919–39', in Jane Lewis, ed., *Labour and Love: Women's Experiences of Home and Family, 1840–1940* (Oxford: Basil Blackwell, 1986), 195–219.

26. An equipped six-room flat cost from $25 to $40 a month in January 1929 and from $18 to $33 in January 1933. A six-room flat without modern conveniences, or only partially equipped, cost between $16 and $25 a month in 1929 and between $15 and $18 in 1933 (Canada, ministère du Travail, *La Gazette du Travail*, février 1929, 256, and février 1933, 257).

27. In this period, most shops stayed open until 11:00 on Saturday night.

28. White sauce was made of water and flour, also used to make wallpaper paste.

29. The number of removals in Montreal was in fact on the rise throughout the initial years of the Depression: 54,000 in 1930, 55,000 in 1931, 65,000 in 1932, and almost 82,000 in 1933, according to figures supplied by Montreal Light, Heat and Power (*La Patrie*, 17 avril 1931, 3, 17 avril 1933, 3). Moreover, the economic situation meant that the majority of families were looking for low-cost housing. . . .

30. It should be recalled that Montreal Light, Heat and Power enjoyed a virtual monopoly in the Montreal region, which permitted it to maintain high rates and to disconnect with impunity clients who failed to pay their bills. According to Robert Rumilly, more than 20,000 families were cut off from electricity in the depths of the Depression [cited in Claude Larivière, *Crise économique et contrôle social: le cas de Montréal, 1929–1937* (Montreal: Éditions Saint-Martin, 1977), 175].

31. The unequal distribution of resources in poor households has been noted on numerous occasions by feminist historians and sociologists. In this regard, see the works listed in note 25 as well as Ruth Lister, 'Women, Economic Dependency and Citizenship', *Journal of Social Policy* 19, 4 (1990): 445–67.

32. There have been a number of studies of this discourse. See Andrée Lévesque, *La norme et les déviantes. Des femmes au Québec pendant l'entre-deux-guerres* (Montréal: Éditions du Remue-ménage, 1989).

33. *Assistance maternelle* provided a layette, bed linen, food, and fuel, and sometimes even furniture. It also paid for the costs of the delivery and for a month's supply of milk following the birth [Denyse Baillargeon, 'L'Assistance maternelle de Montréal: Un exemple de marginalisation des bénévoles dans le domaine des soins aux accouchées', *Dynamis. International Journal of History of Science and Medicine*, Special number, *Mujeres y salud. Prácticas y saberes/Women and Health* 19 (1999): 379–400].

34. That is, a little over half the fertile couples, as two of the 30 in the study had no children.

35. Three of the couples using contraception

employed condoms, eight engaged in with-drawal, and four used the rhythm method ('Ogino-Knauss'). The first two methods seem to have been the most frequently employed throughout Canada [Angus McLaren and Arlene Tigar McLaren, *The Bedroom and the State: The Changing Practices and Politics of Contraception and Abortion in Canada, 1880–1980* (Toronto: McClelland & Stewart, 1986), 22)].

36. In this connection, see Andrée Fortin, *Histoires de familles et de réseaux. La sociabilité au Québec d'hier á demain* (Montréal: Éditions Saint-Martin, 1987); Marc-Adélard Tremblay, 'La crise économique des années trente et la qualité de vie chez les mon-tréalais d'ascendance française', Académie des sci-ences morales et politiques, *Travaux et Communications* 3, *Progrés Techniques et qualité de vie* (Montréal: Bellarmin, 1977), 149–65.

37. Recent studies reveal similar attitudes. See Lister, 'Women, Economic Dependency and Citizenship'.

# 6

# What Makes Washday Less Blue?
# Gender, Nation, and Technology Choice
# in Post-war Canada

Joy Parr

The way Canadian women did their wash confounded the appliance managers of American branch plants in the late 1950s. In 1959 wringer washers—a technology little altered in 20 years, and by contemporary engineering standards a technology entirely superseded—outsold automatics three to one in Canada. This was exactly the reverse of the pattern in the United States, where automatics that year accounted for 75 per cent of sales.[1] 'Theoretically there is no market for ordinary washing machines as everyone should be buying the automatic type', a senior official at Canadian General Electric asserted counterfactually. He added in a bemused attempt at explanation, 'I suppose, however, that the big market for ordinary washing machines lies in less developed countries.' E.P. Zimmerman, who ran the appliance division at Canadian Westinghouse, yearly through the 1950s forecast a breakthrough for automatic machines in Canada, as did his counterparts at Kelvinator and Frigidaire, and yearly found that sales of wringer machines remained strong. 'This is strange,' he affirmed (implicitly

rejecting the underdeveloped countries explanation), 'because usually Canada is much closer to US trends than this.'[2]

Readers familiar with the literature on domestic technology might share this puzzlement, because the fine work published in the early 1980s by Strasser and Cowan on the United States case has served as the template for understanding household technology in the North Atlantic world. United States production of automatics surpassed wringers definitively in 1951. Although Strasser and Cowan are attentive to distinctions between the priorities of makers and users, in the case of washing machine technology they report not conflict but a quick convergence of interest.[3] They find that automatics were accepted into American households as soon as they were made available by US manufacturers.[4]

Cowan's justly famous parable about how the refrigerator got its hum, which has the giant electrical apparatus and automobile manufacturers successfully championing the condenser cooling technology over which they commanded proprietary rights, only makes the prolonged failure of

Joy Parr, 'What Makes Washday Less Blue? Gender, Nation, and Technology Choice in Postwar Canada', *Technology and Culture* 38 (1997): 153–86. © Society for the History of Technology. Reprinted with permission of The Johns Hopkins University Press.

automatic washers in the Canadian market seem more inexplicable.[5] For it was these same American makers, and for the same reasons, who intended to have Canadian women of the 1950s do their washing in automatic machines. In fact, it was not until 1966, 15 years later than in the United States, that Canadian automatic sales passed those of wringer washers.[6]

. . .

Household technology is centrally different from industrial technology. An industrialist commissions a machine from a producer goods manufacturer, as he might commission a suit from a custom tailor. The machine and the suit, having been made to the user's specifications, upon delivery, are promptly put to use. In household technology, this smooth transition cannot be assumed.[7] Makers, as Mme Renee Vautelet, a past president of the Canadian Association of Consumers, noted in 1958, tended to think of consumers as 'the buying side' of themselves.[8] In certain conjunctures, the cultural similarities between domestic machine makers and domestic machine users may transcend those differences made by the market economy and gender. Machines offered for sale then may be accepted unproblematically by women seeking tools for their household work. In the United States, for automatic washers, this appears to have been the case, at least for middle-class urban women.[9] But generally the culture of makers and the culture of users are very different. Machinery which is not made to the specifications of the users, as household technology almost always has not been, often does not satisfy.[10] Here gender, but also class and national differences are at play. . . .

. . . To understand why women have refused apparently excellent new machines, we need to pay attention to users and include 'an examination of the *details* of women's lives' as part of the history of technological change.[11] To understand the effects of machines which were put to use, we need to consider how 'the form of the household, and the sexual division of labour within it' might actively have shaped domestic technol-

ogy.[12] A discussion of household technological choice must reckon not only how women's technological preferences as users differed from men's technological preferences as makers and sellers, how engineering and commercial priorities came to prevail, but the possibility that *men, as makers and sellers, did not always get their way*. Here I try to set such a broad context for technological choice, considering how traits of the Canadian political economy and of makers and marketers worked with and against the internal politics of households and perceptions of well-being and waste to determine which man-made laundry technology women would (agree to) use.

A wringer washing machine consists of a steel tub, either galvanized or porcelain enamelled, upon which the wringer, a pair of wooden or rubber rollers, is mounted. An electric or gas motor suspended beneath the tub drives an agitator to move laundry through the wash water and revolve the rollers, clamped in tension, to express water from the goods being laundered. The machine was not self-acting. The tub was filled by the operator from a hose or bucket with water heated to the required temperature and then soap or its successor, detergent, and the clothing and linens were added. The woman operating the machine filled a separate tub or pair of tubs with rinse water and then manually lifted the items being washed from the soapy water. She fed them individually through the wringer into the rinse tubs in turn, moving the clothing through rinse waters with a stick. At each rinse she again lifted each piece by hand from the water. After the last rinse she guided the completed washing once more through the wringers, this time into a basket to be carried to the line to dry. After being used for several loads, the soapy water was either siphoned from the tub or disgorged into a floor drain. This process was hard on women's hands and their backs, and except for the 10 or so minutes when the agitator was running, required the operator to be actively at work. All in all, this does not seem a technology to inspire devotion among its users.

But by comparison with the technology it replaced in most Canadian homes, the wringer washer was a real improvement. You definitely noticed the difference, Lily Hansen recalled. 'I wasn't very good at scrubbing clothes on the washboard, and wringing them at all. You know, you're trying to wring sheets.' 'When my kids complained about the inconvenient malfunctioning wringer,' Martha Watson wrote, 'I told them they didn't know when they were well off.'[13]

But few denied the limitations of the technology. In rural homes, the machine was stored outside and in winter had to be dragged into the kitchen before washday could begin. In city homes the wringer washer was usually in the basement, and because the machine was not self-acting, 'You were running up and down stairs all morning doing this washing.' In machines without pumps, 'getting the water out of these big tubs, it was heavy work.' Even in the best of circumstances, with a nearby pair of concrete tubs, separate hoses from hot and cold taps, and a mechanical siphon to empty the tub, the routine—washing white, coloured, and then heavily soiled work clothes in sequence, and returning each load in turn to the machine tub for rinsing with the aid of the agitator—was physically demanding. Clothing with buttons or zippers and larger linens had to be folded carefully while still soaking wet before they could be passed through the wringer. Metaphorically, many reported, doing laundry 'was a pain'.[14]

. . .

Yet for all this, the transition from wringer to automatic technology was not swift in Canada. Allison Smith, a Commerce graduate from the University of Alberta, spent the fifties in remote northern villages where her husband was posted as a Royal Canadian Mounted Police officer. In winter she melted ice for the wash on a wood stove, brought the water to a boil in her electric kettle, regretting her accountant's habit of counting as her sons' 54 diapers went through each stage of the wash and out onto the line. In her Meadow Lake, Saskatchewan, kitchen in 1955 she

tacked up a picture cut out of a magazine of a Bendix duomatic. Four years later she returned to urban life of modest prosperity, but not until 1973 did she acquire an automatic washing machine.[15]

To understand why, right up until the mid-sixties, more Canadian women each year bought wringers than automatics, why more considered the wringer the proper machine for the job of doing the wash . . . , we need to look beyond the relative convenience of the machines. We need to consider the broader context in which the consumption decision was made—what Ruth Schwartz Cowan has called the consumption junction.[16] The washer was not a single machine but an integral part of the mechanical system of the house. The buying decision was similarly complex and political. In the home, major household purchases had opportunity costs. They presented opportunities to some household members and denied them to others. Within the Canadian political economy, wringer and automatic machines had very different locations. Wringer and automatic machines both washed clothes, but each of the technologies was built upon and had built in distinct assumptions about the relationships between machines and other resources, both human and natural, made in response to their succeeding contexts, assumptions to a degree coherent and common among technologies of their time, as we think of people as bearing affinities of a shared generation. These differences were readily apparent to women of the time, although they are more elusive to us now some 40 years distant. . . .

. . .

Marketers met the concerns and fantasies of real Canadian women best with ads which highlighted the self-acting capacities of the automatic machine. . . . Unlike the displays for contemporary wringers (which showed women looking towards the machines), the graphics in advertisements for automatics more frequently showed a woman turned away from the washer, to smile not at the machine but at the child with whom she was playing or the husband with whom she was about to depart.[17] The claim that the automatic 'ended washday' by making it more feasible to do 'two or three small washes through the week' may have been the Hobson's choice Susan Strasser describes, between 'a weekly nightmare' and an 'unending task'.[18] Yet Ontario Hydro's promise, 'a few things each day keeps "washday" away', of a machine which would 'do all the hard work' of the wash and promote busy mothers to the position of 'supervisor in the laundry department' could not but tempt women in the home.[19]

Visions of automatics must have danced in the heads of most mothers of infants, for pungent pails of diapers could not be held for a single weekly washday. The woman who owned only two dozen diapers would have been washing them most days by hand. Whatever one's reservations about owning an automatic, who would not have been ready and willing to dream the advertiser's fantasy of a magical machine which all on its own made dirty into clean? Thus, many ads for automatics targeted new mothers. To launch their new washer-dryer set in 1953, Westinghouse worked on the nightmares raised by the thought of arriving twins. Once again the machines were imagined as, and introduced to consumers as, people, in this case as baby twins. This 'Blessed Event' campaign used ads showing storks delivering new washer-dryer twin sets. . . . Dealers provided birth certificates, tastefully printed in black and gold, to each buyer who took the mechanical twins home. The firm fused the images of the twins they had manufactured and the twins who would create dirty diapers by offering a free pair of machines to every mother in Canada who bore twins on the launch day of the new model, the 17th of March of that year.[20] There were echoes of the 1930s Stork Derbies and the celebrated Dionne Quintuplets in the Westinghouse letters to 15,000 doctors, hospitals, and nurses' associations, asking for their intervention to discover lucky candidates and authenticate the births. But the campaign captured well the shared current of pleasure and desperation which flowed about mothers in the midst of the Canadian baby boom. The campaign would also have appealed to a singular predisposition among contemporary manufacturers, at once to feature users in the image of their machines, and to feature the machines they made as human.[21]

Most advertisements for washers addressed a female audience. Men were invoked infrequently in any capacity in ads to sell wringers, but they began to appear now and then in the late 1950s in campaigns for automatics. The man in a checked hunting shirt an Ontario Hydro ad showed loading an automatic washer, 'so easy even a *man* can do it', had only a walk-on part, for the accompanying text quickly turned to address a female reader. But Inglis pitched ads to men twice, first in the 'Wife-Saver' campaign of 1958, which attempted rakish double entendre, urging husbands to 'save' their wives by 'trading them' in on new Inglis washers and dryers. The ads the next year—'Is your Bride still waiting for her Inglis?'—proceeded more cautiously, combining copy written for husbands—'We know you are just as anxious as any husband to save work for your bride but honestly . . . hasn't the family wash been a labour of love too long?'— with an illustration of a young bride holding a large laundry basket rather than a bouquet, intended to catch women's attention (Figure 1). The timing is interesting here. Men portrayed as patriarchs and providers were targeted directly as buyers in 1958 and 1959 as a recession deepened in Canada and manufacturers found sales in replacement markets more difficult to make.[22]

. . .

. . . The product engineering and merchandising of automatic washers presumed mass consumption, that washers could be offered relatively cheaply so that both a conversion and a replacement market would rapidly develop. But the costs of carrying the technology across national boundaries, which made automatic washers relatively more expensive in Canada (and other jurisdictions) than in the United States, made automatics implausible and impractical as objects

**Figure 1.** 'Is your Bride still waiting for her INGLIS?' *Marketing*, 3 Apr. 1959, p. 6.

of mass consumption. For makers, the washer was an object for sale, reaching out towards an imagined consumer. For prospective users (who may or may not have featured themselves as consumers), neither the price nor the promise was as alluring as the makers assumed.[23]

. . .

Early automatics often were bought by men as gifts for their wives. 'To purchase gadgets that relieve . . . drudgery and thus promote domestic affection', as Marshall McLuhan observed in 1951 in *The Mechanical Bride*, could be seen as a duty, a species of moral choice. The other leading male commentator on technology of the day, George Grant, was generally critical of American influences upon Canada and wary of transnational technology as a threat to liberty. But he made an exception for 'the wonderful American machines' he believed let his wife, Sheila, lead a freer life, acknowledging that 'the practical worth of modern technology' was demonstrated 'every time Sheila washed the clothes in her machine'.[24]

The men who presented their wives with the first automatics were often professionals—geologists or engineers worried about the peripatetic lives their careers imposed upon the family, or university professors who encouraged their wives' dedication to pursuits other than housewifery. They had the income to afford the automatic, enough control over the family budget to make the decision alone, the conviction that manufacturers' promises for the machine would be fulfilled. Beverly Newmarch, in 1948 the wife of a newly hired geology Ph.D. in a British Columbia coal-mining town, remembers how she came to have an automatic in her company duplex: 'Chuck decided that with what I had had to use, I should now have an automatic. He began to look at want-ads! I was horrified, since automatics were so new, I didn't want to start out with one that had experience! He persevered, however, and found himself a new Bendix, still in the wooden crate. The American consul had brought it up to Victoria and for some reason or other they had not been able to obtain permission to install it in their home—something about the plumbing not being adequate.' Ann Brook, married to a navy man frequently away from home, returned from work one day to find the automatic she had declined ('Hum, don't need an automatic washing machine, who needs an automatic washing machine?') already installed. Her husband had conferred once more with their customary appliance salesman, Mr Beeton, and he and Mr Beeton had agreed, 'maybe you should try it and see.' Mrs Brook did not decline the gift.[25]

If for the men who bought them in the forties and early fifties automatic washers were unambiguously desirable objects which bespoke affection and a better life, for children they are recalled as mesmerizing entertainments. The rare front-loading automatics somewhat resembled the even rarer televisions about which most Canadian youngsters had only heard tell before 1955. Most women who got automatics in the early post-war years tell stories of lines of small spectators gathering to watch the wash.[26] Women as equipment users had a more complex appraisal to make. Some were persuaded early on. Margaret Shortliffe had first seen an automatic Bendix at Cornell University in 1939, noted the merits of its alternating drum technology, and refused agitator substitutes, either wringer or automatic, washing by hand until her husband got a Bendix to Kingston, Ontario, in 1946. Winnifred Edwards, like Shortliffe, got along without a machine until the kind of equipment she had seen in hospital laundries was available for sale in 1952. The consequences of investing in a particular durable tool delayed their purchase of any machine, as it delayed many women's purchase of automatics, for deliberating on an investment takes longer than choosing to consume an object of either personal or altruistic desire.[27]

In such deliberations, price is plainly an important factor. Automatic washers cost more than wringer machines. In 1950, the gap was wide. Standard wringers could cost as little as $90, some automatic models as much as $370. In 1956 the Chatelaine Institute reported best-selling wringer prices ranging from $129 to $259, and automatics from $325 to $469. Over time the gap narrowed, but still in 1966 the average price of wringers advertised in Eaton's mail-order catalogue was $146; automatics at an average of $234 cost half as much again.[28]

This was not a negligible difference, particularly in the first decade after the war when couples were equipping homes for the first time. Personal incomes in Canada were not high in this period, in 1947–50 about two-thirds of incomes in the United States.[29] Prices for Canadian consumer goods in nominal and real terms exceeded those in the United States. Hard choices had to be made. The consumer credit controls that applied to washers until 1953 required down payments of one-third and full payment within a year.[30] Getting everything at once by running into debt was not an option. Deciding what to get first required considerable juggling. For how long should the household get by without a stove, a mechanical refrigerator, or a washer?

. . . Buying a wringer rather than an automatic washing machine was a sensible economy. The savings, for example, would have bought a vacuum cleaner or a radio, and the wash would still be done. The washer was the one place in the basic household consumption package where there was a little discretion. Among the 8,611 Toronto women Eaton's interviewed about their purchases of furniture and appliances between January 1949 and August 1952, the amount paid for refrigerators ($343–$348) and for stoves ($205–$219) varied little. For washers the range was considerable. Women under 24 paid on average $152, women over 35 on average $188. More older than younger women were buying automatic machines. New equipment for keeping food cold and making it hot took a relatively fixed amount out of every household budget. A younger homemaker, with more household equipment to acquire at once, could more easily make do with a wringer washer, than do without a stove or a mechanical refrigerator.[31] The Central Mortgage and Housing Corporation surveyed 6,600 families who had purchased houses between January and May of 1955 in Halifax, Montreal, Toronto, Winnipeg, and Vancouver. The amount spent varied between cities, on stoves by $62, on refrigerators by $45, but on washers (on average the least expensive of the three appliances) by $127. Only on washers could the new home buyers with the least to spend accrue appreciable savings.[32]

Among the much smaller group of women with whom I spoke and corresponded, a similar pattern emerges. A washer was important, often important enough to risk going into debt for, especially important once children began to arrive.[33] But the choice was not posed in the post-war years as between two laundry technologies, between an automatic and a wringer. Rather, women spoke about the other tasks which might be mechanized and the other obligations of the home. The decision about a washing machine was part of these other decisions about equipping the household and the household's relationship to the wider world. Buying the automatic, the more expensive machine, when a cheaper satisfactory alternative existed could easily seem to foreclose more opportunities than it opened, to be less about liberty than constraint.

In rural homes, the needs of the barn and of the house had to be met from the same purse. Investment in labour-saving equipment for the farm took priority, partly because men made these decisions on their own.[34] Perhaps also, in some parts of Canada as in Iowa and the Palouse region of Idaho and Washington, women saw investments in farm equipment as saving domestic labour because they eliminated the need for hired men.[35] The priority of the barn is plain in the detailed study of 352 Ontario farm families Helen Abell conducted in 1959. On the most prosperous farms, where investment in all labour-saving equipment exceeded $13,000, less than 10 per cent of this investment was in domestic technology. Paradoxically and surprisingly, the proportion of the farm family's resources invested in household appliances rose among poorer farmers, to 20 per cent for the house when all equipment was valued at less than $7,000.[36] Because there were few satisfactory substitutes in domestic technology, the least mechanized of farm families had to allocate the largest share of their equipment budget to the kitchen and laundry basics, at least in Ontario. Choosing a wringer over an automatic reduced these pressures and might, for example, have brought an electric cream separator into the kitchen.[37] In more highly capitalized operations, a farm woman may more readily have been able to justify the purchase of an automatic machine to free her for farm work outside the house. Jellison finds Iowa women used this argument in the 1950s. The same reasoning may account for why automatic washers more quickly became commonplace in the farms of Quebec, where dairy predominated, than in other Canadian markets.[38]

. . .

Even in good times, the $100–$200 gap between the cost of a wringer and an automatic machine made Canadian women hesitate and consider other household needs. In the late fifties, as manufacturers were expanding their production of automatics, a five-year-long recession began. Many a 'wife's pay cheque' was 'merely replacing that of a laid-off husband'. Marketers began to suspect what researchers later would document, that economic uncertainty had an exaggerated effect upon the purchase of major durable goods. In lean times households were 'likely to be cautious about replacing any machine which wasn't actually breaking down', and likely to see the best new machine as the one which put least pressure on other aspects of the family budget.[39]

Makers who featured users making the choice between wringer and automatic washers on the basis of the laundry technologies alone made a more elemental misjudgement. In the early 1950s, the fantasies of Canadian young people were inhabited less by shiny white boxes lined up on showroom floors than by plumbing, wiring, and pipes. The year automatic sales first exceeded wringers in the United States, electrification and running water systems were the stuff of which young Canadians' dreams were made.[40] As a leading Canadian home economist noted in

1946 and was still noting in 1954, it seemed 'impractical to discuss the dream houses of the future . . . until more of our houses, urban and farm, have running hot and cold water.'[41]

. . .

Important as these straightforward economic and infrastructural constraints were, they do not wholly explain the Canadian preference for wringer washers. By the early sixties, many of the economic and infrastructure considerations which favoured wringer washers over automatics had faded. Wages and salaries were rising. Women remembered feeling more prosperous and more confident that prosperity could be sustained.[42] The price gap between wringers and automatics had narrowed. Almost every household had electricity and more than four out of five had hot running water. Yet in 1964 wringers still were outselling automatics by a considerable margin. There was still a mass market for wringers even among Canadian higher-income groups. Women who owned wringers still were more likely to replace them with wringers than with automatics.[43] While producers and marketers asserted that replacing a wringer washing machine with an automatic was 'trading up', it is not at all clear that women doing the wash saw the matter in the same way.

Cultural values attach to goods offered for sale. Product engineers build cultural assumptions into the machines they design. Marketers set out to find or to forge a constituency to whom these assumptions make sense. But their sales prospects will not necessarily share makers' values, or make their determination on the basis of marketers' assumptions. The purchase of goods is self-implicating. Thus, as David Nye notes, the possession of electrical appliances 'engages the owner in a process of self-definition'; in their operation 'the self and object are intertwined.' But the cultural current flows two ways. The machine may remake its user ('I was born to use an automatic'), but the user may also refeature the machine ('The automatic is a wasteful extravagance'). Once the constraints of price, plumbing,

and income had begun to fall away, it was still not for makers and marketers alone to define how Canadian women would do the wash, or what for them constituted an excellent machine.[44]

Machines are located within moral economies. The tools we use embody values. They may also constrain the field within which we can make moral choices. They 'expand or restrict' our 'actions and thoughts', reveal or conceal the implications of our decisions.[45] Some machines, by their design, seem to operate with resplendent technological autonomy; others, by design, constantly disclose and allow their operator to monitor the demands of the machine upon the provisioning system of which it is a part. Automatic washing machines are of the first sort, wringer washers are of the second. Canadian women making the choice between them in the 1950s plainly distinguished the two kinds of machines in these terms, and gave this signification to the distinction.

A woman filling a washer by hauling water, or working a hand pump, or standing by a running hose knew how much fresh water she was drawing for the task. She saw the character and the quantity of the waste she was disposing into the yard, the septic field, or the sewer mains when the job was done. A homemaker who relied upon a well and septic system knew she must monitor the capacities of these systems and adapt her domestic routines daily and seasonally to accommodate their limits. Any woman who had run a wringer machine had a clearer sense of the relationships between washing, water, and waste, than those of us today who have only used automatic machines that fill and drain through discrete piping, leaving volumes drawn and disposed unobservable and unremarked. For rural women in the 1950s, the new automatics that promised to put each load of laundry through several rinses in fresh water presented an immediate hazard to operation of the farm home. But city women as well had experience with which to recognize the automatics as prodigal, of fuel to heat water, and of water itself. In response to a request for ideas for better washers, Mrs H.G.F. Barr of London, Ontario, wrote thus in 1955: 'I have been appalled at the amount of water that seems necessary to do a normal family wash in the new spin-dry type of machine. I believe one brand boasted that it rinsed clothes seven times, and all of them threw the water out after one use. There is hardly a city or town in Canada that does not have some water shortage in summer months. Large sums are being spent on reforestation, conservation and dams. It would appear that this trend towards excessive use of water should be checked now.' Through the 1960s such negative consumer commentaries upon automatic washers remained common, homemakers' rhetoric to describe the new machines more evocative of the manic sorcerer's apprentice in the contemporary Disney film *Fantasia* than of the regulated modern domestic engineering manufacturers and marketers sought to portray.[46]

Manufacturers, in both their design decisions and marketing strategies, treated the washer as an isolated object rather than as one element in a production process called 'doing the wash'. It was, after all, the washer alone they had to sell. By contrast, women consumers thought of doing laundry as a task rather than a machine. They appraised the process in the way production processes conventionally are construed, considering their own management priorities and skills and all the non-capital inputs required, as well as the traits of the machinery they might put to work.[47]

In these terms, manufacturers' emphasis on the gadgetry raised alarms among consumers. The early automatics were fragile machines, prone to break down and repairable only by specialized technicians who were not always nearby. 'In the search to provide more and more automatic features', Mrs W.R. Walton of the Consumers Association warned, makers were producing washers 'so sensitive and complex, it will take an engineering expert' to fix them.[48] By contrast, in 1958 many wringer washers were being sold with long guarantees, and supported by a dense network of local dealers who by pref-

erence specialized in wringer sales. In an economy where all household appliances lately had been in short supply, where couples still were aspiring to an adequate rather than affluent standard of living, buying a delicate automatic seemed both short-sighted and frivolous.

The promise that an automatic machine would do the wash all on its own seemed a threat. Even when intervention was required, the self-regulating features of the automatics defied operator intervention. Tubs that filled by a timer ran half empty when water pressure was low. Loads that became unbalanced under lids that locked for the duration of the wash cycle caused the machine to jostle uncontrollably about the room. Women who in the 1950s expressed a preference for simpler machines over which they could exercise a greater measure of control spoke from well-founded technical, managerial, and resource concerns about the operation of the new automatic laundry equipment.[49]

Between the engineering of the wringer and automatic washing machines lay a generational divide. Wringer washers were made in batches, durable and simple to repair. These product characteristics happily complemented a consumer culture habituated to scarcity and schooled to value conservation and thrift. Automatics were mass produced, designed for a consumer culture which would value innovation over durability and be willing to place convenience for the machine operator ahead of household water and fuel costs and the social costs of creating more waste. For domestic appliances, at the core of this change was a redefinition of what constituted an excellent machine, a narrowing of the purchasing decision to give priority to labour-saving features over other resource concerns. Many Canadian women in the fifties and sixties were unwilling to cross this generational divide. Their loyalty to the wringer washer technology and their skepticism about the new automatics is a sign of this resistance. The choice between wringer and automatic machines implicated Canadian homemakers in forming distinctions between consumer and user, between gratification and prudence, between production and conservation, between built to last and built to replace. In the circumstances in which they then found themselves, and with the knowledge they then had, it is not hard to see why, red hands and aching back and wet floors notwithstanding, so many resisted the chromium promises of the new machine.

In the post-war years household technologies increasingly were characterized as consumer goods. The rapid rise of a culture of mass consumption and the more central place consumer goods came to hold in the definition of personal identities and civic values is well documented for the United States. Sometimes popular knowledge about these goods effected cultural changes, even when the goods themselves were not widely owned. This is the case Robert Frost makes for interwar France.[50] But the process can also work the opposite way.

Consumer goods can be, and have been, refused because of the cultural values they embody. The degree to which mass consumption became institutionalized differed between regions and nations and across classes. In the decade following World War II, these differences varied with the pace of post-war recovery, the precedence given to export or domestic markets, and household versus industrial needs. Centrally, the plausibility of mass consumption was tied to perceptions of plenty and to beliefs about how the national wealth should be husbanded and shared. For consumer goods that are also working tools this dialogue was vigorous and many-faceted. In measure, manufacturers and marketers remade the material and symbolic functions of their machines to address the resistance of consumers. But as long as the purchasers of household equipment continued to think of themselves centrally as users appraising tools, they were declining to be defined solely as consumers. Their choices of what goods to buy bespoke deeper concerns about how much was enough, and for whom, framed in the politics of

the households and the communities to which they belonged.

## Notes

This article was first presented at the Technological Change Conference at Oxford University in September 1993. The author is grateful to Shirley Tillotson, Marilyn MacDonald, James Williams, Bea Millar, R Cole Harris, and Anthony Scott for comments on an earlier draft, and to Ingrid Epp and Margaret-Anne Knowles for research assistance.

1.  Canadian Westinghouse Hamilton, Employment Forecast Interview Report (EFIR), 5 May 1959, RG 20 767, National Archives of Canada (NAC); 'Thor Gathers Speed after US Agreement', *Marketing*, 24 Apr. 1959, 8. *Marketing* was the Canadian equivalent of *Printer's Ink*.

2.  Canadian General Electric, 7 Oct. 1958, EFIR, 6 Dec. 1962, RG 20 765 23–100–C27, NAC; Zimmerman's comments are in Canadian Westinghouse, EFIR, 6 May 1959, RG 20 767, NAC; for Kelvinator, see RG 20 773, NAC.

3.  Judy Wajcman suggests in her study of refrigerators, however, that Cowan reduced housewives to the role of consumers, responsive only to price, and told the story as a rivalry between manufacturing interests in which user preferences did not figure. Judy Wajcman, *Feminism Confronts Technology* (University Park, Penn., 1991), 102. It is worth considering whether the precedence of price over use values in consumer decision-making may have been more marked in the United States than in other North Atlantic economies in the 1950s.

4.  Susan Strasser, *Never Done: A History of American Housework* (New York, 1982), 267–8; Ruth Schwartz Cowan, *More Work for Mother: The Ironies of Household Technology from the Open Hearth to the Microwave* (New York, 1983), 94.

5.  Cowan, *More Work for Mother*, 128–43.

6.  *Home Goods Retailing* (HGR), 23 Jan. 1967, 1, 7, 23. *Home Goods Retailing* addressed in Canada roughly the same market as *Electrical*

*Merchandising* in the United States. Domestic Appliances—Canadian Manufacturing + Imports-Exports for 1965 and 1966, RG 20 1755 8001–404/34, NAC.

7.  There is a fine discussion of this issue in Wajcman, *Feminism Confronts Technology*, ch. 4.

8.  'Are We "Selling" the Company to the Consumer?', *Industrial Canada* (July 1958): 140.

9.  Peter J. McClure and John K. Ryans Jr, 'Differences between Retailers' and Consumers' Perceptions', *Journal of Marketing Research* (Feb. 1968): 35–40; the discussion of retailers' understandings of consumer valuation of automatic washers is on pp. 36–7.

10. For example, see the discussion of product engineering in a 1980 Spanish washing machine firm in M. Carme Alemany Gomez, 'Bodies, Machines and Male Power', in Cynthia Cockburn and Ruza Furst Dilic, eds, *Bringing Technology Home: Gender and Technology in a Changing Europe* (Buckingham, 1994), 132–3.

11. Christine Zmroczek, 'Dirty Linen: Women, Class and Washing Machines, 1920s–1960s', *Women's Studies International Forum* 15 (1992): 183.

12. Wajcman, *Feminism Confronts Technology*, 102.

13. In 1993 and 1994, through columns in Victoria and Vancouver, British Columbia, newspapers I recruited 23 women, married between 1945 and 1955, to interview about the furniture and equipment they used in their homes up until 1968. These columns were picked up by national news services, and I received additional letters from across the country in response. All interviews were tape-recorded and then transcribed. The interview transcripts and letters will be deposited in the Simon Fraser University Archives, Burnaby, British Columbia. Lily Hansen (pseud.), interview by author, New Westminster, BC, 25 May 1994; Tina Wall (pseud.), interview by author, Victoria, BC, 16 June 1994; Martha Watson, Alma, Ont., letter to the author, 24 July 1993; Irene Newlands, Surrey, BC, letter to the author, 12 Oct. 1993.

14. Allison Simpson, interview by author, Delta, BC, 18 May 1994; Joan Coffey, interview by author, Coquitlam, BC, 17 May 1994; Mary Paine

(pseud.), interview by author, Delta, BC, 17 May 1994; Patricia Cliff, interview by author, Victoria, BC, 16 June 1994; Marjorie Barlow, interview by Margaret-Anne Knowles, North Vancouver, BC, 3 Mar. 1994; Lynn Stevens, interview by author, Langley, BC, 26 May 1994; Nettie Murphy, interview by author, Mission, BC, 24 Nov. 1994; Gerry Kilby, interview by Margaret-Anne Knowles, Vancouver, BC, 1 Feb. 1994; 'Better Care Longer Wear', *Canadian Homes and Gardens* (Oct. 1950): 68–9; Jane Monteith, 'Planning a Laundry for Today and Tomorrow', *Chatelaine* (Feb. 1949): 37.

15. Simpson, interview.

16. Ruth Schwartz Cowan, 'The Consumption Junction: A Proposal for Research Strategies in the Sociology of Technology', in Wiebe K. Bijker, Trevor Pinch, and Thomas P. Hughes, eds, *The Social Construction of Technological Systems: New Directions in Sociology and the History of Technology* (Cambridge, Mass., 1987), 263, 278.

17. 'Change Washday into Playday! The New Easy', *Canadian Homes and Gardens* (*CHG*) (Nov. 1956): 45; 'Now the New Beatty Washer Saves You', *CHG* (June 1952): 34; 'Bendix Introduces '53 Line', *Marketing* (Jan. 1953): 1; 1958 ad for automatic washer showing mother with toddler in high chair, washer behind them and cover line, 'Less time for your laundry, more time for your family', Live Better Electrically file 570, Ontario Hydro Archives.

18. Marie Holmes, 'Look What's Happening to Washday', *Chatelaine* (May 1953): 78; Strasser, *Never Done*, 268.

19. Ads for automatic washers 1959 and 1960, Live Better Electrically file 570.1, Ontario Hydro Archives. The advantages Australian women found in daily laundry are described by Kereen Reiger, 'At Home with Technology', *Arena* 75 (1986): 115–16, 117–18.

20. '"Twins for Twins" Promotion', *Marketing*, 21 Feb. 1953, 1; 'Practical and Emotional Appeals Feature This Consumer "Contest"', *Marketing*, 21 Mar. 1953, 2; 'Laundry Dealership Told "Babies Mean Business"', *Marketing*, 5 Sept. 1958, 46.

21. Marshall McLuhan ponders this conflation in *The Mechanical Bride: Folklore of Industrial Man* (New

York, 1951). Dianne Newell pointed out to me this aspect of these essays, particularly apparent in McLuhan's choice of illustrations; see similarly, Richard Sennett, *The Fall of Public Man* (New York, 1974), 20; Mariana Valverde, 'Representing Childhood: The Multiple Fathers of the Dionne Quintuplettes', in Carol Smart, *Regulating Women* (New York, 1992), 119–46; special Dionne issue of *Journal of Canadian Studies* (Winter 1994–5).

22. 1959 automatic washer ad, Living Better Electrically 570.1, Ontario Hydro Archives; 'Buy a Washer, Save a Wife: Promotion Soaps Up Husbands', *Marketing*, 11 July 1958, 30; 'After the Wedding, a Washer Inglis Ad Aimed at Husbands', *Marketing*, 3 Apr. 1959, 6. The latter campaign ran in both *Maclean's* and *La Patrie*. The *Marketing* stories describe the advertising campaign and the advertiser's rationale for its design.

23. For a discussion of the different ways in which manufacturers using mass and batch production methods feature and attend to consumers, see Philip Scranton, 'Manufacturing Diversity: Production Systems, Markets, and an American Consumer Society, 1870–1930', *Technology and Culture* 35 (1994): 476–505.

24. McLuhan, *Mechanical Bride*, 32, 33; William Christian, *George Grant* (Toronto, 1993), 177, 250. Grant's best-known writings are *Lament for a Nation: The Defeat of Canadian Nationalism* (Princeton, NJ, 1965) and *Technology and Empire: Perspectives on North America* (Toronto, 1969).

25. Shortliffe, interview; Ann Brook, interview by author, Abbotsford, BC, 24 Nov. 1994; Susan Taylor (pseud.), interview by author, Victoria, BC, 10 May 1994; Joan Niblock, interview by author, Langley, BC, 25 May 1994; Bev Newmarch, Calgary, Alberta, letter to author, 6 Sept. 1993.

26. Olive L. Kozicky, Calgary, Alberta, letter to author, 14 Sept. 1993; Newmarch, letter to author; Elizabeth Perry, Calgary, Alberta, letter to author, 12 Sept. 1993.

27. Shortliffe, interview; Edwards, interview; Liz Forbes, Duncan, BC, letter to author, Nov. 1993.

28. 'Laundry's No Problem', *CHG* (Oct. 1950): 91; 'How to Choose Your Next Big Appliance',

*Chatelaine* (Nov. 1956): 22; Canadian General Electric, EFIR, 9 June 1965, RG 20 765 23–100 C27, NAC; Tanis Day, 'Substituting Capital for Labour in the Home: The Diffusion of Household Technology', Ph.D. dissertation (Queen's University, 1987), 185. The 1966 prices cited from Day are in 1971 dollars.

29. Jean Mann Due, 'Consumption Levels in Canada and the United States, 1947–50', *Canadian Journal of Economics and Political Science* 21 (May 1955): 174–81.

30. Department of Finance, 'Control of Consumer Credit, PC 1249', 13 Mar. 1951, RG 19 E2C, vol. 32, NAC.

31. The least spent for refrigerators was $342, the most $353; for stoves the range was between $205 and $219, both narrower differences on larger sums than the $35 gap for washers. 'Purchasing of Furniture, Household Appliances and Home Furnishings—Toronto—By Age Groups, 1949–50–51 and 32 weeks of 1952', Market Research 1953–60 S69, v. 25, T. Eaton Company, Archives of Ontario.

32. 'Purchasing of home furnishings and appliances by new home owners', Controller's Office, 2 Sept. 1958, series 165, box 2, file 5.1, T. Eaton Company, Archives of Ontario.

33. Pam McKeen, interview by author, Victoria, BC, 15 June 1995; Niblock, interview; Coffey, interview; Gerd Evans, interview by Margaret-Anne Knowles, Burnaby, BC, 6 Apr. 1994; Mrs A.B. Botham, Ganges, BC, letter to author, 16 Oct. 1993; Hazel Beech, Lake Cowichan, BC, letter to author, 22 July 1993.

34. This seems to have been the case for Ontario in the 1950s. See Nora Cebotarev, 'From Domesticity to the Public Sphere: Farm Women, 1945–86', in Joy Parr, ed., *A Diversity of Women: Ontario 1945-80* (Toronto, 1995), 203, 207. In Quebec, aspiration for domestic comfort took greater precedence; Yves Tremblay, 'Equiper la maison de ferme ou la ferme, le choix des femmes québécoises, 1930–1960', *Bulletin de l'histoire de l'électricité* 19–20 (1992): 235–48.

35. Katherine Jellison, *Entitled to Power: Farm Women*

*and Technology, 1913–63* (Chapel Hill, NC, 1993), 109; Corlann Gee Bush, '"He Isn't Half So Cranky As He Used To Be": Agricultural Mechanization, Comparable Worth, and the Changing Farm Family', in Carol Groneman and Mary Beth Norton, eds, *'To Toil the Livelong Day': America's Women at Work, 1780–1980* (Ithaca, NY, 1987), 228.

36. 'Report of Findings Concerning Consumer Information; Crafts and Hobbies; Housing (The Farm Home)', Progress Report #7, 'Special Study of Ontario Farm Homes and Homemakers 1959', 11, 12, 28, AOS6076, Helen Abell Papers, University of Guelph Archives.

37. J.K. Edmonds, 'Keep a Sales Eye on the Farmer's Wife', *Marketing*, 24 May 1957, 28.

38. Ibid. Proportion of automatic washing machines among electric washing machines in Quebec homes (%): 1960 (13); 1961 (15.6); 1962 (18.4); 1963 (21.6); 1964 (25.4); 1965 (28.3); 1966 (32.7); 1967 (38.8); Dominion Bureau of Statistics, *Household Facilities and Equipment* (Ottawa, 1960–7). Jellison, *Entitled to Power*, 180, 185.

39. 'The Working Wife—Appliances Target', *Marketing*, 24 Dec. 1958, 8; J.K. Edmonds, 'An Expanding Durable Goods Market: Aim Ad Pitch to Working Wife', *Marketing*, 28 Oct. 1960, 42; Lee Maguire, 'Canadian Consumer Buying Intentions: A Study of Provincial and Socioeconomic Differences', Master's thesis (University of Windsor, 1967), 34. A copy of this thesis is in the University of Guelph Library.

40. Helen Abell and Frank Uhlir, 'Rural Young People and Their Future Plans, Opinion and Attitudes of Selected Rural Young People Concerning Farming and Rural Life in Alberta, Ontario and Quebec 1951–52', Canada, Department of Agriculture, 1953, in Helen Abell Collection, University of Guelph Archives.

41. Margaret McCready, 'Science in the Home' (typescript, Feb. 1946) and 'Whither Home Economics' (typescript, Nov. 1954), in Margaret McCready Collection, A013518 and 13519, University of Guelph Archives.

42. F.H. Leacy, *Historical Statistics of Canada*, 2nd edn (Ottawa, 1983), E49. Women who remembered the fifties as a time when they struggled to get by retrospectively often dated their own post-war prosperity from 1962.

43. In 1964, three-quarters of wringer sales were to households with incomes greater than $5,000; see G.D. Quirin, R.M. Sultan, and T.A. Wilson, 'The Canadian Appliance Industry', working paper, University of Toronto, Institute for Quantitative Research in Social and Economic Policy, 1970, 36, 77. Also in 1964, sales of wringer washers amounted to 203,000, while sales of automatics came to 162,900; 75.3 per cent of wringer sales were to replace wringers, 59.6 per cent of automatic sales were conversions from wringers. See 'Major Appliance Study, 1964 Study: 1964 sales by types of transactions', Major Appliance Study, RG 20, vol. 1755, P8001–4404/46, NAC.

44. Penny Sparke, *Electrical Appliances* (London, 1987), p. 6; Rosemary Pringle, 'Women and Consumer Capitalism', in Cora Baldock and Bettina Cass, eds, *Women, Social Welfare and the State in Australia* (Sydney, 1983), 100; Susan Strasser, *Satisfaction Guaranteed: The Making of the American Mass Market* (New York, 1989), 15; David Nye, *Electrifying America: Social Meanings of a New Technology, 1880–1940* (Cambridge, Mass., 1990), 281; John Fiske, *Reading the Popular* (Boston, 1989), 2.

45. Nye, *Electrifying America*, 281; Mihaly Csikszentmihalyi and Eugene Rochberg-Halton, *The Meaning of Things: Domestic Symbols and the Self* (Cambridge, 1981), 53.

46. The comment from Mrs Barr and another similar by Mrs G. F. Grady of Peterborough are in 'Housewives' Ideas for Better Washers', *CHG* (June 1955): 66; the filling system of the seven-rinse Inglis automatic is described in Mrs R.G. Morningstar, 'Survey of Time and Motion Studies for Household Equipment', Report 23, 1952, Canadian Association of Consumers, MG 28, 1 200, vol. 1, NAC; 'Look What's Happening to Washday', *Chatelaine* (May 1953): 79, 81; 'Today's Household Equipment', *Chatelaine* (Nov. 1951): 90; 'Buying Public Loves Laundry

"Automation"', *HGR*, 25 Mar. 1963, 18; 'Laundry Market Accelerating Fast in Canada', *HGR*, 7 Mar. 1966; Nye, *Electrifying America*, 303; Mrs Cindy Bolger, Ariss, Ontario, letter to author, 25 July 1993; Forbes, letter to author.

47. Suzette Worden, 'Powerful Women: Electricity in the Home, 1919–40', in Judy Attfield and Pat Kirkham, eds, *A View from the Interior: Feminism, Women and Design* (London, 1989), 140; Pringle, 'Women and Consumer Capitalism', 100–1.

48. T.A.B. Corley, *Domestic Electrical Appliances* (London, 1966), 136; Sigfried Giedion, *Mechanization Takes Command* (New York, 1948), 570; Mrs W.R. Walton, paper presented before CEMA, 1962, in *Proceedings 5th Annual Appliance Marketing Seminar* (n.p., Canadian Electrical Manufacturers Association, 17 May 1962), 16; Greta Nelson, interview by Margaret-Anne Knowles, Burnaby, BC, 5 Mar. 1994; Botham, letter to author; Newmarch, letter to author.

49. Perry, letter to author; for reactions to Canadian women's 'doubts and prejudices' about automatics, see Margaret Meadows, 'What To Look for When Buying an Automatic Washer', *Chatelaine* (May 1951): 84; 'Working Up Sales Lather—Market Was Made Sure It Was, Westinghouse', *Marketing*, 22 Feb. 1957, 7; 'Guarantees Washer for Twelve Years', *Marketing*, 28 Mar. 1958, 1; 'Consumer Attitude Survey—Fuels and Household Appliances', May 1961, British Columbia Electric Marketing Division, British Columbia Hydro Archives, 5, 39, 41; Bea Millar, interview by author, notes only, Vancouver, BC, 8 May 1996. . . .

50. Robert Frost, 'Machine Liberation: Inventing Housewives and Home Appliances in Interwar France', *French Historical Studies* 18 (1993): 128.

# 7

# Finding a Place for Father:
# Selling the Barbecue in Post-war Canada

Chris Dummitt

Daily household chores do not figure prominently in images of 1950s manliness. Domesticity enters our remembrance of men's lives at that time as an absence; a point of wry humour for women, sly humour for men. But post-war men and women did label some household tasks as masculine; this paper looks at one such task, outdoor cooking. Men were central to the image of barbecuing, which advertisers introduced into the Canadian market and backyard during the late 1940s and 1950s. In this new form of household cookery the chief steak griller was male.

What should we make of men and barbecuing? In an era known for its strict gender division of labour, men's barbecuing transgressed normative gender roles.[1] Typically, preparing the evening meal was considered part of a homemaker's responsibilities. Why, then, did women not become the spatula-toting barbecue chefs of popular imagination? Certainly male cooks were not unknown. The army cook and the gourmet chef are two possible precedents. But both World War Two and the Korean War had ended by the mid-1950s and the backyard barbecue was not often celebrated as *haute cuisine*. And although hunting and fishing were popular pastimes,

men's outdoor cooking in these areas need not have translated into their position as the family backyard cook. So why did men become the family barbecue chef? What made barbecuing different from other forms of post-war cookery?

In this paper, I argue that barbecuing's masculine status arose out of broader changes in both post-war gender relations and notions of fatherhood; namely, an increased expectation that fathers be more involved in family domestic life. Men occupied an ambiguous place in post-war Canada's renewed cult of domesticity. Being a distant breadwinner was no longer sufficient, but a gender division of labour which assumed fatherly absence for much of the day remained unchecked.[2] It is within this narrow cultural space, a search for an appropriately modern place for men in 1950s domestic life, that we should read the emergence of the male barbecue chef.

## Masculine Domesticity

Besides barbecuing, men were central participants in a wide assortment of family leisure activities in the 1940s and 1950s. Along with family outings, coaching youth sports, and hob-

Chris Dummitt, 'Finding a Place for Father: Selling Barbecue in Postwar Canada', *Journal of the Canadian Historical Association* 9 (1998): 209–23. Reprinted by permission of the Canadian Historical Association.

bies like model-train building, barbecuing was one of a variety of masculine endeavours amidst the relative cornucopia of post-war family leisure. The period's increased time for, and emphasis upon, leisure fit in with longer-term changes in ideologies of fatherhood. In these narratives, the 'new father' took more interest in matters of daily family life, including leisure-oriented child care and the psycho-sexual development of sons and daughters. Such developments did not represent a change in men's position as breadwinners, but expanded fatherhood's realm into new, more domestic, areas.[3]

In fact, the post-war father was not altogether 'new'. Increasingly, gender historians have been lured towards men's household activities, towards tantalizing and perplexing evidence of what Margaret Marsh has labelled 'masculine domesticity'. This historiographical movement follows the work of Catherine Hall and Leonore Davidoff. Their study of the early nineteenth-century English middle class, *Family Fortunes*, challenges the usefulness of a strict and literal reading of separate spheres ideology to convey the complexity of women's and men's lives. For our purposes, they point towards the interpenetration of public and private as relational categories. They urge us to inquire into the process whereby the public/private dichotomy is created. Americans Robert Griswold and Michael Kimmel follow up these insights in examining the place of domesticity in ideologies of fatherhood and masculinity, respectively. Both recognize that by treating breadwinning as the meta-narrative of fatherhood, we obscure the way fathers have been both public and private figures as well as the power relations that have worked to make this complex social position appear one-dimensional.[4]

Twentieth-century Canadian historians have similarly commented on the inadequacy of breadwinning discourses to wholly capture the history of fatherhood. Historians such as Suzanne Morton and Joy Parr note that men's domestic travails have often been labelled as 'help' to distinguish them from similar activities performed by women. To explain this linguistic posturing in the context of 1920s Halifax, Morton argues that 'there was no language available to recognize the male contribution to domestic production' so men's gardening, hunting, and alcohol manufacturing were said to be 'hobbies' or 'leisure activities'. Morton's and others attempts to understand the relationship between men's wage labour and domestic life are still tentative, certain that there is more to be told, uncertain how to proceed. As one gender historian notes, 'There is clearly something more to the family man than the imagery of economic man can comprehend, something more complicated governing his relations with the others in his household, both female and male, than his relation to the market alone can explain.'[5]

This paper attends to the 'something more' of the family man implicated in barbecuing's commercial speech. Cookbook writers, journalists, retailers, and advertisers packaged a particular image of domestic masculinity to sell along with the barbecue. But bringing men into domestic matters was not straightforward. Men's barbecuing raised eyebrows. Many agreed with the author of a 1955 *Maclean's* exposé on outdoor cooking who described the phenomenon as 'weird' and 'odd'.[6] Even so, sellers of barbecue culture prepared themselves for such doubters. They went to great lengths to convince Canadians that barbecuing was an acceptable masculine leisure pursuit. Barbecuing's commercial speech did not merely replicate a routine designation of some pre-existing masculine essence. The intensity of efforts to masculinize the barbecue belies the naturalness claimed for outdoor cooking's masculinity. Instead, barbecuing's commercial speech presented, to use Foucault's terms, a 'proliferation of discourse'—a veritable orgy of linguistic posturing that linked outdoor cooking to symbols of virile masculinity and manly leisure.[7]

But why did domesticity form such a crucial part of this image of the post-war masculine good life? And how did creators of barbecuing's commercial speech sell masculine domesticity to post-war Canadians? To ask such questions is not to equate commercial speech with daily life. Daily interaction and understanding do not flow unproblematically from ad copy. Yet, to examine how commercial speech envisioned the link between masculinity and domesticity is crucial. Although the promotions of commercial speech could be modified, this discourse formed the basis of post-war Canada's barbecue culture.[8]

## Making the Barbecue Masculine

The barbecue's entry into Canadian backyards followed a two-stage process. The federal government's 1947 *Emergency Exchange Conservation Act* restricted imports of domestic appliances and other allegedly 'luxury' consumer products, barbecues included. Accordingly, Canadians who wished to enjoy outdoor cooking in the late 1940s were largely limited to building their own permanent brick and cement barbecues. 'How to' articles in *Canadian Home and Gardens*, *Home Building*, and *Handy Man's Home Manual* provided substantial promotion of this fad. But although such articles boasted how easily the average family man could build such contraptions, it was not until import restrictions were lifted in the early 1950s that the cultural phenomenon of backyard cooking became firmly established in Canada.[9]

The extent of the move to outdoor cooking is difficult to discern. Unlike electric stoves, census takers and other statisticians of family commodities did not regularly track rates of barbecue ownership. Even if such records were gathered, they may not have included home-built barbecues or the use made of picnic sites and campground firepits. Despite these limitations, we can uncover the barbecue's cultural significance in other areas. Retailers and manufacturers, for example, regularly reported boom sales. An Ontario home barbecue building company reported in 1955 that 'for every barbecue [we] built ten years ago, [we] build a hundred

today.'[10] Cookbooks added new sections on 'Outdoor Cookery' and 'Outdoor Meals' to their regular list of chapters. In 1959, Sears made grilling central to its advertising strategy, devoting the cover of its summer catalogue to the barbecue.[11] It is safe to say that by the late 1950s barbecuing's commercial speech had grilled its way onto the Canadian consciousness.

Journalists, advertisers, and cookbook writers set priorities for certain aspects of barbecuing. In particular, sellers of barbecue culture found its location outside the home to be significant. *Maclean's* writer, Thomas Walsh, suggested a genetic link between masculinity and the outdoors as the reason for men's proclivity to pick up the barbecue tongs. He noted that, 'one theory for the increasing number of male cooks is simply that barbecuing is done outdoors, which is man's natural domain. It's the same inherited impulse that makes him take over at a corn roast.' Many advertisers backed up Walsh, consistently describing outdoor cooking, which primarily included meals served in the relatively domestic suburban backyard, as qualitatively distinct from cooking done inside the home.[12]

The barbecue was also potentially rustic and old-fashioned. The *Art of Barbecue and Outdoor Cooking* went out of its way to note that grilling was 'an age-old method of preparing meat'. Others contrasted this 'age-old' process with the exigencies of modern life. Unlike cooking done by homemakers in a modem kitchen, barbecuing hearkened back to an earlier time. According to Tom Riley, author of *How to Build and Use Your Own Outdoor Kitchen*, 'It seems, along with a rocket soon to the moon, we want the goodness of a simple thing—the heartiness and friendliness of outdoor cooking.' For Riley, the bustle of modern life explained men's barbecuing:

> The time was when a fellow cooked a meal over an open fire just plain and simply because he had to. When he received a chance to eat elsewhere, any kind of chance, he dropped everything and ran—his one fear he might be late. But the world

does change. In these hurried days of supersonic aircraft and pushbutton kitchens, amidst the myriad of marvelous things we possess, the same fellow has no desire to hurry out to dinner alongside the superhighway. Instead, he is tantalized by the idea of donning a chef's cap and leisurely barbecuing a sizzling supper in the backyard.

In this vein, the barbecue represented a brief respite from modern life and, presumably, modern gender roles as well.[13]

Those who sought out historical precedent for men cooking over fire took the imagined nature of barbecuing's rustic lineage to its furthest extremes. Cookbook writers with an eye on the past found no paucity of historical barbecue chefs. The *Canadian Cook Book* credited the cave man for this 'very popular form of cookery'. Then, the culinary expert turned historian went on to trace a more recent, though still distant, ancestry: 'Some of the most efficient barbecues can still be seen in the remains of medieval castles where great spits held suckling pigs, fowl, and all forms of succulent meats over coals of enormous hearths.' Moving south and east, the origins of the shish kebab received similar treatment. *The Art of Barbecue and Outdoor Cooking* told its readers that 'Long, long ago Armenian soldiers and migrating mountain folk speared pieces of wild game or lamb on their swords and roasted it over a roaring camp fire. This they called "shish kebob" meaning skewered pieces of meat.' With a slight geographical twist, another writer claimed the shish kebob was 'a Turkish term for roasting food over a fire on the point of a sword'. What had changed since the ancient Turks and Armenians? 'Today, metal skewers replace swords. And, many more foods such as fish, vegetables and even fruits are skewered to add interest to the menu.' Lest North Americans feel left out of barbecue history, Tom Riley asserted that 'the American Indian of the east coast was doing a fair job with a spit long before Columbus.' Later, Riley brought many of these themes together. 'Luckily for our times,' he mused,

there were some blessed persons throughout the ages of outdoor cooking who took an interest in their campfires. They experimented. The native who first roasted on a spit, his friend who tried a pit. The Chinese epicurean who first basted a fowl in a low chimney, the fellow who first broiled over charcoal, the soldier who stuck a combination of meat and vegetables on his sword for the first shishkebab—slowly throughout the ages they found the rudiments of good barbecuing.[14]

To recall barbecuing's ancient lineage in this way became part of the genre of writing on outdoor cooking. These were not serious attempts to historicize the barbecue. Instead, journalists and cookbook writers made sense of men's outdoor cooking by invoking its history in terms redolent of muscular and military manhood.

Meat was key to such invocations. Throughout the 1950s almost no visual image of a barbecue was complete without the requisite steak, hamburger, or pork chop. Journalists' and cookbook writers' language complemented the visual imagery, suggesting hot dogs, hamburgers, deluxe steaks, individual steaks, and chops as the ideal grilling foods. One cookbook established a hierarchy of food to be served at a barbecue, with meat at the top: 'Usually when a complete meal is being served outdoors, it is the meat course that is barbecued, perhaps with one or more vegetables. When serving a crowd, unless the barbecue is equipped with a spit, it is often impossible to accommodate more than the meat over the fire box.' In this listing, vegetables could be accommodated but only if there was room.[15]

For obvious reasons, Canada Packers sought to strengthen the association between meat and barbecuing. In the summer of 1955, the company offered a free portable brazier to consumers who purchased a specified amount of their canned meat products, including beef stew, bologna, beans with wieners, and Klik pork luncheon meat. In the image accompanying the offer, a smiling apron-clad man serves a Fred-Flinstone-size steak to an appreciative female onlooker, suggesting that Canada Packers could continue its service to the virile, meat-hungry new barbecue owner. Similarly, the cover of Canadian Tire's 1961 summer catalogue unabashedly connected red meat with manly virility. Throughout the 1950s and into the 1960s, Canadian Tire catalogue covers hosted a series of cartoons with the same stock characters and stock plots. Each centred on the efforts of a white, middle-aged man chasing after, and making sexual advances upon, a much younger, 'full-bodied' woman (usually blonde). In the barbecue rendition of this postwar misogynistic male fantasy, the older man serves a large T-bone steak to an admiring younger woman. Two 20-something-year-old men stare on incredulously, looking back and forth between the woman's succulent steak and the hot dogs they had received.[16] Through this overt symbolism, advertisers asserted a direct relationship between meat, barbecuing, and virile heterosexual masculinity.

Advertisers assured potential owners that the physical structure of the barbecue was just as masculine as the meat it was designed to grill. The 'tough' descriptions of barbecue advertisements are noteworthy for their mere repetitiveness. 'Heavy steel', 'sturdy steel', and 'heavy-gauge steel' were the descriptors of choice. An advertisement for Eaton's Spring/ Summer Catalogue provides a representative flavour: 'Top . . . is made of heavy-gauge aluminum to be completely rust proof. Firebox is a durable stainless steel. Grill, spit and supporting uprights are steel finished in gleaming nickel plate. Legs and wheels are of braced steel in baked-on enamel finish with cross braces.'[17] Eaton's promised prospective buyers that this was a sturdy contraption that would hold up under extreme conditions. The type of steel with which a barbecue was constructed was undoubtedly important in determining both its effectiveness and its longevity. But advertisers' rhetoric of strength and durability sought to reassure consumers about more than the equipment's functionality. Eaton's 1954 spring/summer catalogue

boasted that a 'light weight' barbecue, ideal for trips away from home, was still capable of a 'man's sized job of outdoor cooking'.[18]

Advertisers went on to gender the movement of the barbecue's 'heavy' and 'sturdy' parts. Unlike advertisements for the modern electric stove, barbecuing's commercial speech did not describe their product's machine-like functions in easy-to-understand language. Instead, with barbecues, a 'crank mechanism' worked to adjust heat control by raising and lowering the 'extra heavy grid'.[19] Unlike the celebrated easy, modern dials on the electric stove, the barbecue worked with 'cranks'. Sociologist Susan Ormrod found a similar tactic at work in the gendering of technical commodities in 1980s Britain. Jargon-filled language prevailed with allegedly masculine items, while advertisers employed comprehensible and non-expert language to describe products deemed feminine.[20] In our case, barbecuing's pseudo-industrial language differentiated it from stoves and other 'feminine' cooking appliances in the home.

These linguistic devices were also used for barbecue utensils. Such items were often labelled 'tools'. An advertisement accompanying a Canadian Home and Gardens article on barbecue culture listed, 'five members of a gadget set, namely large fork, soup ladle, flapjack flipper, vegetable spoon, spoon for odd jobs. . . . The last item is a real old-fashioned butcher knife for carving steaks. . . .'[21] This description boasts a number of gender assumptions. First, the advertisement labelled the group a 'gadget set' despite the fact that all of its objects were relatively common household items. As well, the butcher knife's 'old-fashioned' status conveyed the image of barbecuing's rusticity. In this way, advertisements inserted a cultural mélange of masculine symbols into the language of barbecuing, they distinguished between a butcher knife used to carve a grilled T-bone from a butcher knife used to carve an oven-broiled T-bone.

Cookbook writers extended these distinctions to include the barbecue cook's clothing.

Advertisements often depicted men clad in apron, chef's hat, and, sometimes, heat-protecting mitts. The inclusion of the chef's hat cast allusions to another acceptable male cook, the fine-dining chef. In fact, writers often used this title in tandem with images of men in the customary duck hat or toque. The *Canadian Cook Book* highlighted protective needs to further distinguish barbecue dress from apparently similar items worn by housewives. It warned that, due to the dangers of cooking over fire, barbecue apparel should consist of 'a large, heavy, non-frilly apron and thick oven mitts'. Such warnings did not normally accompany other sections of the cookbook.[22] Finally, advertisements presented barbecue attire as humorous. Lest readers miss the comical association, manufacturers emblazoned sayings such as 'call me cookie', 'hotdog', or 'wot'll it be' on aprons as a reminder. Sears summed up the appropriate barbecue costume in its 1959 summer catalogue; beside a tiny picture of barbecue garb, the description read, 'Asbestos palm mitts, white duck hat, apron. Humorous.'[23]

Commercial speech presented humour, especially self-deprecating humour, as central to barbecue culture. Irony was the tool of choice. Articles on outdoor cooking overflowed with images of men beaming proud smiles one moment and dousing a raging fire the next. Journalist James Bannerman openly admitted his own incompetence:

> All I know about barbecuing could be tattooed in large letters on the south end of a thick gnat [Barbecuing] sounds easy and I don't doubt it would be to a person of normal intelligence. It so happens, however, that I am not a person of normal intelligence and for a while it looked as if I was never going to get anything more out of my barbecue than the odd puff of pallid smoke.[24]

In taking on this humorous tone, Bannerman fit his work into a wider genre of writing on masculine domesticity in post-war Canada. The image of the hapless father recurred in a variety of 1940s and 1950s media. This genre portrayed men as more than adequate breadwinners but ridiculed their status in the home. For example, in a 1952 *Maclean's* article, 'Timetable of a Father Looking After the Children', a fictitious mother leaves home at 7:25 for a meeting on child guidance, instructing her husband to put the two children to bed 20 minutes later at 7:45. A carnivalesque evening ensues in which hapless dad is stripped of all dignity in a blatantly incompetent, though energetic, attempt to put his children to bed. The kids, the woman next door, and, presumably, the reader, mock father's feeble efforts to assert control in domestic matters. Yet, ultimately, this ritualized mocking did not challenge men's position in the family. Instead, it reasserted that men's 'true' position, the position in which they were not mocked, lay outside the home.[25] By treating men's barbecuing as a joking matter, barbecuing's commercial speech appealed to this wider discourse that linked domestic incompetence with normal masculinity.

## Barbecuing and Post-war Leisure

In order to sell barbecues and barbecue products, advertisers enticed men to try barbecuing because of the enjoyment they would receive. Despite the fact that men would be cooking a meal, something considered work for women, barbecuing's commercial speech maintained that grilling steaks was 'fun'. The language was repetitive: 'Enjoy Outdoor Living', 'It's fun to cook and eat on the patio', 'Outdoor meals can provide enjoyment and good eating. . . .'[26] Yet, in claiming the barbecue as 'fun' entertainment, advertisers employed a gendered strategy to neatly situate the barbecue within post-war family leisure. They incessantly sought to enlarge what could be a very fine distinction between leisure and work in barbecuing.

A number of journalists suggested that barbecuing required an altered, more relaxed, dining etiquette. For one commentator, to eat a meal '"picnic style" included a consideration of all the elements of informality plus a change of atmosphere and even a different type of menu.' Writing in the Halifax *Chronicle-Herald*, Steven Ellingston agreed that the 'relaxed, camp-out, carefree attitude' was key. According to yet another journalist, 'The barbecue has added its weight to the general breakdown of formality in the home, which [has] daily become more functional and less formal. . . . People who a generation ago wouldn't have eaten in their shirt sleeves are now sitting around barbecues in shorts, bathing suits, pedal pushers and blue jeans.' Not all appreciated the new barbecue dining style. *Canadian Home and Gardens* food columnist, Frederick Manning, criticized barbecuing's effect on social mores. 'If it's all the same to you,' he appealed to readers in August 1948, 'I'll cook mine in the kitchen and carry it out, wind and weather permitting, but only if the dining room is knee deep in a paper and painting job. After all, what is wrong with a dining table in summer anyway?'[27] By making dinnertime into leisure-time, barbecuing upset traditionalists like Manning and established its gendered distinctiveness.

To further differentiate barbecuing from the more mundane forms of cookery, journalists and advertisers maintained that the family barbecue was an 'event'; a special, and irregular, occurrence. Advertisers envisioned and promoted a family eating schedule supplemented by occasional bouts of male interest and involvement. For example, in 1958, Simpson's told wives of prospective barbecue cooks that the barbecue appliances they advertised were 'for his outdoor cooking *sprees*'.[28] Others presented the barbecue as an ideal way to entertain guests or celebrate a family outing. The 1957 promotional film, *Barbecue Impromptu*, celebrated the wonders of stainless steel through the fictional occasion of a couple preparing a barbecue dinner party for the husband's business associates. In this simulation, the dinner provided a direct link between the man's public business life and his private home

life. Both husband and wife shared the responsibilities for preparing the meal for the guests. While the husband greeted his guests and operated the barbecue itself, his wife prepared most of the meal.[29] Whether celebrated as a dinner party or a family meal, commercial speech highlighted the specialness of men taking part in meal preparation at a barbecue.

This part-time co-operative spirit exemplified idealized notions of post-war gender relations. A *Canadian Home and Gardens* article suggested Sunday morning as a time to 'gather the home circle around [the barbecue] and have brunch. . . . Somebody can make coffee while dad flips the flapjacks, scrambles the eggs, or grills the bacon and the youngsters take over fixing the table or distracting the pup from too close attention.' Another writer claimed that the 'ideal picnic will be turned into a "family game" if everyone has particular duties and responsibilities. Dad is responsible for the fire and icing of the beverages and perishables: the girls help mom with the food and the young man takes care of the game equipment, bats and balls, portable radio, playing cards and perhaps the paper plates, cups and silverware.' In these scenarios, the barbecue meant more than just the father fixing the fire, it represented collective effort and collective enjoyment. The change in the sex of the cook was, therefore, only one part of a wider narrative of changing values and mores.[30]

As part of this collectivist and informal narrative, advertisers and cookbook writers cast the barbecue chef's responsibilities in a language of sly humour. One cartoon depicted an apron-clad barbecue chef taking care of the after-dinner cleanup by spraying water from a garden hose onto dishes piled up in a children's plastic pool. Thomas Walsh's description of what men did to prepare a meal on the barbecue reflected a similar lackadaisical attitude: 'A man who ten years ago did nothing about supper but sniff under the saucepan lids and who wouldn't dream of setting a table, today doesn't mind building a fire and putting some meat on it.' Walsh played on the assumption that not many men would mind the not-so-arduous task of 'building a fire and putting some meat on it.' Here the discourse on leisure made a double movement; barbecuing was leisure for men but work for women. Walsh went on to quote a suburban housewife on her husband's new-found love of barbecuing:

> My husband takes care of all our barbecue meals. He comes home and starts right in. 'Get me the garlic salt. Hand me the tongs. Get me the fork. Hand me a bay leaf. Put some more charcoal on the fire. Bring the plates over here.' Holy cow! There's more to cooking than holding a couple of pork chops over the fire.[31]

The truncated cooking responsibilities suggested here made barbecuing truly appear, as the advertisements boasted, 'easy'.

## Conclusions

Barbecuing's commercial speech was a prescriptive discourse. We should not expect it to offer realistic descriptions of daily life. And when cookbooks and popular magazines described barbecue culture, it appeared as a uniformly white, middle-class, and heterosexual phenomenon. The visual imagery, especially in high-end publications like *Canadian Home and Gardens*, presented idealized nuclear families in middle-class suburban backyards as the norm. In this way, barbecuing's commercial speech was part of a larger middle-class advertising discourse that offered up a homogenized world of post-war abundance.

We can see that not all participants in barbecue culture accepted unproblematically the rhetorical flourishes of its commercial speech. Certainly, *Maclean's* satirist Robert Allen disputed the benefits of barbecuing as relaxing leisure. In a brief moment of seriousness, Allen decried leisure that focused on 'doing': 'If we're going to keep shortening the work week,' he argued in *Maclean's* in 1957, 'we should start realizing that we can't fill up the other end with hobbies. . . .

Relaxation is a lot like happiness: the harder we chase it, the farther it moves away.'[32] For Allen, barbecuing and other masculine hobbies required too much hustle.

At the same time, Allen still dismissed the significance of the new post-war domestic leisure; he argued that barbecuing was not leisure, but neither did it equal men's real work. Allen's dismissal of barbecuing's significance may lead historians to do the same, to treat the barbecue as an insignificant aside to 1950s masculinity. Certainly, other household items such as cars, lawnmowers, and fix-it tools appear to have been more pivotal in men's lives. But a close reading of barbecuing's commercial speech militates against such an interpretation. The barbecue's insignificance, its status as a humorous sidebar to the 'real' story of men's breadwinning obligations, did not stem automatically from its material conditions. To read the barbecue as an inconsequential aberration is to accept the myth of barbecuing sold by cookbook writers, journalists, and advertisers.

Alternatively, we can read in barbecuing's commercial speech a proliferation of discourse on the subject of masculinity and domesticity in 1950s Canada, not, as popular lore might hold, an absence of such discourse. Taking our cue from Foucault's insights into the fascination behind Victorian sexual repression, we can see that the incitement to speak of barbecuing as humorous and insignificant formed a discourse of disavowal and repudiation. The sellers of barbecue culture were incessantly concerned about domesticity. Advertisements and cartoons may have been lighthearted, but they were also earnest. The creators of barbecuing's commercial speech sought to assuage any anxiety caused by the transgression inherent to barbecue culture by enfolding it in a masculine discourse of dismissal.

What does the existence of this discourse suggest about gender relations in the 1950s? How do we read such refusals? First, our uncovering of the intensity of barbecuing's commercial speech fits into an emerging revisionist history of the 1950s.[33] Here, we find the gendered insecurities of the decade. Where would men fit into the post-war era's domestic life? How could men's changing place in the family be reconciled with normative ideals? Far from being a period of static gender relations, barbecuing's commercial speech demonstrates that cultural negotiation and conflict underlay the decade's social life. We like to remember this period as a time of placid tranquility but contemporaries more often described a world of rapid change.

Barbecuing's commercial speech points out the direction of some of these changes. The Victorian division between public and private, however tenuous and artificial, had supported cultural divisions between masculine and feminine. But as suffragists, women war workers, and others assailed this cultural construct, and the ideology of gender relations it supported, individuals looked elsewhere to shore up their belief in the naturalness of gender difference. If the division between public and private had eroded, what replaced it? Can we view men's involvement in domestic matters as one small step in a progressive evolution? Should we replace the previous history of post-war gender relations that characterized the period as a step backward with a new history emphasizing slow but steady advancement? Our exploration of gender and barbecuing again points in a different direction. Gender hierarchies based on the division between public and private had faltered but new dichotomies took their place. New gendered divisions between leisure and work redefined and rearticulated older divisions between public and private and masculine and feminine. Ultimately, the story of barbecuing and post-war gender relations is not a tale of simple progression or descent, but a complex narrative of cultural change.

## Notes

For both constructive criticism and support during the time I spent revising this article, I thank Joy Parr, Jack Lillie, and Karen Ferguson as well as the audiences at the annual meeting of the Canadian Historical Association and at Simon Fraser University's Border Crossings series. I especially thank my former advisor, Shirley Tillotson, for her commitment and even-handed guidance during my time at Dalhousie and since.

1. On gender relations in the immediate post-war decades, see Mary Louise Adams, *The Trouble with Normal: Postwar Youth and the Making of Heterosexuality* (Toronto, 1997); Doug Owram, *Born at the Right Time: A History of the Baby Boom Generation* (Toronto, 1996); Veronica Strong-Boag, 'Home Dreams: Women and the Suburban Experiment in Canada, 1945–1960', *Canadian Historical Review* 72, 4 (1991): 471–504; Strong-Boag, 'Canada's Wage-Earning Wives and the Construction of the Middle Class, 1945–1960', *Journal of Canadian Studies* 29, 3 (1994): 5–25; Mona Gleason, 'Disciplining Children, Disciplining Parents: The Nature and Meaning of Advice to Canadian Parents, 1945–1955', *Histoire Sociale/Social History* 29 (May 1996): 187–209. Useful counterpoints in the American literature include Elaine Tyler May, *Homeward Bound: American Families in the Cold War Era* (New York, 1988); Joanne Meyerowitz, ed., *Not June Cleaver: Women and Gender in Postwar America, 1945–1960* (Philadelphia, 1994).

2. On the place of fathers in post-war domestic life, see Robert Rutherdale, 'Fatherhood and Masculine Domesticity During the Baby Boom: Consumption and Leisure in Advertising and Life Stories', in Lori Chambers and Edgar André Montigny, eds, *Family Matters: Papers in Post-Confederation Canadian Family History* (Toronto, 1998), 309–33; Rutherdale, 'Fatherhood and the Social Construction of Memory: Breadwinning and Male Parenting on a Job Frontier, 1945–1966', in Joy Parr and Mark Rosenfeld, eds, *Gender and History and Canada* (Toronto, 1996), 357–75; Owram, *Born at the Right Time*.

3. There is some question as to whether notions of fatherhood that Robert Griswold has described for the United States as the 'new fatherhood' also developed in Canada before World War Two. On

the origins of the 'new fatherhood' in Canada, see Cynthia Comacchio, '"A Postscript for Father": Defining a New Fatherhood in Postwar Canada', *Canadian Historical Review* 78, 3 (Sept. 1997): 385–408. For studies which treat post-war parenting and fatherhood more generally see, Neil Sutherland, *Growing Up: Childhood in English Canada from the Great War to the Age of Television* (Toronto, 1997); Owram, *Born at the Right Time;* Mona Gleason, 'Psychology and the Construction of the "Normal" Family in Postwar Canada, 1945–1960', *Canadian Historical Review* 78, 3 (1997): 442–77; Gleason, 'Disciplining Children, Disciplining Parents'; Rutherdale, 'Fatherhood and the Social Construction of Memory'; Rutherdale, 'Fatherhood and Masculine Domesticity During the Baby Boom'; Katherine Arnup, *Education for Motherhood: Advice for Mothers in Twentieth-Century Canada* (Toronto, 1994); Strong-Boag, 'Home Dreams'.

4.  Margaret Marsh, 'Suburban Men and Masculine Domesticity, 1870–1915', *American Quarterly* 40 (June 1988): 165–86; Marsh, 'From Separation to Togetherness: The Social Construction of Domestic Space in American Suburbs, 1840–1915', *Journal of American History* 76 (Sept. 1989): 506–27; Leonore Davidoff and Catherine Hall, *Family Fortunes: Men and Women of the English Middle Class, 1780–1850* (Chicago, 1987); Robert Griswold, *Fatherhood in America: A History* (New York, 1993); Michael Kimmel, *Manhood in America: A Cultural History* (New York, 1996). Other important works that contribute to this literature include John Tosh, 'Domesticity and Manliness in the Victorian Middle Class: The Family of Edward White Benson', in Michael Roper and John Tosh, eds, *Manful Assertions: Masculinities in Britain Since 1800* (London and New York, 1991), 44–73; Nancy Cott, 'On Men's History and Women's History', in Mark Carnes and Clyde Griffen, eds, *Meanings for Manhood: Constructions of Masculinity in Victorian America* (Chicago, 1990); Linda Kerber, 'Separate Spheres, Female Worlds, Woman's Place: The Rhetoric of Women's History', *Journal of American History* 75, 1 (1988): 9–39.

5.  Joy Parr, *The Gender of Breadwinners: Women, Men, and Change in Two Industrial Towns, 1880–1950* (Toronto, 1990), 90–2, 191, 200; Suzanne Morton, *Ideal Surroundings: Domestic Life in a Working-Class Neighbourhood in the 1920s* (Toronto, 1995), 129.

6.  Thomas Walsh, 'How to Cook Without a Stove', *Maclean's* (9 July 1955).

7.  I borrow here from Foucault's insights into the 'repressive hypothesis' of Victorian sexuality. He argues that an excitable and interested 'incitement to discourse' lay behind Victorian prohibitions, warnings, and regulations on sexual matters. See Michel Foucault, *The History of Sexuality: An Introduction*, trans. Robert Hurley (New York, 1978). In the case of the barbecue, we can see that the elaborate rituals, language, and humour of barbecuing's commercial speech worked in a similar fashion. At the same time as this discourse refuted men's incorporation into feminine domesticity, the intensity of its refusal and the meanings of its privilege point both to the existence of men's domesticity and to a language that sought to make it masculine.

8.  In this paper, I examine barbecuing through what I refer to as 'commercial speech'. I include in this definition sources that might not otherwise be considered 'commercial'. My concern is with the manner by which the barbecue was sold as a cultural concept. Advertisements in catalogues and newspapers were one way the barbecue was sold. But cookbooks that added new sections on 'Outdoor Cooking' and journalists who expounded on the eccentricities of the new fad were also essential in the selling process. Together they presented potential buyers and casual onlookers with a language which, although it could be taken up, rejected, or distorted, nonetheless formed the initial framework through which barbecuing was understood.

9.  Joy Parr, 'Gender, Keynes, and Reconstruction', paper presented to the Department of History, Simon Fraser University, 1998; 'How to Build Your Own Barbecue', *Canadian Home and Gardens* (June 1948); 'The Barbecue Anyone Can Build',

*Canadian Home and Gardens* (May 1949); 'Barbecues for Outdoor Living', *Home Building* (June–July 1952); *Handyman's Home Manual* (New York, 1960).

10. 'Barbecue Grills Pace Housewares Sales Rise', *Weekly Retail Memo*, 27 June 1955; 'Food Chains Plan Big Outdoor Eating Promotions', *Weekly Retail Memo*, 4 June 1956; '"Outdoor Dining Room" to Spur Summer Food Sales', *Weekly Retail Memo*, 17 June 1957; Walsh, 'How to Cook Without a Stove'. Published by the *Vancouver Sun*, the *Weekly Retail Memo* was a digest of news from publications in the United States and Canada relevant to retailers who might wish to advertise in the paper.

11. Cookbooks which followed this trend include, *The Ogilvie Cook Book* (Toronto, 1957); Nellie Lyle Pattinson, *Canadian Cook Book*, revised by Helen Wattie and Elinor Donaldson (Toronto, 1961); Agnes Murphy, *The American Everyday Cookbook* (New York, 1955); *Dishes Men Like: New and Old Favorites. Easy to Prepare . . . Sure to Please* (New York, 1952). Although some of these works were published in the United States, all were in use in Canada during the period covered by this paper. All cookbooks referred to in this paper are held in the collections of the Halifax Public Library, the Vancouver Public Library, and in the personal collections of Lynda Laton, Tena Neufeld, and the author.

12. Walsh, 'How to Cook Without a Stove'; See also *Eaton's Summer Catalogue* (1960): 10–11; *Sears Spring and Summer Catalogue* (1959): 448; Halifax *Chronicle-Herald*, 15 June 1956, 14.

13. Tested Recipe Institute, *The Art of Barbecue and Outdoor Cooking* (New York, 1958), 22; Tom Riley, *How to Build and Use Your Own Outdoor Kitchen* (Chicago, 1953), 3–4. Seeming to contradict Riley's argument that families wanted to flee the superhighway at mealtime, Andrew Hurley has traced the transformation and growth of roadside diners into family restaurants in postwar America. See Andrew Hurley, 'From Hash House to Family Restaurant: The Transformation of the Diner and Post-World War II Consumer Culture', *Journal of American History* (Mar. 1997): 1282–1308.

14. *Canadian Cook Book*, 193; *The Art of Barbecue and Outdoor Cooking*, 86; Walsh, 'How to Cook Without a Stove,' 41; Riley, *How to Build and Use Your Own Outdoor Kitchen*, 4–5.

15. 'Let's Have a Picnic . . . and Make it a Success', Halifax *Chronicle-Herald*, 18 June 1954, 16; *Canadian Cook Book*; Halifax *Chronicle-Herald*, 7 June 1955, 7.

16. Halifax *Chronicle-Herald*, 7 June 1955, 7; *Canadian Tire Summer Catalogue* (1961).

17. *Eaton's Spring/Summer Catalogue* (1954): 548. For other examples, see *Sears Summer Catalogue* (1953): 35–6; *Eaton's Summer Catalogue* (1959): 187; Halifax *Chronicle-Herald*, 15 June 1956, 14; Halifax *Chronicle-Herald*, 19 June 1959, 14.

18. *Eaton's Spring/Summer Catalogue* (1954): 548.

19. *Eaton's Summer Catalogue* (1959): 187; *Eaton's Summer Catalogue* (1960): 10–11. Joy Parr explores the gendered tactics of electric range manufacturers and salesmen in Ontario between 1950 and 1955 in her 'Shopping for a Good Stove: A Parable About Gender, Design and the Market', in Parr, ed., *A Diversity of Women: Ontario. 1945–1980* (Toronto, 1995), 75–97.

20. Susan Ormrod, '"Let's Nuke the Dinner": Discursive Practices of Gender in the Creation of a Cooking Process', in Cynthia Cockburn and Ruza Furst Dilic, eds, *Bringing Technology Home: Gender and Technology in a Changing Europe* (Buckingham and Philadelphia, 1994), 42–58.

21. Advertisement accompanies Frederick Manning, 'Summer Eating and Some . . .', *Canadian Home and Gardens* (Aug. 1948).

22. Actually, the section on pressure cooking did give various warnings to housewives about how to avoid an explosion. However, unlike in the section on outdoor cookery, the authors do not suggest wearing protective clothing in case of such an explosion!

23. *Canadian Cook Book*; *Eaton's Summer Catalogue* (1959): 187; Halifax *Chronicle-Herald*, 15 June 1956, 14; Halifax *Chronicle-Herald*, 19 June 1959, 5; *Canadian Tire Summer Catalogue* (1961);

Walsh, 'How to Cook Without a Stove'; *Sears Summer Catalogue* (1959): 448.

24. James Bannerman, 'Me and My Barbecue: Adventures in barbecuing, past and present—a harrowing tale with a happy ending', *Canadian Home and Gardens* (May 1949). On a similar theme, see Robert Allen, 'But I *Don't Want* the New Leisure', *Maclean's* (23 Nov. 1957); Walsh, 'How to Cook Without a Stove'.

25. Barry Mather, 'Timetable of Father Looking After the Children', *Maclean's* (15 Jan. 1952). See also Robert Allen, 'How to Endure a Father', *Maclean's* (31 Jan. 1959); 'You Too Can be a Perfect Parent', *Maclean's* (15 Mar. 1951); 'How Children Remodel Their Parents', *Maclean's* (6 Aug. 1955); Victor Maxwell, 'So Daddy's a Dope!', *Maclean's* (15 June 1947).

26. *Eaton's Summer Catalogue* (1960): 10–11; *Canadian Tire Spring and Summer Catalogue* (1960): 104; *Canadian Cook Book*, v; *The Art of Barbecue and Outdoor Cooking*, 6; *Ogilvie Cook Book*, 219.

27. 'Let's Have a Picnic', Halifax *Chronicle-Herald*; Walsh, 'How to Cook Without a Stove', 43; Steve Ellingston, 'Barbecue Table, Benches Make Eating Out Easy', Halifax *Chronicle-Herald*, 14 June 1958, 11; Manning, 'Summer Eating and Some . . .'.

28. Halifax *Chronicle-Herald*, 14 June 1958, 18 [emphasis mine].

29. National Archives of Canada, ISN-25327, *Barbecue Impromptu*, International Nickel Co. of Canada, 1957. Others have commented upon the distinction between family men and single men both in business and in community affairs. See Parr, *Gender of Breadwinners*; Kimmel, *Manhood in America*; Griswold, *Fatherhood in America*.

30. 'Let's Have a Picnic', Halifax *Chronicle-Herald*; 'Every Meal's a Picnic . . . With a Barbecue!', *Canadian Home and Gardens* (May 1949). On the co-operative nature of barbecuing, see also Manning, 'Summer Eating and Some . . .'; *Canadian Cook Book*; *The Art of Barbecue and Outdoor Cooking*, 149; *How to Build and Use Your Own Outdoor Kitchen*, 12–13.

31. Walsh, 'How to Cook Without a Stove', 43.

32. Allen, 'But I *Don't Want* the New Leisure'.

33. The conservatism of the immediate post-war decades is a point of debate in many recent Canadian works. See Owram, *Born at the Right Time*; Jeff Keshen, 'Getting it Right the Second Time Around: The Reintegration of Canadian Veterans of World War II', in Peter Neary and J.L. Granatstein, eds, *The Veterans Charter and Post-World War II Canada* (Montreal and Kingston, 1998), 62–84; Keshen, 'Revisiting Canada's Civilian Women During World War II', *Histoire Sociale/Social History* 30, 60 (Nov. 1997): 239–66; Adams, *The Trouble With Normal*. In the United States, the debates around this revisionist approach are nicely gathered in Meyerowitz, ed., *Not June Cleaver*.

# 8

## Visualizing Home

The cult of domesticity that arose in the Victorian era (*c.* 1830–1900) produced a wide range of imagery about domestic space, a trend that certainly continues today. Presented here are three different forms of visual culture in which the ideals of home were cultivated: floor plans, photography, and advertisements. Of these three, it is perhaps easiest to acknowledge the subjectivity of advertisements, for they were intended to convince their audiences that they 'needed' to fill their homes with consumer goods. Yet, it is important that we do not privilege floor plans and photographs simply as objective images of domestic space-as-it-was.

As Annemarie Adams and James Opp explained, photographs and floor plans each played active roles in the societies that produced and used them. Indeed, it is hardly coincidental that the advertisements included here used both photographs and floor plans to sell their wares.

While we can 'read' these images to better appreciate how Canadians have historically ordered their domestic spaces, we learn even more from these images about the ideals of domestic space dominant in the period. Keep in mind, then, the content, the form, and the intended audience of these images.

## Series 1: Modernity and Domesticity

Architects designed buildings for both urban and rural Canada, but it was in the exploding cities of the late nineteenth and twentieth centuries where their work changed how public and private spaces were being built (but not necessarily used, as Chapter 5, by Denyse Baillargeon, shows). In doing so, architects were fundamental in constructing urban landscapes and, thus, the face of modern, industrial Canada.

Figures 1 and 2 are floor plans for a middle-class Victorian row house on Jarvis Street in Toronto. This architectural style was imported from Britain, and although rarely found in rural areas or small towns, row houses were common in many Canadian cities. Figure 3 is a photograph of a late-nineteenth-century, middle-class parlour. Interiors of the middle-class Victorian home, featuring a family in the parlour and almost always in front of a fireplace, were prominent in both paintings and photographs. These photographs were considered important markers of identity, both individual and familial. As treasured possessions, they were secured in family albums, framed and hung on walls, or sent to friends and family.

1.  In what ways does the floor plan depict an ideal, Victorian society with respect to gender and class? How is work in the home separated from play and family? What other separations can you see?
2.  Examine the floor plan and note which rooms are located closest to the street and which rooms are located at the back of the house. What is the significance of this distinction? Which rooms are privileged by this organization and why?
3.  What clues are there in the photograph and in the floor plans that the ideal Victorian home featured the parlour as the most important space for family time? Would the architect of the floor plan in Figures 1 and 2 have approved of the scene depicted in the photograph? Consider the setting, the arrangement of bodies, and the poses.

Figure 4 is a floor plan of a Kwakwaka'wakw (Kwakiutl) longhouse and Figure 5 is a photograph of a Kwakwaka'wakw village, both produced in the late nineteenth century. The photograph was taken in 1881 by Edward Dossetter, travelling through by ship. The floor plan was sketched by the anthropologist Franz Boas (1858–1942), who spent much of his professional life studying the First Nations of Canada's west coast and, like many of his fellow anthropologists, was very interested in Native domestic spaces. In the name of science, Boas used rigorous schematic plans, photographs, and material specimens to produce an 'objective' representation of everyday Kwakwaka'wakw life. However, the cultural context of nineteenth-century anthropology indelibly shaped these scientific views, as noted in Paige Raibmon's study (Chapter 2). Therefore, such sources require a careful reading, set against the cultural perspective of the fieldworker.

The legend and symbols on the floor plan are from the original, and the language in the legend is also that of Boas. When a term, such as 'middle forehead', is in quotation marks, this refers to Boas's translation of the Aboriginal term. When there are no quotation marks, such as around bedroom, this means it was Boas's term only and he did not provide the Kwakwaka'wakw term. Also, only the exterior lines on the plan represent walls. The other lines represent beams that were used to frame the longhouse as well as the embankments that were built around the interior to create a separate level in case of flooding.

4.  What would social reformers and missionaries approve and disapprove of in the ordering of domestic space in the longhouse (Figure 4) and the organization of the village (Figure 5)?
5.  How has Boas sought to 'prove' the cultural worth of the Kwakwaka'wakw? Why, for example, does his diagram suggest the presence of walls around the 'bedrooms'?
6.  Compare the arrangement of space in Figures 4 and 5 with that of the first three images and floor plans from urban Canada.

What are the similarities and differences in the organization? What accounts for these differences? How might Boas's reading of the Kwakw̲a̲k̲a'wakw interior space be shaped by an understanding of 'civilized' domesticity as embodied in Figures 1, 2, and 3?

## Series 2: Home and Consumption

The 1921 census was the first to show that as many Canadians were living in cities as in rural areas, and the gap between urban and rural populations only grew in subsequent decennial censuses. Becoming increasingly 'urban' carried with it a number of significant changes for the social history of Canada. For example, a market culture solidified itself even as Canada's economy underwent tremendous upheaval and a debilitating depression during the 1930s. Advertising became more systematic and scientific in its methods, seeking to promote and naturalize consumption as an act of everyday life as both need and pleasure. In both regards, women as consumers were of particular importance. Women's periodicals, such as the fashion magazine *Chatelaine* and the housekeeping magazine *Canadian Home Journal*, provided outlets for these advertisers while also providing advice and instruction for their readers. The following two images (Figures 6 and 7) are examples of how advertisers sought to navigate the urban market culture of the interwar years and speak to the variety of women consumers in this era of changing gender identities and experiences.

1. What does the Lux advertisement suggest about gender and power relations in the 1930s?
2. How does each advertisement lay claim to a 'modern' lifestyle for newlywed women? How do the advertisements appeal to gender roles to encourage consumption in the midst of the Great Depression?
3. Although both advertisements appeared in 1934, what elements in each suggest they were intended for different audiences?

## Series 3: Suburban Landscapes

The post-1945 era gave rise to a new era of suburban living. Empowered by the creation of new financing options, government programs, and a general boom in the economy, a generation who had lived through a massive depression and another world war enthusiastically made their way into the hundreds of thousands of new homes being built on the peripheries of Canada's major cities. As Chapters 6 and 7, by Joy Parr and Chris Dummit, emphasize, this era was defined in part by a return to 'normal' gender relations. Looking back at the turbulence of the Depression era and the upheavals of World War II, many felt that women's roles had strayed too far from the traditional Victorian ideals of home and family. Set against the backdrop of the Cold War, by the mid-1950s a suburban, nuclear family was celebrated as the epitome of the democratic West's superior way of living, a bulwark against the threat of communism. When examining each of these images, including a careful reading of the text in the advertisements, consider the following questions:

1. Examine the floor plans of Figures 8 and 9. What has been the most significant shift in domestic space compared to the Victorian period? What room(s) are located most centrally and would receive the most traffic?
2. How are these houses designed to fit a 'suburban' lifestyle? What are the expectations of the builders in relation to the people who might occupy these homes?
3. How do the advertisements in Figures 10 and 11 produce gendered assumptions regarding domestic space? How do they define or reinforce the proper social roles occupied by men and women?
4. Carefully examine the representations of children in the advertisements. How are the expectations for children gendered? What roles do children play in defining suburban spaces?

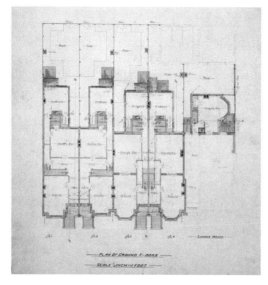

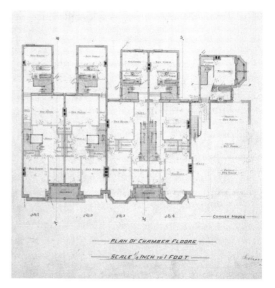

**Figure 1.** Design for dwelling house, Jarvis Street, Toronto, 1887, plan of ground floor, Mathew Sheard. Archives of Ontario, J.C.B. and E.C. Horwood Collection, C11–658–0–1 (628a)7. Also printed in Peter Ward, *A History of Domestic Space: Privacy and the Canadian Home* (Vancouver: University of British Columbia Press, 1999), 32.

**Figure 2.** Design for dwelling house, Jarvis Street, Toronto, 1887, plan of chamber floor, Mathew Sheard. Archives of Ontario, J.C.B. and E.C. Horwood Collection, C11–658–0–1 (628a)8. Also printed in Peter Ward, *A History of Domestic Space: Privacy and the Canadian Home* (Vancouver: University of British Columbia Press, 1999), 33.

**Figure 3.** Pitt family in parlour, Montreal, 1895, photographer unknown. Notman Photographic Archives, McCord Museum of Canadian History, Montreal. MP–0000.300.

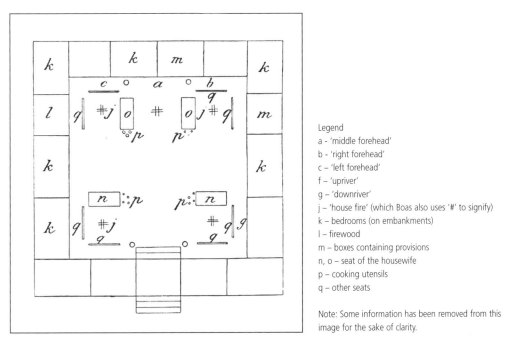

Legend
a - 'middle forehead'
b - 'right forehead'
c – 'left forehead'
f – 'upriver'
g – 'downriver'
j – 'house fire' (which Boas also uses '#' to signify)
k – bedrooms (on embankments)
l – firewood
m – boxes containing provisions
n, o – seat of the housewife
p – cooking utensils
q – other seats

Note: Some information has been removed from this image for the sake of clarity.

**Figure 4.** Plan of a Kwakiutl longhouse, from Franz Boas, *The Jesup North Pacific Expedition*, vol. V, part II (Leiden: E.J. Brill Ltd, 1909; reprint, AMS Press, 1975), 415.

**Figure 5.** Edward Dossetter, photograph of Humdaspe, Vancouver Island, 1881. Image 42298, courtesy the Library, American Museum of Natural History.

**Figure 6.** Advertisement for Lux (laundry soap), 'More Stocking Runs?—You'll Ruin me Babs', *Chatelaine*, Feb. 1934. Reprinted with kind permission of Unilever Archives. Lux is a trademark of Unilever.

*Photograph by "Jay"*

# Meet
# Mrs. Modern

She may be a young newly-wed as
pictured here; or she may be in her
30's or 40's. But it isn't her age that matters;
it's her outlook that counts. She is thoroughly
modern in the way she does things and buys things. She
is a member of CANADIAN HOME JOURNAL's "Cooking
Class", through which she obtains expert counsel in the culinary art and
which, incidentally, guides her in her purchases of nationally advertised food
products.

It is because of the practical way in which CANADIAN HOME JOURNAL deals with the
important subject of cooking, under the skillful direction of Katherine Caldwell that this
magazine leads all Canadian magazines to date this year (as in past years) with 51,387 lines
of food and food beverage advertising.

## CANADIAN HOME
### JOURNAL
*Canada's National Women's Magazine*

# 200,000 Net Paid A.B.C. Every Issue
### CONSOLIDATED PRESS LIMITED - TORONTO, CANADA

**Figure 7.** Advertisement for *Canadian Home Journal* (Consolidated Press, Ltd), 'Meet Mrs.
Modern', *Saturday Night*, 8 Sept. 1934. Reprinted with permission of Chatelaine.

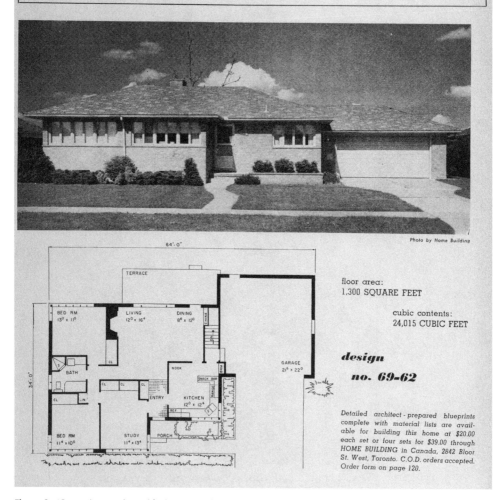

## CONVENIENCE-PLANNED
### *for lasting satisfaction*

THIS home is sure to be a favourite with SH readers for it meets just about every planning requirement of the average Canadian family. Attractively landscaped with well placed foundation shrubbery, the exterior combines bark face buff brick (veneer), brown-and-grey shaded roof, and very light mist green for trim and garage door.

The centre hall arrangement provides ex-cellent traffic circulation. While the room to the left of the entry hall is indicated in the sketch plan as a study, most families will of course use it as a third bedroom. The vanity-equipped bathroom is much above-average in size—boasts a separate shower in addition to the bath.

The 145 square foot kitchen is brought up to the front and comes complete with built-in snack bar, corner sink, broom closet and dining nook. Notice its excellent placement in relation to basement stairs and the garage. A full basement is provided. Plans give full details for all built-ins.

Photo by Home Building

floor area:
1,300 SQUARE FEET

cubic contents:
24,015 CUBIC FEET

*design*
**no. 69-62**

Detailed architect - prepared blueprints complete with material lists are available for building this home at $20.00 each set or four sets for $39.00 through HOME BUILDING in Canada, 2842 Bloor St. West, Toronto. C.O.D. orders accepted. Order form on page 120.

**Figure 8.** 'Convenience—Planned for lasting satisfaction', *Home Building in Canada: Small Homes,* 1960 edition (Toronto: Walkers Publishing, 1960), 100.

## J. E. HOARE, Architect

*Owner S. J. Reid of North Toronto, Ontario, is full of praise for this new ranch-style home. His only regret was that our picture was taken before a flagstone terrace had been added, and the landscaping completed!*

*We agree that the plan is particularly good, and the exterior most attractive. Outer walls are red brick, combined with white vertical boards. Roof is black. House was erected by H. A. Hoare, builder, and contains 25,600 cubic feet, without garage.*

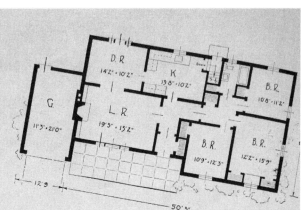

*The home owner says:*

# "It's Comfortable and Convenient"

**Figure 9.** 'The home owner says: "It's Comfortable and Convenient"', *Home Building in Canada: Small Homes*, 1951 edition (Toronto: Walkers Publishing, 1951), 140.

**Figure 10.** Advertisement for Crane Ltd (Montreal), 'To the King's Taste!', *Canadian Homes and Gardens*, Sept. 1952.

This floor is composed of Dominion Jaspé Linoleum tiles. Patterns J-720 and J-72~

# This floor reflects a thoughtful husband!

**"The floor in your kitchen,"** said my husband when we were planning it. "must be the kind that will save you work. I want you to have lots of leisure to enjoy yourself."

That's how linoleum came in. Our dealer told us it was the only answer — easy to keep colourful and clean even on the muddiest days, easy on the feet and — this really pleased my husband — easy on the budget!

I'm delighted with the result. Linoleum has everything!

If *you* are planning to build or renovate, consult your dealer or flooring contractor. Ask for comparative prices of linoleum and other floors. And keep in mind that linoleum is colourful, resilient, easy to keep clean . . . and that its durability has been time-tested by forty year's wear on Canadian floors.

*The kitchen above and breakfast nook here say a cheery "Good morning" 365 days a year. Let us have your name and address so that we can send you colourful FREE literature which will open your eyes as to what is being done to create individual, delightful, durable floors for every room in the house. Sixty-five colours and patterns to choose from.*

**DOMINION** *Jaspé* **LINOLEUM TILES**

BEAUTIFUL · RESILIENT · TIME-TESTED

Also Marboleum · Battleship (plain) in tiles or by the yard . . . products of

**DOMINION OILCLOTH & LINOLEUM COMPANY LIMITED**
MONTREAL

*1952 is our 80th Anniversary*

**Figure 11.** Advertisement for Dominion Oilcloth and Linoleum Co. (Montreal), 'This floor reflects a thoughtful husband!', *Canadian Homes and Gardens*, Sept. 1952.

# PART II

---

# At Work

Work is the most thoroughly studied subject in Canadian social history, and it has also been central to the debates that have swirled around and within the field. In part, this is a reflection of the subject matter. The challenges of everyday life, as well as many of its opportunities, have historically involved questions of labour in one form or another. It is hardly surprising, then, that historians concerned with the study of social life—both its experiences and the structures that shape them—should spend so much time researching, thinking, and writing about the historical conditions of work. Labour, work, and the working-class have been and remain among the most vibrant and innovative fields of social historical scholarship.

Historians of work have reshaped our historical understanding of Canada's transition in the late nineteenth and early twentieth centuries from a mostly rural, agrarian country into a mostly urban, industrial country. Until the 1970s, the study of this 'great transformation' usually focused on broad economic patterns, various government trade policies, and the accomplishments of merchants and businessmen. After 1970, however, historians increasingly called attention to the experience and identities of workers and argued that their blood and sweat had made possible a more industrial Canada. Epitomized by the now-classic studies by Bryan Palmer and Greg Kealey, historians were especially interested in understanding how workers organized themselves into craft guilds, fraternal orders, and unions.[1] They explored how workers accommodated and resisted such things as the deskilling of labour through new technologies and the reorganization of factory work under the scientific management theories of Frederick W. Taylor. At the heart of these analyses was an argument that a distinct working-class culture was produced in Canada that owed much to worker organizations and to the often tense relationships that existed between workers, their bosses, and a government that was little more than a handmaiden to the interests of capitalists.

The 1980s and 1990s brought some change to the historical study of work. The convergence of this early social history of labour with other areas of social historical research, especially the history of women, the history of families, and the history of education, deepened our understanding of the impact of industrialization in all sectors of everyday life. Feminist scholarship was particularly important in calling historians' attention to unpaid work, especially that done by women and children within the home. Immigration historians demonstrated how work could function as a form of social currency, reinforcing and delimiting the boundaries of community as new arrivals turned to earlier generations of immigrants for assistance in the settlement process. Education historians showed us how the decision to send or not to send children to school was contingent on the work children contributed to the family economy. The sum total of this and other research was that we gained a much more complete understanding that gender, ethnicity, race, age, and sexuality also affected the experience and identities of workers. Awareness of social class remained of paramount importance to these scholars, but it became more complicated, and thus more fragmented, by other categories of analysis. At the same time, this fragmentation has produced some important depth and breadth to our historical understanding of what it has meant to work, including how work spaces were as diverse and complex as the workers themselves.

Among the most enduring contributions made by scholars in the 1970s and 1980s and confirmed in subsequent scholarship has been the importance of regulation to the historical experiences of work. While the sources of regulation have been multi-faceted, including shop foremen, union stewards, co-workers, family members, consumers, and factory inspectors, the overall effect has been similar. Consistently, historians have demonstrated that workers have been subjected to various practices and technologies of discipline. Equally important, though, historians have shown how confronting, resisting, and accommodating discipline have been central to the experiences of work and the formation of workers' identities.

Disciplining worktime and work space, however, took many different forms. It could be overt and sometimes rather brutal, including corporeal punishment, beatings, whippings, verbal abuse, or the threat of withholding wages. Discipline could also be covert. It might include codes of worker conduct, uniforms, punch-clocks, scheduled washroom breaks, or an unspoken threat of social isolation. As intense as disciplining at work could be, in some cases it followed workers away from their site of work and into the domestic and recreational aspects of their lives. While the history of work has most certainly been about more than the disciplining of workers, their time and their spaces, and the resultant response of workers to this regulation, it is a theme that has also cut across different historical eras, situations, and peoples.

We therefore read about work being done in rural kitchens and parlours, mines, forests, hospitals, streetcars, and factories. We hear the voices of men, women, children, white workers, immigrant workers, black workers, foremen, owners, and architects, among others. We travel in time from the cusp of the industrial age in the mid-nineteenth century through to what many now call the post-industrial age of the 1970s and 1980s. We also get a sense of the different ways in which work was regulated, both formally and informally, both overtly and covertly. We see the effects of gender, race, age, family, and community as they modified the strong class relations that existed among workers and between workers and their bosses.

Readers might be well served to keep some questions in mind as they explore the readings and documents in this section. What historical situations have existed where a person worked for reasons other than a wage? Whether people worked for a wage or not, what was this work environment like? What rules did one follow? How was the labour divided up among the workers? How were individuals identified at work? How did work experiences affect other areas of everyday life? Such questions not only connect these diverse stories and documents of work, but they also allow us to see what has historically connected rural women from the mid-nineteenth century to boy miners in late nineteenth-century Cape Breton to black auto workers in post-World War II Ontario. In doing so, perhaps we also learn a little bit more about our own selves and our ideas and assumptions about what it means to work.

## Note

1.    Besides their own individual work, see Gregory S. Kealey and Bryan D. Palmer, *Dreaming of What Might Be: The Knights of Labor in Ontario, 1880–1900* (Cambridge: Cambridge University Press, 1982).

# 9

# Reciprocal Work Bees and
# the Meaning of Neighbourhood

### Catharine Anne Wilson

The reciprocal work 'bee' deserves to be understood as a vital and characteristic element of nineteenth-century rural Ontario. It was as much a part of Ontario folk culture as the potlatch was for west coast Natives, and much more common than the charivari.[1] The bee was an integral part of the farm economy and an important social resource. Through reciprocal work, individual farm families who lacked self-sufficiency in labour and skills were given a measure of insurance against hard times while they established and maintained a workable farm unit. The bee was also a key component in the structuring, operation, and definition of neighbourhood.

The study of reciprocal work bees takes us directly into the construct and concept of neighbourhood. Neighbourhood is not generally understood as part of the larger social system, but tends to be treated peripherally in relation to such categories as class, ethnicity, and gender, if it is not ignored entirely.[2] As such, a disjunction exists between the family unit and the wider world. By examining the structure and process of reciprocal work bees, we reach a deeper understanding of the relationship between the individual, the family, and the larger social order. Neighbourhood, however, is a nebulous idea. Most commonly it is recognized as comprising people at a certain time who live near each other. In this article it goes beyond this spatial and temporal definition to include interaction, process, and a sense of belonging.[3] In the nineteenth century, neighbourhood was not just the people who lived near you but the basis for economic activity, social support, and the organization of day-to-day living. Though some settlements may have been made up of independent and isolated families that kept to themselves, or tightly knit groups united by ethnicity and religion, others used the bee to develop highly effective networks of interaction. At the bee, people from diverse cultural backgrounds came together and were incorporated according to their genealogy, wealth, age, gender, and skills. Thus the bee helped to create a structural and cognitive order in the neighbourhood. Like the potlatch, it was not only an economic and social exchange but also a process through which shared values and a collective identity were created and communicated. Like the charivari, the bee was a mechanism of social integration identifying those who belonged and those who did

Catharine Anne Wilson, 'Reciprocal Work Bees and the Meaning of Neighbourhood', *Canadian Historical* Review 82, 3 (2001): 431–64. © 2001 University of Toronto Press. Reprinted by permission of University of Toronto Press (www.utpjournals.com).

not. As such, neighbourhood might, but did not necessarily, include the generosity and kindness that came with 'neighbourliness'.

. . .

## 'Busy as Bees'

What settlers called a 'bee' was a neighbourly gathering where people worked together industriously with the bustle of bees in a hive.[4] Bees occurred with regularity and frequency throughout the calendar year in early Ontario. In the spring, bees were called for raising houses and barns, shearing sheep, picking the burrs from fleece, ploughing and dragging the land for planting, and piling logs to clear the land. In the hot, dry days of summer, farm folk gathered together at bees to clean water courses, mow and cradle hay, shell peas, and cut grain. Once the busy harvest season slowed down, a new round of bees began. There were bees for spreading manure, husking corn, ploughing fields, picking and peeling apples, and hunting squirrels and pigeons. Fanning and threshing bees were often held in the barn in the winter months. This was also the time when neighbourhoods turned their energies to processing clothing and food. Bees for butchering livestock, plucking fowl, spinning wool, and sewing quilts and carpets enlivened the long winter months, and sawing and chopping bees kept the family warm and ready for the next round of clearing and building in the spring.[5]

. . .

## 'The Still Bee Gathers No Honey': The Economics of the Bee

Reciprocal work was typical of all agricultural communities, but especially frontier areas where land was readily available and capital and labour were in short supply. In early Ontario, few settlers had cash with which to hire labourers. With land readily available, labourers were costly and hard to come by, especially in the backwoods.[6]

Most families, particularly those with young children, were simply unable to perform all the tasks themselves without assistance from neighbours. This was especially true of chopping, logging, and building, which required special skills and immense physical strength. As cultivated acreages increased, it was also true for certain periods of the year such as harvest time, when work demands reached their peak and time was of the essence. By holding a bee, individual farming families who were not self-sufficient in terms of meeting the demands of peak labour periods in the year or possessing all the skills and equipment required to establish a home and farm could attain those ends. The bee was, in effect, an informal labour exchange, part of the hidden economy overlooked by census takers and economic historians. It was a forum for labour in a variety of ways. It served to concentrate labour for those events requiring large numbers. It provided families with extra labour in emergencies that might never be fully repaid. But, most often, it simply redistributed labour over time so that families had more at certain times in the year, in their personal settlement history, or in their life course, a debt that was then fully repaid at a later date.

The beeing phenomenon, therefore, was an essential part of the farm economy. Through reciprocal labour, the farm family was able to create capital. It was also better able to cope with risks. With a low standard of living, no insurance, and the possibility of sudden and unexpected calamities, it was essential to be on good terms with your neighbours. This was especially true in newly settled areas where population was highly dispersed and kin networks were not yet established. If your barn burnt, your fields were flooded, or your husband was killed, you needed to be able to rely on reciprocal aid rather than face these disasters on your own. If you were not part of this neighbourhood exchange system, the backwoods could be a frightening, risky, even hostile place.[7]

. . .

Bees were also an important part of the exchange economy of early Ontario. A tendency exists for scholars of nineteenth-century Ontario to place too much emphasis on wheat exports and, thus, the importance of cash in the economy. The economy was much more complex, involving a system of exchange that included not only cash but also the barter of goods that the family produced and the credit that settlers extended to neighbours and received in return. Indeed, anything that 'earned credit in the local economy . . . would help to sustain farm making.'[8] Certainly the giving and receiving of labour as found in the custom of bees was a part of this exchange system.

Like most significant interaction, an accounting process was at work. It may have been subtle and hidden beneath the rhetoric of neighbourliness, but it was present nevertheless. Participation was part of an exchange of labour, skills, equipment, information, hospitality, and goodwill. Reciprocal work operated much like a bank, in which all made their deposits and were then entitled to make their withdrawals or acquire small loans. One could even attain personal credit for the contributions made by ancestors or close relatives. It was possible to borrow and then abscond, but most settled families probably contributed and received in equal quantities. Was beeing, however, viewed by the participants as a business transaction or, in an attempt to make sense of this phenomenon, are we projecting our twentieth-century capitalist values on the past? The farm diaries do not clarify the mentality at work. On the one hand, the researcher senses that farmers who did not trust a mental system of checks and balances began their diaries as a way of keeping track of bees and other forms of reciprocal labour. Bees were frequently recorded and clearly identified as such. Walter Beatty, near Brockville, carefully noted the participant, the location, and the type of bee his family attended. For example, on 18 September 1849 his entry reads, 'Jock goes to George Toes Dung Bee.' Return labour was just as carefully accounted. For example, on 24 May 1849 he wrote, 'Thomas Davis sent his horses and son to Plow.'[9] When W.F. Munro gave advice to farmers on calculating their costs in the backwoods, he reminded them to 'take into account the "bees."'[10] It was clearly not as strict an accounting, however, as we might expect. When costs were itemized, they were rarely given in monetary terms, but were generally a day's work for a day's work. But the rule had to be flexible. Inequalities were bound to exist—someone would have a bigger field to harvest, a smaller pile of wood to chop. A family raising a frame barn and having 70 people at the bee would not be expected to attend 70 bees in return. The major players might be repaid with labour, the skilled framer paid cash, and the others paid with the feast and frolic that followed. Clearly they did not have a strict accounting, but it was understood that the same effort would be returned and, in the end, a redistribution of skills, equipment, labour, and hospitality would occur.[11]

Reciprocal work, therefore, played an integral role in the exchange economy, assisting individual farm families to establish a workable farm unit and ensure against hard times. In this manner, it contributed to the extensive growth of the larger provincial economy.

## 'He That Handles Honey Shall Feel It Cling To His Fingers': The Influence of Association

Beyond contributing to the economic structure of neighbourhood, the bee was a social resource. In the early settlement period, with a scarcity of religious and educational institutions and with kin networks stretching back generations, this factor was especially important. The need to co-operate brought people of diverse backgrounds and potentially divisive lines of affiliation together. The bee provided the mechanism for social integration and bonding. Each and every individual raising or quilting can be viewed as an interaction episode where patterns of association and meaning were confirmed and sometimes initiated or reshaped.[12] By participating and abiding by the rules as they were understood, people of various ages, classes, genders, skills, and experiences were incorporated into the group.

A code of behaviour developed regarding communal labour that extended beyond a mere accounting system to encompass social relations. Those giving advice to new settlers urged them to take heed that every favour conferred required a return favour. As Catharine Parr Traill, a leading authority on life in the backwoods, told her readers, 'It is, in fact regarded in the light of a debt of honour; you cannot be forced to attend a bee in return, but no one that can does refuse, unless from urgent reasons; and if you do not find it possible to attend in person you may send a substitute in a servant or in cattle, if you have a yoke.' Though this might be an inconvenience, this 'debt of gratitude ought to be cheerfully repaid.'[13] This generalized reciprocity, 'I'll help you with something later', implied a certain degree of trust and closeness. The request to return the effort at another bee could be met in three ways: accept it, discharge the debt later, and reinforce the bonds; accept to return the favour in another form, maybe discharge the debt, and reinforce the bonds; or refuse to attend, renege on your repayment, and risk breaking the social bond. Few risked exclusion from the system altogether because alienating your neighbours could be costly financially and socially.[14]

Because of this obligatory reciprocity, work groups could become highly stable among a core of persistent farmers, or even last for a generation or more.[15] It was unlikely that all labour obligations would be repaid in the same season, but they might linger for years, cementing and lengthening the lines of obligation, especially among people who shared the same values of hard work, neighbourliness, and trust. The stability of the group was essential to mutual aid. As such, the self-interest of individual families conjoined with the shared interests of the neighbourhood.

Constant social contact and mutual dependency did not necessarily imply deep affection, as work groups could be torn asunder by a serious accident or quarrels between families. Tensions simmering beneath the surface of neighbourhood life frequently erupted at bees, especially those where whisky was liberally served. Patrick Dunigan, for example, who had accused a neighbour of stealing his valuable oak tree, was stripped and tortured with hot irons by his neighbours at a bee. Hatred between Patrick Farrell and James Donnelly Sr over possession of 50 acres culminated at a bee in June 1857 when Donnelly killed Farrell with a handspike.[16] Such violence, even verbal disagreements, acquired significance in the rumour mill. Someone drunk, disorderly, unco-operative, or insulting was clearly breaking the code of neighbourliness and was a nuisance, if not a serious liability, to completing the job efficiently and without incident. Such behaviour not only threatened life and property but also jeopardized the working relationship of the group. That person was apt to be ostracized.

In this manner, the bee was a way of asserting community identity and belonging: one either adhered to the shared values of hard work and neighbourliness and belonged or was left out. For example, two young Englishmen who considered themselves above assisting at a logging bee in Douro Township in the 1830s were ridiculed with laughter.[17] In another case, Thomas Niblock, who had gained the reputation of not paying his debts on time and disparaging his neighbours' company, was not included in the beeing circle in Delaware and had to hire men to help him clear and harvest.[18] So important was a 'neighbourly' attitude that responsible, cheerful, and generous effort even took precedence over the actual quality of the work done. The neighbourly quilter was still asked to a quilting even if her stitches were uneven. Sloppy work could always be ripped out and replaced at a later date; a fissure of friendly relations was more difficult, time-consuming, and costly to repair.[19]

Besides the cheerful repayment of labour, hospitality was an integral part of the exchange and one of the most valued virtues of the social code. Just what constituted appropriate, neighbourly hospitality changed over time. In the early days of sparse settlement and rough ways, hospitality took the form of simple food, entertainment, and plenty of whisky. Whisky, in particular, was the measure of hospitality. Commentators were quick to point out in the 1820s that you simply could not raise a barn without it.[20] Generally it took 16 men to raise a building, and five gallons of whisky was the recommended store to have on hand.[21] An inexperienced grog-boss, as at Moodie's bee, inadvertently wreaked havoc by being too generous too early in the day. Susanna Moodie's 'vicious and drunken' guests stayed on after the logging bee with their 'unhallowed revelry, profane songs and blasphemous swearing', and left her to pick up the broken glasses, cups, and strewn remnants of the feast. Not surprisingly, Susanna condemned bees as being 'noisy, riotous drunken meetings, often terminating in violent quarrels, sometimes even bloodshed'.[22] Concern over the accidents, quarrels, expense of provisions, and damage to property occasioned by such drinking brought about a contest between the whisky supporters on the one side and the evangelicals and temperance advocates on the other in many communities. Evangelicals and temperance advocates met with considerable resistance in their attempt to redefine traditional patterns of hospitality as sinful. For example, a Waterdown man wishing to raise a sawmill without whisky had to send to the Indian mission on the Credit before he could obtain willing men.[23] In another case, men turned out to a raising in Nissouri Township, but once the foundation was laid, refused to raise the barn unless whisky was served. When no whisky appeared, the men left.[24] At times resistance could take a nasty turn. For example, when Thomas Brown, who had previously been part of a gang of young men who caroused at any bee within riding distance, took the pledge, he became a target of ridicule. When

he next attended a bee and refused to drink, whisky was forcibly poured down his throat and he was beaten.[25] By the 1870s, however, as the farming population became more established, older, and respectable, and as evangelicalism gained converts, strong drink was either not offered or limited to moderate amounts after the job was done.[26] Though hospitality continued to be a vital component of the exchange, elaborate meals and entertainment replaced generous quantities of whisky.

By reciprocating in the appropriate fashion through hospitality and labour, people demonstrated their support for reciprocal labour and the shared values that supported it. In so doing, they became or continued to be part of the neighbourhood. This process of incorporation worked to integrate newcomers and established settlers, young and old, rich and poor, women and men not as equals, but with clearly defined identities within the larger group. Though Catharine Parr Traill viewed the coming together of the educated gentleman, the poor artisan, the soldier, the independent settler, and the labourer in one common cause as the 'equalizing system of America', it was neither so romantic nor so revolutionary. Although the bee publicly identified people as belonging, it also established, confirmed, and renegotiated their status in the rural hierarchy, whether that standing was based on experience, skills, age, class, or gender.

Bees constituted a rite of passage for new settlers, a time when they were incorporated into the group values and understandings that could make them into useful and valued members of the neighbourhood. Reciprocal labour tied new and established families together. On the one hand, established farmers who expanded their operations needed additional labour. On the other hand, new settlers relied on more experienced settlers for their skill, equipment, advice, and any older children they could spare.[27] When Mr Sinclair arrived in Howard Township (Kent Co.) in the 1830s, for example, he had a neighbour accompany him to summon the locals to his raising. As newcomer, he had no outstanding favours to call upon, no reputation established as a trustworthy and hard worker, and therefore needed William Anderson to provide an introduction. With no house of his own, and his wife sick with lake fever, Sinclair had to rely on another neighbour to assist in preparing for the feast and festivities that followed. In repaying all these favours in the customary way, the Sinclair family could establish its claim to membership in the neighbourhood and the rights and responsibilities that status conferred.[28]

The bee, like the farm operation itself, incorporated people of all ages into its service while publicly acknowledging their status within the group. The very young and the very old, for example, were relegated to the sidelines to watch, cheer, and pass judgement. Those able to participate in the work were given responsibilities according to their perceived capabilities and talents. It was standard practice, for example, for dangerous, strenuous work, such as raising or logging, to get experienced young men. Though an older man might shout the orders to 'heave ho', only someone with a 'steady head and active body' could go out on a beam.[29] On several occasions while raising barns, seasoned men had let a bent slip and someone had been killed.[30] Novices, therefore, had to be kept away from dangerous work. In John Geikie's account of a logging bee at his father's farm in the 1830s or 1840s, John and his brother (who were under 15 years of age) were allowed only to watch on the sidelines and do the 'lighter parts of the business'. They lopped off branches, made piles of brush, brought the men pails of water, and kept the animals out of danger of falling trees. The men did the chopping and the 'wild work' of rolling the logs together.[31] As power saws and threshing machines were introduced later in the century, the specialized knowledge required to run the machines and ownership of this technology reinforced the age-based social hierarchy. Boys, or men past their prime, were limited to carrying the logs and pitching blocks at the saw-

ing bee, or pitching grain at the threshing bee. Only experienced, active men in their prime could take their place next to the saw blade or the threshing machine. When a worker was considered to be too old to be trusted with the serious or dangerous work, the meaning of his aging was publicly recognized, his status altered, and he was relegated to the sidelines.[32]

The bee also incorporated people of different classes. Gentlemen farmers such as the Langtons, the Stricklands, and the Moodies invited the educated gentleman, the independent settler, the tenant farmer, and the poor labourer alike to join together in common cause. That such a meeting of classes and temporary laying aside of differences was invariably cause for comment suggests that people were well aware of the social hierarchy. After raising their house in 1833, Traill concluded that, 'In spite of the difference of rank among those that assisted at the bee, the greatest possible harmony prevailed.'[33] Such patterns of dependence cutting across classes did not lessen inequality. As scholars studying festive labour in primitive societies have observed, the exchange was not always between equals and was, in fact, a way of reinforcing or establishing one's place in the social hierarchy.[34]

Gentlemen farmers admitted that bees, especially raisings, were essential and unavoidable. They participated in reciprocal labour, but took pains when possible to distance themselves from the lower classes and express their superiority. Both could be achieved in a number of ways. Usually the host was the work boss when a bee was convened, but where inequality between the host and workers was great, the host hired a foreman. John Thomson, a retired half-pay officer who held several properties in the Orillia area, did so when he ordered his hired hand to invite neighbours and Natives, procure supplies, and conduct the raising. It was only when workers threatened to leave because of rain and poor preparation that Thomson got involved and set about cajoling and flattering them to stay for another day.[35]

A typical way to use the bee to express one's place in the social hierarchy was through conspicuous giving—to serve a lavish feast and throw a better party than most participants could afford. Settlers expected the well-to-do to throw a good bee. To live in a commodious frame house and serve your guests only pork and peas outside was not meeting the code of hospitality. It was a challenge for most settlers to acquire and prepare enough simple fare for their guests, given the primitive storage and cooking facilities of early settlement life, but they were all expected to do their best, even if it turned out to be a very modest affair. At the Sinclairs' raising in 1831, for example, the men sat on the beams, ate bread, butter, and meat, and drank water and whisky. They had no plates, only their pocket knives.[36] In contrast, the Stewarts, gentlemen farmers in Douro Township, threw a splendid affair at their raising. The guests sat down in the kitchen and parlour to a feast of roast pig, boiled and roast mutton, fish pie, mutton pie, ham, potatoes, and a variety of vegetables, followed by puddings and tarts. In the afternoon, when rain broke up the work, tea and cakes were served. Guests were entertained by a pianist throughout the afternoon, danced to fiddle music throughout the evening, and, at 11, sat down to another feast of a wide variety of meat, desserts, and decanters of currant cordial. Dancing continued thereafter, and everyone was bedded down for the night under buffalo robes and bear skins. At the end of it all, Frances Stewart was able to look back in satisfaction and conclude, 'Altogether it looked very respectable.'[37] The Stewarts had succeeded in meeting their guests and their own expectations of fitting hospitality, given their station in life, and had confirmed their position of superiority in the neighbourhood.

On such occasions it was expected that the host would at least temporarily cast aside class differences and condescend to rub shoulders with his workers. Such had been expected of the landed class in the Old World at festive occasions.[38] It was the host's way of demonstrating his goodwill, mutual respect, generosity of spirit, and appreciation towards workers. These were integral parts of the concept of hospitality and necessary components of a continuing social relationship. When a well-to-do host was not forthcoming, guests might demand festivities fitting his station. For example, when an owner of 500 acres called a raising, but hadn't planned any entertainment, a large group of young women cornered him during the proceedings and forced him to consider how the evening should be spent.[39] When the host succumbed, dancing and games were organized. Likewise, after rain postponed John Thomson's raising, he and two gentlemen friends retired to his dining room while the remaining workers were relegated to the kitchen for the rest of the day. This division caused 'some envious feelings among certain yankiefied personages' of what Thomson called the 'no-Gent' class. To keep the workers satisfied and willing to stay overnight, Thomson and his friends had to be 'mixed up among them' as they did all they could 'to do away with any bad impression'.[40] Thereafter, Thomson resumed his distance.

In the months that followed, Thomson, like other gentlemen, paid his return labour not by attending what was deemed an 'odious gathering', but by sending his hired hands or a yoke of oxen.[41] The gentleman class participated in reciprocal labour only as long as it was necessary. As an ex-settler flatly stated, 'A gentleman . . . has no business with it—the idle riff-raff are they who will surely come, getting drunk, eating up all your pork and flour, and fighting like Irishmen.'[42] John Langton considered establishing a gentleman's logging association to avoid bees altogether, and Moodie simply stopped going or even sending anyone or anything in his place.[43] Clearly the bee was not the democratizing agent it was sometimes characterized to be.

The bee incorporated people of different age, background, and gender. The view of farm men as commercialists working alone for exchange and profit, while women worked together building neighbourhood and kin ties, needs further examination.[44] The study of bees suggests that both men and women were part of the world of mutuality. Reciprocal work has generally been viewed from the separate spheres ideology. A tendency exists to see logging, raising, and threshing bees as purely male events, and as examples of a 'male community' from which women were excluded.[45] In contrast, feminist scholars have viewed quiltings and other forms of female reciprocity as part of a 'female community' of empathy, spirituality, support, and non-hierarchical arrangements.[46] Scholars now recognize, however, that gender is best understood as a relational system. Through the interaction of men and women, the meaning of gender is created, reinforced, and transformed. More attention is now given to the construction of gender in everyday experience and in settings where men and women operate together. Scholars of rural communities recognize that, unlike urban men and women, who were increasingly defined by their differences from one another, rural men and women continued to share many of 'the tasks which produced their income and sustained their families'.[47] Bees viewed as interaction episodes are exceptionally good opportunities to examine men and women working together, because this form of reciprocal work rarely occurred without the participation of both sexes.

Men were the principal actors in reciprocal labour that involved physical strength and danger. They also exchanged labour among themselves. Women were the principal actors in reciprocal labour that involved the preparation of clothing and food. They also exchanged labour among themselves. Rarely did men and women exchange labour with each other. Beyond these significant differences there was much commonality. Both men and women were involved in bees for the capital development of their farming operation (cleared fields, buildings, household goods), for market (grain, fowl, cloth), and for basic family sustenance (food and clothing). A successful bee—where work was done well, no incidents occurred, and guests were pleased with the hospitality—required the participation of both men and women. Their work, responsibilities, and space intersected at various points throughout the event. Even though they were main actors in different kinds of bees, men and women shared the values and experience of diligence, skill, competition, hierarchical working structures, and neighbourliness. Gender, nevertheless, was an essential variable in understanding their lives.

Logging bees were substantively about men and the rituals of manliness. The loggers formed gangs in different parts of the field and competed to see who would finish logging their section first. It was very strenuous work shifting and heaping logs. In the hottest days of summer, the hours were dreadfully long, the logs terribly heavy, the work tiring and dirty, the grog foul-tasting and plentiful. It took physical stamina to last the day. It took bravery to run the risk of breaking a leg or losing one's life. And it took a great deal of self-control to keep a clear head. As Munro explained in *Backwoods Life*, logging was what 'tries a man's mettle.'[48] Just to participate as a main actor (one who rolled and piled the logs) was a mark of one's prowess. Being allowed to drive the oxen marked the beginning of manhood, and, by participating and observing, boys soon learned what was expected of them once they graduated to the status of main actors. Strength, speed, and energy were all valued, and skill was deeply appreciated and critically evaluated. Lives were at stake. Save for the skill of a good axeman, a tree might fall on man or beast. Men gained and lost reputations at these events as the strongest, the fastest, or the most skilful. Such identities were created in the heat of work and confirmed in the competitive sports that often followed. As Geikie recounted after attending a logging bee in Bidport Township in the 1830s, there was much bragging about chopping prowess, much comparison between men regarding their skills, and much laughing at those who had accidents or used inferior equipment.[49] Heavy drinking, smoking, and fights were part of the equation too, though the 'rough back countryman' style of manhood exhibited by Monaghan, who attended Moodie's bee on a hot July day in 1834 'in his glory, prepared to work or fight', gradually lost favour to the more morally upright male who was esteemed for his strength, skill, stamina—and his self-restraint.[50]

Women played a supporting role at bees where men held centre stage and were a valued audience. As anthropologists who study spectacles argue, the role of spectator is not passive or neutral, as spectacles require exchange between actors and audience.[51] At barn raisings, for example, women cheered the men on as they competed to see which team raised their side first. As Russel Clifton recalled from his barn-raising youth, he was often one of the first lads to ride up with the bent, and 'usually there was some girl among the women that I hoped would worry about my falling.'[52] Even at logging bees, the dirtiest and roughest events of all, women might participate as spectators. For example, Anne Langton and her kitchen helpers walked down and took 'a view of the black and busy scene' at their logging.[53] At hunting bees, women swarmed the fields, supporting their teams by bringing the hunters provisions and relieving them of their game.[54] In the exchange, men and women confirmed their own and each other's gendered identities. To defy these identities was to court disapproval.[55]

Even more important than their valued role as spectators was women's role in preparing and executing the feast and festivities; these were essential components of any successful bee, the first instalment in the pay-back system, and an integral part in developing the farm.[56] Women were indispensable in this capacity. If a family could not supply enough female labour itself, additional women were hired or, more commonly, neighbouring women gave their labour, crockery, cooking utensils, and, on occasion, their kitchens, with the understanding that they would receive help in return.[57] It was hard work. For most women, even with help, it took two to three days to prepare the house and food, in order to set out what was considered 'a respectable table' and to make room for the dancing or games that followed. Great activity then ensued on the day of the event, with cooking, keeping the fires going, serving food, minding children, and being the cheerful hostess.[58] Once the festivities were over, the cleanup began.

In a sense, the roles of actor and spectator were reversed at the feast, as the hostess took centre stage. As fictional accounts portrayed it, 'supper was the great event to which all things moved at bees.'[59] Considerable pressure existed for women to perform. Isabella Bishop concluded in *The Englishwoman in America* (1856) that the 'good humour of her guests depends on the quantity and quality of her viands.'[60] Being hostess to a bee gave women a rare occasion to exhibit themselves, their skills, and their homes. Though men might eat with a 'take what you have and you won't want fashion', they nevertheless took stock of the meal. In their accounts of bees, men carefully and, if the host, proudly itemized the menu and often evaluated the hostess. Wilkie, for example, after attending a chopping bee, noted [of] Mrs Webb [that she was a] 'provident dame [who] had busied herself to some purpose.'[61] Women, however, were the most exacting critics when it came to the meal. As men competed with and assessed each other while logging, women evaluated each other at the feast. As Stan Cross recalled of his parents barn raising, senior women eagerly offered their assistance so that they could 'see first-hand how my mother, who was one of their peers, would approach such an undertaking especially with three babies in tow.'[62] So great was the competition and the pressure to prepare a fine feast that M.E. Graham, in an article entitled 'Food for Bees', urged Ontario farm women not to give themselves 'dyspepsia preparing bountiful, fancy and varied threshing feasts'. She went on to say, 'I know for truth that we simply cook that we may equal or excel the other woman in the neighbourhood.'[63] A lot was at stake, for the quality of the hospitality could determine the family's reputation and its continuing membership in the ring of reciprocity. It was only after the feast and the festivities were over and the guests had gone away happy that the host and hostess could relax and congratulate themselves on having held a successful event.

The quilting was the female counterpart of the male logging bee. As men were the central actors at a logging bee and women played a supporting role, the reverse was true of quiltings. It was an event organized and held by and for women which combined work with socializing. For days the hostess prepared the house and the food for the event, made arrangements for the children, and pieced scraps together to form the top of the quilt. Whereas a general call might be sent out for a barn raising, women were individually invited to a quilting. The guests would secure the top, wool, and backing to a frame, quilt it, and remove it from the frame, ready for use, in the same day. To be invited to a quilting generally meant you were not only a member of a particular social circle but also accomplished in sewing skills. Whereas men were esteemed for their strength, stamina, and bravery, women were praised for their detail and dexterity. The good seamstress sewed fast, short, even stitches and wasted no thread. The hostess was evaluated on her hospitality, and the artistry and skill exhibited by her quilt top. As experienced men took the lead at loggings, experienced women took the lead at quiltings and were known as the 'queen bees'. Young girls learned how to sew from their mothers and grandmothers on doll quilts. Once they were experienced enough, they would be invited to participate in their first bee. In this manner, quilting skills were passed down through the generations, reaffirming the female role and female connectedness.[64]

Usually we think of the quilting bee as a female-only affair, but in the nineteenth century, though women held centre stage, men played significant supporting roles. When young women were present, the hostess, who controlled the social space of the marriage market, invited young men too.[65] A.C. Currie, a young bachelor in Niagara, got invited to several quilting bees over the winter of 1841. Sometimes he had two a week.[66] While the women sat around the quilting frame, the men, under the supervision of the queen bees, would sit on the sidelines and aid by threading needles, chatting, and flirting. As spectators, they were to appreciate the women's domestic skills and social charms; as supporting actors, they were to mingle with the young women at the 'frolic' of charades, dancing, singing, and flirtations that usually followed. Such flirtations at apple-paring and corn-husking bees, where men and women participated as equals, took priority over the actual work accomplished, at least in the retelling. At paring bees, men might peel apples and throw them to the women, who cored, quartered, and strung them. Once the old folks retired for the evening, the young people kissed, danced, and played all sorts of games. Wilkie excitedly recounted his experiences at such a bee when, alone in a moonlit room, amid much whispering and gentle tittering, a game of forfeit ensued and he found himself holding a 'bonnie lass' on each knee.[67] In this manner, bees provided an opportunity for courtship under the supervision of the community.

At the bee, one's identity was confirmed within the neighbourhood. Though people might work together in harmony like bees in a hive, they took their place within a non-egalitarian and differentiated group. While initiating, reshaping, and confirming patterns of association between individuals, the bee also served a variety of functions for the neighbourhood as a whole. One contemporary deemed it to be 'the fete, the club, the ball, the town-hall, the labour convention of the whole community'.[68]

. . .

## 'To Bee or Not To Bee'

What the bee actually meant to participants can only be judged from their actions and the evaluations they have left. Contemporary accounts repeatedly revealed that if a bee functioned well—the job got done, money was saved, people had fun and knew their place—the communal effort was applauded. Participants, however, were well aware of the exchange system that underlay this event and were reluctant to depict reciprocal work as selfless behaviour.[69] They knew that both the communal and the individual ethic were in operation. While selfish ambition and the man who did not do his share were clearly frowned upon, individual gain had an acknowledged place in the system. The barn raising, for example, was a momentous achievement in an individual family's measure of material success. It symbolized not only their reasons for emigrating and their years of saving and planning but also their material wealth, social improvement, and independence. Indeed, private property and individual ownership were never in question. Though people agreed to share their labour, tools, and time, it was always clear whose field had been logged, whose cattle would use the newly raised barn, and who could sleep under the quilt. Most participants would have been baffled to find twentieth-century writers casting the bee as the embodiment of the selfless communal ideal and the polar opposite of the capitalistic spirit of individualism and material gain. Instead, most farm families understood that work was a commodity and also a means to foster neighbourly relations. Their lively networks of reciprocal labour fostered both individual prosperity and mutual reliance. This social reality flies in the face of a number of dichotomies that have been developed by scholars, such as use versus exchange, sufficiency versus commercialization, and the moral economy versus the market economy.[70] That reciprocal work often resulted in a warm sense of generosity, belonging, and security within a larger community was an important by-product deeply appreciated by people at the time and lamented later when lost. When given the opportunity to be released from the constraints of scarce labour

and capital, however, many people chose to leave the obligations and inconvenience of co-operative work behind for other ways over which they had greater control.

The main complaints levelled against bees had to do with managing people. Co-operation is not easy. As with any kind of communal work, industrious workers had to share with the idle, and individual decisions were constrained by the decisions of the group. One common complaint was that it was difficult to control the workers. Some came with the attitude that the host was lucky to have them and they drank and ate heartily while leaving little in the way of quality workmanship. Farmers felt they had more control over their workers and the quality of work if they hired labourers. Furthermore, bees could be costly if the work was shoddy, yet the host was bound to feast and entertain the workers. After her logging bee had gone wrong, Susanna Moodie went out of her way to declare, 'I am certain, in our case, had we hired with the money expended in providing for the bee, two or three industrious, hard-working men, we should have got through twice as much work, and have had it done well, and have been the gainers in the end.'[71] The main disadvantage with the bee was being called upon at an inconvenient time for return work. Just when a farmer needed to seed or harvest his own fields, he was called upon by others to work theirs.[72]

Given the difficulties in managing people, it is not surprising that once other viable alternatives arose, bees declined. Bees persisted in remote areas where hired labour was hard to find and the price of labour was high. They also continued to operate in situations such as the Middaughs' where persistent farm families of similar status had a tradition of reciprocal work firmly established. In other populous and longer-settled areas, however, where farmers were expanding their operations and entering into a cash economy, it was more convenient to hire workers, and the cash payment—an immediate reciprocity—took into consideration the quality and quantity of the work done.[73] Farmers were then free of the obligations of reciprocal labour and could attend to their own farms—and according to their own schedule. The growing availability of cash and hired labour removed the necessity of relying on bees.

Technology was not as central as some have argued in the decline of bees.[74] The introduction at mid-century of patented iron apple peelers, the self-raking reaper, and, later, cross-cut saws reduced the need for bees by cutting the time and labour needed in processing apples, harvesting, and sawing.[75] Some of the new technology, such as threshing machines in the 1880s and later silo-filling equipment, did not alter the tradition of collective work, but was often co-operatively owned and operated. Threshing bees and silo-filling bees continued well into the twentieth century. Only after the First World War, with the introduction of combines and tractors, was one man able to do the work that had previously taken a neighbourhood.[76]

The need for bees also declined with the rise of more formal strategies for security and new forms of entertainment. Insurance companies offering compensation for damage done by fire, fraternal orders offering sickness and death benefits, and eventually the welfare state all played their part in reducing the effect of hard times and families' reliance on traditional networks of neighbourhood support.[77] Furthermore, bees now competed with lodge meetings, Sunday school picnics, school concerts, and agricultural fairs for the visiting and courtship opportunities they provided.

As the economics, technology, and social aspects of farm life changed, bees slowly became a thing of the past.

## Conclusion

Though often idealized as the epitome of the selfless communal ideal, participants in bees behaved as though there was no inherent or insurmountable conflict between individual and communal goals. Both men and women participated in reciprocal labour using the ties born of geography and genealogy to build their resources, increase their own productivity, and shape their future opportunities. Through this sharing, many individual farm families were able to acquire the extra labour, skills, and equipment necessary for capital improvements, so that profitable farming could proceed. Such structural dependence on neighbours reduced the risk of life in the backwoods. Many people found that, through reciprocal work, they could succeed individually and that it was in their own material and social interests to be neighbourly. The network of labour exchange, in effect, produced individual prosperity and mutual reliance. In the process, neighbourhoods were created that could be defined by their spatial dimension, membership, shared values, and collective identity. Such neighbourhoods were dynamic entities, with fluid patterns of interaction particular to each family and responsive to the social networks and social space that individual participants brought to bear on the network as it developed. Finally, though the bee facilitated neighbourhood and often neighbourliness, it did so in a way that incorporated differences in class, age, gender, and skill and acknowledged the importance of private property and social hierarchy.

## Notes

I would like to thank my research assistants, Karen Kennedy and James Calnan. The helpful comments of my colleagues Terry Crowley, Kris Inwood, Jamie Snell, and Richard Reid on earlier versions of this article are greatly appreciated. A version of this article was presented at the 2001 annual meeting of the Canadian Historical Association in Quebec City.

1.   Bryan D. Palmer, 'Discordant Music: Charivaris and Whitecapping in Nineteenth-Century North America', *Labour/Le Travail* 3 (1978): 5–62; Allan Greer, 'From Folklore to Revolution: Charivaris and the Lower Canadian Rebellion of 1837', and

Tina Loo, 'Dan Cranmer's Potlatch', both in Tina Loo and Lorna R. McLean, eds, *Historical Perspectives on Law and Society in Canada* (Mississauga, Ont.: Copp Clark Longman, 1994), 35–55, 219–53; Pauline Greenhill, 'Welcome and Unwelcome Visitors: Shivarees and the Political Economy of Rural-Urban Interaction in Southern Ontario', *Journal of Ritual Studies* 3, 1 (1989).

2. Studies such as those done by Bradbury, Parr, and Marks come close to examining neighbourhood, but still link families only with the larger urban area and economy and bypass the neighbourhood as a unit of analysis. See Bettina Bradbury, *Working Families: Age, Gender and Daily Survival in Industrializing Montreal* (Toronto: McClelland & Stewart 1993); Joy Parr, *The Gender of Breadwinners* (Toronto: University of Toronto Press 1990); Lynne Marks, *Revivals and Roller Rinks: Religion, Leisure, and Identity in Late-Nineteenth-Century Small-Town Ontario* (Toronto: University of Toronto Press 1996). So far the study of neighbourhood has been the preserve of sociologists. For example, for the study of neighbourhood helping exchanges in modern Toronto, see Barry Wellman, 'The Community Question', *American Journal of Sociology* 84 (1979): 1201–31.

3. A vast literature exists on community. For the most recent overview of this literature in a Canadian context, see John Walsh and Steven High, 'Re-thinking the Concept of Community', *Histoire Sociale* 23 (Nov. 1999): 255–73. . . .

4. Samuel Strickland, *Twenty-Seven Years in Canada West*, vol. 1 (Edmonton: Hurtig Publishers, 1972 [1853]), 35; Martin Doyle, *Hints on Emigration to Upper Canada* (Dublin: Curry, 1832), 61; George Easton, *Travels in America* (Glasgow: John S. Marr & Sons, 1871), 89. . . .

5. Queen's University Archives, Walter Beatty Papers, Walter Beatty Diary, 1838–92, box 3057; ibid., Ewan Ross Papers, John MacGregor Diary, 1877–83, series 3, binder 94, no. 2504; ibid., Ewan Ross Papers, James Cameron Diaries, 1854–1902, series 3, binders 25–33, no. 2504; Lucy Middaugh Diary, 1884–7, private possession of Jean Wilson; John Tigert Diaries, 1888–1902, private possession of Tigert family; Joseph Abbott Diary, 1819, reprinted in his *The Emigrant to North America* (Montreal: Lovell & Gibson, 1843); James O'Mara, 'The Seasonal Round of Gentry Farmers in Early Ontario', *Canadian Papers in Rural History* 2 (1980): 103–12

6. For the most comprehensive study of rural labour in nineteenth-century Ontario, see Terry Crowley, 'Rural Labour', in Paul Craven, ed., *Labouring Lives: Work and Workers in Nineteenth-Century Ontario* (Toronto: University of Toronto Press, 1995), 13–102. For frontier labour, see Daniel Vickers, 'Working the Fields in a Developing Economy: Essex County, Mass., 1630–1675', in Stephen Innes, ed., *Work and Labor in Early America* (Chapel Hill: University of North Carolina Press, 1988), 60.

7. Immigrant guidebook writers were well aware of the necessity of reducing risk in the backwoods and urged their readers to take part in bees. See William Hutton, *Canada: Its Present Condition, Prospects, and Resources Fully Described for the Information of Intending Emigrants* (London 1854), 42–3; Catharine Parr Traill, *The Backwoods of Canada* (Toronto: McClelland & Stewart, 1929 [1836]), 121; Easton, *Travels in America*, 90–3, 168.

8. Doug McCalla, *Planting the Province: The Economic History of Upper Canada, 1784–1870* (Toronto: University of Toronto Press, 1993), 82, 146

9. Beatty Diary; see also Tigert Diary and Middaugh Diary. . . .

10. W.F. Munro. *The Backwoods Life* (Shelburne: The Free Press, 1910 [1869]), 38

11. A day's work for a day's work was generally the custom throughout North and South America. See Basil Hall, *Travels in North America, in the Years 1827–1828* (Edinburgh: Cadell & Co., 1829), 311–12; Charles Erasmus, 'Culture Structure and Process: The Occurrence and Disappearance of Reciprocal Farm Labour', *Southwestern Journal of Anthropology* 12 (1956): 445. For what happened when inequalities existed, see Erasmus. 'Culture Structure and

Process', 447; Solon T. Kimball, 'Rural Social Organization and Co-operative Labor', *American Journal of Sociology* 55 (1949): 42. . . .

12. I first came across the use of 'interaction episode' as an analytical tool in Rhys Isaac's *The Transformation of Virginia* (Chapel Hill: University of North Carolina Press, 1982), ch. 'A Discourse on the Method'. My thanks to Richard Reid for drawing my attention to this work. . . .

13. Traill, *Backwoods of Canada*, 122

14. Contemporary writers urged new settlers to repay the favour: Hall. *Travels,* 312; Edward Allan Talbot, *Five Years' Residence in the Canadas* (London: Longman, Hurst, Rees, Orme, Brown & Green, 1824), 69; Doyle, *Hints on Emigration*, 45. See also Paul Voisey, *Vulcan: The Making of a Prairie Community* (Toronto: University of Toronto Press, 1988). 147; Jane Marie Pederson, *Between Memory and Reality: Family and Community in Rural Wisconsin, 1870–1970* (Madison: University of Wisconsin Press, 1992), 154.

15. Kimball, 'Rural Social Organization', 47; Erasmus, 'Culture Structure and Process', 447; Anthony Buckley, 'Neighbourliness—Myth and History', *Oral History* 2, 1 (1983): 49.

16. *Globe*, 10 Sept. 1880, 6; 6 Feb. 1880, 1. For other examples, see Ray Fazakas, *The Donnelly Album* (Toronto: Macmillan of Canada, 1977), 10–14. For a similar tension between a local social order that stressed harmony and the undercurrent of violence brought on by frontier conditions, see Susan Lewthwaite, 'Violence, Law, and Community in Rural Upper Canada', in Jim Phillips, Tina Loo, and Susan Lewthwaite, eds, *Essays in the History of Canadian Law* (Toronto: University of Toronto Press, 1994), 353–86. . . .

17. James Logan, *Notes of a Journey Through Canada* (Edinburgh: Fraser & Co., 1838), 46.

18. National Archives of Canada (NAC), Niblock Letters, MG 24, 180, microfilm A-304, Thomas Niblock to Edward Niblock, 27 Jan. 1850. For those who broke the code and were considered divergent or outsiders, see Kimball, 'Rural Social Organization', 41; Conrad M. Arensberg and Solon T. Kimball, *Family and Community in*

*Ireland* (Cambridge, Mass: Harvard University Press, 1948), ch. 12.

19. Interview with quilters at a quilting bee, Martin House, Doon Village, 1 July 1996

20. Thomas Brush Brown, *Autobiography of Thomas Brush Brown (1804–1894)* (private printing by Isabel Grace Wilson, 1967, available at the Oxford County Library), 17–18. For the importance of whisky and hospitality, see also David Wilkie, *Sketches of a Summer Trip to New York and the Canadas* (Edinburgh: J. Anderson Jr & A. Hill, 1837), 173, 176–7; Hall, *Travels*, 2: 311; James M. Young, *Reminiscences of the Early History of Galt and the Settlement of Dumfries* (Toronto: Hunter, Rose & Co., 1880), 61; Strickland, *Twenty-Seven Years*, 1: 37; William Thompson, *A Tradesman's Travels in the United States and Canada the Years 1840, 41 and 42* (Edinburgh: Oliver & Boyd, 1842), 103.

21. Patrick Shirreff, *A Tour through North America* (Edinburgh: Oliver & Boyd, 1835), 125. For the usual amount of whisky per man, see Rev. T. Sockett, ed., *Emigration: Letters from Sussex Emigrants* (London: Phillips, Petworth and Longman & Co., 1833), 28; Centennial Museum, Judicial Records, Peterborough County, Peterborough. MG-8-2V, Inquest of Charles Danford, Smith Township, Accession No. 71–007, box 5, 1876, no. 30.

22. Susanna Moodie, *Roughing It in the Bush* (Toronto: McClelland & Stewart, 1962 [1852]), 156–62; and also Wilkie, *Sketches*, 176; Shirreff, *A Tour*, 125.

23. Emily Weaver, *Story of the Counties of Ontario* (Toronto: Bell & Cockburn, 1913), 165; Pederson, *Between Memory and Reality*, 142, 217, 219.

24. Brown, *Autobiography*, 25.

25. Ibid., 23–4.

26. Charles Marshall, *The Canadian Dominion* (London: Longmans, Green, 1871), 63; see also Easton, *Travels in America*, 169.

27. Doyle, *Hints on Emigration*, 60–1.

28. Alexander Sinclair, *Pioneer Reminiscences* (Toronto: Warwick Bros & Rutter, 1898), 11–12.

29. Frances Browne Stewart, *Our Forest Home*

(Montreal: Gazette Printing, 1902 [1889]), 174, 177; *Canada Farmer* 2, 9 (15 Nov. 1870).

30. Trent University Archives, Court Records of the United Counties of Northumberland & Durham, Coroners' Inquests, Inquest of James Hill, 84–020, series E, box 49; Judicial Records Peterborough County, Inquest of Charles Danford. A bent was made of two posts connected with a beam. It was laid on the foundation and then raised to form the frame of the barn.

31. John C. Geikie, ed., *Adventures in Canada: Or Life in the Woods* (Philadelphia: Porter & Coates, 1882), 40–4, 47–8; see also Logan, *Notes of a Journey*, 45.

32. Jim Brown, 'Memories of Work Bees', *Up the Gatineau!* 21 (1995): 9; Royce MacGillivray, *The Slopes of the Andes: Four Essays on the Rural Myth in Ontario* (Belleville, Ont.: Mika Publishing, 1990), 90.

33. Traill, *The Backwoods*, 135; see also Moodie, *Roughing It*, 156; Logan, *Notes of a Journey*, 46.

34. Erasmus, 'Culture Structure and Process', 458.

35. Archives of Ontario, John Thomson Diary, MU-846, part 2, 22–4 Apr. 1834. This was done elsewhere as well; see Erasmus, 'Culture Structure and Process', 448.

36. Sinclair, *Pioneer Reminiscences*, 12; see also Wilkie, *Sketches*, 177; Strickland, *Twenty-Seven Years*, 35-6.

37. Stewart, *Our Forest Home*, 174–6.

38. Catharine Anne Wilson, *A New Lease on Life* (Montreal and Kingston: McGill-Queen's University Press, 1994), 110.

39. *Canada Farmer* 2, 9 (15 Nov. 1870).

40. Thomson Diary, 22–4 Apr. 1834.

41. For example, see Thomson Diary, July, Oct., and Nov. 1833, June 1834. John Langton and Moodie sent their hired men to bees also. Anne Langton, *A Gentlewoman in Upper Canada* (Toronto: Clarke Irwin, 1964), 167; Moodie, *Roughing It*, 162.

42. Ex-Settler, *Canada in the Years 1832, 1833 and 1834* (Dublin: Hardy, 1835), 115.

43. Langton, *A Gentlewoman*, 166; Moodie, *Roughing It*, 162.

44. Nancy Osterud goes further than most historians in understanding the rural family and community as gendered relationships. While she acknowledges that men participated in co-operative work, she still tends to see men as part of the commercial world and argues that women were the ones who sustained co-operative relations. In fact, she goes as far as to argue that women advocated a model of interdependence as an alternative to male dominance and capitalist social relations. She states that women used mutuality as a strategy of empowerment. Nancy Grey Osterud, *Bonds of Community: The Lives of Farm Women in 19th Century New York* (Ithaca, NY: Cornell University Press, 1991).

45. John Mack Faragher, *Women and Men on the Overland Trail* (New Haven: Yale University Press, 1979), 112, 116.

46. Carroll Smith-Rosenberg, 'The Female World of Love and Ritual: Relations between Women in Nineteenth-Century America', *Journal of Women in Culture and Society* 1, 1 (1975): 1–29; Marjorie Kaethler and Susan D. Shantz, *Quilts of Waterloo County* (Waterloo, Ont.: Johanns Graphics, 1990), 12; Ruth Schwartz Cowan, *More Work for Mother* (New York: Basic Books, 1983), 112.

47. For gender as a relational system, see Joan W. Scott, 'Women's History', in Peter Burke, ed., *New Perspectives on Historical Writing* (University Park: Pennsylvania State University Press, 1995); for rural communities, see Pederson, *Between Memory and Reality*; Osterud, *Bonds of Community*; Royden Loewen, *Family, Church, and Market: The Mennonite Community in the Old and the New Worlds, 1850–1930* (Toronto: University of Toronto Press, 1993).

48. Munro, *Backwoods Life*, 55.

49. Geikie, ed., *Adventures in Canada*, 41-3.

50. Moodie, *Roughing It*, 158; and for similar accounts of logging bees, see Logan, *Notes on a Journey*, 45; William Johnston, *Pioneers of Blanchard* (Toronto: William Briggs, 1899), 188–9, 227; Wilkie, *Sketches*, 174–5. See also Mark Carnes and C. Griffen, eds, *Meanings for Manhood* (Chicago: University of Chicago Press, 1990); Pederson, *Between Memory and Reality*, 142–3.

51. Bonnie Huskins, 'The Ceremonial Space of Women: Public Processions in Victorian Saint John and Halifax', in Janet Guildford and Susanne Morton, eds, *Separate Sphere: Women's Worlds in the 19th Century Maritimes* (Fredericton: Acadiensis Press, 1994), 147.

52. Cited in West Oxford Women's Institute, *The Axe and the Wheel: A History of West Oxford Township* (Tillsonburg, Ont.: Otter Publishing, 1974), 17.

53. Langton, *A Gentlewoman*, 94.

54. Abbott, *The Emigrant to North America*, 42.

55. An extreme, but nonetheless suggestive, case occurred in 1918 when a young Quebec girl dressed in male attire participated in a log-driving bee, and, when exposed, was sentenced to two years at the Portsmouth Penitentiary in Kingston. Original 11 June 1918, reprinted in *Toronto Star*, 19 May 1992.

56. Elizabeth Jane Errington, *Wives and Mothers, School Mistresses and Scullery Maids: Working Women in Upper Canada, 1790–1840* (Montreal and Kingston: McGill-Queen's University Press, 1995), 96.

57. Catharine Parr Traill, *The Female Emigrant's Guide and Hints on Canadian Housekeeping* (Toronto: MacLear, 1854), 40; Sinclair, *Pioneer Reminiscences*, 12; Geikie, ed., *Adventures in Canada*, 44.

58. Munro, *Backwoods Life*, 55; Stewart, *Our Forest Home*, 172–6; Wilkie, *Sketches*, 176–8; Isabella L. Bishop, *The Englishwoman in America* (London: W. Clowes & Sons, 1856), 205–6; Louis Tivy, *Your Loving Anna: Letters from the Ontario Frontier* (Toronto: University of Toronto Press, 1972), 89.

59. Ralph Connor, *The Man from Glengarry* (Toronto: Westminster Co., 1901), 211.

60. Bishop, *The Englishwoman in America*, 205–6.

61. Wilkie, *Sketches*, 176.

62. Stan Cross, 'The Raising', *Up the Gatineau!* 21 (1995): 7.

63. M.E. Graham, 'Food for Bees', *The Farming World* 18 (11 Sept. 1900): 104.

64. Strickland, *Twenty-Seven Years*, 2: 295–6; Thompson, *Tradesman's Travels*, 37; and for a wool-picking bee that was similarly arranged, see Munro, *Backwoods Life*, 57.

65. Peter Ward, 'Courtship and Social Space in Nineteenth-Century English Canada', *Canadian Historical Review* 68, 1 (1987): 35–62.

66. University of Western Ontario, Regional Collection, William Leslie Papers, box 4178, A.C. Currie to Richard Leslie, 25 Dec. 1841; see also Strickland, *Twenty-Seven Years*, 2: 296; Munro, *Backwoods Life*, 57; Thompson, *Tradesman's Travels*, 37.

67. Wilkie, *Sketches*, 182–6; see also Canniff Haight, *Country Life in Canada Fifty Years Ago* (Toronto: Hunter, Rose & Co., 1885), 67–8; Geikie, ed., *Adventures in Canada*, 326–7; Traill, *Female Emigrant's Guide*, 75; Gavin Hamilton Green, *The Old Log House* (Goderich, Ont.: Signal-Star Press, 1948), 109.

68. Marshall, *Canadian Dominion*, 62.

69. Doyle, *Hints on Emigration*, 61–2; Traill, *The Backwoods*, 122.

70. See Stephen Innes for his insightful discussion of the need for greater caution when using such dichotomies to describe the past. 'John Smith's Vision', in Innes, ed., *Work and Labour in Early America*, 36–40.

71. Moodie, *Roughing It*, 13; see also the Diary of William Proudfoot, 12 June 1833, cited in Edwin Guillet, *Pioneer Days in Upper Canada* (Toronto: University of Toronto Press, 1975 [1933]), 127; Ex-Settler, *Canada*, 115.

72. John J.E. Linton, *The Life of a Backwoodsman; or, Particulars of the Emigrant's Situation in Settling on the Wild Land of Canada* (London: Marchant Singer & Co., 1843), 14; Langton, *Gentlewoman*, 155, 166; *Canada Farmer* 2, 12 (12 Dec. 1870); Traill, *Backwoods*, 122. For a scholarly discussion of the problems associated with bees or other forms of co-operative work, see Erasmus, 'Culture Structure and Process', 456–61; Cowan, *More Work for Mother*, 117; Pederson, *Between Memory and Reality*, 149.

73. Traill, *Backwoods*, 121; Strickland, *Twenty-Seven Years*, 1: 37.

74. Kimball, 'Rural Social Organization', 42, places significant weight on technology as a factor in the decline of co-operative labour. Erasmus disagrees, placing more emphasis on the growth of a money economy and on more intensive agriculture that

makes co-operative work inconvenient and inefficient in terms of the costs and quality of work done. 'Culture Structure and Process', 456. See also Pederson, *Between Memory and Reality*, 154–5.

75. *Farmer's Advocate* 59 (10 Apr. 1924): 548; McCalla, *Planting the Province*, 225; Lois Russell, *Everyday Life in Colonial Canada* (London: B.T. Batsford, 1973), 90.

76. Pederson, *Between Memory and Reality*, 151–4.

77. McCalla, *Planting the Province*, 161; Peter G. Mewett, 'Associational Categories and the Social Location of Relationships in a Lewis Crofting Community', in Anthony P. Cohen, ed., *Belonging* (Manchester: Manchester University Press, 1982); James E. Taylor Calnan, '"A Home Not Made with Hands": National Voluntary Associations and Local Community in Prince Edward County, Ontario, at the Turn of the 20th Century' Ph.D. dissertation (University of Guelph, 1999).

# 10

# The Shantymen

Ian Radforth

During the first half of the nineteenth century the forest industry was among the most important sources of waged employment in Ontario, and for countless farm families it was a crucial source of cash income. Even during the second half of the century, the forest industry continued to play an important role as an employer in Ontario's large, rural economy, and the output of the shantymen[1] provided raw materials for the manufacturing employees in hundreds of sawmills. As the distinctive resource economy of the north began to develop from the 1880s, forest work had a leading part there, too. And in terms of legends and images, the shantymen were no less important. The exploits of that colossal fighter and woodsman of the Ottawa, Joe Muffraw, inspired generations of woodsmen. When the Prince of Wales visited Ottawa in 1860, he rode the timber slide at the Chaudière Falls in the company of raftsmen and was greeted by hundreds of colourfully clad voyageurs and shantymen—the quintessentially Canadian occupational groups of the era.[2]

. . .

Recovering the history of the shantymen means more than simply providing coverage for an important but neglected occupational group in nineteenth-century Ontario. By giving the shantymen their rightful place in the broader history of Ontario labour, we can help to correct the bias in the literature, one that has given disproportionate attention to craftsmen, a comparatively small group compared to the seasonal and day labourers in the forests and on the farms, construction sites, docks, schooners, and steamships. Furthermore, a study of woodsmen brings to light a fascinating way of life—that of men working and living for a whole season in camps away from their families and communities. The shantymen lived and toiled in an all-male environment, where many of the tasks usually done by women were here arranged by the companies and done by other men. The unusual way of life in shanty and rafting operations has long had a romantic appeal celebrated in the songs of the shantymen themselves and in histories, both popular and scholarly. In many respects, it *was* a colourful occupational group whose ways ought not to be forgotten—although there is little danger of that. Yet woods operations also had their businesslike side, and the work routines were exactly that: routines that could grow monotonous. Both aspects of that way of life need to be recalled and reconstructed.

This chapter surveys the history of the shantymen and their work throughout the nine-

Ian Radforth, 'The Shantymen', in Paul Craven, ed., *Labouring Lives: Work and Workers in 19th-Century Ontario*. © 1995 University of Toronto Press. Reprinted by permission of the publisher.

teenth century and in several parts of the province, but most notably in the Ottawa Valley and on the Canadian Shield. It draws selectively, and critically, on the secondary literature, and it presents the results of new research, notably in hitherto little-used archival sources. The records of quite a few lumber companies that operated in nineteenth-century Ontario have been preserved, and some have proved to be quite rich and to provide an unusual vantage point. To be sure, the company sources seldom record directly the voices of the woods worker himself, but they do offer a perspective that is remarkably close to the ground. In some cases, camp foremen and backwoods supervisors reported almost daily on activities in the woods, on the river, or during labour recruitment drives. I have relied heavily on some of the best of these kinds of records.

This research has led me to the conclusion that the work lives of the shantymen in nineteenth-century Ontario were characterized both by variety and movement and by stability. The work itself drew on many kinds of skills and offered the workers great variety—the carefully defined responsibilities of members of felling gangs, the co-operative spirit of the mid-winter sleigh haul, the frantic rush and motion of the spring river drive. Similarly, the shantymen's contact with the world beyond the workplace changed with the season; most spent the winter in remote districts, cut off from families and taverns, whereas in spring and summer the drivers and raftsmen had access to liquor and opportunities for conflict in the towns and villages they passed through as they moved downstream. Those who found jobs in the woods and on the river came from a wide range of backgrounds— French-Canadian, Irish, Scottish, German, Polish, and Aboriginal—and they integrated woods work into their lives in a number of ways. Some were specialists who worked year-round in the industry; others came from various walks of life and stayed in the woods for a few weeks or several months. The recruiting of seasonal workers was virtually a continuous activ-

ity for employers. Yet stability prevailed as well. Over the course of the century there were few technological or managerial innovations that disrupted the well-understood methods of conducting a logging campaign. Similarly, once a crew was on the job, instances of overt conflict between men and bosses were rare. Furthermore, throughout the entire century, woodsmen were immersed in an intensely masculine world, and their dangerous work and crude living conditions always encouraged them to project an image of rugged masculinity.

. . .

## The Seasonal Round of Work

All commercial woods work was based on the labour of gangs of men working from shanties, that is, camps in the woods, located within walking distance of the timber. A gang usually had five men, and a shanty was made up of two to ten gangs, the number depending on such factors as company resources, local traditions, and, especially, the amount of accessible timber of the species, quality, and size desired. Lumbering methods became well established early in the century. They were second nature to the experienced man, and he taught the ropes to greenhorns. That well-understood way to proceed changed remarkably little over the course of the century. In the woods end of the business at least, this was a thoroughly conservative industry.

During the nineteenth century, employers made no formal attempts to innovate, either as individual firms or in co-operation with one another, as their successors did in the next century.[3] To be sure, dramatic innovations in related forest industries such as sawmilling and pulp and paper affected logging, mainly by increasing the demand for timber and making it profitable to enter remote or hard-to-reach forests that had hitherto been too expensive to exploit. Such developments had little direct effect on lumbering methods, however. Small improvements in basic logging methods were sometimes made, including the odd advance introduced from the outside. Boat builders, for instance, tried to develop a market among firms operating on the river.[4] Men and firms that had logged in the even bigger timber of Michigan brought modest innovations with them. Generally, however, I want to stress that once the methods were established, lumbering firms preferred to stick to the methods that worked for them.[5] What worked was a system that relied heavily on nature to facilitate each step in the lumbering process. The activities had a distinctly seasonal rhythm.[6]

Crews for the annual lumbering campaign began to assemble about the beginning of September. At that time of year, there were men available (rafting having been completed shortly before), the worst of the heat and fly season was over, and there still remained enough time to fell and prepare plenty of timber before the snow became too deep. Once a shanty had been built—and that didn't take long because they were crude temporary structures—then the felling gangs, usually of five men each, would set out every day to cut timber.

The cutting gangs came under the authority of the shanty boss, sometimes called the camp foreman. A good boss was an experienced shantyman whom the owners had singled out for his skill at handling logs and men. Before cutting began, he helped cruise the timber limit, assessing the quality and location of the timber, and he chose the site for the shanty and planned a network of roads and trails for bringing in supplies and transporting timber out. During the cutting season he assigned the gangs to specific sites and rotated them to new ones once the timber had been felled. In the woods the shanty boss was in charge. To be sure, he corresponded with headquarters regularly, perhaps daily where and when access was good, and was visited from time to time by an owner or by a woods superintendent, or 'walking boss', who moved among the company's camps. Nevertheless, the foreman was *the* day-to-day authority at the shanty. He had the power to hire and fire, and he did much to set

the tone for relations among the men and the spirit of the shanty.

During the felling season, the head of the gang, or 'head chopper', was responsible for selecting the best trees for the purpose—generally, tall, straight ones that appeared to have little or no rot. He made the undercut, which largely determined where the giant would fall. Since placing the tree in the right spot facilitated the subsequent steps and helped ensure safety on the job, this was an important task requiring experience and sound judgement. A pair of choppers usually worked together making the deep cut that would bring the tree down. Until the 1870s they did so using single-bit or double-bit axes, taking pride in the accuracy of their blows and learning to trust a partner not to break the rhythm and cause an accident. During the 1870s the two-man cross-cut saw was introduced to Ontario woods operations for the purpose of felling. When the saw was properly filed and set with raker teeth that removed sawdust, a pair of skilled sawyers, one hauling on either end of the saw, could fell a tree more quickly and with less energy than two axemen. It is worth noting that this innovation, perhaps the most significant in woods work during the century, involved a new use for a fairly simple hand tool that had been in the tool kit of workers in wood since Biblical times.[7]

Once the tree had been laid low, then the choppers (always using axes) would 'top' the tree, removing the crown, and hack off every branch of the trunk. For crews in sawlog operations, the next steps were straightforward. The trunk was made, or 'bucked', into log lengths, usually of 16 feet with an extra half foot in case the ends were damaged in transport. Here, too, the two-man cross-cut saw replaced the axe during the 1870s. The bucking crew of two men completed the five-man felling gang. Output was about 60 logs a day for one gang.[8] The work demanded strength and stamina, as well as some experience with axe and saw.

For gangs making square timber, the work at this stage was more complicated because it was at the stump that the wood was put in its final form for export. To convert a rough log into a smooth stick of square or waney timber, the crew worked together, each member doing a specific job. The 'rosser', using a rossing iron that resembled a short hoe, scraped a two-inch-wide strip of bark off the tree, from one end to the other—some 30 to 60 feet. The liner then used a chalk line to draw a straight line the length of the cleaned strip. The scorer swung his axe, making notches that would guide the work of the highly skilled 'hewer'. Using his broad axe, a special tool with a 12-inch blade, the hewer gave the side of the log a flat surface. This was the most skilled task of all, for he had to hew the surface perfectly smooth. Once one side had been made flat, the crew rolled the log, repeating the process on all four sides until the stick was square. A talented hewer could strike his blows so accurately that the stick ended up as smooth as a table top, looking as though it had been planed. The final result was a stick or 'balk' of square timber that was at least 12 inches square (and sometimes much more) and 30 to 60 feet long.

Some indication of the way in which the skill required for the positions in a square timber gang was valued is given by the pay assigned the various positions. In October 1870, Mossom Boyd and Company, a long-established and large firm operating in the Kawarthas and Haliburton, paid hewers $30 per month, liners $20, and scorers $15–$18. In the fall of 1877, Gillies Brothers, a major operator in the Ottawa Valley, paid its hewers $38 per month, liners $22, scorers $17.50–$19, and teamsters and general hands $14–$16.[9]

. . .

In sawlog operations, backwoods transportation was more elaborate, and it grew somewhat more so towards the end of the century. The work was divided into two distinct phases. From late October through December, teamsters would arrive to skid the logs along trails cut from the stump to 'skidways', that is, a type of 'landing' or place where wood was piled temporarily.

In sawlog skidding, a horse pulled one or two logs, depending on their size, by means of a skidding chain that ran around one end of the logs, lifting them above the ground. The other end of the chain was hooked onto a crossbar, or 'whippletree', which was attached to the horse by chains and leather straps. The teamsters followed skidding trails cleared early in the autumn either by themselves or by comparatively inexperienced (and lower-paid) men and boys hired specifically for the task. As the snow fell on the ground it helped to reduce friction and to speed operations, and it buried stumps and other obstructions on which logs might snag. Once the teamster reached the skidway with his load, he stopped to pile it, sliding the logs up poles leaning on an angle from the ground to the top of the skidway. Again, in some of the larger operations, especially later in the century, inexperienced men were hired as 'general hands' to perform the back-breaking grunt work of piling.

On sawlog operations the second phase of backwoods log transportation was known as the sleigh haul. It began shortly after New Year's, once freezing weather had set in and the snow conditions were optimal. Sawmill employees who generally had been laid off in December were available to supplement the shanty crews. From the skidways, crews loaded a dozen or more logs onto wooden, horse-drawn sleighs with iron (later steel) runners. The loading equipment was simple. A 'decking line', or rope, was looped around the log, and a horse pulled on it, raising the log above the ground to the sleighs, while men steadied it as it moved. A cant hook was often used for the purpose—a simple wooden pole, three inches in diameter and four feet long with an iron hook on the end. Once the sleigh was loaded, a teamster standing on top of the load drove a team of powerful horses that pulled the sleigh along the haulways or roads.

The main hauling roads were carefully prepared at the beginning of the season, and maintained each night, by a crew that made sure the ruts carved out for the sleigh runners had a rock-hard, glare-ice surface. Once again, on larger operations later in the century, greater care was taken to maintain the roads and ensure the rapid and safe movement of the sleighs. Young lads known as 'chickadees' cleared the roads of manure throughout the day. 'Sandpipers' poured hot sand on downhill slopes to slow down the sleighs and prevent their toppling over. Towards the end of the century, most shanties had a blacksmith to maintain the chains, whippletrees, and other paraphernalia in top working order. Just before New Year's he toiled long hours re-shodding the horses in clogs designed to grip the ice of the haul roads.

Once the teamster and sleigh reached the dump site, the logs were unloaded by crews using a decking line and cant hooks. Yet again the logs were piled, this time in 'rollways' on the banks of streams or on the flat, frozen surface of a lake. Hauling ended about mid-March, once the warmer weather had made sleighing less efficient or all the logs had been moved.

At the end of the hauling season the crews usually enjoyed a hard-earned rest or broke up. The next step in the seasonal round required the high water of springtime, and that usually meant waiting until mid-April. Many men returned home, while others sought pleasure in lumbermen's hotels until their work resumed.

. . .

## In the Shanties

An integral part of the work of the men in the woods was shanty or camp life. Unlike workers in many other occupations, who left their workmates at the end of the day, woodsmen stayed together, sharing accommodations, food, and free-time amusements. The essential features of shanty life—the close, all-male community, the considerable isolation, the traditional routine—changed remarkably little during the course of the nineteenth century.

Accommodations in the woods were invariably primitive. From the earliest shanties to the more elaborate camps of big operators during the last decade of the century, the buildings were crudely and inexpensively constructed by the shantymen themselves. The companies' aim was to keep costs to a minimum. The essentials were supplied by the materials that came immediately to hand in the backwoods from logs for walls to fir boughs for mattresses, thus the expense of transporting large quantities of goods into remote locations was eliminated. A minimum amount of care was taken with construction because the camps were used only for a season or two until the timber within walking distance had been depleted. The shantymen expected primitive conditions when they set off for the bush each fall. In the nineteenth century, as opposed to the twentieth, it appears Ontario woodsmen put little or no pressure on their employers to improve the basic accommodations.

In all small operations and even most large ones, at least until the last decade of the century camboose shanties were the norm. Charles Macnamara, a head office employee of McLachlin Brothers of Arnprior, made a point of documenting camboose shanties in words and photographs. The typical shanty housing 50 to 60 men, he wrote, 'was a low log building about 35 feet by 40 feet, with side walls six feet high and gables about 10 feet at the peak.' The walls were built of logs notched so as to interlock at the ends. Gaps between the logs were chinked with moss. The shanty was roofed 'with "scoops" that is, logs hollowed out like troughs . . . The joints between them were covered with other scoops turned hollow side down, and the ridge of the roof, where the scoops butted together, was also covered with inverted scoops.' There was a single door. In rare instances, there were windows, but usually it was thought that enough light (and more than enough ventilation!) came from the large (12-foot by 12-foot) opening in the roof. It also allowed smoke to escape from the central fire pit, or 'camboose'.[10]

The heart of the shanty was the camboose, a 12-foot by 12-foot area that was built up a foot or two from the ground with logs and filled with sand. There a large fire burned day and night to heat the shanty and allow for cooking. Bread was baked, salt pork boiled, and pea soup simmered in large iron kettles and pots suspended over the open fire or set in the hot sand. Around the edge of the camboose stood simple benches, where the men could sit to eat, warm themselves, or mend their clothing and sharpen their axes by the light of the fire. Along three walls of the shanty were bunks roughly constructed of saplings. They ran two tiers high and were built as muzzle-loaders; that is, the men shoved themselves into the bunks so their heads were against the wall and their feet to the fire. The men slept two to a bunk, sharing a double grey woollen blanket. Along the wall with the door stood the woodpile, wash basins and water barrel, the cook's work table, stores and utensils, and a rough desk for the clerk with handy shelves to hold 'van' supplies—mittens, tobacco, moccasins, longjohns, red flannel sashes, and so on, that would be sold to the men.

In the case of camboose shanties, the only other building in the camp was a log barn for the oxen or horses and their fodder. During the 1890s, big operators, perhaps borrowing from Michigan, tended to opt for a new kind of camp composed of a cluster of buildings, each with a special purpose. Thus, in addition to the barn, there was usually a blacksmith's shack; a cabin where the clerk kept accounts, sold van goods, and slept along with the foreman; a separate cookery where the cook worked and slept along with his assistants, and where they served meals to the men; a cellar for storing root vegetables and salt pork; and perhaps two or three sleep camps or bunkhouses. These bunkhouses were as crude as the camboose shanties and similarly built of logs, but they were heated by a wood stove, usually a tin barrel turned on its side. A tin chimney replaced the large opening in the roof. In the cookery stood a big, wood-burning cook stove and many long tables with benches where the men ate sit-down meals.

These new arrangements represented a modest step towards a further division of labour, most notably the addition of cookees who assisted the cook by peeling potatoes and the like, serving meals, and washing up. The changes also increased the social space between some members of the camp. At night the foreman and clerk, and the cooking staff retired to their respective quarters outside the main sleep camps. Nevertheless, what should be stressed is the close quarters and shared experience of the shantymen. However firm the hierarchy on the job, it was partly offset by the propinquity and fraternity of the shanty. From chore boy to shanty boss, all ate from the same pot and drank from the same dipper.

The shanty diet was determined by both tradition and remoteness. Though the food was not always appetizing or of good quality, it was usually plentiful. It was also rich, as was believed to be suitable for men doing heavy labour. The basis of the diet was salt pork, which was easier to store than beef and usually cheaper. During the second half of the century most of it was imported from Chicago, although local sources were not unimportant. It was fried in strips or, more commonly, simmered as part of a stew, pork and beans, or pea soup. Bread was also a staple. Macnamara remembered the bread baked in sand as being 'particularly fine', and having 'a delectable nutty flavour'. Dried foods—peas, beans, apples, currants, and biscuit or hard tack—were light to transport and kept well, and so they provided the other basic ingredients. Sometimes there was also pickled herring or dried cod. Molasses, sugar, and tea were considered luxuries even at mid-century, but later they became commonplace, as did mustard, cloves, and cinnamon for flavouring. Scurvy, or 'black-leg', was known in some camps; it was caused by the lack of vitamin C in the diet.[11]

. . .

Every shanty worthy of the name had a cook. Only small shacker operations—that is, those conducted on a more or less ad hoc basis by fewer than a dozen men—tried to get along without one. Naturally, it took the time of at least one person to cook meals for a standard shanty of 50 men. Moreover, cooking was acknowledged to be a skilled occupation and was paid accordingly. Cooks were virtually always male, not because of the job itself, which, after all, closely resembled tasks designated as 'women's work' in the home, but because the rest of the crew was male and the camp was far removed from what were considered to be the necessary moral restraints of family and church. Moreover, male cooks guarded their well-paid jobs from women competitors. Female cooks or cookees were sometimes found at the depot camp (the base camp) if there were farms and hence farm families nearby. Even early in the century, it was recognized that company farms were best run by families and that the women might play a role in feeding shantymen at the depot camp. When John Donnally took over responsibility for Hamilton and Low's Rouge River operations in 1835, he was told to consider having a family at the depot because the firm was 'convinced in cooking affairs & Cows that a woman is of service and profit.'[12]

Each fall, camp life soon settled into a routine. During the autumn felling season, the work day lasted until dusk, and in mid-winter, when the rush was on to haul the timber before the thaw, hauling crews worked by torchlight until the mid-evening. Most evenings, the men were so exhausted that once they had eaten they tumbled into their bunks. Sunday provided a day off—at least when the urgency of completing the sleigh haul wasn't stronger than the sabbatarian inclinations of the owners. It was a time to restore energies by taking it easy or by going hunting or fishing. Clothes were repaired, axes and saws sharpened.

Was sex a part of the nightly shanty routine? Probably not for the vast majority, but this question is difficult to answer. Sexual relations and practices in the lumber camps are hard to document and assess. Given the scarcity of evidence

so far come to light, it seems likely that among camp mates there was no openly acknowledged subculture of sexual intimacy in the all-male shanties. Nevertheless, furtive same-sex liaisons did occur; we have evidence of at least one charge of buggery involving two Ontario shantymen. Without further evidence, it is open to speculation whether this kind of incident hints at widespread but well-hidden practices, or whether it was an example of rooting out unusual behaviour. The only sexual relations among the shantymen that were discussed openly were with female prostitutes. In the press of the day, such activity was regarded as a safety valve that released tensions pent up during long periods of celibacy in the shanties.[13]

The routine of shanty life was sometimes interrupted by a visitor. In some camps a priest made a brief appearance to hear confessions and say mass or a preacher would turn up to deliver a sermon and lead a hymn sing. Priests and preachers alike asked the men to subscribe to missionary and hospital work, and the clerks would deduct the designated amount from the season-end pay. In the surviving company records such subscriptions are not noted with much frequency. In all likelihood, clerical visits were rare in many camps and unknown in others. During the late 1870s and 1880s a few reports in the *Canada Presbyterian* indicate some commitment to the shantymen's mission, an endeavour given support by Presbyterian congregations at Ottawa. But such outreach must have been limited. One missionary based at Mattawa emphasized the difficulties in reaching a large population scattered among remote shanties, and he admitted that even where contacts were made, the results varied: 'Frequently the Word is listened to earnestly and a deep impression is made', but other times 'through prejudice or ignorance little good will be accomplished.' Fundamentalist and moral reform organizations that specifically targeted bushworkers were not formed until shortly after 1900.[14]

Physicians' visits, too, were virtually unknown in camps until the new century. When a man became seriously ill, his camp mates were apt to take up a subscription (docked from their final pay) in order to send him home. Thus, when Christof Bernier fell ill in November 1869 in Britten's shanty, the superintendent informed Mossom Boyd that the men had 'together subscribed $14 to defray his expenses back to Quebec.' But doctors might make a special trip to a camp where typhoid or smallpox had broken out in order to deal with the sick and attempt to arrest the disease before it spread beyond the camp. At the time of the smallpox epidemic of 1885, all men living in lumber camps in Ontario were required to be vaccinated—a rare instance of state intervention in the lives of the shantymen.[15] The idea that doctors might make regular checkups of the men in the camps was broached during the nineteenth century. Dr C.A. Duke wrote Gillies Brothers from Baie de Pères in July 1889 suggesting that all the men in his district subscribe 25 cents a month each, and that in return for that payment, the doctor would visit all shanties once a month and tend to any emergencies. As a precedent he cited a system adopted by the Canadian Pacific Railway. Gillies did not accept the suggestion at that time. However, after smallpox spread widely from the lumber camps in 1900, the province required that a similar system be imposed throughout the logging districts.[16]

Rather than being broken by outsiders, the camp routine was more apt to be broken by the men themselves. Saturday night was the time for lively diversions. Nearly every camp had a fiddler, and singing and buck dances were popular pastimes. James Hillis, who in 1883 at the age of 16 got his first woods job with Boyd Caldwell and Company, recorded his experiences in later life.[17] He notes 'how proficient some of those log-rollers were with the violin when they couldn't read a note of music', and he recalls that 'community dances provided a background for their agility at square dancing as well as clog.' Singing was the specialty of men who had a voice and a knack for remembering long ballads and

adapting them to their crew's experiences. Singalongs could be times for exuberance, and the lively tunes of many a shanty song, melodies drawn from Irish, French-Canadian, and American folksongs, as well as those of sailors around the globe, express a great zest for life.

In his recollections, Hillis vividly recalls some of the Saturday-night tricks played on him that first season as part of his initiation into shanty life. When he played one of the popular test-of-strength games, it was rigged so that he fell backwards into a tub of icy water. 'This trick raised my Irish blood', he says, and he was about to raise a ruckus until he was assured that every newcomer had the same trick played on him. On another occasion, when playing hit-ass, a popular game where a blindfolded man had to guess who had walloped him on the rear, unbeknownst to Hillis, his face had been blackened with soot, much to the amusement of his senior camp mates. Hillis also describes the elaborate preparations made in order to terrify young greenhorns. For several evenings running, men would return to the shanty from the dark woods saying they had glimpsed a bizarre animal. Then, on Saturday night, after various horror stories had been told around the camboose fire, the cook would say, '"Listen!" Sure enough, there would be a queer noise on the roof near the smokestack. Everyone in the group would become excited and jump to his feet as the racket above grew worse. Then, in an instant, they would all behold a large, dark furry animal with huge eyes tumble from the chimney to fall with a thump at their feet.' The terrified lads had been tricked by a man dressed in a bull hide.

These kinds of initiation rites denote a strong sense of group identity among the shantymen. When a young lad signed onto a crew, he was doing more than merely taking a job; he was joining a fraternity that had its own rules and ways of doing things and a sense of boundaries between itself and others. Internal discipline prevailed, as did outward conformity. Charles Macnamara put it this way: 'There was a code of conduct and even rules of etiquette to which the newcomer had to conform or he was soon "given his time" and sent down. The men who did not fit in were eliminated, and the gang settled down for the winter as a more or less harmonious community.'[18] At the camp level, the process of winning conformity was probably straightforward, as Macnamara indicates. But for some individuals it must surely have been painful. Precisely how a man was made to conform is a matter that has not been much explored by historians, and the sources are extremely scanty. It is reasonable to assume, however, that ethnic differences must have made for difficulties. Poles from Renfrew County and many a lone French Canadian must have had trouble being one of the boys. Where men from such minorities were numerous enough, it was common practice to make up a Polish shanty or a French *chantier*, and in this way the problems of fitting in were circumvented. The Polish and French camps then set their own standards for conformity (although in many respects the patterns of camp life varied little from those in the camps of the English-speakers).

. . .

## Shantymen, Raftsmen, and Conflict

As we have seen, once the men were on the job, lumbering entailed a set of routines that were familiar to shantymen, season after season. The routine was seldom broken by conflicts. In their accounts of day-to-day activities in the shanties, bosses rarely noted a disruption caused by disputes with or among their men. They did report on other kinds of disruptions. Daily they worried about the weather—would the cold hold long enough, the storms soon depart? Equipment breakdowns and shortages of hay and oats created frequent snags that threatened to set their plans askew. There is no reason to suppose that shanty bosses suppressed news of trouble with the men, given that they reported other difficulties, even ones resulting from their own mistakes. Certainly employers of shantymen and

raftsmen in nineteenth-century Ontario never had to deal with the labour–management conflict that developed when collective bargaining broke down, since there was no collective bargaining. In fact, unions were unknown in the bush and on the river, although some people must have encountered the Knights of Labor when sawmill workers in Muskoka and at Ottawa organized and struck in the late 1880s and early 1890s.

To be sure, there were instances of conflict, and it is worth scrutinizing a few of them, bearing in mind that they were exceptions. Woodsmen and raftsmen did not always get along among themselves, and inevitably there were clashes between individuals. Particularly during rafting, when men could get liquor more easily, fights sometimes broke out. One such incident was reported in the *Bytown Gazette*, probably because it involved a local clerk who bested his raftsman assailant in court. The accused was convicted and fined $10. Another dispute entered into the public consciousness because [one man] died. In early September 1847 the *Bathurst Courier* reported that Hyacinthe Blachette had stabbed Pierre Aubichon in a fight at William Morris's camp on the Petawawa. The men had arrived in the camp two days before, bringing alcohol with them. Drinking had led to fighting and eventually to the murder of Aubichon.[19]

Some of the disputes among workers involved larger numbers of men. The *Canada Lumberman* reported in February 1882 that two rival camps at Hubbard Lake claimed the same landing, that is, the same dump site for their logs. Group pride and a competitive spirit evidently played their parts: 'The result was a kind of guerrilla warfare, until the men at one of the camps cleaned out the other—the foreman of the vanquished camp taking to town in his shirt-sleeves.' In some of the clashes there was an element of ethnic differences. In the summer of 1876 it was reported that a fight had broken out between rival gangs of raftsmen when a crew of

French Canadians discovered that a raft run by Indians had arrived at Ottawa a day sooner than theirs. Such ethnic clashes entered into the folk tradition of the woodsmen. The ninth verse of the song 'The New Limit Line' depicts an incident on the Gilmour limits in Muskoka. The crew of local boys hauling timber behind their lead teamster were confronted by a defiant outsider, a French Canadian who challenged the pecking order:

> Our lead was St. Thomas, from Nogies Creek mouth,
> But a Frenchman called Sweenor he tried to run him out,
> But our Bobcaygeon boys they all got combined—
> They ran Sweenor to hell from the New Limit Line.[20]

The most notorious clash involving ethnic groups was the Shiners' War among Ottawa raftsmen, which reached a climax during the period 1835–7. Observers at the time contended that it was in large part an attempt by organized Irish raftsmen to raise their wages by driving French Canadians from the river. Curiously enough, those same observers pointed out that certain employers were inciting the Irish, who were said to act as the employers' troops in battles that had their origins in clashes over timber limits.[21] Historian Michael Cross accepts both arguments, but he believes that in the frontier situation where there were virtually no forces of social control, one employer in particular, Peter Aylen, cynically manipulated the Irish raftsmen as part of his bid for social prestige.[22] A more compelling explanation for the violence has recently been advanced by Richard Reid.[23] He casts serious doubt on the claim that this was a fight over jobs, by noting that at the peak of the violence local employment opportunities were expanding. He also points out that the Irish cannot have been victorious, as is usually said, for both Irish and French Canadians continued to

work in large numbers on the river, and their relations were generally harmonious. Reid suggests that the Shiners' War makes sense only when partisan political rivalries are taken into account. Peter Aylen was a Reformer who rallied Irish Catholic raftsmen as part of his political campaign to win power and defeat the Conservatives, who relied on Orange and French-Canadian bullies. It is at least clear that this exceptional moment of widespread violence among lumberers was no straightforward instance of class conflict. The alliances were cross-class, and the divisions were essentially ethnic and, quite possibly, partisan.

These were conflicts among workers, but sometimes, of course, a boss clashed with an employee or two. In 1881 a woods superintendent for Gillies Brothers reported that one of his foremen was so fed up with the incompetence of greenhorn teamsters that he had discharged them, because he could not 'get them to do fair work'. A woods boss wrote from Glanmorgan in 1898 to Mossom Boyd expressing his impatience with a clerk with whom he found 'it very difficult to get along'. What's more, the clerk was 'continually making mistakes, and ha[d] no memory.' One employer, a Mr Findlay, succeeded in having charges laid against Baptiste Laframboise, an allegedly insubordinate raftsman who had been hired to run the Chatts Rapids. The story according to a police court reporter was as follows: 'When in the midst of a number of islands, where if every man does not do his duty, the chances are that the raft will be knocked to pieces, Laframboise refused to row. He also made an attempt to assault the foreman.' Fortunately for the raftsman, the magistrate held that as the offence had not been committed within the city of Ottawa, he had no power to act.[24]

The records of lumber companies reveal several cases where men were disciplined for being drunk on duty. A walking boss for Wright docked one such man a half day's pay. When drunks caused fights they were more likely to be fired. Writing from Usborne Depot in 1873,

James McEvoy reported that he 'was obliged to discharge James Smith for getting drunk and raising disturbance.' Moreover, on the Monday morning he was still so drunk 'he could Scersly waulk.' Charles R. Stewart, bush superintendent with Mossom Boyd, wrote from Haliburton in 1869 complaining about a shanty cook by the name of Ingram who had gone on 'a two days drunk'. Stewart believed he 'should have discharged him', but there was no one to take his place (and a cook was essential). Furthermore, Stewart considered Ingram 'a good cook'. And so Stewart had scolded him, saying that 'if he was not sober in the morning [he] would kick him out of the township, and forbid the tavern keeper to give him more drink.' On the morrow, the cook was reported 'penitent' and he 'solemnly promise[d] he w[ould] not take whiskey until next spring.'[25]

. . .

When groups of workers took action against their bosses, they usually appear to have been objecting to the quality of shanty fare. In November 1883 W. Ritchie, camp foreman for Mossom Boyd, wrote from South River reporting on 'a break up in the gang of men—concerning the Board'. The men had 'refused for to work without having Beef.' Five log makers had left as a result, and 'the Balance of the gang remain at their work on conditions that I will get Beef for a chainge when I can.' Ritchie thought the company should approve his purchase of beef, even at high prices, because replacements for the men would have had to be paid higher wages. Since there is no follow-up correspondence, it appears likely that the foreman was given permission to buy the beef and the remaining men were satisfied.[26]

Another dispute over camp fare was not resolved as easily. In 1854 John Egan and Company had 25 shantymen arrested and charged for quitting work and thus breaking their contracts. In the Ottawa police court the defendants explained that 'the pork with which they were supplied in the shanty was unsound, and unfit for use; so much so, that they could not eat it, and had lived for several days on nothing but bread and tea.' Although the men complained several times, the foreman did not get better pork, and so they refused to work. According to the men's testimony the foreman then told them 'that if they could not work on such victuals they might leave.' The magistrates decided that according to the Master and Servant Law they had no power to inquire into the reason for the employees' departure. By leaving before the end of their contracts, the men had broken them. Each of the workers was fined one shilling or sentenced to a week in jail.[27]

Another cause for the occasional labour–management conflict involving whole crews was an employer's attempt to alter the terms of an existing contract. It was well understood that trouble was likely to result from such attempts. In December 1847 Thomas Graham, a Quebec timber dealer, wrote Douglas Cameron, a small lumberman operating out of Glengarry County, regarding the need to reduce shantymen's wages in mid-season. Graham complained that business was slack, he was losing money, and unemployment was so bad at Quebec there were 'Plenty of men here just now would be glad to work for their board.' He instructed Cameron as follows: 'You must make a Second arrangement with your men. They may think it hard but it is worse on me to be paying money for nothing. So you had better mind what you are about.' Unfortunately, we do not know how Cameron fared.[28]

. . .

In his book *Up to Date; or, the Life of a Lumberman*, George Thompson includes a chapter entitled 'Trouble with the Men', where he describes 'the first and only big strike that ever occurred in the bush'.[29] The dispute happened one October (probably in 1873) among the men Thompson was superintending for a large concern operating on a tributary of the Trent River. Towards the end of the month, the manager or head of the firm wrote to instruct Thompson to cut the shantymen's wages by 20 per cent, because of the falling price of labour that autumn. 'Now such a thing as a cut in the men's wages had never before been heard of in the bush', writes Thompson, and he continues:

The view the men took of it was that they were being imposed upon, for they knew that they could have obtained the same rate of wages from other firms when they engaged with men, and being away back in the bush they knew nothing of the drop that had not only occurred in wages, but in timber and lumber; neither did they care. They claimed a bargain was a bargain; they had signed papers for the run or until the shanties closed in the spring, and they were prepared to carry out their part of the contract.

As Thompson tells the story, he knew there would be trouble, and so he insisted that the head of the firm himself come to the headquarters camp to announce the wage cut. On 1 November, the manager did appear with 'a big force of men' who had agreed to take the lower wage and the jobs of the workers. Work stopped for several days as the strikers came to realize the cut would go through; then they insisted they be paid their back wages. Altogether about two-thirds of the workforce were paid off, and then the climax came.

Thompson, the manager, and the camp clerk were sitting in the office at headquarters camp when a group of the men who had just been paid off came in, asking how they were supposed to transport their trunks 10 miles down the lake. The author continues: 'His nibs replied that he did not care a ——— how they got them down. Quick as a flash his nibs got a blow on the neck from one of the men, and then I knew we were in for it.' The manager was incapacitated with terror, and in an unmanly way 'did not speak or attempt to get up from his seat or in any way try even to defend himself.' Not surprisingly, given whose account this is, it was Thompson himself who sprang to the rescue and saved the day:

I instantly drew my revolver and fired in among the men, being careful not to hurt anyone. This had the desired effect; the men tumbled out of the office in short order, and immediately got their trunks, emptied their clothes out and made a bon fire of the trunks right in front of the office, and with curses and yells took their departure.

To complete the story, Thompson reports that the firm lost a fortune on its timber that season because the replacement workers were incompetent and the original men that remained on the job put rotten timber into the raft so that it could not be sold. 'It was a lesson to his nibs,' concludes Thompson, 'for never after did he mention anything about reducing the men's wages. The timber that season was the last our firm ever put on the Quebec market.'

Now, this is a well-told story, but one wouldn't want to give too much credence to certain details concerning the heroism of the author himself. Nevertheless, the essentials of the account have a ring of authenticity. Here were men determined to resist a wage cut and to see their contracts fulfilled. When that proved impossible, two-thirds of them insisted on their wages, got what was owing, and expressed their anger. The other third swallowed the wage cut but used their control over production and quality to sabotage the operation. For the firm, the grim results of an ill-chosen policy were only too evident. It is quite possibly for this reason that firms almost never tried to reduce wages in mid-term.

What of the men themselves? Did they tend to live up to the terms of their contracts? Indications are that shantymen and raftsmen did so, although admittedly the evidence is fragmentary and difficult to interpret. An important source for shedding light on the issue of desertion is the *Bytown Gazette*, which published the paid notices of woods employers regarding runaway employees, as well as police court reports of breaches of the Master and Servant Act. The employers' notices were intended to prevent the runaway from securing a job from another employer in the trade and perhaps to recoup expenses incurred by the employer in hiring him. Some announcements also included a warning to any employer who was found to be harbouring the man in question. A typical notice reads:

> Lumberers on the Ottawa and elsewhere are hereby cautioned from taking into their employment Louis Charout and Theofile LeClair, my hired men, they having left my shanty without my knowledge or consent, and are considerably indebted to me. Any person found employing them or continuing them in their service after the date of this notice will be prosecuted, John Thompson. Nepean, 26th September, 1846[30]

During the 26-year period from 1846 to 1872, the *Bytown Gazette* published 16 notices concerning a total of 78 men who had broken their contracts by quitting their jobs in mid-term. Three of the announcements concerned large groups (18–20 men), possibly whole crews that had deserted; the remainder announced alleged desertions of from one to five employees. The incidents were spread more or less evenly throughout the period. To be sure, the notices indicate that some men did leave their jobs against their employers' wishes and probably in violation of their contracts. Yet 16 alleged incidents involving just 78 men over 26 years are not many, given that during the same period tens of thousands of contracts must have been made in the trade.

. . .

Notwithstanding the evidence regarding these few dozen runaways, it appears likely that desertions were in fact rare. Certainly in the surviving records of lumber companies, where there are countless detailed reports of day-to-day mishaps and difficulties, there are almost no reports of employees quitting their jobs and breaking their contracts. For woodsmen, there were strong disincentives to quitting in midstream. They might lose their back wages, and because so many of the shantymen were paid

only at the end of their contracts, the amounts owing would have been too large to forgo.

The runaways that employers pursued were mainly those who quit early in the game, before they had worked off the cash advances or the expenses their employers had incurred for hotel bills or transportation. Employers had another advantage in that because hiring was concentrated at Ottawa they had a fair chance of finding runaways when they came to town in search of work. So it was with two woodsmen hired by J.R. Booth who were said to have broken their contracts in November 1869. It was reported that Police Sgt Davis had succeeded in apprehending them at Ottawa, where they awaited trial. Once caught, the alleged deserters could then be brought to court and their employers could have the satisfaction of seeing the men fined or jailed. Many convicted runaways were fined $20—more than a month's wages for many of them—or sentenced to 21 or 30 days in jail. A typical report from the police court concerned 'a little shanty cook of the name of Bouchette, about three feet in his boots'. Convicted of breaking a contract with lumberman Peter McLauren, he was given a fine of $20 or 21 days in jail. 'Minus the needful,' the reporter commented wryly, 'he was sent to limbo.'[31] In this way, then, the state helped employers to discipline even that small minority of woods workers who believed they had something to gain by quitting a contract. The substantial fines and jail sentences must have deterred others from lighting out from their camps.

## Looking Back, Looking Forward

This chapter began by arguing that the world of Ontario's shantymen in the nineteenth century was one of variety and movement, as well as remarkable stability. Many of the fundamental patterns of woods work endured well into the next century, although eventually—mainly after the Second World War—there were to be sweeping changes.[32] Throughout the nineteenth century, the workforce came from diverse sources. For many young men and immigrants, working in the woods was a way of earning cash so that they could settle on the land. For farmers on marginal lands, woods wages meant the difference between permanency and migration, making a go of a farm or having to move elsewhere. For some fellows—mainly single labourers—the timber camps provided jobs in winter, a time of year when there was little other work. And for still others, woods work, river-driving, and rafting made up a year-round job and defined who they were. It was not until the second half of the twentieth century that the logging labour force came to consist mainly of a stable population of men who lived permanently in the logging districts and who thought of lumbering as a career.

. . .

The work of the shantymen involved a variety of tasks and distinct seasonal rhythms. In terms of skill the men ranged from the masterful hewer, well paid for his expert handling of a broad axe, to the men who did the grunt work of piling logs. During the mid-winter sleigh haul, the pace could be furious and the hours long, because the ideal cold weather lasted for only a short season. When the timber rafts were passing down smooth stretches of river, life seemed easy; at rapids, there was hope of survival only with strenuous effort. A heavy dependence on natural conditions and seasonal changes has remained characteristic of the industry to this day, although mechanization during the third quarter of the twentieth century reduced the extent of the dependence.

. . .

Labour relations, too, held their basic shape throughout the century. Unions were unknown in the woods and on the river. They did not come to the industry until the next century, when there developed acute labour shortages, a core of radical activists, and state policies that helped to promote collective bargaining. Even spontaneous group protests or strikes—aimed at bad food or wage cuts—were exceptional events.

Individual protest, however, was never absent from logging. But throughout the nineteenth century a man wanting to challenge a boss or quit his job had to weigh the advantages against the fact that by doing so he would lose back pay and might be charged and convicted for having broken his contract.

Through the years the shantymen have retained a reputation for toughness, bravado, and, when in town, carousing. Hard work in remote places, very dangerous jobs, and the all-male life of the camps contributed to the shantymen's image and culture. And yet for many men, lumbering was simply a job at a time of year when jobs were scarce. The work was demanding but familiar, even monotonous. A sojourn away from home was less a means of escape from family life than a chance to advance the well-being of the family. Today, logging continues to provide men with a range of experiences and opportunities, even as rugged masculinity remains the hallmark of the woodsman.

## Notes

For helpful advice, I thank Paul Craven and the other authors of this volume, the Toronto Labour Studies Research Group, and the Early Canadian History Group.

1. A note on terminology: 'Shantyman' in nineteenth-century Ontario referred to any worker engaged in lumbering, although it sometimes referred only to those working in the woods as distinct from river drivers and raftsmen, who worked on the waterways. 'Lumberman' always meant an owner or top manager. 'Lumberer', 'logger', and 'woodsman' were used interchangeably with 'shantyman', but 'woodsman' was much more common. 'Lumberjack', 'woods worker', and 'bushworker' were virtually never heard in the province during the nineteenth century.

2. The economic importance of the forest industry is evaluated in Douglas McCalla, 'Forest Products and Upper Canadian Development, 1814–42', *Canadian Historical Review* 68 (1987), 159–98;

and Peter W. Sinclair, 'The North and the North-West: Forestry and Agriculture', in Ian Drummond, *Progress without Planning: The Economic History of Ontario from Confederation to the Second World War* (Toronto: Ontario Historical Studies Series and the University of Toronto Press, 1987), 77–8. On Muffraw (also Montferrand), see Gerard Goyer and Jean Hamelin, 'Joseph Montferrand', *Dictionary of Canadian Biography* (*DCB*), vol. 9, 562–3. On the Prince of Wales, see *Bytown Gazette*, 15 Aug. 1860.

3.  Ian Radforth, *Bushworkers and Bosses: Logging in Northern Ontario* (Toronto: University of Toronto Press, 1987), chs. 4 and 9.

4.  Ontario Ministry of Natural Resources Library, 'The Pointer Boat', typescript prepared by the Operations Branch, Department of Lands and Forests, 1963; R. John Corby, 'The Alligator or Steam Warping Tug: A Canadian Contribution to the Development of Technology in the Forest Industry', *Industrial Archaeology* 3 (1977): 15–33.

5.  See Graeme Wynn, *Timber Colony: A Study in the Historical Geography of Early New Brunswick* (Toronto: University of Toronto Press, 1981), 54; A.R.M. Lower, *The North American Assault on the Canadian Forest* (Toronto: Ryerson Press, 1938), 27.

6.  The description of lumbering techniques is based on Wynn, *Timber Colony*; Lower, *North American Assault*; Donald MacKay, *The Lumberjacks* (Toronto: McGraw-Hill Ryerson, 1978), passim; James T. Angus, *A Deo Victoria: The Story of the Georgian Bay Lumber Co., 1871–1942* (Thunder Bay, Ont.: Severn Publications, 1990), ch. 7.

7.  Lower, *North American Assault*, 33.

8.  Ibid.

9.  National Archives of Canada (NAC), MG 28 III I, Mossom Boyd and Company Records (Mossom Boyd Records), A1(b) Shanty Operations, 1. Letters from foremen, 1869–1912, vol. 99, Charles Thomson to A. Elliot, 20 Oct. 1870; Archives of Ontario (AO), Gillies Bros. Lumber Company Records, D–10, Misc., 1875–1924, MU 3270, Engagements, 1877.

10. Charles Macnamara, 'The Camboose Shanty',

*Ontario History* 51 (1959): 74. See also Bernie Bedore, *The Shanty* (Arnprior, Ont., private, 1975). For a wider view, see Randall E. Rohe, 'The Evolution of the Great Lakes Logging Camp, 1830–1930', *Journal of Forest History* 30 (1986): 17–28.

11. Macnamara, 'Camboose Shanty', 76; Canada, Royal Commission on the Relations of Labour and Capital, *Report—Evidence, Ontario*, vol. 5, 1189.

12. AO, Hamilton Brothers Records, Outgoing Correspondence, 1835–40, 'Instructions from Messrs. Hamilton & Low to Mr. John Donnally for Management of Rouge business', Oct. 1835, cited in Richard Reid, ed., *The Upper Ottawa Valley to 1855: A Collection of Documents* (Toronto: Champlain Society, 1990), 123.

13. The case of buggery is noted by Steven Maynard, who suggests that court records may prove revealing about sexuality in the logging camps; see his 'Rough Work and Rugged Men: The Social Construction of Masculinity in Working-Class History', *Labour/Le Travail* 23 (1989): 159–69.

14. *Canada Presbyterian*, 3 June 1885. (My thanks to Christine Burr for this and subsequent references to this journal.) Radforth, *Bushworkers and Bosses*, 95–6, 102–3.

15. NAC, Mossom Boyd Records, vol. 102, Charles Stewart to Mossom Boyd, 26 Nov. 1869. Physicians' reports include: vol. 99, Dr Macdonald to A. Elliot, 30 Aug. 1870; vol. 105, Dr D. Williams to Mossom Boyd, 7 Dec. 1900. A copy of the government order may be found in AO, RG 10, Department of Health Records, I B4, vol. 464, scrapbook #1, item #50. The wider context is given in Barbara Lazenby Craig, 'State Medicine in Transition: Battling Smallpox in Ontario, 1882–1885', *Ontario History* 75 (1983): 319–47.

16. AO, Gillies Bros Records, MU 3258, 15 July 1889. For context, see Radforth, *Bushworkers and Bosses*, 104–5; Paul Bator, 'The Health Reformer versus the Common Canadian: The Controversy over Compulsory Vaccination against Smallpox in Toronto and Ontario, 1900–1920', *Ontario History* 75 (1983): 348–73.

17. James M. Hillis, 'Life in the Lumber Camp: 1883', *Ontario History* 59 (1967): 157–62.

18. Macnamara, 'Camboose Shanty', 78.

19. *Bytown Gazette*, 9 Aug. 1870, 28 Aug. 1847. See also *Bathurst Courier*, 7 Sept. 1847, reprinted in Reid, ed., *Upper Ottawa Valley*, 70–1.

20. *Canada Lumberman*, 1 Feb. 1882; *Bytown Gazette*, 3 Aug. 1876; Edith Fowke, *Lumbering Songs from the Northern Woods* (Toronto: NC Press, 1985 [1970]), 'The New Limit Line', 55.

21. NAC, Upper Canada Sundries, vol. 152, George Hamilton to Lt.-Col. Rowan, 1 June 1835, G.W. Baker to Rowan, 15 June 1835.

22. Michael S. Cross, 'The Shiners' War: Social Violence in the Ottawa Valley in the 1830's', *Canadian Historical Review* 54 (1973): 1–26.

23. Reid, ed., *Upper Ottawa Valley*, xxxvi–xl.

24. AO, Gillies Bros Records, MU 3250, George Gordon to William Gillies, 13 Nov. 1881; NAC, Mossom Boyd Records, vol. 96, William Creswell to Mossom Boyd & Co., 8 Feb. 1898; *Bytown Gazette*, 13 June 1865.

25. NAC, MG 24 D 8, Philemon Wright and Family Papers (Mfm. M–234), unsigned diary, 18 Mar. 1859; AO, Gillies Bros Records, MU 3246, James McEvoy to Gillies Bros, 5 Jan. 1873; NAC, Mossom Boyd Records, vol. 102, Charles R. Stewart to Mossom Boyd, 26 Oct. 1869.

26. NAC, Mossom Boyd Records, vol. 105, W. Ritchie to Mossom Boyd, 7 Nov. 1883.

27. *Bytown Gazette*, 17 June 1854.

28. AO, Douglas Cameron Papers, MU 466, Thomas Graham to D. Cameron, 20 Dec. 1847.

29. George Thompson, *Up to Date: Or the Life of a Lumberman* (Peterborough, Ont.: private, *c.* 1895), ch. 6.

30. *Bytown Gazette*, 10 Oct. 1846.

31. Ibid., 6 Nov. 1869, 28 July 1864.

32. Twentieth-century developments are discussed in Radforth, *Bushworkers and Bosses*.

# 11

# Boys in the Mining Community

## Robert McIntosh

> Boys in coal towns are 'particularly rough and uncultivated'.
>
> Nova Scotia teacher, 1886

At the centre of the boy's life in coal towns and villages was the mine. He was raised within sight of it; the smell of coal dust was as familiar to him as the sounds of steam pumps and hoists. The boy may have seen for years his father and older brothers leave for the pit. For most boys raised within these communities, the day arrived when they too surrendered their childhood to it. In the nineteenth century, boys raised in coal-mining towns and villages were expected to enter the mine. The class, gender, and cultural identities the community defined for boys encouraged them in this aim. But as childhood was reconstructed in the urban centres of late nineteenth-century Canada, reservations over child labour filtered into coal communities. Teachers and school and mines inspectors arrived to enforce the new laws reflecting emerging views of childhood. Although they were seldom numerous, they helped to constitute a respectable, reforming middle class in coal towns. Organizations dedicated to the reconstructed childhood also entered coal towns and villages: the Woman's Christian Temperance Union (WCTU), Bands of Hope, Boy's Brigades, and the YMCA in the nineteenth century; in the twentieth, the Scouting movement, Children's Aid Societies, and public health nurses. More importantly, early trade unionists were also drawn to the emerging new standards of appropriate childhood. Advocates of compulsory education and restrictive mining legislation, they were instrumental in enforcing the legal redefinition of childhood in the coalfields. By the early twentieth century, the mining community was clearly ambivalent about boys' presence in the pit.

The coal community was marked by the mine, literally overshadowed by the prominent bankhead at the top of the pit housing its hoisting, dumping, and screening equipment. In close vicinity were pump and winding-engine houses, their large smokestacks and engines 'blowing and snorting away most furiously', the lamp cabin, the fan house, stables, carpenter's and blacksmith's shops, and mine offices.[1] Various storehouses were also distributed about the mine surface, the one for explosives at a distance from the rest. Huge mounds of coal, awaiting shipment out, were adjacent to the bankhead, as were the substantial mounds of waste removed from the coal at the picking table. Piles of lum-

Robert McIntosh, 'Boys in the Mining Community', from *The Boys in the Pits*. McGill-Queen's University Press, 2000. Reprinted by permission of McGill-Queen's University Press.

ber to buttress the roof of working places and underground roads were collected prior to transport into the mine. A pond or reservoir to supply water for the steam engines was in the vicinity, as was a waste pond to collect the water pumped out of the mine. Also on the mine surface was the transportation infrastructure to ship coal out: rail lines inland, loading wharfs at the seaside. By the turn of the twentieth century, compressor sheds, coal-fired electrical generating stations, with their large chimneys, and wash houses for miners had been added to the colliery landscape.

Never far from the mine were the community buildings: churches with their adjacent cemetery, a schoolhouse, the company store, possibly independent retailers beyond company property, the temperance hall, and drinking establishments. Other community halls were erected by fraternal societies or trade union locals. The manager's residence, commonly on a hill overlooking the community, was a prominent landmark. The miners' far more modest dwellings clustered closer to the pit. Larger communities would have a town hall, hotels and restaurants, a bank, a post office, a variety of merchants, perhaps even a newspaper office or a small hospital.[2]

. . .

. . . [A]t least to the end of the nineteenth century, boys were raised in these coal towns with the strong expectation that they would enter the pit at some point in their life. Far more than elsewhere in Canada, boys were bred to the mine in Nova Scotia. Coal mining was a way of life, a lifelong occupation. Dan J. McDonald recalled: 'I was just a boy when I first went down in the pits. I never thought much about it one way or another because it was natural for all the miners' sons in those days. You just followed on.'[3] As late as 1927 a Springhill miner complained to the UMWA [United Mine Workers of America] local that 'he got three boys laying around and eating every thing and the Company won't give them work.'[4] Coal companies made a practice of hiring on a preferential basis men and boys inhabiting company dwellings—and

indebted at the company store—for mine employment.[5] F.C. Kimber, manager at the Reserve Mine on Cape Breton Island, indicated in 1888 that he took boys when they reached the age of 13—'They are always our own boys who live in the place.'[6] Of the 937 boys 12 years of age and older resident in Dominion Coal-owned housing in 1907, an estimated 811 were working in the mines.[7] These coal towns and villages were generally able to reproduce the mining labour force, although in periods of rapid growth, such as from 1900 to 1914, demand far outstripped the local supply of boys.

## Class in the Coal Community

Class profoundly marked coal towns and villages. In single-industry coal communities, there were few merchants, professionals, or clergymen to form an intermediate class between mine management and mine workers. Coal companies exercised wide authority within the community, as employers, as landlords, and as merchants. 'Everybody in Glace Bay', reported the *Canadian Mining Journal* in 1908, 'is either the servant of the Coal Company, or the servant of the servant of the Coal Company.'[8]

Considerable investment in community infrastructure was required to draw and retain a workforce, particularly if the mine was located in an isolated or remote district. Companies built and maintained schools and encouraged the construction of churches by providing free land.[9] Most importantly, coal companies built houses. The General Mining Association [GMA] erected company housing on a large scale, setting a pattern for Nova Scotia, where the construction of company houses continued throughout the nineteenth century, particularly in Cape Breton. By the turn of the twentieth century, the Dominion Coal Company owned twelve hundred houses.[10] In the isolated mining communities of the western interior, companies typically erected bunkhouses.[11] On Vancouver Island, single-family dwellings were built by coal companies from the time of the Hudson's Bay Company.[12] James Dunsmuir was so wedded to the company town that when he opened the Extension mine a few miles south of Wellington in 1897, he insisted that miners employed there, many of whom had built houses in the vicinity, move (at their own expense) to the company village of Ladysmith, better isolated from unionized Nanaimo.[13]

The class gulf was clearly expressed in housing. Mount Rundell, a two-storey building constructed by the GMA for its manager at the Albion Mines in 1827, contained 22 large rooms. Situated on a 75-acre property overlooking the mine and entered by a long curved carriage drive, the estate had a cricket pitch, a fruit orchard and gardens protected by a wooden palisade, stables, servants' quarters, and outbuildings for guests.[14] The slightly smaller Beech Hill was built at Sydney Mines in 1829 for manager Richard Brown.[15] Miners, in contrast, inhabited tenements.[16] Typically, these were brick houses built in one-storey terraces on an English model. The smallest houses had one room and a kitchen, the largest two or three rooms, a kitchen, and sleeping space in the attic. The backyard would usually have an outhouse and large garden, with perhaps a cow, pigs, and chickens.[17] Although by the twentieth century 'miners' rows' were no longer built, having been supplanted by 'cottages' comprising two homes, company houses were reputed for their dilapidation and overcrowding. . . .[18]

Whatever its quality, company-owned housing was an effective tool of corporate control. In a sequence of events frequently repeated in coal communities throughout Canada over the years, a strike at Sydney Mines in the spring and summer of 1876 was followed by evictions from company-owned houses. The arrival of strike-breakers at the end of July led to violence along the picket lines and the arrival of militia units.[19] The coal operators most likely to employ these tactics were the Dunsmuirs, on Vancouver Island. Participation in a strike led to prompt eviction. And efforts to resist eviction led to prompt calls for the militia.[20]

In addition to owning housing, coal companies frequently operated retail outlets. Company stores were originally established to offer merchandise to miners that might otherwise have been unavailable; to offer credit to miners to carry them over periods (during winter especially) when there was little work at the colliery; and, crucially, to ease financial pressure on coal companies by paying workers in goods rather than cash. A store was established at Sydney Mines as early as 1809.[21] GMA manager Richard Brown alleged that the early mine owners on Cape Breton Island 'made more profit by the sale of their stores than of their coal.'[22] The Hudson's Bay Company operated what was effectively a company store, but its successor, the Vancouver Coal Mining and Land Company, instead encouraged independent merchants to establish themselves at Nanaimo.[23] Alberta mining camps, in contrast, typically contained a company store.[24]

Where they persisted, company stores emerged as a lightning rod for controversy. A slow mining season could rapidly inflate the extent of a miner's indebtedness to the company store and deepen his subjection to the coal company.[25] As a resident of Cape Breton observed in 1881, company stores 'are a fertile source of disease. It is true they keep on hand all articles the men require, but the prices are most exorbitant. Such being the case, when work is slack, the workmen, especially if they have large families, are soon head and ears in debt, hopelessly I might add, and completely under the will of the agent [manager], who uses the men as one uses a football. Under these circumstances if the workman sees a chance of bettering his position and pay, he requires to ask permission of his lord and master, which request is often met with a point blank refusal, or a declaration to the effect that he *may* leave *when* the store debt is paid.'[26] The requirement to pay wages in currency—rather than, for instance, in credit at the company store—was not legislated in Nova Scotia until 1899. Company stores persisted into the twentieth century.[27]

The nineteenth-century manager wielded wide power in the community. He ruled on access to company housing and to consumer goods in the company store; he determined the nature of local services, including streets (frequently named after corporate officials), policing, and schooling.[28] Small wonder that Pictou County boys doffed their caps when the manager of the Acadia Company drove by in his carriage or sleigh.[29] As late as 1946, the Royal Commission on Coal condemned closed camps in the western interior, where 'the local coal operator controls all land within convenient distance of the mines, owns all housing and controls all stores, hotels and service facilities.'[30]

The power of the colliery manager was tempered by the authority that miners retained underground, for at least as long as board-and-pillar mining continued, and the need for ongoing negotiation of working conditions in the mine. It was also mediated by paternalism: a relationship marked by mutual obligations whereby the powerful offer protection and direction; the weak, obedience and loyalty. Even at the largest nineteenth-century mines managers knew all employees by name. R.H. Brown noted in his diary in 1874 that the '[b]oy Alex McAskill [was] hurt in pit today, driving tubs on No.1 Level. One tub got off road and jambed [sic] his leg. [N]o bones broken.'[31] Similarly, when a boy broke his leg at Springhill in 1890, manager Henry Swift reported this event in his regular correspondence with company officials.[32] Reinforcing paternalist relations were the ties of family, which frequently bound miners and mine officials. Into the twentieth century, the majority of mine officials were former working miners.[33]

Paternalist overtures gave mine managers a more compliant workforce. As one correspondent wrote in 1881, 'I know of no instance where an employer has displayed a concern for the social well being and improvement of his workmen, in which he has not been amply repaid, by their increased respect and zeal on his behalf.'[34] Paternalism offered employees a range of bene-

fits. Companies might provide coal free or at cost to employees.[35] The Hudson's Bay Company offered miners at Nanaimo in 1862 a house, fuel, and medical attendance.[36] In Pictou County, the General Mining Association purchased uniforms for a volunteer rifle company in the 1860s.[37] Boys at the Caledonia Mine received a traditional Christmas treat, which they forfeited in 1888 when one of their number inadvertently broke a piece of mine machinery.[38] In the twentieth century, coal companies commonly provided sports fields and open-air rinks.[39]

Paternalist gestures in the mining community extended to a contest run by the Provincial Workmen's Association [PWA] in 1884 for the most popular mine manager in Nova Scotia.[40] Respected officials could expect periodic tokens of the miners' regard. G.M. Appleton, engineer at the Vale Colliery, was presented in 1885 with 'a very valuable box of Drawing Instruments and a Writing Desk'. Shortly before mine manager Leckie left Springhill it was suggested that '[o]n the eve of his departure there should be a big meeting of the workmen and the presentation of something tangible that he might take away with him—as a memorial of the good wishes of the men—and be able to show his friends.'[41] As Ian McKay has pointed out, gift-giving carried significance both as a 'gesture of subordination' but also as reflecting notions of 'reciprocal rights and obligations'.[42] Paternalism placed limits on the powerful by embodying expectations about how power could legitimately be exercised.

Only gradually was corporate strength within the company town eroded. Fraternal orders, whereby miners combined to provide mutual death, disability, or medical benefits in exchange for the payment of dues, carved out a niche for mine workers outside of the ambit of the company (although members of the lodge of Freemasons formed at the Albion Mines in 1860 asked permission of the local manager before they marched through the town).[43] Miners also established co-operatives. As early as the 1860s, co-operative retail stores were organized in the

Nova Scotian coalfields. A store established at Albion Mines (later Stellarton) in 1861 may have been the first in Canada. Some, including stores at Stellarton and Sydney Mines, enjoyed considerable longevity.[44] The British Canadian Cooperative Society in Cape Breton, with nearly 3,500 members and $1.5 million in annual sales by the 1920s, was a significant counterweight to the extensive chain of company stores operated by the Dominion Coal Company in Cape Breton.[45] Retail co-operatives were also formed in western Canada: at Nanaimo before the end of the nineteenth century and in the Crowsnest Pass in the first decade of the twentieth.[46]

Miners also organized for electoral politics. They formed political clubs, including one in Stellarton in 1882.[47] In 1886 the PWA entered provincial politics, unsuccessfully running two candidates for the House of Assembly.[48] The incorporation of mining towns from late in the nineteenth century and the extension of the franchise to miners in company housing in Nova Scotia in 1889 encouraged political organization.[49] But the political education the PWA attempted to provide only slowly overcame a tradition of deference to the company in mining towns. 'For a long time,' David Frank quoted a former miner, 'the miners themselves wouldn't vote for a miner. They'd figure he wouldn't know enough.' It was not until the 1910s that numerous trade union municipal councillors were elected, determined to restrict company police and evictions from company housing and to review the modest levels of municipal taxes paid by mining companies. A miner was elected mayor of Glace Bay in 1918.[50] During the 1920s, four Farmer-Labour candidates were elected to the provincial legislature from Cape Breton County.[51] Paralleling the changing political orientation of Nova Scotian miners, a Socialist Young Guard emerged in provincial coalfields in the early twentieth century.[52] Coal miners enjoyed more success in electoral politics in western Canada. In Alberta, they were represented in the provincial legislature between 1909

and 1913, and from 1921 to 1930.[53] And in British Columbia, labour candidates were repeatedly elected: in fact, with the exception of the years 1894 to 1898, miners were represented in the provincial legislature continuously from 1890 to 1930, a unique accomplishment, as Allen Seager observed, for working-class constituencies of the period.[54] Nanaimo even sent miner Ralph Smith to Parliament in 1900.[55]

Most importantly, corporate domination was challenged by the growth of unions in the coalfields. . . . Trade unions allowed mine workers to carve out a margin of manoeuvre. As part of this process, they allowed them to re-examine child labour in light of class, to question its value to the boy, and to explore options, such as the acquisition of formal education that would open broader opportunities, both within and outside of coal communities, for their sons. Organized miners . . . were strong advocates both of compulsory education provisions and of laws restricting child labour in the mines. Mine owners, in contrast, resisted these legislative initiatives. . . .

Boys raised in coal towns and villages learned their class identity in various ways. During the UMWA recognition struggle of 1909–11 in Nova Scotia, few non-union children ventured to attend school, where they were subjected to scorn, even blows.[56] At the same time, children boycotted one of Glace Bay's Sunday schools because it was led by a Dominion Coal manager.[57] Similarly, the UMWA recognition strike on Vancouver Island produced a boycott of school classes in 1912.[58] Two boys were among those jailed after the riots of 1913 at Nanaimo.[59] At the times of greatest industrial conflict, class identity was most keenly felt.

## Gender in the Mining Community

If class was the basic social division boys encountered in coal towns and villages, gender also divided the residents of coal communities. Manhood was defined most fundamentally against women. A miner unhappy about his pay, yet not voting for a labour candidate, was told to give his wife 'the pants' and 'go home with the children and wear the skirt.'[60] The sexes were distinguished in other ways. Men were rugged. Women were not. A manager at Springhill, Henry Swift, remarked favourably on a badly cut young boy: 'He never flinced [flinched] . . . being a smart, handy little fellow.'[61] Sydney Mines manager R.H. Brown recorded in his diary that his wife was 'bled in the right arm by the Doctor for her giddy head.'[62] Men fought. Women swooned. 'The excursion of the athletic association [at Springhill] ended in a row. I believe the boys had the best of it although some of the women fainted.'[63] Most importantly, men worked for wages in the mines; women did not. A man was a breadwinner.

Masculine identity, based in men's work, shifted over the turn of the twentieth century. In the nineteenth-century coalfields, the model for manliness was the craftsman, an independent contractor, paid on the basis of the quality and quantity of coal he produced. He took pride in his ability to produce large coals efficiently and safely. Victor Belik, a Crowsnest Pass miner, observed: 'You know, a coal miner is just like a fisherman with his fish tales. In the bar, we dig more coal than in the mine, because everyone brags about what they do.'[64] But masculinity, when defined around craftsmanship, was exclusive.[65] Thomas Keating, a British immigrant miner, considered the mine labourer 'in the light of the weak brother, unskilled, requiring all our aid'.[66] Similarly, the elderly mine worker, no longer capable of work as a miner, was no longer a complete man. An expression current in the anthracite coalfields of Pennsylvania at the turn of the twentieth century held that 'twice a boy and once a man is a poor miner's life.'[67]

Boys learned that their masculine identity— their integrity as men—hinged on their ability both to acquire a craft and to earn a living. To linger at school was effeminate—even disreputable. Boys looked forward to their start in the mine as a mark of approaching manhood, assur-

ing them added respect in the family and within the community. Their initiation to the mine consisted largely of 'pit-hardening', the acquisition of the required toughness. The *Springhill News and Advertiser* wrote admiringly about a 'young lad who walked uncomplainingly for a good mile from the mine with a severe scalp injury, which was ultimately treated with 11 stitches.'[68] After the explosion at Springhill in 1891, only a handful of survivors were able to stagger out of the stricken pit unaided. Two boys particularly distinguished themselves in the eyes of journalist R.A.H. Morrow. Fifteen-year-old Dan Beaton, 'on hearing the explosion, immediately ran to the place where he knew his younger brother was working, and found him burnt, wounded, and his clothes on fire. After extinguishing the fire he put him on his shoulder, and would not give up his charge to any one who offered assistance until he had taken him out of the mine and laid him on a lounge in his own home.'[69] Fourteen-year-old driver Dannie Robertson only survived the explosion because his horse, Jenny, absorbed the brunt of the blast, which threw Robertson back into a box. Momentarily dazed, he was aroused by the noise of timber cracking as the roof collapsed. Almost delirious, with bad burns on his head, face, arms, and side, he started to make his way out of the pitch-black mine. Hearing the cries of 12-year-old trapper Willie Farris, he groped his way to his side. Because of his burns, Robertson could not take hold of the boy to assist him out. Instead, he instructed Farris to climb on his back, and supporting him as best he could, he ran out of the mine. Once on the surface, Robertson asked the men carrying him home on a sled 'that he be allowed to walk into the house, so that his mother might not be alarmed.'[70]

The craft-based definition of manliness— hard-working, respectable, bread-winning, reasonable—was challenged in its day by 'rough' behaviour in the coal towns—hard drinking, gambling, improvident. But it was also under increasing stress as the transformation of mine work and skills lessened miners' autonomy and scope for independent judgement, and as the crisis in the coal industry threatened miners' livelihood. If one pillar of manhood in nineteenth-century coalfields was the miner's skill, a second was his ability to bring home a living family wage. A resident of Glace Bay underscored to the Nova Scotia premier in 1924 the humiliations of economic distress 'that rob a man of his last ounce of self-respect he possesses.'[71]

The transformation of the skilled miner's work from the 1890s and the decline of the coal industry after the First World War produced a crisis in the definitions of masculinity carried over from the nineteenth century. The new basic 'test of manhood' was reconstructed less around skill than around class loyalty.[72] Trade unions built support by appeals to manliness. Strikebreakers were excoriated as effeminate (or female-dominated).[73] But long strikes created a dilemma for the miner, torn between his loyalty to fellow workers and his responsibilities as the family breadwinner. As one New Waterford miner pointed out in a letter to the Sydney *Post* during the lengthy Cape Breton strike in 1925, 'The miners can stand the gaff [strain] far better than their wives and little children can.'[74] Employers were quick to apply pressure to this tender point. 'As between the wives and families on the one hand and the Western Federation of Miners on the other,' Vancouver Island miners were lectured in 1903, 'I should think the families have the highest claim upon the husband.'[75] Likewise, a striking Glace Bay miner was told by the mine manager in 1909 that if he 'thought more of the United Mine Workers than he did of his wife and family, then he had better pack his traps and leave the country.'[76]

Unlike the male role, women's place in the community did not change. Girls were raised to be wives. The miner's wife's status was based on her ability to 'make do', her demonstrated capacity to maintain a home. Within this sphere, women could exercise considerable influence.[77] In addition, women were the mainstay of the community's social and religious networks, as Bill Wylie has observed, 'keeping up the ties within families and with neighbours, ensuring the observance of religious traditions, and pulling together with other women in times of crisis.'[78] Women shared the stress of uncertainty, the possibility faced daily that their husband and sons might not live to return home from the mine.[79] They also bonded together to support male trade unionists in women's auxiliaries, where they organized dances, dinners, picnics, excursions.[80] They also embarked on limited self-organization through participation in Women's Labour Leagues, which sponsored educational programs.[81]

Women also learned of wage-earners' superior entitlements. Unequal consumption patterns within mining communities are most clearly illustrated with respect to alcohol. Like mine work, alcohol consumption was gendered. If accounts of drunken men and boys were common in mining communities, there were none of women.[82] These reports are emblematic of more than merely the rough aspects of the colliery town; they also illustrate males' superior access to leisure and drink.[83]

Corporate challenges to family livelihood forced women into unusual roles. At times of industrial conflict, they paraded, demonstrated, and appeared on picket lines. During a strike at the Albion Mines in 1842, miners' wives and children attacked the mansion of the company agent, smashing kitchen windows, hurling insults at him.[84] At Wellington in 1877, women 'discouraged' strikebreakers, meeting them at the pit with their infants, jeers, and missiles.[85] A generation later, miners, their wives, and their children collectively harassed strikebreakers at Nanaimo.[86] Women took a prominent part in the riots of 12 August 1913 on Vancouver Island, shouting 'Drive the scabs away', throwing stones, urging others on.[87] On Cape Breton Island, women participated in the riots and looting that followed decisions on the part of company stores during the major strikes of the early 1920s first to suspend the sale of anything but basic foodstuffs and then to cut off credit sales altogether.[88]

Women's public role was recognized very reluctantly. Their voices were seldom if ever heard before the numerous government commissions of inquiry that toured the coalfields.[89] Newspapers hesitated to report their role in riots, preferring to depict women (and children) as victims. The police did not arrest or charge women, and consequently the courts did not try them.[90] Miners too may not always have accepted a public role for their wives. Striking miners at Minto, New Brunswick, for instance, distanced their wives from the conflict in 1937 by failing to inform them of picket locations.[91]

Women did not share the intimate relation with the mine that their menfolk had. Marking the distinction within the family between those who earned wages in the mine and those who did not was 'pit talk', conversation about the experience of the mine which—to their frustration—excluded women.[92] There is some evidence to suggest that women were the first to resist boys' entry into the mine.'[93] Alberta miner Frank Wheatley, for instance, acknowledged in 1919 that although he advocated boys' traditional apprenticeship to the craft, his wife was 'keen that [their sons] don't go into the mine.'[94]

## Culture in the Coal Community

Nineteenth- and early twentieth-century coal towns and villages were also marked by a cultural divide that reflected contested views of class and gender identity. In these communities, a traditional culture characterized by irregular work habits, tolerance of disorder, superstition, and questionable leisure activities—such as the 'rum-hole' and fist fights, the brothel, gambling, and blood sports—had become the target of an emergent liberal ethic, one that found the coarse, turbulent behaviour within the coal community abhorrent.[95] Early trade unionists, who congregated at the 'respectable' end of the cultural spectrum, devoted considerable energy to hectoring miners to counter a public perception that they were '[r]ough in speech, in mind and in manners;

reckless of reason and right; regardless of law, of order, and morality'.[96] Traditional, rough culture in coal towns and villages tolerated child labour. Respectable culture grew increasingly intolerant of boys' early start to work in the mines.

Most characteristic of traditional culture—and a target of early trade unions—was miners' irregular mode of working.[97] 'What our miners should aim at', the PWA urged in Nova Scotia, 'is to be steadily industrious.'[98] Sydney Mines manager R.H. Brown, searching for means of 'making them work steadily', noted in 1874 the number of occasions when the majority of mine workers were absent, severely curtailing or even stopping coal production: on the twelfth night of Christmas 'many men and boys were off work', on St Patrick's day 'not half the men [were] out', on Good Friday, and on May 1st, when the 'Queen Pit night shift [was] idle, [because] only 9 pair men and no boys came out.'[99] Because 'the pits were very frequently idle owing to the number of holy days or saints days that were celebrated', mine managers requested the assistance of the PWA. Robert Drummond suggested that they enlist the aid of the clergy, 'telling them that commemoration days were abused and offering to collect church dues through the office in return for their intervention'. The clergy was amenable and was rewarded with the check-off.[100]

Absenteeism was also related to superstition. Arbitrary death in the pit, while spurring organized miners to lobby for safety measures, including miner certification, also encouraged folk beliefs. At Springhill, it was held that a life was lost whenever company owners visited.[101] Madame Coo, an Aboriginal Nova Scotian credited with predicting the explosions at the Foord Pit in 1880 and at Springhill in 1891, wielded influence with many Nova Scotian miners.[102] On one occasion, even the pits at distant Sydney Mines were closed, as their manager complained, 'on acc[oun]t of [a] prophesy [of a mine disaster] of [an] old woman at New Glasgow'.[103] This manager protested a few years later to the local Roman Catholic and Presbyterian clergy about their superstitious congregations after a very low turnout at work one day because 'one foretold for an explosion.'[104]

There were other causes of absenteeism. When a death occurred in the mine, work ceased immediately and did not resume until after the deceased was buried. Companies resisted these pit closures, and by 1887 the tradition of suspending work from death to burial was not always respected.[105] In 1909 C.O. MacDonald observed that whereas miners might remain idle on the day of an accident, they would be at work on subsequent days 'unless the number of men desiring to actually attend the funeral prevents its being worked on that day.'[106] But the tradition of closing a pit for a funeral continued at least into the 1920s.[107]

The lure of pleasant weather also took mine employees from work. Spring led to a 'picnic scourge', when high levels of absenteeism were 'not unusual'.[108] 'The miners are strong on picnics', reported the trade publication the *Canadian Mining Journal*, 'preferring a day's picnicking to a day's pay at any time, and this year the month of August was prolific in picnics.'[109] Much absenteeism was closely linked to the traditional 'idle spell' after payday to attend to chores around the house, in the garden, or to do some shooting or hunting.[110] The lure of a circus or a game of baseball also periodically drew enough boys away from smaller mines to force a temporary closure.[111]

Absenteeism was also the child of a binge. According to a report from Westville, Nova Scotia, in 1883, 'Things were lively round the streets on pay Saturday. All the Rumholes were in full blast.'[112] A Stellarton correspondent observed that '[a]ny stranger coming into our village last Saturday night would have said "Well I've heard that miners were rough and thriftless, but I never thought they were quite so bad."'[113] A description of Joggins in 1885 included 'one general store . . . and twenty grog shops'.[114] Nearby Springhill boasted 40 rum-holes.[115] Neil A. McDonald, a PWA official from Glace Bay,

wrote candidly in 1882: 'Work is very brisk and there is plenty of Shipping, but the output is often very short of what it should be. Too much rum the cause.'[116] The issue of absenteeism began to be raised with greater insistence by mine managers in the twentieth century. An industrial publication claimed in 1914 that on post-payday Mondays up to fifteen hundred Nova Scotian miners were absent from work.[117] Senior British Empire Steel Corporation officials condemned miner absenteeism, which they alleged to reach 10 per cent on Mondays, before the Duncan Royal Commission in 1925, linking it with drinking.[118]

Drink produced irregular work habits. It also led to violence. Although the claim of local Salvation Army converts that Westville was 'the worst place this side of Hades' was likely exaggerated, coal towns and villages were notorious for their rough behaviour.[119] In one account, 'The first public pugilistic exhibition, for a long time, was held on the street [in Westville] last Friday night, and some say it was splendid, and I'm sure it must have been refreshing after such a long interval of quiet; and especially after so much Scott Act [prohibition by local option] talk. What would the village, or in fact any place, be without the "wee drop" that gives us more than school or college, that wakens wit, and kindles lore, and bangs us full of knowledge.'[120] A correspondent sent this report from Springhill in 1883: 'Last Saturday, pay day, there was considerable drink and noise. Quiet drunks before dark, raging ones after dark. . . . Big bloody fight in Rogues corner [a popular local gathering point].'[121] Druggist John D. Higinbotham, newly arrived in Lethbridge from Ontario in 1885, remarked of payday brawls that '[i]t was a surprise . . . that any of the eighteen saloons were still standing.'[122] Drink also led to domestic violence. An immigrant to Nanaimo from Scotland early in the twentieth century remarked that 'a lot of the men would get drunk to drown out their troubles and come home and sometimes would beat up the wife and kids.'[123] On occasion it drew a public response. The *Trades Journal* referred in January 1885 to a 'wife beater [who] got quarters in the jail.'[124] More commonly, domestic violence was privately endured.[125]

Drink and disproportionate numbers of young single men encouraged other coal-town vices. Efforts in one Nova Scotian coal town to close a brothel were recounted in the *Trades Journal*: 'There is one house that has a very questionable name, and which a large number of the young men visit. It is kept by a fair charmer and goes by the name of "Over the Garden Wall." It is a pest to the neighborhood.'[126] When a citizens' vigilante group assembled to destroy the Garden Wall, its female proprietor threw a brick, striking the leader of the group bent on tearing it down. Her assailants withdrew.[127] Informal mechanisms for the maintenance of propriety were more successful in Springhill. A disreputable house at 'Rogues' Corner' was raided between four and five one Sunday morning. The crowd 'horse-whipped a temporary lodger up the street to his boarding house.' The residents of the house were told to leave town.[128] Prostitution flourished less in the settled communities of Nova Scotia than in the frontier camps of western Canada.[129]

Gambling was a popular leisure activity.[130] One PWA lodge meeting in Springhill was particularly poorly attended because of the number of miners 'having to at[t]end the preformance [sic] of a Card Sharper and patent med[icine]s hack'.[131] Races of all varieties also drew wagers.[132] So did traditional blood sports. 'The barbarous custom of dog fighting prevails largely at present', reported one indignant coal-town journalist. 'When people are coming from Church on Sunday, it is common to see large crowds running madly hither and thither to witness a dog-fight.'[133] Cock-fighting was also reported.[134]

For boys, the cultural divide in coal communities revolved on school attendance, increasingly the badge of youthful respectability. By the late nineteenth century, if the family had money for appropriate clothing and books, children were spending some time in school. Nineteenth-century schools were generally of poor quality and teachers of uncertain qualification.[135] Information was drawn from textbooks, memorized by sing-song chant, and reproduced on demand in overcrowded primary classrooms that grouped several dozen children in perhaps six or eight grades.[136] The harassed teacher, increasingly female, soon discovered that if she could keep children in their seats and teach them to read, 'she would be safe from interference on the part of parents and trustees.'[137] The relevance of the curriculum to working children was unclear and the lasting legacy of the school years uncertain.[138] While Robert Drummond claimed that of the hundreds of pit boys in Nova Scotia 'we would be surprised, if told that more than a dozen could not read or write', the federal labour commissioners repeatedly encountered illiterate boys in 1888.[139] A Cape Breton miner, testifying that the youngest pit boys were nine or ten years of age, was asked if they could read and write. 'I think they have a small chance', he responded.[140] The experience of the mine distinguished the pit boys of the mining community from those boys who did not work. Hostility between pit and school boys was embodied in an event as innocuous as a snowball fight. When 'missiles' broke school windows in the course of an exchange of snowballs between pit and school boys at Stellarton, the responsible pit boys were brought before a justice of the peace and fined 50 cents apiece. Such was the price of the pit boys' probable triumph.[141]

Pit boys' participation in rough culture demarcated them from schoolchildren. Wage-earning relieved them from the domestic chores that had previously had the first call on their time outside of school. It also liberated them of the more circumscribed behaviour required of the schoolchild. Once boys started to work, parental control of their leisure activities was substantially diminished. 'Now that I was a wage-earner,' recalled one English pit boy in writing his autobiography, 'I could go out at night for as long as I liked and where I liked.'[142]

The community offered a range of attractions. A Halifax journalist observed of Springhill's pit boys that 'they meet in little groups on street corners or wherever there happens to be an attraction, and make things as lively as possible.'[143] They would lounge, exchange news, chew tobacco, stare at girls and women, and observe other street activity. Street-corner idling was free and, as Lynne Marks has underlined, one of the few alternative leisure pursuits to uncomfortable, overcrowded homes.[144]

Other sites of boys' activity included the bowling alley (when Springhill's burned down, the Trades Journal reported that 'mothers of boys . . . are heartily glad') and the shooting gallery.[145] Although the youngest pit boys' leisure activity did not generally involve girls, older boys might be drawn towards them. One censorious journalist noted in 1885: 'Dance-Halls are the rage. Morality is at a discount.'[146] The ubiquitous rum shops led to frequent accounts of intoxicated boys[147]—'Last Saturday there were quite a number of drunks to be seen on the streets, a few of whom were boys.'[148] In 1888 two particularly 'drunk and disorderly' boys aged 12 and 14 were jailed in the course of their merry-making.[149] Similarly, a year later, '[s]everal small boys not more than ten to twelve years, were seen paralyzed through drink.'[150] '[T]he rum fiends', complained the Canadian Mining Review in 1894, 'serve the devil by dispensing liquid poison to the miners, boys as well as men.'[151] When driver Malcolm Ferguson was asked if boys were 'generally sober', he responded, 'Some of them.'[152] The drunken and blasphemous boys reported at Springhill in 1887 were the despair of Robert Drummond.[153]

By the 1880s, the charivari, a mock serenade to a couple on their wedding night, belonged to the young.[154] 'Of all the forms, kinds, species and degrees of blackmail,' complained one writer in 1884, 'certainly the worst kind of all is that which goes by the name of charivari.' He told of a couple on their wedding night 'being bombarded by tin tea kettles, bake pans, old dinner horns, bone crackers and old horse pistols.' He advised: 'Boys give it up once and for ever. Don't be a charivarist.'[155] His advice was unheeded. One charivarist rashly used a two-dollar bill as wadding for a gun salute later in the decade. 'After the salute had been successfully fired, he recovered consciousness and bethought him of the bill. Parts of it were found but the glory of the whole had faded.'[156] Hallowe'en demanded its rituals of youth also. The Trades Journal commended boys on their behaviour on that evening in 1887: 'They contented themselves with waving torches and doing a little shouting.'[157]

Boys' views of organized religion were evident when they disrupted church services. 'Young Rowdies' disturbed a Primitive [Methodist] service in 1870, and another service at Stellarton in 1885.[158] Two lads were fined two dollars apiece and costs after disturbing a Salvation Army meeting in 1888.[159] Three boys were fined the following year in Springhill for the same reason.[160] 'Unruly' boys attempted to burn the Presbyterian Mission at Nanaimo in 1900.[161] Temperance groups were similarly targeted. The Trades Journal complained in 1889 that boys in Sydney Mines 'make what they think great sport by tearing away [the] doorsteps' of the new temperance hall.[162]

Lynne Marks has observed that, in late nineteenth-century Ontario, regular church attendance and participation in church organizations were the 'central focus of local respectable culture'. She also noted that this culture—in contrast to local rough culture—was dominated by women, who had far higher rates of church attendance than men.[163] Church groups and temperance associations were further hallmarks of respectability in the coalfields. Associated with the Protestant churches were a great range of temperance societies. The Sons of Temperance, the Church of England Temperance Society, the Cadets of Temperance, the International Order of Good Templars, and the Juvenile Templars were all active in coal communities.[164] In the 1880s, an active Vigilance Society prosecuted liquor-sellers in Springhill.[165] The PWA, a strong advocate of temperance, denied membership to any-one engaged in illicit liquor-selling.[166] It readily acquiesced in the allotment of punishment by mine managers to mine workers for liquor offences.[167] Robert Drummond repeatedly urged that miners be paid on some day other than Saturday, in light of the ensuing drunkenness.[168]

Fraternal societies, with some reservations on account of the alcohol consumed on certain occasions, were deemed respectable. Commonly organized on ethnic lines, they were the most popular form of voluntary association. Major ones included the Masons, the Loyal Orange Lodge, the Odd Fellows, the Knights of Pythias, and the Ancient Order of Foresters. Using the Masons as the model, these groups developed elaborate rituals and degrees of hierarchy, and their rhetoric centred on a brotherhood of male virtues such as independence. Initiation into a fraternal order was seen as a rite of passage into manhood.[169] Fraternal orders had a significant place as means of working-class self-help, spon-soring a variety of insurance programs.[170] They also encouraged occasions of community socia-bility: parades, balls, dinners, and picnics. Although women were not members of fraternal orders, much of the activity these groups spon-sored—unlike 'rough' pastimes within the min-ing community—included women. The Orange Society of Westville, after parading through the town behind the lodge banner, retired to a sup-per and ball in November 1882.[171] Fuller Lodge, of the Independent Order of Odd Fellows, marked the arrival of the New Year of 1885 with a 'Supper and Ball'—described in the local press as 'a most recherché affair'.[172] On other occa-sions, the activities of fraternal orders could be marked by heavy drinking. The revelry associ-ated with the Orangemen's Glorious Twelfth pic-nic in 1904 led to considerable absenteeism in Pictou County the following day.[173]

. . .

Into the twentieth century, a traditional view of boys dominated coal communities: they were competent to labour, their early initiation to work

was valuable to them and their families, schooling was of uncertain worth. Gainful employment was fundamental to male respectability: to remain a schoolchild was effeminate, even disreputable. C.W. Lunn, a railwayman, journalist, and labour advocate, contributed a serialized story to the Halifax *Herald* over several months in 1905 about a young boy, Tommy Barnes, who entered the mine at the age of 10 as a trapper to support his widowed mother. Diligent in his studies at home in the evening, a fine sportsman, organ-izer of a boys' junior PWA lodge while still an adolescent, committed to 'wise councilling and clever negotiating', Barnes was distinguished as a youth who was going 'to make a mark'.[174] The pit boy was not offensive to the respectable min-ing population.

But shifting notions of respectability and the new views of appropriate childhood led to changing commentary on the pit boy. A growing commitment to children's schooling among the mining population put into question a boy's early start to mine work in coal towns and villages. Their behaviour, as child wage labour was defined ever more commonly as a social prob-lem, led to frequent claims that the mine brutal-ized boys. While O.R. Lovejoy offered an extreme opinion in claiming that the pit boys of his experience were 'so tainted by vicious habits that an almost insuperable obstacle to a maturity of virtue and intelligence is presented', his views were widely shared within the urban reforming classes.[175] Boys in coal towns and villages were 'particularly rough and uncultivated' claimed a teacher in 1886; another educator affirmed in 1912 that pit boys were 'chiefly interested in learning how to chew tobacco and in acquiring an extensive vocabulary of picturesque profan-ity.'[176] With increasing frequency, pit boys were defined as violating liberal society's new and universal prescriptions for childhood.[177] Respectable society was increasingly hostile to the employment of boys in the mines.

Within the mining community, new views of class interest led organized miners to scrutinize boys' early start to work at the mine. At the same time, women began to raise doubts about sending their boys into the pits. Concern also arose among men about the integrity of their craft, about whether it was a suitable basis of earning a livelihood. The redefinition of respectable culture in coal communities also undermined the popular view that local boys' appropriate place was the mine. By the early twentieth century, the expectation had weakened that boys raised in coal towns and villages would work in the mines.

## Notes

1.  Victoria *Daily British Colonist*, 27 Jan. 1861.
2.  Bertha Isabel Scott, *Springhill, a Hilltop in Cumberland* (Springhill, NS: n.p., 1926); E. Blanche Norcross, *Nanaimo Retrospective: The First Century* (Nanaimo, BC: Nanaimo Historical Society, 1979); A.A. Den Otter, *Civilizing the West: The Galts and the Development of Western Canada* (Edmonton: University of Alberta Press, 1982), 161–96; 238–65.
3.  Bill McNeil, *Voice of the Pioneer* (Toronto: Macmillan, 1978), 61.
4.  See Angus L. Macdonald Library, St Francis Xavier University, United Mine Workers of America, Local 4514, *Minutes*, 8 Jan. 1927.
5.  C. Ochiltree Macdonald, *The Coal and Iron Industries of Nova Scotia* (Halifax: Chronicle Publishing Co., 1909), 57.
6.  LC, *Evidence*, 459.
7.  Macdonald, *Coal and Iron Industries*, 72.
8.  *Canadian Mining Journal* (*CMJ*), 11 June 1908, as quoted in David Frank, 'Company Town, Labour Town: Local Government in the Cape Breton Coal Towns, 1917–1926', *Histoire Sociale/Social History* 14, 27 (May 1981): 178.
9.  James M. Cameron, *The Pictonian Colliers* (Halifax: Nova Scotia Museum, 1974), 103–4. The Hudson's Bay Company provided a teacher at Nanaimo as early as 1853. Norcross, *Nanaimo Retrospective*, 40–6.
10. *Canadian Mining Review* (*CMR*), June 1902, 166.
11. See David Bercuson, ed., *Alberta's Coal Industry* (Calgary: Historical Society of Alberta, 1978).
12. Charles Forbes, *Vancouver Island, Its Resources and Capabilities as a Colony* (Victoria: Colonial Government, 1862), 57.
13. John Douglas Belshaw, 'The Standard of Living of British Miners on Vancouver Island', *BC Studies* 84 (Winter 1989–90): 53.
14. William N.T. Wylie, *Coal Culture: The History and Commemoration of Mining in Nova Scotia* (Ottawa: Historic Sites and Monuments Board of Canada, 1997), 172; Cameron, *Pictonian Colliers*, 24–5; Joseph Howe, *Western and Eastern Rambles*, ed. M.G. Parks (Toronto: University of Toronto Press, 1973), 159.
15. Wylie, *Coal Culture*, 182.
16. Ian McKay, '"By Wisdom, Wile or War": The Provincial Workmen's Association and the Struggle for Working-Class Independence in Nova Scotia, 1879–97', *Labour/Le Travail* 18 (Fall 1986): 18–19.
17. Stephen J. Hornsby, *Nineteenth-Century Cape Breton: A Historical Geography* (Montreal and Kingston: McGill-Queen's University Press, 1992), 103–5, 178; LC, *Evidence*, 412.
18. LC, *Evidence*, 412; *CMJ*, 1 July 1914, 442.
19. These events were also commonly followed by legal action against striking miners. Ian McKay, 'The Crisis of Dependent Development: Class Conflict in the Nova Scotian Coalfields, 1872–1876', in Gregory Kealey, ed., *Class, Gender, and Region: Essays in Canadian Historical Sociology* (St John's: Committee on Canadian Labour History, 1988), 37–9.
20. Jeremy Mouat, 'The Politics of Coal: A Study of the Wellington Miners' Strike of 1890–91', *BC Studies* 77 (Spring 1988): 8.
21. Macdonald, *Coal and Iron Industries*, 219.
22. Richard Brown, *The Coal Fields and Coal Trade of the Island of Cape Breton* (Stellarton, NS: Maritime Mining Record Office, 1899), 53.
23. Belshaw, 'Standard of Living', 50–1.
24. See Bercuson, ed., *Alberta's Coal Industry*, 127, 133.
25. Hornsby, *Nineteenth-Century Cape Breton*, 171.
26. *Trades Journal* (*TJ*), 16 Mar. 1881, cited in McKay, '"Wisdom, Wile or War"', 20.
27. Macdonald, *Coal and Iron Industries*, 219–22.
28. Frank, 'Company Town, Labour Town', 181.
29. Cameron, *Pictonian Colliers*, 103.

30. Canada, *Report of the Royal Commission on Coal, 1946* (Ottawa: Edmond Cloutier, 1947), 599. Similar concern over company towns in Cape Breton had been expressed earlier. See Nova Scotia, Royal Commission Respecting the Coal Mines of the Province of Nova Scotia, *Report* (Halifax: Minister of Public Works and Mines, 1926), 10.

31. Public Archives of Nova Scotia (PANS), RG 21, series A, vol. 38, no. 10, Richard Brown diary, entry for 7 Feb. 1874.

32. PANS, RG 21, series A, vol. 32, Letter Books, Henry Swift to J.R. Cowans, 24 Nov. 1890.

33. In 1903 nearly all Nova Scotia's colliery managers were former workmen. Even at the massive Dominion Coal Company, in 1910 virtually all officials 'were ex-miners trained in the mining schools.' See Donald MacLeod, 'Colliers, Colliery Safety and Workplace Control: Nova Scotian Experience, 1873–1910', Canadian Historical Association, *Historical Papers* (1983): 251. Mine-owner Robert Dunsmuir first entered the mines as a boy of 16. See Daniel T. Gallacher, 'Robert Dunsmuir', *Dictionary of Canadian Biography* (*DCB*), vol. 11 (Toronto: University of Toronto Press, 1982), 290–4.

34. *TJ*, 20 Apr. 1881.

35. Companies would levy a charge, for instance, just for the cost of delivering the coal. Macdonald, *Coal and Iron Industries*, 59.

36. Forbes, *Vancouver Island*, 57.

37. Cameron, *Pictonian Colliers*, 104.

38. *TJ*, 9 Jan. 1889.

39. A.W. Macdonald, 'Notes on the Work of the Industrial Relations Department of the Dominion Coal Company Ltd. and the Dominion Iron and Steel Company Ltd.', *Transactions of the Canadian Mining Institute* (1916): 326; Scott, *Springhill*, 51.

40. McKay, 'Wisdom, Wile or War', 31.

41. *TJ*, 28 Jan. 1885, 27 Mar. 1889.

42. McKay, 'Wisdom, Wile or War', 31.

43. Cameron, *Pictonian Colliers*, 122.

44. Macdonald, *Coal and Iron Industries*, 223–5. Others, such as the Pioneer Co-operative at Springhill, lasted only a few years. See *TJ*, 21 June 1882, 4 May 1887. On reasons for the failure of co-operative stores in mining communities, see

45. Ian MacPherson, *Each for All: A History of the Co-operative Movement in English Canada, 1900–1945* (Toronto: Macmillan of Canada, 1979), 23.

45. Ian MacPherson, 'Patterns in the Maritime Cooperative Movement, 1900–1945', *Acadiensis* 5, 1 (Autumn 1975): 68–70.

46. Lynn Bowen, *Boss Whistle: the Coal Miners of Vancouver Island Remember* (Lantzville, BC: Oolichan Books, 1982), 197–8; Sharon Babaian, *The Coal Mining Industry in the Crow's Nest Pass* (Edmonton: Alberta Culture, 1985), 77–8.

47. *TJ*, 8 Jan. 1882.

48. McKay, 'Wisdom, Wile or War', 43.

49. Ibid., 45.

50. Frank, 'Company Town, Labour Town', 181–6.

51. Wylie, *Coal Culture*, 121.

52. David Frank and Nolan Reilly, 'The Emergence of the Socialist Movement in the Maritimes, 1899–1916', *Labour/Le Travailleur* 4 (1979): 99.

53. Allen Seager, 'Miners' Struggles in Western Canada, 1890–1930', in Deian R. Hopkin and Gregory S. Kealey, eds, *Class, Community and the Labour Movement in Wales and Canada, 1850–1930* (n.p.: Society for Welsh Labour History and the Canadian Committee on Labour History, 1989), 176.

54. Ibid., 176–7.

55. Allen Seager, 'Socialists and Workers: The Western Canadian Coal Miners, 1900–1921', *Labour/Le Travail* 16 (Fall 1985): 37–42; Carlos A. Schwantes, *Radical Heritage: Labor, Socialism, and Reform in Washington and British Columbia, 1885–1917* (Seattle: University of Washington Press, 1979), 73–4, 100–1.

56. Halifax *Herald*, 26 Sept. 1910.

57. Ibid., 31 July 1909.

58. Nanaimo *Free Press*, 28 Nov. 1912, cited in Alan John Wargo, 'The Great Coal Strike: the Vancouver Island Coal Miners' Strike, 1912–1914', BA essay (University of British Columbia, 1962), 94.

59. *CMJ*, 1 Nov. 1913, 690.

60. *Maritime Labour Herald*, 15 Apr. 1922, cited in Steven Penfold, '"Have You No Manhood in You?": Gender and Class in Cape Breton Coal Towns, 1920–1926', *Acadiensis* 23, 2 (Spring 1994): 27.

61. Cited in Ian McKay, 'The Realm of Uncertainty: The Experience of Work in the Cumberland Coal

Mines, 1873–1927', *Acadiensis* 16, 1 (Autumn 1986): 52.

62. PANS, RG 21, series A, vol. 38, no. 13, Richard Brown diary, entry for 24 Feb. 1894.

63. *TJ*, 29 May 1889.

64. Lawrence Chrismas, *Alberta Miners: A Tribute* (Calgary: Cambria, 1993), 29.

65. As one woman wrote to the PWA's official newspaper in 1882, 'I am precluded by sex from joining your society.' *TJ*, 11 Oct. 1882.

66. Labour Canada Library, Annual Meeting of the PWA Grand Council, *Minutes*, 1907, 611.

67. Quoted in Harold W. Aurand, *From the Molly Maguires to the United Mine Workers: The Ecology of an Industrial Union, 1869–1897* (Philadelphia: Temple University Press, 1971), 37.

68. Cited in McKay, 'Realm of Uncertainty', 52.

69. R.A.H. Morrow, *The Story of the Springhill Disaster* (Saint John: R.A.H. Morrow, 1891), 83–4.

70. Ibid., 84–6; Scott, *Springhill*, 72.

71. PANS, MG 2, box 675, folder 1, F1/15295, A.M. MacLeod to E.H. Armstrong, 26 Jan. 1924.

72. Penfold, '"Have You No Manhood"', 21.

73. Ibid., 27.

74. Sydney *Post*, 4 Apr. 1925, cited ibid., 29.

75. 'Minutes of Evidence, Royal Commission on Industrial Disputes in the Province of British Columbia', Canada, *Sessional Papers*, 1904, vol. 38, no. 13, 36A, 4.

76. Halifax *Herald*, 31 Mar. 1909.

77. See Penfold, '"Have You No Manhood"', 30–2; David Frank, 'The Miner's Financier: Women in the Cape Breton Coal Towns, 1917', *Atlantis* 8, 2 (Spring 1983): 137–43.

78. Wylie, *Coal Culture*, 133–4. Lynne Marks observed that church groups offered the only organized associational life in small towns for married women in contemporary Ontario. See Marks, *Revivals and Roller Rinks*, 137.

79. David Alan Corbin, *Life, Work, and Rebellion in the Coal Fields: The Southern West Virginia Miners, 1880–1922* (Urbana: University of Illinois Press, 1981), 92–3.

80. John R. Hinde, '"Stout Ladies and Amazons": Women in the British Columbia Coal Mining Community of Ladysmith, 1912–1914', *BC Studies* (Summer 1997): 44. A One Big Union women's auxiliary was formed in Minto in 1926. Allen Seager, 'Minto, New Brunswick: A Study in Class Relations between the Wars', *Labour/Le Travailleur* 5 (Spring 1980): 110–11.

81. Penfold, '"Have You No Manhood"', 38–42.

82. See *TJ*, 11 May 1883, 21 Nov. 1888, 2 Jan. 1889; *CMR*, Dec. 1894, 237, for references to intoxicated boys.

83. See also *TJ*, 5 Oct. 1887.

84. McKay, '"Wisdom, Wile or War"', 21.

85. Victoria *Daily British Colonist*, 17 Mar., 5 May 1877.

86. Nanaimo *Free Press*, 25 Nov. 1912.

87. Hinde, '"Stout Ladies and Amazons"', 33–4.

88. Penfold, '"Have You No Manhood"', 33–4.

89. See, for instance, LC, *Evidence*; 'Minutes of Evidence, Royal Commission on Industrial Disputes in the Province of British Columbia', Canada, *Sessional Papers*, 1904, vol. 38, no. 13, 36A; Provincial Archives of Alberta (PAA), Royal Commission on the Coal Industry, *Report and Evidence*; Commission on Miners' Old Age Pensions, *Report*; National Archives of Canada (NAC), RG 33, series 95, Royal Commission on Industrial Relations, 1919, *Minutes of Evidence*; Labour Canada Library, Royal Commission Respecting the Coal Mines of the Province of Nova Scotia, *Minutes of Evidence*, 1925.

90. Penfold, '"Have You No Manhood"', 36; Hinde, '"Stout Ladies and Amazons"', 33–4.

91. Seager, 'Minto, New Brunswick', 119.

92. McKay, 'Realm of Uncertainty', 24.

93. C.W. Lunn, 'From Trapper Boy to General Manager: A Story of Brotherly Love and Perseverance', Ian McKay, ed., *Labour/Le Travailleur* 4 (1979): 226; Bowen, *Boss Whistle*, 17.

94. Bercuson, ed., *Alberta's Coal Industry*, 84.

95. See P.C. Bailey, *Leisure and Class in Victorian England: Rational Recreation and the Contest for Control, 1830–1885* (London: Routledge & Kegan Paul, 1978). The *Trades Journal* conveyed an assessment of the relative cultural balance of Nova Scotian coal communities in 1889: 'Considering the occupation of the miner the wonder is not that a third of them drink, but that two-thirds of them are admitted to be sober men.'

*TJ*, 26 June 1889. On the threats to traditional popular culture from industrialization and its associated ethic, see E.P. Thompson, *Customs in Common: Studies in Traditional Popular Culture* (New York: New Press, 1991). On cultural divisions in contemporary small-town Ontario, see Marks, *Revivals and Roller Rinks*.

96. *TJ*, 13 Apr. 1881. The view of the miner as a degraded brute was captured in popular novels such as *Germinal* by Emile Zola and Hugh MacLennan's *Each Man's Son*.

97. On the traditional weekly 'idle spell' of urban craftsmen, often called 'Blue' or 'Saint' Monday, see Gregory Kealey, *Toronto Workers Respond to Industrial Capitalism, 1867–1892* (Toronto: University of Toronto Press, 1980), 54, 68; Bryan Palmer, *A Culture in Conflict: Skilled Workers and Industrial Capitalism in Hamilton, Ontario, 1860–1914* (Montreal and Kingston: McGill-Queen's University Press, 1979), 21.

98. *TJ*, 18 July 1883. Drummond failed to acknowledge that companies operated nineteenth-century mines irregularly.

99. PANS, RG 21, series A, vol. 38, no. 10, Richard Brown diary, entries for 21 Mar., 6 Jan., 17 Mar., 3 Apr., 1 May 1874.

100. Robert Drummond, *Minerals and Mining, Nova Scotia* (Stellarton, NS: Mining Record Office, 1918), 276–7.

101. *TJ*, 1 Aug. 1888.

102. Cameron, *Pictonian Collier*, 215; McKay, 'Realm of Uncertainty', 47.

103. PANS, RG 21, series A, vol. 38, no. 10, Richard Brown diary, entry for 4 May 1874.

104. PANS, RG 21, series A, vol. 38, no. 12, Richard Brown diary, entry for 2 Apr. 1881.

105. *TJ*, 13 Apr. 1887.

106. Macdonald, *Coal and Iron Industries*, 73.

107. David Frank, 'The Cape Breton Coal Miners, 1917–1926', Ph.D. dissertation (Dalhousie University, 1979), 232; McKay, 'Realm of Uncertainty', 55–6.

108. See *CMR*, Dec. 1894, 236; *CMJ*, 15 June 1913, 381.

109. *CMR*, Sept. 1903, 198.

110. *TJ*, 8 Nov. 1882.

111. A circus, which the boys apparently found disappointing, closed the mine at River Hebert for a day. See *TJ*, 13 Aug. 1884. A baseball game once shut the Joggins mine. See Halifax *Herald*, 7 June 1906.

112. *TJ*, 25 Apr. 1883.

113. *TJ*, 17 May 1882.

114. *TJ*, 14 Jan. 1885.

115. *TJ*, 14 Sept. 1887.

116. *TJ*, 11 Oct. 1882.

117. *CMJ*, 15 April 1914, 254.

118. See Labour Canada Library, [Duncan] Royal Commission Respecting the Coal Mines of the Province of Nova Scotia, *Minutes of Evidence*, 1925, 2648–9, 2953.

119. *TJ*, 23 Dec. 1885.

120. *TJ*, 5 Oct. 1887. The Canada Temperance [Scott] Act had been declared in force in Pictou County in 1882. See *TJ*, 27 Sept. 1882.

121. *TJ*, 7 Mar. 1883.

122. Quoted in Den Otter, *Civilizing the West*, 164.

123. Quoted in Allen Seager and Adele Perry, 'Mining the Connections: Class, Ethnicity, and Gender in Nanaimo, British Columbia, 1891', *Histoire Sociale/Social History* 30, 59 (May 1997): 66.

124. *TJ*, 21 Jan. 1885.

125. See Katherine Harvey, 'To Love, Honour and Obey: Wife-Battering in Working-Class Montreal, 1869–79', *Urban History Review* 19, 2 (Oct. 1990): 128–40.

126. *TJ*, 25 Apr. 1883.

127. *TJ*, 24 Oct. 1883.

128. *TJ*, 12 Aug. 1885.

129. On prostitution in the Alberta mining camps, see Den Otter, *Civilizing the West*, 174, 242–8; and Bercuson, ed., *Alberta's Coal Industry*, 190–1.

130. See Daniel Samson, 'Dependency and Rural Industry: Inverness, Nova Scotia, 1899–1910', in Samson, ed., *Contested Countryside: Rural Workers and Modern Society in Atlantic Canada, 1800–1950* (Fredericton, NB: Acadiensis Press, 1994), 129.

131. See Angus L. Macdonald Library, St Francis Xavier University, *Minutebooks*, Pioneer Lodge, PWA, 14 Aug. 1884.

132. Belshaw, 'Standard of Living', 61–2.

133. *TJ*, 12 Aug. 1885. Other reports of dog-fighting are found in the issues of 30 Sept. 1885 and 11 Jan. 1888; and in the Sydney *Daily Post*, 31 July 1909.

134. See *TJ*, 9 Jan. 1889; Nanaimo *Free Press*, 6 Feb. 1901.

135. Katherine I. McLaren, '"The Proper Education for All Classes": Compulsory Schooling and Reform in Nova Scotia, 1890–1930', M.Ed. thesis (Dalhousie University, 1984), 33, 44–6.

136. Ibid., 54–5.

137. Paul Axelrod, *The Promise of Schooling: Education in Canada, 1800–1914* (Toronto: University of Toronto Press, 1997), 57–9.

138. McLaren, '"The Proper Education for All Classes"', 19.

139. *TJ*, 9 May 1888. See LC, *Evidence*, 437, 447.

140. LC, *Evidence*, 454.

141. *TJ*, 1 Apr. 1885.

142. Jack Lawson, *A Man's Life* (London: Hodder and Stoughton, 1932), 74.

143. Halifax *Morning Chronicle*, 4 Dec. 1890.

144. On this point, see Marks, *Revivals and Roller Rinks*, 81–5.

145. *TJ*, 8 Nov. 1882 (bowling alley), 19 Dec. 1888 (on the shooting gallery as a 'drop-in' for boys).

146. See *TJ*, 3 June 1885. On nineteenth-century courting, see W. Peter Ward, *Courtship, Love, and Marriage in Nineteenth-Century English Canada* (Montreal and Kingston: McGill-Queen's University Press, 1990), esp. chs 4 and 5.

147. *TJ*, 18 July, 31 Oct. 1883, 2 Jan. 1889.

148. *TJ*, 11 May 1883.

149. *TJ*, 21 Nov. 1888.

150. *TJ*, 2 Jan. 1889.

151. *CMR*, Dec. 1894, 237.

152. LC, *Evidence*, 437.

153. *TJ*, 24 Aug. 1887.

154. See Bryan Palmer, 'Discordant Music: Charivaris and Whitecapping in Nineteenth-Century North America', *Labour/Le Travailleur* 3 (1978): 5–62; E.P. Thompson, '"Rough Music": Le charivari anglais', *Annales. Economies. Sociétés. Organisations* 27 (1972): 285–312. Philippe Ariès remarked on how activities at one time common to all age groups eventually came to be confined to the young. See Ariès, *Centuries of Childhood: A Social History of Family Life* (New York: Knopf, 1962), 62–99.

155. *TJ*, 10 Sept. 1884.

156. *TJ*, 15 May 1889.

157. *TJ*, 2 Nov. 1887.

158. New Glasgow *Eastern Chronicle*, 30 June 1870; *TJ*, 28 Oct. 1885.

159. *TJ*, 6 June 1888.

160. *TJ*, 22 May 1889.

161. Nanaimo *Free Press*, 24 Mar. 1900.

162. *TJ*, 24 Apr. 1889.

163. Marks, *Revivals and Roller Rinks*, 15, 230–2 (Tables 3–5).

164. *TJ*, 2 Nov. 1887, 7 Mar. 1888.

165. Scott, *Springhill*, 50.

166. Labour Canada Library, Annual Meeting of the PWA Grand Council, *Minutes*, 1894, 281.

167. Labour Canada Library, Robert Drummond, 'Recollections and Reflections of a Former Trades Union Leader', unpublished manuscript (*c.* 1926), 198.

168. He first made the suggestion in *TJ*, 21 July 1880, when he observed that payday at Stellarton had been switched to Thursdays with considerable success, 'there being much less dissipation than has followed Saturday pay-days.'

169. Marks, *Revivals and Roller Rinks*, 109.

170. Lynn Bowen, 'Friendly Societies in Nanaimo: The British Tradition of Self-Help in a Canadian Coal-Mining Community', *BC Studies* no. 118 (Summer 1998): 67–92.

171. *TJ*, 15 Nov. 1882.

172. *TJ*, 7 Jan. 1885.

173. Cameron, *Pictonian Collier*, 328.

174. Lunn, 'From Trapper Boy to General Manager', 233.

175. O.R. Lovejoy, 'Child Labor in the Coal Mines', *Annals of the American Academy of Political and Social Science* 27 (1906): 297.

176. *The Bulletin* (Dartmouth), 15 Dec. 1886, cited in McKay, 'Realm of Uncertainty', 27; Frederick H. Sexton, 'Industrial Education for Miners', *Transactions of the Canadian Mining Institute* (1912): 594.

177. A Nova Scotian 'new model boy' is presented in Lunn, 'From Trapper Boy to General Manager', 211–40.

# 12

# 'The Case of the Kissing Nurse': Femininity, Sexuality, and Canadian Nursing, 1900–1970

Kathryn McPherson

On a lazy Sunday afternoon in January of 1959 Mrs Bew and Mrs Sulman discovered they had a problem. Right in front of their office window sat a parked car in which a young couple were engaged in passionate kissing. As matrons of the Vancouver General Hospital nurses' residence, Bew and Sulman were responsible for ensuring that more than 500 student nurses adhered to the residence rules and thereby maintained a sterling reputation for the school and hospital. Here lay the dilemma. Owing to the nature of the activity in the car, the matrons could not see the woman's face. If she was a Vancouver General Hospital student, the school representatives could interrupt the couple and insist that the woman return to her residence. After all, not only was her behaviour unseemly, but it was past 2:30 p.m. and all student nurses were expected to be back in the hospital a half-hour before their 3 p.m. shift began. If she was *not* a Vancouver General Hospital student, could the matrons rightfully request the couple to move to another location? Just as the diligent overseers had decided to take action, the car door slammed and the young woman—a senior nursing student—sauntered towards the residence. The matrons intercepted the student, reported her to the school authorities, and the student was suspended for two weeks.

To be sent home for a fortnight was a stern penalty, though not unusually so. Yet the prospect of the student having to return home to explain to her parents why she had been reprimanded was severe enough to prompt immediate sympathy from her colleagues in the nursing school. Protesting what they considered harsh and inconsistent punishment, the student nurses threatened to strike if the errant nurse was not reinstated. News of the conflict leaked to the press and by the end of the week was receiving not only local but national coverage. Faced with public humiliation and the potential loss of 500 bedside attendants, the hospital administration met, first with the vigilant matrons to sort out the details of the case and then with the student council to negotiate the rules governing residence life and nurses' leisure time.[1] Meanwhile, newspapers, radio stations, and television networks debated the 'Case of the Kissing Nurse' to understand why, as the *Toronto Daily Star* put it, 'are certain women's professions discriminated against in romance?'[2]

Kathryn McPherson, '"The Case of the Kissing Nurse": Femininity, Sexuality, and Canadian Nursing, 1900–1970', in McPherson et al., eds, *Gendered Pasts: Historical Essays in Femininity and Masculinity in Canada.* © 1999. Reprinted by permission of University of Toronto Press.

The high public profile this conflict garnered was unprecedented, but in other ways events at Vancouver General Hospital in 1959 revealed long-standing social and occupational tensions over how nurses' sexuality, femininity, and respectability would be defined. This chapter unravels those tensions as they played out in three historical contexts, beginning in the late nineteenth and early twentieth centuries, when the 'modern' trained nurse first appeared, through the interwar years, and then into the post-World War II decades. In spite of the many changes in the structure and content of nursing work, throughout the era under study most nurses received their training in hospital apprenticeship programs. For two or three years, apprentices were schooled in the many rules and regulations they were to carry into paid work, and thus the educational process was a dominant factor in shaping nurses' social role. Drawing on historical documentation from institutional records, oral interviews, and popular culture, this essay explores how ordinary or 'rank-and-file' nurses, during their apprenticeship and as graduates, negotiated their occupational identity. Sexuality was a central component of that identity. Although same-sex relations constituted an important, and woefully understudied, dimension of nursing's past, this discussion focuses on the dominant regulatory regime of heterosexual symbol and practice.[3]

To do so, this essay employs Judith Butler's theoretical framework of gender as performance. Butler likens the gendered roles of men and women to those of theatrical performance. She argues that there is no core gender or sexual identity expressed through social roles. Rather, men and women develop or put on masculine and feminine identities through the 'stylized repetition of acts' performed daily. But not just any set of acts will do. Gendered acts are developed within specific social and historical contexts: women and men learn and develop their roles within the confines of social taboos and expectations. Because, as Butler states, 'the gendered

body acts its part in a culturally restricted corporeal space and enacts interpretations within the confines of already existing directives',[4] individuals may make gendered roles 'their own' but performing one's role wrong incurs the wrath of social censure. In Butler's conceptualization the human body is critical not only as the vehicle for gendered performances but also as the site where sexuality or 'desire' is socially constructed. Bodies 'do' gender in part to 'do' desire.[5]

This framework is useful for understanding nursing's relationship to social definitions of appropriate femininity in several ways. First, Butler's assertion that there is no core or 'essential' femaleness (or maleness) being expressed through gender stands as a reminder that there is no core or essential 'nurse' being expressed in the workplace. The category of 'nurse' is wholly a social creation, a role being played, not an essentialized nurturing identity being expressed. Like actors, nurses had to learn their part, not only in terms of the occupationally specific skills and responsibilities they took on, but also in terms of the behaviour and attitudes they had to exhibit. Playing the part wrong invoked powerful social sanctions. And like actors, nurses had to dress the part. The modern nurse donned an occupationally specific uniform, a costume that distinguished her from other women or other caregivers. As well, Butler's focus on sexuality is particularly germane for nursing, an occupation bedevilled by its members' intimate knowledge of the human body.

Finally, Butler's emphasis on the historical specificity of gender roles underscores the importance of identifying how nurses' occupational identity was created, contested, and constrained according to the specific social rules operating at a given point in time. For rank-and-file nurses, the workplace identities they developed, over time and through repetition, were scripted by several potent forces: social definitions of respectable femininity, the political economy of health care, and the legal and social norms developed by nursing leaders, administrators, and educators—what I call the nursing elite. These three scripts were not always autonomous; when any one of these factors changed with time, so, too, were the other sets of influences reconfigured.[6] And while the focus of analysis here is the relationship between gender and sexuality, class and race were equally powerful influences on nursing's occupational identities.[7]

## The 'Modern' Nurse

The 'modern' nurse stepped onto Canada's historical stage in the late nineteenth and early twentieth centuries, when hospitals implemented a radical restructuring of institutional staffing. As part of the wider campaign to make institutions respectable and reliable providers of modern scientific medical treatment for all classes of patient, hospitals established nursing schools. There, apprenticing students laboured on the wards for three years in exchange for training and certification as 'graduate' nurses. Under the supervision of small staffs of graduate nurse supervisors, students offered hospitals cheap, subordinate, and flexible patient care staff. Unlike the working-class widowed or married women who preceded them, the young, single, white women from a range of class and ethnic backgrounds who filled the ranks of apprenticeship programs were expected to embody the social standards of bourgeois femininity.

The first stage of this grooming process was the introduction of standardized uniforms. While each institution added its own distinctive features, most adopted the basic design of a long blue dress, covered by a white apron and crowned with a cap. The uniform was inspired by that worn by domestic servants in elite households and, like domestic servants, nurses endured uniform styles that were slightly out of style. Trained nurses were expected to dress differently from other working women, but not the same as their patients.[8]

Uniforms promised to fulfill several symbolic functions. Standardized dress eradicated differences of class or ethnicity or even personality that distinguished young recruits from one another. Whatever features differentiated the uniforms adopted by individual schools, the commonalities were sufficient to create an occupationally specific code that indicated nurses' status as 'on duty'. And while the uniform represented the work that nurses performed, it simultaneously identified nurses as different from any other female wage-earners. Especially important was the clear demarcation between nurses and the only other group of working women who had intimate contact with the bodies of strangers—prostitutes. Like religious habits, nurses' uniforms signified the desexualized status of the women wearing them, simultaneously containing female sexuality even as the bodies wearing the uniforms learned about the human body.

The uniform, then, located nurses symbolically as workers, as women, as serving society, and as sexually contained. In doing so, the uniform drew on gender-specific images—after all, only women were nurses—but at the same time distinguished nurses from other women. Given the complexity of this symbolic order, it was not surprising that women who donned the nurses' costume found their role difficult to learn. Efforts to entice trained nurses to comply with the Victorian ideology of middle-class femininity and sexual respectability underscored the fundamental contradiction that tending the bodies of strangers created for working women, as events at Halifax's Victoria General Hospital in 1896 revealed. That year, the Lady Superintendent of the Hospital and of the Nursing School, Miss Elliot, introduced a 'new rule' mandating that apprenticing students assume the tasks involved in cleaning and treating male patients' private parts. The possibility of direct contact with male genitalia provoked substantial discontent among the nurses, as well as among the patients, who found themselves waiting for long periods to receive attendance. The situation peaked when one well-to-do male patient complained so vociferously that a commission was struck to investigate the matter.

The commissioners' report highlighted the difficulty nursing faced drawing clear lines between appropriate occupational behaviour and the broader social standards of feminine behaviour upon which nursing rested. The commissioners reiterated the hospital's general principle that 'Nursing is a woman's work, for which she is peculiarly fitted', but conceded that 'there are obviously limitations to her usefulness, imposed both by modesty and her want of physical strength.' But the commissioners were unequivocal that the students' insubordination contravened both the occupational and social standards to which the young women were expected to comply.[9]

> A young woman entering the profession of nursing ought to make up her mind to the discharge of a great many unpleasant and even repulsive duties for patients, irrespective of sex. If she cannot, then she has no business in the profession, either in a hospital or in private practice. What is wanted is the proper spirit of the profession. . . .

To inculcate the 'proper spirit of the profession' nursing elites endeavoured to distinguish professional from carnal knowledge. They did so by establishing two sets of complex rituals, one that shaped therapeutic treatment performed at the bedside, the other that shaped social behaviour on duty and off. The former defined nurses as skilled in modern scientific therapeutics. The latter played on an exaggerated vision of Victorian femininity to claim an asexual status for working nurses. Mary Poovey has described this occupational image as the 'sexless, moralizing angel',[10] but nursing's reliance on both femaleness and sexuality was never completely denied. After all, the modern nurse was born out of the gender division of medical labour, and her position within the health-care system was premised on heterosexual complementariness, as the 'wife' to the male doctor or administrator. Even hospital residences did not serve to cloister students: the weekly 'theatre leave', provisions

for 'receiving' male guests in the residence lobby, and school-sponsored dances all accommodated heterosexual activity within strict limits.[11]

Rather than try to deny nurses' sexuality or the gendered nature of the occupation, nursing leaders sought to reformulate what Mariana Valverde terms the 'ethical subjectivity' of student and staff nurses by not merely repressing desire but redefining it.[12] Building on the symbolism of nursing uniforms, the professional elite developed a vision of femininity that overstated contemporary standards of social deference, sexual passivity, and ladylike gentility. The key element of ladylike behaviour was restraint: from being noisy, from smoking, from drinking alcohol, from gossiping, or from challenging hospital authorities. Sexual behaviour was central to this regulatory regime. Student nurses were warned not to flirt, 'pose', or show 'familiarity' towards male patients, orderlies, or medical staff.[13] In a crucial inversion of the chivalric code, nurses were instructed to 'stand at attention' or give up their seat or place in an elevator when in the presence of any doctor or senior nursing staff.[14] These various elements of social and sexual restraint were considered as a single goal. As late as 1935 a superintendent of nursing disciplined her charges for smoking, on the basis that 'smoking leads to alcohol and progresses to promiscuity.'[15]

For three years, six and a half days per week, twelve hours per day, apprenticing nurses were encouraged, corrected, and chastened in the details of this regulatory regime. The performative ritual began each morning when students had to assemble in the foyer of the nursing residence to participate in morning prayers and have their uniforms inspected. After a brief breakfast they went on the wards, wherein their therapeutic and social behaviour was monitored by staff nurses or even senior students. Successful adherence to the prescribed rituals was rewarded with promotion to the next rank of student. Punishment for transgressing school rules usually involved some public display of discipline, such as having late leave revoked or being denied the right to wear the nursing cap when on duty.[16] Serious or frequent flaunting of rules would result in the errant apprentices being summoned to the nursing superintendent's office.

At the end of each workday, a shift change also signalled an identity change. Student nurses took off their uniforms (and, indeed, were forbidden from wearing their uniform off duty), donned civilian clothes, and then, no longer asexual nurses, were obliged to adhere to the rules of respectable femininity that residence life demanded.[17] For several short hours, between the end of their shift and residence curfew, students could participate in the social pursuits enjoyed by other young women. In this way, the entire system of regulation developed by hospitals was designed to constrain female sexuality off duty and to neutralize it completely on the wards. After three years, students had learned the clear demarcation between them and other women, in terms of skills they had acquired but also in terms of the sexual scripts they performed.

Understandably, some students interpreted the nuances of this occupational script with ease, others with anxiety. Hospital records indicate that nursing administrators regularly admonished their students for failure to conform to the behaviour norm. Students who chose not to participate in their occupation's performative rituals resigned, sometimes because of marriage and in other cases due to conflicts with school administrators.[18] Despite these actions, relatively few apprenticing nurses abandoned their training, in part because in the years before World War I the Victorian image of respectable femininity did not appear old-fashioned or outmoded compared to that being prescribed for other women. If anything, the model devised within nursing reinforced Victorian notions of bourgeois femininity, so that nurses simply performed a more extreme version of the model of femininity and sexuality being advocated for all women, especially those of the middle class.

## Challenges to Victorian Femininity, 1920–1942

By the 1920s, however, nursing's vision of respectable sexuality began to stand in contrast with the liberated sexual mores being advocated for the new woman. Christina Simmons, a historian of sexuality, has examined how in the 1920s the 'Myth of Victorian Repression' was constructed to signal what was wrong with American gender relations and why a sexual revolution was needed to revise them. The new woman of the 1920s was sexually liberated and actively pursuing heterosexual relations. By condemning the repression of pre-World War I gender relations, social commentators indicated that healthy sexual lives demanded expression, not repression. Within this context, nursing appeared anomalous. The feminine persona reinforced by nursing leaders and educators in the 1920s and 1930s was emblematic of the Victorian sexual restraint that by the 1920s was considered outmoded and dangerous.[19]

The most obvious symbol of this disparity was nurses' dress. Throughout the 1920s and 1930s, nursing schools across the country maintained the traditional uniform style and continued to rely on it to signify their occupational identity. Blue dresses with tight bodices, full skirts, high collars, and long sleeves constituted the standard apparel. White aprons and bibs were worn over the blue dress, with starched white collars, cuffs, and ties added according to student status and school style. Each day students donned their costume, and each day that dress was inspected. As students progressed through their years as probationer, junior, intermediate, and then senior nurse, additions to their uniform signified the maturation process. Upon graduation, practitioners were permitted to wear an entirely white costume—dress, cap, stockings, and shoes. The symbolic inversion of traditional female imagery, wherein the colour white signified nurses' workplace experience rather than a bride's sexual inexperience, was

reinforced by the elaborate graduation ceremonies (modelled after wedding ceremonies
and, to a lesser degree, religious initiation rites)
sponsored by training schools and alumnae
across the Dominion. Such rites of passage also
reaffirmed the asexual status of trained nurses:
they graduated out of the cloistered world of
hospital apprenticeship sexually and socially
pure, driven by vocation and profession, not by
marriage or sexuality.

Given the power of the symbolism, it is not
surprising that nursing educators and administrators vigorously defended the dress code they
had established. Only on the question of hair did
supervisors fail to impose their standards. As
bobbed hair became all the rage with North
American women, superintendents of nursing
resisted the fashion, punishing students who
bobbed their locks and insisting that students
wear their hair long, in a bun on the back of the
head, with the cap perched on top. One student
nurse at Halifax's Victoria General decided to use
her day off to acquire a bob. When she returned
to the ward the nursing superintendent
demanded that the student retrieve her shorn
hair and pin it back onto her head so that she
might continue to conform to the conventional
look.[20] In this battle, the older generation lost
and bobbed hair became the standard coiffure,
but on other issues the old guard held fast. In the
fashion world of the flapper, hemlines were rising and waistlines dropping, but within nursing
the uniform remained pinched at the waist, and
seven inches off the floor.[21]

Nursing leaders were not unaware of the dif-
ferential that had developed between their staffs
and the dress and ethos of other women, but
maintained that the 'problem' of modern femininity had not penetrated their ranks. As one
superintendent of nursing put it: 'In spite of the
criticism given the so-called "flapper" of today. . .
there is a large proportion amongst our pupils
who measure up to the best in the past not only
of our own school but of the nursing world in
general.'[22] Emboldened by the limited job oppor-

tunities available to potential recruits, nursing
leaders clung tenaciously to the asexual feminine
persona fashioned by their predecessors.

Working nurses were less decided that the
scripts defining their occupational identity
needed to differ so dramatically from that of
modern femininity. Clearly, some rank-and-file
nurses sought to integrate elements of a more
modern, sexualized feminine persona into their
workplace identity. Graduates modernized their
dress as soon as they were liberated from training programs,[23] while students openly defied
institutional rules by breaking curfew, flirting
with patients, and dating male hospital personnel.[24] Tensions between modern femininity and
occupational standards emerged as a central
theme in nurses' popular culture of the interwar
years, as students used their publications to
mock regulatory regimes. Vancouver General's
1939 Nurses' Annual included a cartoon depicting morning roll call. Although students in the
front row were conforming to the military discipline of this morning ritual, those in the back
row were finishing their morning toilet, which
included getting dressed and applying
makeup.[25] The 'stylized repetition of acts' that
constituted morning roll call was undermined
by an equally 'stylized' set of acts derived from
modern femininity, such as putting on lingerie
and lipstick.

Nurses' popular culture also subverted the
sexual sanctity of the uniform by linking nurses'
heterosexual conquests to their occupation and
dress. The cheeky 1928 poem, 'The Nurse's
Chance', began:

> It seems to me a nurse has got
> A most delightful life
> Since she has many chances
> To become a rich man's wife

Their 'slick' uniform offered nurses a 'mean
advantage' over 'mushy' male patients on the
mend. Advising nurses to 'strike while the iron is
hot', the poem concluded:

Roll Call — and so on "Behind Scenes"

SOURCE: Vancouver General Hospital, *Nurses' Annual*, 1939.

For men assume the wife will be
Just like the nurse who cooled
Their fevered brow so patiently
But oh! how men are fooled[26]

Bedside labour permitted nurses to improve their class position by becoming 'a rich man's wife' but also to undermine conventional gender relations within marriage.

Such articulation of the sexual tension inherent in bedside care served to challenge the conventional occupational identity endorsed by nursing educators in schools across the country. At the same time, the contradictions inherent in the political economy of interwar health care prompted many working nurses to foster the traditional nursing image. Most graduate trained nurses made their living in the private health-care market, caring for individuals in the patients' homes or private hospital rooms. A small minority of practitioners were employed as public health nurses, travelling from house to house or working in local, sometimes mobile, health clinics. As women not contained in home, factory, or office, nurses had to negotiate daily with male doctors, administrators, patients, and members of the community. To mediate their position as women traversing the 'public' world of private or community health services, many nurses accommodated themselves to the traditional asexual image of nursing.

For instance, to secure work, nurses often relied on recommendations from male doctors and often travelled unchaperoned with male doctors to attend patients. Adhering to carefully delineated rules of personal and sexual propriety helped nurses defend against unwanted sexual advances, rumours of sexual impropriety, or allegations of professional advancement through sexual relations.[27] Relations with patients could prove equally challenging to negotiate. In her 1920 *The Girl of the New Day*, feminist author Ellen Knox acknowledged the perils to purity that private health care posed: 'what are you to do', she asked rhetorically, if a patient 'flatters you or says low, common things, better left unsaid.'[28]

That such transgressions might well result in allegations of improper behaviour and dismissal were alluded to in a poem reproduced several times in nursing publications:

Some people think that nurses
Fall in love the very day
They come to count a sick man's pulse
Or bring his dinner tray.

Insisting that invalid males were far from attractive and that 'fair romance' was not inspired by a 'man without a collar who's as cranky as a bear', the poem concluded:

> So cheer up, wives and sweethearts,
> Because it is not true
> That artful vampires in white caps
> Would wish to steal from you
> To tell the truth, before a week
> The poor nurse is a wreck:
> The love for your man is only this—
> The love to wring his neck.[29]

Critiquing the sexual appeal of male patients, the poem denied that nurses were 'artful vampires in white caps' and assured 'wives and sweethearts' that nurses posed no sexual threat. The poem's humorous conclusion, which made light of the dangerous image of nurse as sexual predator, recognized the reality that in private practice any threat to domestic and marital relations might cost nurses their jobs.

The poem's denial of the potential sexuality symbolized by the uniform was echoed in working nurses' interpretation of their place in the public sphere. Nurses working in public health and private duty often found themselves alone in rough neighbourhoods in the middle of the night, travelling on the outskirts of a city or in an isolated rural district, or accepting rides from strangers. In such contexts, nurses were proud to report, as did a nurse working for Winnipeg's Margaret Scott Nursing Mission (MSNM): 'I am not afraid to go anywhere at any time in my uniform as all our friends and patients know us.'[30] Men from all classes could be counted on to treat MSNM staff with respect. Riding home on the streetcar, 'tired, wornout workmen . . . offer us their seats if we are in uniform', while 'truck drivers . . . private cars, the doctors and anyone going in our direction' would offer nurses rides to patients in outlying districts. For these women, conforming to the behavioural and dress restrictions of the nursing establishment held tangible rewards. The asexual persona served to neutralize even the most sexually dangerous

men, turning working-class and bourgeois males alike into gentlemen. Clearly, there were limits to the symbolic work a uniform could do, as one nurse learned when, walking home from a patient's house in the middle of the night, she was harassed by a local man. But her response to the man revealed the depth of nurses' confidence in their occupational identity: she chastised her harasser, 'If you don't respect me you might have respected the uniform.'[31]

Maintaining boundaries between the more sexualized persona of modern femininity and the traditional asexual occupational image proved a potent means for working nurses to negotiate their daily lives. The occupational identity acquired, however painfully, as apprentices was certainly open to critique. Graduating students used their school publications to mount that critique, albeit often in humorous terms. But nurses' place within the interwar political economy of health also necessitated that ordinary practitioners deploy the asexual feminine persona if they were to serve the public health and private homes safely and respectably. The performative rituals that shaped nurses' occupational identity were re-enacted daily as working nurses sought to legitimate their presence in the world of work.

## Compulsory Heterosexuality: Nursing in the 1940s and 1950s

Just as the political economy of private health care shaped the stage on which interwar nurses played their parts, so, too, did changes to the health-care system during and after World War II influence the dominant definition of nursing that developed. Wartime and post-war economies provided, for the first time, a stable funding base for Canadian hospitals and with it both a dramatic growth in institutional health services and the decline of the private health-care market. Nursing administrators, recognizing the new occupational options young women enjoyed, tried to increase dramatically the numbers of staff and student nurses by making nursing an attractive occupational option. To do so, they modernized nursing's sexual and social feminine image, thereby ensuring that the occupation would remain, in this era, women's work.[32]

Changes in nurses' uniforms served as the most telling evidence of the new feminine ideal being promoted. During World War II nursing schools moved to bring nurses' official dress into line with other uniformed women. This time it was not domestic servants who inspired nurses' costume but women in the military.[33] While it is unclear whether this was a self-conscious manoeuvre to capitalize on the positive image of service women or simply part of the larger fashion trend of the day, nursing schools raised the hemlines, tailored their skirts, shortened the sleeves, relaxed the collar, and, eventually, removed the apron.[34] Leaders were anxious to publicize the makeover their occupation was undergoing. When, for example, the Toronto General Hospital decided to redesign its institutional costume, it consulted an 'internationally known designer who has definite ideas concerning the uniforms'. The designer's advice, that 'a charming appearance in every field of activity is a helpful tonic and especially so in nursing', obviously struck a chord in the health-care world. When the all-white uniform was introduced the *Canadian Hospital Magazine* reported its debut in the language of a model's runway and fashion show.

> This Class wore smart white uniforms with short sleeves and deep inset side pockets, thus doing away with starched cuffs, collars, bibs and aprons. The all-white uniform is a departure which will establish a precedent at the Hospital. Not only is it attractive in appearance but it is practical and should prove very popular.[35]

Whatever concessions to modern fashion nursing leaders were willing to make, they still hoped to signify heterosexual possibility, not experience. This became clear in the 1950s, when many hospitals introduced uniforms with full, soft skirts, a design that conformed to what

historian of fashion Maureen Turim has termed the 'sweetheart line' of female dress design. With respect to Hollywood's uses of the sweetheart line, Turim argues that this shape was able to 'annex the connotations of princess, debutante, or bride that became attached to this exaggerated feminine' appearance and that it contrasted with the 'slinkier tight skirt . . . [that represented] women as sexual warriors and gold diggers'.[36] Like debutantes, not gold diggers, nurses were represented as conforming to feminine norms, available for heterosexual relations if not yet experienced in them.

The image of the 'exaggerated feminine' was central to nursing leaders' recruiting efforts in the post-war decades. High school girls learned that nursing offered more than a job: parties, travel, and socializing all accompanied an occupation 'studded with opportunities and adventure'.[37] Part of the adventure was romance. No longer portrayed as an occupation women pursued until marriage or in place of marriage, nursing was promoted as an occupation that prepared women for, and could be pursued after, matrimony. Leaders campaigned to resolve the dichotomies between heterosexual pursuits and paid work by emphasizing that nursing training enhanced not only women's marital prospects but also their skills at making a marriage successful. As one promotional article declared: 'it's not surprising that the matrimonial rate among nurses is higher than in any other profession.'[38] Thus, the renovation of the occupational dress did not only serve to expose more leg and accentuate more curves, it also served as a powerful symbol of the fundamentally heterosexual status of nurses.[39]

Once again, the nursing uniform served a symbolic function. Through it nursing leaders articulated the highly stylized public persona nurses were expected to embody, a persona that signified the sexual possibility that nurses, like all young women, possessed. The contradiction, of course, was that nurses' actual heterosexuality was to be developed or practised only when they were out of uniform. At no point did occupational leaders expect that the rituals of deference that governed patient care would be replaced by rituals of flirtation or romance on the wards. It was the hours after work, in residence, wherein apprentices were encouraged to fuse contemporary sexual and social norms with their occupational identity.

Nursing schools facilitated heterosexual contact through dating, class formals, and seasonal dances, sometimes organized in conjunction with engineering students at the local university. A 1958 Vancouver General yearbook photograph of a young woman, decked out in a full-length, sleeveless 'sweetheart' gown, walking down the steps of the nurses' residence holding the hand of a dapper young man wearing a tuxedo, reminded nursing and non-nursing readers that apprenticeship training did not insulate nurses from the wider heterosexual culture of post-World War II Canada.[40]

At the same time, residence rules were relaxed to facilitate young nurses' participation in modern cultural forms. Institutions like the Winnipeg General Hospital established a 'smoker' wherein nurses could enjoy cigarettes without having to sneak onto the roof or into a nearby café as they had done in the previous generation. One Winnipeg alumna recalled that until she enrolled, 'I don't think I'd ever seen a woman smoke.' But because 'the smoking room was where all the fun was . . . all the student nurses went in that room, usually after every shift, that's where the people got rid of their tensions, and told all the jokes', the student realized that if she wanted to be part of the after-hours socializing she had to 'smoke in self-defence'.[41] Activities that in a previous generation were defined as deviant were now part of the normative socio-sexual self. Just as the rituals of nursing education had done in the past, the daily rituals of convening in the smoker allowed nurses to socialize and be socialized, to participate in the domain of contemporary femininity even as they met as working women.

The popular culture created by nursing students clearly articulated the heterosexual femininity of their occupation. The 1949 Calgary General Hospital yearbook included the following cartoon. The student's mind wandered from her gynecology text to her romantic fantasies, while the cobwebs growing in her desk suggested that she spent more time dreaming than at her studies. That the student wore pajamas, the uniform of leisure and bed, rather than a nursing garb located her firmly within a gendered rather than vocational role. Within the new political economy of health care, the closer alignment

SOURCE: Calgary General Hospital, In *Uniform and Cap*, 1949.

between nursing and heterosexuality was possible precisely because all nurses, staff and students, were now contained within institutional walls. As hospitals emerged as the primary location of employment, nurses were less frequently called to individual homes where private doctors, family members, or men on the street might harass them or misinterpret their behaviour. In hospitals, institutional structures overrode the specific dynamics of private households and familial employment, and the 'low common things' said to nurses were less likely to compromise their employment status.

Of course, as nurses' heterosexuality became part of public discourse, the pendulum threatened to swing too far. Non-nurse publications and commentators picked up the question of nurses' sexuality and the image of the sexually knowledgeable nurse began to appear. For example, a 1945 cartoon from the *Halifax Herald* depicted two nurses at the bedside of a young male patient. As the patient, not terrifically attractive himself, sucked on a thermometer his eyes bugged out at the big-chested 'Betty Boop'-like nurse. The second, older, grey-haired, bespectacled nurse requested her colleague to leave the bedside because she was causing the patient's temperature to rise unnaturally high. Scientific medicine was being interrupted by female sexuality.

SOURCE: *Halifax Herald*, 1945.

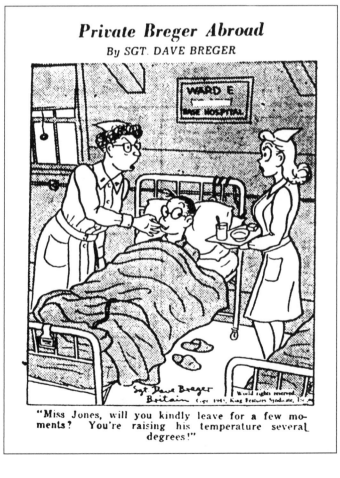

## Private Breger Abroad
### By SGT. DAVE BREGER

"Miss Jones, will you kindly leave for a few moments? You're raising his temperature several degrees!"

At the same time, the fact that the patient was a young man who was clearly more responsive to the ministrations of the curvaceous young nurse suggested that sexuality and science could be combined in powerful ways. When, for instance, a 1950 issue of the University of Manitoba Students' Union newspaper, *The Manitoban*, announced that the Red Cross would be on campus that week the article began: 'Roll up your sleeve and smile for the cute little blonde nurse, boys—she wants some of your blood for her collection.'[42] The nurse's professional mandate to administer a blood bank was recast *à la Dracula*, as if it was *her* collection and her sexual appeal lured potential victims. In this context, it was the public, not nurses, who capitalized on the image of nurses as 'artful vampires in white caps'.

By the late 1960s and early 1970s, the sexualized image of the nurse would be carried one step further. Within American popular culture characters like *M.A.S.H.*'s 'Hot Lips' Hoolihan and Ken Kesey's 'Big Nurse', Nurse Ratched in *One Flew Over the Cuckoo's Nest*, were depicted by left-liberal writers as symbolic of women's heterosexual and socially damaging power. At a more grassroots level, popular culture positioned nurses as more sexually knowledgeable than other women, as nurse-characters' frequent appearances in pornographic films and novels suggested.[43]

Given these circumstances, nurses sought to locate themselves as feminine, sexual, *and* respectable. Many accomplished this by marrying—in fact, this new sexual-social occupational paradigm legitimated the decision made by many women in the post-war era to combine nursing careers with marriage. But the unmarried women, who still comprised the majority of graduates, confronted a definition of femininity in which sexual space was in some ways even more difficult to negotiate than it had been before. Nurses were encouraged to participate in the youth culture of heterosexual and heterosocial activities, but at the same time they had to avoid crossing the line into promiscuity.

The 1959 'Case of the Kissing Nurse' exemplified this tension. When the Vancouver General administrators met to resolve the conflict, their discussion centred not on whether the kissing had occurred but whether it had continued past the point of the respectable. One matron proclaimed, 'I'm not a prude but 25 minutes is too long.' Another administrator asked, 'Who initiated the contact?' and another queried, 'Were his hands in evidence at all times?'[44] Yet while hospital administrators worried that the 'kissing nurse' had gone too far, news reporters queried whether nurses were not allowed to go far enough: Was nursing 'discriminated against in romance?'[45]

Nurses' claims to respectable femininity hinged on their ability to negotiate the mixed messages and ambiguous limits they encountered. Not surprisingly, then, the essence of student complaints at Vancouver General was not about rules regarding deportment per se but about the inconsistency with which those rules were applied. Facing powerful social sanctions if they performed their gender wrong, the students demanded what Butler would call a clearly delineated script. This point was not lost on all observers. Mr McNaughton, second vice-chairman of the Hospital Board, commented that at 10:30 at night he had often seen seven cars lined up outside the residence as students said goodbye to their boyfriends, and asked, 'was it a crime to kiss your boyfriend at 2:30 in the afternoon but not one at 10:30 at night?'[46] Here McNaughton captured the crux of the problem. Heterosexual desire was to be applauded and encouraged in daylight, but practised only after dark, preferably with a man who would become your husband.

Within the new political economy of health services that developed after World War II, nursing leaders scripted a subtle change in their occupational identity. As in previous eras, nurses were encouraged to use their leisure time to pursue 'normal' heterosexual options, but unlike during the pre-war decades, nursing work itself was heralded as enhancing women's sexual appeal. In doing so, leaders were able to capitalize on the powerful youth culture of the post-war era wherein 'innocent' sexual encounters between the sexes were considered healthy and women's sexual possibility was highly visible. As Canadian nursing elites emphasized the heterosexual complementariness of their occupation, they had to come to terms with the possibility of open displays of heterosexual activity—whether in front of the nursing residence or in popular representations of nurses. Meanwhile, working nurses had to navigate the narrow path between being 'kissing nurses' and 'artful vampires'.

## Conclusion

In recent years, historians of nursing have reckoned with the gendered contours of the occupation's past. Emphasizing the asymmetrical division of labour and authority that has ordered relations of power between nurses and the male medical profession, historians have confronted the ways gendered notions have infused the structure and content of nursing work. Such historiographical shifts in interpretation speak to the success of women's history, especially in making gender visible within an occupation that has been so shaped by notions of femininity that it has at times been taken as natural. Much less scholarly attention has been paid to the ways that sexuality shaped nursing's gendered reputation. As the research presented here demonstrates, nurses' close working relationship with the bodies of strangers signalled their potential as 'artful vampires'. To contain or capitalize on that potential, occupational leaders and working nurses scripted specific workplace identities, learned through the highly 'stylized' repetition of acts.

If nursing history has much to learn from gender history, so, too, can studies of femininity and masculinity benefit from the lessons offered from nursing's past. Researchers frequently assert that gender is 'socially constructed', but articulating the precise mechanisms whereby such constructions occurred in the past is often complicated by unavailability of sources. As a thoroughly gendered occupation with a rich primary resource base, nursing offers a site wherein 'normative' sexuality can be interrogated. Historians of Canadian women have tended to address the question of sexuality by examining regulatory regimes or prescriptive codes and then considering the 'deviants' who transgressed those rules. The implication of such studies is that fear of being 'deviant' inspired 'normal' women to adhere to the prescriptive code: heterosexual monogamy emerges as the default position women adopted if they wanted to resist being labelled sex radical, prostitute, or lesbian.[47]

The example of nurses reveals, however, that normal sexuality was not simply a function of expression/repression, but rather a complex process whereby particular combinations of acceptable behaviour were scripted and then learned through occupationally specific rituals of performance in the workplace and during leisure hours. And, as Butler warns, the process of learning normative sexual and gendered identities was often painful: 'Gender is what is put on, invariably, under constraint, daily and incessantly, with anxiety and pleasure.'[48] The nursing identities developed by apprentices took three years and often involved a great deal of negative reinforcement, but once formed they proved powerful. The power of those identities lay in the authority nursing educators and leaders held over apprentices and in the political economy of health that shaped working nurses' conditions of employment. Rejecting the dominant occupational definition held very real consequences for student and graduate nurse alike. At the same time, the occupation could not exist too far outside contemporary heterosocial and sexual norms for fear of public censure or trouble attracting new recruits.

Feminist theorists have also challenged us to think about gender not only as the experiences of women and men, but also as a system of signifying power—that gender can be at work even if real women, or men, are not.[49] And, theorists assert, gender identities are relational—they are formed against or with their socially constructed opposite. There is no doubt that for nurses in [the twentieth] century different and sometimes competing versions of masculinity were constantly lurking about: the sexual partner, the sexual predator, and the supportive gentleman were powerful images invoked to signify the legitimacy or logic of nurses' various occupational scripts. Hypothetical male behaviour was indeed a potent system of signifying power. But it is equally important that however much nurses used masculine imagery to construct their social roles, the actual cast of characters was entirely female. Women with substantial occupational power scripted a social identity that less powerful women embraced, resisted, or modified. In the effort to chart the relations between the genders, historians must not lose sight of the substantial power women wielded over each other or the potential for self-definition they sometimes realized.

## Notes

This article was originally prepared for this volume of essays [Kathryn McPherson, Cecilia Morgan, and Nancy M. Forestell, eds, *Gendered Pasts: Historical Essays in Femininity and Masculinity in Canada* (Toronto: Oxford University Press, 1999)]. Much of the research presented here was subsequently reworked for inclusion in my 1996 book, *Bedside Matters: The Transformation of Canadian Nursing, 1900-1990* (Toronto, 1996), especially material presented in ch. 5, 'The Case of the Kissing Nurse'. I would like to thank Oxford University Press (Canada) for permission to use material presented in *Bedside Matters* for this article. Thanks are also extended to John Lutz, Adele Perry, and Cecilia Morgan for comments on earlier drafts. York University Faculty of Arts Fellowship support made possible the time to draft the original version of this article.

1.  Vancouver City Archives (VCA), Vancouver General Hospital (VanGH), Minutes, Meeting, 15, 16 Jan. 1959.

2.  Jeannine Locke, 'Nurses Denied Romance by Prudish Profession', *Toronto Daily Star*. See also 'Hospital to "Kiss, Make Up" With its Student Nurses', *Vancouver Sun*, 16 Jan. 1959 (VCA, VanGH collection.)

3.  I consider the homosocial space created by nursing's occupationally specific gender and sexual identities in McPherson, *Bedside Matters*, ch. 5.

4.  Judith Butler, 'Performative Acts and Gender Constitution: An Essay in Phenomenology and Feminist Theory', in Sue Ellen Case, ed., *Performing Feminisms: Feminist Critical Theory and Theatre* (Baltimore, 1990), 277.

5.  Judith Butler, *Gender Trouble: Feminism and the Subversion of Identity* (New York, 1989).

6.  For an overview of the changing structure and content of nursing work over the twentieth century, see McPherson, *Bedside Matters*.

7.  See McPherson, *Bedside Matters*; McPherson, 'Carving Out a Past: Canadian Nurses Association War Memorial', *Histoire sociale/Social History* 29, 58 (Nov. 1996): 417–39; McPherson, 'Working With Whiteness', paper presented to the Canadian Association for Medical History, Ottawa. June 1998.

8.  Elizabeth Wilson, a historian of fashion, argues that 'By the 1890s it had become customary for maid-servants to wear black, and, like nurses at the same period, to have women's caps from an earlier period.' Wilson, *Adorned in Dreams: Fashion and Modernity* (London. 1985), 36. . . .

9.  Provincial Archives of Nova Scotia (PANS), Victoria General Hospital (VicGH), 'Report of Commissioners Appointed to Enquire into Management', *Nova Scotia Journal of the Legislative Assembly*, App. 15, 1896.

10. Mary Poovey, *Uneven Developments: The Ideological Work of Gender in Mid-Victorian England* (Chicago, 1988), 14.

11. At the Winnipeg General Hospital (WGH), students were granted late leave until 11:30 once per week, and once a month that could be extended to midnight for 'Theatre Leave'.

12. Mariana Valverde, *The Age of Light, Soap, and Water: Moral Reform in English Canada, 1885–1925* (Toronto, 1991).

13. Winnipeg General Hospital Nurses Alumnae Association Archives (WGHNAAA), WGH, *Student*

*Register*, 1903–6, uncatalogued. See also PANS, MG 20, vol. 1000, no. 1, VicGH, *Chronological Record of Ward Service*, Mar. 1912–Mar. 1920.

14. See, for example, Brandon General Hospital Archives (BGHA), Brandon General Hospital (BGH), *Rules and Regulations for Nurses,* 1906, Box 55.

15. St Boniface General Hospital School of Nursing Alumnae Room Archives, unpublished history of the St Boniface School of Nursing, n.d. *(circa 1976)*, 14–15.

16. When one Vancouver General student was caught smoking in her room she lost her cap for six months. Nora Kelly, *Quest for a Profession: The History of the Vancouver General Hospital School of Nursing* (Vancouver, 1973), 36. At the Royal Jubilee in Victoria one student lost the right to wear her cap for a week when she failed to report a patient's death right away. Anne Pearson, *The Royal Jubilee Hospital* (Victoria, n.d.), 24.

17. In the nurses' home, students had to entertain visitors in the reception room and could not have visitors, other than perhaps mothers and sisters, in their own rooms. Permission had to be sought if nurses wanted to receive a male patient or ex-patient at the residence. Provincial Archives of Manitoba (PAM), WGH collection, 'House Rules for Nurses approved by the board August 1920', WGH, House Committee, Minutes, 25 Aug. 1920.

18. WGHNAAA, WGH, Register, 1903–6. See also PANS, VicGH, *Ward Register*, 1900–20.

19. Christina Simmons, 'Modern Sexuality and the Myth of Victorian Repression', in Kathy Peiss and Christina Simmons, eds, *Passion and Power: Sexuality in History* (Philadelphia, 1989), 157–77. See also John d'Emilio and Estelle Freedman, *Intimate Matters: A History of Sexuality in America* (New York, 1988). In the Canadian context, Veronica Strong-Boag's *The New Day Recalled: The Lives of Girls and Women in English Canada, 1919–1939* (Toronto, 1988) and Andrée Lévesque's *Making and Breaking the Rules: Women in Quebec, 1919–1939* (Toronto, 1994) focus on the continuing prescriptive emphasis on motherhood. . . .

20. Martha Stewart, interview by author, Halifax, 1981. The many references to bobbed hair in stu-dents' yearbooks suggest the degree of contro-versy over the new fashion in hair.

21. For a discussion of the influence of 'American' fashion on images of female sexuality in Quebec, see Lévesque, *Making and Breaking the Rules*, 55–7.

22. WGHNAAA, 'Miss Grant Addresses the Alumnae Association', WGH *Nurses' Alumnae Journal* 18, 23 (1927): 13–14.

23. 'Are Uniforms all Alike?', MGH *Blue and Gold*, 1928, 57. See also *Blue and Gold*, 1933, 'New 1933 Styles in Crisp White Uniforms'. Some agencies, hoping to attract graduate nurses onto their staffs, pro-vided uniforms that, like the images in the Eaton's advertisements and yearbook cartoons, were dis-tinctly modern. The Victorian Order of Nurses uniform, for example, included a drop-waisted dress, a tie, and a cloche hat.

24. PANS, RG 25, Box 10, VicGH, *Ward Nursing Register*, 1920–4.

25. VanGH, *Nurses' Annual*, 1939, 45.

26. 'The Nurse's Chance', WGH *Blue and White*, 1928, 45.

27. For an example of one nurse whose appointment was questioned because of allegations of sexual relations with her employer, see Provincial Archives of British Columbia, GR 496, A.D. Lapp, Superintendent of Tranquille Sanatorium, to Mr P. Walker, Deputy Provincial Secretary, Victoria, 9 Jan. 1936.

28. Ellen Knox, *The Girl of the New Day* (Toronto, 1920), 51.

29. 'Love', WGH *Blue and White*, 1931, 61; VanGH, *Nurses' Annual*, 1928, 84.

30. PAM, MSNM file, *Report*, Dec. 1935, 1503–4.

31. Mary Shepherd, tape-recorded interview by author, Winnipeg, 18 June 1987. . . .

32. Concerns about shortages of graduate nurses abounded throughout the post-war era. See, for example, VicGH, *Annual Report*, 1948, 23–5, and 1953, 30. See also John R. Smiley, Isabel Black, Andrew Kapos, and Boyde G. Gill, *The Untapped Pool: A Survey of Ontario Nurses* (1968); Registered Nurses Association of British Columbia, *Submission to the Royal Commission on Health Services* (1962), 11–24.

33. In her 'They're Still Women After All', Ruth Pierson has demonstrated that the wartime propaganda campaign to recruit women into military and civilian production hinged on the depiction of women in uniform—whether a CWAC dress or a welder's suit—as uncompromisingly heterosexual and feminine. Ruth Roach Pierson, 'They're Still Women After All': The Second World War and Canadian Womanhood (Toronto, 1986).

34. Hamilton General Hospital School of Nursing (Hamilton, 1956) describes that school's efforts to modernize their uniform. See also 'Trends in Nursing', Canadian Nurse (CN) 49, 3 (Mar. 1953): 209, for a discussion of the Demonstration School at Windsor that eliminated the capping ceremony and allowed students to wear the full uniform from the first day of training. . . .

35. 'Toronto General Hospital Student Nurses' Uniform', The Quarterly 7, 6 (Winter 1949): 1. See also 'New Uniforms', In Cap and Uniform, 1952, 44, Calgary General Hospital Nurses' Alumnae Association Archives, uncatalogued.

36. Maureen Turim, 'Designing Women: The Emergence of the New Sweetheart Line', in Jane Gaines and Charlotte Herzog, eds, Fabrications: Costume and the Female Body (New York, 1990), 225–6. . . .

37. Canadian Nurses' Association, 'What Nursing Holds For You', (n.d.). . . .

38. 'Woman in Service', Vancouver Daily Province, 8 July 1944, 8.

39. See Jane Gaines, 'Costume and Narrative: How Dress Tells the Woman's Story', in Gaines and Herzog, eds, Fabrications.

40. VanGH, Nurses' Annual, 1958.

41. Marjorie McLeod, tape-recorded interview by author, 6 Sept. 1992.

42. 'Red Cross Seeking Students' Red Blood', The Manitoban 37, 14 (10 Nov. 1950): 1.

43. For analyses of the sexualized image of nurses in American popular culture, see Philip A. Kalisch and Beatrice J. Kalisch, The Changing Image of the Nurse (Menlo Park, Calif., 1987); Barbara Melosh, 'Doctors, Patients, and "Big Nurse": Work and Gender in the Postwar Hospital', in E.C. Lagemann, ed., Nursing History: New Perspectives, New Possibilities (Philadelphia, 1984).

44. VanGH, Minutes, Meeting, 15, 16 Jan. 1959.

45. Locke, 'Nurses Denied Romance by Prudish Profession'. See also 'At Hospital: "Kissing Nurse" Case Put on Ice', Vancouver Sun, 17 Jan. 1959, 9; 'New Rule for Nurses', Vancouver Sun, 27 Jan. 1959. . . .

46. VanGH, Minutes, Meeting, 15, 16 Jan. 1959.

47. For example, see Lévesque, Making and Breaking the Rules.

48. Butler, 'Performative Acts', 282. Butler emphasizes the coercive or non-volitional dimension of identity formation and acquisition in 'The Body You Want: Liz Kotz Interviews Judith Butler', Artforum International (Nov. 1992): 82–9.

49. Joan Scott, 'Gender: a useful category of historical analysis', American Historical Review 91, 5 (1986).

# 13

# Privilege and Oppression:
# The Configuration of Race, Gender, and Class in
# Southern Ontario Auto Plants, 1939 to 1949

Pamela Sugiman

Over the last few decades, attempts to theorize the relationship of race, gender, and class, and discussions of the centrality of these forces in shaping our lives have become increasingly sophisticated and passionately debated. . . .

There is a need then for social historians and social scientists to rethink some of the old conceptual categories, with an eye to understanding the ways in which race, gender, and class, as historically configured, have structured the economic institutions that govern our lives. How, for example, has this nexus organized wage-earning and shaped workers' experiences in this country? Moreover, what is the link between the gendering and racialization of capitalist workplaces and the politicization of the worker, the development of a worker consciousness, and the collective mobilization of the working class? Importantly, how can we theorize this link between structure and lived experience without reverting to old additive or multiplicative analyses based on the equation race + gender + class or race x gender x class?[1]

This paper offers an examination of the ways in which the matrix of race, gender, and class has

structured the automobile manufacturing industry of southern Ontario, a work setting that has long been racialized and gendered. Since the beginnings of the industry, white men have dominated the auto manufacturing workforce. Anyone who was not white and male was in the minority, different, an intruder, treated as unequal. In the auto plants of southern Ontario, two such 'minorities' existed. One, small groups of women, many of whom were born in Canada of Anglo-Celtic and Eastern European descent, worked in McKinnon Industries of St Catharines, Ontario, and the General Motors Company of Canada's (GM) manufacturing facility in Oshawa, Ontario.[2] Two, even smaller pockets of black men, mostly Canadian-born, were concentrated in janitorial jobs and various types of foundry work in McKinnon Industries and the Ford Motor Company of Canada, as well as some smaller auto foundries in Windsor.[3]

In earlier research, I documented the experiences of white, women auto workers, tracing changes in both their position in the industry and their perceptions and politics over the

Pamela Sugiman, 'Privilege and Oppression: The Configuration of Race, Gender, and Class in Southern Ontario Auto Plants, 1939 to 1949', *Labour/Le Travail* 47 (Spring 2001): 83–113. © Canadian Committee on Labour History.

course of several decades.[4] This study is an attempt to reconstruct a small part of the lives of black men, on the job and in their union, at a time when their numerical presence in the auto plants was at its peak, throughout World War II and into the post-war period.[5] It is based on a review of union documents, as well as the oral testimonies of 12 black men who were employed in the industry during these years.[6] . . .

Oral testimony is a valuable methodological tool to unearth the histories of invisible groups who, by virtue of their small number, have escaped scholarly attention.[7] Due to the hegemony of whiteness in the auto plants, black auto workers have almost no place in Canadian labour history. Jobs in auto manufacturing have been viewed as 'naturally' white (and male); analyses of the racialization and gendering of workplaces have been confined to those settings in which women and people of colour are numerically dominant.[8] Yet in spite of the scant numbers of black men in the plants, auto manufacturers drew on widespread cultural beliefs about race and gender, and exploited and reinforced the structural inequalities that working-class blacks faced in wartime southern Ontario. Employers manipulated these beliefs in hiring workers, allocating them to jobs, and establishing the terms of their employment. In doing so, management was central to the construction of difference among workers—a notable achievement given the striking social homogeneity of the workforce as a whole.

Considering the industrial backdrop that employers had set in place prior to the emergence of the United Automobile Workers' Union (UAW), I also comment on the ways in which black men, as individual workers and subsequently as trade unionists furthering collective goals, coped with, and at times resisted their racial subordination. . . . . Industrial unionism played a central role in shaping these strategies of coping and resistance. Yet the UAW posed contradictions. While the union served as an ally, offering both a philosophical commitment to

social (racial) equality and justice, and the material resources and tools with which to seek it, the UAW also contained the struggle to racialize worker resistance.[9] Union leaders lacked an adequate understanding of racial and sexual discrimination, and they typically reduced both to class relations between workers (as a homogeneous entity) and their employers. Furthermore, the union constructed a false dichotomized 'choice' between racial (and sexual) *difference* on the one hand and *equality* on the other. Believing in the importance of a unified 'workers' consciousness', UAW leaders, at times, posited difference or divisions within the working class as a threat to the labour movement.

An understanding of the social meaning of racial and sexual difference is central to an analysis of the workplace, working people, and their struggles. When we recognize these differences, we uncover many parallel, but separate working-class realities. The distinctive experiences of black men in the industry can be attributed to the particular ways in which race, gender, and class, both as subjectivities and social processes, have converged at different moments and touched the lives of workers, as well as shaped the larger historical scenario.

. . .

## Constructing Difference among Auto Workers

Though data on the demographic composition of auto plants in Canada is based largely on anecdotal evidence, it is undeniable that employers used race and sex as criteria in filling jobs. Prior to World War II, in the pre-union period, sizable communities of black families lived in the auto towns of St Catharines and Windsor. St Catharines, a small city near Niagara Falls, was the home of McKinnon Industries. Windsor, a mid-sized city that is situated across the river from Detroit, was the location of the Ford Motor Company of Canada, Chrysler Canada, and a number of affiliated auto foundries such as Auto Specialties, Walker Metal Products, and Malleable Iron.

Despite the strong presence of the auto companies in their communities, however, most blacks understood that auto employment was unattainable to them. Before World War II, only a handful of blacks worked in auto [plants]. . . . In the 1920s, two black men, members of the Nicholson family in St Catharines, poured iron in the McKinnon foundry. They may have been the only two 'coloured men' employed by the company at this time. In the 1930s, McKinnon Industries hired a large number of Armenians. These men, most of whom were recent immigrants to Canada, lived in company housing on Ontario Street, which was located opposite the plant. They occupied many of the jobs that increasing numbers of blacks would later fill. In the 1920s, some black men also found work in the Ford Motor Company, though their exact number is not known. Auto employees Lyle Talbot and Rod Davis, respectively, had a father and grandfather working in Ford.[10] Talbot's father was hired in 1919 and worked as a machine operator in the transmission department until 1947.

With the outbreak of World War II, employers were forced to alter their hiring policies in response to stepped up production demands and the temporary departure of many prime-age, white, male employees. Thus, the doors to the auto plants opened a crack for some of those workers who had long been on the outside. For instance, during this time, Ford hired a number of Chinese men in its Windsor plant. Proud of this move, company publicists featured a photograph of each of their 56 Chinese workers in its monthly magazine, *Ford Times*. Ford described the employment of these men as a patriotic gesture in the context of war.[11]

During these years, the company also continued to hire black men in relatively small, but growing numbers. In the United States, the well-known industrialist Henry Ford had established a reputation for providing jobs to 'Negroes', a move indicative of his paternalistic relationship with the African-American community.[12] In 1941, blacks constituted roughly 10 per cent of the workforce (11,000 workers) in the Ford Motor Company in the US.[13] While Henry Ford also upheld this reputation in Canada, the numbers of blacks in the Windsor plant seem almost insignificant in comparison to those in the US. For example, when Lyle Talbot began to work at Ford (Windsor) in 1940, he joined roughly 200 black men.[14]

McKinnon Industries was the other major employer of black men in the auto industry. In 1938, the company hired approximately 80 men, many of whom were black, in its foundry division.[15] Richard Nicholson, relative of the two Nicholsons who worked at McKinnon in the 1920s, was one of these recruits. Shortly after joining the company, he witnessed the entry of several more blacks. According to Nicholson, roughly 15 to 20 black men were hired in McKinnon Industries during World War II. By 1943, there were at least 40 to 50 black men out of a total workforce of 4,500.[16]

Of the 'Big Three', Chrysler Canada had the most overtly racist hiring practices.[17] In fact, the company did not hire a black worker until it was pressured to do so by law in the 1950s. In 1951, the Ontario Fair Employment Practices Act[18] was passed and in 1953, a federal Fair Employment Practices Act was set in place. According to the latter piece of legislation, any company that had a contract with the Canadian government was prohibited from engaging in racially discriminatory hiring practices. Thus, in October 1953, for the first time in its history, Chrysler Canada hired three black men to work on its assembly lines.[19]

None of the companies, however, offered employment to black women. According to a report by Lyle Talbot, former Ford employee and president of the anti-racist organization, the Windsor Council on Group Relations, at a time when many employers badly needed to replenish their diminishing supply of workers, 'the doors of virtually every factory in the Windsor area were closed tight against coloured girls and women.'[20] In fact, of the 50 shops in Windsor that were under UAW contract, not one employed a black woman in either office or factory. Talbot noted that, '[i]t was common knowledge of the coloured people of Windsor that their women-folk were hardly ever sent to factories, stores or offices' by the federal government wartime agency, the National Selective Service (NSS), because of a 'gentlemen's agreement'. In those few cases where the NSS did send black women for jobs, the employers had apparently repri-manded NSS officials. World War II 'broke the barrier' for 'coloured *men*' only.[21]

On the whole, personnel managers asked job applicants few questions about their employ-ment experience or other personal qualifications. (In men of all races, employers overlooked the unique talents of the worker, i.e., skills for the job.) In working-class men, auto employers sought 'human machinery' to perform labour that had been organized for profit-making only.[22] Yet in specifically pursuing 'coloured men', on occasion, management was underlining the salience of race in this class context. Richard Nicholson worked in the foundry in St Catharines for 36 years. He remembers his entry into the company.

> I heard the rumour . . . that McKinnon Industries was hiring blacks. . . . They were looking for *coloured people* to work in the foundry so I went down there to Ontario Street and 'bingo!' I got hired right away because I was a big lad and everything [emphasis mine].

During the war years, auto manufacturers recruited black men through various govern-ment and community networks. Many men found their jobs by way of either the NSS, district service clubs, or ministers of black Baptist churches. When neither the NSS nor the neigh-bourhood rumour system yielded sufficient numbers of black males, however, employers resorted to more active and direct means of recruiting, reaching out beyond local communi-ties. Local folklore tells us that years ago, recruiters for McKinnon Industries went to Toronto to find black men. Then in 1940, under the exigencies of war, they travelled to Nova Scotia as part of a further recruitment drive.[23] The NSS paid the men's passage from Nova Scotia to St Catharines, a distance of close to 2,000 kilometres. At various points in time, McKinnon managers also recruited black men from Fort Erie and Niagara Falls.[24]

## 'Foundries Is Made for Black Men'

Automakers took special measures to locate black male labourers largely because they wanted them to fill the most undesirable jobs in the plants—jobs that few white men wanted. In the auto plants of Ontario, racial segregation was never enforced as a matter of company policy nor was it written into collective agreements (as it had been in the US). Yet management used informal, unspoken means of exclusion to place blacks in one of three areas: the heat treat, the powerhouse, or the foundry. Within various departments or divisions, some black men could also find work as janitors.[25] According to Lyle Talbot, who temporarily worked in each of these jobs, they were all bad places to be. The power-house was dirty.

> [T]hey'd get all kinds of soot from the smoke. . . . In the powerhouse, there was a big pile of coal out in the yard, and big transformers that were run by coal, heat. Black men worked in a tunnel where the coal was brought in on a conveyor from the coal pile into the big furnaces that gen-erated the heat for the power. The men had to make sure that the coal did not fall off the con-veyor going through.

The 'heat treat's the same thing', Talbot added. This is where they treated the metal with heat in long ovens. The worst of the three areas, how-ever, was the foundry—'where all the heavy, slugging, dirty work' went on.[26] The vast majority of the black workforce was situated in the foundry.[27] And there, along with Armenians, they typically performed the least desirable job of iron pouring.

> The men poured their own iron and you had to go out and shift the moulds—had a plate on top about that thick and go on top of the moulds for them to pour the iron. Sometimes they'd be pouring and the mould would be bad and as they poured in the iron would burst out the side and sometimes, as soon as that iron, just a drop, would hit . . . the concrete it would look like fireworks.[28]

GM worker Richard Nicholson commented on the relationship between race and job allocation:

> In 1938 . . . when I went to General Motors, they hired us blacks for one reason. They didn't lie to you. When they hired me, they told me . . . 'We got a job for you in the foundry. It's a hot job. It's a hard job.' . . . [T]hey kept calling in blacks, more blacks. They would've hired more blacks if they could have got 'em because that was where you were supposed to be—right there in the foundry.

Black working-class men had little choice but to accept these hot, hard jobs. Typically, prior to finding employment in the auto industry, these men worked as bellhops or elevator operators in local hotels, and general labourers on railroads, in carnivals, and on farms. They also washed cars by hand, peddled wares on the streets, and collected metal in alleyways for resale.[29] Most of this work was seasonal. Auto employment not only offered higher wages, but more importantly, it was comparatively steady work. The black community faced intense racism in the labour market, a situation that resulted in extreme economic hardship.

Compounding the labour force requirements of auto manufacturers and the dire economic straits of most black workers, employers upheld a particular vision of black masculinity that rested in part on the belief that a 'coloured man' was most suited to hard, dirty, and physically demanding jobs.[30] Before foundries became highly automated, many of the operations required enormous physical strength (lifting castings and pouring iron, for example). And the dominant cultural image of a black man was that of a strong, robust, and muscular worker. Moreover, foundry work was performed at extraordinarily high temperatures and thus demanded tremendous physical stamina. Some company officials claimed that coloured men, in particular, could endure these excesses because of a genetic predisposition to withstand heat.[31] According to auto worker Cassell Smith,

> At that time the foundry there was smoky and dusty and the workers they'd get in there wouldn't stay long. . . . So they decided, we [black men] could stand it . . . that was the purpose of it because they figured, being black, you know, you could stand the heat . . . that they're all the same . . . people in Africa stand a lot of heat.

Exhibiting a racialized paternalism, some managers publicly showcased 'their' hard-working black employees. In doing so, they presented black masculinity in a hyperbolic form—using a racial stereotype to magnify the image of the unskilled working man.[32] In the eyes of some observers in the plants, these men were little more than powerful, labouring bodies. GM foundry employee Richard Nicholson recounted,

> . . . quite a few white people come over and watch you work. Take pictures. They've got pictures of me down there now. Take pictures of us doing this heavy job. And they'd just sit back and say, 'Look at them guys work!' Visitors . . . the foremen or the general foreman [would] bring people in and say, 'Let's show you how we do it—how our boys do it.' They all look at one another and they used to be taking pictures of us guys all the time—the kind of work we was doin.'[33]

These men were highlighted for displaying manly brawn and to some extent they themselves expressed pride in their ability to perform work that involved remarkably high levels of physical exertion.[34] Yet at the same time, black men were objectified by employers. Managers who put the men on public display for performing hard, dirty, hazardous labour—work that they had little choice but to perform—paradoxically reinforced the notion that black males possessed a heightened masculinity while at the same time they emasculated these men in denying their 'humanness', in constructing them as 'beasts of burden'. Employers contributed to the construction of a racialized masculinity, a masculinity that embodied racial and class subordination.

## The Privileges of Manhood

Being a man, however, did bring with it some privileges. It was because of their *sex* that these men were hired in the auto industry. As noted, even during World War II, black women faced formidable obstacles in finding any kind of factory employment in Windsor and elsewhere in Canada. Their sexual status furthermore ensured that black men would possess specific job rights, rights that were denied the small numbers of white women who had been allowed to work in some auto plants largely because of their privilege as a race.

Sexual inequalities were blatant in collective agreements between the UAW and auto manufacturers. Notably, contracts upheld sex-based job classifications and non-interchangeable, sex-based seniority. Moreover, it was not until 1954 that UAW leadership in Canada formally challenged company restrictions on the employment of married women.[35] Unlike their union sisters, men (of all races) were rewarded for being married. Assumed to be breadwinners, black men held departmental, and ultimately plant-wide seniority rights, received the same wages and piece rates, and in theory, could occupy the same job classifications as all other male auto workers. There is no evidence that during these years, any of the local collective agreements between the UAW and the Big Three automakers in Canada openly made distinctions among workers on the basis of *race*. GM worker Richard Nicholson explained that in the past, differences in monetary rewards among the male workforce were based on an employee's family responsibilities only:

> The white boys I worked with and the black boys, we'd always see one another's cheque. . . . We all get the same [pay]. . . . The only difference would be in deductions. If you have more kids than the other guy, you have a dollar or two more because they didn't take as much money off ya.

Married or single, male auto workers received higher than average wages for working-class men because of the successful efforts of the UAW to secure a family wage. The family wage demand was premised on the assumption that workers (men only) must be paid a relatively high rate because of their responsibility, as head of a household, for the economic welfare of a wife and children.[36] It was this ideology of the male breadwinner that in turn provided the rationale for women's lower rates of pay. In the words of Windsor-based auto worker Howard Olbey, in the Ford Motor Company, 'it was all man to man.'

Manhood, of course, is historically contingent. In the United States, black men encountered brutal and overt forms of racism both in the plants as well as within their own union locals.[37] Between 1944 and 1946 alone, the UAW International Fair Practices Department (IFPD) reported 46 complaints at 41 different American UAW locals throughout its jurisdiction. Rank-and-file members lodged 27 of these complaints against management exclusively. These centred around the company's refusal to hire certain persons. In addition, workers filed 14 complaints directly against both management and the local union for failing to act on grievances. They directed five complaints concerning racially segregated meetings and the like against local unions exclusively. Most Fair Practices cases were racial, with a few based on religion and political affiliation and one made on the ground of nationality.[38]

In Canada, however, the racialization of the automotive workforce did not have the same implications as it did south of the border. Because black men in both the plants and in the wider communities of St Catharines and Windsor were so few in number, employers did not use them to undercut white men by paying them lower wages or hiring them as strikebreakers.[39] Thus, the political and economic positioning of Canadian black men was significantly different than those in the United States. In the Canadian plants, white working men consequently did not seem to perceive black workers as a serious threat. One could surmise that white unionists opposed racially discriminatory contracts in an effort to ensure that employers never would use black men as a cheaper, politically docile labour source. There is no evidence, though, to suggest that management in Canada either attempted to use black men as such, nor that UAW leaders weighed this possibility in any kind of public forum. In this particular historical context, and specifically in this sphere of social life—the paid work setting—the social meaning of gender (manhood) and race (blackness), and their configuration, permitted the elevation of black men to the *formal status* of white working-class men.

## 'We're All Brothers with the Union'

The vehicle by which all male auto workers secured various rights and entitlements in the workplace was the UAW, and there was a strong connection between belonging to the union and being a working-class man. Masculine bonds strengthened union ties and, in turn, union affiliation and masculinized class-based allegiances played an important part in reinforcing gender-based solidarities among these groups of men. Indeed, it is difficult to disentangle unionism from 'brotherhood' during these years. The industrial trade union was very much a masculine institution, not only because the vast majority of UAW members and leaders were men, but also because these men built their unionism around a place in the sexual division of familial labour, recreational pursuits, cultural forms of expression, strategies of resistance, and a political agenda that spoke to many of the shared experiences of working-class men.[40]

. . .

Black men . . . had an ambivalent relationship to the UAW. After all, the upper echelons of the union bureaucracy were dominated by white men, few of whom challenged the informal discriminatory measures that kept black workers in perilous foundry jobs and out of the preferred skilled trades.[41] Yet black men's awareness of racist undercurrents within the labour movement did not diminish their strong commitment to industrial unionism and (unlike women members) they became actively involved in mainstream union politics at the local level. In fact, during World War II, their level of UAW officeholding was notably high in proportion to their numbers in the plants.

Of the 12 men interviewed for this study, nine had once held an official position in the local union structure. This finding is striking given that these men were not selected for study on the basis of union involvement.[42] . . .

To the UAW, racial discrimination was a serious matter with clear moral, political, and economic ramifications. The union's critique of racial segregation and inequality rested on several interrelated themes, each of which highlighted the deleterious consequences of racism. First, UAW discourse on race was highly moralistic, and was expressed in passionate, emotional language. Appealing to workers' basic sense of right and wrong, and underscoring the moral authority of industrial unionism, official UAW statements espoused an essential immorality of racism in industry. In policy statements and public addresses, UAW International leaders posited racial discrimination as 'cancerous', 'evil', 'infectious', a 'poison', and 'an act against humanity'.[43] They argued that any good trade unionist should take a stand against racism as a matter of good conscience and out of a commitment to one of the most fundamental philosophies of their union—that of 'brotherhood'.

Second, in statements about race, representatives of the UAW International often delivered an ideological message about the union's interests and responsibilities beyond the walls of industry. Reflecting the larger wartime political context, as well as their own factional interests, UAW President Walter Reuther and his caucus linked racism to Nazism and Communist influence on American society. They furthermore defined racial discrimination, especially segregation, as a threat to North American patriotism and standards of 'freedom and justice'. Proponents of racist attitudes and acts were often referred to as 'defilers of democracy' and thereby 'un-American'.[44]

At the same time, the union addressed race as an economistic/industrial relations issue, a view that had been promoted by Reuther since the late 1930s.[45] UAW records contain a series of diatribes by leaders asserting that it was 'illogical' and 'stupid' for trade unionists to foster or maintain racial divisions between workers because of the potential impact of such divisions on the economic security of white male workers, the future bargaining power of the union, and labour solidarity.[46] The doctrine of the UAW International was that racial discrimination and divisions were rooted in class-based economic inequalities and thus racial harmony necessitated a critical examination of the actions of employers. UAW statements on racial discrimination during the 1940s largely targeted the companies, if not in instilling racial hatred, then at least in exacerbating and profiting from it. Industrial strife and racial strife, according to UAW leaders, went hand in hand. One problem could not be solved apart from the other. Often, such arguments of economic and political expediency were used to reinforce appeals to workers' moral conscience. In a 1941 union publication,

for instance, a black worker in the US stressed the value of unity among workers, if not for decency, then at least for the paycheque.[47]

Admittedly, the UAW was not an oasis of racial harmony. The UAW Fair Employment Practices Department had only limited authority to intervene in regional affairs,[48] the myriad UAW policy statements and public addresses of the war and post-war years were largely rhetorical and were in fact dismissed by many local and regional union leaders,[49] and in any case, these messages most likely conveyed far greater meaning in American plants than in the Canadian Region. When regional directors or rank-and-file members proved unco-operative, however, the UAW International could take decisive action and they did promote the general view that the United Auto Workers union stood in strong support of social justice—especially racial justice—and unequivocally opposed racial discrimination.[50] Notably, official UAW discourse identified racial discrimination, unlike sexual discrimination, as a social/economic/political problem rather than an unfortunate, but largely taken for granted, feature of the times. The official UAW position was that all *male* union members must be treated the same.

Importantly, in Canada, this philosophical commitment to racial equality was reinforced by contract clauses that were premised on a commitment to impartiality and the broadly defined goal of equal opportunity among male members. Many black workers were aware that their UAW representatives were likely to play out their own racial prejudices on the shop floor and in the union. According to GM foundry worker Richard Nicholson, 'there's a lot of things goes on behind your back.' Nicholson believed that union reps would sometimes tell a worker that they had looked into a grievance when they clearly had not. In his view, such inaction made the grievant himself responsible for taking the initiative. Most interview informants, therefore, placed a strong emphasis on the theme of self-determination. At the same time, however, they highlighted the union's role in putting in place the machinery for equity. And this machinery, they believed, could be mobilized in attempts to secure either the hard-won rights of black workers or racial justice on a collective-scale.

Many black men were aware of the limits of such contract clauses and, as previously mentioned, they recognized the informal barriers to equal outcomes. This knowledge undoubtedly circumscribed their 'choices' as auto workers. Over the course of many decades in the auto plants, most black men remained where they had started—in the foundry. According to former Ford and Auto Specialties employee Elmer Carter, '[T]heir idea was, "well, the white man don't want you up there no how, so why . . . put yourself in a position where you know you're not wanted."'

A small number of men, however, protested vociferously about these hurdles and they turned to the *collective agreement* to support their claims. In particular, black auto workers in Canada attributed their ability to move out of a bad job and into a better one to the UAW's commitment to the seniority principle, as well as union-negotiated rules about job posting and transfer rights. Elmer Carter further commented,

> [W]hen I left Auto Specialties and I went to Ford's, there was a lot of different jobs that there was all white people on. . . . There was a lot of coloureds that worked at Ford's. . . . I had a couple of jobs at Ford's that a lot of coloured fellas didn't have and they'd say, 'How did you get that job?' I said, 'Well, I just put in for it' and I got it because by then see jobs would have to be posted in the shop . . . they went by seniority.

Lyle Talbot made similar observations about his 30 years at the Ford plant. He stated,

> The only changes I saw were the changes the union brought about, like equal pay, equal opportunity. For instance, if a job came open, that's in the bargaining unit. . . . If you had the qualifications, they had a phrase. The union had a phrase called 'willing and able'. If you were willing and

able to do the job, the company had to give you a chance on it. I can think of . . . four jobs that I got that the company said I wasn't able to do . . . but the union insisted that they give me a chance.

Most black workers believed that the union contract could be used as a tool to protect their rights, in spite of the actions or inaction, prejudices or indifference, of individual men. The collective agreement was a tool for the achievement of a better life, a measure of dignity, and equal opportunity at work—an instrument that, when pressured, some (white) union leaders would put to use. Given that the formal equal status that black auto workers had in the workplace did not extend into the community, it seemed reasonable to believe that the trade union was an imperfect but important ally. According to John Milben, a foundry worker for 31 years, '[t]he union was a hundred per cent behind us. . . . Fairness. We're all brothers with the union.'

## Race, Brotherhood, and Resistance

The UAW, however, played a contradictory role. While the union served as an ally, its philosophy of *brotherhood* was restrictive in its emphasis on *sameness* among workers. Likewise, the UAW definition of *equality* was narrow, not accounting for (racial or sexual) *difference*. Like women members, black men thus faced many dilemmas. They recognized the need for a separate forum for organizing yet they feared ghettoization and accusations of fostering divisions within the working class and threatening worker solidarity. While class-based and gender-based solidarities were openly celebrated, bonds based on race remained unspoken. This workplace/union scenario had significant implications for race consciousness and black workers' resistance.

Throughout the 1940s and 1950s, many black auto workers in Canada adamantly denied difference on the basis of race, and this clearly impeded efforts to mobilize in protest of racial discrimination. The denial of racial difference was most likely a means of coping with the hegemony of whiteness. Within a predominantly white setting, it represented an attempt to shield oneself from racist attacks, to avoid exacerbating racial tensions, and to assimilate (and thereby become invisible), or at least escape further marginalization in the plant and union. According to Richard Nicholson,

> The blacks never all gathered together 'cause we used to say to one another, 'We're not gonna all sit in a huddle—all of us together.' Like, it looks like you're discriminating yourself. Like you're all together. You know what I mean? I would talk to more white people than I did black people, really because I worked with white people and my boss was white.[51]

Living and working in communities in which racial difference and equality were dichotomized, and where 'Canadians' were perceived as 'white' and not foreign-born, many workers were caught in a dilemma between calling attention to their 'blackness' on the one hand—something that must have been at the core of subjectivity—and being a Canadian, a good trade unionist, and equal to their white brothers on the other. Auto foundry employee Howard Wallace rejected the designation 'black', equating it with American civil rights activists. Wallace preferred to be called 'coloured', something which he, in a seemingly contradictory way, associated with acceptance into mainstream respectable Canadian society. He remarked,

> I never heard tell of no 'black' man in the 1940s. Never heard tell of no black man. We always wanted the name of 'coloured' man. . . . The only time you hear 'em say a black man, it started in the United States. They started it. There's a lot of fellas over there the colour of you but they call themselves black men. Why? I do not know. Well, educated and everything . . . I'm no black man. . . . [A] lot of people like to call themselves black 'cause they call themselves black over the

> River. . . . Either call me a coloured man or call me a Canadian. But I'm just what is anybody else in Canada.

Wallace's reflections make a potent statement about black identity in Canada.

It is impossible, however, for a 'visible minority' to achieve invisibility or complete assimilation. Very few black workers escaped *informal* displays of racism within the plant. Some men recollected that supervisors and co-workers alike participated in a variety of overt racist acts, largely in the form of derogatory jokes and name-calling. In retrospect, though, these men minimized the importance of such acts in shaping their workplace experiences. Some even bragged about their ability, as individuals, to counter and ultimately develop an immunity to such racist behaviour. According to Lyle Talbot,

> . . . you could handle those guys. You know. I've had guys call me 'black bastard' on the job. It didn't bother me at all because I knew that whatever my comeback was, it was just as good as theirs. . . . I had fellows that didn't like working with me, but there was nothing they could do about it. I knew it and they knew it.

> . . .

Individual resistance of this kind helped black workers to invalidate racial harassment and restore some dignity—dignity lost by a host of insults and injuries experienced both within the factory and in the wider community.

Racial prejudice was sometimes brutal and openly expressed, and racial boundaries were strongly upheld in the towns of Windsor and St Catharines. Blacks faced blatant discrimination in housing, schools, churches, recreational facilities, the job market, and in intimate relationships. They were, for example, barred from certain residential areas and ghettoized in others, turned away from restaurants, hotels, and bowling halls, and in some drinking establishments they were placed in a separate area called the 'jungle room'.[52]

Given the extent and impact of racism in their lives as a whole, it is striking that the men had so little to say about its effect on *workplace relations*. It is especially remarkable that most informants claimed that on the whole there were no racial tensions whatsoever among auto workers.[53] An Auto Specialties foundry worker for over 30 years, Howard Wallace, stated, 'you'd see some white fellas or some foreign fellas. They all worked, you know. They all worked together. . . . They all got along. What gets me is they all got along good together.'

Many black men viewed the workplace as separate from the rest of the community, and claimed that the factory was one of the only arenas in which they could exercise their rights and even feel a camaraderie with white men. Auto Specialties worker John Milben related how he would 'feel bad' when he was forced to drink beer in a back room, sit apart from white soldiers in a restaurant, and live on a 'black street' in Windsor. Yet in contrast, 'it was nice in the foundry [he said]. Everybody was treated good. They had a cafeteria there. We sat and ate together. . . . And we'd drink beer together.'

Admittedly, direct racism on the shop floor did not reach the same level of intensity in Canada as it did in the American auto plants. And it is likely that to these men, racial tensions in southern Ontario plants seemed insignificant in comparison to the racial strife they heard about through the American popular media and UAW International press. The scale and intensity of racism in the US most likely denied many black workers in Canada a sense of entitlement to public and collective outrage against the racism that touched their own lives. Given this, UAW leaders and local civil rights activists would occasionally remind Canadian Region members that while racial discrimination had taken a different form in Canada than south of the border, it nevertheless existed and should be challenged.

Moreover, the workers' descriptions of racial harmony within the plant underscore the fluidity of the concept of discrimination itself.

Perceptions of discrimination are products of historical negotiation and as such are always changing. In the past, workers' conceptualization of racial discrimination did not encompass 'workplace harassment'. According to foundry employee Mahlon Dennis, during the war years and into the post-war period, racial harassment was simply 'not an issue'. Harassment is 'more of a recent thing', explained Dennis. 'I can't recall during the period I was involved in human rights, whether there was anything mentioned about harassment . . . mostly . . . it dealt with the employment situation and housing accommodation.' Racial slurs, jokes, put-downs, even the occasional physical assault by another man, were not only part of the masculine culture of the auto plants, they were also endured as part of the everyday experience of people of colour in Canada—one of the hardships of the times. As Lyle Talbot's . . . remarks suggest, it was up to individual men, manly men, to handle this.

Furthermore, the impact of the random racial attack by a co-worker or supervisor was softened somewhat by the men's formal equal rights and place in the industry. For the small group of black men who were 'privileged' to find work in the auto plants, the outcomes of racism were not directly economic. Formal contract rights (which secured economic equality) mediated the informal, day-to-day experience of racial prejudice.

Many black workers lamented the unrelenting power of racist oppression but reasoned that in light of the small but significant gains that they had made in the course of their own lives, it was best to 'turn the other cheek' to it. Getting a job in a car plant was among the most notable of these gains. Just as it mediated the impact of direct racial prejudice on the shop floor, the 'privilege' of auto employment and equal status as a UAW member, paradoxically, set limits on the racialization of black men's collective resistance. As Mahlon Dennis explained, coloured people couldn't complain about racial discrimination in employment during World War II because they were being hired. Former GM core-maker Cassell Smith stated,

> nothing's happening, so don't go throwing your strength. . . . You're going to aggravate something that way. . . . Be prepared for it but as long as things are quiet, let them stay. That's my opinion. I'm not saying I'm right. . . . A person can go and stir up a lot of trouble where there isn't any. . . . So as long as it's quiet and all, leave it. . . . This fighting. They talk about equal rights. This fighting for equal rights is going to be a lifetime thing.

. . .

The position of black men in auto plants was ambivalent. While they recognized that UAW leaders often failed to advocate their specific concerns as a race, most black auto workers exhibited a strong commitment to the ideological principles of industrial unionism. The UAW reinforced in them a sense of their own legitimacy in the union and industry, and this was something on which a handful of individual men would ultimately draw in their attempts to uphold their equal rights as *workers*. It was the UAW philosophy of social justice, class-based solidarity, and brotherhood, along with the privilege of holding a relatively well-paying automotive sector job, that furthermore bolstered unity among these male industrial workers. Most importantly, it was the union that provided black male workers the equity machinery (namely, the collective agreement) with which to challenge employers in their fight against multiple oppressions. The collective agreement, however, is an instrument that took white working men's experiences as the standard for the industry and it therefore left untouched and unremarked upon, the many elusive dimensions of racial oppression.

## Conclusion

From the beginnings of the auto industry in Canada, employers have contributed to the *construction of difference* within the working class.

These differences were based on race, gender, and family status, as well as skill. While auto manufacturers hired white male breadwinners to fill the vast majority of jobs in the industry, they also recruited extremely small numbers of black men (and white women) to perform work that many white men either rejected or were temporarily unavailable to perform. While these two groups of workers met a need on the part of capitalists, management clearly regarded each as marginal to the industry, different, and unequal to the core workforce. Both black men and white women were defined as the 'other', a socially created category that was itself broken down along lines of race and gender.

The history of black men in auto work is one of many contradictions. Such contradictions are the outcome of the changing configuration of race, gender, and social class. While black men were intruders in the homogeneous white world of the auto plants, their status as wage-earning men/union brothers accorded them various rights and entitlements that were denied (white) women workers. Given their positioning in the industry during the war and throughout the post-war years, black men did not constitute a political or economic threat to white workers in Canada. There is no evidence that management attempted to use blacks to lower wage rates, replace white employees, or to act as 'scab' labour during strikes. Moreover, racial segregation and exclusion were so pervasive and strictly upheld in the wider society—in intimate relationships, recreation, housing, education, and religious institutions—that the presence of scant numbers of black men in the foundries was not raised by white trade unionists as a matter of serious consequence. Race acquired a particular, distinctive meaning in man-to-man relations—in the masculine worlds of auto manufacturing and the UAW. The social and political implications of race in these settings permitted black men to be elevated to the formal status of white men, a status that was based on gender privilege, and class, and gender solidarities.

Formal equal rights in union contracts (equal wages and equal seniority rights), though, did not shield black men from face-to-face indignities on the plant floor, nor did they protect the men from the hazards of working in bad jobs, or the economic impact of stunted opportunities within the firm. Gender and class shaped the content of the racism that these men experienced; they did not protect them from it.

Moreover, racialized and gendered experiences have played an important part in configuring the resistance strategies adopted by this group of workers. Black auto employees faced an elusive form of discrimination. At work, they possessed formal 'equal rights', but found themselves confined to the worst jobs in the plants. As UAW members, they were committed to class-based struggles, relying heavily on equal opportunity and brotherhood as guiding principles, and the collective agreement as an instrument of justice. Yet at the same time, they participated in a union politics that at the local and regional levels was lacking in racial content. In both spheres, black men denied racial difference, though daily they were confronted with the hegemony of whiteness. A tiny group of black auto workers thus concentrated their efforts in challenging racial inequalities outside the workplace, particularly in housing and recreation. These activists emerged from a workplace politicized by industrial unionism, yet their struggles were not factory-based, and thereby left unchallenged an important element of their oppression as workers. In a sense, within the factory, equal opportunity served a defusing, perhaps depoliticizing function.

Race and gender shape working-class experience. Whiteness and masculinity were undeniably central features of auto work. The primacy of one of these constructs over the others has sometimes been debated, but this is not at issue here for there is no neat formula that can be consistently applied to understand their alliance. It is more useful to observe how the racialization of gender and the gendering of race have changed over time, and have taken on meaning in differ-

ent spheres of social existence. When we examine the ever-changing nexus of race, gender, and class, we understand the relationship not merely as one of multiple oppressions, but as something more complex—one in which people can be simultaneously victims and agents, privileged and oppressed.

. . .

## Notes

This is a revised version of a paper presented at the annual meeting of the American Historical Association, 2–5 January 1997. For comments on earlier drafts of this paper, I would like to thank Robert Storey, Joan Sangster, and Alice Kessler-Harris, and four anonymous reviewers for *Labour/Le Travail*. Thanks also to Hassan Yussuff, students in the CAW Workers of Colour Leadership Training Programme, and the many workers who graciously agreed to share with me their stories. This research was funded by an Arts Research Board grant and a Labour Studies Programme research grant at McMaster University.

1. R.M. Brewer, 'Theorizing Race, Class and Gender', in R. Hennessy and C. Ingraham, eds, *Materialist Feminism* (New York, 1997), 238.

2. McKinnon Industries was originally a subsidiary of General Motors and later became a General Motors plant.

3. Small numbers of Armenian, Chinese, and Chinese-Canadian workers were also employed in the southern Ontario auto industry during World War II. However, I have chosen to focus here on black workers because they represented the largest minority, with the longest history in the plants.

4. P. Sugiman, *Labour's Dilemma: The Gender Politics of Workers in Canada, 1937–1979* (Toronto, 1994).

5. Unlike their American counterparts, these workers were so few in number, so seemingly marginal to either the company or the union, that their unique histories have never been traced.

Paradoxically, they are workers whose difference made them highly visible in the workplace; yet this difference has rendered them largely invisible in Canadian labour history. Currently, there are no published scholarly accounts of the ways in which race has been used in structuring the auto industry in Canada. . . .

6.  It was extremely difficult to locate black men who had worked in the auto industry during the period of study. Given the harsh conditions of their work, a sizable number of these workers left the auto industry after World War II. Also, many of the men who remained in the plants suffered from serious health problems such as silicosis. Many of these men had died before this project was undertaken. By the time all of the interviews for this study were completed, several participants had died.

7.  For an insightful discussion of the use of oral testimony, see C. Van Onselen, 'The Reconstruction of a Rural Life from Oral Testimony: Critical Notes on the Methodology Employed in the Study of a Black South African Sharecropper', *Journal of Peasant Studies* 20, 3 (1993): 494–514.

8.  See D. Roediger, *The Wages of Whiteness: Race and the Making of the American Working Class* (London, 1991); D. Roediger, *Towards the Abolition of Whiteness* (London, 1994).

9.  I wish to thank Joan Sangster for bringing this point to my attention.

10. Rod Davis was a participant in a session of the CAW Workers of Colour Leadership Training Programme.

11. 'Gung Ho', *Ford Times* 3, 5 (Oct. 1943): 12–14; 'Heart Strings Stretch from Windsor 'Round the World . . .', *Ford Times* 2, 2 (Nov. 1942): 3–4. . . .

12. For a discussion of the relationship between Henry Ford and the African-American community, see L. Bailer, 'Negro Labor in the American Automobile Industry', Ph.D. dissertation (University of Michigan, 1943); K. Boyle, '"There Are No Union Sorrows That the Union Can't Heal": The Struggle for Racial Equality in the United Automobile Workers, 1940–1960', *Labor History* 36, 1 (Winter 1995): 5–23; A. Meier and

E. Rudwick, *Black Detroit and the Rise of the UAW* (New York, 1979); B.J. Widick, 'Black Workers: Double Discontents', in Widick, ed., *Auto Work and Its Discontents* (Baltimore, 1976), 52–60.

13. Widick, 'Black Workers: Double Discontents', 53.

14. Interview #2, 30 May 1994.

15. Archives of Labor and Urban Affairs (ALUA), UAW Canadian Region Series III, box 70, Report of UAW Local 199, District Council Minutes (1939).

16. ALUA, UAW Research Department, acc. 350, box 11, 'Questionnaire on Employment in UAW-CIO Plants, Employment, Women and Negroes, UAW Regions 4–9A' (Apr. 1943).

17. In September 1949, Canadian Region Director George Burt reported to the Region 7 Staff that the Chrysler Corporation of Canada 'does not hire Negroes' and that 'in Windsor most of the Negroes are in foundries.' ALUA, UAW Canadian Region Collection, box 39, file 1, 'Minutes, Region 7 Staff Meeting' (1947–50). . . .

18. The Fair Employment Practices Act, 1951 was enacted to prohibit discrimination in employment on the grounds of a person's race, creed, colour, nationality, ancestry or place of origin. The Act covered application forms and advertisements. It did not include 'sex' as a prohibited ground of discrimination.

19. ALUA, UAW Region 7 Toronto Sub-Regional Office Collection, box 9, 'Minutes, Staff Meeting' (26–7 Oct. 1953), 6.

20. Lyle Talbot Private Collection, untitled document (Mar. 1950). . . .

21. Interview #12, 20 Feb. 1995.

22. I wish to thank *Labour/Le Travail* reviewer #2 for bringing this point to my attention.

23. This finding was generated through a series of informal classroom discussions that I held with participants in the current CAW Workers of Colour Leadership Training Programme. . . .

24. Interview #1, 18 Oct. 1990; Interview #12, 20 Feb. 1995; for example, as well as private conversations with various black CAW members who are currently living in St Catharines and Windsor.

25. *Ford Graphics* 6, 13 (15 July 1953): 6.

26. For a discussion of foundry work in early

twentieth-century Canada, see C. Heron, 'The Craftsman: Hamilton's Metal Workers in the Early Twentieth Century', *Labour/Le Travailleur* 6 (Autumn 1980): 7–48. . . .

27. Black men in the US were also concentrated in foundry work, as well as wet-sanding operations, material handling, and janitorial assignments. See Boyle, '"There Are No Union Sorrows"', 8; Widick, 'Black Workers: Double Discontents', 53.

28. Interview #12, 20 Feb. 1995.

29. Richard Nicholson, Mahlon Dennis, Howard Olbey, John Milben, Clayton Talbert, Elmer Carter, and Howard Wallace all reported to have performed at least a couple of these jobs before securing auto employment. Many men had worked four or five such jobs.

30. For a discussion of race and images of masculinity in the contemporary period, see among others, R. Staples, 'Masculinity and Race: The Dual Dilemma of Black Men', *Journal of Social Issues* 34, 1 (1978): 169–83.

31. Interview #1, 18 Oct. 1990; Interview #7, 3 Aug. 1994.

32. This idea was articulated by *Labour/Le Travail* reviewer #2.

33. Interview #1, 18 Oct. 1990.

34. In his account of metal workers in Hamilton, Ontario, during the early twentieth century, Heron argues that the pride of moulders in steel foundries 'fed on the physical demands of the work, which was notoriously heavy, dirty, and unhealthy.' See Heron, 'The Craftsman', 11.

35. In the GM Oshawa plant, before, during, and after the war, most women were confined to either the sewing department or the wire and harness department. For the duration of the war, some women also worked in GM's aircraft division, a makeshift facility that was designed exclusively for the production of war materials. In McKinnon Industries, women worked in a wider range of departments. Nevertheless, they too were confined to far fewer jobs than men. . . .

36. For a more detailed discussion of the family wage, see B. Bradbury, *Working Families: Age, Gender, and Daily Survival in Industrializing* *Montreal* (Toronto, 1993), ch. 3; N. Gabin, *Feminism in the Labor Movement: Women and the United Automobile Workers, 1935–1975* (Ithaca, NY, 1990); M. May, 'Bread before Roses: American Workingmen, Labor Unions, and the Family Wage', in R. Milkman, ed., *Women, Work, and Protest: A Century of U.S. Women's Labor History* (Boston, 1985), 1–21; R. Milkman, *Gender at Work: The Dynamics of Job Segregation by Sex during World War II* (Urbana, Ill., 1987); J. Parr, *The Gender of Breadwinners: Women, Men, and Change in Two Industrial Towns, 1880–1950* (Toronto, 1990); B. Palmer, *Working-Class Experience: Rethinking the History of Canadian Labour, 1800–1991* (Toronto, 1992).

37. . . . Boyle, '"There Are No Union Sorrows"'; K. Boyle, *The UAW and the Heyday of American Liberalism, 1945–1968* (Ithaca, NY, 1995); Meier and Rudick, *Black Detroit and the Rise of the UAW*; Widick, 'Black Workers: Double Discontents'.

38. ALUA, Emil Mazey Collection, box 11, file 11–6, FEPC 1946–47–2, 'First Annual Summary of Activities, International UAW-CIO Fair Practices Committee' (15 Oct. 1944 to 15 Feb. 1946). See also ALUA, UAW Research Department Collection, box 18, file: Minorities, 1942–47, 2 of 2, 'Fair Practices and Anti-Discrimination Department', UAW-CIO to UAW-CIO International Board Fair Practices Committee (10 Dec. 1946); ALUA, UAW Research Department Collection, box 18, file: Minorities, 1942-47, 1 of 2, 'UAW Fight Against Intolerance', Address by George W. Crockett (4 Nov. 1945); ALUA, Emil Mazey Collection, box 11, file: 11–6, FEPC, 2, 'Fair Practices Committee Decisions' (1946–47); ALUA, UAW Fair Practices Department—Women's Bureau, box 2, file: 2–17, Quarterly Reports (1946), 'Report of UAW-CIO Fair Practices and Anti-Discrimination Department to the International Executive Board, 10 Dec. 1946; AULA, UAW Research Department Collection, box 11, file: 11–20, UAW Fair Practices and Anti-Discrimination Department, 1947–58, 'Summer School Course in Workers Education'.

39. There is evidence that employers used black workers as 'scabs' in some UAW plants in Canada.

For example, at the Walker Metal Foundry, black men were first hired as a result of a strike by a white male workforce. Interview #5, 29 June 1993. However, these cases were rare. There is no evidence that this was a serious consideration at General Motors, Ford, or Chrysler during the period of study.

40. See Sugiman, *Labour's Dilemma*, ch. 2.

41. See Boyle, '"There Are No Union Sorrows"', for a discussion of the opposition of skilled trades to African Americans.

42. The level of participation of workers of colour, however, dropped in the following decades. To this day, workers of colour remain under-represented in the Canadian Auto Workers Union, especially in local office.

43. See, for example, ALUA, UAW Research Department Collection, box 9, file: 9–24, Discrimination Against Negroes in Employment, 1942–47, 'R.J. Thomas to All UAW-CIO Executive Board Members and Department Heads, 25 Nov. 1943'; ALUA, UAW Research Department Collection, box 18, file: Minorities, 1942–47, 1 of 2, 'UAW Fight Against Intolerance', Address by George W. Crockett, Director, UAW-CIO Fair Practices Committee, 4 Nov. 1945.

44. For example, ALUA, UAW Research Department Collection, box 18, file: Minorities, 1942–47, 1 of 2, 'UAW Fight Against Intolerance', Address by George W. Crockett, Director, UAW-CIO Fair Practices Committee, 4 Nov. 1945.

45. See Boyle, '"There Are No Union Sorrows"', 109.

46. For example, ALUA, UAW Research Department Collection, box 11, file: 11–20, Fair Practices and Anti-Discrimination Department, 1947–58, 'Summer School Course in Workers Education'; ALUA, Emil Mazey Collection, box 11, file: 11–6,

FEPC, 1946–47–2, 'First Annual Summary of Activities of the International UAW-CIO Fair Practices Committee'; 'UAW Seeks to Prevent Hiring Discrimination', *Michigan Chronicle*, 8 Sept. 1945.

47. 'UAW Seeks to Prevent Hiring Discrimination', *Michigan Chronicle*, 9 Aug. 1945.

48. See Boyle, '"There Are No Union Sorrows"', 114.

49. Boyle, *The UAW and the Heyday of American Liberalism*.

50. Ibid., 118.

51. This position stands in contrast to black immigrants, largely from the Caribbean, who began to secure employment in the auto industry during the 1960s and 1970s.

52. For example, W.A. Head, *The Black Presence in the Canadian Mosaic: A Study of Perception and the Practice of Discrimination against Blacks in Metropolitan Toronto*. Ontario Human Rights Commission (Toronto, 1975); B.S. Singh and Peter S. Li, *Racial Oppression in Canada*, 2nd edn (Toronto, 1988), ch. 8; W.S. Tarnopolsky, *Discrimination and the Law in Canada* (Toronto, 1982); R. Winks, 'The Canadian Negro: A Historical Assessment', *Journal of Negro History* 53 (Oct. 1968): 283–300. Extensive accounts of racial discrimination in Ontario were also given in Interview #1, 18 Oct. 1990, Interview #2, 30 May 1994; Interview #8, 5 Aug. 1993.

53. Among others, Rick Halpern documents a history of interracial co-operation among some groups of industrial workers. . . . See R. Halpern, 'Interracial Unionism in the Southwest: Fort Worth's Packinghouse Workers, 1937–1954', *Organized Labor in the Twentieth Century South* (Knoxville, 1991), 158–82. . . .

. . .

# 14

# A Platform for Gender Tensions:
# Women Working and Riding on Canadian
# Urban Public Transit in the 1940s

Donald F. Davis and Barbara Lorenzkowski

Canadian use of urban public transit peaked during the 1940s. So too did Canadians' frustrations with it. With people fully employed and automobile use suppressed by tire, gasoline, and vehicle shortages, the overcrowding of buses and trams was so intense that even the 'language of the ladies' had become 'awful'. As the Toronto *Telegram* reported in 1946, one lady 'told another lady to shut her mouth', during an altercation begun by the one climbing up the other's back 'in striving to enter the street car'. The *Telegram* fretted that the 'gnawing neurosis' induced in the women passengers by excessive crowding would soon require streetcars to carry the notice: 'Ladies will kindly refrain from using abusive language.' Overcrowding was having dire implications for traditional gender roles.

As millions of riders competed for physical space, they were also redefining the meaning of public space and the appropriate behaviour within it for 'ladies and gentlemen'. Public transit in Canada had always been a socially contested terrain: in the past it had been a public forum for the debate over industrial discipline, as the burnt and overturned streetcars of 1880–1920, a totem for the 'labour question', attested. On the buses and streetcars of the 1940s, by contrast, Canadians fought over such issues as sexual harassment and the rights of smokers and shoppers, as well as the employment of women drivers and conductors. In short, public transit provided a platform for negotiating and modifying Canadian gender relations.[1]

. . .

The war . . . created opportunities for women in an industry in which they had before then (with some exceptions during the First World War) been employed strictly to type, take dictation, and roll coins.[2] Now they became transit guides and conductors, moving into jobs that admittedly did not require much of a shift in the gender stereotype of woman as man's helpmate. The women who worked in transit garages and repair shops more obviously challenged traditional gender roles. As for female bus drivers and streetcar 'motormen', they had one of the most public plat-

Donald F. Davis and Barbara Lorenzkowski, 'A Platform for Gender Tensions: Women Working and Riding on Canadian Urban Public Transit in the 1940s', *Canadian Historical Review* 79, 3 (1998): 431–65. © 1998 University of Toronto Press. Reprinted by permission of University of Toronto Press (www.utpjournals.com).

forms in 1940s Canada on which to mount their challenge to the sexual division of labour.[3]

At war's end, women transit workers were let go. By 1949, women retained only one important public role in Canada's urban transit industry, that of passenger guides for the Toronto Transportation Commission (TTC), selling tickets and helping travellers to find their way into the vehicles and around the system. This occupation was so stereotypically 'feminine' that one is tempted to concur with historian Ruth Roach Pierson that, while 'the war effort necessitated minor adjustments to sexual demarcations in the world of paid work, it did not offer a fundamental challenge to the male-dominated sex/gender system.' Yet the temptation to dismiss the survival of the TTC Guide Service into the post-war era as a non-event in the history of both public transit and Canadian women should be resisted, for as historian Jeff Keshen has argued, after the war it was impossible for 'things to return to square one'.[4] Nor was the partial 'feminization' of the transit system in English Canada's national metropolis all that minor a change. This article contends that the guides helped to assure the remarkable post-war success of the TTC. As long as their role lasted, the guides made public transit a more welcoming place for women—a more 'feminine' system in effect. Some readers may balk at the notion that 'mere' guides could have played an important role in the evolution of Canadian transit systems after the war. After all, these women were not system managers; they were hourly rated employees. Yet the work of sociologists Michel Crozier, Michel Callon, and Bruno Latour tells us that 'actors' at all levels of a bureaucracy or technological network have the capacity to shape it socially.[5]

In sum, this article discusses three main themes: first, a crisis in gender relations on public transit triggered by unprecedented wartime crowding; second, the employment of women as drivers and conductors (that is, as platform workers) as well as passenger guides; and third, the exceptional decision of the Toronto Transportation Commission to preserve those values, labelled 'feminine', that women workers *and* riders brought to its wartime system. The goal here is to shed light not only on Canadian gender relations and on a group of women workers hitherto in the historical shadows, but also on the evolution of urban mass transit during the 1940s and on the collective Canadian decision to forsake public transit after the Second World War.

. . .

Canadians described urban transit in the 1940s in dehumanizing terms. They called the streetcars 'cattle cars', and the passengers who perennially blocked the entrance, a 'herd of stupid oxen'. Commuters felt like sardines. 'In the street car there's standing room only', Gwen Lambton, a Toronto war worker, recalled; 'we're packed like sardines. . . . The used smell of people who have been up all night, their sweat (and mine) is nauseating, but at least I can't fall.'[6] Canadians were urged to grin and bear this crush. Worse, they were told that, contrary to their actual experience, they were already grinning and bearing it. The Vancouver *Sun* on 9 October 1943 ran a large advertisement entitled 'The Greatest Democracy in the World', asserting that the Vancouver public had accepted the necessity of changes to their working hours; they had 'accommodated themselves to fewer stops; . . . speeded up their use of the street car; . . . filled both ends of the cars.' Yet those upbeat words were accompanied by a downbeat drawing that showed weary, miserable-looking people. The drawing, captioned 'OMNIBUS', came with a subtext that explained the stoic, long-suffering looks:

> The word 'Omnibus' in Latin meant 'for all.' So the modern street car and bus are 'for all.' People of every class, worker and professional man, woman welder and club woman, automobile owner and pedestrian rub shoulders on their way downtown and home. There are no classes among street car riders and bus riders. Everyone is equal. Everyone is sharing his ride in their great common vehicle of the time.[7]

The *Sun* asked its readers to 'carry the spirit' of democratic equality into every other aspect of the war effort.

By acknowledging the extraordinary nature of the class mixing and egalitarianism of wartime public transit, the newspaper was actually pointing to the heaviest burden imposed by the crush: the psychological loss of 'cultural privacy'. Cultural privacy was defined in 1971 by transportation critic Tabor Stone as the 'need and desire of individuals to be among other persons who share their values, norms, beliefs, and standards of behaviour, and to exclude from their presence individuals with other norms and standards.' In the 1940s, Canadian women and men often resented intrusions into their physical and cultural space by people of different age, class, ethnicity, culture—and sex. With vehicles too crowded for men and women to stake out separate spheres by congregating in front or by pushing through to the rear—or even by travelling at different hours—a struggle for social space was inevitable.[8]

Two groups found the crush loading especially vexatious in the 1940s: the 'shoppers', gender-typed as female; and the 'smokers', gender-typed as male. Both became acceptable targets for abuse as each sex vented its resentments about crowding. Attitudes towards shoppers and smokers were complex. Let us start with the female 'shoppers' who used public transit to carry home their purchases. For many, shopping by public transit was a new and unwelcome necessity, the wartime rationing of gasoline and tires having eliminated both home delivery and the family automobile as options. As 'shoppers' did their unaccustomed errands along unfamiliar routes, they found that their cultural privacy was threatened.[9] The time and space that women could call their own were greatly reduced. By 1943, the evening rush 'hour'—traditionally between 5 and 6 p.m.—had lengthened to three hours or more, as the major employers in a dozen or more Canadian cities joined the domin-

ion government's plan to 'stagger' the start and end of the workday of 424,000 workers.[10]

It became difficult for shoppers to find a time when they were not competing with commuters for space. In Windsor, by December 1942 there were standing passengers 'at almost any hour'. Windsor was, to be sure, especially crowded. Elsewhere, seats were still sometimes available during the off-peak hours. Yet shoppers, especially those with jobs or children, were not always able to complete their journeys between 10 a.m. and 3:00 p.m., because they had responsibilities that might prevent an optimal travel schedule. Wartime shortages also made shopping more inefficient and time-consuming. Working women 'became used to buying their groceries after work and then taking the homeward tram after 5:30 p.m., by which time passenger volumes had fallen sufficiently for them to have a shot at a seat. Staggered hours made it extremely difficult for working women to find either the time or the private space for shopping. Stigmatized by their boxes and bags, they became 'shoppers', their right to ridership in clamorous dispute.[11]

. . .

Gendered notions of politeness generally took a beating in the 1940s. As Mrs D.B. White of Ottawa remarked in 1943, 'The cars and buses are so crowded these days, that even the men have to stand!' She added that although a few men would surrender their seats, those who did were 'looked upon by their fellows as particularly odd specimens of the prehistoric animal; and by the ladies with a surprise bordering upon insult.'[12] In 1943 Ottawans could still joke about this 'standing' issue between the sexes. However, by the sultry summer of 1944 tempers had reached the boiling point. A flurry of letters in the Ottawa press that August attested to the frustration and fury with which men and women observed changing gender relations on the very public, very crowded platforms of mass urban transit. Helen Scott set off Ottawa's debate over gender roles in public transit with a letter on

18 August describing boorish behaviour that included sexual harassment:

> I can stand to have men sit right in front of me and not bother to offer a seat, but what I can't stand is when they eye every girl standing within the general vicinity, up and down and back again. Besides making me so angry that I would love to slap them, this is most embarrassing. But they don't even stop there. I've seen elderly women, laden down with parcels, get on the street-car and then have to stand and be jostled by the crowd . . . Numerous times I have been just going to get on the street-car when a man came rushing up, elbowed me aside, and rushed madly down the aisle to grab the first available seat.[13]

This letter hit a nerve, not least among those men who addressed the allegation of sexual harassment in their reply to the editor. None denied harassment. They either justified it or placed the onus on women to avoid it. Gerald Birch, though he endorsed equal rights, did so in order to argue that with rights came duties, one of which it seemed was to compete on equal terms for a streetcar seat. Birch countered: 'And so the girls are being stared at and it really peeves Miss Scott. Would she then kindly tell me why the girls spend hours beautifying their body beautiful for the apparent purpose of attraction and when they do get it, scorn it?' If they want to be ignored, let them 'wear something more concealing.'[14] W.L. Farmer claimed to sympathize with Miss Scott, 'one of the few refined ladies among our very young modern generation', yet described her letter as 'pathetic to say the least'. He further accused women, who had won many rights, of taking for themselves habits that belonged exclusively to men:

> Smoking, drinking, wearing slacks and shorts (the latter so brief), a loose kind of conversation, yes and all this . . . on street-cars. And in all women have acquired more masculinity in the past twenty years than men were able to lose in a thou-

sand years. Oh! for the days of feminine charm, when tobacco and beer dared never so much [as] to skim the sweet innocence of a maiden's lip; when conversation and dress were modest, when manners were the order of the day . . . Aye! men had an eye for feminine charm. But the sparkle has been dulled by the sight of a lot of high-ball guzzling, cigar toting mamas parading everywhere in shorts with the utmost disregard for the next fellow's feelings. Women tried competing with the opposite sex and they've got the competition with all its consequences . . . Now, tell me *why* should a man give his seat to an equal?[15]

In effect, Farmer was asserting that women should count themselves fortunate to attract male attention, considering how unsexed they had become. Or was it oversexed? Those 'shorts' obviously bothered him in the hot summer of 1944. Of course, because of gender roles in the 1940s, women could not announce their sexual availability. If they did, or if they smoked, or if they insisted on sexual equality, they apparently should not expect respect.

. . .

Many male commuters were angry during the 1940s—definitely about transit crowding, and probably also about feminine intrusion into their cultural privacy and social space. The bitter, defensive tone of men's remarks about women's traditional priority in seating also revealed anxiety over their own failure to meet traditional gender expectations, an anxiety that inevitably surfaced in civilian male circles in wartime. (Interestingly, none of the males who complained to the press claimed to be a soldier.) They were undoubtedly also bothered, to varying degrees, by the platform that public transit provided for growing numbers of women workers to make known both their existence and their claims to equal treatment. Nevertheless, the wartime discourse about women transit riders did not focus on the workers among them. It targeted instead the hapless shoppers, women who were being condemned for remaining faithful to pre-war gender roles. For decades women had been prized for being domestic consumers. Now their consumer role interfered with the war effort. While historians have emphasized the positive reinforcement to homemakers from government propaganda extolling their role in the war effort, one must wonder whether insults hurled their way for doing their family's shopping did not outweigh any flattery from the elites.[16]

Shoppers were not the only riders to incur the wrath of fellow passengers, for smoking had also become a flashpoint for gender tensions. In the 1940s smoking was still considered a gendered habit, even as Canadians recognized that women increasingly indulged in it. Smoking areas on trams were a man's world. Calgary males, for example, later became nostalgic about their 'smokers', as these enclaves disappeared with the trams themselves after the war. A long retrospective in the Calgary Herald of 18 February 1956 acknowledged that the 'smoking compartment was filthy, most of the time', and that it 'smelled of stale smoke.' And yet, 'the ride in the smoking compartment was a social occasion, particularly in the morning.' As the men gossiped about the weather, politics, exotic travel experiences, and the transit service, 'time passed quickly as well as pleasantly.'[17]

The 'stern of an Ottawa street car' was also a 'sort of travelling club for smokers' for five months a year, concluded the Ottawa Journal in October 1945. It editorialized: 'Especially is the morning smoke appreciated by those who have a short interval between breakfast and the office, and the man who sets out at the same time each day finds acquaintances in the back of the car. As the smoke billows out the open windows there is talk of fishing, of gardening, of politics . . . and world affairs are given a going-over.'

The Journal thought that women could enter this space: 'Sometimes a woman sits there, but it is assumed that she likes smoke, or at least doesn't object to it.'[18] But, like most men's clubs in the 1940s, Calgary's smoking compartment was 'strictly a male preserve', according to the Herald:

> Occasionally a woman tried to take a seat in the smoker, when the rest of the car was perhaps overloaded . . . Once in a while there would be some frustrated suffragette, who wanted to show that women were smoking too and entitled to the same rights as men, who would barge in and try to make as though she was really enjoying herself. But the atmosphere, both the smoke and the heavy chill that descended when she entered, discouraged the girls.[19]

Realistically, women must have felt unwelcome anywhere the air was 'blue' with smoke. Indeed, in Ottawa they clogged the front of streetcars, a newspaper editorialist remarked, rather than 'move farther down the aisle because, perhaps, by so doing they eventually land[ed] in the bay at the back which is usually occupied by men'— that is, by smokers.[20]

The male tobacco privilege, whether it existed by law or by neglect, came under attack as transit became more crowded during the Second World War. By May 1945, 21 of the 33 transit operators polled by a bus journal had banned smoking. They all reported cracking down on the practice, but men were resisting. Twenty-six of the systems reported difficulty in making their rules stick, especially in cities like Hamilton and Port Arthur (Thunder Bay) which had many manual workers and servicemen. The Sudbury-Copper Cliff Suburban Railway said that it had failed to suppress smoking because 'most of the passengers are miners who have not been able to smoke all day.' The Calgary Municipal Railway complained that it had difficulty restricting smoking to the rear vestibules of streetcars, despite periodic checks by police officers, because its 'own employees [were] offenders to some considerable degree.'[21]

The smoking debate in Edmonton had a distinctly gendered dimension: indeed, the increase in opportunity for female workers on its municipally owned tram system was explicitly linked to the decrease in opportunity for male smokers. Until the war, Edmontonians had agreed to restrict smoking to the rear compartment, but wartime crowding brought confrontation. In September 1940 the Woman's Christian Temperance Union urged city council to ban smoking on trams 'during such time as the windows have to be closed'. Their letter asked for 'a just recognition that non-smoking patrons have some rights, and that young children who use the street railway service have a right to tobacco-free air.' In October the police, in confirmation that smokers were invading the main body of the cars, promised a crackdown. Yet a city commissioner reported in January 1942 that women were still 'especially annoyed' by the large number of men puffing away well forward of the smoking compartment.[22]

. . .

. . . An 8 October [1943] news report announcing majority support on city council for prohibition pointed out that it was not only the rear entrance that doomed smoking, but also the hiring of the 'conductorettes'. They could not be expected to do their work enveloped in smoke. On 25 October 1943 Edmonton council finally prohibited smoking on urban public transit. This particular gender struggle for space had a clear victor.[23]

It might be expected that Edmonton's men would vent their anger over lost privileges at the women conductors, who were literally supplanting the smokers. Yet women *shoppers* took the brunt of male frustrations in Edmonton, as elsewhere. Women *workers* apparently bothered men less in the 1940s than is often assumed, unless of course the women in question threatened a man's *own* job.

While male and female passengers frequently defamed each other, they almost always had a kind word for women streetcar staff. As a public platform for gender conflict, Canadian mass transit displayed more a battle over gendered space than over occupational roles. This

pattern becomes clearer as the experience of other cities with women conductors and drivers is examined. In the next section the narrative shifts perspective, as the nature of the sources requires the story to be told from the companies' point of view rather than, as would be ideal, from that of the women workers who 'invaded' (as the Winnipeg *Free Press* put it) 'one of the last jobs held exclusively by men in Canada'. These women workers, like the smokers and shoppers, reshaped public transit as a social space as they entered it, experienced it, and even as they left it. Glimpses into their lives appear in the next few pages, but much of their history is yet to be learned.[24]

Canadian transit operators were as slow as one of their vintage trams to move towards hiring women platform workers. In most cases, they hired their first female conductors in the summer of 1943, by which time the number of gainfully employed women in the nation had already neared the million mark (rising from 638,000 in August 1939).[25] In January 1943, when 94 per cent of American transit companies were already employing more than 11,000 women, of whom 718 were operating vehicles, Canada still had not a single woman platform worker. Canadian transit companies explained their lack of interest in female help by pointing to the age profile of their male employees; to the fact (as a Montreal Tramways executive put it in June 1941) that 'no new transportation employees [had] been engaged or trained, in many properties, for almost ten years.' Consequently, Canadian transit was, as the TTC's general superintendent remarked later that year, 'particularly fortunate in the respect that the average age of its employees [was] relatively high and not many [were] likely to be enlisted in the armed forces or be attracted to other employment by promise of temporary advantage.' Yet the manpower situation was similar in the United States: a substantial number of American transit employees were too old for the draft. Even so, it is possible that one major difference in the conscription policies of the two countries—the fact that the United States initiated its military draft in September 1940 while Canada waited until June 1942—explained the keener American interest in hiring female platform workers. An alternative explanation would point to the sheer conservatism of Canadian transit operators, a conservatism that had made them slower than Americans to embrace the trolley coach in the 1930s.[26]

. . .

. . . [T]ransit companies appeared to regard the decision to hire female operators and conductors as radically innovative and inherently risky. In August 1943 Winnipeg Electric told its passengers that the original reaction to the proposal to put women on the streetcar platform had ranged from 'mild scepticism to outright scorn'. To ease such qualms, transit journals ran a series of positive articles on the performance and reception of women transit employees in the United States and, later, in Canada.[27] Meanwhile, the dominion government's manpower policies were pressuring Canadian operators to hire womanpower. By mid-1943 the men being sent to transit companies were over 45 years old and, in the opinion of the transit association's Special Sub-Committee on Manpower, of 'very poor' calibre. It advised companies to hire women, paying them on an equal basis with the men. Union opposition had in the meantime collapsed, since the only realistic alternative to hiring women was a much longer working day for the remaining men. Consequently, systems in Victoria, Vancouver, Winnipeg, Windsor, Kitchener, Toronto, and Sydney had committed themselves by July 1943 to hiring women for platform or garage work. Before the end of the year, women were working as conductors, streetcar motormen, or bus drivers in Edmonton and St Catharines, Ontario, as well. As of March 1944, 12 Canadian transit companies were employing 263 women as streetcar operators and conductors, 70 women as bus drivers, and 154 women in maintenance work. As most of these women worked in just four cities, the numbers suggest that, in the 1940s, Canadians remained more hesitant than Americans to give women a public role in public transit.[28]

After some discussion, the principal transit operators in Montreal and Ottawa both decided against hiring women. Montreal Tramways announced that it was not considering the use of women even to sell tickets on street corners. Presumably, the company was still mindful of French-Catholic reservations about women working in as public a sphere as mass transit. It also dared not upset its unions, especially after a strike in March 1943 proved that it had backed the losing side in their jurisdictional disputes. In Ottawa the street railway, apparently fearful of being permanently saddled after the war with platforms requiring two operators, refused to hire women as conductors. As for Toronto-style passenger guides to ride the cars on an ad hoc basis and keep order as needed, the company may have shared the opinion of Ottawa's *Evening Citizen* that 'Lady Hostesses . . . would simply get in the way of squeezing one more passenger on board.' Ottawa and Montreal had plenty of company in spurning women transit workers: only a minority of Canadian transit systems hired female conductors and drivers. There must have been a generalized resistance to giving women such a public platform on which to demonstrate their ability to do 'man's work'.[29]

What resistance there was seems to have been restricted to the corporate boardroom and the union hall, for the public manifestly welcomed 'the feminine twist' in transit wherever women were employed. This positive response should have been expected, given the widespread recognition that women workers were performing an important wartime duty. Female conductors in Toronto interviewed in September 1943 said that there was 'hardly any trip' during which 'some one doesn't congratulate us.' For example, an elderly man told TTC conductor Elsie Waterford, 'I have been riding these street cars for twenty-five years and I think you girls are doing a wonderful job.' According to a Toronto transit executive, 'the people [were] taking . . . splendidly' to female bus drivers in that city. Vancouver's 'electric guides' quickly garnered 'several letters of commendation' from the public. Women conductors were praised in Edmonton for noticeably speeding up loading and unloading. There seems, then, to have been little public resentment of female platform staff.[30]

Transit companies generally gushed over the women's performance: in August 1943 the Winnipeg *Free Press* quoted the transit company's instructor, E.F. Hales, as stating that he had 'found no trainees quicker to learn than the women employees. He noted that they listened very attentively to what is said, and demonstrate themselves as very apt and quick to learn.' Hales further said that 'the advantage a man might have in his natural mechanical ability is more than made up for by the women in their quickness and ability to learn.' Women actually listened, Hales said, 'they don't just say "yes! yes!" all the time when they really don't know what I'm talking about', as men apparently did. The female conductors were 'doing a splendid job', Winnipeg Electric affirmed the following October. In late September 1943 the Toronto Railway Club quizzed transit executives about the performance of the new female workers. H.W. Tate, assistant manager of the TTC, responded: 'There have been no problems as far as women are concerned . . . At the present time they are very satisfactory—in fact more so than we expected.' Transit companies consistently reported that women operators had at least as good an accident record as the men—a significant virtue, given the shortage of replacement vehicles and parts. In late 1944 the TTC revealed that its 'women operators [had] been found highly satisfactory, and their accident ratio [had been] even somewhat less than that of the men bus drivers with the same length of service.' Though Winnipeg Electric stated in December 1943 that female streetcar drivers had more accidents than men, it affirmed that the 'men [had]

been involved in more serious accidents than the women.' In 1945 it praised women operators for being as 'good as, and in some respects better than, male employees'. In June 1944 the Niagara and St Catharines system reported that women bus drivers were 'more courteous' than its men, and as 'accident free'.[31]

These sorts of direct, favourable comparisons obviously threatened males, and they often came with a negative qualifier. Thus, Niagara and St Catharines added that women took longer to train. It was also reported in Windsor that the work of women bus cleaners had not been 'entirely satisfactory' until the company had hired 'two older women to act as matrons'. As for those Toronto women bus drivers with the exemplary accident record, it was pointed out that they were also said to be 'on the cautious side' (which did not sound entirely complimentary); and their male rivals were depicted by TTC's superintendent of traffic as being of low calibre, not the 'type of individual' who would have been hired 'before the war'. Assistant manager Tate elaborated: 'At the present time, the men we are getting into the organization are the last selection and the women are the best of the women; so if you make a saw-off of the two, I think you are on the good end.' In other words, the 'best' woman was as good as the 'last' man. And even then, Tate said, women performed well because 'their reputation [was] at stake'—that is, the reputation of their entire sex. No wonder they were overachievers.[32]

This perception—that they had the pick of Canadian womanhood—must have influenced the attitudes of transit managers towards their female staff. They could admire the performance of exceptional individuals without having to revise their opinions about women's overall suitability to work on the public platform. Ironically, women fostered this prejudice by the high numbers in which they sought—and were rejected for—transit work. For example, 'some 200 women' responded to Winnipeg Electric's first appeal in mid-July 1943 for women streetcar and bus drivers. Of these, the company 'selected ten as suitable applicants for traffic work' and another ten as bus cleaners. Subsequent praise for the work of the first four women operators to emerge from this winnowing process did not, therefore, outweigh the company's public conclusion that 'there was a lack of first class [female] applicants for traffic work.' Similarly, the TTC, in reporting on the attrition rate among its female hirings, chose not to emphasize that 86 per cent of its streetcar staff were still working for it on 1 April 1944 (which meant that women had about the same persistence as wartime men in these jobs), but rather commented on the fact that only 70 per cent of its qualified women bus drivers had stuck with the job. They were quitting, the TTC figured, 'probably due [to] the more strenuous physical demands of that work, and partly due to the proportionately greater amount of rush hour work'.[33]

. . .

Managements clearly were displeased with the costs incurred in training platform workers during the war. The extra week or so must have been especially irksome, given the fact that they had not hitherto deigned to pay their trainees. Undoubtedly, the training experience reinforced the managers' prejudices against both middle-aged men and women. These two groups had, of course, the misfortune to serve their apprenticeships at a time when service conditions made it exceptionally difficult to impress their masters. While one could emphasize the positive—that women platform workers received superb training during the war, with even conductors being required in Toronto, Vancouver, and Winnipeg to qualify as drivers—realism demands recognition that transit managers probably looked forward to the day when they could trim their training budgets by hiring young, male workers once again. In the meantime, they hired women. Winnipeg appears to have had 53 platform workers at the peak, just under half of them operating streetcars, the rest conductors; as well, 29 women cleaned and tidied its vehicles. Although Victoria had three such cleaners (in January 1944),

Vancouver had none; it did, however, have 40 'conductorettes,' with 15 more in training. Edmonton, like Vancouver, used women primarily as conductors—there were 60 of these in April 1944—but an unknown number of women (and men) were also hired during the war to stand by the track switches, turning them manually for approaching cars. Taken together, these cities probably had fewer than 200 women working for them at anyone time. A scattered few worked on smaller systems such as those in Sydney, Kitchener, St Catharines, and Windsor.[34]

The numbers suggest that the majority of Canada's female transit workers had jobs in Toronto, inasmuch as its Transportation Commission hired 721 women during the war to do 'work usually done by men'. At the high point, the Toronto system had 340 female street railway and bus drivers, according to the press. Some sense of the overall distribution of its female workforce can be obtained from the TTC's own count in October 1945 . . . of the women it had employed to do 'men's work'. The count omitted female secretaries, stenographers, and receptionists at head office. The omission suggests that the TTC was not so much interested in determining how many women it was employing (a number it did not publish and perhaps did not compile) as in charting the female incursions into male space.[35]

Toronto's data indicate that transit women prized some jobs more than others, notably those which required technical skills and offered a diversity of challenges (repairwomen, handywomen, and the mechanics' helpers). They also had a preference for trams. On the other hand, women tended to leave jobs that reminded them of housework (the three sorts of 'cleaners') or involved especially heavy work, as did truck driving in the 1940s. Since many buses operated only during peak hours, driving them was exhausting work, the stop-and-go traffic requiring constant wheel and gear play; consequently, bus drivers had the second highest turnover of any of the female occupations reported by the

TTC. If women themselves had arrived at a mutual conclusion with their employers that bus driving was not 'women's work', this finding would have eased the conscience of male managers as they pressured women at war's end to retire from male-gendered jobs or to transfer to 'positions more suitable for women'. Moreover, every transit company expected soon to scrap all or most of its streetcars.[36]

Transit men seem to have regarded bus driving by women as particularly invasive of their space; at least, it was the most threatening to their own masculinity. A bus driver commanded a free-wheel vehicle, alarmingly liberated from the steel and electric network that had hitherto guaranteed due subordination to the centralized, hierarchical, and male system; and unlike trams, buses could leapfrog each other. One male driver in 'a certain Canadian city' complained of a woman driver who had been running behind him: 'These dames aren't so dumb. She's been tagging behind me since 7:30 this morning so that I can pick up all her passengers and she doesn't have to risk getting tangled up. She's supposed to be 12 minutes ahead of me, but what can you expect?' A bus journal concluded that his complaints proved that 'man's feeling of security is a precious thing . . . not to be trifled with.' Like most urban bus drivers in the 1940s, this man had probably started out as a streetcar motorman, his security already 'trifled with' by orders to qualify on the new type of vehicle or retire. He may have had doubts about his suitability for his new occupation even before women entered it. In any case, the most hostile remarks towards transit women typically involved buses. For example, a representative of Toronto's electric railway and motor coach union told the National War Labour Board in November 1944: 'We hear lots of sarcastic remarks about women doing our jobs, but I can tell you that women operators are not satisfactory. They are wrecking equipment . . . They haven't the strength to shift gears and handle heavy buses.'[37]

It was rare for a transit man to broadcast such views, for it was unnecessary to denigrate women to ease them out of transit jobs at the end of the war. The women themselves were supposed to realize that they had been temporary replacements in, as the Toronto *Globe and Mail* described the TTC in October 1945, a 'strictly a "for-men-only" organization'. Winnipeg Electric, having told the Canadian Transportation Association in November 1943 that it was 'not hiring women with any idea of employing them permanently', justified its 1945 decision to *stop* hiring them with the simple justification that men were now available. In Edmonton the street railway simply stopped hiring conductors in 1944, as it looked towards a return to one-man operation. Meanwhile, the TTC, having never disguised its belief that women's employment was 'of an emergency character', and that the jobs were 'for the duration' only, saw no contradiction in praising women for their 'emergency duty' and 'sacrifices', even as it claimed that women now 'were all eager and willing to step aside and let the boys have their jobs back again.'[38]

Were they indeed 'eager and willing'? Certainly, some female transit workers considered, as did Clara Clifford, their job to be 'a war measure'. Yet Clifford worked into 1946, deciding to leave (the TTC did not lay off its female employees) only after an inebriated passenger had accused her of 'taking a job now from a man'. 'This gave me food for thought', she recalled. Yet she resented the drunk's double standard: 'He did not think . . . [of] the four years that I went through this cold to get him to where he wanted to go.' Some women also pressured female platform workers to leave; a 'middle-aged lady' in December 1945 expressed the widely held sentiment: 'It's time a lot of these girls were sent back to the farms. The war's over . . . Let the girls get themselves husbands, stay home and make room for men to get jobs.' The women workers who refused to heed this cultural message were transferred to more 'fitting' work at war's end on the TTC. Elsewhere, they were laid off.[39]

It is not known how many female platform workers actively resisted their gendered 'destiny'. There must have been some who fought to stay in 'male' jobs, inasmuch as few, if any, women entered the paid labour force primarily out of a sense of patriotic 'sacrifice'. When Canadian women were asked what motivated their entry into the transit industry, they stressed the personal satisfaction they derived from their work. Streetcar operator Elsie Waterfield responded: 'They didn't want to depend on their children. They wanted to be independent.' The work also suited their interest in 'mechanical work'. Some women said that they had always wanted to drive a streetcar or that they enjoyed meeting the public. Others pointed out that work on the tram platform gave them an opportunity 'to show all the men who thought they couldn't do it that they could'; these women saw themselves as pathfinders for their sex through men's space. Personal improvement also showed up in the reminiscences: 'I was so withdrawn before I went to work', recollected an erstwhile conductor. 'It gave me all the confidence in the world. I was able to cope with everything—including drunks.'[40]

Money also mattered, as companies advertising 'Good jobs at good wages' understood. Women platform workers emphasized the financial benefits of their jobs: 'I put in every hour I could work because I wanted to buy a home for a family', recalled TTC conductor Clara Clifford. Urban transit was one of the few wartime occupations in which women got equal pay for equal work, thanks to the street railway unions having made their co-operation conditional on the sexes being treated equally, with respect not only to wages but also to seniority and shift work. The unions wanted to ensure that their employers had no economic reason to prefer female to male labour. Pay equity made transit work attractive to women, especially since the typical platform worker was married, and her husband in the military. These women looked to their job to supplement their dependant's allowance, and some of them undoubtedly had

to be told at war's end to resign. Hints about their feminine 'duty' to cede their job to a returning veteran would not have sufficed.[41]

The Toronto Transportation Commission had been unusually open to women workers, and so its efforts at war's end to shut the door on them must have been especially unsettling to the organization. Or the TTC management may have had more opportunity than smaller systems to appreciate the contribution that female employees could make as a *social class*—rather than as *exceptional individuals*—to the well-being of their system. Whatever the motive, it was apparently only on Toronto transit that women retained a role on the public platform in the two decades after 1946. The first TTC guides had started work in April 1942 at busy spots in the downtown area, standing on the sidewalks to sell tickets, make change, and give information on routes and destinations, in order to speed up the service by reducing the number of transactions and inquiries at the fare box. In November 1945 'a new group of girls was formed, to work at points radiating from the center of the city during the . . . rush hours.' The 23 new 'passenger guides' (thus named to distinguish them from the more stationary 'information and ticket guides' working downtown) were not tied to a specific location; they had 'considerable latitude', as *Canadian Transportation* reported the following February, to ride the cars and buses 'within their prescribed' areas, looking for congestion and opportunities to 'be of service' to the passengers. Once on board, they continued to sell tickets and give out information while simultaneously persuading women to move to the back and men to stub out their illicit cigarettes. The guides were praised in February 1946 for having helped lost children to find their school or mother, an army nurse to carry her 'heavy suitcases', and a soldier to retrieve a typewriter forgotten on a tram.[42]

The TTC prized its guides, considering them a prime asset to be featured on ceremonial occasions. For example, in June 1947 it was a guide who held the official ribbon that Toronto's mayor cut to inaugurate the city's first modern trolley coach service. And in March 1954 two files of guides and male inspectors lined the path leading 'dignitaries', including the provincial premier, to the ceremonies that marked the opening of Canada's first subway line. Two smiling guides were at the head of the file, visually in charge not only of the women but also of the male inspectors, who were the company's most senior and respected employees in traffic operations.[43]

. . .

Although the post-war viability of Canadian transit depended on retaining the loyalty of female riders in off-peak hours, only in Toronto did the system actively cater to their needs. The TTC guides made travel more pleasant for women—and for male non-smokers. They reduced shoving and enforced queues, to the obvious advantage of the very young, the elderly, and the small of frame. They persuaded women to move back in the cars, thereby reducing the buffeting they took from men pushing to the rear. They 'sweetly' told men to stop smoking. They patrolled the interior of vehicles, giving women a greater sense of security on the one-man trams and buses of the post-war era. They gave travel directions, to the advantage of women who, as shoppers or mothers, were more likely than their husbands to be venturing into unknown territory. Finally, it is crucial to note that most of the reported instances of special courtesy and generosity on the part of the guides involved other women. There must have been many women (as well as men) whose fidelity to the TTC was reaffirmed by experiencing or witnessing one of the passenger guides perform an act of basic human kindness such as this one, recorded by *Canadian Transportation* in February 1946:

> A very poorly dressed woman got off a car with heavy bundles on a bitterly cold evening. She seemed ill and tired. The guide took off her own rubbers and gloves and put them on the woman, and ascertaining she lived only two blocks from the main thoroughfare, she carried the parcels

and took the woman home. At the door, while the woman was returning the rubbers and gloves, she burst into tears and said, 'I never had anything as nice as this done to me before.'[44]

Only the TTC provided service of this quality to urban commuters in Canada. It had 'feminized' its system the most during the Second World War, and remained easily the most feminized afterwards. The TTC's embrace of 'feminine' values, personified in the tact, cheerfulness, helpfulness, and kindness of its passenger guides, must have been an important asset in transit's post-war struggle to retain enough female patronage to remain economically viable. To be sure, the TTC was doing a lot of things right in the immediate post-war era (including its modernization program), and its regendering in the 1940s was not the sole explanation for its success. Still, the guides did constitute an outreach to women and an attempt to ease the gender tensions among its passengers that overcrowding had produced. On other Canadian systems, passengers were left to fend for themselves.[45]

It is surprising that the wartime crowding does not figure more strongly in accounts of the decline of public transit, and the explosive growth in auto sales in the late 1940s. After all, even a Winnipeg Electric engineer had advised the Canadian Transit Association in late 1944 that he had been 'on our cars when they were so crowded that I felt that a personal indignity had been visited upon me by our own company.' He then added: 'If I had any choice I would not have chosen our service.' Post-war prosperity actually gave Canadians that choice, and they opted for the motor car *en masse*.[46]

Public transit in the 1940s was indeed an 'indignity', and until historians fully assimilate this fact into their accounts, their explanations of transit's post-war decline will be incomplete and unpersuasive. It was not just the economics of transportation or the politics of subsidies that determined the decision to ride; it was also deep-felt, individual attitudes towards privacy and social space. To understand the widespread rejection of public transit, we must be able to imagine ourselves a reviled, wartime female 'shopper' laden with parcels, one of 65 standees in a 45-seat streetcar, with one man beside her blowing smoke in her face, another two men pressed against her nether regions, and a dozen people blocking her path to the exit. Our historical imagination must also encompass the beleaguered male smoker and the 'hapless male' described in a plaintive letter from an Ottawa man in 1947:

> One has only to board a crowded car today to see how some women will out-do themselves to make some harried male feel small and cheap so that he is more or less obliged to give up his seat to the triumphant female . . . Some women—the obviously independent type—do not expect a man to give up his seat to them. When a tired young man stands up and graciously offers his seat to one of them, she turns him down and remarks with a superior smile, 'I'd rather stand, thank you.' Men, viewing a spectacle like this, have reason to think twice before standing up to be the target for amused glances and sly comments from sitting passengers.[47]

. . .

Not surprisingly, Canadians . . . had difficulty getting past the idea of transit work as strictly 'men's work'. The ideology of women's and men's 'proper' sphere resurfaced in 1944–5, as a powerful 'reconstruction' discourse demanded women's post-war return to the home. The story of the women platform workers who were forced out of the paid labour force or into lower-paid, less satisfying work told a familiar tale. The individuals involved clearly paid a high price for the nation's gender bias. So too did Canada, as transit's failure to listen to the women of Canada before 1941 or to give women a working role in the system after the war (outside of Toronto) contributed to public transit's post-war slide into subsidy and senescence.[48]

## Notes

1.  Toronto *Telegram* editorial reprinted in Ottawa *Morning Journal*, 12 Feb. 1946. All Ottawa press items come from the City of Ottawa Archives (COA), Ottawa Electric Railway Scrapbooks. . . .

2.  An exception to the rule were female bus entrepreneurs in North America. See Margaret Walsh, 'Not Rosie the Riveter: Women's Diverse Roles in the Making of the American Long-Distance Bus Industry', *Journal of Transport History* 17 (1996): 43–56. . . .

3.  There exists a well-developed body of studies on the gendered construction of skills. See, for example, Joy Parr, *The Gender of Breadwinners: Women, Men, and Change in Two Industrial Towns, 1880–1950* (Toronto: University of Toronto Press, 1990); Ava Baron, ed., *Work Engendered: Toward a New History of American Labor* (Ithaca, NY: Cornell University Press, 1991).

4.  Ruth Roach Pierson, *'They're Still Women After All': The Second World War and Canadian Womanhood* (Toronto: McClelland & Stewart, 1986), 216; Jeffrey Keshen, 'Revisiting Canada's Civilian Women during World War II', *Histoire Sociale/Social History* (Nov. 1997). . . .

5.  Michel Crozier, *The Bureaucratic Phenomenon* (Chicago: University of Chicago Press, 1964); John Law, ed., *Power, Action, and Belief: A New Sociology of Knowledge?* (London: Routledge & Kegan Paul, 1986); Wiebe Bijker et al., eds, *The Social Construction of Technological Systems: New Directions in the Sociology and History of Technology* (Cambridge, Mass.: MIT Press, 1987); Wiebe Bijker and John Law, eds, *Shaping Technology/Building Society: Studies in Sociotechnical Change* (Cambridge, Mass.: MIT Press, 1992).

6.  Montreal *Gazette*, 24 Sept. 1948; Ottawa *Morning Citizen*, 7 Dec. 1948, 12 Nov. 1942; Gwen Lambton, 'War Work in Toronto', in Ruth Latta, ed., *The Memory of All That: Canadian Women Remember World War II* (Burnstown, Ont.: General Store Publishing House, 1992), 33.

7.  Vancouver *Sun*, 9 Oct. 1943.

8.  Tabor R. Stone, *Beyond the Automobile: Reshaping*

*the Transportation Environment* (Englewood Cliffs, NJ: Prentice-Hall, 1971), 100.

9. Modern prejudice envisages the 1940s shopper as someone with hatbox in hand, but she was more likely to have the evening's meal or a scarce commodity like sugar or coffee in her bag. . . .

10. *Chatelaine*, 22 Nov. 1942, 72, 75; City of Calgary Archives (CCA), City Clerk's Fonds, box 245, file 2245, City Clerk of Winnipeg to City Clerk of Calgary, 16 Aug. 1943; National Archives of Canada (NAC), RG 28, vol. 270, file 196–17–4, Department of Munitions and Supply, Press Release 593A, 19 Sept. 1945. . . .

11. *Bus and Truck Transportation in Canada* (*BTT*), Dec. 1942, 29, Feb. 1944, 40–1.

12. Ottawa *Morning Citizen*, 17 May 1943. . . .

13. Ibid., 18 Aug. 1944.

14. Ibid., 21 Aug. 1944. Birch was using the 'potent weapon of humiliation'. This weapon, as Karen Dubinsky has argued, 'touched all those who went public with their stories of sexual conflict.' Karen Dubinsky, *Improper Advances: Rape and Heterosexual Conflict in Ontario, 1880–1929* (Chicago: University of Chicago Press, 1993), 164.

15. Ottawa *Morning Citizen*, 22 Aug. 1944.

16. The widespread negative attitudes towards female shoppers contrasted markedly with government propaganda efforts to recognize women's traditional domestic services (i.e., thrift and price monitoring) as socially necessary. See Pierson, 'They're Still Women', 41; *Chatelaine*, Nov. 1942, 72, 75, June 1944, 76. . . .

17. *Saturday Night*, 30 Nov. 1912, 29, 4 Nov. 1922, 23; Edmonton *Journal*, 31 Jan. 1942; Centre d'archives Hydro-Québec, file F6/16173, 'Rules and Regulations for the Government of Employees of the Hull Electric Company' (1913); Calgary *Herald*, 6 Dec. 1949, 18 Feb. 1956. . . .

18. Ottawa *Morning Journal*, 5 Oct. 1945.

19. Calgary *Herald*, 18 Feb. 1956. This article was prompted by the elimination of the last smoking vestibules. The 'clubhouse' theme also appeared in a *Herald* article of 6 Dec. 1949.

20. Ottawa *Morning Citizen*, 18 Nov. 1942.

21. *BTT*, May 1945, 72; City of Halifax Archives. City Council Minutes, 12 Nov. 1943, 338 (thanks to Kimberly Berry for this reference); CCA, City's Clerks Fonds, box 386, file 2532, 19 May 1947; CCA, Calgary Transit, Series III, box 82, file 859, Superintendent's Office Bulletin, 27 Oct. 1947. . . .

22. Edmonton *Journal*, 24 Sept., 10 Oct. 1940, 31 Jan., 30 Sept. 1942.

23. Ibid., 18 Aug., 4, 8 Oct. 1943; Edmonton *Bulletin*, 4, 8 Oct. 1943; City of Edmonton Archives (CEA), City Council Minutes, 25 Oct. 1943.

24. Winnipeg *Free Press*, 14 Aug. 1943.

25. C.P. Stacey, *Arms, Men and Governments: The War Policies of Canada, 1939–1945* (Ottawa: Queen's Printer, 1970), 416. This number did not include the 750,000 women working on family farms and the 43,000 women in the armed forces.

26. *Canadian Transportation* (*CT*), Feb. 1942, 90, May 1943, 245; *Proceedings of the 37th Annual Meeting of the Canadian Transit Association*, 1940–1, 110.

27. Canadian transit executives apparently had forgotten or chose not to recall that 12 women had served as streetcar conductors in Halifax for a year after the explosion of 6 December 1917. They were paid off 'when the men came home'. . . . See *Canadian Railway and Marine World*, Feb. 1933, 71; Provincial Archives of Nova Scotia, MG 9, vol. 229, Nova Scotia Tramways and Power Company Ltd, *Annual Report of the President and Directors for the Year Ended Dec. 31st, 1917*, 1–2; Halifax *Mail-Star*, 2 Dec. 1958; George Dillon and William Thomson, *Kingston Portsmouth and Cataraqui Electric Railway* (Kingston: Canadian Railroad History Association, 1994); Vancouver *Province*, 17 July 1917 (Moose Jaw). (Thanks to Kimberly Berry and Steven High for the Great War references.)

28. *BTT*, July 1943, 37; Aug. 1943, 20; Vancouver Public Library, Harold Till, *Vancouver's Traffic History, 1889–1946* (n.d.), 60; Public Archives of Manitoba, P608 Amalgamated Transit Union, Minutes of 13 Apr. 1943; *CT*, July 1943, 378, Aug. 1944, 441; Toronto *Globe and Mail*, 12 July 1943; Winnipeg *Free Press*, 15 July 1943; Vancouver *Province*, 11 Aug. 1943; Kitchener *Daily Record*, 12 June, 7 July 1943. . . .

29. Montreal *Gazette*, 17 May, 19 June 1943; The

Clio Collective, *Quebec Women: A History* (Toronto: Women's Press, 1987), 277–84; Alison Prentice et al., eds, *Canadian Women: A History* (Toronto: Harcourt Brace Jovanovich, 1988), 299; Ottawa *Evening Citizen*, 29 Nov. 1945; NAC, MG 28, I103, vol. 230, file 7, A.R. Mosher, 'A Public Statement on the Montreal Tramways Strike', 5 Apr. 1943

30. Toronto *Daily Star*, 22 Oct. 1943; *CT*, July 1943, 378, Nov. 1943, 590, Jan. 1944, 30; Toronto *Globe and Mail*, 10 Sept. 1943; Ottawa *Morning Citizen*, 18 Oct. 1943; Ottawa *Evening Citizen*, 30 Nov. 1943 (latter two for Edmonton); Kitchener *Daily Record*, 7 July 1943; NAC, AV, tape R8547, Elsie Waterford reminiscences.

31. *CT*, Oct. 1943, 542, Nov. 1943, 590, Jan. 1944, 28–30, June 1944, 330, June 1946, 328; Winnipeg *Free Press*, 14 Aug. 1943; *BTT*, June 1944, 42.

32. *BTT*, June 1944, 42; *CT*, Nov. 1943, 590, Dec. 1943, 653.

33. *CT*, Dec. 1943, 653, Jan. 1944, 27, June 1944, 330; Winnipeg *Tribune*, 15 July, 5 Aug. 1943; Winnipeg *Free Press*, 14 Aug. 1943. The male turnover was 2.3–2.5 per cent per month in 1943.

34. *CT*, Jan. 1944, 30, Feb. 1944, 82, June 1946, 328; NAC, MG 30 B137, Norman D. Wilson Fonds, vol. 18, file 19, Thomas Ferrier to Edmonton City Commissioners, 19 Apr. 1944; Colin K. Hatcher and Tom Schwarzkopf, *Edmonton's Electric Transit* (Toronto: Railfare Enterprises, 1983), 116; Edmonton *Journal*, 10 Jan., 29 Mar. 1944.

35. *CT*, Nov. 1945, 637; Toronto *Globe and Mail*, 6 Oct. 1945. The TTC's reliance on women workers was not unusual for a Toronto company: in October 1943, more than 40 per cent of Toronto's manufacturing workers were female— the highest percentage for any Canadian city. NAC, MG 28 I103, vol. 362, General Part I, 1942–57, Department of Trade and Commerce, Dominion Bureau of Statistics, Employment Statistics Branch, 'Sex Distribution of the Persons in Recorded Employment at Oct. 1, 1943' (Ottawa: King's Printer, Dec. 1943).

36. *CT*, Nov. 1945, 637.

37. *BTT*, Sept. 1943, 25; Ottawa *Evening Citizen*, 1 Nov. 1944.

38. Toronto *Globe and Mail*, 6 Oct. 1945; *CT*, Oct. 1943, 542, Dec. 1943, 654, June 1946, 328, 334; Edmonton *Journal*, 10 Jan., 7 Dec. 1944, 21 Nov. 1945.

39. NAC, AV, tape R8546, reminiscences of Clara Clifford; Ottawa *Morning Citizen*, 1 Dec. 1945.

40. Winnipeg *Free Press*, 5 Aug. 1943; Toronto *Daily Star*, 22 Oct. 1943; Winnipeg *Tribune*, 5 Aug. 1943; NAC, AV, tapes R8546–7, reminiscences of Elsie Waterfield and Clara Clifford.

41. NAC, AV, tape R8546, reminiscences of Clara Clifford; *CT*, Jan. 1944, 27–9, Feb. 1944, 82, June 1946, 328; *Bus Transportation*, Dec. 1944, 35; Edmonton *Journal*, 10 Jan. 1944; Vancouver *Province*, 11 Aug. 1943; *BTT*, July 1943, 37. . . .

42. Only single women were employed as passenger guides, in keeping with the post-war trend against hiring married women. See NAC, AV, tape R8546, reminiscences of Clara Clifford; *CT*, Feb. 1946, 84, 86, Jan. 1949, 30; Toronto *Globe and Mail*, 19 Jan. 1943; Ottawa *Morning Journal*, 30 Nov. 1945; *BTT*, Aug. 1949, 42. . . .

43. Mike Filey, *The TTC Story: The First Seventy-five Years* (Toronto: Dundurn Press, 1996), 72, 89. The TTC guides lasted until March 1995, when the service ended for budgetary reasons. Information from Ted Wickson, the former TTC archivist.

44. *CT*, Feb. 1946, 86.

45. This conclusion raises the question of whether any American transit system had female guides immediately after the war and whether its ridership also held up unusually well. Unfortunately, the sources used here, including *Transit Journal* and *Bus Transportation*, allow us only to pose, not answer, this question. . . .

46. *CT*, Dec. 1944, 663. Motor vehicles in Canada rose in number from 1.5 million in 1945 to 2.6 million in 1950. F.H. Leacy, ed., *Historical Statistics of Canada*, 2nd edn (Ottawa: Statistics Canada, 1983), T147–78.

47. Ottawa *Evening Citizen*, 24 Nov. 1947.

48. Transit's story must have been repeated in countless other industrial sectors. Yet historians have

tended to assume rather than prove that the post-war departure of women from entire occupations damaged society and the economy. In effect, there has been a liberal and individualistic focus, rather than a communitarian one, to the research. Among the few studies to examine the economic damage resulting from women's return to home and hearth in North America are Lewis Humphreys, 'Women and Government Intervention in the Canadian Labour Force, 1941–1947', MA thesis (Dalhousie University, 1986); Sherrie A. Kossoudji and Laura J. Dresser, 'Working Class Rosies: Women Industrial Workers during World War II', *Journal of Economic History* 52 (1992): 431–46.

# 15

# Back to the Garden:
# Redesigning the Factory for a Post-Industrial Era

Steven High

> There is an image of the 19th century industrial economy, familiar from a hundred history textbooks: the coal mine and its neighboring iron foundry, belching black smoke into the sky, and illuminating the night heavens with its lurid red glare. There is a corresponding image of the new economy that has taken its place in the last years of the twentieth century, but it is only just imprinting itself on our consciousness. It consists of a series of low, discreet buildings, usually displaying a certain air of quiet good taste, and set amidst impeccable landscaping in that standard real-estate cliché, a campus-like atmosphere.
>
> Manuel Castells and Peter Hall,
> *Technopoles of the World*[1]

In their juxtaposition of the old economy against the new, Manuel Castells and Peter Hall clearly prefer the latter. For them, the idyllic surroundings of Silicon Valley exemplify the triumph of post-industrialism over industrialism. The ascent of a new high-technology and service economy, and the simultaneous decline of an older manufacturing one, is widely interpreted to be as inevitable as sunrise and sunset. Left in the shadows, however, has been another dimension of industrial transformation: the emergence of a post-industrial aesthetic.[2]

This post-industrial aesthetic was born out of deeply rooted environmental values and sensibilities. Historian Samuel P. Hayes has termed the post-Second World War period of rising standards of living and levels of education the environmental era.[3] In the decades between 1945 and 1984 planners incorporated environmental values into factory exteriors, by removing the factory from its former industrial landscape and placing it in 'natural' surroundings, either in industrial parks or in the countryside. These greenfield sites—as opposed to older brownfield ones—represented a return to the beginnings of industrialism. Just as rural locations had set apart early North American factory sites from the degrading industrial cities of Great Britain, greenfield sites promised to purge the factory system of its reputation for human and environmental degradation. In effect, this was a return to the pastoral ideals of the factory.

Much like the nineteenth-century tableaux depicting workshops in the wilderness, factories built after the Second World War reflected public concern over the adverse effects of industrialism on the natural and human environment. In order to trace changing concepts of plant design, this chapter delves into the image worlds presented in four trade publications: *Architectural Record*, *Industrial Development*, *Site Selection Handbook*, and *Industrial Canada*. The post-industrial facade did not so much reflect changing corporate attitudes as it did changing societal values about the environment and the nature of progress.[4] In the process, imaginative boundaries between industrial and post-industrial economies, blue-collar and white-collar workers, factory and office, industrial land and park land became blurred.[5] Behind this new facade, however, the old rational factory persisted, smaller, more sanitized, and more disposable than before.

## Industrial Pastoralism and the Rational Factory

The ideology of early American industrialism differed sharply from that of Great Britain, the cradle of the Industrial Revolution. Americans did not want to bring the British factory system—with its reputation for 'human depravity and wretchedness'—to North America.[6] There would be no 'dark satanic mills' in the New World. Indeed, in the early nineteenth century, the image of America as a new Garden of Eden permeated both American and European thought. In an often-cited passage from *Notes on the State of Virginia* (1785), Thomas Jefferson mused that the young Republic would be better served if industry 'let our workshops remain in Europe.'[7] Jefferson nonetheless came to the conclusion that manufacturing could be introduced without disturbing America's rural landscapes and republican ideals.[8]

This ideal was not without its inner contradictions: the garden image was itself a product of the Christian imperative to put the land to work for humanity.[9] Europeans coming to North America did not wish to preserve the wild landscape but rather to create a cultivated one that

proclaimed the values of order and taste.[10] The garden would be a controlled environment where nature served people's every need. In his study of early views of the Acadian landscape of maritime Canada, historian Ramsay Cook found that 'when Europeans set about transforming the wilderness into a garden, they were engaged in taking possession of the land.'[11] Thus, the New World's environment would be purified even as it was being taken into possession.

At first, industrialization seemed to conform to the 'machine in the garden' ideal. In Jefferson's time, American factories were powered by water. Long after Great Britain had converted to steam power and developed great industrial cities such as Manchester, mills and factories in North America remained in the countryside, located near falls or rapids. Abundant water-power sites in North America ensured that—at least initially—industrialism was a largely rural phenomenon.[12]

European visitors often recorded their astonishment at seeing New England textile mills. Visiting the mill town of Lowell, Massachusetts, Alexander MacKay 'looked in vain for the usual indications of a manufacturing town . . . The tall chimneys and the thick volumes of black smoke.'[13] His surprise was shared by many. Historian Marvin Fisher concluded from an analysis of published travel diaries that 'unlike the factory areas of the Old World, Lowell seemed essentially rural; the most frequent descriptions stressed such words as "clean," "open," "airy," "fresh," "new," "young," and "different."'[14] Even the system of using mill girls from surrounding rural areas as the chief source of labour was widely acclaimed. No less of an authority than Charles Dickens compared these healthy-looking New England women favourably with the 'waifs' who laboured back in England.[15]

It was only the introduction of steam power and the emergence of the urban factory at mid-century that American industrialism began to resemble its European counterpart. For nearly a century—from the 1850s to the 1940s—industrialization and urbanization, and later suburbanization, went hand in hand. The so-called machine age saw the rise of mass production and the idealization of the machine, with industrial engineers and factory owners seeking to construct the ever-elusive rational factory. By the 1920s, new technological advances in material handling, reinforced concrete, and the application of electricity had revolutionized factory design and layout. Electricity in particular permitted far more flexibility in arranging the plant and manufacturing process. As Henry Ford himself pointed out: 'The provision of a whole new system of electric generation emancipated industry from the leather belt and line shaft, for it eventually became possible to provide each tool with its own electric motor . . . The motor enabled machinery to be arranged according to the sequence of work, and that alone has probably doubled the efficiency of industry, for it has cut out a tremendous amount of useless handling and hauling. The belt and line shaft were also very wasteful of power—so wasteful, indeed, that no factory could be really large, for even the longest line shaft was small according to modern requirements.' Factories became rationalized and grew to unprecedented size.[16] The new rational factory was realized with the construction of Ford's mammoth River Rouge complex in 1927, where iron ore and other raw materials were shipped to one end of the huge complex and Model A automobiles rolled out the other.[17] The ubiquitous cult of the machine even found artistic expression in the paintings of Charles Sheeler in the 1930s. After spending six weeks at Ford's new factory, Sheeler painted 32 views of the complex that would become prime examples of industrial pastoralism.[18] The characteristic American landscape had by this time become an industrial one, and the metaphor of the machine had been imposed on things social, cultural, and religious.

Virtually every major study of factory design ends at River Rouge, enabling scholars such as Manuel Castells and Peter Hall to contrast monolithic industrial complexes with the discreet buildings of the new economy. In doing so, however, they overlook another half-century of change in factory design. Just as suburban homes promised middle-class families clean living in peaceful green surroundings, industrial parks and the countryside promised manufacturers a fresh new start reminiscent of the earliest phase of New World industrialization. This transmutation was made possible by three technological developments: the rapid diffusion of the automobile and increased worker mobility; rural electrification in the 1930s, which allowed the factory to move beyond the industrial suburbs; and the invention of the computer and the resultant feasibility of decentralized production. In addition to these technical considerations, industrialists increasingly wanted to rid themselves of newly unionized workforces in the cities and to cleanse the stain of human and environmental degradation.

## Building the Post-Industrial Facade

Even though the notion of post-industrialism had surfaced as early as in the 1960s, the term did not become common usage until sociologist Daniel Bell published *The Coming of Post-Industrial Society* in 1973.[19] Bell interpreted the vast changes sweeping the industrialized world as evidence of an emerging knowledge-based economy of computers and telecommunications. While the belief in technology as a key governing force in society was nothing new, technological progress in an environmental age took on a new form.[20] No longer did the billowing black smoke from factory chimneys signal prosperity and progress. Instead, a more suburban landscape of progress resurfaced.[21]

The mills and factories of the industrial age had released a great deal of hazardous waste, causing extensive pollution of air, water, and land.[22] In the course of a century of industrial activity, old greenfield mill or factory towns had turned brown. Assisted in no small part by spectacular ecological disasters such as the Cuyahoga

River fire and the poisoning of people's homes in Love Canal, environmentalists and consumer-rights advocates put large corporations on the defensive in the late 1960s and early 1970s. In 1972, the editors of the trade journal *Industrial Development* warned their corporate subscribers to consider 'changing socio-economic priorities' to avoid tarnished corporate images and financial loss. Three years later, the editors claimed that years of 'environmental hysteria' had severely battered the image of large corporations: 'Golden Boy had gone bad and had to be regulated and watched via permits, reports and approvals of his activities.'[23] US senator Daniel Patrick Moynihan credited anti-business and anti-growth attitudes for a policy shift in the early 1970s from a 'war on poverty' to a 'war on dirty air'.[24]

The tarnished image of industrialism was such that local elites did not wait for plants to close to re-engineer their city's image as post-industrial. Hamilton's long-standing association with the steel industry became a matter of intense embarrassment to civic leaders during the 1970s and 1980s. The city's reputation as a 'lunch-bucket town'—a label that had graced David Proulx's 1971 coffee table book, *Pardon My Lunch Bucket: A Look at the New Hamilton*—was downplayed by urban boosters such as Mayor Victor Copps: 'I don't particularly mind Hamilton being called a lunch-bucket city. It's no crime to take your lunch to work. There's nothing indecent in getting your hands dirty in the foundry or rolling mill, making a decent living so you can bring up one of those large families that steelworkers are so fond of.'[25] Yet in due course, Copps claimed, the old lunch bucket was destined to 'become a museum piece, something that us old-timers can take our grandchildren to see one of these days to point out the way it used to be.'[26] In the new Hamilton a set of post-industrial values and images displaced the pride of place that industrialism had once engendered.

The precariousness of life in Canada's industrial towns and cities, combined with an ascendant post-industrial economy, worked to undermine people's self-worth. A 1982 survey of 300 Windsor residents, and a focus group of 35 'opinion leaders', uncovered many people's embarrassment at living in a blue-collar town. Even though 7,000 area auto workers had just been laid off, most residents pointed to the working-class image rather than the unemployment problem as the main reason for Windsor's poor image. Fully 67 per cent of respondents believed that the city had developed a negative reputation in the rest of Canada.[27] Blue-collar workers thus faced the problem of diminishing status and prestige. As one scholar observed, a 'factory job is not a station that is often aspired to.'[28]

In responding to the growing force of environmentalism, industrial firms set out to remake their smokestack image. To that end, many development agencies dropped the word 'industrial' from their names in favour of 'community' or 'economic'. During the 1970s and early 1980s, large industries such as US Steel and National Steel eliminated 'steel' from their names or, in the case of the Steel Company of Canada, adopted the less noxious-sounding acronym Stelco. As 'factory' became associated with environmental and human degradation, the word gradually disappeared from the corporate vocabulary. Instead, the environmentally correct vocabulary included 'facility', 'real estate', 'building', 'operation', and 'plant'.[29] These words could just as easily have described an office building as a factory.

Evidently, post-industrialism was more than semantics, with flexible production displacing mass production in many manufacturing sectors. In the process, the main centres of technological innovation shifted from industrial cities to post-industrial spaces, from Detroit to the Silicon Valley. Certain critics even likened universities such as Stanford and MIT—the powerhouses of the new economy—to the coal mines of an older industrial era.

Yet the boundary between the old and new economies remains vague. How different is the manufacture of computer hardware components from the manufacture of appliances? In this sense post-industrialism refers as much to innocuous physical surroundings as it does to the nature of the economic activity. A growing number of enterprises once identified with industrial smokestacks have successfully made the transition to the new economy not by manufacturing different products, but by changing factory design, image, and location.[30] As a result, old industrial landscapes such as the Steel Valley of northeast Ohio that once towered over their communities have given way to new post-industrial spaces designed to blend into suburban surroundings. These new spaces are rational factories in all but name.

## Factory Design and Location

How were new ideas and values incorporated into factory design and location? Companies have been very conscious of their 'obligation to present an attractive face to the community'.[31] In the late 1940s and early 1950s, an appealing exterior increasingly came to mean pleasant landscaped surroundings, as illustrated in the trade journal *Architectural Record*. General Robert Johnson, head of the Johnson and Johnson Company, declared at the end of the Second World War that the vast majority of American factories were obsolete and ought to be razed to the ground. However, Johnson found that his small factories, located in rural areas, induced pride in work and a sense of loyalty to the company. F.N. Manley, director of construction, described the ideal plant: 'It will be a one-story building . . . It will be out away from congested city areas, away from any "industrial slums." Johnson does not want to operate in industrial slum conditions.' In pursuing this goal, the company expected employees to drive to work and walk in, with management, through the front doors: 'The general rule is to enclose everything possible in clean, colorful coverings, hiding all possible working parts and oily bearings. Usually an industrial designer is retained to modify machine designs and work out color schemes, all

to the end that girls can operate them safely and simply, without soiling the nurses' uniforms that management provides for them.'[32] As early as 1948, then, Johnson and Johnson employed a mainly female workforce, a source of cheap, non-unionized labour, and had begun the process of redesigning factory work as white-collar.

With larger parcels of land available in the countryside or in industrial parks, post-Second World War designers had a considerable amount of freedom. Writing in 1953, Frank L. Whitney noted that the 'architectural concept of the industrial plant has in the past decade been radically revised.' Once designed to stand 50 years and to possess a dignified institutional quality, factories became increasingly functional.[33] Industrial firms proved more willing to 'enlarge it, change it, sell it, or abandon it entirely, whenever it begins to hamstring the operations. We expect a certain fluidity in manufacturing operations, and we design for it as we can.' In abandoning the masonry that had formerly symbolized distinction and longevity, Whitney encouraged prospective clients 'to think of the industrial plant more as a shell over a mechanical process than as the ancestral home of a corporation, and try to design for fast changing times.'[34] Post-war factory designers discouraged corporate executives from 'institutional monumentality' and instead promoted factories designed for 'flexibility'. Michael F. Roberts, a partner in the Toronto-based architectural firm Wilson Newton Roberts, informed the readership of *Industrial Canada* that 'an industrial building is an envelope wrapped around a manufacturing process.'[35] In light of this new-found concern for flexibility, older factories became inefficient and therefore disposable.

By the 1950s, multi-storey factories had lost out to single-storey ones, in part because vertical material-handling proved to be far less efficient. In the late nineteenth and early twentieth centuries, factory designers had built narrow industrial buildings, then shaped like the letters I, L, E, T, U, H, or F, to allow in natural light and ven-

tilation.[36] Inexpensive electricity not only eliminated the need for natural light, but also made
redundant the belts and shafting that had made
the multi-storey factory desirable.[37] As a result of
technological improvements, a 1954 survey of
manufacturers found a strong demand for single-
storey buildings.[38] At the same time, the trend
was towards constructing smaller plants with
less than 50,000 square feet of floor space.

Did anything distinguish Canadian-designed
factories from American ones? In a series of articles on 'The Canadian Plant of the 70s', the editors of *Industrial Canada* admitted there was 'no
such animal'.[39] The label proved useful, they suggested, only as it alluded to progress, innovation,
and change. The comforting allusion to a
Canadian plant at a time of intense economic
nationalism in the country was unspoken.
Beyond the rhetoric, there was little about the
theoretical 1970s plant that could be described as
distinctly Canadian. New plants on either side of
the border shared many commonalities of design,
location, ownership, and post-industrial image.[40]

Even so, the post-industrial facade was further embellished by local association. Most companies named new manufacturing facilities after
their locality. When the Acme Cleveland
Corporation relocated its Providence plant to
nearby Cranston, Rhode Island, in 1978, it initially retained the old name. The corporation
later succumbed to the idea that the plant should
be renamed. Corporate executive Harry Leckler
justified the change with an assurance that the
plant's name presented 'a vital link to the community that will provide us with services and
political cooperation.'[41] This rhetorical link was
particularly important for American multina-
tional corporations operating in Canada. The
plant manager of Canadian Mechanical
Engineering, an American subsidiary operating
in Canada, gave in to demands by workers in
Windsor and erected a flagpole to fly a Canadian
flag in front of the plant.[42] By adopting local and
national symbols, big corporations attempted to
blend in to their environment.

The industrial park was another concept
that took a firm hold in post-industrial America.
Although manufacturers had sought greener pas-
tures in industrial suburbs long before 1945,
industrial parks proved different from suburbs in
that they promised manufacturers a greenfield
site in perpetuity through the strict regulation of
aesthetics.[43] As a result, the number of industrial
parks multiplied 'as if by magic', in the words of
one American booster.[44] In 1970, the trade journal *Industrial Development* counted 2,400 industrial parks in the United States, a 78 per cent
jump from 1965. Many of these new developments were situated along transportation arter-
ies, major highways, and airport hubs, making
aesthetics especially important. An author writing in *Industrial Development* claimed:
'Developers, tuned in to the national clamor
against environmental quality, are paying
increasing attention to controlling the industrial
park environment through such requirements as
ample setbacks; architectural approval of plant
design and construction materials; underground
utilities; wide streets and off-street parking;
screened outdoor storage.'[45] The trend towards
the regulation of industrial landscapes was partly
related to the national clamour against industrial
pollution.[46] In the case of the Bramalea Industrial
Park near Toronto's Pearson Airport, the promise
of lower taxes, full-service lots, and a central geographic location attracted investors.[47] In addition, many parks had strict regulations barring
obtrusive industry.[48] The industrial park was
therefore the destination of choice for light-man-
ufacturing industries ready to reorient their businesses as post-industrial.[49]

The post-industrial facade in plant design,
together with the inclination to locate plants in
suburban areas, small towns, or rural areas, grew
out of changes in corporate thinking since the
Second World War. This trend surfaced in 1958
when the magazine *Factory Management and
Maintenance* singled out 10 plants for special
praise, all of which were located in the countryside.[50] Corporate executives readily conceded

that the search for pleasant surroundings and cheap labour tended to be one and the same. Pete J. Barber, head of Honeywell's real estate department, noted that real estate was 'a means to an end, that end being specifically sales and profit. Real estate is only a tool to arrive at those ends.'[51] Del Morgano, the manager of facility planning at UARCO, a medium-sized manufacturer of business forms with nine factories, was even more blunt. His company located a new plant in Brockville, Ontario, reflecting UARCO's corporate policy to locate all its production facilities in towns with populations ranging from 5,000 to 10,000. Morgano also noted that small towns had low unionization rates.[52] Numerous studies have called attention to the shift in industrial production from older areas to newer ones that enabled companies to escape unionization and high taxes. While these two factors were undoubtedly major considerations in the corporate boardroom, there was also an awareness that environment played an 'ever-increasing role in facility planning'.[53]

## Factory Image

If plant design and location underwent significant revision in the decades following the Second World War, the representation of mill and factory went even further in redefining these as post-industrial spaces.[54] Corporations considering a change in factory location or the building of a new facility were helped in their decision by the *Site Selection Handbook*. Published three times annually, the *Handbook* surveyed state and provincial industrial incentives and plant financing programs, environmental regulations, and rates of unionization. As its readership included many of the corporate real estate executives and facility planners involved in plant location decisions, the *Handbook* was chock-full of advertisements for places for sale in every corner of Canada and the United States. It is thus an ideal resource for examining the changing image of the factory. An analysis of the advertisements

appearing in the 1972, 1977, and 1982 *Handbooks* confirms the re-emergence of the 'machine in the garden' ideal.[55]

One of the ways that local or state industrial commissions sold property in their areas was to stress the park-like surroundings. Pastoral landscapes awaited the smart corporate manager. One attractive advertisement in this genre was placed by Canadian National Railways. The CNR's ad featured a briefcase-holding executive gazing in wonder down a picturesque river valley towards the snowcapped mountains in the distance. Amid the brilliant oranges and yellows of the autumn landscape, several factories and a dam blend into the idyllic setting. The same message was delivered—though less colourfully—in an advertisement for the Port of Lake Charles, Louisiana, that displayed a factory surrounded by a field of flowers. The caption was as blunt as the image: 'Plants thrive here . . . all year. Give your company roots—here! A growing plant, even a plant branch, needs plenty of fresh water, a healthy warm climate, ample room to grow, and lots of Tender Loving Care!' Both of these advertisements promised firms an industrial location clearly set apart from the traditional industrial landscape.

In other cases, advertisers transformed the relocating factory itself into a plant that formed part of the metaphorical garden. Money may not grow on trees but factories did. San Joaquin County, for example, claimed that, 'We grow all kinds of plants in California where distribution is the key.' This particular variety of vegetation, though, had a cog wheel and an oil barrel as leaves and various transportation networks as its roots.[56] In many advertisements, a natural-looking plant or tree came to represent the factory. Just how hard advertisers worked to cultivate environmentally friendly images is illustrated by captions in the *Site Selection Handbook*: 'We're involved in ecology . . . At Raritan Center it is an integral part of our planning. At Raritan Center it is a pleasure to come to work and watch your business grow. We set out to build an environment for business and industry with a true park-like atmosphere . . .'[57]; and' Among the Nation's Finest Parks . . . Are some we've Reserved for Industry!'[58] In an environmental age the selling of places to industry meant promising a new life in a fresh, green landscape.[59] But once the idea had been planted, how would it grow?

Changing notions of progress in factory design become readily apparent in the corporate images conveyed in *Industrial Development*'s regular 'Million Dollar Plants' column.[60] The editors showcased single-storey, light manufacturing facilities pictured behind beautifully landscaped lawns. While photographic images may have been the ideal medium of corporate self-representation at the beginning of the twentieth century, it was not particularly well-suited to record the beauty of the new generation of post-industrial factories. As a result, many companies turned towards architectural site renderings.

These architectural sketches often situated pale industrial buildings amid rows of trees and bushes and immaculate lawns.[61] Graphic artists usually located these factories and mills in summer's splendour and, whenever possible, invoked high-tech/low-wage 'Southernness' by the kind of vegetation shown.[62] The horizontal lines of the factory flowed into the natural landscape around it,[63] and no other industrial buildings were ever in view, to avoid negative associations with other industrial landscapes. Architects proved so successful in their efforts to distance plants from past associations with 'dark satanic mills' that it is virtually impossible to decipher whether the buildings depicted were actually designed for industrial use. Their large windows and other design features made them indistinguishable from office complexes. The boundaries between factory and office became veiled as the post-industrial aesthetic relocated the factory from an urban, industrial landscape to a rural, natural one.[64]

The absence of human activity was another distinguishing feature of the post-industrial factory depicted in architectural drawings. A great stillness pervades the hundreds of drawings surveyed in *Industrial Development*. Apparently, a post-industrial manufacturing firm no longer needed employees as nearly empty parking lots were common.[65] Even though a drawing of a $7.2 million food-processing plant in Vineland, New Jersey, included space for dozens of cars, there are only six automobiles depicted in the employees' parking lot and three others in executive spaces near the front door (the proportion of cars owned by managers was nothing if not miraculous). For obvious reasons, it proved harder to visually reconfigure an assembly plant or a steel mill as an office complex. Yet the natural bearing of these industrial developments did not prevent imaginative graphic artists from trying. Caterpillar's 585,000-square-foot Mount Joly, Illinois, plant, for example, was cloaked in tree-lined avenues and landscaped lawns.

The cover of the March 1975 issue of *Industrial Development* dedicated to industrial parks presented a similar picture. In the campus-like setting of the industrial park, industrial buildings were obscured by a tree-lined avenue with attractive street lights at the centre of the drawing. Again, the absence of workers is striking. Other sketches of industrial parks such as the one depicting Lusk Industrial/Business Park in Newport Beach, California, showed orderly rows of square, one-storey buildings with tree-lined streets and a handful of cars.[66] Shown from a bird's-eye view, the Orange County, California, airport-industrial park evoked an image of prairie homesteads, with trees circling each building.[67] Conversely, the proposed Airpark at Dallas/Fort Worth appeared almost stately with its treed avenues and impressive buildings. Industrial land was being reinvented everywhere, at least in the imaginative realm.

## Behind the Facade of the Post-Industrial Factory

An important internal dialogue of images and text exists in *Industrial Development* that researchers such as David Nye have not considered in their own studies of image world.[68] A close reading of the text that accompanied architectural sketches and photographs reveals a world view that differed dramatically from the modesty of the images. Much like the booster rhetoric of the 1910s, the written descriptions of the modern 'Million Dollar Plants' stressed their physical grandeur (the bigger the better) and the size of investment (the more the mightier):

> New modular housing production facility at Gulfport, Miss., for Stirling Homex Corp., will have world's largest capacity, producing 100 units daily.

> Progresso Foods has a $7.2 million food processing plant under construction in Vineland, New Jersey.

> Union Bottling Works of Houston recently opened a 197,000-sq. Ft. Plant on a 20-acre tract for bottling Pepsi-Cola products. The $3.8 million facility, largest soft drink bottling plant in the world, will turn out 1.7 million soft drinks per day.

As the subtext to these images reveals, the editors of *Industrial Development* continued to measure progress in quantifiable terms by showcasing the number of mills or factories, their assessed value, and the value of manufacturing. While the images seemed to illustrate that factories had broken with their past negative associations, the texts continued to emphasize the size of investments. Evidently, the philosophy of growth remained intact behind the facade of the post-industrial factory.

Beneath the mantle of green, the rational factory persisted, save that its ownership was more distant than ever before. In fact, the twentieth-century shift from civic capitalism to national or global capitalism profoundly altered the world view of corporate executives. In the early twentieth century, business had been rooted in the local community and looked for status, honour, and brides from that community.[69] While these locally derived and intensely personal relationships had not prevented conflict, 'they bounded and channelled it, humanized it, and obstructed that abstraction and generalization from experience that could constitute class consciousness.'[70] By the 1960s, however, civic capitalism became moribund as the locus of ownership shifted. The result proved disastrous for industrial cities such as Trenton when the entrepreneurial owner of an earlier era was replaced by absentee capitalists.[71] One by one, the Trentons of the world lost control over their economies.

Concurrently, the locus of power and influence within industrial enterprises shifted from operational managers to 'finance men'. These splits are revealed through the business philosophies of W. Lawrence Weeks, who worked his way up the corporate ladder over 31 years to become vice-president of operations at Republic Steel, and David Roderick, the head of US Steel. In an oral history interview recorded in 1990, Weeks expressed his disillusionment with the upper echelons of Republic that increasingly consisted of 'legal-minded' or 'numbers-minded' individuals rather than persons with steel-making experience. Indeed, he came to use the label 'steelmen' to differentiate those like himself from the new breed of 'top managers' with no operating experience.[72]

The situation obviously appeared altogether different from the perspective of those at the top. Interviewed by Ralph Nader in his spacious office on the sixty-first floor of the US Steel building in Pittsburgh's Golden Triangle, David Roderick freely admitted that he did not consider himself to be a 'steelman'.[73] Instead, he claimed to be in the business of making money. Roderick's distance from the factory floor surfaced repeatedly in the interview. When closing steel mills and terminating tens of thousands of employees, Roderick took into account neither employees' loyalty nor their personal attachment to the company. Instead, he insisted that the interest of 'the steelworker' took a back seat to that of 'the shareholder': 'He's not looking at it from the standpoint of management, which has to manage assets in the best interests of the shareholders, but with total sensitivity to employees. To, in effect, sell them and reinvest them in a business that is earning four percent when I can take them and put them in a business that is earning twelve percent . . . I mean, why would I do that? I don't get paid to do that. That's not what shareholders expect.'[74] The differing viewpoints of Weeks and Roderick confirm historian Alfred Chandler's contention that top managers' lack of experience with technological processes such as steel-making contributed to a breakdown in communication between head office and the operating divisions of conglomerates.[75] Sharon Zukin likewise found that the removal or sidelining of steel men from the upper echelons of the big American steel companies cleared the way for radical restructuring and diversification out of steel.[76] Shareholders wanted a bigger return on their investment than traditional steel men could deliver. As a result, the origins of industrial decline lay in the long-term processes of abstraction and internationalization.[77]

The accelerating pace of change and the expanding scope of social relations have transformed how individuals view the world. Anthony Giddens sees social relations being transformed by global interconnectedness and the 'grip of local circumstances' over people's lives being diminished, disembedded through the process he calls social 'distanciation'.[78] Geographer David Harvey and historian Stephen Kern have examined how sweeping changes in technology and culture have resulted in time-space compression and created 'distinctive modes of thinking about and experiencing time and space'.[79] And yet, as British geographer Doreen Massey rightly points out, globalization affects people in unique ways. For corporate executives used to instant communication and jet-setting the world might indeed have become a smaller place. However, those on the factory floor in North America were in no position to benefit from the global changes occurring around them.[80]

By the 1970s, the social divide and physical distance between corporate executives and hourly wage workers had grown as social relations became more distant. The development of industrial capitalism cut the ties between corporations and localities, as managers expanded into new markets and new product lines, making the single-unit manufacturer an oddity in most industries.[81] Behind the more agreeable mask of the post-industrial plant hid a corporation increasingly unwilling to put down roots. Portrayed as a plant or a tree in a suburban garden, the post-industrial factory had in fact become much less rooted than an earlier generation of polluting factories.

## Conclusion: Greening the Factory

In the past two centuries, North American industrialism has come full circle, from the garden to the city and back again. This shifting metaphor of production reveals a lingering belief that the factory system can be redeemed through close contact with nature. Manufacturers hoped to regenerate their faded reputations by designing new factories to look like low-lying office buildings. Managers of industrial parks adopted strict environmental regulations requiring that these areas look like suburban landscapes and not industrial ones. In addition, visual images published by industrial firms and development agencies presented the manufacturing plant as part of the natural landscape. Historian Stephen V. Ward observed that this shifting location has been accompanied by a new iconography of industry: 'The factory chimneys have finally gone; the cog wheels very nearly so. A new manufacturing imagery based on the computer and the electronic circuit has taken their place.'[82] Corporations redesigned the public face of the factory in the second half of the twentieth century to conform to an emerging post-industrial aesthetic often associated with the new economy of high technology and service. It may be useful to consider industrial transformation in terms of a new aesthetic of industry, rather than simply a shift from an old industrial economy to a new post-industrial one. Even though this aesthetic paid tribute to environmental concerns, the subtext continued to emphasize the size of factories and the return on investments. It appears that this image of quiet good taste camouflaged, and perhaps even legitimated, corporate efforts to abandon unionized labour in the cities. Behind the post-industrial facade, the growth ideology maintained its hold on a new generation of corporate managers who had little loyalty to people, place, or product.

## Notes

1. Manuel Castells and Peter Hall, *Technopoles of the World: The Making of 21st Century Industrial Complexes* (London: Routledge, 1994), 1.

2. Changes in production in earlier eras have sometimes produced 'a new aesthetic of industry'. See David E. Nye, *American Technological Sublime* (Cambridge, Mass.: MIT Press, 1994), 107. A post-industrial aesthetic thus infuses Castells and Hall's judgement of 'quiet good taste'.

3. Samuel P. Hayes, *Beauty, Health, and Permanence: Environmental Politics in the United States, 1955–1985* (Cambridge: Cambridge University Press, 1987), 2–3.

4. Progress has often been understood as the conquest of nature. See, for example, Richard White, 'The Nature of Progress: Progress and the Environment', in Leo Marx and Bruce Mazlish, eds, *Progress: Fact or Illusion* (Ann Arbor: University of Michigan Press, 1996), 121.

5. The collapsing of the division between the new and old economies has its antecedent in the various attempts at an urban-rural synthesis. James L. Machor, *Pastoral Cities: Urban Ideals and the Symbolic Landscape of America* (Madison: University of Wisconsin Press, 1987).

6. The American Society for the Encouragement of Domestic Manufacturers (1817) quoted in Thomas Bender, *Toward an Urban Vision: Ideas and Institutions in Nineteenth-Century America*

(Lexington: University Press of Kentucky, 1975), 19.

7. Thomas Jefferson quoted in Bender, *Toward an Urban Vision,* 19.

8. Americans in the early republic apparently saw no contradiction between their 'professed love of nature' and their 'passionate embrace of the machine'. See John F. Kasson, *Civilizing the Machine: Technology and Republican Values in America, 1776–1900* (New York: Hill & Wang, 1999 [1976]), 8, 174.

9. Donald Worster, *Nature's Economy: A History of Ecological Ideas* (Cambridge: Cambridge University Press, 1994), esp. ch. 2.

10. A connection between the 'garden setting' and the ascendant English middle class is drawn in Leonore Davidoff and Catherine Hall, *Family Fortunes: Men and Women of the English Middle Class, 1780–1850* (Chicago: University of Chicago Press, 1987), 370.

11. Ramsay Cook, '1492 and All That: Making a Garden out of a Wilderness', in Chad Gaffield and Pam Gaffield, eds, *Consuming Canada: Readings in Environmental History* (Toronto: Copp Clark, 1995), 62, 69–73.

12. Daniel Nelson, *Managers and Workers: Origins of the Twentieth-Century Factory System in the United States, 1880–1920* (Madison: University of Wisconsin Press, 1995). An outstanding study of the environmental effects of this early phase of industrialization can be found in Theodore Steinberg, *Nature Incorporated: Industrialization and the Waters of New England* (Amherst: University of Massachusetts Press, 1991).

13. Traveller Alexander MacKay quoted in Marvin Fisher, *Workshops in the Wilderness: The European Response to American Industrialization, 1830–1860* (Oxford: Oxford University Press, 1967), 93.

14. Ibid., 92.

15. Marianne Doezema, *American Realism and the Industrial Age* (Cleveland: Cleveland Museum of Art, 1980), 36.

16. For a discussion of rationalization, see Lindy Biggs, *The Rational Factory: Architecture, Technology, and Work in America's Age of Mass Production*

(Baltimore: Johns Hopkins University Press, 1996), 6. Biggs writes that: 'rationalization in industry has a more specific meaning: it refers to the introduction of predictability and order—machinelike order—that eliminates all questions of how work is to be done, who will do it, and when it will be done. The rational factory, then, is a factory that runs like a machine.'

17. The massive River Rouge complex on the outskirts of Detroit was comprised of 23 main buildings, 93 miles of track, 53,000 machines and 75,000 employees. David L. Lewis, *The Public Image of Henry Ford: An American Folk Hero and His Company* (Detroit: Wayne State University Press, 1976), 160. The two other major studies of factory design are Grant Hildebrand, *Designing for Industry: The Architecture of Albert Kahn* (Cambridge, Mass.: MIT Press, 1974), and David A. Hounshell, *From the American System to Mass Production: The Development of Manufacturing Technology in the United States, 1800–1932* (Baltimore: Johns Hopkins University Press, 1984). Unfortunately, there is still no equivalent study of factory architecture in Canada.

18. For more on Charles Sheeler, see Miles Orvell, *After the Machine: Visual Arts and the Erasing of Cultural Boundaries* (Jackson: University Press of Mississippi, 1995) and Karen Lucie, *Charles Sheeler and the Cult of the Machine* (Cambridge, Mass.: Harvard University Press, 1991).

19. Daniel Bell, *The Coming of Post-Industrial Society: A Venture in Social Forecasting* (New York: Basic Books, 1976 [1973]), 37. The post-industrial label was further popularized by Alvin Toffler's best-selling *The Third Wave* (New York: William Morrow, 1980). However, the post-industrial idea is not without its critics. Fred Block has concluded that the post-industrial label is mainly used as a 'relatively empty synonym for modernity'. See *Postindustrial Possibilities: A Critique of Economic Discourse* (Berkeley: University of California Press, 1990).

20. The origins and implications of technological progress are explored in Merritt Roe Smith and Leo Marx, eds, *Does Technology Drive History? The Dilemma of Technological Determinism* (Cambridge, Mass.: MIT Press, 1994).

21. Michael L. Smith, 'Recourse of Empire: Landscapes of Progress in Technological America: in Smith and Marx, eds, *Does Technology Drive History?* For a cross-disciplinary discussion of the iconography of landscape, see Denis Cosgrove and Stephen Daniels, eds, *The Iconography of Landscape: Essays on the Symbolic Representation, Design and Uses of Past Environments* (New York: Cambridge University Press, 1988). Sharon Zukin has noted that an industrial landscape was a 'moral order' in *Landscapes of Power: From Detroit to Disney World* (Berkeley: University of California Press, 1991), 254–6.

22. Joel A. Tarr, *The Search for the Ultimate Sink: Urban Pollution in Historical Perspective* (Akron: University of Akron Press, 1996), xxx.

23. Editorial, *Industrial Development* (Nov.–Dec. 1972), 2–6.

24. Daniel Patrick Moynihan, 'The Federal Government and the Economy of New York State' (15 July 1977), 6.

25. David Proulx, *Pardon My Lunch Bucket: A Look at the New Hamilton . . . With a Bit of the Old Thrown In* (Hamilton: City of Hamilton, 1971), i.

26. Ibid.

27. Windsor was hurt by its reputation as a 'Blue Collar' town according to 30 per cent of respondents, by 'No Jobs' in 29 per cent, by being 'Too American' in 16 per cent, by 'Bad Press' in 2 per cent, and by people 'Leaving City' in 5 per cent. The city's opinion leaders were even more likely to point to the city's 'lunch bucket' image than ordinary residents. Donald J. MacTavish, ed., *Windsor and Essex County Blueprint for a Brighter Tomorrow* (Windsor: Windsor Star, 1982).

28. Allison Zippay, *From Middle Income to Poor: Downward Mobility among Displaced Steelworkers* (New York: Praeger, 1991), 2–3.

29. Stuart Hall, 'The Question of Cultural Identity', in Stuart Hall, David Held, and Kenneth Thompson, eds, *Modernity: An Introduction to*

*Modern Societies* (Oxford: Blackwell Publishers, 1997), 596.

30. In a commissioned history of Eaton Corporation, the old alienating urban factories of the 1960s were compared to the 'new environment' created at the company's plant in rural Nebraska. As the company president notes in his preface to the book, Eaton was 'constantly creating, and recreating, the workplaces'. Donald N. Scobel, *Creative Worklife* (London: Gulf Publishing Company, 1981), ix, 1–3.

31. Gordon B. Carson, ed., *Production Handbook* (New York: Ronald Press, 1958), 32. See also Nye, *American Technological Sublime*, 107–12.

32. 'An Enlightened Look at a Factory' (c. 1948), reprinted in Architectural Record, *Building for Industry: An Architectural Record Book* (Westport, Conn.: Greenwood Press, 1972), 15.

33. See, for example, Frank L. Whitney, 'Newer Trends in Industrial Buildings', in ibid., 3.

34. Ibid., 2.

35. Michael F. Roberts, 'Building For Industry', *Industrial Canada* (Dec. 1970), 31.

36. James M. Moore, *Plant Layout and Design* (New York: Macmillan, 1962), 71.

37. K.G. Lockyer, *Factory and Production Management* (London: Pitman, 1974 [1962]), 92–3.

38. 'Factors Affecting Industrial Building Design' (c. 1954), reprinted in Architectural Record, *Building for Industry*, 8–9.

39. 'The Canadian Plant of the 70s: No.1—Plant Engineering', *Industrial Canada* (Feb. 1970): 15.

40. The post-industrial facade was very much on display in the pages of *Canadian Architect*. See, for example, 'Levi Strauss Manufacturing Plant, Stoney Creek, Ontario', *Canadian Architect* 26, 10 (1981).

41. Minesinger to H.H. Leckler and Leckler to Minesinger, 6 Sept. 1978, Acme Cleveland Corp. (1969–1982), container 5, folder 76, Western Reserve Historical Society Archives (WRHS).

42. Ian Duke, interview by author, Windsor, 27 Feb. 1998.

43. Robert Lewis, 'Running Rings around the City: North American Industrial Suburbs, 1850–1950', in Richard Harris and Peter J. Larkham, eds, *Changing Suburbs: Foundation, Form and Function* (London: E. & F.N. Spon, 1999), 148.

44. David C. McNary, 'Industrial Parks: If They're Well-planned, They're Profitable', *Industrial Development* (Mar.–Apr. 1970): 7–11.

45. Ibid., 10.

46. A survey of industrial park owners found that nine in ten regulated the aesthetics of industrial buildings and property. Linda Liston, 'Proliferating Industrial Parks Spark Plant Location Revolution', *Industrial Development* (Mar.–Apr. 1970): 7–11.

47. Advertisement, 'A "Custom-Made" Industrial Site?', *Industrial Canada* (Apr. 1969): 69.

48. 'See How They Grow: A Survey of Industrial Park Development Trends', *Industrial Development* (July–Aug. 1978): 13.

49. A 1975 survey found that manufacturers in the following sectors were most likely to relocate to industrial parks: food, electrical, appliances, tires, and distribution warehouses. Van G. Whaler, 'What Are Today's Industrial Parks Like?', *Industrial Development* (July–Aug. 1975): 21–3.

50. Moore, *Plant Layout and Design*, 37.

51. Pete J. Barber, 'The Site Selection Process at Honeywell', *Industrial Development* (Nov.–Dec. 1982): 9.

52. Del Morgano, 'Organizing for Facility Planning and Real Estate Management, part 1, The One Man Operation', *Industrial Development* (Mar.–Apr. 1979): 18–19.

53. Editorial, *Site Selection Handbook* (1972), 2.

54. Early twentieth-century factory owners used the common artistic formula of exaggerated edifices to convey 'heroic size' in their publicity. See Dominic T. Alessio, 'Capitalist Realist Art: Industrial Images of Hamilton, Ontario, 1884–1910', *Journal of Urban History* 18, 4 (1992): 442.

55. In 1972, the editors of the *Handbook* began a separate and unique volume covering environmental factors and design. *Site Selection Handbook: Industry's Guide to Geo-Economic Planning* (1972), 2.

56. Advertisement, *Site Selection Handbook* (1972), 43.

57. Advertisement for Raritan Center Industrial Park in Newark, New Jersey, ibid., 124.

58. St Louis-San Francisco Railway Company advertisement, ibid. (1977).

59. Other selling points included the availability of reliable non-union workers, a central location (often used by representatives of older industrial areas), and great historical events and icons. Thus, Boston pilgrims vied with Daniel Boone and coonskin-capped pioneers for the attention of corporate executives.

60. An image analysis of factories showcased in this column between 1969 and 1984 was conducted. Virtually identical visual images can be found in *Industrial Canada*, the newsletter of the Metropolitan Toronto Industrial Commission, and the photographic archives of Windsor's Industrial Commission. Windsor-Essex County Development Commission Records, MS 42, Windsor Municipal Archives (WMA).

61. See the architectural drawing of the Applied Devices Corporation plant in Orlando, Florida. *Industrial Development* (Mar.–Apr. 1976): 27.

62. See the drawing of the Westinghouse Electric Corporation plant in Coral Springs, Florida. Ibid. (May–June 1978): 25.

63. Ibid. (Mar.–Apr. 1970): 29.

64. Historian Bryan Palmer wryly observed that the proposed Goodyear Tire plant in Napanee, Ontario, was depicted as a kind of resort. Landscaped lawns and trees made the atmosphere 'deceptively congenial'. Bryan D. Palmer, *Capitalism Comes to the Backcountry: The Goodyear Invasion of Napanee* (Toronto: Between the Lines, 1994), 147.

65. *Industrial Development* (Mar.–Apr. 1971): 30.

66. Ibid. (Jan.–Feb. 1975): 30.

67. Ibid. (Jan.–Feb. 1974): 26.

68. David E. Nye, *Image Worlds: Corporate Identities at General Electric, 1890–1930* (Cambridge, Mass.: MIT Press, 1985).

69. Donald F. Davis, *Conspicuous Production: Automobiles and Elites in Detroit, 1899–1933* (Philadelphia: Temple University Press, 1988), x; John N. Ingham, *The Iron Barons: A Social Analysis of an American Urban Elite, 1874–1965* (Westport, Conn.: Greenwood Press, 1977), xviii; Philip Scranton, 'Large Firms and Industrial Restructuring: The Philadelphia Region, 1900–1980', *Pennsylvania Magazine of History and Biography* 116, 4 (1992): 419, 461–2.

70. Philip Scranton, *Proprietary Capitalism: The Textile Manufacturer at Philadelphia* (Cambridge: Cambridge University Press, 1983), 418.

71. John T. Cumbler, *A Social History of Economic Decline: Business, Politics and Work in Trenton* (New Brunswick, NJ: Rutgers University Press, 1989), 7.

72. W. Lawrence Weeks, interview by Donna DeBlasio, Youngstown, 1991. See also interview with Tom Cleary, vice-president of operations by Youngstown Sheet & Tube, 20 Sept. 1991. The videotapes are held at the Youngstown Historical Center for Industry and Labor.

73. Ralph Nader and William Taylor, *The Big Boys: Power and Position in American Business* (New York: Pantheon Books, 1986), 13.

74. Ibid., 60–1.

75. Alfred Chandler, *Scale and Scope: The Dynamics of Industrial Capitalism* (Cambridge, Mass.: Belknap Press of Harvard University Press, 1990), 622–3.

76. Zukin, *Landscapes of Power*, 74.

77. Ibid., 256.

78. Anthony Giddens, *The Consequences of Modernity* (Stanford, Calif.: Stanford University Press, 1990), 16–19.

79. Stephen Kern, *The Culture of Time and Space, 1880–1918* (Cambridge, Mass.: Harvard University Press, 1983), 2–3. David Harvey, 'On the History and Present Condition of Geography: An Historical Geography Manifesto', *Professional Geographer* 36 (1984): 1–11.

80. Doreen Massey, 'A Global Sense of Place', *Marxism Today* (June 1991): 25–6.

81. Chandler, *Scale and Scope*, 607.

82. Stephen V. Ward, *Selling Places: The Marketing and Promotion of Towns and Cities, 1850–2000* (London: Routledge, 1998), 182.

# 16

# Visualizing Work

From the late nineteenth century to the present day, employers have used photographs and other visual materials for a wide variety of purposes. Public relations departments employed such images not only to sell products or services, but also to project their own workers and work spaces as healthy, happy, and inviting. Since the vast majority of historical images of waged work are handed down to us from company archives or originated as commissioned material by employers, historians need to be aware that such representations of labour are inherently problematic. All of the images in this section share this concern, since all of them are formal representations of waged work. Although such illustrations can shed some light on the organization of work space, it is important to be aware that whether these images are embodied in advertisements or photographs, it is the company's point of view that is being presented to the public.

In addition to the specific questions below, it is worthwhile considering some of the broader issues of absence in these images. What kinds of work were not typically photographed or advertised? How might workers themselves have represented their own work differently? Where does unwaged labour fit into our visual understanding of work?

## Series 1: Industrial Spaces

The process of industrialization transformed the Canadian economy in the late nineteenth century, but industrial work spaces continued to evolve well into the twentieth century. The scale of industrial production expanded dramatically as industries consolidated, built increasingly larger factories, and turned to 'scientific' management techniques that 'rationalized' the workforce. Rather than being dispersed across many different sites, work was centralized by industrial architects who designed large-scale workplaces that brought together power plants, machine shops, manufacturing, and transportation facilities.

The following images were published in a glossy corporate brochure promoting Algoma Steel, based in Sault Ste Marie, Ontario. Very little text accompanied the images, which were intended to portray the company's extensive assets and demonstrate large-scale capacity for potential investors and customers. Since the company commissioned all of these photographs, it is important to consider how the camera directs our view, and what principles are being embodied by the cultural aesthetics of the photographer.

1. In its 1938 promotional material, the majority of images published by Algoma Steel were external images of buildings, as shown in Figures 1 and 2. Carefully examine the perspective and camera angles of these two images. What message is being presented about the company?
2. Figures 3 and 4 offer different perspectives on the interior working spaces of Algoma Steel. What purpose do these images of interior spaces serve?
3. Examining all of the photographs in this series, what role do workers play? Where do they appear and how is their relationship to the machinery of the industrial workplace portrayed?

## Series 2: Selling Service

With the introduction of Pullman sleeping cars in the late nineteenth century, Canadian railways started to employ black porters to offer service to first-class passengers. While some were recruited from the United States and the Caribbean, many African Canadians also found employment in this position. Porters were responsible for cleaning, stocking, and heating or cooling the cars, as well taking care of the needs of their passengers. Their duties could range from polishing shoes to mixing drinks to caring for those suffering motion sickness. Although black railwaymen performed a wide variety of jobs for Canadian railways, their most public role was as porters, a position that was racially defined by the turn of the century.[1] Black porters remained a significant presence on railways even after World War II, as demonstrated by these four photographs taken in the late 1940s or 1950s as publicity material for Canadian National Railways.

1. How can you tell that these photographs (Figures 5–8) are staged, rather than simply snapshots of everyday life?
2. Examine the sequence of the four photographs. What is the narrative or story that the company is trying to portray? Why would CN want to link the porter's home life with his work?
3. In these photographs, how are the spaces of home and work gendered? How do these representations of black porters compare with Pamela Sugiman's analysis of masculinity and black auto workers?
4. What was the audience for such images? How might people have read these photographs differently in the 1950s from how we might interpret them today?

## Series 3: Business at Work

In the first decades of the twentieth century, a revolution in corporate management and administration led to a dramatic expansion of paperwork, from general records and book-keeping to marketing and investment management. Although Canada's population rose by one-third between 1901 and 1911, clerical workers as a profession grew by more than 80 per cent and numbered over 100,000. Such a rapid growth was only possible by allowing large numbers of women into what had formerly been a male work space. As the 'feminization' of clerical work proceeded, men found themselves struggling to define new codes of masculinity that stressed the 'rationality' of business.

Women did not, however, enter on equal terms. Employed for less pay and blocked from career advancement, women clerical workers were often viewed as transitory, entering the workforce as young adults but expected to withdraw once they were married. As Kathryn McPherson points out in her study of nurses and nursing (Chapter 12), the public visibility of office workers also raised questions regarding sexuality, dress, and outward appearance.

Figures 9 and 10 offer contrasting images of two Montreal offices, one from 1924 and one from the late 1950s or early 1960s. The changing technologies of the workplace are evident in both photographs, and are the subject of Figure 11, an advertisement for Gestetner.

1. Comparing Figures 9 and 10, what similarities and differences do you find in the physical layout of office space?
2. From Figures 9 and 10, how is the physical space within the office gendered? How does the spatial ordering of the office reflect the hierarchical relations between those who work within it?
3. In its advertisement (Figure 11), how does Gestetner use body language and positioning to sell copy machines? How are the roles of office workers and managers gendered, both in the image and in the text?

## Note

1. Sarah-Jane (Saje) Mathieu, 'North of the Colour Line: Sleeping Car Porters and the Battle against Jim Crow on Canadian Rails, 1880–1920', *Labour/Le Travail* 47 (Spring 2001): 9–41.

**Figure 1.** 'New Coke Oven Battery', *Algoma Steel Corporation Limited: Its Works and Properties, June, 1938* (Sault Ste Marie: Algoma Steel, 1938), 25.

**Figure 2.** 'Machine Shop and Tool Room', *Algoma Steel Corporation Limited: Its Works and Properties, June, 1938* (Sault Ste Marie: Algoma Steel, 1938), 49.

**Figure 3.** 'Teeming Heat of Steel into Ingot Moulds', *Algoma Steel Corporation Limited: Its Works and Properties, June, 1938* (Sault Ste Marie: Algoma Steel, 1938), 34.

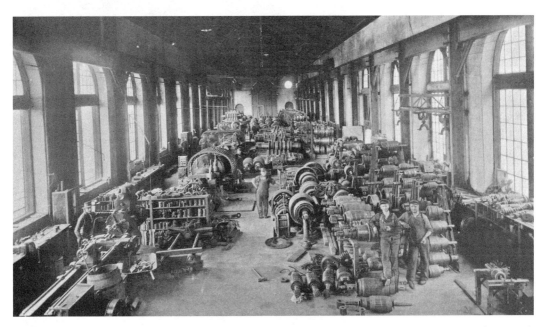

**Figure 4.** 'Roll Shop', *Algoma Steel Corporation Limited: Its Works and Properties, June, 1938* (Sault Ste Marie: Algoma Steel, 1938), 53.

**Figure 5.** CN porter and family at table. Canadian Science and Technology Museum, CSTM/CN collection/Musée des sciences et de la technologie du Canada, MSTC/CN collection, image 49315-2.

**Figure 6.** CN porter and family at doorstep. Canadian Science and Technology Museum, CSTM/CN collection/Musée des sciences et de la technologie du Canada, MSTC/CN collection, image 49315.

**Figure 7.** CN porter on train. Canadian Science and Technology Museum, CSTM/CN collection/Musée des sciences et de la technologie du Canada, MSTC/CN collection, image 49315-8.

**Figure 8.** CN porter at work. Canadian Science and Technology Museum, CSTM/CN collection/Musée des sciences et de la technologie du Canada, MSTC/CN collection, image 39403.

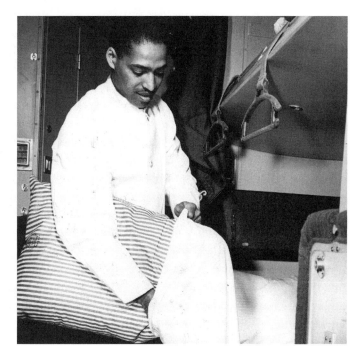

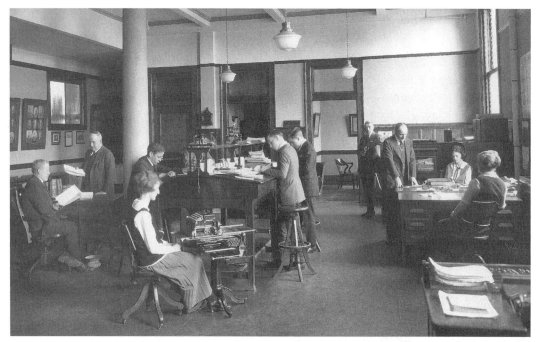

**Figure 9.** An office in Montreal, 1924, Wm. Notman & Son. McCord Museum, Montreal, VIEW–21089.

**Figure 10.** Office, c. 1950s–1960s. Canadian Science and Technology Museum, CSTM/CN collection/Musée des sciences et de la technologie du Canada, MSTC/CN collection, image 55246.

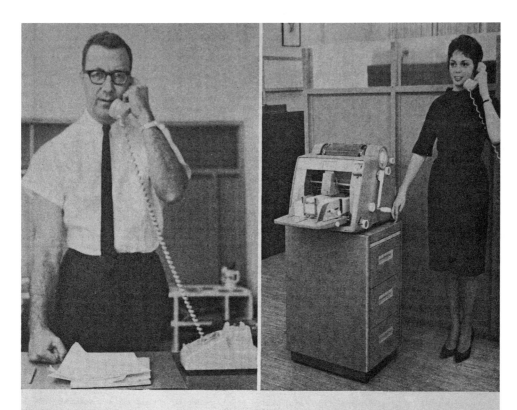

## Clean, Clear Copies?

### Spotless. Clean Fingers, too!

Boss and Girl-Friday both like Gestetner—and that's important! He likes its clear, "printlike" reproduction.  She likes running it without getting ink on hands or dress.

Anyone can get good results with Gestetner. Setting up the job—from a one-page letter to a price list illustrated in colours—is easy and clean.  Operation is so automatic that she can "set it and forget it".  But don't you forget to use our coupon!

*Gestetner*

1924 · Forty Proud Years in Canada · 1964

Makers of the **complete** duplicating line

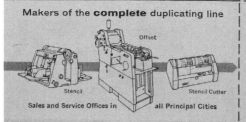

Offset

Stencil

Stencil Cutter

Sales and Service Offices in    all Principal Cities

GESTETNER  849 Don Mills Road, Don Mills, Ontario

☐ Please send me your new Portfolio of Specimens of Gestetner work, applicable to my business.

☐ I would like to see your machines for myself. Please arrange.

Name_____

Address_____

_____

Business_____  ME-1-8-64

**Figure 11.**  Gestetner, 'Clean, Clear Copies?', *Macleans*, 8 Nov. 1964.

# PART III

# At Play

While the social history of home and work emerged as serious fields of research in the 1970s, the social history of play only moved into the mainstream of scholarly study in the late 1980s and early 1990s. Historians of home and work had certainly mentioned leisure activities, such as sport and tavern life, but these were considered only a part of some other history of family, class, gender, or ethnicity. Indeed, it is significant that the history of sport in Canada emerged from university kinesiology and physical education programs rather than history departments. In the 1990s, the history of play moved from the background to the foreground of Canadian social history. This was a move inspired, in part, by the work of cultural anthropologists who convinced historians that the ways in which a society plays and the rules that govern that play reveal much about the structures of social organization. By the end of the 1990s, our understanding of Canadian social history was enriched by the study of spaces such as roller rinks, exhibitions, tourist destinations, and sporting fields.[1]

This historiographical development now makes it both possible and necessary for a reader of Canadian social history to suggest answers to what might appear to be a rather basic question: what has it meant, historically, for Canadians to 'play'? In the articles that follow, the social history of 'play' refers to the social history of leisure, of recreation, of having fun. This might include a wide range of activities, such as attending boxing matches or putting on community theatre. But the meanings of 'play' are far more complex and deep than the pure joy of fun. For example, small-town lacrosse fields, gaming houses, and pubs were all spaces subjected to the anxious watching of those who worried about what these spaces were doing to the moral, spiritual, and physical health of both individual bodies and the nation.

The concept of play as a social space is complicated by the fact that it overlaps many of the areas of study we have already examined. What functioned as leisure for some people served as work for others, while some forms of recreation were framed as proper pursuits within the home. These essays, therefore, offer an opportunity for readers to question the very division of these worlds, and to examine how play was constituted by the shifting relations between home and work.

This section covers the period 1870–1970, for this was a century of historical change that reorganized the daily lives of Canadians in such a way that leisure time became something scheduled on official and personal calendars. The change was most dramatic for Canada's working classes. In this period, unions advocated and obtained nine-hour work-days, then 40-hour weeks, and finally paid vacations, accomplishments that increasingly and explicitly set aside time for activities not based at work or home. The invention of the 'week-end' and the transformation of summer from a season of intense labour to one of mixed labour and recreation, in addition to the transportation revolution of rail and then the automobile, saw an increasing number of Canadians go to the beach, take a trip, attend a hockey game, and become more visible in the popular culture of Canadian towns and cities. This should not be construed, however, as a golden era of working-class recreation. While access and opportunity certainly grew between the late nineteenth and late twentieth centuries, so, too, did surveillance and regulation.

From 1870 to 1970 there was much hand-wringing by the governing classes about the leisure activities of workers and youth. In the last decades of the nineteenth century in particular, 'good' activities, such as amateur sport and strawberry socials, were expected to ward off the potential immorality and evils of 'bad' activities, such as drinking, smoking, and masturbation. The concern of middle-class reformers in this period was primarily for the bodily and moral health of individuals. By the early twentieth century, however, the distinctions made between moral and immoral forms of recreation and leisure increasingly involved the state, as governments at all levels—federal, provincial, and local—introduced new forms of laws, licensing, and inspection in an effort to govern who was playing, when they were playing, and where they were playing. Unlike the late 1800s, when 'good' activities were perceived as a means for improving individuals, after 1900 reformers and the state increasingly sought to improve the moral and physical health of the social body as a whole. As the readings included here demonstrate, recreation and leisure were taken very seriously by government throughout the twentieth century, a pattern we still see in our own lives today.

While the authors in this section are attuned to the importance of gender, ethnicity, race, class, and age as social variables, they also demonstrate that the spaces of 'play' brought together peoples of different backgrounds and social positions. While not everyone engaged in recreation and leisure the same way, one could make the argument that, more so than home and work, 'play' seems to have been more socially inclusive. But how open were spaces like fishing holes and pubs? How did leisure and recreational activities create boundaries of community that included but also excluded at the same time? What did contemporaries think about these communities of play, especially those that featured people of different ethnic or racial identity, from different classes, and from both sexes? Such questions help make clear that having fun in Canada has been fundamental to the experience of social history, but it has also been central to the formation of and struggle over Canadian identities.

## Note

1.   See, for example, Colin Howell, *Northern Sandlots: A Social History of Maritime Baseball* (Toronto: University of Toronto Press, 1995); Lynne Marks, *Revivals and Roller Rinks: Religion, Leisure, and Identity in Late Nineteenth-Century Small-Town Ontario* (Toronto: University of Toronto Press, 1996); Ian McKay, *The Quest of the Folk: Antimodernism and Cultural Selection in Twentieth-Century Nova Scotia* (Montreal and Kingston: McGill-Queen's University Press, 1994); Keith Walden, *Becoming Modern in Toronto: The Industrial Exhibition and the Shaping of a Late Victorian Culture* (Toronto: University of Toronto Press, 1997).

# 17

# Lacrosse: Idealized Middle-Class Sport for Youth

### Nancy Bouchier

In June 1871, the neophyte players of Ingersoll's Shamrock lacrosse club devoted themselves to learning their new fast-paced sport. As if out of nowhere, lacrosse arrived in town as the first wave of local baseball mania floundered. The Shamrocks practised assiduously, learning the difficult throwing, catching, and dodging skills needed to play lacrosse. Pleased with their progress, but realizing that they didn't have anyone to play against, they challenged the baseball players from the then-retired Victoria baseball club, taunting them 'to awake from their lethargy and take up the lacrosse stick' for a Dominion Day match.[1] Accustomed to having good holiday sport, townspeople relished the chance to get a glimpse of their old heroes and the new sport of lacrosse at the same time. Some three thousand townspeople thronged to the unusual event to witness their town's newest representative team, a good-looking group of young athletes dressed in smart blue and white uniforms donated by local merchants Holmes and Gillespie.

What townspeople saw on the playing field, however, looked more like a bloodbath than respectable sport. Being totally unfamiliar with lacrosse, the more competitively experienced Victorias resorted to violent physical force to van-quish the younger though more highly skilled opponents. This brutish modus operandi, labelled 'a gross libel upon lacrosse, and an outrage upon common sense', drew criticism from community members and the press for being 'cowardly and unmanly'.[2] Directing harsh words at the offenders, a writer in the *Chronicle* commented sarcastically, 'We would suggest that lacrosse is a game entirely distinct from either football or shinny, and that it has certain rules, the strict observance of which are the very essence of the game.'[3] The bewildered Victorias learned this essence at the expense of their competitive pride. They found organized lacrosse quite unlike their more familiar game of baseball, a game for which they had—briefly—won the Silver Ball and Canadian championship. Many people—males and females alike—knew the popular childhood game of baseball well, having experienced it as players or spectators. Lacrosse, however, seemed to appear out of the blue, carried along on the momentum of baseball mania stirred up by sports reformers and urban boosters. Picking up where baseball left off, lacrosse captivated the hearts of local sporting enthusiasts in both towns eager to be entertained through sport: as the *Sentinel* observed, 'with the loss of the late lamented Silver Ball lacrosse seems

Nancy Bouchier, 'Lacrosse: Idealized Middle-Class Sport for Youth', in *For the Love of the Game: Amateur Sport in Small-Town Ontario, 1838–1895*. McGill-Queen's University Press, 2003. Reprinted by permission of McGill-Queen's University Press.

to be favoured game this season.'[4] That lacrosse had none of the stigma associated with cricket helped its appeal to urban boosters and sport reformers alike.

Despite its lengthy tradition in North American Indian religion, tradition, and society, lacrosse's organized form appeared in Ingersoll and Woodstock as a sport without a past.[5] Montreal sportsman Dr W. George Beers virtually reinvented and codified the traditional Indian game, popularizing it through his treatise *Lacrosse: The National Game of Canada* (1869). His sport carried a specific social agenda: to cultivate Canadian nationalism, manliness, and respectability in male youth, and to keep the leisure activities of males in check, so to speak.[6] With such idealistic trappings, lacrosse quickly found popularity in Ingersoll, Woodstock, and other Canadian towns and cities. Due to its newness, sport reformers considered it a socially clean and morally pure sport, having none of the 'debasing accompaniments, the bar room association' that other sports with roots in popular social traditions possessed.[7] In 1871, just as local sport reformers introduced it to the townspeople of Ingersoll and Woodstock, lacrosse had its own governing body, the National Lacrosse Association (NLA), to provide rules and codes of behaviour governing the structural, strategic, and moral aspects of the game.[8] The NLA worked to ensure that *its* way of playing the game would become *the* way.

People in Ingersoll and Woodstock adopted the sport in ways that built upon the growing local connection between team and town. Town boosters who sought locally feasible ways in which to play sport considered lacrosse a respectable sport that enhanced the physical and moral health of local male youth; honourable pursuits like lacrosse ultimately turned boys into men. The repeated themes of boyish sport and young manhood, echoed in early writings on lacrosse, became central to its promotion locally and nationally.[9] Locally, social and sport reformers held great concerns over the

problem of how male youth should spend their leisure time. With high school enrolments increasing, and with a decline in the apprenticeship system, middle-class boys and youth depended upon their families for longer periods than before.[10] By the turn of the century, 80 to 90 per cent of 5- to 16-year-olds in Ingersoll and Woodstock attended school 200 days a year.[11] They increasingly came under female scrutiny—both in schools and in the home—prompting some social observers to fear for the loss of male role models. Under female influences, would local male youth become more feminine?[12]

Historians David Howell, Peter Lindsay, and David MacLeod point out the intricacies of the 'young boy problem' of the day. Social critics of the times argued that, unchecked, this situation would cause males to become physically weak and therefore powerless and unmanly.[13] Keenly concerned about this, parents and social reformers sought appropriate spare-time activities to occupy male youth, ones that, as Steven Riess observes, defined manliness and created ways to achieve it.[14] Organized lacrosse aimed to expose young males to respectable versions of masculinity while teaching them the importance of physical activity for their physical and spiritual health in an increasingly sedentary world. George Beers offered a list of those who would do well to pick up a lacrosse stick—socialites, sissies, and unmanly men: 'Fellows who "spree," who make syphons [sic] of their esophagi, and who cannot make better use of their leisure than to suck mint juleps through straws, those model specimens of propriety who think a man on the road to perdition unless he is always reading good books, and making himself a bore to his friends by stale, hypocritical conversation. Those nice young men in black broadcloth who never can take a joke, [and] those whining schoolboys who creep unwillingly to school.'[15] All of them would do well to take up lacrosse.

Keeping local crime rates down and keeping youth off the streets motivated Ingersoll and Woodstock community boosters to promote organized lacrosse for local boys. Truancy and street crime in the towns paled by comparison with the province's large cities, yet many townspeople knew well that these problems affected local males; as one Ingersoll social observer cried, 'the wheels of our social mechanism are out of order!'[16] Local newspapers reported sensational tales from the cities, where the young boy problem became a fixture.[17] But they didn't just happen far away in big cities: local people saw loafers hanging around, haunting street corners on evenings and, worse, on Sundays. These 'dirty wretches' insulted passersby, spitting out tobacco juice and obscenities.[18] Where did people like this come from? The local press fingered the toughs as those living near the railway tracks on the north side of town, where, not coincidentally, many workers and their families lived. Asked by the Commission Appointed to Enquire into the Prison and Reformatory System about potential cures for such idleness, Woodstock's gaoler offered a simple solution: 'I would keep children employed at something or other', he proclaimed, and give them 'good honest play, a game of lacrosse or similar amusement'.[19] Woodstock's chief constable, T.W. McKee, held the nickname 'Tzar of the Beavers Club' for his efforts to keep boys suitably occupied and on the right path.[20]

Lynne Marks argues cogently in her book *Revivals and Roller Rinks* that late nineteenth-century Protestant ministers in small-town Ontario did what they could to promote rational recreation, using the mostly male worlds of leisure and associational life to accomplish this aim; however, their social agenda found resistance on several fronts.[21] Sermons given in Ingersoll and Woodstock repeatedly stressed the relationship between manliness and male leisure. Their titles reveal local preoccupations: 'How Does Physical Welfare Affect Moral Conduct?', 'Young Man's Leisure', 'Where Do You Spend Your Time?', 'True Manhood', and 'A Manly Man'.[22] Marks shows that oftentimes most young men weren't in church to hear them.[23] Providing reprints of sermons that could be clipped out of local newspapers gave clergymen, social reformers, teachers, and parents another opportunity to impress important messages upon youth. Aiming squarely at the community's young men in 1872, Ingersoll's Reverend P. Wright claimed that local boys lacked a conception of true manhood, a 'fruitful source of failures in young men'.[24] Yet, with a grasp of this idea, he assured all who heeded his words, 'evil has no chances for young men.' Strength and courage needed to be suitably controlled for a lad to be considered manly. Public places like lacrosse playing fields and the streets, as well as more private spheres such as the home, provided opportunities to display this control. Sermons reminded Ingersoll boys of their social responsibility to females: 'Don't make a great bluster and be rough and hard, thinking to be manly. Be a little quiet in the house, gentle with your little sisters, and not tiring mother with a great deal of noise. . . . When your work is over and it is the right time for sport kick up your heels and have lots of fun outdoors.'[25]

Even the most private matters regarding male sexuality needed suitable control, according to sermons from local clergymen. In a sermon given to the Brantford YMCA, Woodstock's Reverend Dr Nichol warned boys against the evils lurking in the hearts and bodies of young males. He spoke 'very strongly against practices that were destroying the manhood of thousands and supplying our insane asylums with occupants.'[26] This thinly veiled reference to masturbation, popularly known as the 'curse of Onan' or 'the secret vice', doubtless shocked many. By the turn of the century, however, the notion that healthy physical activity expended vital energy in morally appropriate ways became a standard claim for advocates of sexual science as well as promoters of youth sport, who worked to create an 'athlete of continence, not coitus, continuously testing his manliness in the fires of self-denial'.[27]

Local sport promoters knew well that at its outset lacrosse superbly embodied the idea that games build character, a key ingredient in muscular Christianity.[28] Through lacrosse they aimed to instill the valued character traits such as team-work, self-sacrifice, courage, manliness, and achievement that they believed could be trans-ferred from playing fields to other, real-life situa-tions. These high motives for the sport distinguished it from rowdy, idle diversions, making it seem a morally uplifting activity, an able contender against the social upheavals that plagued small towns changing because of their urban and industrial growth.[29]

The National Lacrosse Association's premier award for amateur competition, the Claxton Flags, was donated by a charter member and sometime president of North America's first Young Men's Christian Association.[30] Montreal millionaire, phi-lanthropist, and social reformer James T. Claxton's intent for the flags, valued at $250, aimed to fos-ter 'clean, amateur athletics amongst the youth of Canada'.[31] This occurred long before the YMCA became known chiefly as a sports institution.[32] The flags, like Woodstock's Silver Ball baseball tro-phy, awarded winners in challenge competition. Nevertheless, while Woodstock's Silver Ball rules laid out only the technical rules for baseball matches, the Claxton Flags lacrosse competition had a deep moral imperative written into its cod-ified rules. Soon after Woodstonian amateur sport promoters created a lacrosse club locally, the town's Ladies Benevolent Society graced the Beavers with their own lacrosse pennant, an impressive piece painstakingly made by local women, 'worked in gold, surmounted by a Beaver, with *BLC* embroidered underneath'.[33] Like the Claxton Flags, it reminded people of the Beaver club's social and moral aspirations.

Lacrosse playing rules kept sharply focused on the moral intent behind the sport's organiza-tion. They demanded that players develop a rational, educated strength, with the idea of 'right action' restricting physical and social play.[34] The key to this approach rested in the strenuous phys-ical exertion bordering on combat required by the sport, coupled with its potential for violence. Twenty players on the field, sticks in hand, needed to be careful when charging after a single

ball. The Ingersoll Victorias' approach and the reaction it provoked at that Dominion Day match in 1871 showed that players had to downplay brute force to avoid the kind of physicality that scraped bodies and broke bones. On the game's scientific approach, George Beers wrote, 'that there is a science in the game is proved by the fact that many throws, dodges, checks, etc., are explained by fixed principles, from which no one can deter and be successful.'[35] Still, physics alone did not make for good lacrosse; the science also stressed the concomitant development of social and sports skills on the playing field. According to such beliefs, a sense of fair play needed to rule the day. Only unmanly men turned to brute force to vanquish their opponents.

Ingersoll and Woodstock's organized clubs reinforced the social and moral learning experi-ences believed to be inherent in the game. To accomplish this they built what Beers called a sporting freemasonry, a term aptly intended to appeal to his middle-class male audience.[36] Both masculine enclaves, lacrosse and nineteenth-cen-tury freemasonry alike emphasized camaraderie, an esoteric body of knowledge, and rituals of play and costume. Both boasted sub-communi-ties within national and provincial networks. To cultivate this freemasonry Beers admonished lacrosse players everywhere to 'learn by heart and practice in conscience that beautiful verse of Thackeray's': 'Who misses or who wins the prize, / Go, lose or conquer as you can, / But if you fail, or if you rise / Be each, pray God, a gentleman.'[37]

The spirit of gentlemanliness encouraged club members to express their sense of hon-ourable camaraderie.[38] Woodstock's Beavers did this in 1879 when they honoured their club sec-retary, local merchant Edward W. Nesbitt, on the eve of his wedding. They presented him with an exquisite silver tea service along with a beautiful parchment scroll at a testimonial dinner. Elaborately detailed in gold, the scroll's inscrip-tion speaks volumes about the club's social and moral goals for training young males for success in sport and life:

We feel it is no empty boast when we say that it is an honour to belong to the *Beaver Lacrosse Club* of Woodstock. The Young men who organized this Club nine years ago have retired and now occupy positions of trust and honour in our community leaving their places in the Club to be filled by other and younger men who bid fair to follow in the footsteps of their predecessors. At home and abroad the name of the *Beaver Lacrosse Club* has been and is now a synonym of honesty, uprightness, and fair dealing. Taking defeat in the same good natured and gentlemanly manner that they have scored victories, and on all occasions, recognizing the golden rule, *To do to others as they wished to be done by.*[39]

Through lacrosse clubs, middle-class men like Nesbitt and other community members in positions of trust and honour carried out a specific social agenda. They believed that they could lead local male youth to develop respectable values that would help them along life's journey and that the success of local lacrosse teams would be the town's success as well. Nesbitt would carry on his crusade for years to come, eventually taking the helm of the Canadian Lacrosse Association, a high accomplishment for someone from small-town Ontario.

Men of similar social and economic backgrounds masterminded this agenda for lacrosse in Ingersoll and Woodstock. Of the 72 men governing local amateur clubs in the towns between 1871 and 1890, 69 had Protestant religious affiliations, even though Roman Catholics comprised as much as one-third of the local populations. As with others involved in sport reform, these men's occupational backgrounds united them and differentiated them from other local males. All but five of the lacrosse club organizers held non-manual occupations, working in local banks, law offices, stores, publishing offices, and the like, where roughly only one-quarter of the jobs in town could be found. Only five working men— skilled ones at that—governed local lacrosse clubs, even though they came from the largest

occupational sector, one-half of all local occupations, recorded on local manuscript censuses. Although unskilled workers accounted for another one-quarter of the local workforce, none could be found among lacrosse organizers. The local voluntary association and political involvement of lacrosse club organizers also provide highly suggestive glimpses into the world views shared by these socially prominent local men. Clearly men on the go, one in every three lacrosse organizers at some time sat on town council, while one in six belonged to the board of trade.

While club organizers possessed remarkably similar social backgrounds, club members held diverse ones. This suggests co-operation, presumably based in consent, from community members from other social groups. Junior lacrosse clubs far outnumbered senior, representative ones, as in baseball.[40] Between 1880 and 1889, three-quarters of 147 lacrosse club members in Ingersoll and Woodstock fell between the ages of 15 and 21 years, where just 15 per cent of the local populations came from. As with baseball, lacrosse players came from a broader social base than did Woodstock's old cricket club. Sons of skilled manual workers played beside those of non-manual workers, a strategy that Gillian Poulter points out helped transmit desired values through a more socially diverse population.[41] Lacrosse promoters, focused upon shaping these boys into manly men, drew male youth from middle- and working-class homes alike.

Baseball could not be beat as an activity rooted in popular culture, yet, as an activity geared towards youth as earnestly designed by sport reformers, nothing beat lacrosse, in its heyday *the* game of boys and young men locally. Club leadership positions brought public approval and recognition to young males: 'The boys who are envied are the captains of the lacrosse teams', praised a writer in the *Sentinel*.[42] Field captains, chosen on their own merit, held an office that was 'no sinecure'.[43] Junior clubs played matches against other teams in town. With its own national association, lacrosse began locally within an already established non-local organized sport framework, with rules already codified and a national governing body already in place. A writer in the *Chronicle* once opined of this quintessentially organized sport, 'no one who ever heard of lacrosse would suppose for a moment that it could exist without a head to govern it, to form rules, etc. There is not in Canada one club that could really be called a lacrosse club that does not belong to some one of the associations.'[44] NLA rules stipulated that member clubs could not compete against non-members, closing the ranks of competition by design and working to control the sport's development, presumably to keep a tight rein on its moral imperative and behavioural restrictions laid out in club constitutions and bylaws. While baseball held a resilient tradition in the informal culture of shop and factory, not to mention the culture of children, the game of lacrosse created by sport reformers seemed to be a sport without a past, holding no such roots for the first generation of local boys who played the game in the 1870s.

If one looks at the well-publicized intermediate and senior divisions of play where teams represented the town, however, one can see reform ideals falling quite short of their mark. Local senior lacrosse clubs, like Ingersoll's Dufferins and Woodstock's Beavers, both charter members of their local AAAs [Amateur Athletic Associations], lasted for decades. The two competed in regional divisions of senior and intermediate play in the NLA and, after 1887, in the newly formed Canadian Lacrosse Association (CLA).[45] As in baseball, representative inter-urban lacrosse competition provided a way in which the two communities could puff themselves up and bring glory to the hometown—a serious business indeed. To perfect their game, Woodstock's players trained carefully, restricting their diet and practising three times a week at the ungodly hour of 6 a.m. Neighbours from the village of Norwich poked fun at their earnestness and the intensity of their regimen: 'they are already feeding on dried beet and drinking milk and raw eggs for their "wind." We hardly think that they need any extra supply of that commodity.'[46]

As in baseball, community members ardently supported winning teams. In 1888 Ingersoll's citizenry petitioned the mayor to declare a half-holiday to watch the Dufferins' match for the Southern District championship.[47] In 1901, for Woodstock's birth as a city, the *Sentinel Review's* Inaugural Edition reflected upon that town's sporting past, proclaiming that the town's Beavers club had given Woodstock 'an enviable reputation in the realm of sport'.[48] The characteristic Woodstonian drive and determination that had made the team such a success, it argued, also led to Woodstock's rise to city status. There, as in other small communities throughout Canada, team uniforms, symbols of order and respectability, and team names reinforced hometown ties, providing myth-makers with opportunities to tell stories about themselves and their reality.[49] To them, lacrosse fields provided symbolic battlegrounds.

Community organizations, mayors, local professional men and merchants, families, and friends all found ways to support their town's team. Hoping to mould a winning team, they offered rewards for players' social and sport skills. Of course, rewards would be needless if players always behaved in desired ways. In 1871, following the tradition established by local baseball teams, Ingersoll citizens banded together to offer a $10 prize for the best team in the local Dominion Day match; however, symbolic prizes and rewards—some opulent, some simply sentimental in nature—displaced cash prizes soon thereafter.[50] The prominent local jeweller, H. Richardson, for example, offered a gold pencil prize for the Dufferin benefit garden party, while a local firm, Mason and Company, handed out a gold-lined silver cup for a throwing competition.[51] In 1888, James Vance, the local barrister and town councillor who became president of both the IAAA [Ingersoll Amateur Athletic Association] and Dufferin lacrosse club as well as the CLA, commissioned a gold medal to award a running competition.[52] Woodstonians also did their share of rewarding the efforts of local lacrosse players. In 1874, Dr Turquand, a well-known civic leader, temperance man, and some-time mayor, donated a silver cup for the best all-round local player.[53] A few years later, local jeweller Samuel Woodroofe, an active sport pro-moter of the local bicycle and football clubs and executive member of the WAAA [Woodstock Amateur Athletic Association], handed out a sil-ver medal for a running competition between club members. A shrewd businessman, he placed the medal in his store window for a week, calling attention to the team while bringing curious cus-tomers into his store.[54] Local grocer E.W. Nesbitt, whose impending wedding had prompted the Beavers to throw him a testimonial dinner, also got into the act of rewarding local youth for their effort and expertise on local lacrosse fields. A sometime president of both the WAAA and the CLA, he gave a diamond pin for the best all-round player who attended practices punctually.[55]

The town and its lacrosse team had a well-cultivated connection. From the early 1870s on, club and holiday organizers in both towns fea-tured lacrosse matches for their Dominion Day celebrations some 19 times between them over a span of 20 years. Thousands of holiday-goers flocked to view these sport spectacles and the other holiday events—noontime parades, speeches from local dignitaries, track and field events, and community picnics. The profits made from 10-cent admission fees to holiday matches alone funded a club's entire season. At a time when Wild West shows were all the rage elsewhere, Woodstock's clubs, like clubs from Montreal and Toronto, arranged holiday exhibi-tion matches against Native Indian teams from nearby reserves.[56] The matches sparked the interest of George Gray, an Ingersoll school-teacher, who saw two of them in Woodstock and recorded them in his diary.[57] Unfortunately, Gray didn't describe the spectacles that followed the matches in any detail, something that newspaper reports of the time suggest consisted of the

Indians dancing a 'war dance' to the beat of cer-emonial drums. Face-painted, wearing head-dresses and other ethnic garb, they played a tightly choreographed role, but whatever they themselves thought of that role, or even who had gotten the spectacle up, remains to be discov-ered. While Native Indian teams never visited Ingersoll, local people still went along with the theme, dressing up as Indians for their Dominion Day nighttime torchlight procession in 1879.[58] Lacrosse propagandists and local civic leaders used the extravaganzas and their images to juxtapose symbolically and celebrate what they viewed Canada *had been* against what it *had become*. The productions fortified their pride in their locality and in the Canadian nation in a way that evoked images of the sport's distant origins in Native culture, a theme also highlighted in the 1876 and 1883 Canadian lacrosse tours to Britain.[59] In 1893 a sketch published in the *Sentinel Review*'s Dominion Day tribute showed a crest with symbols for each province surrounded by scenes of the Canadian wilderness (including a Native Indian standing on a rocky shore) and a well-placed lacrosse stick lying across it, suggest-ing that lacrosse, geography, and climate together united the nation.[60]

While local sanctioning came from middle-class community leaders, lacrosse clubs received substantial grassroots support from local fans. Intent upon making team victories their own, fans were often just way too boisterous, some-thing that town leaders and lacrosse organizers abhorred. This residual element of rowdiness could be found within the connection between team and town that capitalist boosterism fostered. With its tremendous popularity in the late 1870s and 1880s, and with the increasing associations between lacrosse teams and the corporate urban community, the gap between what sport reform-ers hoped to achieve through lacrosse and what actually happened widened significantly.[61] Pressures for victory, coupled with intense fan and player identifications with the home team, undermined reformers' efforts.[62] So, too, did greater player commitment to winning for the glory of the team and the honour of the town. An earnestness to win at times displaced earnest people's desire for self- and social improvement.

Despite prohibitions, newspapers frequently reported money won and lost on the games, showing that fans loved to bet on the representative matches of their hometown team.[63] In 1879, Simcoe's team and their backers arrived for a match in Woodstock 'supplied with heaps of wealth' that Beaver supporters 'readily took up'.[64] As had happened in local baseball, only short steps separated betting from game fixing and under-the-table payments to amateur players. In July 1887 the Brantford Brants courted Beaver players Kennedy, Kelly, and Laird with offers of jobs, guaranteeing a sizable $20 per week playing season salary.[65] Certain Brantford fans also reportedly offered Beaver player and Patterson Factory worker Ed Kennedy $20 to throw a game.[66] A writer for the *Sentinel* decried the action, praising Kennedy's apparent refusal to take part in it and claiming, 'this is the sort of thing that is ruining lacrosse, it is the betting spirit that leads to such attempts at fraud. Unless betting and the influence of betting men is stamped out, amateur lacrosse is dead—in fact it don't deserve to live.'[67]

Sport reformers' efforts to clean up betting and other bad behaviours at local lacrosse playing fields just didn't seem to work. Obviously, many resisted them. Some flatly refused to abide by the behavioural regulations of amateur clubs at the town's athletic grounds. Others refused to participate in the community event, finding other spots, like the cemetery hill overlooking the WAAA grounds, where they could watch the performances free.[68]

Ingersoll and Woodstock lacrosse organizers also had a hard time constraining other forms of resistance, like the violence that accompanied senior-level matches, something that was nothing new, as historians Alan Metcalfe and Barbara Pinto show about Shamrock team competition around the same time in Montreal.[69] Like hockey

today, the sport bred player violence during emotion-packed competition. Ironically, this enhanced the sport's appeal to those inclined that way. During one visit to Ingersoll in 1888, for example, heavily charged competition put Woodstock players under attack.[70] During the match—refereed by what the Woodstock press called 'daisy umpires'—one Woodstock player body-checked his opponent and sent him flying. Hundreds of outraged Ingersoll fans charged the field, mobbing him and his teammates. The mêlée lasted 15 minutes. After the field cleared and play recommenced, one obscenity-screaming spectator chased down a rough Woodstock player and, catching him by the throat, thrashed him. Strangely enough, the rowdy spectator needing to be restrained happened to be the town's police chief.

Lovers of the sport throughout southwestern Ontario knew how playing-field antics led to antipathies between the two towns. Commenting on this state of affairs, the Embro *Courier* pointed a harsh finger at overzealous fans who took the game personally, with the connection between team and town going too far: 'if the spectators of these two towns would keep quiet and not interfere so, much of the bad feeling between the boys would die out.'[71] The Tillsonburg *Liberal* similarly blamed local spectators, who, it instructed, should 'keep their mouths shut and not interfere with the players disputes which occur on the field.'[72] A reporter from Ingersoll's *Chronicle* responded to the indictment, acknowledging the displaced rowdiness inherent in intense inter-urban competition: 'if you expect the spectators in rival towns to keep quiet you make a great big mistake.'[73] With fans 'howling like maniacs', lacrosse competition, encouraged by boosterism, undercut images of respectability in the sport.[74] While rowdiness occurred often in the stands, rather than at the centre of public display, sport reformers nevertheless had a hard time with its high visibility.

Local newspapers often stepped into the battle, admonishing locals to act in a gentlemanly, respectable way. Yet members of the press, too, exhibited elements of displaced rowdyism. After a riotous Woodstock match, a writer in the *Chronicle* suggested, 'had the spectators stepped in and hammered some of them and maimed them for life the punishment would be no less than they deserve.'[75] This situation, although testifying to lacrosse's immense popularity as a form of action-packed competition and entertainment, undercut the reforming of local sport. With its rising popularity and its intricate ties to urban boosterism, lacrosse emerged by the turn of the century as an antithesis to the vision of Canadian youth and sport first expounded by middle-class sport reformers. As the gap between ideation and behaviour widened, it clearly did not live up to expectations as a truly national, respectable game that could unite social groups under the leadership of a small, select group of local men.

## Notes

1. Ingersoll *Chronicle*, 6 July 1871.
2. Ibid.
3. Ibid., 13 July 1871.
4. Woodstock *Sentinel*, 16 June 1871.
5. I use the terminology used by lacrosse writers of the era. For a view of the game from the Native Indian oral tradition, see *Tewaarathon (Lacrosse): Akwesasne's Story of Our National Game* (North American Indian Traveling College, 1978). On European interpretations of lacrosse in Indian cultures: Stewart Culin, 'Games of the North American Indians', *Twenty-fourth Annual Report of the Bureau of American Ethnology* (Washington: Government Printing Office, 1907); George Catlin, *Letters and Notes on the Manners, Customs and Condition of the North American Indians*, vol. 2 (London: The Egyptian Hall, 1871); Michael A. Salter, 'The Effects of Acculturation on the Game of Lacrosse and on Its Role as an Agent of Indian Survival', *Canadian Journal of History of Sport and Physical Education* 3, 1 (May 1972): 28–43. See also Gillian Poulter, 'Playing the Game: The

Transformation of Indigenous Cultural Activities and the Creation of National Identity in Victorian Canada', paper presented to the Canadian Historical Association, 1997.

6. W.G. Beers, *Lacrosse, the National Game of Canada* (Montreal: Dawson Brothers, 1869); Alan Metcalfe, *Canada Learns To Play: The Emergence of Organized Sport, 1807–1914* (Toronto: McClelland & Stewart, 1987), 181–218; Don Morrow et al., *A Concise History of Sport in Canada* (Toronto: Oxford University Press, 1989), 45–68; Christine A. Burr, 'The Process of Evolution of Competitive Sport: A Study of Senior Lacrosse in Canada, 1844 to 1914', MA thesis (University of Western Ontario, 1986); Alexander M. Weyand and M.R. Roberts, *The Lacrosse Story* (Baltimore: H. & A. Herman, 1965).
7. Beers, *Lacrosse*, 35.
8. Don Morrow, 'The Institutionalization of Sport: A Case Study of Canadian Lacrosse', *International Journal of History of Sport* 9, 2 (Aug. 1992): 236–51.
9. W.G. Beers, 'Canadian Sports', *Century Magazine* 14 (May–Oct. 1879): 506–27; Goal Keeper, *The Game of Lacrosse* (Montreal: Montreal Steam Press, 1860); 'The Ocean Travels of Lacrosse', *Athletic Leaves* (Sept. 1888): 42; 'A Rival to Cricket', *Chambers Journal* 18 (Dec. 1862): 366–8; W.K. McNaught, *Lacrosse and How To Play It* (Toronto: Robert Marshall, 1873).
10. Susan E. Houston, 'Politics, Schools, and Social Change in Upper Canada', *Canadian Historical Review* 53 (Sept. 1972): 249–71; Houston, 'Victorian Origins of Juvenile Delinquency: A Canadian Experience', *History of Education Quarterly* 20 (Fall 1972): 254–80; Houston and Alison L. Prentice, *Schools and Scholars in Nineteenth Century Ontario* (Toronto: University of Toronto Press, 1988); Prentice, *The School Promoters: Education and Social Class in Mid-Nineteenth Century Upper Canada* (Toronto: McClelland & Stewart, 1977); R. Gidney and W.P.J. Millar, *Inventing Secondary Education: The Rise of the High School in Nineteenth Century Ontario* (Montreal and Kingston: McGill-Queen's University Press, 1990).
11. I have gleaned this information from the *Annual*

*Report of the Normal, Model, Grammar and Common Schools in Ontario* found in the Ontario Sessional Papers Report of the Minister of Education (No. 3) 1893.

12. Steven A. Riess, 'Sport and the Redefinition of Middle Class Masculinity', *International Journal of the History of Sport* 8, 1 ((May 1991): 5–27; Mangan and Walvin, eds, *Manliness and Morality*; E. Anthony Rotundo, 'Body and Soul: Changing Ideals of American Middle Class Manhood', *Journal of Social History* 14 (1983): 23–38; Joseph Maguire, 'Images of Manliness and Competing Ways of Living in Late Victorian and Edwardian Britain', *British Journal of Sports History* 3, 3 (Dec. 1986): 265–87.

13. David Howell and Peter Lindsay, 'The Social Gospel and the Young Boy Problem, 1895–1925', *Canadian Journal of History of Sport* 17, 1 (May 1986): 75–87; David I. MacLeod, 'A Live Vaccine: The Y.M.C.A. and Male Adolescence in the United States and Canada, 1870–1920', *Histoire Sociale/ Social History* 11, 21 (1978): 5–24.

14. Riess, 'Sport and the Redefinition of Middle Class Masculinity', 5.

15. Beers, *Lacrosse*, 42–3.

16. Ingersoll *Chronicle*, 10 Apr. 1873.

17. For example, ibid., 23 Mar., 24 Sept. 1868, 10 Apr. 1873, 16 May 1878, 27 Nov., 4 Dec. 1884. To keep its readers abreast of criminal happenings, the *Chronicle* instituted a new regular column, 'Crimes of the Week'.

18. Ibid., 27 Nov. 1884.

19. Ontario, *Report of the Commissioners Appointed to enquire into the Prison and Reformatory System*, 1891, 529. Thanks to Susan Houston for bringing this item to my attention.

20. Woodstock *Sentinel*, 19 Apr. 1880.

21. Lynne Marks, *Revivals and Roller Rinks: Religion, Leisure, and Identity in Late Nineteenth-Century Small-Town Ontario* (Toronto: University of Toronto Press, 1996).

22. Reprints of sermons, in whole or part, found in Woodstock *Sentinel*, 20 Nov. 1887; Woodstock *Herald*, 14 Mar. 1845; Ingersoll *Chronicle*, 25 Oct. 1888, 30 Jan. 1868.

23. Marks, *Revivals and Roller Rinks*, 122.

24. Ingersoll *Chronicle*, 7 Nov. 1872.

25. Ibid., 20 June 1867.

26. Woodstock *Sentinel*, 29 Jan. 1889.

27. As cited in Riess, 'Sport and the Redefinition of Middle Class Masculinity', 11; Donald J. Mrozek, *Sport and American Mentality, 1880–1910* (Knoxville: University of Tennessee Press, 1983); B.G. Jefferis, *Light in Dark Corners: A Complete Sexual Science* (Toronto: J.L. Nichols and Co., 1895).

28. Peter McIntosh, *Sport in Society* (London: C.A. Watts, 1963), 69–79; Gerald Redmond, 'The First Tom Brown's Schooldays and Others: Origins of Muscular Christianity in Children's Literature, 1762–1855', *Quest* 30 (Summer 1978): 4–18; Guy Lewis, 'The Muscular Christianity Movement', *Journal of Health, Physical Education and Recreation* (May 1966): 27–30.

29. Beers, *Lacrosse*.

30. On the development of lacrosse generally, see Metcalfe, *Canada Learns To Play*, 181–218; Peter Lindsay, 'A History of Sport in Canada, 1807–1867', Ph.D. dissertation (University of Alberta, 1969), 114–32.

31. Claxton's obituary from *Sunday World*, 1908, as cited in Harold Cross, *One Hundred Years of Service with Youth: The Story of the Montreal YMCA* (Montreal: Southam Press, 1951), 144.

32. See Cross, *One Hundred Years of Service with Youth*. Local connections between lacrosse and the YMCA in Woodstock also predated the association's full-scale involvement in sport. At its outset in 1871 the Woodstock YMCA's aim, 'the improvement of the religious, mental, and social conditions of young men in Woodstock', overlooked sport, but within two years the Beavers and the YMCA were contemplating combining their energies to form a gymnasium. By 1874 the Beavers used YMCA club rooms for lacrosse meetings. Woodstock *Sentinel*, 24 Oct. 1873, 29 May 1874; W. Stewart Lavell, *All This Was Yesterday: The Story of the YMCA in Woodstock, Ontario, 1868–1972* (Woodstock: Talbot Communications, 1972).

33. Woodstock *Sentinel*, 7 July, 28 Nov. 1871. Today the pennant is kept in the Woodstock Museum.

34. John Weiler, 'The Idea of Sport in Late Victorian Canada', in Michael Cross, ed., *The Workingman in the Nineteenth Century* (Toronto: University of Toronto Press, 1974), 228–31.

35. Beers, *Lacrosse*, 52; Burr, 'The Process of Evolution of Competitive Sport'.

36. Beers, *Lacrosse*, 50; Christopher J. Anstead, 'Fraternalism in Victorian Ontario: Secret Societies and Cultural Hegemony', Ph.D. dissertation (University of Western Ontario, 1992); Lynn Dumenil, *Freemasonry and American Culture, 1880–1930* (Princeton, NJ: Princeton University Press, 1984); J.S. Gilkeson, *Middle Class Providence, 1820–1940* (Princeton, NJ: Princeton University Press, 1986).

37. Beers, *Lacrosse*, 42.

38. Ingersoll *Chronicle*, 7 July 1887; Woodstock *Sentinel*, 30 June 1887.

39. 'Testimonial to Edward W. Nesbitt. Woodstock 26 November, 1879' [my emphasis]. Woodstock Museum.

40. The number of senior and junior baseball and lacrosse clubs in Ingersoll and Woodstock, 1860–89:

41. Poulter, 'Playing the Game'.

42. Woodstock *Sentinel*, 20 June 1887.

43. McNaught, *Lacrosse and How To Play It*, 19.

44. Ingersoll *Chronicle*, 13 Sept. 1888.

45. On the founding of the CLA, see Toronto *Mail*, 8,

46. *Norwich Gazette*, 15 July 1886.

47. *Chronicle*, 14 Sept. 1888.

48. Woodstock *Sentinel-Review*, Birth of the Industrial City Edition, 9 July 1901.

49. On the relationship between team and town, see Morris Mott, 'One Town's Team: Souris and its Lacrosse Club, 1887–1906', *Manitoba History* 1, 1 (1980): 10–16; Carl Betke, 'Sports Promotion in the Western Canadian City: The Example of Early Edmonton', *Urban History Review* 12, 2 (1983): 47–56.

50. Ingersoll *Chronicle*, 13 July 1871.

51. Ibid., 30 June 1885, 19 May 1887.

52. Ibid., 10 May 1888.

53. Woodstock *Sentinel*, 1 Apr. 1874.

54. Ibid., 21 May 1880, 21 Nov. 1884.

55. Ibid., 16 May 1888.

56. In 1871 the Beavers paid the Grand River Indians $60 to compete against them in the May 24th match. Ten-cent admissions covered this outlay and brought a $159 profit to the club (Woodstock *Sentinel*, 7 July 1871). Other Native Indian teams were the Tuscaroras, Onondagas, Muncitown, Sioux, and Six Nations. *Sentinel*, 7 July 1871, 31 May, 23 Aug. 1872, 26 June 1874, 23 May, 4 July 1879, 30 Apr. 1880, 23 June 1882, 25 May 1887; Ingersoll *Chronicle*, 9 May 1877. See Daniel Francis, 'Marketing the Imaginary Indian', in *The Imaginary Indian: The*

9, 13, 15, 18, 20, 23, 26 Apr. 1887. More generally, see Metcalfe, *Canada Learns To Play*, 206–8.

**Table for Note 40**

| | Jr baseball | | Jr lacrosse | | Sr baseball | | Sr lacrosse | |
|---|---|---|---|---|---|---|---|---|
| | Ing. | Wdsk. | Ing | Wdsk. | Ing. | Wdsk. | Ing. | Wdsk. |
| 1860–4 | 0 | 0 | – | – | 1 | 1 | – | – |
| 1865–9 | 2 | 2 | – | – | 1 | 1 | – | – |
| 1870–4 | 5 | 5 | 1 | 6 | 2 | 2 | 3 | 4 |
| 1875–9 | 8 | 11 | 2 | 4 | 2 | 2 | 0 | 3 |
| 1880–4 | 7 | 2 | 7 | 12 | 1 | 2 | 4 | 7 |
| 1885–9 | 5 | 16 | 13 | 15 | 2 | 2 | 5 | 5 |
| Total | 27 | 36 | 23 | 37 | 9 | 10 | 12 | 19 |

Source: Ingersoll and Woodstock sport database in author's possession.

*Image of the Indian in Canadian Culture* (Vancouver: Arsenal Pulp Press, 1992), 173–90; Poulter, 'Playing the Game'.

57. George A. Gray Diaries, 3 July 1871, 24 May 1872, Woodstock Museum.

58. Ingersoll *Chronicle*, 3 July 1879.

59. Kevin Wamsley, 'Nineteenth Century Sport Tours, State Formation, and Canadian Foreign Policy', *Sporting Traditions* 13, 2 (1997): 73–89; Poulter, 'Playing the Game'; Don Morrow, 'The Canadian Image Abroad: The Great Lacrosse Tours of 1876 and 1883', in *Proceedings of the 5th Canadian Symposium on the History of Sport and Physical Education* (Toronto: University of Toronto, 1982), 11–23; David W. Brown, 'Canadian Imperialism and Sporting Exchanges: the Nineteenth Century Cultural Experience of Cricket and Lacrosse', *Canadian Journal of History of Sport* 18, 1 (May 1987): 55–66.

60. Woodstock *Sentinel-Review*, 1 July 1893.

61. On escalating violence and rowdyism in lacrosse, see Metcalfe, *Canada Learns To Play*, 192–203; Alan Metcalfe, 'Sport and Athletics: A Case Study of Lacrosse in Canada, 1840–1889', *Journal of Sport History* 3, 1 (Spring 1976): 1–19; Burr, 'The Process of the Evolution of Competitive Sport'.

62. Barbara S. Pinto, '"Ain't Misbehavin": The Montreal Shamrock Lacrosse Club teams, 1868 to 1884', MA thesis (University of Western Ontario, 1990).

63. Woodstock *Sentinel*, 22, 29 Aug. 1879, 25 Aug. 1882, 15 Sept. 1886, 28, 30 June 1887; Ingersoll *Chronicle*, 23 June 1887.

64. Woodstock *Sentinel*, 22 Aug. 1879.

65. Ibid., 20 July 1887.

66. Ingersoll *Chronicle*, 23 June 1887.

67. The editorial went on to say, 'Betting, slugging, and professionalism follow in natural order. Suppress the first and the other evils are easily dealt with.' Woodstock *Sentinel*, 30 July 1887.

68. Ibid., 3 July 1885.

69. Pinto, '"Ain't Misbehavin"'; Metcalfe, 'Sport and Athletics'.

70. Woodstock *Sentinel*, 6 Sept. 1888.

71. Reported ibid., 7 Aug. 1885. Related to the incident, see ibid., 7, 14 Aug. 1885; Ingersoll *Chronicle*, 6 Aug. 1885.

72. Tillsonburg *Liberal* editorial reprinted in the Woodstock *Sentinel*, 30 July 1887.

73. Tillsonburg *Liberal* editorial reprinted with comments, Ingersoll *Chronicle*, 28 June 1888.

74. Ingersoll *Chronicle*, 28 June 1888.

75. Ibid., 30 July 1885.

# 18

# 'Care, Control, and Supervision': Native People in the Canadian Atlantic Salmon Fishery, 1867–1900

Bill Parenteau

It was June 1886 and 'the ladies' had come to Camp Harmony a few weeks into the season to join the gentlemen of this Restigouche River Fishing Club in the annual rite of salmon angling and communing with nature. On this occasion, club member Dean Sage recalled in a published account, the men had prepared a special treat; the ladies were to witness a bloodless simulation of the 'primeval' Mi'kmaq custom of spearing salmon by torchlight. The 'Indians entered heartily into the idea', Sage explained, and set about binding the birchbark *flambeaux*, all the time 'chanting . . . a recital of an old chief's former prowess with the spear.'

With darkness approaching, the party and their guides took to the canoes, in anticipation of experiencing the mysteries of nature. The *flambeaux* were lit and stuck crossways in the canoes, which were formed in a line across the river. As the guides poled the canoes upriver, the line between water and atmosphere vanished. 'Every pebble on the bottom was as distinct as if nothing but air lay between us and it, the canoes seemed to be floating on air and the small fish, trout, suckers and parr looked like flying machines, so perfect was the delusion.' The illusion became even more mesmerizing as the party passed over the salmon pools and large fish, up to 40 pounds in weight, began 'in a dazed way' to dart under and follow the canoes.

The spell was broken only 'when the Indians began to get excited'. They became 'half-crazed', the sportsman-naturalist remembered, 'by the likeness of this to their old expeditions when the river was free to them.' Even the trusted head guide Jacques had shed the trappings of civilization. 'Ef we spearin' now we git couple dis time, den pole back, an run over 'em again, an' git couple more meebe', Jacques was said to have suggested, as he stood up in the bow of the canoe, poised to bludgeon the passing salmon with his blunt pole. '[O]nly by a strong effort and my repeated warnings', Sage proudly recalled, did Jacques 'restrain himself from driving at each fish that crossed his path.' 'Alexis Vicaire, a cousin of Jacques', in another canoe, couldn't control his natural instincts, and at last, with a wild yell, struck at a passing salmon, fortunately missing him.' This most unsporting display, and the prospect of similar acts, forced the club members

Bill Parenteau, '"Care, Control and Supervision": Native People in the Canadian Atlantic Salmon Fishery, 1867–1900', *Canadian Historical Review* 79, 1 (1998): 1–35. © 1998 University of Toronto Press. Reprinted by permission of University of Toronto Press (www.utpjournals.com).

to intervene. 'We were obliged to assert our authority very strongly', Sage lamented, 'to check the growing desire of the Indians to kill the salmon with their poles, which they easily could have done.' The *flambeaux* were extinguished and the party headed back to camp. The 'repressed spirits of the Indians', according to the author, were vented in a race back to the camp, at the end of which all members of the party were soaked with river water. Then 'the Indians gradually calmed down, under the influence of the hearty meal, which their exertions gave them the excuse for taking.'[1]

The story told by Sage makes an excellent starting point for understanding the ongoing restructuring of harvesting patterns of Atlantic salmon in Canada as well as the emerging power relationships between sportsmen and other resource users. During the second half of the nineteenth century, Native people in Nova Scotia, New Brunswick, and Quebec were systematically excluded from the Atlantic salmon harvest. The agency primarily responsible for their exclusion was the federal Department of Fisheries, which after 1867 enacted conservation measures banning the modes of harvesting used by Native fishers and instituted an administrative regime for enforcement. The fisheries department was strongly influenced by elite salmon anglers both in constructing its conservation program and in enforcing regulations. The regulations banning spearing and other Native harvesting methods were aggressively pursued by the angling fraternity and, in fact, had grown out of the 'code of the sportsman', which viewed these fishing methods as 'villainous practices'.[2] After 1870, elite sport fishermen solidified their position at the top of the hierarchy of resource users by contributing to the rehabilitation of salmon rivers and paying for surveillance and the prosecution of poachers. Participation in the state conservation and administrative program allowed anglers to extend their control over salmon rivers and, progressively, to restrict harvesting by other groups of commercial and subsistence resource users.[3] On

the watersheds of eastern Canada, the process of eliminating Native salmon fishing was lengthy and often uneven; not surprisingly, it involved a great deal of resistance and accommodation on the part of Native people. The morality play that featured Sage and his fellow sportsmen of Camp Harmony heroically subduing the 'natural instincts' of the Mi'kmaq demonstrated how far the process had progressed on many salmon rivers by the 1880s.

The story can also be seen as a metaphor for the transformation of Native people from active resource users to cultural commodities—there to enhance the wilderness experiences of the fly fishermen. If Native people were demonized as destroyers of the salmon fishery, they were also highly valued by the elite angling fraternity. Native men were generally competent fishing guides and, in some instances, the only ones available. The Native guides who accompanied salmon anglers also served an ideological/cultural function. An integral part of the code of the sportsman was that each 'true sportsman' should be a naturalist, that he fully understand the habits of his quarry as well as the environment. For the elite angler, Native people were part of the environment. Virtually without exception, the sporting literature of the period 1850–1900 that concerns salmon fishing also contains information on the racial characteristics, living habits, customs, and mythology of Native people. Sportsmen of the Victorian era were fond of comparing their modern existence with the supposed primitive world of Native people. What many elite anglers wanted was not simply someone to help them catch fish, but an authentic 'primitive' man to guide them into an imagined world of primeval wonder—someone to legitimize their adventure as a true wilderness experience. Elite anglers paid dearly, sometimes thousands of dollars, to fish for salmon in the rivers of eastern Canada; they also expected for their money the privilege of experiencing such perfect illusions as that enjoyed by the members of Camp Harmony.
. . .

The development of natural resource management and an elite male sporting culture in North America in the late nineteenth century were complementary and, in significant ways, interrelated phenomena. As John Reiger and Richard Judd have shown, there was an almost natural affinity between the two groups. Fish and game officials relied on elite sportsmen to push for increased funding and an expanded resource management bureaucracy, and, in turn, the sporting interests counted on a regulatory regime favourable to recreational hunting and fishing. 'Such organizations', Judd notes, 'linked arms with state fish and game commissions and helped turn the conservation movement in the direction of sporting, as opposed to commercial or subsistence activity.'[4]

Perhaps nowhere was this intimate connection between elite sportsmen and government officials more evident than in the Atlantic salmon fishery of the eastern Canadian provinces. The sport-fishing industry provided key political support for the expensive hatchery program, which received a surprising amount of criticism from other resource users. In addition, salmon leases by 1890 were generating tens of thousands of dollars in revenue. Most important, under the terms of the leases, salmon clubs provided guardians to protect the rivers from poachers. Both the federal and the provincial salmon leases contained clauses that specifically outlined the number of guardians to be employed and the time period in which they were to protect the waters on which the club had exclusive fishing rights.[5] By 1890 the exclusive Restigouche Salmon Club, for example, was spending in excess of $5,000 each year to protect its leasehold.[6] The addition of scores of private guardians, many of them vested with magisterial powers, provided an immense boost to the chronically underfunded department in its efforts to control the salmon harvest. Not surprisingly, the needs and desires of the salmon clubs received a sympathetic hearing in the formation of regulations and resolution of disputes between resource users. The numerous high-ranking officials in the federal and provincial fisheries bureaucracies that were avid members of the angling fraternity reinforced the influence of the clubs.[7] Thus, the sport-fishing interests were able to exert a measure of control even over user groups with considerably more political power than Native peoples, particularly the commercial net fishers.

## Care, Control, and Supervision

Among the earliest initiatives undertaken by the fishery department was prohibiting the spearing of salmon in upriver pools and on spawning beds. As was the case with some colonial legislation, the federal Fisheries Act passed in 1868 recognized the tradition of Native spearfishing. An exemption was included in the clause prohibiting spearfishing that allowed the Minister of Fisheries to 'appropriate and license or lease certain waters in which certain Indians shall be allowed to catch fish for their own use in and at whatever manner and time are specified in the license or lease, and may permit spearing in certain localities.'[8] These privileges were extended by the minister in only a few instances during the late 1860s and early 1870s, although some of the bands in New Brunswick and on the north shore of the St Lawrence River were allowed to operate or share the proceeds of net-fishing stands on waters that ran through their reserves. The intention of the federal government was to 'civilize' the Native people by encouraging them to establish permanent agricultural communities; this initiative formed part of the underlying logic behind prohibiting the spearing of salmon, which was seen by Fisheries and Indian Affairs officers as part of the wandering life characterized by indolence and vice.[9] The paternalist attitude of the government was summed up by one Indian agent who, when commenting on the agitation of the band on Burnt Church Reserve (Miramichi River) for the extension of fishing rights, suggested that 'the Indians need care, control and supervision.'[10] All three of these administrative imperatives were demonstrated by the Department of Fisheries during the late nineteenth century; overwhelmingly, the emphasis was on control and supervision.

The impact of the initiative to remove Native people from the salmon fishery was felt unequally by the bands that resided near the rivers of Nova Scotia, New Brunswick, and Quebec. In Nova Scotia and the Bay of Fundy shore of New Brunswick, obstructions to the salmon run, pollution, and overfishing had so degraded the resource that it was no longer a central component in the Native economy. In the places where salmon did still run—the Saint John and Margaree rivers, for example—competition from white settlers significantly reduced the opportunities for Native people.[11] The impact of the legislation was particularly hard felt on the New Brunswick shore of the Baie des Chaleurs, the Gaspé Peninsula, and the tributaries on the north shore of the St Lawrence. The new fisheries policies placed the Montagnais bands of the St Lawrence River 'in a very precarious condition', observed Théophile Tétu, captain of the government schooner *La Canadienne*. The solution to the problem, the fishery officer believed, was to increase the annual relief allowance given to the Native people of the north shore and to provide seed and agricultural implements to the bands on the Baie des Chaleurs. 'Those people would come to understand that the Government is friendly to them', Tetu concluded, and, within a few years, he predicted, 'the increase of fish in our rivers would repay the expense incurred for the attainment of the desired object.'[12]

. . . The primary recourse of people around the world who fail to recognize the legitimacy of state regulations that infringe on traditional patterns of hunting and fishing is, of course, 'poaching'. Not surprisingly, the annual reports of local fishery officers and the published narratives of sportsmen in the late nineteenth century abound with references to poaching by Native people. Most Native people were certainly not restrained by moral considerations, as the salmon fishing laws were widely held to be unjust, and the practice of fishing at night lent itself to engaging in such furtive activities. However, the extent of Native poaching may have been exaggerated. White settlers throughout the region, particularly in New Brunswick, were equally ill-disposed towards the federal salmon fishing regulations and fished illegally in large numbers.[13] It is likely that Native people sometimes became the scapegoats for other poachers, particularly when *flambeaux* and other signs of spearing were in evidence. The attitude of riverine residents of European descent was suggested by Sage: 'The white settler on the Restigouche and its tributaries "drifts" for salmon with great persistence and success. He is, however, dreadfully shocked at the idea of an Indian taking a salmon with a spear.'[14] In addition, many stories of Native poaching in sporting narratives were embellished to serve as morality plays for promoting sportsmanship and reaffirming the intellectual/racial superiority of Europeans. In reality, Native people, when on the reserves at least, were more closely watched and monitored than settlers. The successful Native poacher had to contend not only with fishery officers but also with Indian agents and resident missionaries, who routinely invaded their privacy in search of alcohol or other illicit products.

Patterns of poaching were diverse and were influenced, among other factors, by the level of surveillance on a particular river and by the needs and proclivities of Native residents. Poaching activities ranged from the individual who speared a single fish when afforded the opportunity, to well-organized groups of Native fishermen filling several canoes with salmon. The observations of Napoleon Comeau, who served as guardian for the leaseholders of the renowned Godbout River from the late 1860s until after 1900, are instructive for understanding patterns of illegal salmon fishing. He divided poachers into two groups, the first being 'professionals', who needed a considerable outfit (canoes, nets, etc.) and connections with a merchant who would buy the illegal fish and protect their anonymity. The second group he classified as the 'poacher through necessity', who could not cause 'any serious damage' but was difficult to control and 'sometimes very annoying'. 'Their outfit is very light,' he noted, 'and may consist of only a landing net, spear, gaff, or snare, easily hid on the person, and frequently thrown away, when danger is scented. They also have the sympathy of the community and no evidence can be had against them.'[15] This statement about community support was a near-universal condition that stood as one of the primary barriers to the eradication of poaching throughout the Atlantic salmon fishery. As Comeau and other fishery wardens reported, it was commonplace for their movements to be closely monitored by Native people and white settlers alike.[16] Overall, with the leasing of an ever-increasing number of salmon rivers after 1875, poaching became more difficult for both Native people and white settlers. From just a few prized salmon waters being leased at Confederation, the number of rivers in New Brunswick and Quebec on which anglers held exclusive fishing rights increased to more than 60 by the early 1890s.[17] Poaching was certainly not eliminated, but the addition of hundreds of private guardians to protect the rivers on behalf of anglers had a marked restrictive impact.

The removal of Native bands in Nova Scotia, New Brunswick, and Quebec from the salmon harvest hastened their entry into the sport-fishing industry as guides. This transition was looked upon with favour and was even promoted by fishery officers, as it meant, from their perspective, that the segment of the Native population most likely to spear salmon would be under the supervision of people who understood the importance of conservation.[18] The economic 'benefit' of guiding over fishing was neatly stated by a local officer in 1895, when the Mission Point band began to demand that it be compensated for the removal of its fishing station: 'While the absorption of the Mission Point Station by the Department may be made to appear to be a great loss to the Indians financially, it is really a benefit, because the rental paid for the net, even had it judiciously been distributed would have only amounted to $0.50 per annum to each family, while the removal of the net from a critical position at the entrance to the north channel on the middle ground of the river was a great benefit to the upper waters, and anglers, consequently a great advantage to the Indians as the better the angling the greater the amount to employment at $3.00 per day.'[19] It was an unequivocal admission that the fishing station was never an adequate replacement for spearfishing. The officer also failed to mention that one successful night of spearing would have easily netted more income than a few weeks of poling a canoe for 10 or 12 hours per day, watching some 'sport' struggle with the delicate art of fly fishing.

## Guiding in the Ideal World of the Sportsman

By virtue of their skills with the birchbark canoe and their knowledge of rivers and forests, Native people served as guides from the earliest days of recreational sporting in the North American colonies. As the sport-hunting and sport-fishing industries expanded after 1870, Native men from Nova Scotia, New Brunswick, and Quebec entered the guiding profession in increasing numbers. Exact figures for the number of Native men employed as guides are not part of the historical record; however, it is clear from the records of the Department of Indian Affairs that men from nearly every band in the three provinces were engaged in this work. Frequent statements by Indian agents to the effect that 'the greater portion of the male population during the summer season hire themselves as guides to sportsmen' suggest that, for a considerable number of bands, guiding was a vital economic activity.[20] With regard to the salmon fishery, hundreds of Native men served as guides, and they were both pushed in this direction by fishery policies and pulled in by economic incentives. Compared with the other wage-labour opportunities open to Native people—woods work and farm labour, for example—the pay for guiding was high. Salmon guides were particularly well paid, earning as much as three dollars per day in the 1890s, while wages for common labourers were rarely more than one dollar.[21]

Although there were often long stretches of time during the day, particularly on hot afternoons in midsummer, when guides could lounge in their quarters adjacent to the angling lodge, salmon guiding generally involved long hours of work and could be physically demanding. Guides attached to salmon fishing lodges, which were common on the best rivers, such as the Restigouche and the Casapedia, were at the disposal of anglers at any time during daylight hours and occasionally for moonlight cruises. Those who worked for travelling fishing parties were saddled with the additional duties of hauling gear, making camp, and preparing meals. From a physical standpoint, the most difficult part of the job was poling upriver. The sporting narratives of the period frequently comment on the amount of skill needed for poling and the stamina of their Native guides:

> It is a very difficult accomplishment to pole a canoe at all, and still more difficult to do it well. There is a certain kind of swing that has to be learned in order to make the pole leave and enter the water correctly, and the centre of gravity must be maintained on the very small base afforded at the narrow end of the canoe so exactly, that the frequent slipping of the pole from the round stones at the bottom shall not effect it, nor the unexpected twists and dodges of the light bark as it encounters some sudden turn in the current or puff of wind. The skillful poler meets all of these emergencies successfully as if by instinct, and without apparent effort.[22]

Poling was only one of many skills, both physical and social, needed to be a competent salmon guide. Guides, naturally, needed to know

the spots where a fly cast would have the greatest chance of meeting with success and how to approach the easily spooked salmon. These requirements of the job were vital in serving the inexperienced salmon angler, but less important with club members who fished the same pools year after year. With the exception of some small rivers, anglers generally hooked salmon while in the canoe, at which time they were paddled or poled to a convenient and safe landing place. The contest between angler and salmon could go on for up to two hours, depending on the size of the fish and the strength of the rod and line used; lengthy battles often demanded that the angler get in and out of the canoe two or more times, as the salmon emptied the reel of line and the party was forced to give chase. In such situations, the angler had to be guided in and out of the canoe quickly, smoothly, and safely, so that he might give all his attention to keeping the salmon on the line. The guides also needed to keep track of the location of the fish, so as not to get the canoe in an unfavourable position or allow the salmon to break the line by wrapping it around a rock or sunken tree. At the end of the contest the salmon needed to be gaffed, which, if not performed with a steady hand, could jar the fish off the hook and set it free. Many fishing stories ended sadly with the loss of a salmon at this critical juncture.[23] As anglers often travelled hundreds of miles and spent considerable sums for the privilege of salmon fishing, it was important for guides to avoid even the appearance of responsibility for losing a fish.

From the perspective of the salmon angler, a good salmon guide was a companion who gave assistance and shared in the thrill of the catch, without being intrusive or too pointedly giving directions. Personality traits, such as stoicism, a sense of humour, and the ability to recount Native folk legends, could enhance the reputation of a guide and bring further opportunities.[24] In addition to being relatively well paid, salmon guides also had a more stable clientele than other Native guides. In contrast to canoeing guides attached to the so-called watering places, where the relationship with a group of tourists was most often a one-time affair, individuals and crews of guides frequently returned to service the same salmon fishing lodges each year. Here guides could establish a reputation for good work and, within fairly rigid boundaries defined by class and race, forge more intimate relationships with their clients. A good guide was akin to a trusted domestic servant—reliable, competent, and able to understand his place. It was a relationship with which a great many salmon fishermen were familiar in their domestic lives.[25]

Understanding the systematic exclusion of Native peoples as active resource users in the salmon fishery is a fairly straightforward proposition, compared with examining the relationship to the anglers who set up sporting enterprises near their reserves. The historical record of salmon guiding in the late nineteenth century consists mainly of scattered, passing references in government documents and the published narratives of sportsmen. Native people left few, if any, unadulterated accounts of their experiences as guides; therefore, any assumptions about how they perceived the job or their interactions with anglers must be filtered through the thick lens of these narratives. Ultimately, any discussion of guiding that uses sporting narratives must be as much about elite anglers as it is about Native salmon guides.[26]

Overall, the pursuit of sporting activities in Canada became more inclusive in the decades after Confederation, but salmon fishing remained an exception. Virtually all the major salmon rivers in New Brunswick and Quebec were colonized by the wealthy and politically connected by 1890. Secure access to good salmon fishing required buying waterfront property and/or leasing a stretch of river from the New Brunswick or Quebec government. Groups of elite angling enthusiasts quickly formed into clubs and took control of the best salmon waters in the 15 years after Confederation. The exclusivity of these clubs was epitomized by the

'wealthy and aristocratic' Restigouche Salmon Club, which was dominated by well-heeled members of the New York financial community and, by 1890, had an initial membership fee of $7,500. Beyond this initial fee, the average cost for a 20-day fly-fishing trip on the Restigouche in 1890 was estimated to be $450, not counting rods and other personal gear.[27] Although not all salmon clubs were as exclusive, there were precious few opportunities for good salmon fishing open to even the middle-level executive.[28]

One of the by-products of the wealth of salmon anglers and of their closer, more protracted contact with Native people was that Native guides and their bands were more often than others favoured by the noblesse oblige of sportsmen. Starting in the mid-1870s, the salmon clubs on the Restigouche River began making periodic grants to the Mission Point Reserve, which contained the largest single contingent of salmon guides, for specific projects, or when the conditions on the reserve appeared particularly bad.[29] More often, charity came in the form of salmon. While some anglers salted or pickled the salmon that could not be consumed while at camp, many others routinely gave a portion of the catch to Native people. It was also the practice of some camps to donate perishable food items to the guides at the end of the season. On a practical level, Native people needed and even came to depend on the charity of salmon anglers.

On a cultural level, such acts were a way of reaffirming the power relations between the anglers and the local Native people and of distinguishing salmon angling as a sportsmanlike endeavour. In examining big-game hunting in India and Africa within the context of British imperialism, J.M. MacKenzie and others have suggested that when elites reverted from industrial modernity and brought their sentimental version of the hunting phase of social development to other places, they also projected social relations on the host people.[30] With its wealthy patrons buying and leasing riparian rights and building luxurious lodges, the salmon-angling industry certainly had the same imperialist profile as big-game hunting. Salmon fishing was also similarly ritualized and guided by a chivalric code. Giving away a portion of the catch was a way of legitimizing the sometimes enormous catches of the anglers, separating the true sportsman from the 'game hog', who turned the noble arts of hunting and fishing into a crass and uncivilized quest for meat. The ideological underpinnings of such acts were well represented in the statement of the poet Charles G.D. Roberts about a fishing trip on the Tobique River in New Brunswick: 'We imagined the mahogany youngsters at Tobique mouth reveling in the fruits of our prowess; and we imagined them so vividly that the artist forthwith made a sketch of our imaginings. And thus we felt no scruples on the abundance of our catch.'[31] Thus, in part, salmon anglers participated in the sometimes brutal exclusion of Native people from the resource, paid extraordinary amounts of money to catch salmon, and then gave a portion of the catch away, 'to make class and race divisions, and hierarchical rule, seem immemorial'.[32]

As the preceding statements suggest, the code of the sportsman, increasingly adopted in North America after 1850, played an important role in determining the relationship between anglers and guides. The core of the sportsmen's code was a set of rules about proper methods of taking fish and game and the appropriate seasons for killing each species. These aristocratic notions, which could be traced back to the seventeenth-century writings of Izaak Walton, the patron saint of anglers, had a profound effect on harvesting patterns in the Atlantic salmon fishery. However, the code was more than a guide to sporting etiquette. To be fully accepted as a member of the sporting fraternity, the individual hunter or angler had to be a naturalist, knowledgeable of the habits of fish and game as well as the habitats in which they thrived. For many salmon anglers this meant an intimate knowledge of 'woodcraft', an integral part of which were the customs, language, technology, and hunting and fishing methods of Native people.[33]

The sportsmen's interest in Native culture was related to and stimulated by the growing wilderness cult of the late nineteenth century. In Europe the search for the unadulterated character of man through an examination of supposed primitive cultures dated back to at least the late Middle Ages; modern notions of the 'wild man' or 'noble savage' began to take form in the mid-eighteenth century with the writings of Rousseau and the Romantics. With the closing of the American frontier, the acceleration of urbanization, and the passing of Native people as a perceived threat, eastern North Americans also began to reassess the long-held negative images of wilderness and indigenous peoples. Wilderness, in the North American mind, was slowly transformed in the nineteenth century from being a barrier to civilization to being a positive influence—a foundation of national character.[34] In addition to being represented as a symbol of savagery, the wild man—in this case the Native peoples of North America—became also a symbol of freedom, nobility, and vitality, as increasingly oppressive urban environmental conditions forced a reassessment of the process of 'civilization'.[35] In ever larger numbers in the last decades of the nineteenth century, middle- and upper-class North Americans began to seek out rather than avoid wilderness experiences and contact with Native people.

It was this 'anti-modern' impulse that fuelled the sporting tourism industry, creating guiding opportunities and transforming Native culture into a commodity to be consumed by curious visitors.[36] Already by the 1870s, provincial governments, railroads, and the popular press began to cater to the search for authentic wilderness experiences, advertising Native culture as a tourist attraction, with emphasis on the primitive qualities most cherished by the traveller. The feelings of sporting and travel writer C.H. Farnham, as he first entered the Montagnais village on the Betsiamits River in the mid-1880s, was indicative of the manner in which these agencies catered to the growing numbers longing to be 'released from the iron cage of modernity into a world re-enchanted by history, nature and the mysterious.'[37] 'As I walk through an Indian village I am startled by seeing my aboriginal self', Farnham informed the readers of *Harper's Magazine*:

> We rarely meet our prehistoric ancestors, but here I sit down on the earth with my disconnected forefathers; I talk with men and women who still are absolutely a part of nature. Here I see how far we have come since my family left the woods . . . I met yesterday on the beach an Indian coming from a seclusion of two years in the heart of the continent. He lived without any of what we call the necessities of civilization, and yet he was quite like other men in flesh and limb. The shyness and quietness of his nature were upon him so strongly that I would not break into his reserve, nor dissipate the awe I felt in his presence. He had a very different feeling for me; he knew a hundred men, even a whole tribe, far more skillful at getting a living out of the wilderness, so he had no wonder to waste on an inferior.[38]

As in other places, the organization of what scholars have referred as the 'tourist gaze' had political, economic, and cultural implications.[39]

The transforming capacity of the tourist gaze was exemplified by broad changes in the Native economy of eastern Canada after 1860. Thousands of Native people abandoned other economic pursuits to produce handicrafts for the tourist market. By 1890 there were so many Native people making seasonal visits to tourist venues to sell moccasins, necklaces, baskets, and other 'Indian curiosities' that the market had become glutted and it was no longer a viable means of subsistence.[40] Native men also entered the guiding industry during the same period. Tourism promoters naturally ignored any negative consequences of the transformation in the lives of Native people, as the tourist gaze did not allow for such complications. Thus, even the Montagnais, who suffered and died of starvation as a result of fishery policies that promoted recreational fishing, could be reconstructed and packaged as a simple, happy people, willing to assist the sporting tourist. 'In addition to the magnificent sport afforded to salmon fishermen by many of the streams upon the north shore of the Lower St Lawrence', a government pamphlet noted, 'there is the added attraction of the romance and glamour that connect themselves with the peculiar folk-lore of the aboriginal inhabitants of the country through which they flow—the dusky Montagnais who make such splendid guides and canoe men for the anglers who fish these waters.'[41]

Sportsmen, even more than other wilderness tourists, were fascinated by all aspects of Native culture. Their closer contacts with Native people, and the pretensions of many sportsmen that they were experts on the increasingly popular subject of natural history, prompted them to speak as authorities on the Native *mentalité*. Many salmon anglers truly believed that their wilderness experiences and contacts with Native culture were more authentic than those of mere tourists; they used sporting narratives as a means of establishing their credentials as sportsmen and legitimizing their experiences as true wilderness adventures. Sporting narratives frequently used Mi'kmaq, Maliseet, or Montagnais words to describe commonly used camp items and translated the names of rivers, mountains, and other places from their Native language into English. When Native guides were given speaking parts in salmon-fishing stories, it was common for the authors to attempt to reproduce their broken English. Words such as 'urn', ''em', and 'mebbe' appear over and over again as representations of Native use of the English language.[42] Even more common in sporting narratives was the assignment of particular personality and character traits to all Native people. Native guides were often portrayed in salmon-fishing narratives as physically imposing, capable of great feats of stamina and of enduring weather, heat, the wrath of insects, and other hardships without complaint. 'The strength and endurance of these guides are marvelous', one sportsman commented. 'I have known them to carry over 300 pounds of baggage each over a portage.'[43] Accounts of the virtues of individual guides were not infrequently accompanied by sketches and pictures. The mythologized Native guide was a man of instinct, 'lazy and generally worthless at any regular labor', but 'indefatigable in avocations containing an element of sport'.[44] Normally taciturn and retiring, the Native guide of sporting narratives was animated by the thrill of the chase.

Sporting writers paid especially close attention to what they perceived as the naïveté of guides, their ignorance of social graces, and their clumsiness when stepping out of the natural environment. 'They have a charming disrespect for persons and personages', Sage explained, as he told the story of 'old Larry Vicaire' who, 'annoyed' by the refusal of 'Princess Louise' to listen to her husband and sit down in the canoe, 'placed his hands on the royal shoulders, and forced their owner into a sitting position, with some allusion to the wishes of the "ole man"'.[45] Roberts, in a similar vein, delighted in telling the story of his Maliseet guide's misadventure in attempting to fish with a fly rod.[46] Informed by Victorian notions of race and class, stories that revolved around the naïveté of guides constituted the principal form of humour in salmon-fishing narratives. They served to reconfirm for elite sportsmen that Native men, while they might possess attractive masculine character traits and assert a measure of authority on the river, were impotent when confronted with civilization and best confined to their proscribed role as domestic servants of the wilderness.

There were intellectual contradictions to sport tourism, beyond the realities that sporting tourists were simultaneously idealizing traditional Native culture and aggressively participating in its destruction. Principal among these contradictions was that the glorification of Native woodcraft ran counter to the code of the sportsmen with respect to methods of taking fish and game. While sporting tourists wished to be in communion with Native people, they also desired membership in the fraternity of sportsmen who adhered to the code, which, in its condemnation of such Native practices as snaring, baiting, and spearing, separated the civilized gentleman from the base pot hunter or poacher. The fixation of sporting writers with spearing illustrated the contradictory tensions between the code of the sportsman and the cult of wilderness.

Native poachers using the traditional *negog* were used in some salmon-fishing narratives as a foil for demonstrating the moral superiority of recreational modes of fishing and the ingenuity and intelligence of the civilized angler. One such morality play featured prominent American sporting writer Charles Hallock and the degenerate 'half-breed' Indian Joe, matching wits on a river in Nova Scotia. When the indiscretion was detected, Joe was hiding in the bushes. He was lured out with the promise of 'a little whiskey' and goaded into revealing the location of his illegally caught fish by the suggestion that a member of the angling party wished to purchase a salmon. The story ended with Joe being shown mercy (he was let off with stern warning) and the obligatory diatribe against barbarous fishing practices.[47] In another probably fictional scenario, two teenage boys, who were taken to a noted salmon river on the Gaspé Peninsula as part of a wilderness 'summer school', stumbled upon the notorious 'half-breed' poacher Pete Labouisse night fishing with spear and *flambeaux*.[48] The two adolescents chased Pete until his canoe was shattered in a set of rapids; Pete, who couldn't swim and had broken his leg, was thrown into the churning water. Jumping into the water, one of the boys made a daring rescue. In returning to camp with the injured prisoner, the two boys further demonstrated their humanity by insisting that Pete not be imprisoned.[49] In this instance, showing a revulsion to destructive fishing practices and a willingness to take action is represented as an initiation to the elite sporting fraternity. Indeed, the triumph of the civilized boys over primitive Pete is held up as a rite of manhood.

While spearing was vilified as the most destructive of all forms of salmon fishing, it was also idealized as a grand spectacle of Native culture, an event that brought into full view the glories of primitive masculinity. J.E. Alexander, for example, who bitterly condemned the practice, could still admire spearing as a ritual that stirred what he and so many other sporting tourists saw as the natural instincts of the Native hunter. 'The native love of excitement in the chase has something to do with their pertinacious pursuit of salmon by spears and flambeaux . . . Nothing can exceed the wild excitement with which these men pursue it . . . The flame and the shadow, swayed by ripples, conceals the spearers' forms, and bewilder the doomed salmon. Their silvery sides and amber coloured eye-balls glisten through the rippling water. The dilated eyes, the expanded nostrils, and the compressed lips of the swarthy canoe men, fitly picture their eager and excited mood. A quick, deadly aim, a violent swirl, and some momentary convulsive struggles all tell the rest.'[50] The identical language used in describing the physical attributes of the salmon and the fishermen, in this and other sporting narratives, underscored the supposed primitiveness of Native people and the extent to which their actions were instinctual rather than conscious and considered. It followed that these instincts needed to be controlled.

Contextualized within the cultural politics that surrounded representations of the traditional Native practice of spearing salmon, the significance of the 'staged authenticity' of the ritual undertaken by the members of Camp Harmony in 1886 comes into full view.[51] Underneath the frequent professions of admiration and brotherhood, the relationship between salmon anglers and Native guides was about power and control. Perhaps even more than other sporting tourists, salmon anglers sought to reconstruct the 'contact zones' between the two groups—to produce a wilderness environment that included Native people but was relatively free from the inherent conflicts that character-ized the history of Native-white relations over natural resources.[52] Sporting tourists wanted to consume Native culture at a comfortable level and at a safe distance. The mock spearing party was essentially a cultural experiment, containing just the ideal amount of primitive danger and excitement deemed appropriate for 'the ladies' but never beyond control of the so-called civilized sportsmen. It demonstrated the extent to which salmon anglers by the late 1880s were controlling both the salmon harvest and the content of the Native culture to which they were exposed. Sage and his fellow club members had found, or, rather, created a satisfactory resolution to the contradictions between the code of the sportsman and the cult of wilderness.

## Conclusion

The removal of Native people from the Atlantic salmon harvest was part of a larger process of economic, political, and social change in the last decades of the nineteenth century. Resource depletion from growing competition with white settlers, sport hunters, and commercial interests hastened the destruction of a hunting and gathering economy that had long been in decline. Central to the acceleration of this process was the advent of more comprehensive state administration, in the form of changes in fish and game laws that favoured recreational over subsistence and commercial exploitation. Also vitally important, but beyond the scope of this study, were the policies of the Department of Indian Affairs, which were founded on idealized notions of 'civilizing' Native people and consolidating them into communities of independent yeoman farmers, oftentimes in areas where environmental conditions made this goal unrealistic. Policies prohibiting salmon fishing for subsistence and, especially, commercial purposes were in direct contradiction to the developing policy of forcing Native people to become more self-sufficient and individualistic; they served to underline the duplicitous nature of the administrative initiatives undertaken by the Department of Marine and Fisheries and the Department of Indian Affairs in the late nineteenth century. It is important to recognize that in an era when Native people were, for the most part, prevented from mounting legal challenges, state policy could have devastating consequences. In particular, the alienation of the Montagnais on the north shore of the St Lawrence River from the salmon harvest contributed to severe deprivation and even starvation in the region during the 1870s and 1880s. The threat of starvation was not uncommon among the bands on the Godbout, Saint John, and Mingan rivers, for example, where 13 salmon anglers caught slightly over 16,000 pounds of salmon in 1871.[53] In hindsight, at least, the true sportsmen of the nineteenth century were less civilized than they appeared in the self-congratulatory sporting literature of the time.

The exclusion of Native people as active resource users coincided with their entry into the guiding profession in larger numbers in the second half of the nineteenth century. Native men possessed the requisite skills, and salmon guiding provided relatively high wages, at a time when other opportunities were diminishing. The transition was also stimulated by cultural forces, namely the growing cult of wilderness and the anti-modern impulse sweeping through North America during the second half of the nineteenth century. Whether they were sightseers or 'sports', what the wilderness tourists of the nineteenth century wanted was to journey into the past, in the hope that gazing upon 'primitive culture' would help them cope with and understand their own increasingly complex and divisive society. After 1850 this demand was increasingly met by an organized tourist industry, complete with its own literature, which advertised and sold Native culture as part of the wilderness experience and was predicated on the economic dependence of Native people. Necessity and imagination created a class of Native seasonal workers who served both as conduits, to lead elite anglers into the spiritual realm of the wilderness, and as domestic servants, to provide comforts in the temporal world.

## Notes

The research and writing of this article were made possible by a postdoctoral fellowship from the Social Sciences and Humanities Research Council of Canada. The author would like to thank David Frank, Kerry Abel, Delphin Muise, Colin Howell, and the anonymous *CHR* referees for their helpful comments and suggestions.

1.  Dean Sage, *The Restigouche and Its Salmon Fishing, with a Chapter on Angling Literature* (Edinburgh: D. Douglas, 1888), 216–23.

2.  This phrase was used by renowned American sportsman Charles Lanman in his *Adventures in the Wilds of the United States and British North America* (Philadelphia: J.W. Moore, 1856). On the code of the sportsman, see John Reiger, *American Sportsmen and the Origins of Conservation* (Norman: University of Oklahoma Press, 1977); James A. Tober, *Who Owns the Wildlife? The Political Economy of Conservation in Nineteenth Century America* (Westport, Conn.: Greenwood Press, 1981); Richard P. Manning, 'Recreating Man: Hunting and Angling in Victorian Canada', MA thesis (Carleton University, 1994).

3.  It should be recognized that Native people were by no means the only resource users affected by this process. The Atlantic salmon fishery had a significant commercial net-fishing sector; and thousands of farmers, settlers, and other residents along the rivers of eastern Canada also used the resource, fishing for salmon by various means, including the spear. Efforts by the sport-fishing industry and the government to control the harvesting activities of these groups resulted in local political struggles and numerous incidents of social violence, which are beyond the scope of this study. For an elaboration of the larger picture, see Bill Parenteau, 'Creating a Sportsman's Paradise: Salmon Fishing Regulation and Social Conflict in New Brunswick, 1867–1900', paper

presented at the biennial conference of the American Society for Environmental History, Las Vegas, Nevada, March 1995. For a case study of the conflicts between non-Native resource users, see Neil S. Forkey, 'Anglers, Fishers and the St Croix River: Conflict in a Canadian-American Borderland, 1867–1900', *Forest and Conservation History* 37, 4 (1993): 160–6.

4. Reiger, *American Sportsmen and the Origins of Conservation*; Richard Judd, *Common Lands, Common People: The Origins of Conservation in Northern New England* (Cambridge, Mass.: Harvard University Press, 1997), 283.

5. After Confederation, angling leases were issued by the federal government. The New Brunswick legislature in the late 1870s, however, challenged the legal right of the federal government to hold such powers over the non-tidal portions of the province's rivers. In 1882 the Supreme Court of Canada ruled in favour of New Brunswick, and thereafter all salmon-angling leases were issued by the provinces. For obvious reasons, government leases could only be issued for stretches of river running through Crown land. Because there was very little Crown land on salmon rivers in Nova Scotia, as well as public resistance, the province did not adopt the leasing system.

6. National Archives of Canada (NAC), Records of the Department of Marine and Fisheries, RG 23, vol. 167, file 610, Arthur D. Weeks, secretary, Restigouche Salmon Club, to Sir Herbert Tupper, 26 Feb. 1894.

7. On the participation of political elites in salmon clubs, see Parenteau, 'Creating a Sportsmen's Paradise'.

8. Canada, *Statutes of Canada*, 31 Vict., 1868, c. 60, 183.

9. For a good statement of this notion, see *Sessional Papers*, 1872, no. 5, Annual Reports of the Department of Marine and Fisheries, Napoleon Lavoie, 'Report of the Cruise of the Government Schooner *La Canadienne* in the River and Gulf of St Lawrence', appendix, 23–4.

10. NAC, Records of the Department of Marine and Fisheries, RG 23, vol. 298, file 2331, R. Mitchell to L.H. Davis, Minister of Marine and Fisheries, 'Report on Burnt Church Indian Fishing', 31 May 1897.

11. *Sessional Papers*, 1867, no. 43, 'Reports of the Fisheries of the Dominion, 1867', 'Mr. Venning's Report'.

12. Ibid., 'Reports of the Fisheries of the Dominion, 1867', and Théophile Tétu, 'Some Remarks on Our Sea and River Fisheries', appendix, 27–8.

13. Parenteau, 'Creating a Sportsmen's Paradise', 42–55.

14. Sage, *The Restigouche*, 22.

15. Napoleon Comeau, *Life and Sport on the Lower St Lawrence and Gulf*, 2nd edn (Quebec: Telegraph Printing Company, 1923), 108–10.

16. The cat-and-mouse games played between Comeau and the residents of a nearby reserve are recounted ibid., 110–13. On the monitoring of fish and game wardens, see the North American Fish and Game Protective Association, *Minutes of the Proceedings of the First Meeting* (Montreal, 1900), 23–4.

17. For a listing of the leased rivers in the early 1890s, see Charles G.D. Roberts, *The Canadian Guide Book: The Tourist's and Sportsman's Guide to Eastern Canada and Newfoundland* (New York: D. Appleton, 1891), 264–7.

18. On this logic, see, for example, 'Editorial', *Rod and Gun in Canada* 3, (1901): 10.

19. NAC, Records of the Department of Marine and Fisheries, RG 10, vol. 298, file 2331, Alexander Mowat to E.E. Prince, commissioner of fisheries, 16 Nov. 1895.

20. *Sessional Papers*, 1893, no. 26, 14, Annual Report of the Department of Indian Affairs, 'Report of V.I.A. Venner, Indian agent', 30.

21. NAC, Records of the Department of Marine and Fisheries, RG 23, vol. 298, file 2331, Alexander Mowat to E.E. Prince, commissioner of fisheries, 16 Nov. 1895. Information on wages in the late nineteenth century can be found in various volumes of the *Report on the Royal Commission on the Relations of Capital and Labour in Canada* (Ottawa, 1889). On the opportunities for guides to earn additional money by providing other services or

goods, see J. Michael Thoms, 'Illegal Conservation: Two Case Studies of Conflict between Indigenous and State Natural Resource Paradigms', MA thesis (Trent University, 1995).

22. Sage, *The Restigouche*, 20.

23. For a particularly good account of a lengthy struggle with a salmon and the importance of an expert guide, see Henry P. Wells, *The American Salmon Fisherman* (London: S. Low, Marston, Searle and Rivington, 1886), 155–62. See also T.R. Pattillo, *Moose Hunting, Salmon Fishing and Other Sketches of Sport, Being a Record of Personal Experiences of Hunting Wild Game in Canada* (London: S. Low, Marston, 1902), 24–57.

24. See, for example, the character study of 'Pierre Joseph' in *Rod and Gun in Canada* 2, 6 (1900): 364; Roberts, *The Canadian Guide Book*, 165–6; Sage, *The Restigouche*, 22–32; E.T.D. Chambers, 'Among the Northern Lakes', *Rod and Gun in Canada* 2, 5 (1900).

25. The attributes of a particular guide could be known to a surprisingly wide circle of sportsmen. Even the early modern sporting/travel guides recommended specific guides to their readers. See Robert Barnwell Roosevelt, *Game Fish of the Northern United States and British Provinces* (New York: Carleton, 1869); Charles Hallock, *The Fishing Tourist: Angler's Guide and Reference Book* (New York: Harper, 1873).

26. The topic of Native guides in eastern Canada has not been studied to any great extent. On the methodological and conceptual problems of examining the relationship between sportsmen and guides, see Patricia Jasen, 'Who's the Boss: Native Guides and White Tourists in the Canadian Wilderness, 1850-1914', unpublished paper, presented at the annual meeting of the Canadian Historical Association, Ottawa, June 1993; Patricia Jasen, *Wild Things: Nature, Culture and Tourism in Ontario, 1790-1914* (Toronto: University of Toronto Press, 1995), 133–5.

27. *Sessional Papers*, 1891, no. 24, 8a, Annual Report of the Department of Marine and Fisheries, 'Report of Salmon Fisheries on the Bay des Chaleurs', appendix, 30–1. On the exclusivity of clubs in Quebec, see L.Z. Joncas, *The Sportsmen's Companion, Showing the Haunts of Moose, Caribou and Deer, also of the Salmon, Ouananiche and Trout of the Province of Quebec* (Quebec, 1899), 101–2.

28. An exception to the general pattern could be seen in Nova Scotia, where the rivers were more open to local people and the occasional fishing tourist of modest means. However, the fishing was much less consistent and usually not as good as in places like the Gaspé and the North Shore of New Brunswick. Salmon fishing in Nova Scotia could also be a contentious affair, with rival parties in dispute over the best pools. See Pattillo, *Moose Hunting, Salmon Fishing and Other Sketches of Sport*; Richard Lewes Dashwood, *Chiploquorgan, or Life by the Camp Fire* (London: Simpkin, Marshall, 1872).

29. NAC, Records of the Department of Indian Affairs, RG 10, vol. 1991, file 6653, 'Report of Napoleon Lavoie, Progress of the Mission Point Indians, 1876'; *Sessional Papers*, 1884, no. 16, 4, Annual Report of the Department of Indian Affairs, 'Report of Octave Drapeau, Mission Point Reserve', 31.

30. See John M. MacKenzie, *The Empire of Nature* (Manchester: Manchester University Press, 1987); MacKenzie. 'The Imperial Pioneer and Hunter and the British Masculine Stereotype in Late Victorian and Edwardian Times', in J.A. Mangan and James Walvin, eds, *Manliness and Morality: Middle Class Masculinity in Britain and America* (Manchester: Manchester University Press, 1987), 176–98; Dennison Nash, 'Tourism as a Form of Imperialism', in V.L Smith, ed., *Hosts and Guests: The Anthropology of Tourism* (Philadelphia: University of Pennsylvania Press, 1977), 37–52; Martin Green, *The Adventurous Male: Chapters in the History of the White Male Mind* (University Park: Pennsylvania State University Press, 1993).

31. Roberts, *The Canadian Guide Book*, 177.

32. Green, *The Adventurous Male*, 68

33. On adoption of the code of the sportsman in North America, see Reiger, *American Sportsmen and the Origins of Conservation*; Manning,

'Recreating Man: Hunting and Angling in Victorian Canada'; Tober, *Who Owns the Wildlife?*

34. The classic statement on this subject is Roderick Nash, 'The Wilderness Cult', in his *Wilderness and the American Mind*, 3rd edn (New Haven: Yale University Press, 1982). An excellent discussion of these issues can be found in Jasen, *Wild Things*, 13–20; see also Nelson H.H. Grayburn, 'Tourism: The Sacred Journey', in Smith, *Hosts and Guests*, 21–35.

35. Jasen, *Wild Things*, 17–19. On representations of Native people in Canada, see Daniel Francis, *The Imaginary Indian: The Image of the Indian in Canadian Culture* (Vancouver: Arsenal Pulp Press, 1992); Terry Goldman, *Fear and Temptation: The Image of the Indigene in Canadian, Australian and New Zealand Literature* (Montreal and Kingston: McGill-Queen's University Press, 1989); Leslie Monkman, *A Native Heritage: Images of Indians in English-Canadian Literature* (Toronto: University of Toronto Press, 1981).

36. The classic statement on anti-modernism is T. Jackson Lears, *No Place of Grace: Antimodernism and the Transformation of American Culture, 1880–1920* (New York: Pantheon, 1981); see also Ian McKay, *The Quest of the Folk: Antimodernism and Cultural Selection in Twentieth Century Nova Scotia* (Montreal and Kingston: McGill-Queen's University Press, 1994).

37. McKay, *The Quest of the Folk*, xv.

38. C.H. Farnham, 'The Montagnais', *Harper's Magazine* (Aug. 1888): 379–80; for another excellent comparison between 'primitive' and 'civilized' man, see Edward A. Samuels, *With Rod and Gun in New England and the Maritime Provinces* (Boston: Samuels and Kimball, 1897), 23–6.

39. John Urry, *The Tourist Gaze: Leisure and Travel in Contemporary Societies* (London: Sage, 1990); McKay, *The Quest of the Folk*; Dean MacCannell, *The Tourist: A New Theory of the Leisure Class*, 2nd edn (New York: Shocken, 1989)

40. Abundant evidence of the pervasive trade in Native handicrafts and the eventual saturation of the market can be found in the synoptic reports of Indian agents in the annual reports of the Department of Indian Affairs. On the decline of the trade, see, for example, *Sessional Papers*, 1892, no. 14, Annual Report of the Department of Indian Affairs, 28, 35, 37, 39.

41. Joncas, *The Sportsmen's Companion*, 105.

42. Dashwood. *Chiploquorgan, or Life by the Camp Fire*; Wells, *The American Salmon Fisherman*; Hallock, *The Fishing Tourist*; Sage, *The Restigouche*.

43. E.T.D. Chambers, 'The Ouananiche and Its Canadian Environment', *Harpers's Magazine* 93 (June 1896): 119; on the physical attributes of guides, see also Roberts, *The Canadian Guide Book*; 'Pierre Joseph', *Rod and Gun in Canada* 2, 6 (Nov. 1900); St Croix, 'Second Sight and the Indian', *Rod and Gun in Canada* 4, 3 (Aug. 1902): 103–4; Heber Bishop, *Guide Book to the Megantic, Spider and Upper Dead River Regions of the Province of Quebec and the State of Maine* (Boston: Megantic Fish and Game Club, 1897).

44. Sage, *The Restigouche*, 23.

45. Ibid., 23–4.

46. Roberts, *The Canadian Guide Book*, 98

47. Hallock, The *Fishing Tourist*, 36–8.

48. The fact that both Indian Joe and Pete Labouisse were 'half-breeds' was by no means a coincidence. Like other Victorians, sporting writers were fixated with issues of racial purity. The assignment of mixed-race lineage to poachers was, in some respects, a way of maintaining idealized, romantic notions of the character of 'primitive man' (i.e., racially pure Native people). On the importance of racial purity to nineteenth-century tourists, see Jasen, *Wild Things*, 107–12.

49. Robert Grant, *Jack in the Bush, or a Summer on Salmon River* (New York: Charles Scribner's Sons, 1893), 297–331.

50. J.E. Alexander, 'Fishing in New Brunswick and etc.', in W. Agar Adamson, *Salmon Fishing in Canada: By a Resident* (London: Longman, Green, Longman and Roberts, 1860), 330.

51. The concept of 'staged authenticity' is elaborated in MacCannell, *The Tourist*, 98–100.

52. Mary Louise Pratt defines 'contact zones' as 'the space of colonial encounters, the space in which peoples geographically and historically separated

come into contact with each other and establish ongoing relations, usually involving conditions of coercion, radical inequality, and intractable conflict.' Pratt, *Imperial Eyes: Travel Writing and Transculturation* (London: Routledge, 1992), 5.

53. Complete statistics are available for the year 1871. The average for the three rivers combined was probably closer to 10,000 pounds per year. Still, it does not seem unreasonable to suggest that five tons of salmon may have been put to good use by the Montagnais. *Statements of Salmon Fishing On the River Godbout, from 1859–1875* (Ottawa: A.S. Woodburn, 1876), 10; Comeau, *Life and Sport on the Lower St Lawrence*, 368, 375, 386.

# 19

# 'Not Merely for the Sake of an Evening's Entertainment': The Educational Uses of Theatre in Toronto's Settlement Houses, 1910–1930

Cathy L. James

It is only recently that the power of the drama as a living force in daily life has been appreciated. Not only is it an educational force along intellectual and spiritual lines, but it offers first hand to the individual, a vision of the possibilities of self development and self equipment for the positive business of everyday existence. . . . It is of great educational value to witness the acting of a good play, but to walk upon the stage, to speak to hushed audiences is to awake to a consciousness of power generally unsuspected within the self.[1]

In early January 1916, in the midst of the First World War, Toronto's Central Neighborhood House presented Maurice Maeterlinck's play *The Blue Bird*. It was indisputably an amateur production, yet it was a remarkably lavish one, especially for Toronto. Staged at the Orde Street School, where the settlement operated a social centre, the play showcased the dramatic talents of 50 adolescents and children from among the settlement's membership and involved countless other members as crew. The show also drew on the labour of innumerable volunteers—including at least half a dozen up-and-coming members of Toronto's professional arts community. According to the reminiscences of the play's director, Dora Mavor Moore, who was herself to become an important figure in Canadian theatre, the production profoundly inspired many of those who helped to mount it, both among the cast and the crew.[2] Local newspapers reported that it made a favourable impression on its audience as well, not just on the approximately 800 parents, friends, neighbours, and local residents who attended, but also on the 400 invited guests and journalists from 'uptown'. The staging of this play was, in fact, something of a minor sensation in the city, and it heralded the evolution of what was to be one of the most successful programs of Toronto's settlement movement in the post-First World War era—the theatre program.[3]

The period between 1910 and 1930 can be described as the heyday of community theatre in North America. It blossomed in this period in forms ranging from the children's Christmas concerts and pageants mounted at public schools and local churches to the professional-quality

Cathy L. James, 'Not Merely for the Sake of an Evening's Entertainment: The Educational Uses of Theatre in Toronto's Settlement Houses, 1910–1930', *History of Education Quarterly* 38, 3 (1998): 287–311. Copyright by History of Education Society. Reprinted by permission.

productions of the Little Theatre movement.[4] The intention of this paper is to explore the many roles that the theatre played in Toronto's settlement houses. Its aim is to demonstrate that settlement workers in Toronto, like their counterparts in cities south of the border, attempted to use the power of the theatre to influence, inspire, and inform—in short, to educate—both their clientele and the broader community. Toronto's settlement workers and their sponsors attempted to put the theatre's capacity to stimulate and uplift to work for them in a variety of ways: as a means to supplant working-class culture; as a tool of assimilation and spiritual elevation; as one strategy in their bid to create a cohesive community untroubled by class, ethnic, or religious tensions; as an emotional and physical outlet for settlement members; and as a means of maintaining the settlement movement's original commitment to voluntarism at a time when its staff members were participating wholeheartedly in the professionalization of social work. Overall, in Toronto's settlements, the theatre was at least for a brief time a dynamic, effective, and versatile educational tool, one which settlement workers believed would reach the widest possible audience with the lessons they sought to instill.

## The Roots of the Toronto Settlement Movement

The settlement house movement began in England in 1884 with the founding of Toynbee Hall. The idea quickly spread throughout England and to the United States; in 1911 there were at least 46 settlement houses in Britain and over 400 in the United States, of which Jane Addams's Hull-House was the most famous.[5] By the turn of the century Canadian activists had adopted the movement as well; American settlement worker Sara Libby Carson established the first Canadian settlement, Evangelia House, in Toronto in 1902, and the movement caught on to such an extent that by

the mid-1910s settlements had been founded in major cities from British Columbia to Quebec. Toronto alone boasted six settlement houses by 1914: Evangelia House; University Settlement; Central Neighborhood House (CNH); St Christopher House; Memorial Institute; and Riverdale Settlement.[6] . . .

Inspired by the British Idealist school of thought, early proponents of the settlement movement argued that social regeneration in the urban industrial milieu could best be accomplished if members of the middle class created islands of 'enlightenment' in the midst of urban slums—that is, they should establish institutions where those who had the benefit of higher education and cultural refinement could live for a time in order to provide the urban poor with 'constructive' recreational and educational opportunities. . . . Settlement advocates hoped that by living as neighbours in working-class districts they might, through role-modelling and through direct instruction, inculcate working people and their children with a love for what were considered to be the highest forms of art, literature, and philosophy. Settlers maintained that these cultural endowments had the power of spiritual and social redemption, and furthermore, that people who lacked exposure to the highest cultural attainments were likely to become both intellectually and morally degenerate. As one Toronto settlement advocate asserted, without the encouragement of educated and cultured mentors, working women in particular were likely to sink 'unconsciously . . . into the slough of sordid toil and foolish pleasure'.[7]

Settlement workers saw their institutions not only as recreational and educational centres, however. Rather, they also used the settlements as sites from which to launch social investigations and to test innovative schemes aimed at promoting the welfare of the poor on a very pragmatic level.[8] To this end, settlement staff pioneered many social programs, such as children's libraries, well-baby clinics, supervised playgrounds, and employment bureaus, which were later adopted by civic, provincial, and federal agencies. But beyond the provision of needed educational, recreational, and welfare services to the poor, settlers had an even wider purpose for this aspect of their work; they hoped ultimately to recreate a sense of community in their districts and in their nations, a sense, they believed, which had existed throughout the English-speaking world prior to the commencement of the Industrial Revolution. Settlers wanted to act as 'bridges' between the classes, and between members of different religious and ethnic groups, in order to aid in their 'reconnection'. They hoped also to stimulate interest in the poor among the prosperous, and to provide the latter with opportunities to use the knowledge and skills they had gained while in university or college in meaningful, socially significant ways. It is important in this context to recognize that while they were sympathetic to the plight of the working class and the immigrant, and often acknowledged that these groups had much to contribute, settlement workers remained convinced of the intrinsic superiority of middle-class Anglo-Celtic culture, and continued to worry that, if left alone, the working class and the immigrant might pose a very real threat to bourgeois cultural hegemony.[9]

Their concern sprang from a series of rapid social and economic changes taking place within turn-of-the-century Canada as a whole, and within Toronto in particular. From the late nineteenth century onward, Toronto found itself increasingly confronted with the problems faced by most contemporary industrial centres in the 'Western' world. The city's rapidly expanding population taxed its rudimentary services, such as water and sanitation, beyond their limits. Frequent layoffs, low wages, unsafe working conditions, and the lack of support for unemployed workers put intense pressure on Toronto's already faltering private and public poor relief system. Land speculators exploited the working poor's need to live close to their workplaces by charging exorbitant rents and by refusing to maintain low-income rental properties. In the absence of an efficient and affordable transit system which might allow them to live on the outskirts of the city and commute to work, most working-class families had little choice but to minimize their housing costs by crowding into lodgings with other families or by taking in boarders. As housing conditions deteriorated in downtown areas, the city became increasingly segregated into rich and poor neighbourhoods; the middle class and wealthy began moving to newly established suburban residential developments, abandoning downtown districts to businesses, workers, and factories. These trends served to increase a sense of social fragmentation and alienation between Toronto's affluent and indigent.[10]

. . .

All this provided the impetus for the creation of Toronto's settlement houses, which were scattered among the 'neglected' ethnic communities throughout the city, cheek-by-jowl with smoke-belching factories, with cramped, grey sweatshops, and with struggling storefront businesses and decaying housing on busy, sometimes unpaved streets. Because of the proximity of ethnic quarters to each other, all settlement memberships in the city were incredibly diverse—ethnically, linguistically, and religiously; most institutions claimed to have representatives from 20 or more nations among their members. The groups which utilized Toronto's settlements most frequently, however, were Eastern European Jewish, working-class British, and Italian immigrants, along with a sizable minority from Slavic and Balkan regions. In addition to the difficulties inherent in addressing the needs of such an eclectic clientele, settlements also had to compete with the attractions of local saloons, dance halls, vaudeville theatres, and nickelodeons for the leisure time of the working poor. Yet while uniformly suspicious of these and other expressions of popular culture, settlement workers' views, at least on the latter two, were far more equivocal than one might initially suspect.

## Popular Theatre in the Edwardian Age

Many settlement advocates and other social reformers in early twentieth-century North America believed that because of its powerful mass appeal, the theatre had, like the settlement itself, great potential as an agent of assimilation, spiritual uplift, and social rejuvenation.[11] As Jane Addams pointed out, '"Going to the show" for thousands of young people in every industrial city is the only possible road to the realms of mystery and romance; the theater is the only place where they can satisfy that craving for a conception of life higher than that which the actual world offers them. . . . [it] becomes to them a "veritable house of dreams."'[12] The problem was, according to the critics, that this power was being squandered; the theatre which was generally available to the working class was, as one observer asserted, 'at the best trivial and at the worst salacious'.[13] Addams herself argued that 'the only art which is constantly placed before the eyes of "the temperamental youth" is a debased form of dramatic art, and a vulgar type of music.'[14] Rather than elevating its audience to a higher moral and intellectual plane, she maintained, the 'cheap theatre' was destroying the home life of many working-class families and driving some youths to crime and even insanity, while on a lesser scale it was corrupting the eyesight, the physical health, and the moral judgement of countless viewers.[15] She acknowledged that much of the attraction of the 'cheap theatre' lay in the way that it reflected its audiences' own experiences, but as historian Mina Carson has pointed out, Addams regretted the 'emergence of a new "folk" art in this context . . . because the commercial structure of urban entertainment precluded active audience involvement in its development.'[16] Popular forms of the theatre, in other words, encouraged their audiences to be passive and idle—and this was a pressing concern for reformers, the majority of whom were anxious to prevent the 'pauperization' of the masses.[17] Moreover, Addams and other middle-class observers argued that working-class audiences were vulnerable to exploitation through the 'cheap' commercial entertainments that mushroomed in cities all over North America from the turn of the century onward. Toronto was no exception to this phenomenon; indeed, historian Carolyn Strange has determined that between 1900 and 1915 alone the number of commercial entertainment enterprises in the city expanded from nine to 112.[18] In Toronto, as in Chicago and New York during these years, the 'cheap theatre' became immensely popular among the working class, much to the chagrin of many reformers of the day.[19]

What was it about the 'cheap theatre' that observers in Canada and the United States found so invidious? In part, it was the plots themselves; Addams noted that a survey conducted in the winter of 1908 of over 460 theatres in Chicago determined that the leading theme in the majority of them was revenge. This was bound to be an unpopular motif among settlement, civic, and religious leaders who were concerned about inter- and intra-ethnic rivalries and tensions.[20] Moreover, Addams claimed, the cheap theatre sensationalized robbery, sexual molestation, assault, and murder, and she warned that given the power of the medium to influence youthful morality, this posed a serious potential threat to social order.[21]

The assessment that the pursuit of revenge and the glamorization of crime were significant themes in many productions was no doubt correct;[22] yet historian Kathy Peiss has demonstrated that American popular theatre was not entirely preoccupied with dark and malevolent motifs. She notes that vaudeville comedy acts were also very popular among working-class audiences, although the admission price for vaudeville theatre was usually too high to allow most low-income wage-earners, and particularly women, to attend very frequently. As for the general nature of vaudeville, Peiss notes: 'Working-class vaudeville was a mixture of the sentimental and the suggestive. Songs and monologues explicitly expressed the Victorian construction of gender, celebrating domesticity and women's virtue, while tests of strength affirmed men's virility and power. . . . These were juxtaposed, however, with sexual innuendo and raucous familiarity.'[23] One settlement worker reported that in some of New York's vaudeville theatres 'the songs are suggestive of everything but what is proper, the choruses are full of double meanings, and the jokes have broad and unmistakable hints of things indecent.'[24] Other observers also condemned the ribald nature of most vaudeville theatre.[25] Apparently, middle-class commentators were as distressed by overt references to sexuality in commercial entertainment as they were to its sometimes violent themes.

By the 1910s the popularity of live vaudeville theatre was beginning to fade as silent motion picture shows captured an ever-increasing proportion of the working-class audience. At a nickel for an evening's entertainment, the cinema was particularly popular among women, including mothers and children, and these groups came to comprise the bulk of the audience in most motion picture theatres. Peiss notes that the nickelodeon had much the same attractiveness for working-class women in New York as the saloons had for their male counterparts; they were also a more widely accepted form of entertainment for young, working women than . . . dance halls. . . .[26] This had an interesting result, for according to contemporary journalist Rollin Hartt, movie producers and theatre owners who wanted to appeal to the widest possible audience found themselves obliged to avoid 'improprieties' and ensure that 'a uniform decency' prevailed throughout their offerings.[27]

Yet while proponents like Hartt maintained that a 'uniform decency' prevailed in silent films, many middle-class reformers remained unconvinced. Their suspicions were provoked by the fact that most early movies were either melodramas or filmed versions of vaudeville variety acts. Stories of intrigue and romance were common fare, as were serialized tales which featured plucky young women successfully manoeuvring around bizarre and implausible threats to their virtue, or happily indulging in 'risqué' pleasures and flamboyant lifestyles.[28] Through the 1910s and 1920s the vast majority of motion pictures glorified youth, heterosexual romance, and conspicuous consumption—thus, according to some observers, raising working-class expectations to an absurd level and impairing the character development of working-class young people. Moreover, the darkness and intimacy of the theatres made parental and neighbourhood supervision of heterosocial relations in these contexts more difficult, and this increased reformers' apprehensions concerning the possibilities thus afforded for sexual misconduct.[29]

Despite these concerns, most North American settlement workers viewed the popular theatre in a much more positive light than they did other commercial amusements. In Toronto, settlement workers occasionally treated their members to carefully selected shows at local vaudeville theatres, even as they encouraged participation in settlement activities as a means to keep their clientele out of the commercial playhouses. Overall, their clientele's passion for the stage was something that settlers sought to encourage, not restrain. But it is important to note that they attempted to encourage that passion along carefully circumscribed lines, and usually towards active rather than passive forms of participation. As Norman J. Ware of Toronto's University Settlement explained, 'drama is a vital part of the Settlement. Self-expression isn't a thing to which we can or wish to say "no": but we can guide it and make it to move in worthy channels where undirected it would perhaps wander in the paths of burlesque.'[30] Settlement users continued to embrace the role of passive audience members at the popular theatre, however, and many settlement workers sought to guide even this form of participation. For example, in 1926 the staff of Toronto's St Christopher House persuaded their board of directors to purchase a movie projector so that they could show films on Saturday afternoons. St Christopher's workers hoped that by charging only a nominal admission, they might gain some control over the movies their members saw, but this was a vain ambition; instead, this settlement's membership continued to frequent commercial cinemas in addition to attending St Christopher's weekly screenings.[31]

## The Settlement Theatre

There were several very good reasons for settlement workers to introduce theatre programs to the slate of activities they offered. Perhaps the most important was the opportunity for 'uplift' they believed these programs might provide. Like Jane Addams and other settlement activists, Canadian settlement workers frequently argued that performing in plays developed the imaginations and characters, as well as the aesthetic and artistic sensibilities, of settlement members.[32] As Addams contended, 'there is no force so powerful as that of the drama in awakening and stimulating an interest in intellectual and beautiful things.'[33] Arthur C. Holden, an American settlement critic, maintained that '[t]hrough pronouncing words of genius, which are put into one's mouth, one learns the attributes of genius and begins, unconsciously at first, to equip oneself for a fuller and more purposeful part in society.'[34] For Holden, watching the performance of a 'good' play was educational, but acting in such a play awakened within the performers a sense of their own power and ability.

Canadian advocates, moreover, claimed that encouraging their members to put on plays demonstrated to the general public the mostly untapped talents of immigrant youth, talents which some commentators believed were innate to Southern and Eastern Europeans particularly. These gifts, settlers argued, could form the basis of a considerable contribution to Canadian culture as a whole. As a journalist for the Toronto *Globe* noted in a review of Central Neighborhood House's 1917 production of *Peter Pan*, 'In provid-

ing outlets for the expression of the artistic nature which is the rich endowment of the little ones of the stranger races who have come to live among us[,] the workers in Central Neighborhood activities are not only doing great things for these children of deep-souled peoples, but they are developing something that, by and by, will bring an immeasurable enrichment to the country's life.'[35] By showcasing the thespian aptitude of immigrant youth, settlement workers hoped to raise the status of all non-Anglo-Celtic immigrants in middle-class Anglo-Canadian eyes. Settlers frequently argued that the newcomers' enjoyment of settlement plays, so like the love of play-acting exhibited by their middle-class counterparts in clubs, private schools, colleges, and universities, proved that love of the theatre, along with love of the classics of English literature, was universal among all people.[36] Thus, as another reporter noted of Central Neighborhood House's *Peter Pan*, 'This charming play of Barrie's is, of course, familiar to you. And now it is just as familiar to the dwellers in the Allies' ward.'[37] The implication was that this familiarity drew 'us' and 'them' closer together. For most champions of the settlement movement in Canada, a shared culture was essential to the development of a truly cohesive community. It should be emphasized, however, that the sharing most settlers had in mind was almost entirely the endowment of Anglo-Canadian cultural icons on immigrants. Regardless of their admiration for the 'innate talents' of Southern and Eastern Europeans, settlers apparently assumed that these immigrants had few dramatic works of their own to offer.

Settlement workers' views of immigrants' artistic tendencies were not entirely positive. Rather, they sometimes warned that immigrant children's inherently dramatic natures could easily develop potentially dangerous and destructive propensities for 'histrionics' unless they were channelled through the theatre into more positive and productive expressions.[38] Many middle-class activists assumed that working-class immigrants had a particular proclivity for disorder. An important aspect of settlement theatricals, therefore, was that they helped keep the children off the streets and out of mischief. Furthermore, settlement workers believed that 'good' plays would inculcate moral lessons and inspire patriotic fervour among new Canadians; participating in dramatic programs could thus prevent settlement members from even *wanting* to indulge in unruly or subversive behaviour.[39] Acting in plays also encouraged a facility in English among non-English speakers, and this, too, helped to advance their assimilation into Anglo-Canadian society. . . . One anonymous writer to an Anglican newspaper, the *Canadian Churchman*, spoke for many moderates on the issue of immigration, including many settlement workers, when he argued that nations which think, speak, and dream in the same tongue, and feed impressionable minds with the same masterpieces 'are bound to approximate towards each other in the essentials.' 'Language', he asserted, 'is thicker than blood.'[40]

For settlement workers, another positive aspect of a strong drama program was that the plays produced in the settlements gave both the players and their working-class audiences some wholesome, and sorely needed, pleasure—transporting them for a time outside their otherwise 'drab' and 'miserable' existence.[41] This sharing of pleasure brought cosmopolitan communities together in a fellowship which, many observers believed, reached across lines of ethnicity and religion, as Jewish, Italian, Slavic, and British parents sat side by side, glowing in the reflected glory of their offspring on stage. Moreover, some newspaper reviews of settlement plays emphasized how friendly, even to strangers, the audiences were at these productions. These reports contrasted the behaviour of settlement audiences with that of the more aloof middle-class theatre audiences and went on to marvel at how these hard-working, beleaguered wage-earners were able to remain so cheerful and welcoming. In addition to all this, settlement workers thought that performing on the stage might contribute to the overall mental and physical well-being of immigrant families, since acting, singing, and dancing allowed overburdened youngsters to be children again, while watching them allowed their parents and neighbours a measure of benevolent happiness and vicarious pride.[42]

But settlers thought their theatre programs did more, even, than this for settlement clientele. According to authorities like Jane Addams, acting in plays also provided urban children and young people with important role models and with the opportunities for the adventure, romance, and excitement that the young so desperately craved.[43] Addams remarked, 'The drama provides a transition between the romantic conceptions which [working-class children] vainly struggle to keep intact and life's cruelties and trivialities which they refuse to admit.'[44] This made it all the more important that the overworked and downtrodden children of the slums have access to the best plays which, she asserted, were generally unavailable to them in the cheap commercial theatres. . . .

. . .

## All the Settlement's a Stage . . .

In addition to public performances, settlement staff and members practised their acting, directing, and producing skills before in-house audiences as well. Toronto settlements staged performances at practically every special event they celebrated, as well as for no particular reason at all. One-, two-, and three-act plays, in addition to scenes or adaptations of larger productions, were regular features of winter and spring festivals at the settlements. Settlements celebrated holidays like Christmas, Easter, St Patrick's Day, and Halloween with plays, and they also staged them for annual intra-settlement gatherings.[45] Furthermore, the settlements organized drama competitions, and in the 1920s the best play from each institution was entered in annual inter-settlement contests; the settlements also presented many of these to the general public.[46] The local school social centres that some settlements operated with the financial assistance of the Toronto Playgrounds Association usually provided the venues for these large productions. In this regard, most of the press reports about settlement productions either began or ended with an appeal for further extending the use of schools as social centres; the city's space-starved settlement houses contended that they lacked the capacity to handle the numbers of young people who wanted to participate in the shows, let alone the numbers who wanted to attend them.[47]

Not all settlement dramatics were large-scale efforts, however. In fact, self-governing clubs within the settlements produced most settlement plays. The majority of these clubs did not centre on dramatics; rather, they included drama as just one part of their regular activities. Nearly all settlement clubs staged plays, with the exception of the men's groups, most of which preferred staging concerts or musical variety shows. Most women's club members also appear to have had less interest in the theatre than did their children, but some adult women participated in settlement productions on occasion, and a few women's clubs even presented plays of their own.[48] Cultural strictures, shyness, a perception that play-acting lacked dignity, and for many, discomfort over their lack of facility in English, no doubt contributed to this lower participation rate among adults.

Whatever its cause, the result was that settlement workers focused most of their resources on facilitating the dramatic work of clubs for 10- to 20-year-olds. Settlement workers expected each of these clubs to produce a play, or some other entertainment, for general meetings of the membership at the very least. Many clubs staged independent performances as well, often charging 10 or 15 cents admission in order to raise funds for special projects or other club activities. For example, at the 1913 Mid Winter Festival at CNH the children in the settlement's dramatic club produced 'Red Riding Hood'. They gave four performances to audiences of about 50

each, and managed to raise $10 towards the purchase of baseball uniforms for the settlement's teams.[49] Settlers encouraged such efforts, in part due to their strong conviction that the children learned from them several important lessons in self-reliance, teamwork, and initiative.

Perhaps the attraction of dramatics in regular settlement club activities did not lie just in the fact that it provided young people with entertainment, illustrations of certain moral paradigms, or a vehicle for fundraising for settlement clubs. Drama training could also, after all, furnish settlement members with the practical skills of elocution and of self-presentation, and regular performances before a variety of audiences were a means to help these young people gain confidence in their abilities. Certainly at least some settlement members learned these skills very well; as one reporter noted after viewing CNH's *Peter Pan*, 'the purity of the English spoken on the stage would have put to shame most of the English that goes by that name in the city.'[50] Those skills could empower settlement members, for working-class children who could express themselves well and could move with confidence while in the public eye had a much better chance of 'getting ahead', in middle-class terms, than did their untrained counterparts. Dramatics programs were not merely recreational, therefore, but also contributed to settlement members' practical skills and the development of their 'best selves'.

Most Toronto settlements had special drama clubs in addition to regular boys' and girls' clubs, but the drama clubs were not exclusive, especially if non-members wanted to participate in larger settlement productions. In fact, the settlements attempted to include as many as possible in performances presented to the general public. Program organizers, for example, asked sewing clubs to help make costumes and asked athletic clubs for older boys to act as ushers.[51] When they did not participate directly in the play, arts and crafts and other special interest clubs sometimes displayed their handiwork during theatre nights. Settlers no doubt hoped to develop public appreciation for the depth of talent present in settlement memberships, as well as to indicate the multi-faceted nature of settlement work.[52] In this way, theatre nights were as much showcases for the settlements as they were for the cast and crew of the plays.

The gendered aspect of Toronto's settlement theatre deserves special comment, for while the drama programs were popular among children of both sexes through the 1910s, the number of boys involved in them gradually began to diminish in the 1920s. A number of factors account for this trend. To begin with, Toronto settlements began to extend their theatre programs during wartime, when funding for standard 'boys-only' athletic and recreational programs had been cut. Boys, with few other choices available to them, embraced settlement theatre with enthusiasm. After the war, however, settlements reinstated and expanded boys' athletics and recreation programs, and this extended range of options contributed to the decrease in the number of boys participating as actors in public presentations. By contrast, girls who wanted more active forms of recreation within the settlement had few alternatives even after the end of World War One, and of those available, dramatics may well have seemed the most attractive. Settlement workers certainly argued that both drama and organized sports provided excellent physical and emotional outlets for overworked young people of both sexes, but the fact remains that they organized fewer sports teams for girls than they did for boys. Nevertheless, given that organized athletics for girls was still a relatively new concept,[53] it is not certain that large numbers of girls would have chosen sports over dance and drama even if they had been offered the same opportunities their brothers had. For many, the settlement theatre, safe and sanitized, may well have seemed a much more suitable way for girls to blow off steam.

Moreover, the content of many of the plays may also have encouraged more girls to take part than boys, since the storylines were often variations on the classic heterosexual romance saga, which was not likely the most captivating subject for the 10- to 14-year-old set that comprised the bulk of the settlements' male clientele. The preponderance of fairy stories may also have been a deterrent to boys' participation; although fairies, elves, and sprites were essentially asexual in most plays, it would still be easier for a girl to play one of these characters than a boy. Indeed, there were not only many more parts for girls than for boys, but girls could also play masculine roles without social penalty, whereas it would be difficult under normal circumstances for boys to play feminine characters except perhaps in a farce. Thus, when Central Neighborhood House produced *Peter Pan*, girls played most of the characters, including Peter Pan and the Lost Boys, while boys played the pirates and the Piccaninny warriors (and did so with great gusto, according to the newspaper reviews).[54]

. . .

## The Play's the Thing . . .

The volunteer club leaders most often selected the plays that the settlement clubs performed, and their choices are illuminating. Most of the plays they chose were either dramatizations of fairy tales like 'Little Red Riding Hood', 'Hansel and Gretel', and 'Snow White', or they were stories which featured fairies, like 'The Elf Child', 'Peter Pan', and 'A Midsummer Night's Dream'. 'Alice Through the Looking Glass' and, in the 1920s, 'Winnie the Pooh', as well as similar plays by well-known British children's authors were also common, as were other stories about toys coming to life, as in the operetta 'The Doll's Wedding', or the one-act Christmas story 'The Land of Lost Toys'. While settlement workers wrote the scripts of some of these plays, most were simplified adaptations of published works. For example, when Central Neighborhood House presented 'A Midsummer Night's Dream', the script writer stripped the story down to the feud between Titania and Oberon over the changeling boy, focusing on Oberon's successful efforts to humiliate his unsubmissive consort.[55] In their simplified form the moral of these plays became very clear; most often, it focused on illustrating the ideals, roles, and behaviours considered appropriate in middle-class Canadian society. Thus at the end of CNH's version of 'Midsummer Night's Dream', a humbled Titania replies to Oberon's reiterated demand for the changeling boy by saying, 'Take him, my lord; thy will is all my joy', and the story ends happily, with the fairies dancing off together.[56] The message is plain; Titania refused to submit to the 'rightful' authority of her husband, and had to be 'disciplined' by him. Once she acquiesced, 'proper' relations between the fairy king and queen were restored and their kingdom was again harmonious. The moral is particularly pointed in view of the fact that a number of social workers complained that immigrant wives were insufficiently submissive to their husbands and other authority figures.[57]

Club members themselves sometimes wrote and produced their own plays, but when they did, they usually followed the fairy tale motif. Only one apparent exception to that rule has come to light—a play entitled 'The Lost Twins', which was a melodramatic tragedy written and performed in 1917 by some 10- to 14-year-old girls in CNH's Sunshine Club. The settlement presented that play to the general public, together with several other short playlets, and it is interesting to note that while newspaper reviewers, distanced from the story by class, age, and personal experience, found it merely 'delightful', for some of the children 'The Lost Twins' was, apparently, cathartic.[58] Tragedy was, after all, not unknown in their young lives.

Some settlement workers enjoyed play-acting as much as their youthful clients did; for example, on two occasions staff members of St Christopher House took lead roles in settlement plays.[59] This seems not to have happened at the other settlements, but on one occasion, Mary Joplin Clarke, headworker of Central Neighborhood House from 1915 to mid-1917 (and also, not incidentally, the daughter of a noted Canadian eugenicist), wrote a play which she and her colleagues presented at the 1916 Canadian Conference of Charities and Correction as part of the National Welfare Exhibit on Feeble-mindedness. The characters in 'Mental Milestones', a half-hour dramatization of the evils of permitting feeble-minded women to live on their own without social and reproductive restrictions, were all played by settlement workers or volunteers; given the subject matter and the circumstances, having settlement members perform such a play might have presented some troublesome repercussions. In any case, Clarke and her cast performed the play twice a day for the three days of the conference, reportedly to rave reviews from the conference participants.[60]

It seems significant that Toronto's settlement workers encouraged their members to perform fairy plays but did not, apparently, want them involved in more 'serious' sketches, such as the one presented at the National Welfare Exhibit. In fact, settlements in Toronto staged no adult-oriented 'serious' dramatic presentations in the entire 20 years covered by this study. This may have had mainly to do with the youth of the players, but it also indicates that in this city settlement theatre was not seen as a means to help settlement members and their neighbours to explore pressing issues which had a direct impact on their lives. It was, rather, intended to distance 'reality' at the same time it taught moral lessons and ideals, as well as the roles and behaviours considered appropriate by the dominant group in Anglo-Canadian society. This approach varied significantly from that of Hull-House and a few other American settlements which did encourage long-standing dramatic clubs to perform more mature works.[61]

It is important to note that the choice of plays itself tended to confirm the cultural hegemony of the Anglo-Canadian middle-class, and provided little acknowledgement of the value of working-class, non-Anglo-Celtic cultural heritages.[62] Thus, the plays not only tended to emphasize dominant gender roles and attitudes, but they also seemed at times to imply that peasant cultures, from which many settlement members came, were inherently inferior. For example, in the play 'Pastorella' the narrator relates the following:

> Pastorella grew up thinking the shepherd and his wife were her real parents. As soon as she was old enough she had to learn how to spin the wool, to make her own dresses, and to help in the field with the sheep. Here she made friends with the other shepherds and shepherdesses[,] but strange to say she always seemed to be ten times prettier and sweeter than any of them. They learned to love her very dearly, and when work was done and the sheep were resting, they would make a crown for Pastorella of flowers, then they would dance around her singing, 'Pretty Pastorella is our Queen.'[63]

Of course, it turns out that Pastorella *is* in fact their queen who, like Sleeping Beauty, must be hidden among the peasantry in order to keep her safe until she is grown. Unaware of her identity, Pastorella is just naturally superior, which is to say she is hard-working, good, and obedient. After some adventures (which she does nothing to initiate), it comes time for her to marry her rescuing prince, but she is reluctant until she is informed of her royal origins. The message seems clear—girls who upheld the hegemonic ideals of virtuous femininity were innately superior, and would be 'handsomely' rewarded.

\* \* \*

As the staging of Mary Joplin Clarke's 'feeble-mindedness' play indicates, settlement members and their neighbours in the local community were not the only targets for education through the settlement theatre; settlement leaders wanted to impress certain lessons on middle-class Anglo-Canadians as well. What those lessons were was best summarized by the program notes for CNH's *Blue Bird*:

> more hearts than we dream are turning wistfully towards the times that are waiting to be born. . . . And so some of us are . . . working quietly at the weaving of the New Song, weaving the word NEIGHBOR into the hearts of men [*sic*], by moulding thought to a broader, freer pattern, leading local, civic, insular and group prejudices to a more universal outlook, preparing the way for the Children of the Future. . . . We are producing our play to-night not merely for the sake of an evening's entertainment, but for the permanent good that comes from following Maeterlinck's thought.[64]

Advocates of Toronto's settlement movement were intent on inculcating the middle class with a sense of their interdependence with the working class and on encouraging them to embrace an ideal of co-operative citizenship similar to that illustrated by *The Blue Bird*. It is important to recognize that the principles that the settlements were attempting to impress upon their clientele were also being taught to the children of the middle class through their youth organizations. By convincing middle-class young people to come to the settlement and teach the principles of democratic citizenship to immigrants, settlement leaders underlined the relevance of those principles to the instructors themselves. Proponents of the settlement movement thus encouraged middle-class young people to see themselves as models of democratic values and mores—as representatives, in other words, of what they believed to be the acme of human civilization—and as such to feel a sense of obligation towards the less privileged members of their community. It was a sense they tried, through a variety of means, to instill within the wider public as well. Theatre reviews of settlement productions, and other forms of publicity and fundraising literature, attempted to put a human, individual face on the poor and the immigrant, from whom members of the middle class were often distanced.

As positive as this seems, it is clear that the co-operative community which Toronto's settlement workers hoped to establish wore a middle-class, Anglo-Canadian countenance. It is important to recognize that in the context of early twentieth-century Anglo-Canadian society, the superiority of middle-class Anglo-Canadian culture appeared to be just 'common sense', and thus the unequal gender, class, and ethnic relations within it seemed, and were presented as, normal and just.[65] The content of the plays that the settlements produced provide ample demonstration of this assumption. For the proponents of the settlement movement, the need for non-Anglo-Celtic immigrants to abandon their cultural heritage and to assimilate into capitalist, Anglo-Canadian society appeared self-evident. The co-operative community that settlers envisioned could not exist without it.

In the end, the grand scale of the settlement theatre program did not survive long past the end of the 1920s. With the introduction of the financial oversight of the Community Chest association, the advent of mass consumer culture, the onset of the Great Depression, and the growing popularity of psychiatric social work, Toronto's settlements found it increasingly difficult to maintain the program in its original form. Not that drama disappeared from settlement offerings altogether; clubs continued to prepare and perform in plays for the entertainment of each other and their friends, neighbours, and parents. Community theatre, too, prospered outside the settlement houses of post-war Toronto. But it was a very different kind of community theatre than that which the settlements had offered, and it was oriented towards very different goals.

Ultimately, the settlement theatre was an expression of the complexity and ambivalence of the settlement movement as a whole during the period from 1910 to 1930. It demonstrates the way in which settlements became gathering places where the objectives of individuals, cultural groups, and social classes met and often competed for hegemony. Through their drama programs settlers sought to control what their members saw and did in their leisure time. Yet settlement drama programs, to some extent at least, can be seen as a means to empower those same members by providing them with some useful skills. In some instances these efforts at empowerment were effective; in others they were amended or abandoned as a result of the influence brought to bear by settlement users.

These activities empowered settlement workers themselves as well in their roles as dramatics instructors, as artists, as social workers, and as the acknowledged spokespeople for the poor. Moreover, while they used the settlement theatre as a means to influence their clientele, at the same time they also attempted to provide some leadership to their middle-class Anglo-Canadian peers, encouraging them to modify their behaviours and attitudes in accordance with the ideals of the co-operative community. Far from being mere entertainment, settlement theatre was intended to play a significant role in the (re)creation of what settlement workers envisioned as the cohesive, unified Canadian community.

## Notes

[The author] would like to thank Alison Prentice, Margaret Conrad, Barbara Beatty, and William Westfall for their helpful critiques of earlier drafts of this essay.

1.  Arthur C. Holden, *The Settlement Idea* (New York, 1970 [1922]), 54.

2.  Paula Sperdakos, *Dora Mavor Moore: Pioneer of the Canadian Theatre* (Toronto, 1995).

3.  City of Toronto Archives (hereafter CTA), SC5, box 5, file 2, 'Drama and Music: Programmes', 'The Blue Bird for the CNH'; box 11, file 1, 'Newsclippings, 1911–1930', 'Where We Found the Blue Bird', 'Blue Bird Draws 500', 'Settlement House Success', 'Making Canadians of Little Foreigners', uncredited press clippings, Jan. 1916.

4.  See, for example, Karen J. Blair, *The Torchbearers: Women and Their Amateur Arts Associations in America, 1890–1930* (Bloomington, Ind., 1994), for an account of the range of community theatre

ventures which local women's art associations undertook. . . .

5. See Allen F. Davis, *Spearheads for Reform: The Social Settlements and the Progressive Movement 1890–1914* (New York, 1967), 8; Robert A. Woods and Albert J. Kennedy, eds, *Handbook of Settlements* (New York, 1970 [1911]), vi. . . .

6. See Cathy L. James, 'Gender, Class and Ethnicity in the Organization of Neighbourhood and Nation: The Role of Toronto's Settlement Houses in the Formation of the Canadian State, 1902 to 1914', Ph.D. dissertation (University of Toronto, 1997).

7. 'A[lberta] S. Bastedo, 'A Visit to Evangelia House', *The Varsity* 25, 3 (19 Oct. 1905): 43.

8. Standish Meacham, *Toynbee Hall and Social Reform 1880–1914: The Search for Community* (New Haven, 1987), 34; Jane Addams et al., *Hull-House Maps and Papers* (New York: Crowell, 1895; repr. New York: Arno Press, 1970); James, 'Neighbourhood and Nation', ch. 6.

9. Jane Addams, 'The Subjective Necessity for Social Settlements', in Addams, *Philanthropy and Social Progress* (Freeport, NY: Books for Libraries Press, 1969 [1893]). See also T.J. Jackson Lears, 'The Concept of Cultural Hegemony: Problems and Possibilities', *American Historical Review* 90, 3 (June 1985): 567–93.

10. See Peter G. Goheen, *Victorian Toronto, 1850 to 1900: Pattern and Process in Growth* (Chicago: Department of Geography, Research Paper no. 127, 1970).

11. See, for example, Laurence Irving, 'The Drama as a Factor in Social Progress', *University Monthly* 15, 7 (May 1914): 348–57.

12. Jane Addams, 'The House of Dreams', in Addams, *The Spirit of Youth and the City Streets* (New York: Macmillan, 1909; repr. Urbana, Ill., 1972), 75–6.

13. Irving, 'The Drama', 350.

14. Addams, *The Spirit of Youth*, 87–8; see also Irving, 'The Drama', 350.

15. Addams, *The Spirit of Youth*, 91–3.

16. Mina Carson, *Settlement Folk: Social Thought and the American Settlement Movement, 1885–1930* (Chicago, 1990), 114.

17. The majority of turn-of-the-century social reformers worried constantly about pauperizing the poor—that is, encouraging, through too liberal charity, able-bodied men in particular to abandon their responsibilities to provide for their families, and, through rewarding improvident behaviour, encouraging the wives and children of these men to adopt 'shiftlessness' as a way of life. See, for example, James Pitsula, 'The Emergence of Social Work in Toronto', *Journal of Canadian Studies* 14, 1 (Spring 1979): 35–42.

18. Carolyn Strange, *Toronto's Girl Problem: The Perils and Pleasures of the City, 1880–1930* (Toronto, 1995), 117.

19. Ibid., 122–3.

20. Addams, *The Spirit of Youth*, 84.

21. Ibid., 80–8.

22. See Rollin Lynde Hartt, *The People at Play* (Boston: Houghton Miffin, 1909; repr. New York: Arno Press, 1975), esp. chs 4, 5.

23. Kathy Peiss, *Cheap Amusements: Working Women and Leisure in Turn-of-the-Century New York* (Philadelphia, 1986), 144.

24. Paul Klapper, 'The Yiddish Music Hall', *University Settlement Studies* 2, 4 (1905): 22, quoted ibid., 145.

25. Ibid., 144.

26. Ibid., 151–2.

27. Hartt, *The People at Play*, 122.

28. Peiss, *Cheap Amusements*, 153–8. See also Strange, *Toronto's Girl Problem*, 122–3; Hartt, *The People at Play*, 155–91.

29. Strange, *Toronto's Girl Problem*, 59; Peiss, *Cheap Amusements*, 180.

30. University of Toronto Archives (hereafter UTA), Student Christian Movement, B79–0059, [Norman J. Ware], 'The "Futurist" Number: University Settlement Review' (n.p., n.d. [Sept. 1913]).

31. CTA, SC484, I B 1, box 1, St Christopher House, Headworker's Report, 13 Apr. 1926. . . .

32. See, for example, 'The University Settlement' [Annual Report, February 1925], 7; CTA, SC5, box 11, file 1, 'Newsclippings, 1911–1930', 'Settlement House Success' (n.p., n.d. [Jan. 1916]).

33. Jane Addams, *Second Twenty Years at Hull-House* (New York: Macmillan, 1930), 370.

34. Holden, *The Settlement Idea*, 54.

35. CTA, SC5, box 11, file 1, 'Newsclippings, 1911–1930', 'Applied Art By Young at Orde St. School' ([*The Globe*], n.d. [Spring 1917]).

36. Irving, 'The Drama', 348–9; 'The University Settlement' [Annual Report, Feb. 1925].

37. CTA, SC5, box 11, file 1, 'Newsclippings, 1911–1930', '"Peter Pan" Produced At Orde Street School' (n.p., n.d. [Spring 1917]). The 'Allies ward' was, of course, St John's Ward, more often simply known as 'The Ward', which was Toronto's most notorious slum and the city's most cosmopolitan district. . . .

38. CTA, SC5, box 11, file 1, 'Newsclippings, 1911–1930', 'Making Canadians of Little Foreigners', and 'Settlement House Success' (n.p., n.d. [Jan. 1916]).

39. CTA, SC5, box 11, file 1, 'Newsclippings, 1911–1930', ' "Peter Pan" Produced at Orde Street School', and '"Peter Pan" Abroad in Toronto Again' (n.p., n.d. [Spring 1917]).

40. 'The Melting Pot', *Canadian Churchman*, 7 Apr. 1910, 216.

41. Unlike Jane Addams, Canadian settlement workers did not acknowledge, at least in print, that the popular theatre could also afford urgently needed pleasure to its audiences. See Addams, *The Spirit of Youth*, 75.

42. CTA, SC5, box 11, file 1, CNH 'Newsclippings, 1911–1930', 'Kiddies Much Enjoy', 'Where We Found the Blue Bird', 'Central Neighborhood Children and Their Play'.

43. Addams, *The Spirit of Youth*, 75–7.

44. Ibid., 77.

45. For example, one year a group of older children at Evangelia put on *As You Like It* as a part of the settlement's Christmas celebrations. See Metropolitan Toronto Reference Library—Baldwin Room, S54, 'History of Canadian Settlements', Book B, Evangelia, notes compiled by H.J. and C. Hogg. . . .

46. CTA, SC5 B, box 1, file 3, CNH Headworker's Report, Mar. 1915; SC5 A, box 1, CNH *Annual Report*, 1923; SC14, Toronto Association of Neighbourhood Services (TANS), Federation of Settlements, Minutes, 7 Apr. 1920; SC484, I B 1, box 1, St Christopher House Headworker's Report, 17 Apr. 1923.

47. See, for example, CTA, SC5, box 11, file 1, 'Newsclippings, 1911–1930', 'School Buildings for Social Uses', and 'Central Neighborhood Children and Their Play' (n.p., n.d.).

48. See, for example, Canadian Baptist Archives, vertical files, 'Memorial Institute Annual Report, 1920'; CTA, SC484, I B 1, box 1, St Christopher House Headworker's Reports, 15 Feb. 1921, 14 Nov. 1922.

49. CTA, SC5 B, box 1, file 1, CNH Board of Directors' minutes, Headworker's Report for Mar. 1913; see also Headworker's Report for Apr. 1913; SC5 D, box 1, file 5, E.B. Neufeld, 'Head Worker's Report', CNH *Year Book*, 1913; SC484, I B 1, box 1, St Christopher House, Headworker's Report, 15 Feb. 1921, 30 May 1922.

50. CTA, SC5, box 11, file 1, 'Newsclippings, 1911–1930', 'Fine Social Centre Work' (n.p., n.d. [Spring 1917]).

51. See, for example, CTA, SC5, box 11, file 1, 'Newsclippings, 1911–30', 'Where We Found the Blue Bird' and 'Blue Bird Draws 500'.

52. See, for example, CTA, SC5, box 11, file 1, 'Newsclippings, 1911–30', 'Applied Art By Young at Orde St. School' and 'Central Neighborhood Closing'.

53. Helen Lenskyj, *Out of Bounds: Women, Sport and Sexuality* (Toronto, 1986).

54. CTA, SC5, box 5, file 2, 'Drama and Music: Programmes', 'Peter Pan'; SC5, box 11, file 1, 'Newsclippings, 1911–30', '"Peter Pan" Abroad in Toronto Again', 'Delightful "Peter Pan" at Orde St. Centre', '"Peter Pan" at Orde St. School', and 'Fine Performance By Clever Children'.

55. CTA, SC5, box 5, file 10, 'Script: A Midsummer Night's Dream'.

56. Ibid.

57. See, for example, Paula J. Draper and Janice B. Karlinsky, 'Abraham's Daughters: Women, Charity and Power in the Canadian Jewish

Community', in Jean Burnett, ed., *Looking Into My Sister's Eyes: An Exploration in Women's History* (Toronto, 1986), 75–90.

58. CTA, SC5, box 11, file 1, 'Newsclippings, 1911–30', 'Wee Folk Entertain At Orde St. School'.

59. CTA, SC484, I B 1, box 1, St Christopher House Headworker's Report, 22 Nov. 1921, 11 Nov. 1924.

60. Mary Joplin Clarke, 'Mental Milestones', in Canadian Conference of Charities and Correction, *Proceedings, 1916* (Ottawa: King's Printer, 1916); CTA, SC3, Bureau of Municipal Research, E2, box 1, White Papers, 'Feeble-Mindedness', White Paper Number 12.

61. See Elsie F. Weil, 'The Hull-House Players', in Allen F. Davis and Mary Lynn McCree, eds, *Eighty Years at Hull-House* (Chicago, 1969), 88–91.

62. Again, this contrasts with Hull-House, which did allow the performance of foreign-language plays. See Addams, *Second Twenty Years*, 368.

63. CTA, SC5, box 5, file 11, 'Script—Pastorella'.

64. CTA, SC5, box 5, file 2, 'Drama and Music: Programmes', 'The Blue Bird for the CNH'.

65. Roxana Ng, 'Racism, Sexism, and Nation Building in Canada', in Cameron McCarthy and Warren Crichlow, eds, *Race, Identity, and Representation in Education* (New York, 1993), 52.

# 20

# Celebrating Violent Masculinities: The Boxing Death of Luther McCarty

Kevin B. Wamsley and David Whitson

## Introduction

It has long been argued that sports have sustained and reproduced particular types of masculinity and have served to naturalize a variety of forms of male violence.[1] Historically, the sport of boxing has provoked recurring controversies around these and related issues. Boxing injuries have repeatedly raised important questions about the 'legitimacy' of violence that takes place in sanctioned sporting contests and about public attitudes towards violence as entertainment. Boxing has a long history as a popular form of male entertainment, but with the growth of national media and especially popular tabloids in the late nineteenth century, national and world 'championships' became objects of widespread popular fascination.[2] Some boxing matches, particularly in the heavyweight division, became national, even international, events. In this context, the social meanings attached to boxing, and the popular identifications that were mobilized around particular fighters, became the focus of considerable public debate.

This paper examines some of these issues, with reference to a fight that took place in Calgary in 1913—a fight that was supposed to produce a white challenger for Jack Johnson's world title, but ended in the death of one contestant and manslaughter charges against the winner. One of the ensuing controversies was about the place of the law and the courts in the regulation of sporting violence. Attitudes towards this matter, however, and attitudes towards boxing more generally were closely connected with other social agendas having to do with gender, race, and civic status, as well as with popular ideas about science and modernity. An examination of the public rhetoric that surrounded the Arthur Pelkey–Luther McCarty match and its aftermath offers some insights into the social climate of the early twentieth century and the ideological campaigns that characterized this period.

## Boxing, Public Attitudes, and Social Change

In the popular media debates that developed around boxing, the sport was both widely celebrated and heavily criticized. It is important to understand some of the ways in which boxing

Kevin B. Wamsley and David Whitson, 'Celebrating Violent Masculinities: The Boxing Death of Luther McCarty', *Journal of Sport History* 25, 3 (Fall 1998): 419–31. Reprinted with the permission of the *Journal of Sport History* and the North American Society for Sport History.

became a vehicle for the articulation and valorization of particular, and sometimes competing, social ideas. Boxing has always exemplified what Connell et al.[3] call a 'confrontative sport'. In confrontative sports, it is not only legitimate but necessary for men to dominate opponents by force and violence—behaviour that became increasingly illegitimate outside the ritualized contexts of sports. Thus, champions in confrontative sports became popular exemplars of a rough version of masculinity that was still widely respected, even as they were criticized by moralists and social reformers.[4] However, the models of masculinity that were traditionally valorized in boxing became further complicated, in the late nineteenth and early twentieth centuries, by changing middle- and upper-class ideas about masculinity and by ethnic rivalries and racial tensions. All of these factors affected both official and popular attitudes towards boxing, and some were mobilized by boxing proponents to try to legitimize the sport beyond its core audience of working-class men.

At one level, what was at stake can be illustrated by the struggle between amateur boxing and professional prizefighting, itself an example of the larger struggle for authority and control in sports between 'moral entrepreneurs' who promoted the moral and social instruction of young men through amateur sporting participation, and economic entrepreneurs whose interests lay in the development of commercial spectator entertainment. It is evident that many turn-of-the-century prizefights attracted enthusiastic public interest. Concerns about brutality and corruption were raised in influential sectors, though, and prizefighting was banned in Canada by a federal statute passed in 1881.[5] Yet, despite this legislation, prizefights continued to attract audiences across the country, and although the law legitimized police raids, in most jurisdictions only minor charges were laid, and convictions were few.[6]

This official tolerance, which effectively circumvented the law, deserves some comment. In the first place, it was socially legitimate for boys to learn boxing and compete in amateur bouts under the auspices of organizations like the YMCA. Indeed, boxing at the turn of the century was widely seen as consistent with the moral and social purposes of 'muscular Christianity', and Donnelly argues that for many middle-class men, boxing was understood 'as an activity that would promote manliness and character, morality and patriotism'.[7] Manliness here defined a particular middle-class kind of masculinity, and boxing was considered to offer important socialization for youths into manly ideals, habits, and norms of courage.[8] Thus, support for boxing, often grounded in youthful experience, was not at all uncommon among those men—city officials and police, as well as businessmen and politicians—whose role it was to enforce the statutes.[9]

In addition, from the mid-1890s, boxing clubs and advocates increasingly made the argument that when properly conducted and adjudicated, prizefights should be understood as scientific exhibitions of technical skills and physical discipline. The discipline of the body, of course, had always been central to the Victorian belief in the educational value of sports. When this was articulated with the idea of technique, however, an association was also being claimed with explicitly 'modern' forms of excellence. Ideas about progress through scientific analysis and technical advances were central to popular notions about modernity, and that these ideas would have influential proponents in various sports was entirely consistent with ascendant ideas of the day.[10] The association of boxing with modern technique was usually just rhetoric on the part of fight promoters who sought to widen the social range of those interested in boxing. Yet, it worked because it associated the sport with the new religion of an industrializing society—science. In describing successful prizefighters as exemplars of tactics, technique, and fitness, in other words, of disciplined achievement, this discourse articulated the preferred self-image of newly ascendant middle-class males. The scientifically trained body was something 'the modern man' was proud of and respected in others.

Consequently, boxing came to be socially rationalized through what Early refers to as an 'obsessive quest for more reified technique and rules'.[11]

However, there were other discourses in the promotion of prizefights that spoke to more traditional kinds of identifications and visceral kinds of desires. First, it should be noted that the celebration of violence did not disappear, nor was it confined to the 'rough' working class. Indeed, spectator fascination with violence was as likely to be found among businessmen and professionals as among working men, and Gruneau and Whitson have noted in their discussion of violence in hockey that the celebration of force, as well as skill, in sport has historically brought together, through a widely shared response, men of very different social backgrounds who might have little else in common.[12] This is a point we shall return to later. In addition, prizefights offered obvious focal points for civic rivalries, and fight promotion was often bound up with civic boosterism.

Most important for the events we are about to examine, however, was that after Jack Johnson won the heavyweight title from Tommy Burns in 1908, the rhetoric of race presented itself as a readily exploited discourse of rivalry for fight promoters across North America. Even before this, prizefighters had often been matched so that promoters could appeal to ethnic identifications and rivalries (e.g., Jewish, Irish, Italian). The promoters of interracial bouts took this a step further, building popular support for 'white hopes' and appealing openly to white supremacist sentiments.[13] In the standard storyline that surrounded interracial fights, moreover, the supposed tactics and science of the white man were typically pitted against the 'natural' qualities (including 'brute' force) of his black antagonist.

## Boxing in Calgary and Tommy Burns[14]

The above discussion provides some general background to the Pelkey–McCarty fight promotion of 1913. In spite of the federal statutes

referred to, and the laws of the North West Territories, western Canadian centres like Calgary regularly hosted the matches of local fighters. For town councillors and especially law enforcement officers, these were occasions for ambivalence and contradictions. Some matches were raided, while others received praise in the local papers for their fine displays of athletic skills. It is evident from many reports that prominent city officials, police and firemen, and business leaders regularly legitimated matches with their attendance. In particular, Calgary fire chief Cappy Smart was known to be an avid fight fan and sometimes referee. Historian Grant MacEwan describes some of Smart's escapades:

> Nobody suggested that Cappy Smart was a saint but to most Calgarians, he was a hero and a very human one. He had his fun and sometimes it was dangerously close to the limit of city council's patience and tolerance. His drinking habits didn't escape attention but aldermen knew that any attempt to remove this man from office would have brought public rebellion.[15]

At one match in 1903, Smart is reported to have escaped through a window while police were raiding the event.[16]

By 1910, ex-champion Tommy Burns had 'set up shop' in Calgary, hoping to establish the city as one of the leading fight locations in North America. Burns organized boxing exhibitions, built an arena on the outskirts of the city, and even fought a few times himself. It was soon evident to him that Calgarians were well informed on boxing news, that fans were keenly interested in the current state of the heavyweight division, and that it was with some excitement that they anticipated hosting future bouts in the city. In a letter to his friend Bob Edwards, editor of the *Calgary Eyeopener* newspaper, Burns wrote:

> My present plans are primarily to arrange a ten to twenty round contest with Jack Johnson whom I am confident I can defeat with clean

breaks. A clean break contest is absolutely devoid of brutality and thus [there] should be no reasonable objection to having such an event pulled off in Calgary. . . . Few people seem to think or realize the amount of advertising such sporting events give a young city all over the world. All I ask is permission to stage one contest here. After that I feel sure that the authorities will freely admit that there are no objectionable features to the fighting game when conducted under clean management.[17]

We can see here that Burns appealed to the boosterism and dreams of civic repute that were very much part of the Calgary of that period. However, at the same time, Burns attempted to distance his promotions from the familiar negative stereotypes of brutality and corruption that some associated with prizefighting. A Burns promotion would be a clean fight with clean management. Burns also sought to legitimate his fights, while adding to his audiences, by encouraging women to attend pre-fight exhibitions. Newspaper promotions for Burns's first lecture and exhibition at the Sherman auditorium made it clear that his presentations were always well received by packed houses and the audience was usually composed of at least one-third women.[18] Before a later fight that Burns arranged between himself and Arthur Pelkey, he held a special 'Ladies' Day' for women who had never viewed a boxing contest. As part of Burns's usual campaign style and, more importantly, to position women as the philanthropic and moral guardians of society, all donations collected were to be distributed to local charities. It was obvious that boxing supporters believed that the presence and endorsement of women would enhance the reputation of the sport in the community.

The promotional rhetoric used to interest local men during the lead-up to the championship fight included no references to charity, but did feature repeated assurances that the boxers were in excellent physical condition and that they were men of good character. Reacting to resistance to boxing from some Calgarians, Burns regularly defended what he claimed to be the manly and honourable character of his fighters. In fact, despite his earlier interest in fighting Johnson himself, Burns refused in 1913 to accept the challenge of Jack Johnson to fight Luther McCarty in Calgary:

> There is absolutely no reason why I should make this match. Johnson has not conducted himself in a gentlemanly manner at all since gaining the title, and now that I am a match-maker I am only putting on matches which are between men of good character and clean-living fellows. I have started the game in this city and am doing my very utmost to keep it clean. In refusing to make this match it was not through mere race prejudice but for the good of the game in Calgary. So far it has been clean boxing and clean boys. While I am here it will remain that way.[19]

Clearly, neither Burns nor the local media viewed Johnson as a 'clean boy'. Stereotypical comments about blacks were common in Calgary newspapers. For example, the *Calgary Daily Herald* reported on the 'Colored Ball' that when the music played, 'the musical natures of the colored people would be clamorous for expression' but that 'the blithsome hearts of colored people delight not alone of music—they do like chicken.'[20] The same newspaper had reported the previous year of Jack Johnson, '[the] big tar baby has a new white wife.'[21] Johnson was also made a figure of racist humour in both the *Calgary Daily Herald* and the *Calgary Eyeopener* in what Wiggins refers to as 'Samba' cartoons.[22] Calgary was by no means unique in this open circulation of racial caricatures and attacks.

Indeed, it was evident across North America that in his victories over the top white fighters of the day, in his uncompromising attitude outside the ring, and in his open liaison with a white woman, Jack Johnson had become a symbol for the fears and animosities many whites harboured towards blacks.[23] The desire to see Johnson put back 'in his place' was widespread, and heavy-weight boxer Jim Corbett, for example, announced that '[n]obody who knows boxing is more anxious to see a white fighter at the head of pugilism than I.'[24] Under the headline 'Black Clouds', the *Calgary Daily Herald* stated that '[t]hings are looking very dark indeed when every class of pugilism is threatened with a leader of the Negro race.'[25] Johnson's position as champion was a continuing affront to the well-established notions of white supremacy, and Burns was not the only fight promoter seeking to find a credible contender around whom white hopes could be mobilized. In this context, he was also very aware that his promotion of the Pelkey–McCarty fight could only benefit from the promotion of anti-Johnson, anti-black sentiment, as white fans were invited to participate in the coronation the next 'white hope'.

## Manslaughter

Local interest for the bout of 24 May 1913 at Burns's Manchester arena, just outside the city limits, was overwhelming. Tickets, ranging in price from two to six dollars, were only available at Tommy Burns's clothing store, and it was estimated that 3,000 fans attended.[26] Burns hired special streetcars to deliver fans to the arena. Following some preliminary contests, Arthur Pelkey and Luther McCarty entered the ring with referee Ed Smith, a sportswriter from Chicago. The Reverend William Walker reminded the two boxers that 'the great referee stood over them in this bout, all powerful above the man selected by them to see fair play.'[27] The much anticipated contest lasted only one minute and 46 seconds, however. The men circled, they clinched briefly, a few blows were exchanged, and then Pelkey struck McCarty with an 'arm blow' to the right cheek. McCarty looked at his trainer and winked, the fighters stepped back, and Luther McCarty slumped and fell to the mat.[28] He was counted out, Smith raised Pelkey's arm in victory, and several doctors worked for 30 minutes to revive the fallen boxer. A local photographer captured the moment

as McCarty lay on his back and the sun shone through the glass roof of the arena, briefly forming a 'halo' around the fallen boxer's head before it disappeared back into the clouds.[29] Although McCarty had fallen seconds after a blow he had apparently shrugged off, he never regained consciousness, and Luther McCarty was the first boxer to be killed in a boxing ring in Canada. A coroner's jury exonerated Pelkey from any responsibility for McCarty's death, but he was immediately arrested by the North West Mounted Police and formally charged with manslaughter.[30] Tommy Burns's Manchester arena was mysteriously burned to the ground 36 hours after the match.

Chief Justice Harvey presided over the well-publicized trial, asking the jurors to decide if the contest had been a prizefight and, if so, was Pelkey responsible for the death of McCarty? The medical opinions as to the cause of death conflicted in the courtroom, but doctors agreed from the autopsy that McCarty suffered a blood clot in his brain and a partial dislocation of his neck. Without understanding at the time that the force of the blows exchanged in the bout were not as important as the way in which they were delivered, witnesses denied that any of the punches could have killed McCarty. It was also suggested that McCarty might have injured himself when riding a horse a few days before the fight or that he may have been suffering trauma from previous fights. Despite the inconclusiveness of the medical testimony, however, it was evident that the immediate catalyst to McCarty's death was blows received to his head during the fight.

On the lesser question of whether the bout was an illegal prizefight, it was clearly evident from cross examination that this was the case. The promotion for the fight itself, the advertising, gate receipts, the public proclamation of Pelkey as champion both in the newspapers and in the courthouse rendered the denials of several witnesses as bordering on the ridiculous. All those who organized, participated, or took a genuine interest in the fight were well-versed in the particularities of the law with regard to prizefighting.

They were familiar with popular attitudes, which they themselves had influenced considerably, about the distinction between prizefighting and scientific boxing. Yet, at no point during the trial was the question of the social legitimacy of amateur or scientific boxing raised until, in his closing remarks to the jury, Chief Justice Harvey suggested that the definition of prizefighting:

> would not include boxing when it is carried on as an exemplification of what has been called the manly art of self defence though it might if the contest was typical of what might be designated as the brutal science of attack. It appears that if the purpose is an exhibition of sparring or boxing on its scientific side it is . . . unobjectionable.[31]

It is interesting to note how the members of the boxing community called to the witness stand, and even court officials themselves, trivialized the social implications of violence and implicitly challenged the idea of trying a boxer in a court of law. The Chief Justice himself even suggested that participation in boxing as a manly sport was unobjectionable. The same ideas and language were used to define the issues in the media. The *Calgary Daily Herald*, for example, editorialized that Pelkey's 'arrest after the fight must have been a legal formality, for it is not conceivable that a charge of manslaughter should be proceeded against him.'[32]

The charges against Pelkey represented a direct challenge to some of the popularly held beliefs about sport in the community. Violent sports like hockey, boxing, and lacrosse had been part of local cultural practices for more than 20 years. While it was readily admitted that McCarty's death was indeed a tragedy, few Calgarians argued that anyone had done anything wrong or illegal. The trial, based on a physical assault during a sport contest, raised two related issues for sportsmen and spectators. In the first instance, legal intervention in a properly conducted sporting event was questioned by all those (mostly male) who believed that violence in confrontative sports was simply part of the sport and therefore legitimate. In addition, the intervention of the law implicitly challenged some of the commonly held values that linked participation in rule-bound confrontative sports to the development of manly character. A legal decision would impact all 'manly' sports in the community and the promotion of similar activities among Calgary's young men.

It was argued in defence that this fight and other professional boxing matches were carried out in the same manner as those at the local YMCA, where Tommy Burns had been an honorary president.[33] In this general defence of boxing, it was an article of faith that the sport promoted manliness and character-building among young men in the community.[34] As indicated above, moreover, Burns claimed that he only promoted fights between men of good character; YMCA administrators similarly suggested that boxing programs under their auspices provided Calgary boys 'with healthful recreation, educational features, good companionship, and the opportunity of associating with trained leaders who are picked for their manly qualities.'[35] Chief Justice Harvey himself was revealed to have made annual contributions to the YMCA.[36] What was implied by extension was that any criticism of a Burns's boxing match was also a censure of the valuable programs conducted at the YMCA.

Another theme in the testimonies of witnesses during the trial, and in some of the popular attitudes about violent sports expressed in other Canadian newspapers and courtrooms, was that officials of various sports were quite capable of policing their own problems.[37] Accidents and serious injuries in confrontative sports were positioned as unfortunate but 'natural' occurrences. It was claimed that they were freakish exceptions in activities with adequate regulations and safeguards, and they were viewed as a small price to pay for the development of manly character. What many considered to be the place of the law in sport was made quite clear by Judge Snider during another boxing case in 1911 when he stated that, it will be a long time before Parliament will think it wise to so hedge in young men and boys by legislation that all sports that are rough and strenuous or even dangerous must be given up. Virility in young men would soon be lessened and self-reliant manliness a thing of the past.[38]

These beliefs about the value of sport in the production and reproduction of particular types of masculinity were commonly held in the Calgary sporting community and by some of the city's most prominent men. Members of the courtroom burst into laughter when witness Major Ross testified that the Crown Prosecutor himself had been present at numerous local boxing matches.[39] And when Tommy Burns arrived in 1910, according to the *Calgary Daily Herald*, the dinner given in his honour 'looked more like a professional and businessmen's banquet for practically every seat was occupied by a lawyer or physician, while the remainder of guests were businessmen.'[40] As respected members of the community and spectators at the Pelkey–McCarty fight, many professional men were called to the stand during the trial. Through the course of the proceedings, it was evident that a particular male solidarity emerged when questions about the social value of boxing were raised.

The discourses of science connected to the rational pursuit of manly sport were repeatedly expressed by witnesses and court officials who sought to excuse and obfuscate the tragedy and blatant violence of the event. When the legitimacy of the kind of masculinity that was being promoted in the match, in boxing, and through sport more broadly was occasionally challenged, witnesses tended to humorize and dismiss the whole affair. A Dr Spankle, who admitted to attending at least 25 matches in his lifetime, was asked if he attended the fight and retorted, 'No, I was at the boxing contest.' He further suggested that he would not be afraid to stand up against the heaviest blow struck on the fatal night. When asked if he had ever seen a knockout blow deliv-

ered, he responded amid much courtroom laughter, 'I have delivered one myself once.'[41] Another witness, Dr Ing, was asked to determine which sport was more dangerous, hockey or boxing. He replied, '[w]ell I would rather have six rounds with Pelkey than a game with the Ottawa hockey team.'[42]

Hockey itself was more violent in the 1900s than is widely recognized today, but these testimonies spoke explicitly to codes of masculinity, understood within the sporting community, that identified violent confrontations within sporting contests as legitimate and valuable social interactions between consenting men. At one point during an adjournment in the trial, court sheriff Graham and lawyer E.L. Harvey 'caused much amusement by engaging in a short boxing match' in the courtroom.[43] During the staged exchange, the mock combatants made light of the medical descriptions of McCarty's death. These attempts at humour appeared to provide some sort of relief for the tension that had been created within the sporting community and in the city more broadly. At the same time, however, the relaxed and even skeptical behaviour towards the proceedings on the part of officers of the court demonstrated the ambivalence of these men towards the legitimacy of the intervention of the law into sporting events. It also demonstrated how widely respected among middle-class men were the kinds of masculinity celebrated in confrontational sports.[44]

The Calgary newspapers reported that the entire city breathed a sigh of relief after the jury determined that indeed a prizefight had taken place, but that it was not clear if Pelkey was responsible for McCarty's death. Pelkey was immediately released and charges that had been laid against Tommy Burns for organizing the whole affair were dropped later in the year. After leaving Calgary, the promotional career of Burns and the boxing career of Arthur Pelkey fizzled quietly. Tommy Burns's brother Eddie Brusso continued to offer boxing instruction at the Calgary YMCA after McCarty's death.

## Concluding Remarks

The events leading up to the Pelkey–McCarty boxing match and the manslaughter trial in Calgary raise some interesting questions about the contested meanings of sport in an early twentieth-century community. In a city where sport had quickly become an important part of community life and where, before that, fighting had always been (for men, at least) an accepted practice in a 'Wild West' culture, prizefighting was promoted in particular ways that sought to maximize interest and create business opportunities. Visiting celebrities like Jack Johnson, John L. Sullivan, and Jim Corbett, a series of boxing-related entertainments and championship matches, and extensive newspaper coverage all contributed to constructing a reputation for Calgary as a 'fight town'. In this context, Tommy Burns's promotions brought international attention to Calgary, albeit not, ultimately, as he had intended. His efforts, nevertheless, were appreciated by Calgary boosters who saw publicity for the city in his activities. His efforts were also appreciated, of course, by fight fans. Burns was thus very successful in winning attention and support in the Calgary community. It has been central to our discussion of the Pelkey–McCarty fight that there were important subtexts in boxing promotions in the early twentieth century that spoke to popular ideas about both race and masculinity and invited support among white male workers and professionals, based both in racial and masculine solidarities.

The death of Luther McCarty and the trial that followed, however, brought male solidarity into play in ways that the match itself did not require. What is clear from all accounts is that McCarty's death did not bring about any reappraisal of the attitudes and values that were widely shared among men of all social classes, and that violence in sport was seen as a legitimate masculinizing practice. Indeed, the trial provided a public forum for the expression of support by influential men in the community for boxing in

particular and for confrontative sports in general. It could be argued that during the Pelkey trial, the societal condemnation of violence embodied in law was qualified and even ridiculed by respected community figures. Laws are unlikely to be taken seriously when they are visibly violated by public officials, and when individuals like the Chief Justice, the Crown Prosecutor, and prominent newspaper editors were all involved in sanctioning and valorizing the kind of masculinity that was taught in boxing, it can be argued that men were closing ranks in defence of a masculinity that was deeply rooted in force.

At one level, these events can be read as the story of a specific fight, in a specific city, at a specific time in the history of race relations in North America. As such, they illustrate several recurring themes in the history of North American sport in the early twentieth century. These would include the association of improved sporting performance with technique and science, the mutual interests of sporting promoters and civic boosters, and the several ways that sports promotions sought to trade on ethnic and racial (as well as civic) rivalries. However, perhaps the most interesting and enduring aspect of the Pelkey–McCarty fight, and the trial of Pelkey (and of boxing) that followed it, is how ready men from all segments of society were to come together in defence of the value of confrontative sports.

This can only be understood, we suggest, in the larger context of historical changes in what has been called the gender order, a structure of socially constructed patterns that reproduces, on balance, the social power and privileges of men.[45] However, gender relations involve not only male-female relations but also hierarchies among men and among different ways of being male. There are clearly many ways of being a man, but pride of place in the eyes of many men still goes to the men who embody force and aggression and who show that they can dominate other people physically. Thus, the celebration of violence in sport, like the celebration of toughness of men who excel in body contact sports, is an opportunity to publicly reaffirm the value of physical domination—something that appeals viscerally to many men even as it is constrained by law in social contexts.[46] The male violence that is routinely sanctioned in sport and the aggressive men who are often glorified for their sporting exploits have together made sport one of the few surviving areas of social life that legitimate the use of force and promote respect for 'forceful' men. In the discourse that surrounded the Pelkey trial, a violent act committed under sporting conditions was given social legitimacy, and considerable male solidarity was demonstrated. In the testimony and asides attributed to many of the leading men in Calgary, we can see that the 'modern' respect for skill and competitive achievement did not supplant belief in the value of a more traditional version of masculinity and the value of social practices that reproduced it.

## Notes

The authors wish to thank Terry Jackson for sharing his expertise on Tommy Burns, his insight into the case, and for sharing his research files and photographs.

1. Michael A. Messner, 'When Bodies are Weapons: Masculinity and Violence in Sport', *International Review for the Sociology of Sport* 25, (1990): 203–19; David Whitson, 'Sport in the Social Construction of Masculinity', in Michael A. Messner and Donald F. Sabo, eds, *Sport, Men and the Gender Order: Critical Feminist Perspectives* (Champaign, Ill.: Human Kinetics, 1990), 19–30; Kevin Young, 'Violence, Risk, and Liability in Male Sports Culture', *Sociology of Sport Journal* 10 (1993): 373–96.

2. See Paul Rutherford, *The Making of the Canadian Media* (Toronto: McGraw-Hill Ryerson, 1978); Elliott J. Gorn, *The Manly Art: Bare-Knuckle Prize Fighting in America* (Ithaca, NY: Cornell University Press, 1986).

3. Robert W. Connell, D.J. Ashenden, S. Kessler, and G.W. Dowsett, *Making the Difference: Schools, Families and Social Division* (Sydney: Allen & Unwin, 1982).

4. See, for example, Michael Oriard's discussion on the relationships between sports, masculinity, and violence in *Reading Football: How the Popular Press Created an American Spectacle* (Chapel Hill: University of North Carolina Press, 1993).

5. For brief discussions of this legislation, see Bruce Kidd, 'Capturing the Provincial State for Amateur Sport: The Ontario Athletic Commission in the Interwar Period', in Kevin B. Wamsley, ed., *Method and Methodology in Sport and Cultural History* (Dubuque, Iowa: Brown and Benchmark, 1995), 203–34; Kevin B. Wamsley, 'Legislation and Leisure in 19th Century Canada', doctoral dissertation (University of Alberta, 1992).

6. See Kevin Young and Kevin B. Wamsley, 'State Complicity in Sports Assault and the Gender Order in 20th Century Canada: Preliminary Observations', *AVANTE* 2 (1996): 51–69.

7. Peter Donnelly, 'On Boxing: Notes on the Past, Present and Future of a Sport in Transition', *Current Psychology* 7 (1988–9): 339. On urban sport and moral imperatives, see Steven A. Riess, *City Games: The Evolution of American Urban Society and the Rise of Sports* (Champaign: University of Illinois Press, 1989); Paul S. Boyer, *Urban Masses and Moral Order in America, 1820–1920* (Cambridge, Mass.: Harvard University Press, 1978).

8. On 'muscular Christianity' and the role of sport in promoting 'manliness', see J. Anthony Mangan, *Manliness and Morality: Middle-Class Masculinity in Britain and North America, 1800–1940* (New York: St Martin's Press, 1987). Also on sports and the idea of 'manliness', see Morris Mott, 'One Solution to the Urban Crisis: Manly Sports and Winnipeggers, 1900–1914', *Urban History Review* 12 (1983): 57–70; Morris Mott, 'The British Protestant Pioneers and the Establishment of Manly Sports in Manitoba, 1870–1886', *Journal of Sport History* 7 (1980): 25–36. See also Norman Vance, *The Sinews of the Spirit: The Ideal of Christian Manliness in Victorian Literature and Religious Thought* (Cambridge: Cambridge University Press, 1985).

9. From content surveys of the *Calgary Daily Herald* and the *Calgary Eyeopener* (1895–1914),

it is evident that this is particularly accurate for the city of Calgary during the early twentieth century. Showing support for local bouts, and providing legitimacy for the sport of boxing, newspapers often provided the names of prominent men in attendance.

10. See John Hoberman, *Mortal Engines: The Science of Performance and the Dehumanization of Sport* (New York: Free Press, 1992), 33–61.

11. Gerald Early, *The Culture of Bruising: Essays on Prizefighting, Literature, and Modern American Culture* (Hopewell, NJ: Ecco Press, 1994), 6.

12. Ibid., xiii–xv; Richard Gruneau and David Whitson, *Hockey Night in Canada* (Toronto: Garamond Press, 1993), 189–90.

13. See Randy Roberts, *Papa Jack: Jack Johnson and the Era of White Hopes* (New York: Free Press, 1983).

14. For the most extensive source on Tommy Burns, see Terry Jackson, 'Tommy Burns: World Heavyweight Boxing Champion', Master's thesis (University of Western Ontario, 1985). See also Don Morrow and Terry Jackson, 'Boxing's Interregnum: How Good Was Tommy Burns, World Heavyweight Boxing Champion 1906–1908?', *Canadian Journal of History of Sport* 24 (1993): 30–46.

15. Grant MacEwan, 'The Firehall Legend: Calgary's "Cappy" Smart', in Max Foran and Sheilagh S. Jameson, eds, *Citymakers: Calgarians after the Frontier* (The Historical Society of Alberta, 1987), 73.

16. William M. McLennan, *Sport in Early Calgary* (Calgary: Fort Brisbois Publishing, 1983), 192.

17. *Calgary Eyeopener*, 23 Mar. 1912.

18. *Calgary Daily Herald*, 19 Oct. 1910.

19. Ibid., 17 May 1913.

20. Ibid., 11 Oct. 1910.

21. Ibid., 10 Mar. 1909.

22. William H. Wiggins Jr, 'Boxing's Sambo Twins: Racial Stereotypes in Jack Johnson and Joe Louis Newspaper Cartoons, 1908 to 1938', *Journal of Sport History* 15 (1988): 242–54.

23. See Roberts, *Papa Jack*; Al-Tony Gilmour, *Bad Nigger: The National Impact of Jack Johnson* (Port Washington, NY: Kenniket Press, 1975); Jeffrey

Sammons, *Beyond the Ring: The Role of Boxing in American Society* (Chicago: University of Chicago Press, 1988).

24. *Calgary Daily Herald*, 17 May 1913. See also Michael Dinning, 'The Search for the Great White Hope: Heavyweight Boxing in Canada—1908–1915. Arthur Pelkey—His Rise and Demise', unpublished paper (University of Western Ontario, n.d.).

25. *Calgary Daily Herald*, 26 Oct. 1910.

26. Judge Harvey's Notebooks, 68.302, box no. 3, no. 54, p. 185 (Provincial Archives of Alberta, Edmonton).

27. *Calgary Daily Herald*, 26 May 1913.

28. Judge Harvey's Notebooks, pp. 186–7.

29. Photograph, Copyright 1913, Reeves, Calgary. Copy from The Sports Nostalgia Store, Upper Saddle River, New Jersey, from the personal collection of Terry Jackson, London, Ontario.

30. *Calgary Daily Herald*, 27 May 1913.

31. *R. vs. Pelkey*, Alberta Law Reports, VI, 1913, p. 107.

32. *Calgary Daily Herald*, 26 May 1912.

33. McLennan, *Sport in Early Calgary*, 204.

34. Judge Harvey's Notebooks, p. 208; *Calgary Daily Herald*, 23 June 1913.

35. Letter from W.T. Tait to Chief Justice Harvey, 19 Mar. 1913, National Archives of Canada, MG 30, E-87, vol. 10, W.Y.

36. Letter from W.T. Tait to Chief Justice Harvey, 3 Apr. 1913.

37. See Young and Wamsley, 'State Complicity in Sports Assault'.

38. *R. v. Wildfong and Lang*, 1911, 17, C.C.C.256, Ontario County Court.

39. *Calgary Daily Herald*, 23 June 1913.

40. Ibid., 29 Oct. 1910.

41. Ibid., 21 June 1913.

42. Ibid., 6 June 1913.

43. Ibid., 20 June 1913.

44. For further discussion of this issue, see Young and Wamsley, 'State Complicity in Sports Assault'.

45. Robert W. Connell, *Gender and Power* (Cambridge: Polity Press, 1987).

46. See Gruneau and Whitson, *Hockey Night in Canada*.

# 21

# Trying Again: Regulating Booze in Canada after Prohibition

Craig Heron

After a century of campaigning, Canada's teeto-tallers had to confront failure. They watched their dry utopia collapse in most parts of the country in less than a decade after 1920. The temperance movement, which had been thrown onto the defensive almost as soon as province-wide prohibition was launched, now found itself fighting the less draconian regulatory model of 'government control' as a more workable alternative. State policy-makers, however, were not willing simply to turn back the clock to the freewheeling days of the pre-war era. Instead, they set in place new administrative measures to accomplish some of the same old goals of curbing consumption and controlling behaviour. If full-scale prohibition had failed, there was no reason to give up on the project of moral regulation.

The new watchword was 'moderation'. It captured the yearning of bourgeois Canadians for refined drinking occasions, an end to law-lessness, and a new era of less politically destabilizing extremism. It embraced the proletarian desire for the right to respectable imbibing and an end to class-biased legislation. It was an appeal to greater personal freedom for sensible, orderly behaviour, under the still watchful eyes of the state. It was an acceptable compromise for the brewing and distilling interests, and it made

sense to the majority of the thousands of Canadians who were asked to express an opinion on the continuation or repeal of prohibition between 1919 and 1929.

## The Many Roads to Repeal

. . .

With the exception of Quebec and, for idio-syncratic reasons, Alberta, government control arrived in two distinct, widely separated steps. Government-run cash-and-carry liquor stores appeared to be the easiest policy shift to sell to voters, and most provinces started with that measure alone. There was much more hesitation about reopening public drinking places. That possibility resurrected the menacing image of the pre-war saloon, and usually only brewing interests and working-class wets were willing to champion the barroom. Except for Ontario, the sale of near beer in hotels, pool halls, and lunch counters came to an end with government-control legislation. Full-strength beer in government stores was available only in take-home bottles and, in Ontario and British Columbia at least, only a dozen at a time. Draft beer could not be sold.[1]

The liquor stores alone proved unsatisfactory. 'A great many workingmen don't care to or have

---

Craig Heron, 'Trying Again: Regulating Booze in Canada after Prohibition', from *Booze: A Distilled History* © 2003 Between the Lines. Reprinted by permission of the publisher.

not the means and opportunity, to take a carton of beer home', the Hamilton *Labor News* complained in 1927. 'In any event they prefer to have a glass, or perhaps two, along with friends in congenial surroundings.' Manitoba's veterans agreed: 'What the ordinary man wants is some place where he can lawfully get a glass of beer in decent surroundings.' In his 1928 study of government control in Canada (before most provinces had licensed premises), the British writer Reginald Hose observed, 'It is evident that people who perpetuate the prohibition-time habits of drinking surreptitiously in any convenient meeting place will not be satisfied with store facilities for their buying, and when two or three foregather in a back-room where treating and some sort of service of the kind they like is offered, there will continue to be secret drinking.'[2]

In the end the growing evidence that moonshining and bootlegging continued to exist in full force alongside government-controlled outlets helped to convince governments and voters to make booze accessible in controlled public settings. In most provinces licensed drinking establishments arrived a few years after liquor stores as a result of renewed wet campaigning, especially by labour and war veterans' organizations and the brewing interests. The dynamics of change were somewhat different in each province, and the new experiences under government control increasingly became part of the debate in the other still-dry provinces.

. . .

## Under Watchful Eyes

The new regimes of government control that all these provinces established were considerably less 'wet' than what had been tolerated before the war. They were also openly designed to make access to alcoholic beverages difficult and to educate the drinker in moderation. As the Edmonton *Bulletin* suggested when Alberta introduced its government-control legislation, 'While declaring the sale of beer and wine and liquor to be legal, the bill brands both seller of beer and the user of liquor as doing something that is either morally wrong or publicly dangerous or both.'[3]

Although province-wide prohibition had been repealed, some kind of local-option provision, either provincial law or the old Scott Act, survived in each province to allow municipalities to keep out liquor stores, brewers' warehouses, and/or beer parlours. Even in Quebec in the mid-1920s, for example, 91 per cent of people living in cities and 58 per cent of those in towns had access to licensed premises, but 85 per cent of the rural population did not, so that only half of the province's population lived in wet municipalities. As in the pre-war version of local prohibition, booze could legally be sent into these dry areas by mail or express order, and transportation by automobile now allowed drinkers to travel longer distances to government liquor stores. A 1928 study of government control in Canada concluded, 'The belief in local option is losing weight as a means of arresting excessive drinking.' Although there was little expansion of dry zones, most withstood referendum challenges and held on for many more years.[4]

Each provincial liquor control act also created a powerful provincial regulatory commission of between one and five members, usually known as a liquor control board (or commission), with sweeping powers to set policy for alcohol consumption. Like a growing number of regulatory agencies (such as labour relations boards), these bodies made and enforced law in their own ad hoc fashion, largely outside the purview of legislatures or courts. They were headed by high-profile, widely respected men (such as Ontario's Sir Henry Drayton, a former federal railways minister, and Manitoba's R.D. Waugh, a former League of Nations commissioner). In Quebec they reported to the treasurer, in Saskatchewan and British Columbia they reported directly to the legislature, and elsewhere to the provincial cabinet. The sweeping powers of these boards or commissions took many of the details of public policy around booze out of the hands of legislators and away from close public scrutiny. As a result, most of the related issues gradually faded away from the vortex of political controversy and fell off the agendas of political parties. Politicians were happy to let the new administrators handle the problems.[5]

Each board employed a large, widely scattered but rigidly controlled staff to monitor drinkers and inspect drinking places. Neither the board members nor the staff was rooted in any particular profession, such as medicine, psychiatry, public health, or even the law; their political connections were generally far more important than any kind of professional expertise. The dynamics of this new regulatory regime primarily involved moral policing. The boards saw their role as much more than administering retail outlets and issuing licences; they were moral guardians whose policies and procedures were intended to encourage sobriety and discourage alcohol abuse. As Ontario's Liquor Control Board indicated in its first annual report, 'The Board has endeavoured always to keep in mind that the Act under which it was organized was a control act, and that therefore a proper control of the purchase and sale of liquor should be its aim.' The Ontario board was proud of its initial accomplishments:

> A marked cutting down of the bootlegging evil; a lessening of youthful temptations to break prohibitory laws; the bringing about of greater respect for all law; a decrease if not an elimination of the making of 'home brew' with its dangerous poisonous tendencies; and, it is hoped, a real stimulation to temperance in all things by education and home training rather than by prohibiting which does not prohibit.

Board policies tried not only to curb consumption but also to nudge drinkers towards less alcoholic beverages—beer and wine—which were generally made easier to obtain and less expensive than spirits. As the secretary of the Quebec Liquor Commission put it in 1922, 'The Board is much more anxious to push the sale of beer and wine than of whisky and is importing French wines in large quantities and selling them at small profit to encourage their consumption.' Five years later Alberta's board reported that beer made up nearly 93 per cent of alcohol sales, wines only 3.4 per cent, and spirits only 3.9 per cent. Liquor control boards also kept tight controls over advertising for alcoholic beverages, which was banned outright in Ontario, Nova Scotia, and New Brunswick and closely monitored elsewhere.[6]

The liquor control boards had a monopoly on the wholesale purchase and retail sale of most alcoholic beverages. Building on the much more limited experience of the 'dispensaries' that some provinces had operated during prohibition, each board ran a chain of stores that were the only places in which drinkers could buy booze by the bottle, domestic or imported—and at uniform prices fixed by the board. Beer (and, in Ontario, wine) got special treatment, and could often be sold through other outlets. In Quebec grocers and other retailers were allowed to sell beer (and nothing else) purchased directly from brewers, and several provinces (Quebec, Manitoba, Saskatchewan, Alberta, and British Columbia), as well as Newfoundland, eventually permitted hotels to sell beer in cases for off-premise consumption. In some provinces brewers were permitted to pool their wholesaling in one warehousing operation and to deliver beer directly to customers. Ontario permitted the breweries, brewers' warehouses, and wineries to sell directly to the public from their own government-inspected retail outlets, a practice later introduced by only half the provinces.[7]

Compared to pre-war retail outlets, the government stores themselves were less numerous and convenient. In 1930 there were only 27 across Nova Scotia, 32 in Alberta, 109 in Quebec (85 of them in Montreal), and 124 in Ontario (compared to 211 private shops in 1915, as well as nearly 1,300 taverns and clubs). The outlets were also open for shorter hours. By 1933 stores in six of the eight wet provinces were closed in the evenings, and two provinces closed their stores at 1:00 p.m. on Saturdays. All of them shut down on Sundays, public holidays, and election days.[8]

Customers entering government liquor stores found them to be coldly austere places, more like banks than retail stores. No advertisements or displays adorned the windows or walls. The booze was kept out of reach behind counters, and customers had to hand their written requests to board employees behind wickets. Until 1928 Manitoba required bottles purchased to be delivered directly to the purchasers' homes, but most provinces allowed customers to carry bottles, wrapped discreetly in brown paper, out the door. 'The fact that the sale is confined to sealed packages and that there are no opportunities for "tasting and sampling" has rid the stores of a certain loafing element which frequented the wine and spirit shops of the past', wrote one commentator in 1928. In Saskatchewan's small towns and villages, only beer was available in the government stores; liquor was delivered to homes by mail order. In places where taverns had not been legalized, drinking outside households remained illegal, and even in places where beer was available by the glass, spirits had to be consumed out of sight at home. Some provinces established specific limits on the amount of booze an individual could buy: one bottle of spirits at a time in Quebec and New Brunswick; one case of spirits or two dozen quarts of beer per week in Manitoba; one quart of spirits, one gallon of wine, or two gallons of beer in Saskatchewan. Prices were kept high to discourage drinking (but also, ironically, to help provincial revenues). Even well-paid steelworkers and autoworkers who brought home $25 to $30 in their pay packets each week in 1925 would think twice about laying out $3.50 and up for a 'twenty-sixer' of rye or gin or $5 for Scotch.[9]

In all wet provinces except Quebec and New Brunswick drinkers had to get an annual permit to buy alcohol from these stores, at a cost of one or two dollars. Generally the permits were booklets that had to be presented for each purchase, when the clerk would enter the date and amount obtained. They were, in the words of one commentator, 'a constant if somewhat irksome

reminder to the public that the purchase of liquor, like other drugs, requires proper supervision.' Tourists could get special, short-term permits.[10]

Issuing these permits turned liquor store staff into social workers who had to determine whether a customer should for any reason be denied a permit and whether he or she was consuming too much. Police, municipal welfare authorities, and charity officers could intervene to prevent individuals from getting permits if they were on the dole or otherwise in economic or moral trouble (as in the pre-prohibition era, people could be put on a permanent interdiction list). In 1931 Ontario's board staff co-operated in nearly 27,000 special investigations of relief applicants; the number climbed to over 59,000 in 1932. Few of those investigated had permits, it turned out. Sometimes a permit would be returned to the wife or mother, or to the original male, with a limitation on purchasing power. Aboriginal peoples on or off reserves were to be denied permits categorically. The liquor store staff was expected to watch for excessive consumption and to turn away such bibulous customers (or potential bootleggers).[11]

In its 1928 report, Ontario's board noted that the 'social side' of its work had been largely extended and that many permits had been cancelled—more than 5,000 out of some 400,000. The board believed that cancellation should happen 'not only in cases where liquor has been abused, not only in cases where liquor may be purchased for resale, but also in all cases where the purchases of liquor are made at the expense of the home.' Customers should be allowed to purchase booze only after they had taken care of 'the necessities of life' and paid 'adequate duty to dependents'. Liquor store staff had therefore been instructed 'to render co-operation in the putting down of abuses of the permit privilege, to apply their local knowledge, to collect doubtful permits, and from time to time to invoke Head Office assistance in dealing therewith.' They were regularly reminded that 'the keynote of the law is "control," not sale, that moderation is the best way to support the law, and that satisfactory service by a store is best proved, not by volume of sales, but by prevalence of good social conditions in the surrounding community and absence of drunkenness and of complaints from neglected dependents.' In 1949 the federal government weighed in with a request that liquor stores refuse to cash the new family allowance cheques.[12]

Given that staff positions were all patronage appointments in the local constituency, these front-line workers must have faced a daily challenge in balancing such an earnest moral agenda with their continuing relationships with friends and neighbours. To keep them on their toes, the boards' chief administrators bombarded them with memoranda stipulating rules and procedures to be followed and demanding detailed reporting.

After beer by the glass was legalized, liquor control boards used their power to license 'beverage rooms' or 'beer parlours' to create a rigidly structured drinking environment. (Only Quebec allowed the public drinking of beer in cafés, and Nova Scotia, Ontario, and the four western provinces eventually issued one-occasion banquet permits.) Even the labelling was significant: the terms 'bar' or 'saloon' were forbidden, and only in Quebec could the word 'tavern' be used. Most provinces initially required that the rooms be attached to hotels (or, in some cases, set up in railway cars or steamboats) or, to satisfy the veterans, housed in military messes and social clubs with limited memberships. Would-be proprietors went through rigid screenings to determine that they were fit to run an orderly, respectable operation. 'Tied houses' connected to breweries were explicitly forbidden in some cases, actively discouraged in others, but tolerated in a few. Most beer parlours were former hotel saloons, but hotel-keepers got licences only if they had a minimum number of rooms for rent and adequate dining-room facilities for guests or longer-term residents. The boards' supervision of spatial design and interior decor established a kind of moral architecture to shape customers' (and owners') behaviour. Before opening their doors to the public, the proprietors had to meet stringent architectural requirements, and all alterations had to be approved by the board. New renovations might be demanded at any time if the flow of customers revealed particular problems (such as the location of washrooms). The businesses were not allowed to advertise what they were selling on signs on the street or to accept most forms of advertising from breweries. There was no consensus about whether these places should be concealed from public view: some provinces demanded uncovered windows so that people passing by could see what was going on, while others insisted on blinds or curtains to prevent the innocent from being shocked.[13]

In parts of the United States the post-prohibition regime of public drinking was tied to restaurants, but in Canada, although beer or wine with meals might be permitted in hotel restaurants, the regulations for the main drinking sites moved in the opposite direction. Proprietors of beer parlours could sell nothing but beer (and in some cases wine, though few stocked it), and could offer no food, soft drinks, or tobacco. Customers were forbidden to play games (even checkers or cards) or gamble. Except in Montreal, where licensed nightclubs offered dancing and exotic floor shows under Quebec's more permissive legislation, patrons could see no entertainment and were not even able to amuse themselves by dancing, singing, or playing musical instruments. Even the sound of music from other rooms in the hotel had to be blocked. The idea was that without these extra services and amenities, customers would have less interest in lingering.[14]

The stand-up bar was banished. Customers had to be seated at small tables in clusters of four drinkers (presumably, four men could treat each other without getting too drunk or using up too much of the family income). Glasses or bottles of beer had to be served at these tables one or two at a time, and only the waiter could move drinks between tables. The law forbade someone to stand up with a drink in hand (it was harder to pick fights from a sitting position). The more tightly restricted hours included, in some cases, a compulsory closing at supper time (curiously, although they never had prohibition, pubs in England, Australia, and New Zealand had much more restrictive hours of operations imposed on them). No credit or cheque-cashing was permitted. Lighting was often dim, the decor was simple and utilitarian, and (as in the liquor stores) little adorned the walls.

These new watering holes, then, were purposely made as stark, austere, and unattractive as possible, not just to discourage patrons from lingering and to encourage them to drink less, but also to prevent the places from becoming the free-wheeling, boisterously interactive places of the past. The rules were intended to discipline drinkers to act in a decent, orderly fashion while socializing in this public space. Beer parlours soon took on the characteristic shape and texture that would last for four or five decades in most parts of the country. In the words of one British Columbia waiter, you had to 'sit down, shut up, and drink your beer.' A disgusted Protestant clergyman thought the new drinking place was 'more of an evil than the old saloon, for men will drink more, and more men will get drunk sitting down at a table than uncomfortably standing at a bar.' Many years later a government commission in Manitoba agreed that 'beer parlors are places where men may drink and drink and may do nothing else' and worried that they tended 'rather to encourage than to discourage drinking'.[15]

Regular coercion was built into the dynamics of the beer parlours. Ironically, the immediate impact was not on the individual drinker in a beer parlour but on the proprietor and his staff. In Ontario the term applied to the licence issued to a hotel-keeper was the 'authority', which suggests a legal responsibility to carry out liquor board policy. Bartenders and waiters were the front-line enforcers, regulating the flow of booze and controlling drunks when they got out of control. Inspectors visited the places frequently to check for infractions, watching out for too much drunkenness and assessing the waiters' treatment of customers. The inspectors reported on the

number of glasses in front of each drinker and counted heads to see if the room had more bodies than officially designated. They measured the head in the beer glasses and checked to see that the glasses were filled to the regulation line. They looked hard at young customers to see if they were under the legal drinking age of 21. They evaluated how the proprietor and his staff handled fights. Negative reports on any of these issues would lead to written reprimands from the liquor control board and even temporary suspension of the owner's licence—in effect, an indirect fine in the form of lost revenue. The new liquor control acts said nothing, though, about how much an individual could drink. Although owners could eventually lose their licences if excessive drunkenness was reported, provincial authorities left local police forces to deal with the effects of drunken behaviour—fights, family violence, too much noise, general disturbances. Interdiction of problem cases was also once again an option.[16]

Alongside the beer parlours were a variety of licensed clubs that ranged from the poshest businessmen's meeting places to the far more common veterans' clubs, eventually known in popular parlance as 'Legion Halls'. To qualify for these special licences, the associations had to prove that they had a closed membership and were non-profit, and they were not allowed to sell drinks to non-members (nonetheless, some would try to do so). In Quebec and British Columbia the clubs were initially supposed to be only storing members' alcohol in lockers so that they could enjoy it on the premises, for a small service fee. In practice, especially in the posher clubs, members took to 'pooling' their booze, which allowed them to order individual drinks from the club staff—a legal fiction that the BC board finally regularized in 1940. The liquor control boards generally permitted these clubs to operate on a looser leash. They could have music and entertainment, and the more proletarian of them often got rowdier than the beer parlours. In some cases (such as Manitoba in 1931), revised regulations allowed some clubs to admit guests or 'associate' members, who paid a nominal fee. In practice those places operated as little more than another form of beer parlour.[17]

## Beer Parlour Patrons

The new legal regime of 'government control' thus had two distinct forms of regulation. The liquor stores served a mixed population of people who liked to take their booze home, which was certainly the choice of most bourgeois drinkers who could afford to stock a liquor cabinet or maintain a wine cellar. The beverage rooms or beer parlors and the great majority of the clubs, however, were understood to have a more specifically working-class clientele. Outside the hushed gentility of the businessmen's clubs, the only publicly accessible places to drink had been opened in response to working-class pressure and were designed to be spartan, unattractive sites where only working men, for the most part, would want to gather for a glass of beer. The middle and upper classes would find little to their taste there, and liquor control boards made their decisions about where and to whom to grant licences on that basis. The great majority of beverage rooms were in hotels in the downtown core or in, or near, working-class neighbourhoods.[18]

Workers wasted no time in making use of these new drinking places, and the rooms quickly found a place as part of the overall pattern of working-class life and leisure. But the extent of that place depended, as always, on the level of living standards of Canadian working people and the material resources at their disposal for leisure pursuits. Although the cost of living levelled off in the 1920s and even dropped in the 1930s, working-class incomes remained chronically insecure. The interwar decades were particularly difficult because the deep depression that hit the country late in 1920 did not lift until 1926 and then returned with a vengeance after 1929. As in past business downturns, working-class families might have little or no disposable income for participating in the commercialized

leisure that was expanding during those years. People with young, growing families would also have felt more constraint.

Within this context, working men did what they had always done: they either restrained their leisure-time expenditures or, in a small minority of cases, indulged their patriarchal privilege to drink, with the risk of pushing their families to the edge of abject poverty. Most probably did not need a liquor store clerk to remind them that their booze was a luxury that their families could not afford. Among Canadians over 14 years of age, per capita consumption rose from half a gallon of absolute alcohol in 1923 to .87 gallons in 1930, then tumbled to .46 in 1933 and 1934 and slowly returned to .74 in 1937, the most prosperous year of the Depression decade. Total beer consumption, which made up between 52 and 62 per cent of the absolute alcohol consumed in the 1920s and 1930s, followed a parallel course—from nearly 41 million gallons in 1924 to 62 million in 1930, down to just over 40 million in 1934 and up again to well over 60 million by the end of the decade. The number of liquor permits issued also rose and fell in the same pattern. Drinking was a cheap pleasure, but one that must have been sacrificed often in these years. In contrast, full employment at better wages during the Second World War brought soaring consumption and sales of liquor permits.[19]

There is no question, however, that working men moved into the new public drinking places in large numbers and, within the legal and structural constraints imposed on those rooms, made every effort to use them as the multi-purpose social centres that the old-time saloons had been. Prohibitionists had too often failed to understand that the thirst to be slaked among wage-earners was at least as much a yearning for male conviviality as it was for alcoholic beverages (though many workers certainly thought they needed the latter to get the former). So, once again these rooms became spaces in which workers could relax together, talk politics, gossip, and generally reaffirm their identities as manly working men.

For the many single men who rented rooms upstairs in the hotels to which so many drinking places were attached, or in nearby boarding houses, beer parlours were a communal living room shared with other bachelors. As in the past, many drinking spots took on the flavour of the nearest group of workers—longshoremen, loggers, railwaymen, steelworkers, miners, for instance. Others drew the bulk of their clientele from a specific neighbourhood. As a former Québécois bushworker, Gérard Fortin, remembered, taverns in Quebec City in the 1930s could still be places to pick up news about jobs or meet a recruiter. In some neighbourhoods they were also once again good places to talk about unions or conduct union business.[20]

Workers soon pushed the limits of the liquor control board regulations. They wandered about the room, bursting into loud choruses of popular songs in defiance of the ban on singing, breaking into fights to defend offended honour. 'They were the same old saloons, with the exception that the men sat at tables instead of standing at a bar; and they drank beer instead of whiskey', a Ladies Home Journal writer reported after visiting several Montreal taverns. 'There were the same old smells, same old maudlin songs and laughter, same old vulgarity, same old quarrelling and wrangling, same old drunks.'[21]

Once again it was younger men who seemed to set the tone of these places. 'In these taverns we saw few old men', a Quebec writer noted after visiting 15 taverns. 'Eighty per cent, at least, were young men between the ages of 18 and 30.' The rituals of violence that unfolded echoed the displays of masculine identity that had erupted around taverns and saloons for generations. When the young Gérard Fortin ended up working in a west coast pulp and paper mill in the 1930s, drinking became the occasion for settling scores over ethnic tensions in the local workforce. 'We had spent the evening drinking in the workers' club, and now one fellow who was always trying to provoke us was blasting off on all cylinders', he recalled. 'I just wasn't ready to

put up with it. I jumped him, but before I had a chance to hang one on him, a whole bunch of English guys jumped me.'

Like the pre-war drinking places, beer parlours ranged from the rough and rowdy to the more sedate and affable. In the mid-1920s Sir John Willison found the ones he visited in Calgary and Edmonton 'without exception quiet and orderly' and saw 'no evidence of drunkenness or heavy drinking'. On the whole workers seemed to treat these gathering places as spaces in which they could 'have a quiet beer and tell a few good jokes.' In their reports inspectors might well designate such places as 'decent'.[22]

If these new drinking places had familiar features held over from the saloon era, in some parts of the country they also had a major new element—women. Public drinking was no longer an exclusively male experience, as growing numbers of female drinkers settled into chairs in beer parlours to enjoy a beer. This was not an entirely surprising development, because the prohibition period had coincided with a considerable change in the standards of acceptable public behaviour for women, especially those from working-class families. Even before the war, young women had been staking out more public space within popular culture, showing up in much larger numbers at the various sites of leisure and entertainment, both in groups of single women and in the company of boyfriends. By the 1910s and 1920s young women were challenging conventions about feminine propriety in their appearance and behaviour—including smoking cigarettes in public. They found new role models on the movie screens: women like Mary Pickford or Theda Bara who stepped outside conventional models of femininity in their performances and highly publicized private lives. During the war most women had been granted the right to vote for the first time, and during the 1920s many young women no doubt voted to end prohibition.[23]

Since most provinces waited a few years between opening government liquor stores and licensing public drinking, they forced most drinking into the home, where, according to the moderationist argument, women's power in the domestic sphere would restrain their menfolk from drinking too much. Inadvertently, government policy may have had quite a different effect by breaking down the male near-monopoly on drinking and giving wives easier access to the bottle that their husbands brought home. As *Saturday Night* argued in 1934, when these legal regimes pushed drinking into private spaces, 'It was obviously difficult to exclude women from participation when once they had decided that they were the equals of the lords of creation.'[24]

In Edmonton the first person out the door of the new government liquor store in 1924 was a woman with six bottles of Guinness under her arm. Several women were also spotted in the lineups outside liquor outlets in Ontario cities on opening day in 1927. 'In the days of the saloon only men drank', Halifax's labour paper, the *Citizen*, argued in 1929. 'But now the women are drinking.' Many women no doubt shared the widespread belief that beer in particular was a healthy food and tonic, but they also seemed to want to join in the social life around drinking. Courtship and long-term relationships with men had a new glow of romantic heterosexual companionship, beamed out most powerfully in the Hollywood movies to which thousands of Canadians were flocking in the 1920s. Married couples were spending more leisure time together at home and some no doubt shared a drink, probably most often with friends or kin on special or celebratory occasions—birthdays, seasonal holidays, card parties, or summer outings, for example.[25]

By no means would all these women risk the possible attack on their reputations that visiting a beer parlour might bring, particularly those in non-Anglo-Canadian households, but many evidently saw nothing indecent or disreputable about quiet socializing with female friends or male companions over a glass or two in such places. No feminist organization or women's groups took up this cause, but informally women were asserting a new demand for equal treatment. As the first beer parlours opened up, however, hotel owners were strongly inclined to exclude women, on the assumption that a female in a public drinking place had loose morals and was probably a prostitute. The liquor control boards reinforced that patriarchal concern by consistently refusing to let women serve drinks (in Ontario, even if they were hotel owners). In the face of such resistance, some young women may well have found it easier to visit blind pigs or speakeasies with their dates. A staff writer with the *Ladies Home Journal* said he had seen many such places when he visited Montreal:

> Between midnight and morning, in a cabaret and in a half-dozen bootlegging clubs and joints I saw hundreds of women drinking; many of them were mere girls; and fully one third of them were drunk. A newspaper woman I met that night in a 'blind pig' club where three hundred men and women were drinking, told me she had seen a thousand women drunk in such places in Montreal.

Again, many illicit drinking places were run by women, most often in the informal, less commercial atmosphere of their own homes, where women drinkers probably felt more comfortable. These places were most likely an important lever for prying open a wider, perhaps grudging social acceptance of women amidst the beer glasses.[26]

As more women insisted on their right to participate in the new public drinking culture, space for them eventually opened up in the beer parlours in a few provinces in the interwar period. Quebec, Saskatchewan, and Manitoba shut the door on them completely, but a version of heterosocial public drinking was gradually worked out in the 1920s in British Columbia and was eventually extended to the two other jurisdictions with licensed beer parlours. Initially, with some hesitation, British Columbia's Liquor Control Board allowed women in. They showed up in much smaller numbers than the men, as another group of evangelical snoops discovered when they descended on Vancouver's beer parlours on two weeknights in 1926 to count noses and tallied up only 284 women alongside 2,396 men in 54 establishments one night and 143 mixing with 766 in five parlours on another night (a somewhat smaller proportion than investigators found in British pubs at the end of the 1930s). On the one hand, the disparity in numbers is not surprising, considering that the still pitifully low wages earned by women left them dependent on their beaus or husbands to pay for an evening's entertainment. Most wives and mothers also still had far too much work and responsibility for running the family household to have the time (or the independent income) to take an evening off to visit a beer parlour, and many husbands did not like to see their wives in such a place. On the other hand, the proportions are so much larger than they were in the 1913 surveys that there can be little doubt that many more women wanted some space in the new arenas of public drinking.[27]

By mid-1925 many BC hotel-keepers were nonetheless refusing to serve women, and the next year their provincial association voted unanimously to keep women out. Although the government was sympathetic to the owners, especially because it wanted to deflect some of the heavy criticism pouring down on the beer parlours from moral reformers, it advised the hotel-men that the law was not likely to allow this kind of overt discrimination. With the Liquor Control Board's consent, a gentlemen's agreement among the proprietors led to signs warning female customers that they were not welcome. The Vancouver *Province* liked this move: 'There is no doubt that the presence of women makes it more difficult to conduct beer parlors in a decent and orderly manner.' The paper argued that 'whatever an odd woman here or there may say about it, public opinion and particularly that part of it contributed by women, is strongly averse to women frequenting beer parlors.'[28]

In their quiet, persistent ways, some women nonetheless continued to show up for a drink.

Then, in 1927, after one hotel lost its licence briefly for serving them, the BC Liquor Control Board agreed to a compromise that allowed a completely separate section for women and any men who accompanied them—that is, for 'ladies and escorts' (this was the informal division of space in British pubs at the time, and some version of it had existed in parts of the United States before the war). Men could not enter that side of the beer parlour on their own. This arrangement was not entrenched in law or formal regulation, but other hotels began to follow suit, sometimes simply reserving a part of the main parlour for women and their male friends (only in 1942, in the heat of hysteria about venereal diseases being spread by prostitutes in beer parlours, did the BC Liquor Control Board begin to insist on partitions between the sections).[29]

Next door in Alberta a similar story unfolded. Women drinkers were admitted for two years until the provincial board decided to turn Calgary and Edmonton beer parlours into male-only enclaves, but then, two years later, it allowed proprietors elsewhere in the province to open women-only rooms within their establishments. Apparently few did. Nonetheless, by the time Ontario licensed its first 'beverage rooms' in 1934, the presence of women was so non-controversial that the Liquor Control Board made these specially designated areas for 'ladies and escorts' a requirement in almost all licensed hotels. These spaces typically took up half the beverage-room area, had their own separate entrances and washrooms, and were heavily patronized from the beginning. Informally, some proprietors allowed only one or two men to accompany each woman. Early on, the licensed clubs also wanted to be able to have female guests, but the board made them submit specific requests for 'ladies' nights', which could not be held more than once or twice a month. Small, independently organized clubs of married couples often rented space in the hotels or clubs to enjoy monthly card games or other social activities along with their beer.[30]

Women drinkers had found a new space within working-class culture, but the authorities who regulated public drinking did not lose their suspicions about shady morality. Not only did they agree to co-operate with public health campaigns against venereal disease, but proprietors could also be much less tolerant of women who they believed drank too much than they were of men on the other side of the partition. Gendered constructions of drunkenness lived on. Women excluded from public drinking could nonetheless be deeply resentful. In May 1945 the Victory-in-Europe celebrations saw hundreds of women storm into Winnipeg beer parlours to demand service. Some of them were served, and some were thrown out, and two days later these places were once again male-only bastions.[31]

Clearly, new feminine identities—particularly among single women, but apparently also with many wives—had been worked out in working-class communities in these early decades of the twentieth century; and these identities incorporated booze as part of a more public, less domestically focused lifestyle. Of course, this process had also included the construction of new masculinities that did not require the exclusion of women from male-only environments and allowed for regular heterosexual socializing in leisure time, yet did not fundamentally disrupt patriarchal authority. After all, women still needed the protection of an 'escort'.

Interestingly, though, this mingling of the sexes coexisted with the renewed booze-based solidarities of male-only drinking spaces on the other side of the beer parlour partition. As in the past, many working-class men still preferred to enjoy the experience without women; as one BC observer noted, 'There are many men who can not be happy unless they are telling or listening to lewd stories or punctuating their conversation with a series of oaths, and such men do, no doubt, find their liberty of action circumscribed by the presence of ladies in the parlor.' This tendency was more than a question of personal comfort or individual liberty. Male-

only drinking was an important symbol and reinforcement of male privilege in the working-class household and beyond.[32]

Post-prohibition public drinking had thus allowed for the crystallization of two versions of working-class masculinity side by side in the state-regulated beer parlour: one that replicated the 'boys-only', often misogynistic, bachelor-driven form that had roots all the way back to the earliest days of tavern-going; and the newer form based in public courtship in commercialized spaces and companionate socializing with spouses after marriage.

Women were not the only outcasts from this male social space. People of colour were not always made to feel welcome either. Aboriginal peoples faced the harshest treatment, since the federal legislation governing their lives would continue to deny them legal access to alcohol until 1951. Those who had entered beer parlours might get the same service as whites, particularly if they could 'pass' and drew no attention to themselves, but in practice waiters in some hotels were likely to refuse to serve anyone with recognizably 'Indian' features. Native women might also be more readily targeted as prostitutes. Aboriginal drinkers also had to watch out for the RCMP officers who occasionally showed up to check for violators of the Indian Act. Native people deeply resented the inequitable treatment they faced.[33]

For other groups there was no formal process of exclusion, and, especially by the 1940s, blacks and Asians could usually sit down in the same beer parlours as white drinkers (though Japanese customers were barred during the war). Yet, as in the pre-war saloons, men who gathered in these public drinking places might have distinct ideas about who belonged in their little community, and racially based tensions could erupt, particularly if the non-white drinkers were sitting with white women. Hotelkeepers could arbitrarily refuse to serve mixed-race couples or particular people of colour, and liquor control boards generally refused to intervene to stop such racist practices.[34]

## Lingering Shadows

. . .

Across the country, drinkers looking for alcohol outside the time constraints and watchful eye of liquor stores and beer parlours could easily locate the neighbourhood bootlegger or the more sociable blind pigs (increasingly known as 'booze cans'). In 1925 the Montreal *Standard* reported that there were dozens of such establishments in the heart of the city, and four years later the Quebec government passed legislation allowing police to arrest people found in a blind pig. Over the next 20 years, according to a retired union leader in Welland, Ontario, workers often found their way to such places, especially when they came off a shift after hotel closing hours. 'In order to buy a drink after work, they would sometimes end up at a friend's place', he wrote. 'There were few larger commercial bootleggers; most were family-run places.' He explained that they were known as 'social clubs'. The proprietors and customers, he said, 'were mainly workers who, in most cases, worked together. The price was reasonable, and the bootlegger's wife usually made sandwiches for the customers.' In rural areas especially, moonshine also continued to bubble away in backyard stills, which provincial authorities could not touch (that phenomenon remained a federal responsibility).[35]

Whatever the source of the booze, the bootlegger was probably closer to home than were the widely scattered government liquor stores. It might take several days for an express order from a government store to arrive, while bootleggers could deliver quickly, right to the door. Taxi drivers were often reliable suppliers. A former worker at Toronto's huge Inglis plant recalled how bootleg booze came right into the factory:

People had taken out a brick. It was a double brick because it was a double wall, and you just went to the phone. If you wanted a bottle in the daytime, you would just phone the cab number and just say, 'The hole in the wall,' and you stood there with your money and you passed your money out to the cab driver. He used to drive up to it, roll down the window, and pass the bottle through. And we had a lot of bottles. That was a pretty hot little corner, at times. We had a lot of wine come through that hole.[36]

. . .

What the rigid new regime of government control had created was a dual system of alcohol consumption: one stream flowed through state-regulated stores and public drinking outlets; the other went through the illicit channels that had appeared decades earlier, matured during the prohibition era, and continued to thrive as a result of the strictness of the new laws and regulations. These two systems—the government policies intended to remind customers of liquor stores and beer parlours that they were engaged in a somewhat disreputable activity, and the furtive practices of the illicit underground economy in booze—combined to cast drinking as a disreputable pleasure to be enjoyed quietly and secretively. In the tradition of the speakeasy, patrons of the unlicensed cabarets (outside Quebec) got accustomed to enjoying their booze from a bottle hidden under the long tablecloths, with no objections from the staff of these so-called 'bottle clubs'.[37]

Just how profoundly public policy and popular attitudes had changed became clear after the outbreak of the Second World War. The temperance movement's continued lobbying for tighter controls convinced Mackenzie King to take action, but in the face of his cabinet's considerable resistance the prime minister announced, late in 1942, no more than a program to restrain consumption. Beyond requiring the dilution of spirits to 70 proof, he merely called on the provinces to reduce sales (spirits by 30 per cent, wine by 20 per cent, and beer by 10 per cent), ban advertising, and restrict hours for stores and beer parlours. The provincial governments, angry at not being consulted and concerned about the potential loss of revenue, pointed out the administrative difficulties posed by the measure and railed against the unpopularity of the rationing that was soon necessary. Working men needed their beer to keep them contented, they argued. Indeed, some workers were soon sporting buttons with the slogan 'No Beer—No Bonds'. The restrictions on beer were withdrawn 15 months later after making no appreciable dent in the public's thirst for booze.[38]

Yet prohibition did not discredit all roles for the Canadian state in shaping the moral environment. The repeal campaign was carried in large part on a promise that government control would be more effective in regulating drinking practices than was the uncontrolled behaviour that had emerged in the dark shadows of the illicit underground economy in booze. With governments haunted by the memories of pre-war saloons, the new system of control was explicitly designed to deter easy or heavy consumption of alcohol by regulating both time and space in which drinking was to take place, the activities that were permissible while drinking, and the company people could keep in public drinking places. In many ways the new drinking regime was not so much a completely new approach to moral regulation as a vastly expanded version of what had been evolving before prohibition was introduced. It was a model that US policy-makers examined closely as the campaign for repeal in that country reached its peak in 1933. Some US states borrowed the Canadian version of government liquor stores, though many more simply licensed private retailers. Most states initially allowed public drinking only where food was available, but more of them gradually took up the Canadian beer parlour model of selling drinks only.[39]

A new legal regime had thus set the boundaries of drinking cultures for the next half-century. Although the diversity of public drinking places would increase in most provinces after the Second World War, the fundamentals of this structure of regulation would not begin to change until the 1970s. Within these limits, the

working men and women who filled up most of the licensed establishments made them work as effectively as possible as oases of pleasure and sociability. In some cases, when the legally regulated facilities proved inadequate, they turned back to the underground economy that prohibition had brought to life and that continued to thrive. However they got their booze, many working-class men still treated public drinking places as exclusive bastions of collective male privilege that validated their dominance over women and children in their own families and in society more generally. At the same time, this gendered solidarity operated against a still substantial wall of widespread social disapproval of their behaviour, which was disparaged as a disreputable low-class excess. Class identities hardened in the heat of such scorn.

## Notes

1. Reginald E. Hose, *Prohibition or Control? Canada's Experience with the Liquor Problem, 1921–1927* (New York: Longmans, Green, 1928), 32–43, 66–9.

2. *Labor News* (Hamilton), 29 July 1927, 2 (quotation by Hamilton labour paper); John Herd Thompson, 'The Prohibition Question in Manitoba, 1892–1928', MA thesis (University of Manitoba, 1969), 102 (quotation by veterans); Hose, *Prohibition or Control?*, 30 (quotation by Hose); Gerald A. Hallowell, *Prohibition in Ontario, 1919–1923* (Ottawa: Ontario Historical Society, 1972), 138; Robert A. Campbell, *Demon Rum or Easy Money: Government Control of Liquor in British Columbia from Prohibition to Privatization* (Vancouver: University of British Columbia Press, 1991), 47, 52–3; Campbell, *Sit Down and Drink Your Beer: Regulating Vancouver's Beer Parlours, 1925–1954* (Toronto: University of Toronto Press, 2001), 20.

3. L.W. Moffit, 'Control of the Liquor Traffic in Canada', American Academy of Political and Social Sciences, *Annals* 163 (Sept. 1932): 192; Dianne Kathryn Stretch, 'From Prohibition to

Government Control: The Liquor Question in Alberta, 1909–1929', MA thesis (University of Alberta, 1979), 76 (quotation).

4.  Raymond B. Fosdick and Albert L. Scott, *Toward Liquor Control* (New York: Harper, 1933), 166–77; Hose, *Prohibition or Control?*, 12–21 (quotation at 20); Moffit, 'Control of Liquor Traffic', 191–2; James H. Gray, *Bacchanalia Revisited: Western Canada's Boozy Skid to Social Disaster* (Saskatoon: Western Producer Prairie Books, 1982), 59; Greg Marquis, 'The Canadian Temperance Movement: What Happened after Prohibition?', paper presented to the Canadian Historical Association annual meeting, 2001, 10–11.

5.  Moffit, 'Control of the Liquor Traffic', 189–90; Robert Prévost, Suzanne Gagne, and Michel Phaneuf, *L'histoire de l'alcool au Québec* (Montreal: Editions Internationales Alain Stanke, 1986), 73–83; Daniel Surprenant, 'Une institution québécoise: la Société des alcools du Québec', *Études Canadiennes/Canadian Studies* 35 (1993): 27–52.

6.  Mariana Valverde, *Diseases of the Will: Alcohol and the Dilemmas of Freedom* (Cambridge: Cambridge University Press, 1999), 145–53; Ontario, Liquor Control Board, *Report*, 1927, 5, 7 (quotations by Ontario board); *Canadian Annual Review*, 1922, 706 (quotation by Quebec official), and 1924–5 (388), 1927–8 (532). . . .

7.  Fosdick and Scott, *Toward Liquor Control*, 166–77; Hose, *Prohibition or Control?*, 22–31, 44–54; Dominion Bureau of Statistics, *Control and Sale of Liquor*, 1934, 4–13; Manitoba Liquor Enquiry Commission, *Report* (Winnipeg, 1955), 304–27.

8.  *Canadian Annual Review*, 1930–1, 171, 195, 284; Fosdick and Scott, *Toward Liquor Control*, 166–77; Dominion Bureau of Statistics, *Control and Sale of Liquor*, 1934, 4–13.

9.  Hose, *Prohibition or Control?* (quotation at 23); Prévost, Gagne, and Phaneuf, *L'histoire de l'alcool*, 78; Gray, *Bacchanalia Revisited*, 65; Craig Heron, *Working in Steel: The Early Years in Canada, 1883–1935* (Toronto: McClelland & Stewart, 1988), 92.

10. Fosdick and Scott, *Toward Liquor Control*, 166–77; Gray, *Bacchanalia Revisited*, 40–3; Hose,

*Prohibition or Control?*, 24–6 (quotation at 26), 62–5; Sir John Willison, 'Liquor Control in Western Canada', Archives of Ontario, F8 (Howard Ferguson Papers), MU1029 ('Papers Concerning the Temperance Question in Ontario, 1907–1929'); *Canadian Annual Review*, 1922, 853; 1923, 708–9; 1924–5, 434.

11. Ontario, Liquor Control Board, *Report*, 1931, 8, and 1932, 8.

12. Ibid., 1928, 9–10 (quotations); 1929, 11–13; 1930, 9–13; 1931, 7–8; 1932, 7–8; Moffit, 'Control of the Liquor Traffic', 191; Valverde, *Diseases of the Will*, 166–7; Campbell, *Sit Down and Drink Your Beer*, 67; Craig Heron, 'The Boys and Their Booze: Masculinities and Public Drinking in Working-Class Hamilton, 1890–1946', paper presented to the North American Labor History Conference, Detroit, 2002.

13. Brewers Association of Canada, *Brewing in Canada* (Ottawa: author, 1965), 41, 49; Campbell, *Sit Down and Drink Your Beer*; *Canadian Hotel Review* (Sept. 1934): 7, 22–8; Heron, 'Boys and Their Booze'.

14. Hose, *Prohibition or Control?*, 32–43; Willison, 'Liquor Control in Western Canada'; *Canadian Annual Review*, 1924–5, 433–4; Campbell, *Demon Rum or Easy Money*, 54–5, Robert A. Campbell, 'Managing the Marginal: Regulating and Negotiating Decency in Vancouver's Beer Parlours, 1925–1954', *Labour/Le Travail* 44 (Fall 1999): 109–27; Campbell, *Sit Down and Drink Your Beer*, 15–27; Prévost, Gagne, and Phaneuf, *L'histoire de l'alcool*, 94; John Gilmore, *Swinging in Paradise: The Story of Jazz in Montreal* (Montreal: Vehicule Press, 1988); William Weintraub, *City Unique: Montreal Days and Nights in the 1940s and '50s* (Toronto: McClelland & Stewart, 1996), 23, 33, 52, 121–30; Heron, 'Boys and Their Booze'; Richard Rohmer, *E.P. Taylor: The Biography of Edward Plunket Taylor* (Toronto: McClelland & Stewart, 1978), 73–4.

15. Campbell, *Demon Rum or Easy Money*, 54 (quotation by BC waiter); Ben H. Spence, *Quebec and the Liquor Problem* (Westerville, Ohio: American Issue Publishing Company, n.d.), 48–9 (quotation by

clergyman); Manitoba Liquor Enquiry Commission, *Report*, 398–412 (quotation by Commission at 404). In the mid-1920s, Judge Emily Murphy worried about the seating arrangements of the beer parlours: 'Personally, I would like to see the table abolished in favor of a standing bar', she told Sir John Willison. 'It would prevent people sitting down easefully [sic] and ordering glass after glass of beer.' Willison, 'Liquor Control in Western Canada', Edmonton, 8.

16. Valverde, *Diseases of the Will*, 145–62; Ernest R. Forbes, 'Prohibition and the Social Gospel in Nova Scotia', in Samuel D. Clark et al., eds, *Prophecy and Protest: Social Movements in Twentieth-Century Canada* (Toronto: Gage, 1975), 81; Spence, *Quebec and the Liquor Problem*, 39–46, 135–44; Moffit, 'Control of the Liquor Traffic', 190–1; Campbell, 'Managing the Marginal', 115–16; Campbell, *Sit Down and Drink Your Beer*, 29–49; *Canadian Annual Review*, 1934, 149; Prévost, Gagne, and Phaneuf, *L'histoire de l'alcool*, 95; Willison, 'Liquor Control in Western Canada'.

17. *Canadian Annual Review*, 1922, 708; 1924–5, 434, 449, 500; 1929–30, 523; Willison, 'Liquor Control in Western Canada'; Campbell, *Demon Rum or Easy Money*, 48, 83–6; Campbell, *Sit Down and Drink Your Beer*, 19–20, 112; Heron, 'Boys and Their Booze'; Manitoba Liquor Enquiry Commission, *Report*, 417–26.

18. Heron, 'Boys and Their Booze'; Robert E. Popham, *Working Papers on the Tavern*, vol. 3, *Notes on the Contemporary Tavern*, Substudy no. 1232 (Toronto: Alcoholism and Drug Addiction Research Foundation, 1982), 19. In a 1946 survey in Ontario, two-thirds of those who identified themselves as fairly regular patrons of beverage rooms were skilled, semi-skilled, or unskilled workers; Popham, *Working Papers on the Tavern*, 22. The major exception to the working-class dominance of beer parlours was in the grander hotels, which generally had well-appointed beer parlours for affluent guests or businessmen; the *Canadian Hotel Review* featured some of these in the 1930s. By refusing to serve draft beer and offering only bottled beer (which

at 20 cents a bottle was twice the price of beer by the glass), hotel managers kept out the riff-raff; in this way, the manager of Toronto's posh King Edward Hotel 'restricts his guests to the quieter, more refined type who want to enjoy a good drink in peaceful surroundings.' *Canadian Hotel Review* (Sept. 1934): 10–11; see also ibid. (May 1934): 13, ibid. (Aug. 1934): 10, 27.

19. Robert E. Popham and Wolfgang Schmidt, comps, *Statistics of Alcohol Use and Alcoholism in Canada, 1871–1956* (Toronto: University of Toronto Press, 1958), 24; *Canada Year Book*, 1941, 533; Gray, *Bacchanalia Revisited*, 66–7, 76–92; Campbell, *Demon Rum or Easy Money*, 86–96.

20. Gerard Fortin and Boyce Richardson, *Life of the Party* (Montreal: Vehicule Press, 1984), 46; David Sobel and Susan Meurer, *Working at Inglis: The Life and Death of a Canadian Factory* (Toronto: James Lorimer, 1994), 125; Milan (Mike) Bosnich, *One Man's War: Reflections of a Rough Diamond* (Toronto: Lugus Productions, 1989), 71, 81. For a detailed description of using a tavern in union organizing by structural steelworkers in 1950–1, see Popham, *Working Papers on the Tavern*, 3, 106–8.

21. Spence, *Quebec and the Liquor Problem*, 162–3 (quotation).

22. Ibid., 463–4 (quotation by Quebec writer); Fortin and Richardson, *Life of the Party*, 43–4, 46, 55, 58–9 (quotation by Fortin), 79; Willison, 'Liquor Control in Western Canada', 9 (quotation by Willison); Campbell, 'Managing the Marginal', 117 (quotation by inspector); *Canadian Annual Review*, 1932, 226; Heron, 'Boys and Their Booze'; Mark Rosenfeld, '"It Was a Hard Life": Class and Gender in the Work and Family Rhythms of a Railway Town, 1920–1950', Canadian Historical Association, *Historical Papers* (1988): 262–3.

23. Carolyn Strange, *Toronto's Girl Problem: The Perils and Pleasures of the City, 1880–1930* (Toronto: University of Toronto Press, 1995); Kathy Peiss, *Cheap Amusements: Working Women and Leisure in Turn-of-the-Century New York* (Philadelphia: Temple University Press, 1986); Veronica Strong-Boag, *The New Day Recalled: Lives of Girls and*

*Women in English Canada, 1919–1939* (Toronto: Copp Clark Pitman, 1988).

24. *Saturday Night* (Toronto), 3 Nov. 1934, 2 (quotation).

25. Gray, *Bacchanalia Revisited*, 43, 54–7; Suzanne Morton, *Ideal Surroundings: Domestic Life in a Working-Class Suburb in the 1920s* (Toronto: University of Toronto Press, 1995), 85 (quotation); Andrew Davies, *Leisure, Gender, and Poverty: Working-Class Culture in Salford and Manchester, 1900–1939* (Buckingham: Open University Press, 1992), 55–81; Mary Murphy, *Mining Cultures: Men, Women, and Leisure in Butte, 1914–41* (Urbana: University of Illinois Press, 1997), 42–70; Virginia Wright Wexman, *Creating the Couple: Love, Marriage, and Hollywood Performance* (Princeton, NJ: Princeton University Press, 1993). For the arrival of working-class women in British pubs during the First World War, see David W. Gutzke, 'Gender, Class, and Public Drinking in Britain during the First World War', *Histoire Sociale/Social History* 27, 54 (Nov. 1994): 367–91.

26. Spence, *Quebec and the Liquor Problem*, 131–2 (quotation); *Star* (Toronto), 1 June 1927, 1–2; *Globe* (Toronto), 2 June 1927, 1–2. Our view of the inside of prohibition-era drinking places in Canada remains opaque, because there has been little systematic study of the rooms in Canada.

27. Campbell, *Demon Rum or Easy Money*, 55–8.

28. Ibid., 57 (quotation).

29. Ibid., 55–8; Manitoba Liquor Enquiry Commission, *Report*, 315, 322, 424; Gutzke, 'Gender, Class, and Public Drinking'.

30. Robert A. Campbell, 'Ladies and Escorts: Gender Segregation and Public Policy in British Columbia Beer Parlours, 1925–1945', *BC Studies* 105/106 (Spring–Summer 1995); Campbell, *Sit Down and Drink Your Beer*, 51–77; Campbell, 'Managing the Marginal', 114–17, 125; Willison, 'Liquor Control in Western Canada'; Heron, 'Boys and Their Booze'. Women were kept out of taverns in New Brunswick until 1971, when the first ladies and escorts sections were finally approved. Greg

Marquis, 'Civilized Drinking: Alcohol and Society in New Brunswick, 1945–1975', *Journal of the Canadian Historical Society* (2000): 191.

31. Gray, *Bacchanalia Revisited*, 88–9.

32. Ibid., 44–5; Campbell, 'Managing the Marginal', 116–17 (quotation at 117); Heron, 'Boys and Their Booze'.

33. Campbell, *Sit Down and Drink Your Beer*, 93–105.

34. Ibid., 79–88; Valverde, *Diseases of the Will*, 162–70; Heron, 'Boys and Their Booze'.

35. Ben H. Spence, 'Prohibitory Legislation in Canada', in American Academy of Political and Social Sciences, *Annals*, 109 (Sept. 1923): 243; *Canadian Annual Review*, 1928–9, 389; James H. Gray, *Booze: The Impact of Whisky on the Prairie West* (Scarborough, Ont.: New American Library of Canada, 1972), 197–207; B.J. Grant, *When Rum Was King* (Fredericton, NB: Fiddlehead Poetry Books, 1984), 71; Stretch, 'From Prohibition to Government Control', 85–7; Manitoba Liquor Enquiry Commission, *Report*, 308–9; W.E. Mann, 'The Lower Ward', in S.D. Clark, ed., *Urbanism and the Changing Canadian Society* (Toronto: University of Toronto Press), 39–69; Reginald G. Smart and Alan C. Ogborne, *Northern Spirits: A Social History of Alcohol in Canada* (Toronto: Addiction Research Foundation, 1996), 64; Bosnich, *One Man's War*, 99 (quotations); *Canadian Hotel Review* (Feb. 1934): 19.

36. Sobel and Meurer, *Working at Inglis*, 127. . . .

37. Campbell, *Demon Rum or Easy Money*, 93–4, 127–9.

38. J.W. Pickersgill, ed., *The Mackenzie King Record*, vol. 1, *1939–1944* (Toronto: University of Toronto Press, 1960), 460–4, 485–8, 652–4; Campbell, *Demon Rum or Easy Money*, 86–90; Marquis, 'Canadian Temperance Movement', 11–13; Gray, *Bacchanalia Revisited*, 76–92; Rohmer, *Taylor*, 133–8, 152–3; Michael R. Marrus, *Mr. Sam: the Life and Times of Samuel Bronfman* (Toronto: Penguin Books, 1991), 311–13.

39. David E. Kyvig, *Repealing National Prohibition* (Chicago: University of Chicago Press, 1979), 187–9.

# 22

# A Man's City: Montreal, Gambling, and Male Space in the 1940s

Suzanne Morton

Montreal in the 1940s was a man's city.[1] Guides such as *Montreal Confidential* directed tourists and businessmen to the city's most exciting clubs and districts while the short-lived American tabloid *Pic: The Magazine Men Prefer* offered its readers a photo essay on 'Montreal: Booming Paris of the West' featuring the city's gambling clubs and its most famous burlesque performer Lily St Cyr of the Gayety Theatre.[2] The North American press often drew attention to the exotic nature of Montreal: as a bit of Paris in North America it was touted as one of the most vital centres of male sporting culture to survive on the continent. Its unique position as the only major city in North America where liquor flowed legally and continuously throughout the 1920s and 1930s and its geographic proximity to dry northeast American cities made Montreal a popular destination for parched tourists during prohibition. Moreover, unlike other Canadian and eastern American cities, Montreal was not dominated by the culture of a Protestant elite who demanded the enforcement of legislated forms of morality. The glamour and excitement of

Montreal as an island of European libertine freedom in a generally repressive Protestant continent were widely incorporated into North American popular culture in examples which ranged from early Harlequin romances to Damon Runyon's short stories.[3]

In our attempt to understand the relationship between urban space and gender, much recent work has concentrated on women's or gay men's space in the city. The work of scholars such as Mary Ryan, Christine Stansell, Judith Walkowitz, and George Chauncey have altered the way we see the city as they examine the way women and gay men used urban spaces to create and reinforce their own identities.[4] This paper hopes to borrow from these insights and apply them to a specific Canadian city, Montreal in the 1940s, in an examination of male spaces associated with gambling. I want to argue that although these spaces could be and were further segregated by class, race, language, and age, they provided important settings which preserved a male sporting culture in a period historians have usually associated with the development of heterosocial

Suzanne Morton, 'A Man's City: Montreal, Gambling and Male Space in the 1940s', in *Power, Place and Identity: Historical Studies of Social and Legal Regulation in Quebec*, Tamara Myers, Kate Boyer, Mary Anne Poutanen and Steven Watt, eds. Montral History Group, 1998. An expanded version of this paper appears in *At Odds: Canadians and Gambling, 1919–1969*. University of Toronto Press, 2003.

or mixed-sex commercialized leisure. At the same time urban space was used by marginal women and gay men as a strategy to forge identity and of survival, this examination of semi-public male spaces illustrates the use of space in the city to reinforce privilege and as a form of continuity with older homosocial leisure patterns.

Gambling—in its various forms of book-making, cards, and a popular Montreal dice game called barbotte—was almost completely associated with men. A female reporter who published a series of articles on Montreal gambling in 1946 stated that she had met with her informants over coffee rather than enter their locations of business since she did 'not think women were allowed.'[5] Similarly, a long-time employee of one of the downtown's busiest betting establishments claimed that he had never seen a woman in his place.[6] Of course there were some exceptions, usually in the most exclusive establishments where women could be found on the arms of men at the barbotte table or the roulette wheel. There were also other forms of gambling which appealed specifically to or incorporated women, namely bingo and sweepstakes, but by and large, placing bets, playing cards, and rolling dice were activities men engaged in with other men. These forms of competitive games capitalized on notions of 'macho risk taking', aggressive behaviour, and courage.[7] What is remarkable and most important about gambling as a male activity is that in the words of one Montreal observer it 'extended to all classes, colors, creeds and nationalities.'[8] Gambling linked a diverse group of men and although there might have been particular class, race, or linguistic variations, the common locations of gambling in the city served as male space.

Gambling was one of the activities most associated with what has been described as nineteenth-century male sporting culture. According to Timothy Gilfoyle, male sporting culture linked various forms of gaming with communal drinking, commercial sex, and the celebration of male autonomy through sexual aggressiveness, promis-

cuity, and a renunciation of men's connection with their families. It thus posed a direct challenge to respectable bourgeois Christian morality.[9] Both Gilfoyle in his study of nineteenth-century prostitution and Elliot J. Gorn in his investigation into boxing during the same period argue that the nature of male sporting culture and its emphasis on masculinity diminished divisions based on class, ethnicity, and religion.[10]

Male-sporting behaviour survived in the twentieth century in forms other than gambling. The use of taverns as male space, for example, was regulated by discriminatory provincial laws which permitted women entrance only under specific conditions. Indeed the tavern, along with other examples of exclusively male space such as the locations of professional and amateur sports, and the culture around brothels, frequently overlapped with gambling activity.[11] Moreover, it is also well worth making the obvious point that male segregation within the city was not restricted to leisure activities as most occupations and many industries were in themselves gender-specific.

Although male sporting culture survived in Montreal, by the early twentieth century it was overshadowed by heterosocial forms of leisure. The nineteenth-century celebration of domesticity transformed middle-class and later working-class patterns of leisure and the advent of commercialized mass entertainment such as amusement parks, nightclubs, roller rinks, dance halls, and movie theatres popularized this new ideal and expanded the group of men and women who were likely to socialize together. These new semi-public commercial spaces have been recognized by Roy Rosenzweig and Kathy Peiss to have undermined the working-class tradition of same-sex leisure.[12]

In the 1940s, Montreal was still Canada's largest city, with a population of approximately one million people. This population was divided by many factors, including language, with approximately 65 per cent of the population French-speaking. So, in addition to the North

American pattern of urban division along class and racial lines evident in Montreal in the wealthy districts of Westmount and Outremont or the concentration of visible minorities in Chinatown and black districts, language also divided the city along an east-west axis.[13]

Montreal's distinctiveness also was evident in its experience of the Second World War. Although the Montreal economy was focused on war production, there was greater ambivalence towards and more public dissent directed at Canada's involvement in the war than in other Canadian cities. Local full employment, the influx of a transient male military population looking for pleasure, and a political climate which did not necessitate wartime austerity meant that the licit and illicit branches of the Montreal entertainment industry prospered. One historian of jazz wrote that 'the sheer frivolity and extravagance of Montreal nightlife mocked the extortions [sic: exhortations] of Canadian leaders to sacrifice and sobriety.'[14] Prostitution experienced a crackdown in 1944 after the Canadian Army threatened to make Montreal out of bounds for its personnel unless immediate action was taken to curb the threat of venereal disease.[15] Public pressure to stop gambling was slower to take root and did not occur until after the war, when Montreal gambling kingpin Harry Davis was murdered in broad daylight in August 1946. The temporary enthusiasm for the enforcement of laws against gambling which followed was accompanied by public petitions from various reform coalitions requesting an inquiry into the deficiency and corruption in policing of commercial gambling and prostitution.

Organizations such as le Comité de moralité publique were able to capitalize on similar political pressures and concerns in the United States expressed in the Kefauver Commission into organized crime and were finally granted their own Montreal inquiry in 1950.[16] The Caron Inquiry operated from September 1950 to October 1954 and its mandate covered all aspects of gambling activities in Montreal in the 1940s.[17]

Most illegal forms of gambling were covered under the federal government's Criminal Code.[18] While the law did not prevent any individual from making a bet with another individual, it could intervene into any situation where it might be possible for a third party to make a profit off the wager. Gambling in itself was not illegal but participating in or operating any form of commercialized gambling contravened federal law. The criminal law also contained an implicit class bias as there was a means to bet legally on horse races at the racetrack for those who were able to attend daytime races and use the government-approved parimutuel machines (where the federal and provincial governments took their share of revenue). Conversely, those who could not leave their place of work were breaking the law when they placed bets with a local bookmaker. This exception which allowed commercialized gambling under specific and limited conditions excluded most working-class participants. Thus, it is not surprising that most gambling probably took the illegal route.

Illegal commercialized gambling was thus an important component of the Montreal economy. Some contemporary observers even considered it Montreal's most important industry as it was alleged to gross over $100 million per year in the mid-1940s.[19] It was also an activity that in some sense was understood to be spatially defined. The very word 'underworld' and the common description in reference to the city's loose policing creating a 'wide open city' or 'une ville ouverte' reinforced this geographic and topographical connection. Certainly there was a paradox acknowledged in the description of gambling as simultaneously hidden from view (or underground) and operating in an exposed manner with little fear of police intervention. The importance of space and the feeble attempts to regulate it were also evident in the only tactic police used to control gambling and brothels during the 1940s: the padlock.

While the padlock now has infamous connotations connecting Premier Maurice Duplessis and his attempts to quiet political dissent within the province, the most common use (and misuse) of the padlock law in Montreal was to regulate offenders of public morality. Under the power of a municipal bylaw, gaming and betting houses on their third charge were to be physically closed by padlock for a specified number of days.[20] In order to prevent this potential interference with business, operators responded to potential closures by providing police with fictional addresses or placing apartment numbers on fake doors, broom closets, and even toilets.[21] This unsuccessful strategy for regulating gaming through the control of space was not restricted to Montreal and was implemented with somewhat more success in Toronto and Vancouver.[22]

In 1945, before any serious attempt to crack down on gambling, Montreal reporter Ted McCormack wrote, 'the gaming houses are scattered like raisins through the loaf of the town.'[23] While this was an appealing image and suggestive of the abundant sites available for gaming, it was not quite true. The location of betting and gaming establishments was not random and although there was no single 'men's district' in the city,[24] gambling activities were associated with specific neighbourhoods or districts. During the Caron Inquiry, 248 addresses were provided as locations of repeated raids between 1942 and 1950. Among the addresses cited, not a single address connected gambling to the wealthiest districts of Westmount or Outremont. Instead, the locations were concentrated in the red-light district around the intersection of Ste Catherine and St Laurent, the neighbourhoods immediately adjacent to the main train stations, the downtown theatre and nightclub district, and the area centred around the working-class commercial streets of Mont Royal and St Laurent. In addition to these specific neighbourhoods, prominent bookies and gaming houses also operated close to places where large numbers of men were employed such as the Angus rail yards, munition factories, and the Tramway depot.[25]

The Montreal geographic pattern of gambling conforms with the organizational characteristics noted by David C. Johnson in his study of American cities, where Johnson observes that the 'bright light districts' were embraced by criminal entrepreneurs. Here illicit activities operated beside legitimate enterprises, lending the illegal neighbours a sense of legitimacy and respectability. Proximity to train stations and hotels along with theatres, restaurants, and nightclubs generated a steady flow of sidewalk traffic that might be greeted on the streets with employees trying to hustle men inside.[26]

Not only were there apparent spatial concentrations of gambling in the city but the addresses also shared common legal pretenses such as so-called 'bridge clubs', bowling alleys, barbershops, tobacco stands, and billiards parlours or pool halls. Of the establishments which can be identified in the Montreal city directory as operating some legitimate business as a front for or in conjunction with gambling activities, 54 were listed as bridge clubs, 14 as billiard parlours or pool halls, 11 as barber shops, eight as bowling alleys, and five as tobacco stores. These businesses, where illegal gambling activity repeatedly transpired, were occasionally even combined so that cigar stands also had their own pool tables.

In a day and age when men had their hair cut more frequently and cigarettes were more acceptable yet not available in food stores, barber and tobacco shops appeared on almost every corner. Their high customer turnover and male clientele made them perfect foils for collecting bets on races. An address on Ste Catherine Street West, where a bookie operated for at least 15 years, was listed in the city directory as a barbershop. A witness testifying before the Caron Inquiry stated that clients entered through the front of a barbershop to a larger room upstairs. The shop itself was large enough for three or four chairs but held only one for show.[27]

The link between barbershops and a male gambling subculture had been long established in Montreal. In the report of the 1925 inquiry into municipal policing, Judge Louis Coderre cited the example of a gambling house at the corner of Ste

Catherine and Peel Streets 'camouflaged, and very poorly, as a barber shop'.[28] Coderre continued to draw the connection between betting houses and barbershops and tobacco stores, noting, 'Their doors are open to all, which shows how safely they can be operated.'[29]

Even if barbershops themselves were not the site of illegal gambling, they could be a good source for men looking for information about where to find some 'action'. When reporters for *La Presse* were seeking a barbotte game, they successfully approached the barber across from the Mont Royal Hotel for mere information.[30] These networks went beyond information and could become personal. Montreal gambler Harry Ship stated that he had first met some of his later gambling colleagues hanging about the same barbershop on St Laurent.[31]

The shortage of outdoor play space in the nineteenth-century city generated the need for new forms of participatory leisure activities for working-class men. Leisure historian Steven Riess has described the process by which working-class sporting men and boys were gradually deprived of traditional recreational activities such as playing ball in the street through municipal bylaws which regulated the use of public space with the goal of fostering order and efficient commerce.[32] One of the results was the increased importance of the saloon or 'workingmen's club' which offered various forms of entertainment outside the home. The most famous saloon in late nineteenth-century Montreal was Joe Beef's Canteen located by the waterfront.[33] Entertainment in Joe Beef's Canteen in its most extreme form included watching live bears but this type of excess was gradually replaced with more sedate pleasures such as playing pool. Steven Riess has argued that in the United States, billiard parlours were 'probably more widely distributed than any other commercialized entertainment except perhaps movies.'[34] The number of pool halls continued to grow in the twentieth century as listings in the Montreal city directory increased from 39 businesses in 1920 to 117 in 1940.

Halls and parlours with only a few tables could not succeed as prosperous ventures unless the owner ran the business in combination with another activity catering to male sporting culture such as shoe shines, cigar stands, and lunch counters or he supplemented his income with illicit revenue.[35] Establishments were not usually permanent and the listing of billiard parlours in the Montreal city directory suggests a frequent turnover. The location of billiard halls, even if they were not involved in illicit activities, tended to overlap with the same districts as other gambling activity. The halls and parlours needed male patronage but did not need a great deal of space or capital to operate. This was in contrast to the operation of other leisure activities such as bowling alleys, which required the construction of special facilities for the sport.

In the nineteenth century, billiards and pool were much more of a cross-class male activity than bowling, which attracted only working-class participants. Alan Metcalfe has noted that billiards was very popular in Montreal and received prominent coverage in both the French and English newspapers of the 1870s.[36] The game not only bridged linguistic groups but also class extremes as it was played in the city's 'best' homes and hotels as well as its most seedy districts. Although the game was the same, its respectable status disappeared in its encounter with working-class players whose enjoyment of pool, in the eyes of middle-class moral critics, was inescapably bound with gambling and alcohol.[37] Even when pool halls and billiard parlours became independent from alcohol consumption, they retained their notorious reputation, perhaps because of the way in which these activities brought together men from a broad range of class backgrounds. A Montreal reformer in 1919 described pool halls as 'veritable nurseries of hell where boys as well as younger men congregate and learn the devious ways of vice and crime.'[38]

While billiards and pool remained an exclusively male activity, at least one form of bowling was transformed into a heterosocial and ultimately more respectable pursuit. By the 1940s, not all bowling alleys could be considered male space. Nascent sportswriter Trent Frayne observed in 1943 that on a visit to a bowling alley 'there were so many women there that I thought for an embarrassing moment I was in the lingerie department.'[39] World War II promoted the popularity of bowling among women but the feminization of the activity had begun in November 1909 when a Toronto bowling entrepreneur invented the modern game of five-pin bowling using a three- to four-pound ball. This lighter ball replaced the 16-pound ball used in 10-pin bowling and was intended to attract a more respectable clientele than the 'husky' and 'hairy-chested' working-class men who traditionally played the game. Ten-pin bowling remained a male preserve but five-pin bowling took off in popularity in the 1920s as women were introduced into mixed leagues and companies found the limited physical demands of bowling ideal for bringing together employees of various ages in industrial and commercial leagues. Thus, the influx of women, the presence of non-perspiring men, and the support of corporations elevated the status of the sport.[40] The continued presence of bowling alleys in the Montreal police reports suggests, however, that not all alleys were recreated into respectable homosocial space and certain establishments, probably those continuing to play the 10-pin game, continued to be sites of male sporting culture.

Except for the richest and poorest games, gambling brought together men from across the class spectrum. Crowded around a barbotte table might be 'businessmen, servicemen, playboys with their girlfriends, clerks, theatre ushers, taxi drivers, workers and so on down the line to just plain rummies'.[41] While Montreal police dismissed accusations of the vast numbers of returned soldiers and working-class family men who lost their pay envelopes in the city's illegal clubs, this denial contradicted the more frequent descriptions of the range of men brought together over the tables.[42] An aspect of the variety of men

that gambling united was extreme upward and downward mobility; Montreal gamblers often came from nothing and claimed they quickly lost everything. Reports after Harry Davis's murder dwelled extensively on his impoverished childhood.[43] This unstable world of quick wealth and sudden poverty contrasted with the more rigid conception of status in the respectable world and made cross-class mixing possible.

Gambling could also bring together men across other divisions such as ethnicity and language. Here again there were variations. Certain clubs catered to specific ethnic groups such as the Jewish clientele attracted to the Laurier Bridge Club's pinochle games or the almost exclusively Italian and Syrian clientele of the Montsabre Club on St Denis Street.[44] These ethnic male enclaves were at least a partial reflection of residency patterns, as particular clubs served the men who lived in their neighbourhood. In light of the multi-ethnic character of Montreal, it is remarkable to observe not the existence of clubs serving specific communities but rather, the degree to which gambling brought men together. Male sporting culture in Montreal brought together a mixture of French, English, Jewish, Italian, Greek, and occasionally black men. The group of male gamblers conspicuously absent from this syndicate was the Chinese.

The only segregated gambling clubs in Montreal were those which served Chinese men and it is significant to note that in the petitions to establish the Caron Inquiry, the French and English reformers were largely silent on this issue. Until the concern about commercialized gambling and the peril of organized crime emerged in the 1940s, the gambling problem in Montreal had at times been synonymous with the Chinese community. An extreme gender imbalance in nineteenth-century immigration patterns to Canada and twentieth-century laws which prohibited legal Chinese immigration meant that the Chinese population of Montreal, as in other Canadian cities, was predominantly male. Thus, the particular combination of race and gender created a special meaning associated with Chinese gambling which differentiated it from gaming in the rest of the city. The general discourse against gambling was not applicable in Chinatown as it did not fit into concerns around organized crime or moral apprehension around men squandering family income. Nevertheless, the clubs of Montreal's Chinatown were presented in a particularly negative light, the danger of their racial exclusivity only compounded when they opened their doors to white clientele.[45]

In the minds of some critics, Chinatown itself was nothing more than a front for illicit activities as it harboured restaurants where one could buy lottery tickets but not obtain a cup of coffee.[46] Anti-Asian sentiments meant that the Chinese clubs were among the locations most carefully policed. In the first six months of 1945 before a serious police crackdown on Chinese gambling in the city, 71 per cent of all men charged with keeping a betting or gambling house and 43 per cent of all gambling found-ins were connected to the Chinese communities.[47] This was at a time when the total Chinese population of the Island of Montreal comprised far less than 2,000 men or about .1 per cent of the population.[48] Obviously, police statistics do not reflect the distribution of gambling in the city, but rather the policy of municipal officials at a time when non-Chinese gambling establishment were operating in the open. Moreover, gambling in Chinatown almost disappeared completely after city police instituted a policy in July 1945 whereby any men caught in raids of Chinese clubs were brought to police headquarters, where their identities were verified and they [were] held overnight before being released on bail. In all other cases, gambling 'found-ins', usually hired by operators to be caught in planned raids, were granted bail on the spot and after providing false names would forfeit the bail (the money provided by the club owner or bookmaker) and avoid conviction. The distinct rules for policing Chinese gambling and the racial segregation of their establishments made Chinese gambling culture very

different from that of other forms of male sporting culture in the city. The experience of the Chinese of Montreal challenged the universality of male sporting culture and provided an important exception of its inclusiveness.

In addition to factors such as class and race, time intersected with location to create distinct male space. Locales with a more gender-neutral function such as small groceries, confectionery shops, and lunch counters could be transformed by the time of day, the day of the week, and the season of the year. Bookies and gambling clubs in the downtown area, which catered to both the nightclub clients and daytime employees in offices and small manufacturing, often shared facilities in order to make the most efficient use of expensive rental space. Bookmakers and their agents would open at 10:00 in the morning and would be busiest between three and six in the afternoon. Bookmakers were busiest on Saturdays, which coincided with free time and a new paycheque. In the evenings, barbotte or the card games would begin after the last race had been run. These operations opened around 8:00 pm and would run until 4:00 or 5:00 in the morning.

The daytime operation of betting on horses complemented the hours of small businesses such as barbershops and taverns, which were supposed to close at 10:00 p.m. On the other hand, pool halls and bowling alleys, with their later closing times, and private clubs, with no time restrictions, were more suited to the nocturnal hours of cards and barbotte.[49] The around-the-clock facilities available to men highlight the fact that at least some men were free to move around the city day or night. This temporal freedom meant that specific places could adopt different functions at different times.

The concept of a changing use of place also applied to the transmutation of space in the suburbs. While the notion of male leisure space is bound in our conception of the downtown core, an investigation into gambling also challenges our understanding of suburbs as only domestic space.[50] Elite gambling clubs catering to a male clientele operated just outside municipal police jurisdictions, a strategy which dated from the late 1920s when 'The White House Inn' operated in Lachine and continued in the 1940s when the 'swankiest' gambling club in Montreal attracted patrons to 'The Mount Royal Bridge Club' in the upper-middle-class suburb of Côte St Luc. A crackdown in Montreal policing in the 1940s also drove the city's largest and most important dice games, the barbottes, to the fringe areas of Côte de Liesse and Côte St Michel. These clubs were connected to the downtown by specially commissioned taxis which linked all Montreal gambling districts together through the transportation of clientele.[51] The presence of gambling clubs in areas associated with family life and respectability challenged any rigid or strict denotation of Montreal's moral geography.

Another understanding of Montreal's moral geography was that in the general absence of women, male spaces were frequently identified as dirty. Downtown operations usually had lunch counters, licensed by municipal authorities, which sold sandwiches, soft drinks, coffee, and cigarettes to men while they waited for the results of their races to come in.[52] With no apparent irony intended, municipal sanitary inspectors would occasionally remove or threaten the removal of lunch-counter licences for breaking the municipal code of health. For example, while no concern appeared to be directed towards criminal activities taking place all around, in June 1942 the operators of a large and permanent bookmaking establishment on Ste Catherine Street West received a warning that unless the rat droppings were cleaned up, rat holes filled in, and a sink installed, the lunch counter would lose its municipal licence.[53] Problems with cleanliness of lunch counters reveal a common characteristic of male spaces, which were often identified as dark and dirty.[54] Patrons at 1455 Bleury had to be asked specifically 'not to spit on the floor'.[55] Concerns around cleanliness suggest a level of male sociability, particularly in bookmaking shops, which was dis-

tinct from the act of placing the bet itself. Customers clearly sat around at tables provided by owners, perhaps drinking a Coke and eating a sandwich, while they waited for results to come in. At the Sportsmen's Club on Bleury, there were often informal card games taking place for which owners did not receive any percentage of the money played. This form of comradeship overcame physical conditions and probably added to the pleasure of the gambling experience. Participants were involved in an urban subculture, not strictly a business transaction.

Although male sporting culture was still spatially defined in Montreal in the 1940s, it was evident that it was a world in decline. Riess attributes the demise of the male sporting culture to the rise of suburbia, as the relocation of many families from the city core interfered with easy access to separate male spaces. In Montreal, the Caron Inquiry acted as a springboard for the political career of Jean Drapeau, and the publication of the final report in October 1954 coincided with his election as mayor on a reform platform. Mayor Drapeau instituted 'un grand nettoyage', which curbed the most obvious examples of unofficial tolerance around gambling and prostitution. The Montreal reform administration ran concurrent with organizational changes taking place in commercialized gambling everywhere. By the early 1960s, the provincial gambling squad in Ontario would observe that 'the cigar store and pool room is [sic] vanishing.' Illegal gambling continued to be an important male activity but its space-specific culture diminished as bets were relayed by anonymous telephone contacts to the suburbs where bookmaking enterprises operated out of ordinary-looking houses.[56] Certainly, elements of this Montreal male sporting world of the 1940s still survive today in the city's Italian, Portuguese, and Greek cafés with their male-only clients crowded around card and pool tables. Another version of this bygone male world also survives in the novels of Mordecai Richler and Ted Allan.[57]

What did it mean to create and maintain urban space that excluded women? The persistence of male sporting culture in the twentieth century permitted the survival, reproduction, and reinforcement of this particular version of masculinity. Men continued to own all of the city in a way that was not possible for women. Enclaves associated with male sporting culture appeared to be particularly important for young men who were learning about masculinity. Bookmakers' establishments, pool rooms, bowling alleys, cigar stands, and taverns offered an opportunity to socialize with other men in an environment removed from the domestic sphere and the pressures of heterosocial leisure activities. In doing so, it strengthened notions of participants' masculinity and their power as it recreated a network of privilege and power. Although space could play an important role for the marginalized and the oppressed such as the Canadian Chinese community, it was also important to remember that it was used effectively by those who had power to perpetuate their position and preserve a form of masculinity which existed outside the bourgeois ideal. This need not be romanticized, as the practice reinforced and celebrated male privilege, aggression, and competitiveness. Divisions found in class, ethnicity, or sexual orientation should not be minimized, but the examination of gambling spaces in Montreal in the 1940s in particular suggests that with at least one important exception, men with a variety of identities shared the same physical space and a similar male sporting culture. There were limits to this commonality, as the exclusion of Chinese men reminds us, but placing a bet, staking a hand, or rolling the dice attracted, in the words of a Montreal novelist, 'men of various sizes, shapes, odours and auras'.[58]

## Notes

1. I would like to thank Programme nouveau chercheur, Fonds pour la formation de chercheurs et l'aide à la recherche for funding this project and Mary Matthews, Tanya Gogan, and Tamara Myers for their research on the Enquête Caron.

2. Archives de la Ville de Montréal (hereafter AVM),
P43, Enquête Caron, box 054–06–03–02, E–791; *Pic* (Mar. 1950); Al Palmer, *Montreal Confidential* (Montreal, 1950).

3. Ronald J Cooke, *The Mayor of Cote St Paul: A Harlequin Book* (Toronto, 1950); Damon Runyon, *Guys and Dolls* (Harmondsworth, 1956 [1931]). This Montreal has also been captured in William Weintraub's *City Unique: Montreal Days and Nights in the 1940s and '50s* (Toronto, 1996).

4. Mary P. Ryan, *Women in Public: Between Banners and Ballots, 1825–1880* (Baltimore, 1990); Judith Walkowitz, *City of Dreadful Delight: Narratives of Sexual Danger in Late-Victorian London* (Chicago, 1992); Christine Stansell, *City of Women: Sex and Class in New York, 1789–1860* (Urbana, Ill., 1987); George Chauncey, *Gay New York: Gender, Urban Culture, and the Making of the Gay Male World, 1890–1940* (New York, 1994).

5. AVM, P43, Enquête Caron, box 054–06–03–01, testimony of Jacqueline Sirois, 3 July 1952, 16.

6. AVM, P43, Enquête Caron, box 054–06–03–01, testimony of Izzie Litwack, 6 Oct. 1950, 696.

7. John C. Burnham, *Bad Habits: Drinking, Smoking, Taking Drugs, Gambling, Sexual Misbehavior and Swearing in American History* (New York, 1993); Kathy Peiss, *Cheap Amusements: Working Women and Leisure in Turn-of-the-Century New York* (Philadelphia, 1986), 21.

8. Wilfred Emmerson Israel, 'The Montreal Negro Community', MA thesis (McGill University, 1928), 195.

9. Timothy Gilfoyle, *City of Eros: New York City, Prostitution, and the Commercialization of Sex, 1790–1920* (New York, 1992), 81, 98–9. Male sporting culture is described by Timothy Gilfoyle as centred on a variety of gaming such as 'horse racing, gambling, cockfighting, pugilism and other "blood" sports'.

10. Gilfoyle, *City of Eros*, 102, 104; Elliot J. Gorn, *The Manly Art: Bare-Knuckle Prize Fighting in America* (Ithaca, NY, 1986).

11. Montreal gamblers in the 1940s had close connections to boxing and the operation of city nightclubs, restaurants, and cabarets. Although there were some links between the gambling fra-

ternity and narcotics in the 1930s, with a few significant exceptions, most Montreal gamblers seemed to be distanced themselves from illegal narcotics and prostitution in the 1940s. In the testimony of alderman Frank Hanley, himself a former jockey, he acknowledged a connection with two of the city's most prominent gamblers through boxing connections. AVM, P43, Enquête Caron, box 054–06–02–01, 1952–2Z, testimony of Frank Hanley, 27 June 1952, 20, 56.

12. Peiss, *Cheap Amusements*; Roy Rosenzweig, *Eight Hours for What We Will: Workers and Leisure in an Industrial City, 1870–1920* (Cambridge, 1983).

13. Israel, 'Montreal Negro Community', 185; Paul-André Linteau, *L'histoire de Montréal depuis la Confédération* (Montreal, 1992).

14. John Gilmore, *Swinging in Paradise: The Story of Jazz in Montréal* (Montreal, 1988), 90.

15. Suzanne Commend, 'De la femme dechue à la femme infectieuse: perception sociale et repression de la prostitution montréalaise pendant la Seconde guerre', MA thesis, (Université de Montréal, 1996).

16. William Howard Moore, *The Kefauver Committee and the Politics of Crime, 1950–1952* (Columbia, Mo., 1974)

17. Danielle Lacasse has written on aspects of this inquiry relating to prostitution in *La prostitution féminine à Montréal, 1945–1970* (Montreal, 1994). See also François David, 'Le Comité de Moralité Publique de Montréal', *Cultures du Canada Français* 8 (1991): 84–95.

18. *The Criminal Code and Other Selected Statutes of Canada* (Ottawa, 1951), ch. 36, ss. 225–36.

19. Ted McCormack, 'Gambling in Montreal', *Maclean's*, 15 Sept. 1945, 5.

20. No. 921: 'By-Law to authorize the Recorder's Court of the City of Montreal to order the temporary closing of certain immovables' (17/1/1927), *By-laws of the City of Montreal. Compilation of all By-laws to date* (Montreal, 1931).

21. AVM, P43, Enquête Caron, box 054–04–02–01, testimony Lionel Elie, 3 Oct. 1950, 305–14; box 054–03–03–02, E–19, E–20, E–21, E–22, Padlock Registers 1932–48.

22. *Vancouver Sun*, 18 July 1940, 5.

23. McCormack, 'Gambling in Montreal', 7.

24. Phillip Thomason, 'The Men's Quarter of Downtown Nashville', *Tennessee Historical Quarterly* 41, 1 (1982): 48–66. This district in nineteenth-century Nashville was marked by tailors, tobacco shops, saloons, and barbershops.

25. AVM, P43, box 054–05–02–01, testimony of Omer Dufresne, 2 Feb. 1951, 75; box 054–01–03–01, 1952–94, testimony of Albert Langlois, 15 Sept. 1952. This absence of gambling establishments in Westmount, Outremont, and Notre Dame de Grâce was reinforced by inquiry witnesses.

26. David R. Johnson, 'The Origins and Structure of Intercity Criminal Activity 1840–1920: An Interpretation', *Journal of Social History* 15, 4 (Summer 1982): 596.

27. AVM, P43, Enquête Caron, box 054–04–02–01, Barney Shulkin, 28 Sept. 1950, 363. A parallel example of a billiard parlour with only one pool table but many tables for card games was brought to the attention of the Coderre Inquiry in 1925. *Montreal Star*, 14 Mar. 1925, 55.

28. *Montreal Star*, 14 Mar. 1925, 54; translation of Coderre's judgement.

29. Ibid., 55.

30. AVM, P43, Enquête Caron, box 054–05–02–02, 1952–78, testimony of Raymond Taillefer, 10 Apr. 1951, 28.

31. AVM, P43, Enquête Caron, box 054–06–02–01, 1952–46, testimony of Harry Sharp, 22 July 1952, 357.

32. Steven A. Riess, *City Games: The Evolution of American Urban Society and the Rise of Sports* (Chicago, 1991), 72–3.

33. Peter Delottinville, 'Joe Beef of Montreal: Working Class Culture and the Tavern, 1869–1889', *Labour/Le Travailleur* 8, 9 (Autumn–Spring 1981–2): 9–40.

34. Reiss, *City Games*, 75.

35. Ibid.

36. Alan Metcalfe, *Canada Learns To Play: The Emergence of Organized Sport, 1807–1914* (Toronto, 1987), 138.

37. Reiss, *City Games*, 73–4; Delottinville, 'Joe Beef'.

38. E.I. Hart, *Wake Up Montreal!* (Montreal, 1919), 16.

39. B.T. Frayne, 'Set 'em Up', *Maclean's*, 1 Feb. 1943, 13.

40. Larry Gough, 'Sallys in our Alleys', *Maclean's*, 1 Jan. 1944, 15, 26; Lizabeth Cohen, *Making a New Deal: Industrial Workers in Chicago, 1919–1939* (Cambridge, 1990), 179.

41. McCormack, 'Gambling', 7.

42. AVM, P43, Enquête Caron, box 054–03–03–01, D–147. Handwritten note from Captain O'Neill.

43. For example, see *The Standard*, 27 July 1946.

44. AVM, P43, Enquête Caron, box 054–03–02–02. Complaints, 1947, re: 6968 St Denis.

45. Kwok B. Chan, *Smoke and Fire: The Chinese in Montreal* (Hong Kong, 1991); Denise Helly, *Les Chinois de Montréal, 1877–1951* (Quebec, 1987). See also Kay Anderson, *Vancouver's Chinatown: Racial Discourse in Canada, 1875–1980* (Montreal, 1991). Chinatown held its own particular dangers with concern around opium and mixed-race prostitution.

46. Robert A Percy, 'Dufferin District: An Area in Transition', MA thesis (McGill University, 1928), 106.

47. AVM, P43, Enquête Caron, box 054–03–02–01, Morality Squad Reports, 1945.

48. According to the 1941 census there were 1,844 Chinese living on the Island of Montreal out of a total population of 1,116,800. In 1951 this number had fallen to 1,142 men and 292 women out of a total population of 1,320,232. Canada, *Census*, 1941, vol. 1, Table 32, 'Population by principal origins for census sub-districts'; *Census*, 1951, vol. 1, Table 34, 'Population by origin and sex for counties and census divisions, 1951', 34.9–34.10.

49. Montreal Bylaw 1103 (12/1/1931).

50. Veronica Strong-Boag, 'Home Dreams: Women and the Suburban Experiment in Canada, 1945–60', *Canadian Historical Review* 72, 4 (Dec. 1991): 471–505.

51. AVM, P43, Enquête Caron, box 054–04–02–01, testimony of Lizzie Hitwack, 11 Oct. 1950, 874. Not only were the suburbs an important site of gambling, but testimony before the Caron commission also suggested that at least some gamblers were model family men who commuted into the city each day for work. One of the city councillors representing the predominantly English suburb of Notre Dame de Grâce, which itself had no reported gambling activity, claimed that 'most of the bookies' in Montreal lived in his district with their families. According to the councillor, 'They do business in town and they live in the suburbs.' AVM, P43, Enquête Caron, box 054–06–02–01, testimony of John Edward Lyall, 27 June 1952, 64.

52. AVM, P43, Enquête Caron, box 054–04–02–01, testimony of Edgar Bruce Murdoch, 29 Sept. 1950, 182; testimony of Samuel Hyams, 2 Oct. 1950, 232.

53. AVM, P43, Enquête Caron, box 054–05–03–01, E–420. Inspection reports for 286 Ste Catherine West. This book operated between 1932 and 1946.

54. AVM, P43, Enquête Caron, box 054–05–02–01, testimony of Albert Hotte, 6 Feb. 1951, 17. Sanitary inspector re 327 Ste Catherine East.

55. AVM, P43, Enquête Caron, box 054–03–03–02, E–95. Photos from 1455 Bleury, 5 Sept. 1946.

56. Alan Phillips, 'Gambling the greatest criminal conspiracy of them all', *Maclean's*, 7 Mar. 1964, 15.

57. Ted Allan, *Love is a Long Shot* (Toronto, 1984); Mordecai Richler, *Apprenticeship of Duddy Kravitz* (1959), *Son of a Smaller Hero* (1955), and *St Urbain's Horseman* (1971).

58. Allan, *Love is a Long Shot*, 29.

# 23

# Manipulating Innocence:
# Corruptibility, Youth, and the Case against Obscenity

Mary Louise Adams

In 1949, a Toronto man wrote to the Ontario Government Censorship Bureau (a bureaucratic entity that, in fact, did not exist) to protest the availability of cheap pulp paperbacks. 'These books,' he wrote, 'many of them filthy in the extreme, have alluring colour covers, and any adolescent can buy publications for 25 [cents], that his parents would be shocked to read.'[1] His complaint was one of many received by the Ontario Attorney General's office in the post-Second World War period when, after years of paper shortages and restrictions on trade, Canadian newsstands were opened to a huge range of mass-market publications from the United States. Concerned citizens, as individuals and as members of a wide spectrum of organizations, condemned the 'licentiousness of magazines',[2] the 'flood of objectionable literature',[3] 'porno-graphy for profit',[4] and, among other things, the transformation of Canada into 'an open end[ed] sewer' for filth from the United States.[5] For the most part, these objections were articulated through a discourse of concern for youth who, it was assumed, had relatively unlimited access to inexpensive printed material over which their parents and teachers had little control.

In the 1930s and 1940s, mass-produced literature had flourished, especially in the United States. The creation of new genres and new approaches to marketing and distribution combined with improvements in printing techniques to make the publication of comics and paperbacks increasingly profitable.[6] After the war, Canadian newsstands felt the full impact of this growing sector of the US publishing industry. The market for so-called 'real literature' was swamped by 35-cent pulp novels, 15-cent magazines, and 10-cent comics that were readily available in drugstores and cigar stores. In Ottawa, for instance, a single news and magazine distributor received 3,800 copies of *Women's Barracks*, a 1952 pulp novel title.[7] In 1950, a researcher for the Toronto Board of Education counted 135 different comics for sale in that city, and he estimated their readership at more than 500,000 individuals each month.[8] To put these figures into perspective, the Canadian distribution of hardcover books was limited to 2,000 bookstores, while magazines and pulps could be bought at more that 9,000 outlets.[9]

Alongside this boom in pulp publishing, so-called sexy magazines were also becoming

Mary Louise Adams, 'Manipulating Innocence: Corruptibility, Youth, and the Case against Obscenity', in *The Trouble with Normal: Postwar Youth and the Making of Heterosexuality*. © 1999 University of Toronto Press. Reprinted by permission of the publisher.

increasingly visible. As a 1952 *Reader's Digest* article said, such questionable material was nothing new; what had changed was its accessibility. In the years before the Second World War, 'girlie' magazines had been available only in (male) adult environments like 'barbershops, saloons and army posts'. By the 1950s, however, these magazines were being sold right at the corner drugstore, on the same shelves as family magazines and 'useful books'.[10] In 1953 the launch of the 'tasteful' and expensively produced *Playboy* solidified the trend.

Fears about the power of mass media to divide parents from children were not unique to post-war North America.[11] They had followed the emergence of novels in the nineteenth century, and of silent films in the 1910s and 1920s. They would re-emerge over television in the late 1950s and the 1960s. We see them today in discussions about rock videos, Nintendo games, and the Internet. Writing about the British campaign against horror comics of the mid-1950s, Martin Barker says that 'each rising mass medium in turn has been targeted in the name of revered values.'[12] But, he adds, parental and social concerns are less a factor of the medium that spawned them than they are of the values assumed to be threatened by it. Where turn-of-the-century working-class parents worried that commercial entertainments such as cheap movies undermined traditional gender roles and put their daughters in too close proximity with boys,[13] middle-class parents of the 1950s worried about standards of sexual behaviour and whether the pulps encouraged their children towards deviance. In both cases, the medium was an easier target of popular protest than the general social context which spawned it.

Post-war discourses about the 'corruptibility' of youth, and their need for protection from sex as it was portrayed in various forms of pulp literature, were able to provide the impetus for broad-ranging initiatives of moral and sexual regulation that targeted adults as much as they targeted young people themselves. Discursive

constructions of youthful innocence helped to set the boundaries of normative sexuality, thus marginalizing non-normative forms of sexual expression by people of all ages. Without the concepts of youth they were able to mobilize, these regulatory discourses would never have been so widely circulated.

Post-war discussions about the effects of indecency and obscenity on young people occurred in a variety of contexts. Here I pay particular attention to three of these: efforts in the late 1940s to restrict the circulation of comic books, especially crime and horror comics; the proceedings of the 1952 Senate Special Committee on Salacious and Indecent Literature; and a 1952 trial over obscenity that took place in Ottawa. Each of these illustrates the way 'youth' was used as a rhetorical trope in attempts to maintain dominant sexual and moral standards.

. . .

## The Threat of Indecency, or Why the Concern about Obscenity?

What counted as harmful literature in the late 1940s and the 1950s was a wide range of material, although the exact details of its content is not always easy to ascertain. As they do today, standards of decency and propriety varied widely— even within class and ethnic groupings. Certainly there did not exist agreed-upon definitions— even in law—of either indecency or obscenity. What I am concerned with here, however, is not so much the actual content of materials that were thought to be indecent or obscene, but the language and discursive strategies used to present them as such. How was it that social critics were able to generate concern about particular types of publications? My findings are similar to those of Martin Barker in his analysis of the British campaign against horror comics. Barker found that arguments against the comics were based more on popular ideas about the young people who were assumed to be reading the comics than about the content of the books themselves.[14] In

Canada, post-war debates about the moral effects of mass-market publications crystallized concerns about the nature of youth, their relationship to sexuality, and the place and character of sexuality in Canadian society.

Two distinct, but related, efforts to clean up Canadian newsstands suggest that different media came under scrutiny at different times. In the late 1940s, crime comics were the major concern, until a 1949 amendment to the Canadian Criminal Code almost completely eliminated them from the newsstands. In the 1950s, cheap paperbacks and what were referred to as 'girlie magazines' took their turn as targets of public protest and condemnation. Disapproval of these publications was institutionalized in the 1952 Senate Special Committee. While these two episodes of moral concern exploited a variety of regulatory strategies—some shared, some not—the ideologies that helped to construct them were remarkably similar.

Anti-indecency campaigns (I use the word 'campaign' with hesitation—it suggests perhaps too organized a shape for what were often contradictory efforts) relied heavily on representations of young people as in need of both protection and control, particularly in the realm of sex and morality. Teens were assumed to be impressionable—'born imitators'—in ways that adults were not. Adolescence was seen as a time of both sexual and moral development,[15] the success of the former depending to a great extent on the success of the latter. With the proper guidance, teenagers could learn to control their unfolding sexuality. However, this belief that teenage morality was a blank slate meant that teens were open not only to 'proper' influences but to 'improper' ones as well. Their moral immaturity—or moral innocence, as it was more likely to be called—was said to leave them vulnerable to harmful sexual attitudes that might lead to degeneracy and delinquency. As one magazine journalist claimed, 'The love comics are to the girly magazines what elementary schools are to high schools. If a child's taste is formed by love

and crime comics, he or she will continue to crave lurid, unreal, violent and sexy material in print.'[16] And such material, apparently, could skew an adolescent's understanding of her own social climate: 'The mass production and distribution of sensational novels depicting lewd, repulsive and perverted behaviour of the characters as a normal way of life has superseded all other worthwhile publications offered for sale in Canadian stores. Men and women are portrayed as monsters of perversion and the women pictured as Lesbians and modern Messalinas. Added to this is the continuous suggestion that crime and perversion is [sic] normal. . . .'[17]

More than anything else, it was normality that was deemed to be under threat from the pulp publications. They were accused of making immorality seem normal, of shifting the boundaries of what was seen to be acceptable: perverts might cease to be perverse; abnormality might fail to operate as a negative marker of sexual and moral difference from the norm; monogamous heterosexual marriage might end up as just one of many forms of sexual expression. Arguments about the dangers of indecency suggested that a whole process of moral degeneration would be put into effect if 'immature' teenagers read pulps, absorbed their sordid values, and carried them into the 1960s.

Young people were widely regarded as products in which adults invested sums of time and money, along with material, emotional, intellectual, and spiritual resources. Parents considered it their right to make these investments exclusively or to have them made by other adults of their choosing. In this context, teenagers' reading of comics or dime-store novels turned the publishers of this literature into trespassers and usurpers of parental prerogative. The publishers were guilty of competing with and disrupting the influences of the home, the church, the school. A widely circulated 1952 resolution from the town council of Timmins, Ontario, included the following justification for regulatory measures against obscenity: 'AND WHEREAS, millions have been spent on excellent universities, high schools and public schools to educate our children to become law-abiding, productive and lovable citizens, who are our most sacred investment, and who should not be exposed to an education, through the reading of filthy literature, stories of compromising situations, and details of sex crimes, which tend to undermine our whole educational system. . . .'[18]

Some thought that bad literature was powerful enough not just to threaten but to cancel the efforts of church, school, and home to educate young people about proper forms of sex and family living. Members of the Canadian Committee for the International Conference in Defence of Children worried that indecent literature might turn young people from the goals adults had set for them: 'high ideals, noble emotions and constructive action directed to the general good'.[19] Pulp literature was seen as competition for approved forms of sex education (however limited these were) that promoted the normalization of sexual and moral standards. The outcome of this contest could affect 'the whole moral tone of the nation'.[20] 'Civilized life', 'democracy', and 'freedom' were all thought to be dependent upon a particular, dominant version of morality. As long as this was challenged by the salacious materials on the newsstands, the future itself seemed to be threatened.

During the early years of the Cold War, statements about 'threats' to the nation often concealed fears about Communism, and the discussion about printed indecency was no exception to this. A direct relationship was assumed between a particular version of moral health and Canada's strength as a nation. Demoralization, in both senses of the word, was assumed to be a prime strategy of infiltrating Communists. In their 1953 report, members of the Senate Special Committee on Salacious and Indecent Literature stated that 'in the world-wide struggle between the forces of darkness and evil and those of good, the freedom-loving, democratic countries have need of all the strength in their moral fibre to

combat the evil threat, and anything that undermines the morals of our citizens and particularly of the young is a direct un-Canadian act.'[21]

During the proceedings of the committee, chair J.C. Davis (who took over after the death of J.J. Hayes Doone, the instigator of the project) expressed his own racist version of this position, without any opposition from his colleagues: 'This is a Christian country, and we have to fight the powers of darkness from non-Christian countries. The morals of this country have to be strengthened to keep us strong. We are being attacked at the very roots by the influx of indecent literature and we have to stop it one way or another.'[22]

Notions of 'threat to the nation' operated discursively in much the same way as the more frequently cited 'threat to youth'—by stirring up moral indignation that might lead to calls for protective regulation. Moreover, each of these phrases could be used to underscore the gravity of the other: a threat to the nation was perceived to be a threat to teenagers and youth. Who could not be moved by the vulnerability of young people, struggling towards maturity? Who did not want them to develop to their full potential? Who could abandon the goals of those who had died so recently on European battlefields? Who could abandon their sons and daughters to an atmosphere of immorality and indecency that was assumed to be the antithesis of a democratic society? The crusade against obscenity and harmful literature was built on, and gained its momentum from, these kinds of discursive attachments. Notions of patriotism and 'Christian values' were called on to underscore arguments against the mass-market publications. They lent weight to an issue that might otherwise have appeared to be trivial.

## The Canadian Fight against Crime Comics

In Canada, the fight to ban crime comics, although not entirely cohesive, was broadly based. As the product of well-organized efforts by individuals and groups it certainly had significant effects. The man most often identified with the crime comics campaign was E. Davie Fulton, Tory member of Parliament from Kamloops, British Columbia. Fulton claimed that national interest in the matter had been 'aroused' by the Federated Women's Institutes, the Federation of Home and School Associations, the Ontario Teachers' Federation, Parent-Teacher Federations, and the Imperial Order Daughters of the Empire (IODE)— all of them middle-class and predominantly female organizations.[23]

Comic books were by no means new in the late 1940s, but their content had undergone substantial change since they first appeared in the 1920s as bound collections of newspaper strips. In 1938 readers were introduced to Superman, the first super hero (created by Jerry Siegal and Toronto-born artist Joe Shuster). By 1941, American publishers were putting out 168 different titles, and by the middle of the war, National Periodical Publishers claimed sales of more than 12 million comics per month.[24] At its peak, in the post-war decade, it is estimated that the US comics industry was producing 60 million comics per month.[25]

. . .

After the Second World War, the patriotic superheroes took a back seat to new narrative genres. Crime, horror, and love comics became especially popular, launching a wave of public concern. New titles appeared regularly, and many readers increased their consumption by exchanging copies with friends. As Fulton said, the whole process of buying, reading, and trading could occur outside parents' control. Newspaper and magazine articles frequently played up the fact that comics were not a large part of adult culture. Parents and teachers were often described in the act of 'discovering' a 'hidden stash' in a child's room or school desk. Apparently many were 'shocked' by what they found: drawings of women that emphasized their breasts and buttocks; detailed stories about

crime, including murder and rape; titles like *Tales from the Crypt*, *Haunt of Fears*, *Crimes by Women*, *Heart Throb*, and *Flaming Love*.

Toronto Board of Education trustee W.R. Cockburn was typical of those who spoke out against comics. In 1945 he raised concerns about them with the board's Management Committee, saying they were 'degrading and detrimental to the welfare of our youth'.[26] Complaining that Biblical comics were largely unavailable in Toronto, Cockburn showed his colleagues comic books he had been able to buy in the city— *Daring*, *Human Touch*, *Black Terror*, and *Boy Commandos*—saying, 'They're nothing but a lot of rot about daggers and guns.' A similar argument was endorsed in 1947 by the members of the IODE's National Education Committee, who lamented the eclipsing of funny comics: 'Instead we have "Superman" and gangs of thieves, G-men and sadistic murderers who carve their way through the "funny pages" talking plain talk, and giving people "the works."'[27]

While views like those expressed by Cockburn and the members of the IODE were widely reported on, they were not shared by everyone. In 1949, *Chatelaine* ran a story by Mary Jukes called 'Are Comics Really a Menace?'[28] In an attempt to interrupt prevailing anti-comics discourse she claimed that psychologists, teachers, and parents 'do not look upon this form of entertainment as dangerous [despite] the daily papers continu[ing] to turn up stories tying juvenile delinquency to the reading of certain types of comics.' In a poll of 2,000 of its readers, *Chatelaine* found that 'they are wholeheartedly in favor of real comics; they don't feel that all comics should be scrapped because of the few horror numbers.' Of course, the acceptability of 'real' (funny?) comics was precisely the point the IODE had been trying to make. Fulton, Cockburn, and the others who raised their concerns publicly didn't think all comics should be scrapped; their goal was to influence policies that separated the 'good' (what they called 'real') comics from the 'bad.' . . .

Portrayals of crimes, overly graphic representations of women's bodies, and a rarely defined immorality were the main concerns of the anti-comics crusaders. Today, post-war comics seem an odd mix of provocativeness and predictability. In Canadian titles, at least, the good guys and gals always won—even if it wasn't until the last frame—and, generally, crime didn't pay. But such morally acceptable endings were invariably preceded by fights, killings, and other dirty deeds, depictions of scantily clad women, and graphic or textual sexual innuendo. 'Barry Kuda', a story in a 1946 issue of *Unusual Comics* (Bell Comics, Toronto), shows how these 'dangerous' elements were combined: 'What made the walls of Queen Merma's palace tremble as she held a farewell banquet for Barry Kuda and Algie? Barry was soon to learn, when the banquet hall became a scene of boiling terror and Sato's awful army, with their bodies glowing red hot, fought to brand the Queen's domain with THE SYMBOL OF SIN!'[29]

As Sato's volcanic eruption destroys Merma's palace, the blond and muscular Barry Kuda (wearing a wrestling-type singlet and shorts) carries the slim, white, long-haired Merma (wearing bikini shorts and conical breast-coverings) to safety. Barry returns to the palace to fight the devilish Sato, complete with horns, and to find his friend Algie. But Barry's plan is foiled when he is frozen stiff in his tracks by one of Sato's men.

In the meantime, Sato himself has gone in search of Merma.

> Merma: What do you want, Sato? Keep away! What can you gain by killing me?
> Sato: But—I'm not going to kill you, my dear. It's lonely in Volcania! I'd like a real queen for a wife!
> Merma: No! No! Not that! Barry—Bar—

Her cries are to no avail. Merma gets frozen too. In the next frame, she is lying helpless on a table, Sato's doctor hanging over her scantily clothed body. When her 'frozen flesh is thawed', he gets ready to inject her with the blood of one of Sato's

guards so that she will be able to survive in their underworld. 'Oh. No! No! Barry! Algie! Help!'

The scene shifts to the outside of the palace where Barry has managed to thaw himself out, find his friend, and kill some of Sato's minions. Bodies are flying in all directions. And just in time, Barry and Algie run through the carnage to find Merma, who is about to receive the injection of devilish blood. 'Help No—Oh, Barry! Thank Heavens!' Sato is vanquished, Merma is saved, and Barry and Algie are feted as heroes.

. . .

Opponents said that the comics 'glamorize[d] crime, brutality and immorality'[30] and gave young people 'a wrong idea of the civilized way of life'.[31] Adult commentators tended to take the view that young readers (blank slates that they were assumed to be) passively absorbed whatever the comics put before them and that, once exposed to crime, sex, and violence on the page, children and teens would develop a taste for it and be moved to re-enact it in daily life.

In June 1948, Fulton first introduced the issue into the House of Commons, arguing that crime comics were leading Canadian young people into delinquency. While this flagging of possible moral degeneration got the issue on the government's agenda, it was not enough to convince the Minister of Justice, J.L. Ilsley, of the immediate need for suppression. The minister claimed that his own research, including queries to the provincial Attorneys General, had not uncovered any conclusive evidence of the link between reading crime comics and subsequent delinquent activity. Ilsley quoted Dr C.M. Hincks, general director of the National Committee for Mental Hygiene, who said: 'It has never been scientifically established that crime or thrill stories either in movies, radio or comics have contributed to delinquency. Prohibiting publication is an admission of failure on the part of the family and the educational system in encouraging the development of wholesome and healthy interests.'[32]

Ilsley's stance on comics was a 'scientific' one versus the decidedly moral approach adopted by Fulton. Originally, Fulton had attempted to take a more 'rational' approach. Before introducing his bill, he requested statistics on delinquency from the Minister of Justice. But the figures he received, for crimes committed by people under the age of 18, did little to help his case. In 1945 there had been 3,934 convictions; in 1946 there were 3,682; and in 1947 there were 3,350.[33] Despite Fulton's continued claims to the contrary, the actual incidence of delinquency was falling. According to sociologist Augustine Brannigan, this trend in delinquency rates was consistent for the years 1942 to 1949, and the figures remained 'relatively low' until the mid-1950s.[34] Still Fulton persisted, appealing to common-sense notions of what was good for young people, of how easily they might be corrupted, and of how dangerous the effects of comic books were:

> I just want to give an example from the one [comic book] I have in my hand. It starts off on the inside cover with the picture of a man striking a match and staring at it. The caption over the next picture is, 'Tonight I dreamed of a blazing moon like a fiery wheel in the sky—burning trees were crashing about me,' and the caption is illustrated. The next picture portrays him walking to a slum tenement, and he says, 'I saw an old condemned building. Nobody would care if it burned down.' The next picture shows this man holding a burning match, and the caption says, 'Tonight I stole into the cellar of the condemned building and set my first fire.' That is a fine thing to put before a youngster of twelve or so, who perhaps has just struck his first match.[35]

Eventually, Ilsley conceded that legislation was necessary. Apparently, his change of position came after he received a selection of comics from Fulton—*Crime* and *Crime Does Not Pay*—comics which Ilsley characterized as a flagrant abuse of freedom of the press. But Ilsley wanted to take his time over the new law, and the conclusion of the comics debate was held off until the next par-

liamentary session. By the time that session was underway, Ilsley had retired from politics and been replaced as Justice Minister by Stuart Garson. Fulton introduced his private member's bill once again, and a full-scale debate of crime comics occupied the House for several days.

MPs rallied to the call to protect youth from 'the trash you get in these dime crime comic books'.[36] In a particularly evocative, though not entirely typical, contribution to the Commons debate, Daniel McIvor, MP for Fort William, described the crime comics as a tactic of 'the devil'. He said, 'You can almost hear him saying, "Get them young. That is the time to get them." Our Sunday school teachers can work their heads off and still not succeed in combating an agency such as obscene literature. It is a curse.'[37]

Many of the MPs admitted to having made studies of crime comics at their local drugstore or in their home ridings. They argued their support for Fulton's bill on the basis of personal experience and gut reaction. They waved (unnamed) comics at their colleagues and read statements from concerned constituents. Howard C. Green (Vancouver-Quadra) read from a letter from 'a mother in Vancouver, who, by the way, is the daughter of a distinguished Canadian authoress': 'I know you are as anxious as any conscientious parent to see our Canadian children rescued from the evil effects of these criminal immoral magazines. I believe a big house-cleaning of our magazine and paper-back 25-cent books is overdue. We busy ourselves building youth centres, working in church to show our young people the guide posts to clean living, and all the time a stream of filthy books is allowed to come into our country.'[38] The MPs mobilized common-sense assumptions about shared moral principles: 'I know it would disgust everyone in the House and it would disgust the average man and woman right across Canada.'[39] There was much mutual congratulation on the 'high level' of the debate, and there were commendations for Fulton from the other MPs and for the Minister of Justice for bringing the bill to the House.

Bill 10 was passed in December 1949. It amended section 207 of the Criminal Code, which dealt with obscene literature: 'to cover the case of those magazines and periodicals commonly called "crime comics," the publication of which is presently legal, but which it is widely felt tend to the lowering of morals and to induce the commission of crimes by juveniles.'[40] While the actual wording of the amendment was broad and vague, its inclusion in the general section on 'obscene literature' is telling. Subsection one of section 207 would be contravened by anyone who 'prints, publishes, sells or distributes any magazine, periodical or book which exclusively or substantially comprises matter depicting pictorially the commission of crimes, real or fictitious, thereby tending or likely to induce or influence youthful persons to violate the law or to corrupt the morals of such persons.'[41] Even in law the moral capacities of young people were what set the bounds of decency. Under such a broad definition, fairy tales and news articles might have been subject to prosecution. Of course, they were not. Crime comics, on the other hand, rapidly disappeared from Canadian newsstands. At the end of 1950, a researcher for the Toronto Board of Education claimed to have found no crime comics for sale in the city.[42]

## Fredric Wertham and *Seduction of the Innocent*

One of the main proponents of the theory that comics were dangerous literature—the reading of which could lead otherwise normal youngsters to perform criminal or sexually immoral activities—was Dr Fredric Wertham, senior psychiatrist for the New York City Department of Hospitals from 1932 to 1952. In 1948, the year E. Davie Fulton introduced his bill into the Canadian House of Commons, Wertham published five articles in popular American magazines denouncing comics in general and crime comics in particular.[43] In the House of Commons debates, Fulton referred to Wertham and cited his American 'evidence' as support for the proposed amendment to the Criminal Code.

Wertham outlined his position in detail in his 1954 book, *Seduction of the Innocent*, which was a featured selection for the Book-of-the-Month Club that year.[44] The book mentions E. Davie Fulton and the passage of Bill 10, quotes from *Hansard*, and speaks in glowing terms throughout most of a chapter about the work against comics that had been done in Canada, both in Parliament and among ordinary citizens:[45] 'No debate on such a high ethical plane, with proper regard for civil liberties but with equal regard for the rights and happiness of children, has ever taken place in the United States.'[46]

It is impossible, here, to do a full critique of Wertham. Nevertheless, it is important to consider his work because it was so influential on Canadian activists. He was quoted in the House of Commons debates. He was referred to and cited by people writing to the Ontario Attorney General. He corresponded with members of the British Columbia Parent-Teacher Federation, including a Mrs Eleanor Gray, who was mentioned by name in *Seduction of the Innocent*. In a letter he wrote to thank Gray for a Christmas card, Wertham acknowledged his own importance in the international debate on comics when he wrote, 'P.S: If you wish to, you may quote any part of this letter in any way you wish.'[47]

According to Wertham, comic books affected reading skills, desensitized young people to violence, and led to delinquent behaviour, psychological difficulties, and problems in sexual development. While delinquency, illiteracy, and sex each get their own chapter in *Seduction of the Innocent*, concerns about sexuality appear throughout the book, as does the evocative sexual language that Wertham used to build his case. For instance: 'I have come to the conclusion that this *chronic stimulation, temptation and seduction* by comic books, both their content and their *alluring* advertisements of knives and guns are contributing factors to many children's maladjustment.'[48] At times he was even more blatant, writing, for instance, that children 'give up crime-comic reading like a bad sexual habit.'[49] But what operates as a literary device on one page becomes fact on another—for Wertham, reading comics *was* a bad sexual habit. In a chapter entitled, 'I want to be a sex maniac!' he says that 'an elementary fact of [his] research' is that 'comic books stimulate children sexually.'[50] Wertham took it as self-evidently bad that 'children' should be sexually 'turned on'. Reading comics, he said, impedes 'the free [sexual] development of children' and causes 'sexual arousal which amounts to seduction'.

Wertham's tendency to refer to children, while offering case studies of adolescents, was a rhetorical technique that helped to support his main argument that comics 'seduced' the 'innocent'. To have referred to adolescents would have been to refer to young people who were already in the process of becoming sexual, who were somewhat less than sexually innocent. In invoking 'children', as an imperilled group, Wertham heightened the sense of moral outrage implicit in his writing. The slipperiness between the terms 'child' and 'adolescent' that is evident in Wertham's text is not unique to him, though he manipulates it to his advantage in a remarkable fashion. That adolescence was considered by many to be a transitional 'stage' between childhood and adulthood contributed to the slippery usage. Definitions of adolescence as transitional meant that while adolescents were not children, they continued to be affected by notions about childhood—for instance, the ambiguous concept of childhood innocence.

. . .

Certainly, Wertham was not the only one to believe that comics had a negative effect on children's sexuality, but he was the only one to state his concerns so explicitly. While other commentators spoke demurely of the links between comics and perversion or comics and immorality, Wertham spoke explicitly about masturbation, sado-masochistic fantasies, homosexuality and homoeroticism, prostitution, and sex crime.

Though his concerns were numerous, underlying them all was the risk that young people were being exposed to things of which they apparently had no prior knowledge, things that he felt were not suitable for children (however defined), including, and especially, their own sexual feelings. He cites numerous cases where boys and girls recounted to him masturbatory fantasies which were 'aggravated' by reading comics. Even in those cases where young adults seemed to have emerged from their comics-reading years unharmed, Wertham held steadfastly to his position that they might, nevertheless, end up with sexual troubles: 'But is it not one of the elementary facts of modern psychopathology that childhood experiences very often do not manifest themselves as recognizable symptoms or behavior patterns in childhood, but may crop up later in adult life as perverse and neurotic tendencies?'[51]

Wertham's analysis rested on a simple construction of monkey read, monkey do, based on his clinical observation of troubled youth. He was particularly concerned about what he saw as the tendencies of the various forms of comics to encourage homoerotic attitudes. Would the millions of comics circulating across North America lead to an increase in the number of sex deviates? Wertham claims that certain types of comics tended to fix boys in their pre-adolescent phase of disdain for girls—what other writers frequently called the 'normal' homosexual phase of heterosexual development.[52] It seems that homoerotic attitudes were caused, in part, by 'the presentation of masculine, bad, witchlike or violent women. In such comics women are depicted in a definitely anti-erotic light, while the young male heroes have pronounced erotic overtones.'[53]

Wertham lamented the fate of adolescent boys, who lived with their own fears of becoming homosexual. Apparently such boys were likely to become 'addicted' to the 'homoerotically tinged type of comic book', a habit which could only lead to homoerotic fantasies, followed inevitably by guilt and shame as they learned of social taboos against sexual deviation. Certainly, homosexually inclined boys had few other sources to turn to for acknowledgement of their desires, and, given the social climate, they may have felt shame about their reading habits. But, of course, Wertham was not concerned about the discriminatory social conditions and widespread intolerance that led to those feelings of oppression; he was concerned about the tenor of the comic books. Singled out as exemplary of those needing to be cleaned up were the 'dangerous' chronicles of the Caped Crusader and the Boy Wonder.

Wertham's discussion of Batman is a prime example of 1950s moral panic about sex perversion—four and a half pages of 'expert opinion' on the 'Ganymede-Zeus type of love-relationship'. His arguments about the dangers of Batman drew on the most stereotypical signifiers of homo-ness and on a macho individualist version of masculinity more suited to the receding frontier than to post-war domesticity and middle-class corporate life.

> At home they [Batman and Robin, aka Bruce and Dick] lead an idyllic life . . . They live in sumptuous quarters, with beautiful flowers in large vases, and have a butler, Alfred. Batman is sometimes shown in a dressing gown. As they sit by the fireplace the young boy sometimes worries about his partner: 'Something's wrong with Bruce. He hasn't been himself these past few days.' It's like a wish dream of two homosexuals living together. Sometimes they are shown on a couch, Bruce reclining and Dick sitting next to him, jacket off, collar open, and his hand on his friend's arm.[54]

Moreover, Robin was often shown standing with his legs apart, 'the genital region strictly evident', and Batman, in their crusading adventures, frequently came to Robin's rescue. By Wertham's definition, the stories contained no 'decent, attractive, successful women', evidence of an anti-woman attitude he equated with the homoerotic theme. Boys exposed to this pastiche of codes and signifiers would, no doubt, be incited

to homoerotic fantasies. And, Wertham claimed, he had the case studies to prove it.

While girls are mentioned infrequently in *Seduction of the Innocent*, they too were at the mercy of the comic-book publishers, perhaps even more so than boys. Wertham contends that female character development was more severely affected by comics than was male character development, primarily because of the nature of female superheroes.[55] He considered characters like Wonder Woman so far outside normal constructions of femininity that girls would be thrown into a spin of mental torment if they should ever endeavour to identify with their heroines.

Resting on his claim to 'professional' knowledge, Wertham 'outs' Wonder Woman, asserting that her lesbianism is 'psychologically unmistakable'. Apparently, Wonder Woman 'is always a horror type. She is physically very powerful, tortures men, has her own female following, is the cruel, "phallic" woman. While she is a frightening figure for boys, she is an undesirable ideal for girls, being the exact opposite of what girls are supposed to want to be.'[56] One could make much of the 'supposed to' in this sentence. Is Wertham responding to women's and girls' dissatisfaction with post-war discourses on femininity? Is the powerful Wonder Woman a symbolic foreshadowing of the eruption of 1960s feminism? Is this why Wertham is careful not to make any mention of Wonder Woman's sidekick, the pudgy, bon-bon eating Etta?

In the context of post-war psychological discourse, so-called normal sexuality, as we have seen, was not a given; it needed to be fought for and nurtured. 'Normal' sexuality was thought to be the culmination of a precarious developmental process that might easily be sent astray. Outside influences could stall or preclude the attainment by adolescents of sexual maturity. Comics, at least as Wertham and his followers understood them, were clearly in this category of outside threat. What was thought to make comics especially dangerous was the fact that they were deliberately aimed at a young readership. While their content was 'tame' when compared to, say, sex magazines, the moral imperative to clean comics up was considerable because of the long-term consequences they might have had on the 'immature' characters of their intended young audience. The perceived unambiguous relationship between comics and youth was critical to the success of the anti-comics activists. Certainly the passage of the Fulton bill was a major victory for them. More importantly, concerned citizens were also able to exert tremendous pressure directly on the publishers. In 1954, the publishers developed their own production code, similar to that used in the film industry. Overseen by the Comics Magazine Association of America, the code included guidelines such as the following:

- All characters shall be depicted in dress reasonably acceptable to society.
- Illicit sex relations are neither to be hinted at or portrayed. Violent love scenes as well as sexual abnormalities are unacceptable.
- Respect for parents, the moral code, and for honorable behavior shall be fostered. A sympathetic understanding of the problems of love is not a license for morbid distortion.[57]

While campaigns against the perceived immorality in other types of reading material also drew on discourses about young people's vulnerability to corruption, the frame of the discussion was not the same as it had been in the fight against comics. Unlike the market for comics, the market for sex magazines and pulp novels was not primarily made up of children and teenagers. To talk about protecting young people from the influence of these adult publications was to admit, on some level, a loss of control over young people by adults and a failure to maintain the innocence the campaigns claimed they were protecting. Would the truly innocent youth read such things? It was a contradiction the campaigners never addressed.

. . .

A central feature of the moral panic over indecency was that nowhere in these discussions were the definitions of immorality and indecency at issue, nor was the need of Canadians to be protected from them questioned. Immorality and indecency were assumed to be known and harmful categories; all that needed to be asked—by concerned senators, editorial writers, or parents—was how they could best be dealt with. This limited frame of reference is blatantly obvious in the evidence from an Ottawa obscenity case that ran concurrently with the first round of the Senate hearings. In the trial evidence, one sees how this truncated debate was made possible by ideas about the relationship between youth and sexuality. Indeed, one can also see that had it been possible to step outside prevailing discourses of childhood and adolescence, the trial might never have occurred.

## Lesbianism as Obscenity or *Women's Barracks* as a Threat to Girls

In March 1952, National News Company, an Ottawa distributor, was charged under section 207 of the Criminal Code with 11 counts of having obscene matter in its possession, 'for the purpose of distributing'. Seven 'girlie' magazines and four pulp novels were named in the charges. All were eventually found to be obscene by Judge A.G. McDougall, and National News was fined a total of $1,100.[58]

Among the novels was *Women's Barracks*, written by an obscure French author named Tereska Torres.[59] Its story is similar to the one told in Torres's 1970 autobiography about her time in the women's section of the Free French Army during the Second World War.[60] The novel follows a group of women who spent several years together in a London barracks. We read of their work assignments and drills, of their hopes for France, and their social and sexual lives. The characters are a mixed lot, mostly young heterosexuals, though there are two lesbians and an 'older' (40-year-old), sexually experienced woman named Claude who has affairs with men and women. Several of the heterosexual women have affairs with married men, one of them gets pregnant out of wedlock, all of them drink. In the midst of this, the narrator operates as the moral centre of the book. She distances herself from the other women and their sexual and emotional experiments—engaging in none of her own—trying to maintain her ideals about love, fidelity, and marriage.

To the present-day reader, Torres's prose is far from lurid. Nevertheless, *Women's Barracks* was packaged in typical 1950s pulp style and marketed as 'THE FRANK AUTOBIOGRAPHY OF A FRENCH GIRL SOLDIER'. While the allusions to sex in the book are many, the details of it are few. In her foreword to the book, Torres links the sexual activity and its emotional fallout to the adversities of war; in 'normal' circumstances, she suggests, little of this activity would have taken place.[61]

When the book first came to trial, Crown Attorney Raoul Mercier's strategy was a simple one. He wanted to prove, simply, that the book had been for sale in a particular cigar store, that the store had been supplied by National News, and that copies of the book had been found on the premises of the distribution company. He was confident that the judge would find the text itself obscene when he came to read it.

. . .

Under the law, no one could be convicted on an obscenity charge if they could prove that the 'public good' had been served by the act in question. This was the grounds of the defence strategy pursued by National News's lawyers, G.W. Ford and J.M. McLean. As they put it, even if Torres's book was technically obscene, it still might have fulfilled a social purpose.[62] Expert witnesses were called to explain just what that purpose might have been. The Crown Attorney, wanting equal time, revised his original strategy and called his own experts to prove the first lot wrong. All told, the trial gave rise to a substantial, public, documented discussion of lesbianism.

While lesbianism is clearly not the focus of the novel, it was the focus of courtroom debate. A copy of the novel is filed with the court transcripts at the Archives of Ontario. Inside the front cover are the initials 'R.M.', presumably referring to Crown Attorney Raoul Mercier. Throughout the text are underlinings and annotations in both pencil and black pen. Fifteen pages are marked with tags made out of sticky tape, possibly pages from which Mercier might have wanted to read in the courtroom. On all but two of these pages, there is some reference to lesbianism.[63] In the margins Mercier has written: 'lesbianism' and 'sex act' (each of these is repeated several times); 'lesbian crave' (56); 'ménage à trois' (87); 'homosexual' (32); 'act of lesbianism' (125). The one scene of lesbian seduction is marked 'all previous chapters lead to but this one climax' (46); passages prior to this are marked 'preparation' (34) and 'build-up' (12 and 36), presumably referring to the scene of lesbian seduction. There are no tags on the parts where heterosexual women find themselves pregnant, or where they discuss their plans to sleep with married men, or where they attempt suicide. The definition of immorality at work here is too narrow to include them. For Mercier, what made this book obscene was its discussion of lesbianism.

Even one of the expert witnesses for the defence, Toronto *Globe and Mail* writer J.A. McAree, claimed that lesbianism was the 'theme' of the book.[64] Certainly, he and his colleagues did nothing to challenge the alignment of lesbianism with immorality. In fact, the basis of defence arguments was that Torres's novel served the public good by warning its readers, especially young women, about the dangers of lesbianism.

Allan Seiger, a professor at the University of Michigan, tried to underscore the relationship of the lesbian activity to the war: 'These women are to be regarded, I think, as much casualties of the war as other soldiers.'[65] John Bakless, a journalism professor at the University of New York, stated that the book presented the lesbian episodes as being 'positively repulsive to any normal male or female'.[66] He also said that in 'the context of the book as a whole they clearly point out that the wages of sin is death.'[67] But, asks Mercier, is it not likely that

> a little girl who is not maybe a French woman in the same barracks, but who is in [a] convent or in a boarding school reaching the puberty age, does not know anything about these things, reads this passage from this book, wouldn't you say they would be willing to indulge in this practice to see if it is as described?
> A: I have read that book through, and I wouldn't want to be near a lesbian. Don't forget what happens. . . .
> Q: And you do not think they would be tempted to try lesbianism?
> A: No, sir, there is disaster there too plainly, and it is only with sympathy and regret that you can read it. . . .[68]

What happens is that Ursula, the 16-year-old, sleeps with Claude, the older bisexual woman, and falls in love with her. Claude 'toys' with Ursula emotionally. In her tormented state, Ursula is unable to muster feelings for a male Polish soldier who is pursuing her. Later, she tries to have sex with a male French sailor. But she is not up to it, and he ends up treating her like a little sister during the several days and nights they spend together. After this, Ursula's affections for Claude diminish. She falls in love with the Polish soldier, they plan to marry, they have sex, she gets pregnant, and he goes off to the front and is killed. In despair, she kills herself. It is a disaster, certainly. But the sequence of events is hardly caused by her one night of lesbian sex.

However, it is not Mercier's reading of the plot that stands out here; rather it is his attempt, and that of his opponent, to present the text as having powerful social consequences. What might the book do to young women in particular? Oddly, it is Mercier and his collection of expert witnesses who argue that the picture of lesbianism painted by Torres is an inviting one. Indeed, its attractive-

ness is what makes it dangerous. They refer several times to the passage where Ursula finds herself in bed with Claude—the only explicitly 'lesbian sex' scene in the book. (Not surprisingly, the markings in the margins of Mercier's copy of the book become quite frenzied at this point):

> Ursula felt herself very small, tiny against Claude, and at last she felt warm. She placed her cheek on Claude's breast. Her heart beat violently, but she didn't feel afraid. She didn't understand what was happening to her. Claude was not a man; then what was she doing to her? What strange movements! What could they mean? Claude unbuttoned the jacket of her pajamas, and enclosed one of Ursula's little breasts in her hand, and then gently, very gently, her hand began to caress all of Ursula's body, her throat, her shoulders, and her belly. Ursula remembered a novel that she had read that said of a woman who was making love, 'Her body vibrated like a violin.' Ursula had been highly pleased by this phrase, and now her body recalled the expression and it too began to vibrate. She was stretched out with her eyes closed, motionless, not daring to make the slightest gesture, indeed not knowing what she should do. And Claude kissed her gently, and caressed her. . . . All at once, her insignificant and monotonous life had become full, rich and marvellous. . . . Ursula wanted only one thing, to keep this refuge forever, this warmth, this security. (45)

What would become of a normal teenage girl who read this passage? Adult women, surely, would have the moral strength to resist the temptation such a positive image might hold. But teenagers, their moral characters not yet fully developed, would be less able to distinguish right from wrong. According to Isabelle Finlayson—Crown witness, mother of two, and member of the Ottawa school board and numerous women's groups—teens had not had enough experience to 'be expected to form their [moral] standards, therefore, they would take it [the lesbian sexual activity] as a proper conduct, as conduct accepted generally.'[69] Finlayson seems to be saying that teens had not yet had time to bring their standards in line with socially approved ones. They were still, in a sense, moral works-in-progress who might choose pleasure over indignation and denial.

According to Rev. Terrence Findlay, another Crown witness, the danger of the seduction scene was that a young girl might read such a passage and be enticed to experiment. A young girl, he said, is only 'beginning to form within her' a knowledge and experience of sex and is, therefore, 'intensely curious'. Findlay suggested that if a girl had not already received training about the dangers of lesbianism, the book might 'have a tendency to suggest to that girl that here is a way of satisfying sexual desires without the danger of consorting with male companions.'[70] This kind of literature, he said, tended to sway normal girls towards the abnormal, by making the latter seem both attractive and possible.

Ford tried to counter Findlay's position by emphasizing the 'normality' of most teenaged readers. Is it not likely that the pleasure of the seduction scene would be annulled by the scene where Ursula finds herself unable to have sexual relations with the French sailor? For Ford, these two scenes are intimately linked—lesbian sex leads to frigidity with men. Would not a 'normal teen-age girl' with 'normal sexual reactions' be 'nauseated' by Ursula's 'abnormal relations'—the latter phrase referring both to sex with a woman and an inability to have sex with a man?[71]

Ford wanted Women's Barracks to be taken up as a cautionary tale that might warn young women of the dangers of lesbianism, and in this way might serve the public good. No one disagreed with him over the need for this, although Crown witnesses rejected Torres's book as appropriate to the task. But, asked Ford, were they not all better informed on the subject after having read the novel? Isabelle Finlayson, in particular, claimed she had known nothing about lesbianism before she read the book. How then, asked Ford, could she possibly have

warned her daughter of lesbian dangers? Ford's argument had nothing to do with the book's effects on Finlayson herself; as an adult she was assumed to be beyond its influence, capable of reaching her own conclusions on such a vexing moral issue. Someone like Finlayson, well schooled in popular discourses about sexual deviance and perversion, would have been able to see past the pleasure of the seduction scene to the downfall which would inevitably follow. A teenaged girl, on the other hand, needed to have that downfall made explicit. According to Ford, Torres's novel did just that. It provided the context that schoolgirl gossip and curbside chatter about lesbianism might not.

Judge McDougall did not accept Ford's case. In his judgement he wrote:

> [The book] deals almost entirely with the question of sex relationships and also with the question of lesbianism. A great deal of the language, and particularly the description of two incidents of unnatural relationships between women, is exceedingly frank. The argument advanced before me was that publicity should be given to the question of lesbianism in order that it might act as a deterrent influence and in this respect would be a matter of public good. The dissemination of such information is no doubt a matter that should receive proper attention from a medical and psychological standpoint, but the manner in which the material is presented in this book does not comply with those standards in any manner.[72]

The underlying assumption, on both sides, indeed the basis of the obscenity charge, was that a pulp novel could have a harmful impact on young people who read it. The test of obscenity used by Canadian courts demanded that Davis and Ford take this as their starting point.

In 1953, Women's Barracks was the focus of another trial in St Paul, Minnesota, where notions of the corruptibility of young people were not embedded in the definition of obscenity and therefore had no sway over the final judgement: 'In conclusion, therefore, it is the opinion of the Court that the book, *Women's Barracks*, does not have a substantive tendency to deprave or corrupt by inciting lascivious thoughts or arousing lustful desire in the ordinary reader in this community in these times. It is the finding of the Court that the likelihood of its having such a salacious effect does not outweigh the literary merit it may have in the hands of the average reader.'[73]

Notions of adolescence as a time of rapid and profound change echoed widespread fears about change in the society at large. As the progression of one's adolescence was seen to determine the shape of one's adulthood, so too the collective progress of living, breathing adolescents was thought to indicate the shape Canadian society would take in the future. In this sense, youth operated as a metaphor for the development of the society as a whole: if they turned out all right, it was assumed the nation would be fine, too. But, after two decades of turmoil, such an outcome was not guaranteed.

It is in this context that ideas about the moral and physical capacities of young people were able to help constitute the limits of sexual discourse. The desire to 'protect' youth and the future they were assumed to represent helped to motivate broad-ranging initiatives of moral and sexual regulation—such as the conviction of National News, the banning of crime comics, and the implementation of the Senate Special Committee—that took not only youth but adults as their objects. Common-sense ideas about the nature of adolescent moral and sexual development contributed to the setting of limits on how and where sexuality could be expressed or represented and by whom. Some adults saw teenagers as being under the control of their blossoming sex drives. These adults wanted to set limits on public discussions of sexuality because they feared it would set teens off on an orgy of experimentation. Other adults were less concerned about the impulses of puberty and the exigencies of hormones than they were about teenagers'

moral immaturity. They worried that boys and girls faced with sexual information or images would be unable to distinguish right from wrong and thus might 'innocently' engage in questionable activities. In both perspectives notions of sexuality as potentially dangerous, as destabilizing and morally charged, combined with ideas about the nature of puberty and adolescent development to curtail public discussion of sex.

The relationship between discourses about sexuality and discourses about youth—especially the way these combined to conduct social anxieties around a broad range of issues—was central to the generation of the moral panic around obscenity. At stake in the furor over mass-market publications were accepted standards of sexual morality, standards that affected both young people and adults. Indecent material, in its various guises, offered competing ways of making sense of sex, morals, and relationships. Comics and trashy novels contradicted the many efforts to transform teenagers into 'fine moral citizens' that were commonplace in English Canada during the late 1940s and 1950s. The discourses made available in the pulps threatened the complex of processes through which particular forms of heterosexual expression were normalized. Comics, girlie magazines, and trashy novels suggested alternative ways of organizing sexuality, ones that might upset the dominance of a family-centred, monogamous heterosexuality. At bottom, indecent literature challenged dominant sexual and moral standards and these, as much as individual young people, were assumed to need protecting.

## Notes

1. Letter to 'Ontario Government Censorship Bureau' (a bureaucratic entity which did not exist—the letter was directed to the Attorney General), 20 June 1949, Archives of Ontario (AO), RG 4–32,1949, no. 270.

2. Paul Guay, President of Press and Cinema Services (Canada's equivalent to the League of Decency in the United States), Ottawa

Archdiocese of the Catholic Church, Brief submitted to the Senate Special Committee on Salacious and Indecent Literature; see Canada, Senate, Special Committee on Salacious and Indecent Literature (hereafter Special Committee), *Proceedings*, 3 June 1952, 10.

3.  Letter to Attorney General Dana Porter from a 'citizen' in Stoney Creek, 8 Nov. 1955, AO, RG 4–32, 1955, no. 25.

4.  'Notes taken at a meeting on 24 February 1956, during which a delegation representing a number of [Ontario] civic and religious groups presented a brief to the Attorney General re: salacious literature: AO, RG 4–02, file 91.7.

5.  BC Provincial Congress of Canadian Women, Brief submitted to the Senate Special Committee on Salacious and Indecent Literature, Special Committee, *Proceedings*, 11 Feb. 1953, 41.

6.  For a discussion of the evolution of mass-produced pocket books and the various technologies that have made it possible, see Janice A. Radway, *Reading the Romance* (London: Verso, 1984).

7.  The book was *Women's Barracks* by Tereska Torres, and the distributor was National News Company. See *The Queen v. National News Company*, 514, AO, RG 4–32, 1953, no. 830. There are no records of how many copies were sold.

8.  'Comics as Yule Gift to Clergyman-Trustee, Tely's Palooka Fan', Toronto *Telegram*, 13 Dec. 1950.

9.  Senate, Special Committee, *Report*, 29 Apr. 1953, 243.

10. Margaret Culkin Banning, 'Filth on the Newsstands', *Reader's Digest* (Oct. 1952): 150.

11. James Gilbert. *A Cycle of Outrage: America's Reaction to the Juvenile Delinquent in the 1950s* (New York: Oxford University Press, 1986), 3.

12. Martin Barker, *A Haunt of Fears: The Strange History of the British Horror Comics Campaign* (London: Pluto, 1984), 6.

13. Kathy Peiss, *Cheap Amusements: Working Women and Leisure in Turn-of-the-Century New York* (Philadelphia: Temple University Press, 1986).

14. Barker, *Haunt of Fears*, 87.

15. See Paul Landis, *Adolescence and Youth* (New York: McGraw-Hill, 1947), 47.

16. Banning, 'Filth on the Newsstands', 150.

17. Congress of Canadian Women, Submission to the Senate Special Committee on Salacious and Indecent Literature, Special Committee, *Proceedings*, 25 June 1952, 149.

18. Resolution from the Town of Timmins, Ontario, about indecent literature, AO, RG 4–32, 1952, no. 59. Endorsed by at least 32 other municipalities, it urged the government to survey and censor magazines in order to eliminate 'all that which is undesirable and unfit for consumption by the children of this Province'.

19. Canadian Preparatory Committee, International Conference in Defense of Children, Submission to Senate Special Committee on Salacious and Indecent Literature, Special Committee, *Proceedings*, 25 June 1952, 161.

20. Christian Social Council of Canada, Brief presented to the Senate Special Committee on Salacious and Indecent Literature, Special Committee, *Proceedings*, 17 June 1952, 77.

21. Special Committee, *Report*, 246.

22. Special Committee, *Proceedings*, 25 Apr. 1953, 221.

23. Canada, House of Commons, *Debates*, 21 Oct. 1949, 1043.

24. Patrick Parsons, 'Batman and His Audience: The Dialectic of Culture', in Roberta E. Pearson and William Uricchio, eds, *The Many Lives of Batman: Critical Approaches to a Superhero and His Media* (New York and London: Routledge and the British Film Institute, 1991), 68–9; Bill Boichel, 'Batman: Commodity as Myth', in Pearson and Uricchio, eds, *The Many Lives of Batman*, 6.

25. John Bell, *Guardians of the North: The National Superhero in Canadian Comic-book Art* (Ottawa: National Archives of Canada, 1992), 18. Bell's booklet is the catalogue from an exhibition of the same name at the Canadian Museum of Caricature during the summer of 1992.

26. 'Trustee Calls "Comic" Books "Degrading and Detrimental"', *Globe and Mail*, 26 Sept. 1945.

27. Cited in Brief presented to Special Committee of the Senate by the IODE, 1952, AO, RG 4–02, file 91.7.

28. Mary Jukes, 'Are Comics Really a Menace?', *Chatelaine* (May 1949): 6–7.

29. *Unusual Comics* (Sept.–Oct. 1946), Bell Publishing.

30. 'Comic Book Study Urged for Effect on Children', *Globe and Mail*, 11 Aug. 1950.

31. 'Board Debates Comic Books', *Globe and Mail*, 10 Jan. 1951.

32. Canada, House of Commons, *Debates*, 14 June 1948, 5201.

33. Ibid., 9 June 1948, 4935.

34. Augustine Brannigan, 'Mystification of the Innocents: Crime Comics and Delinquency in Canada, 1931–1949', *Canadian Justice History* 7 (1986): 118.

35. Canada, House of Commons, *Debates*, 8 June 1948, 4932.

36. Statement by G.K. Fraser, MP for Peterborough West, ibid., 6 Oct. 1949, 580.

37. Ibid., 4 Oct. 1949, 517.

38. Ibid., 7 Oct. 1949, 624.

39. Statement by G.K. Fraser, MP for Peterborough West, ibid., 6 Oct. 1949, 580.

40. Canada, House of Commons, Bill 10, 1949.

41. Ibid.

42. 'Comics as Yule Gift to Clergyman-Trustee'.

43. Parsons, 'Batman and His Audience', 71.

44. Fredric Wertham, *Seduction of the Innocent* (New York and Toronto: Rinehart, 1954).

45. Ibid., ch. 11: 'Murder in Dawson Creek—Comic Books Abroad'.

46. Ibid., 282.

47. Copy of letter from Fredric Wertham to Mrs T.W.A. [Eleanor] Gray, 14 Dec. 1953. The letter is appended to a letter from Mrs Gray, on behalf of the British Columbia Parent-Teacher Federation, to the Attorney General of Ontario, 4 Feb. 1954, AO, RG 4–32, 1954, no. 26, box 98.

48. Wertham, *Seduction of the Innocent*, 10; emphasis mine.

49. Ibid., 81.

50. Ibid., 175.

51. Ibid., 177.

52. For an example of this, see Maxine Davis, *Sex and the Adolescent* (New York: Permabooks, 1960), 62.

53. Wertham, *Seduction of the Innocent*, 188.

54. Ibid., 191.

55. Ibid., 99.

56. Ibid., 34.

57. 'Code of the Comics Magazine Association of America', 26 Oct. 1954, AO, RG 4–02, file 76.12.

58. *Regina v. National News Company Limited*, 8 Oct. 1952, AO, RG 4–32, 1953, no. 830.

59. Tereska Torres, *Women's Barracks* (New York: Fawcett, 1950). While published by a New York company, the book was printed in Canada. There is a copy of the novel, with margin notes by the Crown attorney, on file with the court transcripts. AO, RG 4–32, 1953, no. 830.

60. Tereska Torres, *The Converts* (London: Rupert Hart-Davis, 1970). The text on the front cover of the book jacket reads, 'The autobiography of Tereska Torres, author of "Women's Barracks."'

61. Torres, *Women's Barracks*, 5.

62. *R. v. National News*, 16.

63. The other two tags mark a slang reference to prostitution and a scene where a young woman loses her virginity with a man.

64. *R. v. National News*, 29.

65. Ibid., 44.

66. Ibid., 64.

67. Ibid., 54.

68. Ibid., 64.

69. Ibid., 380.

70. Ibid., 361.

71. Ibid., 365.

72. A.G. McDougall, 'Judgment re: Women's Barracks', 22 Nov. 1952, AO, RG 4–32, 1953, no. 830.

73. Judgement from a trial in St Paul, Minnesota, 16 June 1953, quoted in Torres, *Women's Barracks*, 11th printing, June 1958, inside front cover.

# 24

# Honky-Tonk City:
# Niagara and the Post-war Travel Boom

Karen Dubinsky

'There are insane places on the earth, and at one of them I grew up.'

Tom Marshall, *Voices on the Brink* (1988)

By the mid-twentieth century it had become clear that Niagara Falls was endowed with not one but two distinct geographical advantages. One was the spectacular waterfall, but just as important for the tourist industry and the subsequent development of the community was the Falls' position within North America's industrial heartland: southern Ontario and the northeastern United States. By 1967 Niagara Falls lay within 500 miles of 75 per cent of the total population of North America, and it had thus welcomed the post-war travel boom like no place else.

Between 1947 and 1966, according to town historians, the tourist business began to 'grow and blossom out' to 'a multi-million dollar business'. Between 1950 and 1960 alone, over a billion dollars were spent developing tourism and recreation facilities on both sides of the Canada/US border.[1] What happens to a small Ontario industrial town when up to 13 million visitors come to call every summer? Canadian novelist Tom Marshall's fictionalized memoir of growing up in the Niagara Falls of the 1950s provides a clue. To visitors, he makes clear in *Voices*

*on the Brink*, post-war Niagara was a lark, a landmark of affordable pleasure, travel, consumption, and, to newlyweds especially, sex. To residents, it was prosperous bedlam. Mass tourism truly took flight in North America after World War II, and vacations—now formally mandated in labour laws and collective agreements in most jurisdictions—came to represent almost everything good about North American culture. In Canada mushrooming government tourist bureaucracies, politicians, and entrepreneurs fashioned themselves into an effective cultural and political force dedicated to a simple philosophy: that tourism—usually defined narrowly as Americans visiting Canada—was wholly and unquestionably a good thing; and, therefore, the more of it, the better. An especially zealous Arthur Welsh, Ontario's minister of travel and publicity, had no trouble convincing entrepreneurs at a 1946 tourist industry conference to think of Canada as 'a gigantic department store, purveying travel and recreation'.[2]

The growth of mass tourism after the war was remarkable. Out of nowhere appeared mass-circulation travel magazines such as *Holiday*, published in Philadelphia, as well as regular travel features in newspapers and magazines. In Canada a huge amount of money and effort was

Karen Dubinsky, 'Honky-Tonk City: Niagara and the Postwar Travel Boom', in *The Second Greatest Disappointment: Honeymooning and Tourism at Niagara Falls*. © 1999 Between the Lines. Reprinted by permission of the publisher.

spent sprucing up the 'tourist plant', as Arthur Welsh termed his country, to make the place more attractive to US visitors. Training programs for service industry staff and management, such as the University of Toronto's program in institutional management, were quickly instituted, and between 1946 and 1960 the service industry in Canada doubled.[3] Motels, more accessible and affordable than the downtown hotel for working-class or middle-class families, appeared almost overnight. In Ontario the number of motels jumped from 150 in 1951 to almost 500 in 1954 to over 2,000 in 1962.[4]

The rapid growth of the tourist industry had startling implications for national identity, especially in Canada. Canadian tourist boosters were concerned about what they called the 'travel deficit', with many more Canadians visiting the United States than vice versa. At one especially low point, in 1954, every dollar spent by US tourists in Canada was being multiplied 11 times by Canadians in the United States. There was no particular reason to pair Canadian and US vacation habits, and it is certainly arguable that these two variables have little to do with each other. Despite owning three-fourths of the world's automobiles, Americans were homebodies; fewer than 7 per cent of them crossed their borders when they travelled. Canada inherited the lion's share of these visitors, 80 per cent. But when up to 60 per cent of Canadian vacationers crossed into the United States, the Canadian tourist industry panicked.[5] Rather than attempt to make Canadians stay home, through the 1950s and early 1960s the Canadian industry undertook countless promotional and educational campaigns to, as one journalist put it, 'make Canada more attractive to Mr and Mrs US Tourist.'[6] References to Canadian vacations were 'planted' in Hollywood films. Nationally distinctive souvenirs and food were invented and popularized, and Canadians themselves were constantly harangued by the tourist industry to extend a cordial welcome to visitors. For example, Canadians were encouraged to notice licence plates on cars, and when they spot-

ted Americans they were to approach them with a special welcome. They were also invited to learn all they could about local attractions in order to advertise those features, and they were asked to greet excursion steamers with a band and welcoming committee.

The tourist industry tried to convince all Canadians, not just those employed in the tourist or service industry, that US tourist dollars, and hence the courteous treatment of US visitors, were a national as opposed to commercial concern. The industry had a remarkable ability to blur boundaries; imagine General Motors trying to convince anyone other than its own employees that they should sell their cars for them. When the nation had become a gigantic department store or a tourist plant, what was the difference between employment and citizenship, or between citizen and worker? So when the Ontario provincial government asked its employees to become 'salesmen of Ontario' by sending its annual tourist promotion book to friends and family outside the province, those who complied most likely thought they were doing their friends, and perhaps themselves, a favour, rather than acting as unpaid shills for the tourist industry. The tourist industry was able to generate a great deal of enthusiasm for itself precisely because of this ability to recast national goodwill and community spirit into promotion for private industry.

The tourist industry in Niagara Falls was reshaped by these boom years, which in itself helps to explain why the average teacher, autoworker, or housewife became willing, in some ways, to take on double duty as tourist booster. But as we move away from the patriotic pronouncements of the national tourist industry to the experience of life on the front lines, as it were, in a tourist town, the story becomes more complicated. Certainly no one at the Falls required introductory tutorials on the impact or economic potential of tourism. But the relationship of the tourist industry, other kinds of industrial growth, and civic discourse at Niagara Falls was constantly shifting. Sometimes tourism enjoyed favoured status; sometimes manufacturing or hydroelectric development did. Sometimes residents basked in the glory of living at the 'world's most famous address', and at other times the tourist industry embarrassed them. While the region's serendipitous combination of geography and political economy—not to mention its history—guaranteed that the pent-up urge to travel would be unleashed with particular force within its confines, we cannot assume that visitors would always be universally welcomed, or that they would return.

Tourism was hardly a plot foisted upon a pliant or unwilling public. Indeed, it was the apparent democracy and openness of the tourist industry that gave it its appeal. At the same time as travel boosters were proclaiming that anybody could be a tourist, it also seemed as though anybody could be a tourist entrepreneur. From the farmer selling fruit and soft drinks on the roadside to the immigrant mom-and-pop motel operation to the swanky hotel corporation, it appeared that anyone could move into this marketplace and prosper. Yet the long shadow of Niagara's tawdry tourist history still partially crept over this era, and tourist industry rivalries, rocky relations between private and public entrepreneurs, and different ideas about the proper way to care for guests all lingered on.

. . .

## The Town That Was Also a Theme Park

The growth of tourist services—or the 'tourist plant'—at Niagara was staggering. On the Canadian side the number of restaurants, for example, increased from 40 in 1945 to 79 in 1955 to 115 in 1965. Motels appeared almost out of thin air; there were none in 1945, 79 ten years later, and 115 in 1965. By the early 1960s Ontario's Niagara region, with one-eighth of the province's population, contained 20 per cent, or one-fifth, of the province's motels. The local Chamber of Commerce estimated in 1958 that 80 per cent of the overnight accommodation in

town had not existed 10 years previously. Across the river in Niagara Falls, New York, the story was the same: the town boasted the United States' highest concentration of motels outside Miami Beach.[7]

When tourists were not eating or sleeping, they could find plenty of other things to do. Certainly, playing with the waterfall remained an important item on the tourist agenda, and the old standbys—the Cave of the Winds and Table Rock tours, the *Maid of the Mist* boat ride, and the Spanish Aerocar over the Whirlpool—remained popular. But post-war Niagara also featured a catalogue of other amusements that would have made nineteenth-century entrepreneurs like Saul Davis and Thomas Barnett green with envy. By the early 1960s tourist attractions on both sides of the river included two golf courses, replicas of an Indian village and the English crown jewels, an antique auto museum (inexplicably proud of its main attraction, Mussolini's limousine), two children's amusement theme parks, two wax museums, Marine Wonderland and Animal Park, and Niagarama (an 'animated historical funhouse'). Then, too, there was Davis's Niagara Falls Museum (back on the Canadian side of the river in the old Spirella Corset factory), a second museum operated by the Niagara Parks Commission (which also operated a restored eighteenth-century fort at Niagara-on-the-Lake), Ontario Hydro's Floral Clock, a planetarium, and three massive observation towers.[8] The resulting landscape must have been reminiscent of that other great post-war amusement park, Disneyland, which had opened its doors in 1955 in Anaheim, California.

North American entrepreneurs were uncharacteristically slow to recognize and successfully copy the Disney formula. Theme parks did not really proliferate until the 1970s—including Disney World, which opened in Florida in 1971.[9] But in the 1950s and 1960s other popular tourist destinations became fractured versions of Disneyland, offering many of the same sorts of attractions. At Niagara, Storybook Park, for example, invited children to play with Mother Goose characters, and at the Indian Village visitors could stroll through longhouses and teepees and watch what the brochures called 'Real Indians' (from the Six Nations reserve near Brantford) perform dances and manufacture souvenirs. Such attractions were low-budget derivatives of Disneyland's 'Fantasy Land' and 'Frontier Land', but with important differences. Disney's park operated as a miniature state. Disneyland was (and remains) one of the most highly scripted playgrounds in human history, with centralized control entrenched in its design and day-to-day operations. Park designers worked hard to establish a 'coherent, orderly, sequenced layout within which elements would complement each other rather than compete for attention.'[10]

But the attractions of Niagara Falls, which was, after all, a community, were not centrally planned or owned. The diffused and hodge-podge nature of Niagara's amusements made for unique problems and neighbourly difficulties. The Niagara Parks Commission and the New York State Reservation waged a war of words, which eventually ended up in court, with Alice Langmuir, owner of the Burning Springs Wax Museum, located just up the river from both parks. The Wax Museum used a loudspeaker to attract visitors, and park officials complained bitterly of the loudspeaker's 'intensive bombardment', audible to park visitors as well as passersby.[11] Similarly, in 1960, motel owners began to complain to city council about their new neighbour, the Indian Village (owned not by Indians but by Murray Ruta, a local real estate broker). Anthony Solose, owner of the Horseshoe Falls Cottages, complained about the 'continuous smell and smoke of the bonfire' and the 'beating of tom-toms, yelping and hollering'. There was more. 'Tourists with families have always favoured our cottages,' he continued, 'but with Indians peeping over fences the younger children get frightened.'[12]

Things had changed considerably since the days when travellers eagerly sought a glimpse of

their 'first Indian'. In mimicking—on a smaller and more fragmented scale—the sort of amusements that had drawn 10 million visitors to Disneyland within its first two years of business, post-war Niagara stands as a perfect example of the increasing cultural uniformity—what people today call 'McWorld' or 'McDisney'—that was beginning to characterize North America.[13]

## From Mom-and-Pop to Multinational: The Post-war Tourist Industry

. . .

Most participants in the post-war tourist trade were first-generation entrepreneurs, running retail or service industry establishments that required enormous investments of time. Civic affairs and social climbing were probably not high on their agendas. But many of them were also first-generation Canadians and thus culturally in rather a different universe than the business and political elite of small-town southern Ontario. Immigrants owned a sizable portion of the accommodation and restaurant market after World War II.[14]

Emil Badovanic was one such immigrant. In 1940 Badovanic, born in Yugoslavia, left South Porcupine in northern Ontario, where he had been the proprietor of the Goldfields Hotel, to take over the Caverly Hotel, a former public house dating back to the 1860s. Badovanic was joined in this venture by Stojan Demic, a Porcupine miner. The partnership did not work out, so Badovanic and his wife ran the Caverly alone as a 'workingman's hotel' through the 1940s. Although Mrs Badovanic was invisible in the written record of business transactions and liquor licence applications, her labour contributed substantially to the hotel's success. Liquor board inspectors noted through the 1940s that the Caverly's restaurant—which Mrs Badovanic operated—was the hotel's biggest and most popular draw. But the place was a hotel in name only. The travelling public did not patron-ize the place, perhaps because it was located just beyond the main tourist area, and at most four or five workingmen roomed there. The Badovanics' fortunes improved as the post-war tourist boom hit the Falls. They renovated the hotel in 1950, adding 24 new bedrooms, expanding the dining room, and refurnishing the two bars, which were even given names: 'The Cataract Room' and 'The Pine Room'. Through the 1950s the Caverly remained, according to provincial liquor inspectors, a 'clean and well-operated hotel'.

The Badovanics were—at least financially— a classic immigrant success story. They sent their son to university, from whence he returned to take over from his father, and all the while they expanded their real estate holdings.[15] In 1946 they, along with George Sainovich and his wife, purchased another run-down hotel, the historic Prospect House. Allegedly the oldest building in the Niagara Peninsula and, according to local legend, either the headquarters of English War of 1812 hero Sir Isaac Brock or a prison that housed the rebels during the Upper Canada Rebellion of 1837, the Prospect House had, since the 1920s, fallen into disrepair and catered only to long-term boarders. Sainovich and Badovanic quickly turned the place around, 'using history to sell beer', as one commentator put it. By 1955, when Sainovich bought Badovanic out, the place boasted a huge new dining room, two beverage rooms, a coffee shop, and 20 new guest rooms. 'Today,' noted one reviewer approvingly in 1955, 'Americans invade the hotel by the score to revel in its history.'[16] If anyone thought it odd that one of the landmarks of old Tory Ontario was now making Eastern European immigrants rich by catering to US tourists, they kept it to themselves.

Frank Podhorn, a Russian immigrant, was another hotel owner who was able to parlay a good location and prosperous times into a sizable tourist establishment. Podhorn purchased the Falls View Hotel, located on a hill overlooking the waterfall, in 1940, when it was a simple three-storey, eight-bedroom structure. Like the Caverly it had been more a bar than a hotel. Over the next 15 years Podhorn expanded the dining room and increased the number of rooms from eight to 65, adding first cabins and later a sleek motel complex. Inspectors noted that the place's clientele was 'almost 100 per cent American', music to the ears of any tourist entrepreneur of the era. By the end of the 1950s Podhorn had started exhibiting some of the public symbols of small-business success: he became president of the local Hotel Association and started getting his picture in the newspaper.[17]

All of these success stories became so due to a combination of factors, among them hard work, good timing, and good luck. But these establishments also possessed another important and valuable asset—a liquor licence—though a licence alone was not an iron-clad guarantee of financial success. Niagara Falls included plenty of licensed establishments that did not cash in on the post-war tourist boom, remaining instead working-class bars or even, according to the liquor board inspectors who tried to put them out of business, clubhouses for prostitutes, drug smugglers, and gamblers. But for anyone with dreams of entering the tourist market, a liquor licence certainly helped, particularly since on the Ontario side, of all the accommodation possibilities—motels, cabins, tourist homes, and auto-camps—hotels alone could qualify for them.

This necessity led to regular definitional skirmishes. . . . [I]n the early 1930s, when local authorities began regulating tourist homes, some clever tourist-home owners attempted—unsuccessfully, as it turned out—to get themselves classified as hotels to avoid the regulations. Other entrepreneurs followed suit, and from the late 1930s on the Liquor Licensing Board received scores of applications for hotel liquor licences, most of them with the same success as tourist homes had earlier. Sometimes they were rejected because it seemed obvious to the inspector that the application was little more than a clumsy attempt to purvey liquor: a grocery store or a tailor shop with a couple of bedrooms upstairs, for example, stood no chance of convincing anyone that it was a hotel.

But while the category covered a certain material reality—hotels had to conform to regulations concerning fire safety and number of bedrooms, for example—it also evidenced a great degree of subjectivity, and political, class, and ethnic prejudices held great force. Applications from Italians, for example, were often rejected on the grounds that the proposed hotel would serve only an Italian clientele or that the working-class neighbourhood already had sufficient hotel bars. The Woman's Christian Temperance Union occasionally lobbied against applications, particularly those that intended to serve the 'foreign element', and a woman from nearby Fort Erie urged the Liquor Licensing Board in 1946 to 'consider the racial background and character' of permit holders more closely, because 'a great portion of these privileges are finding their way into the hands of foreigners.'[18]

But the most powerful prejudice was politics. Local members of the provincial Parliament intervened for and against would-be hotel owners openly, regularly, and in brazenly partisan ways. One of the most interventionist was William Houck, a former coal merchant who was, for a time, both mayor and Liberal MPP. A cheerful note from Houck would often accompany applications, citing the sterling qualities of the applicant and also mentioning his many years of service and dedication to the Liberal Party. Houck also attempted to use patronage against his opponents. In the late 1930s, Louis Sacco tried to get his licence for the Victoria Inn reinstated. Inspectors had pulled it because, in their view, 'a few cheap beds and mattresses' above his restaurant did not constitute a hotel (one wonders how it qualified to begin with). Sacco was furious, but he knew how the game was played. In his many letters of protest to the Licensing Board he expressed indignation that he was 'being put out of my property by the Liberal Party, for which I have worked and supported all my life.' Houck supported Sacco's reinstatement,

but perhaps not for the reasons the businessman expected. As Houck explained to the commissioners evaluating the case, 'The Niagara Hotel is practically next door but the owner of that is quite a decided opponent of mine and naturally I am not inclined to favour him.'[19]

As Louis Sacco discovered, keeping a licence could be just as difficult as acquiring one, particularly if one was burdened with an unpopular ethnic background or political affiliation. The vigilance of Liquor Licensing Board inspectors was awesome, and during their regular spot visits to establishments they were positively eagle-eyed. The condition of the toilets, whether women had to walk through the men's tavern to get to their washroom, the amount of liquor and food consumed monthly, the question of single women residing in the rooms or, worse still, white women in the company of black men, the condition of the register, women (even wives or daughters of the owner) waiting tables in the men's beverage rooms, loud music playing or people dancing in the dining room, the alcohol consumption of owners or employees and whether waiters were engaged in the nefarious practice of 'double serving' (serving another glass before the patron had fully consumed the first): all of these issues and more came to the attention of the inspectors, and infractions were quickly pounced on. Possessing a liquor licence was a rare and valuable asset in the accommodation business, because only 17 licensed premises existed in Niagara Falls, Ontario, in 1947, and this number included places offering no accommodation, such as the Canadian Legion. As might have been expected, the inspectors' reports for the swanky General Brock and the Foxhead Inn tended to be brief, perfunctory, and seemingly objective.

. . .

Through the 1940s and 1950s, Niagara Falls residents, particularly those who lived near the waterfall, created tourist accommodations from virtually anything they could get their hands on. Backyard garages became 'cabins', and empty lots were quickly transformed into motels. One particularly enterprising soul tried to turn his auto-wrecking yard into a motel. Still the accommodation crisis continued, so much so that before Labour Day weekend in 1949 the Chamber of Commerce issued a stirring appeal, requesting that citizens 'do their community a great service' by 'opening all available facilities' for weekend visitors.[20]

Yet not everyone in town would have agreed that creating comfortable accommodations for tourists constituted a full-fledged crisis, particularly when the Ontario side was, like most Canadian communities immediately after World War II, experiencing an acute housing shortage. Tourist accommodation problems arose during summer long weekends and special events, but for the rest of the year many Niagara residents considered that they had an overabundance of motels, hotels, and cabins. In January 1949, 57 citizens expressed exactly that sentiment to the city council, presenting them with a petition urging them to halt any future tourist accommodation construction in the city on the grounds that the current building boom was 'lowering the prestige and high standards which have been built up over a period of many years'. Opponents of motel development also argued that unrestrained growth was not only ugly but would also glut the market, creating what one man predicted would be 'a condition comparable to the worst slum conditions ever found in any part of the world'. Their opponents had free-market ideology on their side and did not hesitate to use it, terming any attempts at regulation a 'dictatorship' and making eloquent speeches about the sanctity of property rights in the free world. This battle did not pit motel owners against residents, for people involved in the tourist industry could be found on both sides of the debate. Eventually the opponents of accommodation development won the day, and council voted, by a large majority, to put a halt to new development. The ban was officially lifted in 1958.[21]

. . .

## Niagara the Tacky: Ripoffs and Racism

. . . Complaints that had been lodged by travellers for about one hundred years—that it was, in the parlance of the mid-twentieth century, 'tacky', and a giant confidence game—came back to haunt Niagara Falls in the post-war era. The perception of the Falls as an overpriced, overbuilt tourist trap gained a renewed prominence. The fact that the place was now absolutely, unambiguously a mass tourist destination accounted for some of the criticism. As Canadian journalist Larry Krotz observes, modern tourism has a 'flavour-of-the-month' quality, but being 'hot' can be just as much a problem as being 'not'.[22] The distance between new discovery and passé tourist trap is tiny in the modern era, and fame begets disdain with amazing speed. While hardly an undiscovered tourist destination, postwar Niagara exhibited elements of faddishness: intense media exposure, an absurd assortment of tourist attractions, and huge numbers of newly enfranchised working-class tourists swarming the place every summer. Naysayers were bound to emerge.

But it was not only the class snobbery of spoilsports that fuelled complaints, for, in this era as in the past, the tourist industry itself had a good deal to answer for. As tourism became more commonplace it also became, from the perspective of the tourist, easier: standardized, routine, and predictable. But still the hint of corruptibility lingered around tourist towns, as did the insecurities of being what was called in the nineteenth century a 'stranger'. The travel columns of magazines were filled with advice aimed at helping the uninitiated negotiate their way through unfamiliar situations, and especially, confront the apparently rapacious tourist industry. *Holiday* magazine, for example, suggested that travellers wanting to walk around unfamiliar cities 'without being annoyed by street urchins, vendors and others who prey on tourists' should purchase a local newspaper and 'tuck it prominently under your arm.' This trick would instantly recast the stranger as local, allowing 'full freedom to gather local color at will'.[23]

While mistrust was—and remains—a feature of the host/guest relationship, certainly some critics continued to believe that Niagara Falls had cornered the market on fraud. Niagara was regularly lambasted, publicly and privately, for being 'backward', full of fast-buck operators who had fallen out of step with the service-oriented, professional tenor of post-war tourism.

The factional rivalries within Niagara's tourist industry made cheating relatively simple. Canadians blamed crooked Americans, who, they claimed, told lies about Canada in order to keep US visitors to themselves. At different times US tourists came forward with familiar tales told by taxi drivers and motel owners in Niagara Falls, New York: that accommodations on the Canadian side were fully booked due to conventions, that Americans were not allowed to bring their automobiles into the country, that naturalized Americans could lose their citizenship by visiting a foreign country, that the Maid of the Mist boat tour was physically dangerous. Officials on the Canadian side, furious at this slur campaign, retaliated by advertising Canadian attractions more aggressively in the United States.

Niagara Falls, New York, also had to deal with an epidemic of fake 'information booths' that set up shop on the highways into the city. Official-looking uniformed staff at these establishments would not only attempt to keep tourists on the US side by lying about Canada, but also steer them towards particular motels, tour buses, and attractions—the ones that paid them kickbacks. When city officials attempted to crack down on these operations, the entrepreneurs simply moved further and further out of town; one such enterprise was discovered 200 miles from the Falls.[24]

National rivalries and the complexity of crossing a border—even one as permeable as the border at Niagara Falls—could provide just enough confusion to hoodwink strangers. But Canadians were as adept at trickery as their American counterparts. 'Officially' dressed taxi and tour-bus operators continued to flag down motorists to attempt to sell them their services, and some motel owners hit on an inventive way to raise their rates: they left 'No Vacancy' signs on until after dark, and then opened up again, charging desperate travellers higher prices. At peak times some motels would only rent rooms for two or more evenings or would rent rooms on the condition that patrons signed up for a sightseeing tour as well. The fluctuations of the dollar also provided plenty of opportunities to skim a few pennies here and there. Provincial officials constantly warned tourist entrepreneurs that the primary complaint they received from US tourists was being cheated on exchange rates.[25] Tourists also had to contend with garden-variety crime, occasionally aimed specifically at travellers, such as a string of robberies at motels or cabins or the theft of cars with out-of-town plates.

One Niagara Falls Review reporter was so concerned about his town's lingering reputation as a clip joint that he did some investigative reporting. In August 1967, Georgs Kolesnikovs says, he 'slung a camera' around his neck, 'stuffed some tourist brochures in a pocket, asked a blonde friend to come along and played the innocent honeymooner role.' While in general Kolesnikovs found that 'tourists need not worry about being swindled or robbed in Niagara Falls today', he did find what he called 'isolated cases' of tourists being bamboozled, especially in area restaurants. One Lundy's Lane pizzeria no doubt gained a loyal local clientele by charging tourists slightly more than locals for a pizza, and another restaurant added 25 cents to the bill for every visit a tourist made to its washroom.[26]

Black Americans visiting Canada faced an additional problem: Canadian hotels and restaurants did not always confirm Canada's smug sense of itself as an open and racially tolerant society. Openly discriminatory ads from summer resorts—directed against Jews and blacks—were commonplace in Ontario newspapers, especially during the 1930s.[27] Historian Alan MacEachern has discovered that discriminatory practices in the country as a whole continued many decades later, with one especially ironic example: Martin Luther King Jr and his wife Coretta were refused accommodation at a private resort in New Brunswick's Fundy National Park in summer 1960 on the grounds that their presence might prove an 'embarrassment' given the large numbers of white visitors from the US South.[28]

Niagara was, then, hardly alone in using racial criteria to select guests, despite its surprisingly enlightened history. In 1905, for instance, a leading African-American intellectual, W.E.B. Du Bois, had gathered with 29 other black leaders to organize an alternative to the accommodationist leadership of Booker T. Washington. They had intended to have this meeting in Buffalo, but could not find a hotel willing to rent rooms to them. Thus they moved the event across the river and registered, without incident, at the popular Erie Beach Hotel in Fort Erie, just down the road from the Falls. The Niagara region's unprejudiced hospitality was entrenched in the name given to the newly born organization: the Niagara Movement.[29]

Some 40 years later Du Bois and his group would probably have had trouble finding a hotel, or even a restaurant, open to them in the area. Ontario passed legislation in 1944 prohibiting any business from advertising that it catered to 'restricted clientele', the euphemism previously used by whites-only and/or Gentiles-only establishments. Ontario's Travel and Publicity Department monitored tourist industry advertising for such language, though Deputy Minister T.C. McCall did suggest to a resort owner who claimed he wanted to restrict 'drunken parties' that he should use the phrase 'we reserve the right to refuse any reservation' on his advertising. This phrase was perfectly legal and, as McCall pointed out, 'much broader in its effect'.[30]

Some Niagara establishments did not even attempt to play such semantic games. In 1948 a racially mixed group was refused service at a Niagara Parks Commission restaurant in Queenston. 'You met us like we were tigers', said Mrs. E. Whitecotton of New Rochelle,

New York, in an indignant letter to Parks Commission authorities. 'I hate to think you are like the Dixie crackers.'[31]

In 1949 the manager of the General Brock declared at a Chamber of Commerce meeting that his hotel made it a policy not to accept reservations from 'large groups' of blacks, although some tourist homes, and two other local hotels, would. The next year the prize-winning four-thousandth couple to register for a honeymoon certificate were African Americans from Kansas, and they received all the customary honours: guided tours, a welcome from the mayor, and their photo in the local paper. They did not, unlike other prize-winners, get a night, or even a meal, at the General Brock.[32]

By then Niagara Falls was again becoming known as a bawdy, working-class carnival. Extensive and overtly sexual honeymoon promotion was part of this, and so too was the town's resolutely working-class image; not a product of this era, but certainly intensified by post-war changes in leisure and travel. While mass travel after World War II was celebrated as one more example of the good life delivered by North American consumer capitalism, at close range democratized vacation spots looked, to some, rather unappealing. In the original script for *Niagara*, [a 1953 film starring Marilyn Monroe that had a hugely beneficial impact on Niagara Falls as a tourist destination,] Mr Qua, the kindly motel operator, delivered a stout, populist defence of Niagara Falls when he welcomed two of the protagonists to his establishment. 'We sure get folks from everywhere', he said. 'Just catch the license plates: Vancouver, Texas, Mexico City, Iceland. Not the stylish crowd, of course. No sir. To get those folks, them falls there would have to fall up!' But this kind of public tribute to the grassroots tourist was rare; it only happened in the movies.[33] Much more common were complaints.

Some tourists, such as a self-described member of 'the better class' from Toronto, took pen to paper, this one complaining to authorities that Queen Victoria Park was being ruined by ballplayers and beer drinkers. Travel writers also gave the place mixed reviews. A visiting British journalist declared Niagara 'one of the most highly commercialized tourist traps in the world' in 1960, though, like others before him, he softened when he saw the 'awe-inspiring' waterfall, which made it 'all worthwhile'. The US magazine *Saturday Evening Post* concurred, encouraging readers in 1965 to ignore the 'fringe excitement' and 'souvenir stores selling Japanese-made American Indian artifacts'. 'When you stand there on the promontory,' wrote journalist Anne Chamberlain, 'you realize that the falls themselves are still the best show in town.'[34]

Canadian travel writers were much harder on the place. A special travel issue of *Canadian Homes and Gardens* in 1959 created a local controversy when it dismissed the town as 'strictly a tourist place' and warned readers, 'You'll be bombarded by hawkers peddling plastic replicas of the Falls, gaudy ash trays and pennants.' The mayor was especially annoyed that the magazine neglected to place Niagara on its map, which included places like the northern Ontario mining town of Timmins. Even the house organ of the hotel industry, the *Canadian Hotel Review*, usually a relentlessly upbeat booster of tourism, could not resist taking a swipe at the Falls. A favourable story on a new motor hotel and restaurant that opened in 1967 declared, 'It proves that interesting decor and Niagara Falls do go together, an idea many who know the city will find hard to believe.'[35]

Did the problem lie with the poor taste and low standards of the working-class holidaymaker or with the scheming, quick-buck tourist operator? Did tourists get the holidays they deserved (or desired) or were they being manipulated by greedy entrepreneurs? These questions were posed bluntly and answered easily by different players. While provincial tourist department officials could not be as candid as they probably would have liked to be, their collective answer was clear enough. In the eyes of the provincial

government, the Niagara tourist industry had borne an atrocious reputation for about a century, and civic authorities at the Falls were not interested in changing a thing. As one official declared in a private 1950 memo, 'There is nothing wrong with Niagara Falls that their Council could not clean up if they chose.'[36]

In a rare public address on the issue, newly appointed Minister of Tourism James Auld spoke to the Niagara Falls Visitors and Convention Bureau in 1964 about what he called the 'two-sided image' of the Falls. A curious dichotomy of Niagara's tourist industry, which seems, he said, 'as old as history', was the juxtaposition of two Niagaras: the grand waterfall and the 'tawdry, slightly down at the heels image of the publicity stunt—over the falls in a barrel, sleazy honeymoon hotels, the bride's second biggest disappointment and the like.' Even if these images were no longer true, he declared, 'What matters is that people believe them to be true', and he urged tourist entrepreneurs to cease gouging US visitors by shortchanging them on exchange and accommodation rates. His words had little effect. A few years later the Ministry of Tourism was still receiving more complaints from tourists about the Niagara region than any other area in the province.[37]

Some local citizens took these complaints to heart and tried to clean up their image. Niagara's tourist industry implemented many of the national ideas and campaigns initiated after World War II, all designed to remind townspeople that tourism was good for them and thus they should behave politely, even obsequiously, to visitors. As John Fisher, chairman of the Canadian Tourist Association, explained during a visit to the Falls, all of the many attractions of Niagara 'can be wiped out in the shrug of the shoulders of indifference.' The city always commemorated 'Tourist Service Week' in May with newspaper editorials and public lectures on the importance of courtesy to tourists. The Chamber of Commerce and the Niagara Parks Commission sponsored regular 'courtesy schools' for tourist industry staff and the public alike, and in 1961 the city opened the 'Niagara School of Hospitality'. Niagara Falls residents—whether or not directly connected with the tourist industry—were urged to answer a questionnaire designed to test their knowledge of local attractions. Winners received a certificate, free admission to the attractions, and a strong hint that their participation could be the first step to employment in the tourist industry. Even for those without any designs on such employment it became an article of faith that, as one editorialist put it, the 'magic of tourist dollars' was making the whole community prosperous, and thus overcrowded stores, streets, and parks were opportunities, not frustrations.[38]

Along with the stick of continued employment and community prosperity, Niagara residents also enjoyed the carrot of fame and (aside from the occasional trashing by a travel writer) flattery. After all, no other small Ontario towns were visited regularly by movie stars and royalty. In no other place could children amuse themselves by spotting licence plates from all over North America—and indeed, probably see all of them in one summer. Canadian journalist Barbara Frum recalled that growing up in the Falls gave a person an unusual international perspective, because 'Everyone in the world came to Niagara Falls.'[39] Through the 1950s and early 1960s the Niagara Falls Review ran a regular summer column in which reporters gathered comments—almost always folksy and positive—from visitors, who were almost always Americans.

Along with self-congratulations, such encounters with tourists also allowed residents to let off steam by laughing at them, for another popular summer pastime was to swap stories of the silly things tourists said and did. They chuckled at the Americans—again, almost always Americans—who marched into the tourist bureau seeking directions to 'Ontario' or 'Canada', people who expected Niagara Falls residents to speak French, who thought they could

drive to Montreal and back before dinner, who were disappointed that the Maid of the Mist steamboat did not go over the Falls, who thought they had to get their money changed before they travelled from Ontario to Nova Scotia, or who left their false teeth behind in public washrooms. Such stories may have gone some way towards evening out the host/guest relationship.

Whether Niagara Falls had become, in local parlance, 'honky-tonk' was on the minds of some members of the community, and the question drew on the same issues that had haunted Niagara since the nineteenth century. Had the place become 'too' commercial or raucous? Were human-built attractions interfering with the scenic beauty of the waterfall? Were local people acting as responsible custodians? J.R. Matthews, a gift-store owner, took his concerns about the 'general move towards honky-tonk establishments' at Niagara to the Minister of Tourism in 1963. The last straw, for Matthews as well as several members of the city council, had come when a tourist entrepreneur hoisted a gigantic balloon over his establishment, which lay dangerously close to—as the Review put it, 'at the very edge of'—Queen Victoria Park.[40] Memories of Thomas Barnett and Saul Davis lingered, and to be pushing the limits of good taste that close to the waterfall was to invite controversy.

When the Review asked them, 'Is Niagara Falls Honky Tonk?' a number of local residents balked at the phrase, but worried that the place was becoming 'more like Coney Island'. Too much tourist development, according to one resident, was going to 'wreck it for everyone', and another wondered why honeymooners continued to flock to such an unromantic atmosphere. For their part, tourist industry spokespeople claimed they were simply providing what their customers demanded. Ross Kenzie, manager of the Visitors and Convention Bureau, said simply, 'Honky tonk, if it must be called that, is there for those who demand it.'[41]

As it had for the previous century, the Niagara Parks Commission offered everyone the comforting illusion that capital 'N' Nature was being protected where it mattered most. As a Canadian journalist explained, perhaps a bit defensively, because the Parks Commission controlled most of the land around the waterfall, 'There is not much danger of Niagara Falls degenerating into a false-fronted sideshow.'[42]

If Canada was a 'gigantic department store' of travel, Niagara was the bargain basement: cheap and widely accessible, a little bit tawdry, and a lot of fun. Through a happy convergence of geography and history, Niagara was destined to take centre stage as newly enfranchised working-class travellers enjoyed a frantic week or two of paid leisure. The post-war travel boom reinvented Niagara as a fun-filled, populist carnival, and the honeymoon trade—above all else, and as always—gave the place a shady but cheerful tinge.

## Notes

1. Kiwanis Club, *Niagara Falls, Canada: A History of the City and the World Famous Beauty Spot* (Niagara Falls, Ont.: Kiwanis Club, 1967), 195; *Niagara Falls Review* (*NFR*), 15 Nov. 1960, 24 Aug. 1967.

2. Dominion-Provincial Tourist Conference, *Report of Proceedings*, Ottawa, 1946, PAO. I explore the post-war tourist industry in Canada in more detail in 'Everybody Likes Canadians: Americans, Canadians and the Postwar Travel Boom', in Shelley Baranowski and Ellen Furlough, eds, [*Being Elsewhere: Tourism, Consumer Culture, and Identity in Modern Europe and North America* (Ann Arbor: University of Michigan Press, 2001)].

3. F.H. Leacy, ed., *Historical Statistics of Canada*, 2nd edn (Ottawa: Statistics Canada, 1983), D318–28.

4. Hal Tracey, 'Motel Business Is Booming', *Saturday Night*, 11 Sept. 1951; 'Why Tourists Like Ontario', *Financial Post*, 9 Oct. 1954; James Montagnes, 'Motel Owners Step up Investment', *Canadian Business* (July 1959); Ontario Economic Council, *Ontario's Tourist Industry* (Toronto, Dec. 1965), 17; *Canadian Hotel Review* (May 1949): 66. The number of hotels in Canada dropped during the travel

5. boom, from 5,656 in 1941 to 5,157 in 1952. Elizabeth Hay Trott, 'For Hotels, the Boom's Still On', *Monetary Times* (July 1954): 22.

5. Robert Thomas Allen, 'Why U.S. Tourists Are Passing up Canada', *Maclean's* (May 1955); Karal Ann Marling, *As Seen on TV: The Visual Culture of Everyday Life in the 1950s* (Cambridge, Mass.: Harvard University Press, 1994), 132; Kenneth White, 'Is Our Visitor Industry in for Record Year?', *Financial Post*, 16 June 1951; John Maclean, 'Gloom in Playland', *Financial Post*, 20 Oct. 1956. The figures cited for US travel outside the United States pertain to the year 1950. . . .

6. Logan Maclean, 'Needed: Travel Promotion', *Saturday Night*, 25 Apr. 1956.

7. Niagara Falls City Directory 1945, 1955, 1965; Ontario Department of Economics and Development, *Economic Survey of the Niagara Region* (1963), 57, 87; Chamber of Commerce minutes, Niagara Falls, Ont., 19 Nov. 1958; *NFR*, 22 Aug. 1961.

8. *Niagara Falls Gazette* (*NFG*), series on Niagara Attractions, 2 July–13 Aug. 1963, later published by the Niagara Falls, New York, Chamber of Commerce, *Official Guidebook* (1964).

9. Judith A. Adams, *The American Amusement Park* (Boston: G.K. Hall, 1991), 105.

10. Ibid., 94, 97. See also Project on Disney, *Inside the Mouse: Work and Play at Disney World* (Durham, NC: Duke University Press, 1995).

11. Chamber of Commerce minutes, Niagara Falls, Ont., 26 May 1948, 31 Aug. 1949, 12 Oct. 1949; General Manager to Lynne Spencer, 16 Aug. 1948, Niagara Parks Commission, Niagara Falls, Ont. (NPC), correspondence; *NFR*, 12 June 1950.

12. *NFR*, 14, 28 June 1960.

13. On globalization and cultural uniformity, see, for example, Benjamin Barber, *Jihad vs. McWorld: How Globalism and Tribalism Are Reshaping the World* (New York: Ballantine, 1996); George Ritzer and Allan Liska, '"McDisneyization" and "Post-Tourism": Complementary Perspectives on Contemporary Tourism', in Chris Rojek and John Urry, eds, *Touring Cultures: Transformations of Travel and Theory* (London: Routledge, 1997), 96–112.

14. See, for example, *Toronto Star Guide*, 1957; *Travellers Guide*, 1959. Accommodation listings and guidebooks, as well as formal announcements of the opening of hotels and restaurants, indicate that large numbers of Eastern Europeans and Italians owned such establishments; in some listings half the names are non-Anglo.

15. Standard Hotel Files, Caverly; *NFR*, 11 June 1950.

16. Standard Hotel Files, Prospect House; 'Where History Helps Sell Beer', *Canadian Hotel Review* (Aug. 1955).

17. Standard Hotel Files, Falls View Hotel; *NFR*, 3 June 1959.

18. See, for example, Standard Hotel Files, Belleview Hotel, Merview Hotel.

19. Standard Hotel Files, Inspectors' Recommendations against Hotels, Victoria Inn.

20. *NFR*, 2 Sept. 1949.

21. *NFR*, 11 Jan. 1949; Kiwanis Club of Stamford, *Niagara Falls*, 58.

22. Krotz uses Belize in the 1990s as an example of this phenomenon. See Larry Krotz, *Tourists: How the Fastest Growing Industry Is Changing the World* (London: Faber & Faber, 1996), 65–87.

23. 'Tips to Travellers', *Holiday* (Sept. 1946).

24. *NFG*, 26 July 1955, 3 Aug. 1962; *NFR*, 26 July 1955.

25. See, for example, *NFR*, 6 July 1948, 15 Apr. 1950, 7 Aug. 1959, 6 Dec. 1960, 26 Nov. 1963, 21 Aug. 1970; James Auld, Speech to Niagara Falls Visitor and Convention Bureau, 28 Oct. 1964, Minister's Office, Series A-8, RG 5, PAO.

26. *NFR*, 30 Aug. 1967.

27. R.I. Wolfe, 'The Changing Patterns of Tourism in Ontario,' in Ontario Historical Society, ed., *Profiles of a Province* (Toronto: Ontario Historical Society, 1967), 176.

28. *Globe and Mail*, 14 Jan. 1995.

29. Owen A. Thomas, *Niagara's Freedom Trail: A Guide to African-Canadian History on the Niagara Peninsula* (n.p.: Niagara Economic and Tourism Corporation, 1996), 6.

30. McCall memo, n.d., 1947, W. Rourke to T.C. McCall, 7 July 1949, and response, 12 July 1949, Deputy Minister's Office correspondence, PAO.

31. Mrs Whitecotton received a quick apology from the restaurant's manager, who insisted that the problem was not racism but that her party had been queue-jumping. Mrs E. Whitecotton to Manager, Queenston Restaurant, 29 Aug. 1948, and C. Sheldon Brooker, response, 4 Sept. 1948, NPC correspondence.

32. Chamber of Commerce minutes, Niagara Falls, Ont., 25 May 1949; *NFR*, 10 July 1950. Instead, the couple got a dinner at the NPC-run Refectory.

33. 'Niagara' screenplay, Deputy Minister's Office correspondence, RG 5 Series, B-1, PAO. This tribute to the people's Niagara only happened in the movie *script*; it did not make it into the film.

34. NPC, Manager's files, correspondence, 1948; *NFR*, 24 Oct. 1960, 20 Aug. 1959; Anne Chamberlain, 'See America First', *Saturday Evening Post*, 28 Aug. 1965.

35. 'Authentic Decor from English Pubs Big Attraction at Niagara Falls', *Canadian Hotel Review* (Feb. 1967).

36. Interdepartmental correspondence, C.D. Crowe to Thomas McCall, Deputy Minister's Office, 25 Mar. 1950, Series B-4, RG 5, PAO.

37. Hon. James Auld, Speech to Niagara Falls Visitors and Convention Bureau, 28 Oct. 1964, Series A-I, PAO; *NFR*, 27 Mar. 1969.

38. See, for example, *NFR*, 26, 27, 29 May 1952, 26 Apr. 1957, 11 May, 9 July 1961; Niagara Development Committee School of Hospitality Questionnaire, Niagara Falls Public Library, Niagara Falls, Ont.

39. *Globe and Mail*, 16 May 1985.

40. Minister's correspondence, 9 June 1963, Series A-I, RG 5, PAO; *NFR*, 27 June 1963.

41. *NFR*, 27 June 1960; Anne Chamberlain, 'See America First', *Saturday Evening Post*, 28 Aug. 1965.

42. Niagara Falls Public Library Vertical Files, Tourist Industry, *Globe and Mail*, clipping, n.d., c. 1964.

# 25

# Visualizing Play

Since the late nineteenth century, images of play have made their way into a variety of media. Among these are print advertisements, sports and soft news photography for print media, and, of course, on television where entire networks are devoted to the broadcasting of play. Some photographs of play and recreation are taken for family reasons, to memorialize vacations or particular events. Much of our imagery of play, however, has been produced by industries with an interest either in promoting leisure or using the idea of leisure time to sell consumer products and services. Despite this commodification of play (or perhaps because of it), Canadians experienced an expansion of leisure as a component of everyday life, especially among the working and middle classes. As the selections in this section make clear, however, play has historically been an ambiguous site, where power was exercised and social meanings were deeply contested.

The images presented here come from a wide variety of sources. It is worthwhile asking how newspapers, advertisements, public photographs, and private snapshots all constituted different perspectives on the many sites of play that emerged in the twentieth century.

## Series 1: Rough and Respectable

Figures 1–4 are snapshots that, on first glance, might appear to be candid and thus more documentary and factual. The subject matter, men boxing, women playing crokinole, two couples snowshoeing, and a large family gathering at a cottage, in some ways reinforce the apparent 'reality' of the image. But look carefully, for example, at the two men boxing. In the technology of the 1890s, the camera could not stop movement cleanly, and the act of punching someone would appear as a blurred image. The photograph has thus been composed, either by the photographer or by the subjects in the photograph. In fact, all of the photographs in this series are arranged and posed. At a general level, we might wonder what the photographer and/or the people in the photographs were communicating about play? What were they trying to 'say' via the communicative power of the camera?

1.  Compare and contrast Figures 1 and 2. How do these photographs construct gender roles? What is the significance of the social settings in which these activities take place?
2.  Consider the play activities depicted in Figures 3 and 4. What range of recreational pursuits did respectable classes engage in? What is the significance of the outdoors in these images?
3.  Note the ages of the subjects and the physical relations between bodies in all four images. What do these photographs suggest about forging distinct male and female social worlds? How did leisure function as a space for courtship?

## Series 2: Leisure Time

The advertisements in Figures 5 and 6 are examples of how images were historically produced to exploit the expansion of leisure time in the everyday lives of Canadians. In these two examples, both published in *Chatelaine* magazine, Moirs chocolates and General Electric sought to sell their goods by emphasizing how each product enriched play in the lives of women. The meanings the advertisers attached to the chocolates and appliances had nothing to do with the quality of the actual goods, but everything to do with the lifestyle each afforded its owner. In this way, these advertisements resemble the Eveready battery advertisement discussed in the Introduction to this volume.

1.  The products being advertised are both aimed at women consumers, but what are the different assumptions about women and women's lives that are embodied in each? How do these differences reflect changing attitudes towards women from the 1920s to the late 1940s?
2.  Compare and contrast the leisure activities reflected in both advertisements. How do these reflect changes in play between the 1920s and late 1940s? How does class play a role in the intended audience for these products?
3.  In the General Electric ad, what is the significance of the arrangement and number of appliances? Why are no images of kitchens presented?

## Series 3: Consuming Sports

Today, the celebrity status of sports stars is taken for granted. However, the commodification of professional sports evolved in uneven stages throughout the twentieth century, fuelled by shifts in consumerism, leisure, and especially the rise of mass media, including radio and television. The five photographs in this series reflect the public presentation of professional athletes to a wide audience in the 1950s, but they also tell us a great deal about the contested spaces of bodies and athletics in the post-war period.

Figures 7 and 8 are professional public relations photographs of two famous athletes. Maurice 'The Rocket' Richard led the Montreal Canadiens to eight Stanley Cups and was venerated by French-speaking Canadians, who rioted in Montreal when Richard was suspended for hitting an official in 1955. Barbara Ann Scott, an Ottawa-born figure skater, attracted worldwide attention when she became the first North American to win the European and World Championships and followed that feat with a gold medal at the 1948 Olympics. With her face on the cover of *Life* and *Time* magazines, Scott became known as 'Canada's Sweetheart' and turned professional in 1949, travelling in a number of ice revue shows in the 1950s.

The last three photographs offer a different visual perspective on the relationship between media and athletes. All three were taken by newspaper photographer Jack De Lorme for the Calgary *Albertan*. None of the athletes were famous, but all of them were professional: Barbara Baker was an American wrestler travelling through Calgary on tour; Gerry Musetti and Don Bailey were also American imports, who played for the Calgary Stampeders football club; Hiromi Uyeyama was a touring jockey described as a member of the 'only Japanese trainer-jockey combination on the continent' and went by the nickname of 'Spud'. All three of these photographs were cropped and published in the *Albertan* in the same year (1956) and offer a snapshot on how newspapers presented professional sports to their audience. These images, while made to appear spontaneous in nature, were just as carefully posed as the public relations shots of Richard and Scott.

1. Consider the various sports being presented in these five images. Which are considered 'rough' and which are considered 'respectable'? How are athletes' bodies posed to reflect these differences?

2. In the article that accompanied Figure 9, Barbara Baker is described as an athlete who 'packs her 130 pounds into her 5'2" frame with nary a muscle visible anywhere.' Comparing Baker's portrayal with that of Scott (Figure 7), how and why are the two athletes presented differently?

3. How are masculinity and femininity constructed in these photographs? Where do these gendered constructions become ambiguous in the relationship between poses, bodies, and the sports involved?

**Figure 1.** 'A Boxing Match', 1900, Fort Frances, Ontario, by William Hampden Tenner. Archives of Ontario, C 311–1–0–4–1, 10002336.

**Figure 2.** 'Two women playing a game of crokinole', *c.* 1890s, by John Boyd. Archives of Ontario, C 7–2–0–1–55, 10003801.

**Figure 3.** A party snowshoeing and skiing, c. 1905, anonymous. Notman Photographic Archives, McCord Museum of Canadian History, Montreal, MP–0000.25.1023.

**Figure 4.** Picnic party at the cottage of Mrs Wilmot, Woodmans Point, New Brunswick, c. 1895–1900. Gift of Edith Magee, 1988.64.13. Courtesy New Brunswick Museum, Saint John, NB.

**Figure 5.** Moirs chocolates (Halifax), 'Every Hour', *Chatelaine*, Mar. 1928.

**Figure 6.** General Electric (Canadian General Electric), 'More Time for Leisure', *Chatelaine*, Sept. 1948.

**Figure 7.** Barbara Ann Scott, Olympic and world champion figure skater, 1948.

**Figure 8.** Maurice 'The Rocket' Richard. Courtesy of the Hockey Hall of Fame, Toronto, 000038–0094.

**Figure 9.** Barbara Baker, wrestler, 1956, by Jack De Lorme. Courtesy of Glenbow Archives, Calgary, NA–5600–8349a.

**Figure 10.** Hiromi 'Spud' Uyeyama, jockey, 1956, by Jack De Lorme. Courtesy of Glenbow Archives, Calgary, NA–5600–8039d.

**Figure 11.** Gerry Musetti and Don Bailey, Calgary Stampeders football, 1956, by Jack De Lorme. Courtesy of Glenbow Archives, Calgary, NA–5600–8062a.